Game Theory Applications in Network Design

Sungwook Kim
Sogang University, South Korea

A volume in the Advances in Wireless
Technologies and Telecommunication (AWTT)
Book Series

Information Science
REFERENCE
An Imprint of IGI Global

Managing Director:	Lindsay Johnston
Production Editor:	Jennifer Yoder
Development Editor:	Erin O'Dea
Acquisitions Editor:	Kayla Wolfe
Typesetter:	Christina Henning
Cover Design:	Jason Mull

Published in the United States of America by
Information Science Reference (an imprint of IGI Global)
701 E. Chocolate Avenue
Hershey PA 17033
Tel: 717-533-8845
Fax: 717-533-8661
E-mail: cust@igi-global.com
Web site: http://www.igi-global.com

                    Library of Congress Cataloging-in-Publication Data

Kim, Sungwook.
  Game theory applications in network design / by Sungwook Kim.
     pages cm
  Includes bibliographical references and index.
  ISBN 978-1-4666-6050-2 (hardcover) -- ISBN 978-1-4666-6051-9 (ebook) -- ISBN 978-1-4666-6053-3 (print & perpetual access) 1. Game theory. I. Title.
  HB144.K56 2014
  003'.72015193--dc23
                            2014007984

This book is published in the IGI Global book series Advances in Wireless Technologies and Telecommunication (AWTT) (ISSN: 2327-3305; eISSN: 2327-3313)

British Cataloguing in Publication Data
A Cataloguing in Publication record for this book is available from the British Library.

For electronic access to this publication, please contact: eresources@igi-global.com.

Advances in Wireless Technologies and Telecommunication (AWTT) Book Series

Xiaoge Xu
The University of Nottingham Ningbo China

ISSN: 2327-3305
EISSN: 2327-3313

MISSION

The wireless computing industry is constantly evolving, redesigning the ways in which individuals share information. Wireless technology and telecommunication remain one of the most important technologies in business organizations. The utilization of these technologies has enhanced business efficiency by enabling dynamic resources in all aspects of society.

The **Advances in Wireless Technologies and Telecommunication Book Series** aims to provide researchers and academic communities with quality research on the concepts and developments in the wireless technology fields. Developers, engineers, students, research strategists, and IT managers will find this series useful to gain insight into next generation wireless technologies and telecommunication.

COVERAGE

- Cellular Networks
- Digital Communication
- Global Telecommunications
- Grid Communications
- Mobile Technology
- Mobile Web Services
- Network Management
- Virtual Network Operations
- Wireless Broadband
- Wireless Sensor Networks

IGI Global is currently accepting manuscripts for publication within this series. To submit a proposal for a volume in this series, please contact our Acquisition Editors at Acquisitions@igi-global.com or visit: http://www.igi-global.com/publish/.

Titles in this Series

For a list of additional titles in this series, please visit: www.igi-global.com

Game Theory Applications in Network Design
Sungwook Kim (Sogang University, South Korea)
Information Science Reference • copyright 2014 • 543pp • H/C (ISBN: 9781466660502) • US $225.00 (our price)

Convergence of Broadband, Broadcast, and Cellular Network Technologies
Ramona Trestian (Middlesex University, UK) and Gabriel-Miro Muntean (Dublin City University, Ireland)
Information Science Reference • copyright 2014 • 333pp • H/C (ISBN: 9781466659780) • US $235.00 (our price)

Handbook of Research on Progressive Trends in Wireless Communications and Networking
M.A. Matin (Institut Teknologi Brunei, Brunei Darussalam)
Information Science Reference • copyright 2014 • 592pp • H/C (ISBN: 9781466651708) • US $380.00 (our price)

Broadband Wireless Access Networks for 4G Theory, Application, and Experimentation
Raul Aquino Santos (University of Colima, Mexico) Victor Rangel Licea (National Autonomous University of Mexico, Mexico) and Arthur Edwards-Block (University of Colima, Mexico)
Information Science Reference • copyright 2014 • 452pp • H/C (ISBN: 9781466648883) • US $235.00 (our price)

Multidisciplinary Perspectives on Telecommunications, Wireless Systems, and Mobile Computing
Wen-Chen Hu (University of North Dakota, USA)
Information Science Reference • copyright 2014 • 305pp • H/C (ISBN: 9781466647152) • US $175.00 (our price)

Mobile Networks and Cloud Computing Convergence for Progressive Services and Applications
Joel J.P.C. Rodrigues (Instituto de Telecomunicações, University of Beira Interior, Portugal) Kai Lin (Dalian University of Technology, China) and Jaime Lloret (Polytechnic University of Valencia, Spain)
Information Science Reference • copyright 2014 • 408pp • H/C (ISBN: 9781466647817) • US $180.00 (our price)

Research and Design Innovations for Mobile User Experience
Kerem Rızvanoğlu (Galatasaray University, Turkey) and Görkem Çetin (Turkcell, Turkey)
Information Science Reference • copyright 2014 • 377pp • H/C (ISBN: 9781466644465) • US $190.00 (our price)

Cognitive Radio Technology Applications for Wireless and Mobile Ad Hoc Networks
Natarajan Meghanathan (Jackson State University, USA) and Yenumula B. Reddy (Grambling State University, USA)
Information Science Reference • copyright 2013 • 370pp • H/C (ISBN: 9781466642218) • US $190.00 (our price)

www.igi-global.com

701 E. Chocolate Ave., Hershey, PA 17033
Order online at www.igi-global.com or call 717-533-8845 x100
To place a standing order for titles released in this series, contact: cust@igi-global.com
Mon-Fri 8:00 am - 5:00 pm (est) or fax 24 hours a day 717-533-8661

Ad majorem Dei gloriam

Table of Contents

Section 1
Fundamental Ideas of Game Theory

Section 2
Game Theoretic Applications for Network Management Issues

Section 3
Advanced Game Paradigm Topics:
Case Studies in Network Design

Preface

Network Design with its many variants is one of the most active research areas. In addition, new problems in this area are constantly propounded by practitioners working in different aspects of network design such as construction, routing, and staged deployment. Furthermore, many new design paradigms such as ATM, ad-hoc, and telecommunications add rich new flavors to existing problems. Including mobile cellular networks and ad-hoc wireless networks, future generation networks will most likely consist of intelligent devices capable of sensing the environment and effectively adjusting their transmission parameters according to the current network conditions and QoS specifications. These devices will opportunistically use the network resource while selecting the transmission rates, transmission powers, access method, route to final destination for a multi-hop network, etc. This mechanism will greatly influence the performance of all the other users in the network. In addition, most of today's networks are large-scale with lack of access to centralized information, consist of users with diverse requirements, and are subject to dynamic changes. These factors naturally motivate a new distributed control paradigm, where the network infrastructure is kept simple and the network control functions are delegated to individual agents, which make their decisions independently. The interactions among devices sharing a common network resource can be formally modeled as games. The outcome of these games and consequently the overall network performance can be predicted using a game theoretic formulation. Therefore, the interaction of multiple selfish decision-makers necessitates the use of game theory.

Game theory is a mathematical framework to analyze complex interactions of cooperative or competing decision makers taking into account their preferences and requirements. The origins of game theory go far back to the so called *marriage contract problem* in Babylonian times (in the early years of the first millennium). Recent work suggests that the division of an inheritance described in the Talmud predicts the modern theory of cooperative games. Relatively new, in 1713, James Waldegrave wrote out a strategy for a card game that provided the first known solution to a two-player game. Despite these early efforts and many other contributors in the history of game theory, it is widely accepted that the origin of the formal study of game theory began with John von Neumann and Oskar Morgenstern's book, *Theory of Games and Economic Behavior* (published in 1944). This pioneering work focused on finding unique strategies that allowed players to minimize their maximum losses by considering, for every possible strategy of their own, all the possible responses of other players. During the 1940s, game theory emerged from the fields of mathematics and economics to provide a revolutionary new method of analysis. Therefore, originally, game theory was invented to explain complicated economic behavior. The golden age of game theory occurred in the 1950s and 1960s when researchers focused on finding sets of strategies, known as equilibria, to solve a game if all players behaved rationally. The most famous of these is the Nash equilibrium proposed by John Nash. Nash also made significant contributions to bargaining theory and examined cooperative games where threats and promises are fully binding and enforceable. Today game theory provides a language for discussing conflict and cooperation. With its effectiveness in studying complex dynamics among players, game theory has been widely applied in economics, political science (e.g., voter behavior), sociology (network games), law (antitrust), computer science (defending networks against attacks), military science, biology (evolutionary strategies), pure philosophy, with occasional appearances in psychology, religion (recall Aumann's Talmud paper), physics (quantum games), telecommunications, logistics, etc. In these fields, game theory has been employed to achieve socially optimal equilibrium.

Nowadays, game theory has been widely recognized as an important tool in the research area of network design. A promising potential application of game theory in communication networks is the area of congestion control, network routing, load balancing, multi-commodity flow, resource allocation, and quality of service provisioning. Intensive research work has also been devoted to game models in wireless mobile networks. Some of the main issues are power control, bandwidth pricing, incentive mechanism for cooperation between mobile nodes, resource sharing, the access control to a common radio channel, and auctions for wireless bandwidth. In addition, new problems are constantly propounded in various areas such as network security and software engineering. In recent years, these issues have become an increasingly important part of network design.

In applying game theory for wireless communications and networking, wide application examples can be efficiently addressed. The applications are mainly motivated by the inherent characteristics of wireless systems. First, wireless bandwidth is very scarce and limited resource in communications. With the increasing number of wireless access terminals, wireless bandwidth scarcity and hence competition among mobile users becomes more severe. This competition for limited resources closely matches with the concept of game theory. Second, the wireless network systems become more complicated with respect to network size, protocol heterogeneity, QoS sensitive multimedia services, and dynamic interactions. In such issues, game theory is able to significantly help better understand the complex interactions and design more efficient, scalable, and robust protocols. Third, the current-generation wireless systems can provide mobile users with high-speed data services at rates substantially higher than those of the previous generation. As a result, the demand for mobile information services with high reliability, fast response times, and ubiquitous connectivity continues to increase rapidly. Therefore, the effectiveness of network performance has become critically important both in terms of practical utility and commercial viability, and presents a rich area for research. This demands intelligent network management and operation, which may well be solved within the game theoretical framework.

Game theory hopefully will lead to new collaborative research initiatives and help advance the state-of-the-art. The goal of this book is to focus on the active area of applications of game theory to understand current trends, identify understudied areas, and formulate new directions for further investigation. To satisfy this goal, this book will present an introduction on game theory with an emphasis on applications for network design issues. The first section of this book introduces the fundamental concepts of game theory, while the second section explores application fields of game theory, including wireless ad-hoc networks, smart grid, network security, cognitive radio, and network resource management. Finally, the last section of this book discusses advanced applications in network design such as power control, access control, bandwidth adaptation, routing, and game theoretic solutions for the network management. These three sections will be valuable to professionals in the field and researchers in other areas who want an introduction to current game theoretic research frontiers in network design. This book is descriptive and adopts an algorithmic approach. It assumes that readers have some familiarity with algorithms, computer networks, and telecommunications. The unique feature of this book is that it gives algorithmic treatment to all the issues addressed and highlights the intuition behind each of the algorithms presented.

This book specifically treats the recent research and the use of game theoretic techniques that are playing particularly important and distinctive roles in the network design domain. An important component of this book is examples of algorithms, which will give the readers the opportunity to clearly understand to get game theoretic solutions for specific network design issues. The content provided in this book should help readers understand the necessary background, concepts, and principles in using game theory approaches. Therefore, this book is useful for undergraduate and graduate students in computer science and information technology disciplines. In particular, this book can serve as an essential reference for students, educators, research strategists, scientists, researchers, and engineers in the field of network design.

OUTLINE OF THE BOOK

The key challenge in this book is to provide the basic idea of game theory and fundamental understanding the game theoretic interactions among network entities. The research presented in this book focuses on modeling, analyzing, and solving the network design problems. There are two main ways to capitalize game theory in network design. One approach is used to analyze existing systems. After a game model is developed, it can be used to investigate the properties of the systems. The other approach is used to design a new system. Instead of fixing a game and analyzing its outcome, game theory is adopted to get the desired outcome. When a suitable game model is discovered, a system can obtain the properties that are looked for. Nowadays, a lot of models for network design problems have been proposed based on the game theory paradigm.

To provide a didactic approach for studying game theory, this book is organized in three sections. In section 1, we will study the fundamental ideas of game theory. Before we discuss how to apply game theory in different network design problems, the choice of a design technique is crucial and must be emphasized. Therefore, this section presents game theory history, different game models, and solution concepts that can be applied to the design, implementation, and analysis of network design problems. In addition to the explanation of the basic principles, we will also illustrate the limitations and trade-offs of different approaches.

The chapters in section 1 cover the fundamental ideas of game theory. In chapter 1, game theory history and approaches are surveyed. Even though game theory can be traced back to ancient China, the mathematical theory of games was developed in the 1940s. At that time, John Nash transformed game theory into a more general tool that enabled the analysis of win-win and lose-lose scenarios, as well as win-lose situations. In the 1950s-1970s, game theory was developed extensively by many scholars. Lots of game theorists have won Nobel prizes in economics, and John Maynard Smith was awarded the Crafoord Prize for his application of game theory to biology. Nowadays, game theory is used in the social science, economics, biology, engineering, political science, international relations, computer science, and philosophy. In this chapter, game theory applications in various academic fields are briefly presented.

In chapter 2, basic concepts for game theory and game model classification are introduced. Games are classified various criteria as non-cooperative games vs. cooperative games, static games vs. dynamic games, discrete games vs. continuous games, zero-sum games vs. non zero-sum games, n-player games vs. population games, perfect information games vs. imperfect information games, complete information games vs. incomplete information games, pure strategy games vs. mixed strategy games, unitary games vs. hybrid games, egalitarian games vs. hierarchical games, or symmetric games vs. asymmetric games. In addition, famous game solutions are introduced. Solutions for non-cooperative games are Nash equilibrium, Pareto equilibrium, Subgame Perfect Nash equilibrium, Bayesian-Nash equilibrium, -equilibrium, correlated equilibrium, Wardrop equilibrium, and evolutionary stable strategy. Solutions for cooperative games are Pareto optimality, Core, Shapley Value, the nucleolus, Nash bargaining solution, Kalai-Smorodinsky bargaining solution, egalitarian bargaining solution, and Rubinstein bargaining solution. All the issues are covered in chapter 2.

In chapter 3, various game models are presented. As non-cooperative games, static game, dynamic game, sequential game, repeated game, stochastic game, jamming game, potential game, congestion game, Stackelberg game, differential game, Bayesian game, evolutionary game, supermodular game, global game, signaling game, intervention game, negotiation game, minority game, jamming game, and dictator game are explained. As cooperative games, coalitional game, coalition formation game, canonical coalition game, matching game, voting game, and bargaining games, such as Nash bargaining game, Kalai-Smorodinsky bargaining game, Rubinstein bargaining game, are introduced. Special domain of game theory, hybrid games, such as coopetition game and biform game, and reverse game theory, auction game, metagames, and modified game theory are presented.

Section 2 explores application fields of game theory, including wireless ad-hoc networks, smart grid, network security, cognitive radio, and network resource management. The purpose of this section is to study existing game models applied in the field of network design. Through this section, readers can find that game theory is tightly related to network design problems. Using game theory, existing network control approaches cannot only achieve the goal of the flexibility of network resource management and the higher utilization but also greatly facilitate the adjustment of working conditions. Until now, the applications were still in the initial stage of theoretical research; more in-depth research on the game theory in a variety of equilibrium and development of the application of new models are needed in order to ensure a more efficient and flexible network management. From section 2, readers can gain better understanding the existing game theoretic approaches for network design problems and some insights on further research directions.

Chapter 4 provides a tutorial survey and overview of the most recent practical implementations for wireless ad hoc networks. For ad hoc networks, game theory can offer an effective tool to model adaptations that may occur at different layers and also has a strong role to play in the development and analysis of protocols. This chapter shows that game theory can play a significant role to model adaptations that may occur at different layers in wireless ad hoc networks.

Chapter 5 presents game-theoretic approaches for the analysis of smart grid systems. Smart grid is a modernized electrical grid that uses information and communications technology to gather and act on information, such as information about the behaviors of suppliers and consumers, in an automated fashion to improve the efficiency, reliability, economics, and sustainability of the production and distribution of electricity. Since game theory has strong potential for the analysis of smart grid systems, game-theoretic approach presents a promising tool to address several emerging problems in SG systems.

Chapter 6 provides an overview and classifications of existing game theoretic approaches to network security. Network security involves the authorization of access to data in a network, which is controlled by the network administrator. Network security covers a variety of computer networks, both public and private, that are used in everyday jobs conducting transactions and communications among businesses, government agencies, and individuals. This survey highlights important game theoretic applications to network security.

In chapter 7, we classify state-of-the-art game theoretic research contributions on cognitive radio networks and provide a comprehensive overview of game models. A cognitive radio is a transceiver designed to use the best wireless channels in its vicinity. Such a radio automatically detects available channels in wireless spectrum, then accordingly changes its transmission or reception parameters to allow more concurrent wireless communications in a given spectrum band at one location. This process is a form of dynamic spectrum management. By using game theory, the spectrum sharing mechanism can achieve the higher spectrum utilization in cognitive radio networks.

Chapter 8 provides a tutorial overview on game theoretic approaches for the network resource management issues with the most recent practical implementations. Network resource management is one of the most challenging and important aspects of network design to significantly improve network performance. However, a proper understanding of a resource management algorithm often requires an understanding of a number of complex interrelated processes. In this chapter, we classify state-of-the-art research contributions on the network resource management and discuss the fundamental concepts and properties to explain on how to apply the game theory.

In section 3, each chapter covers the advanced game models developed for network design problems. This section deals with the case study of modeling, design, and analysis of game-theoretic schemes in communications and networking areas. Different game models have been applied to solve a diverse set of network design problems. In addition, under different practical constraints, some applications for different network scenarios are given as examples. By considering the technical challenges of a variety of networks, we will show how to employ different game models for different scenarios in cellular networks, wireless networks, ad-hoc and sensor networks, femto-cell networks, and wired communication networks.

In chapter 9, game-based network routing schemes are introduced; Cooperative Game Theoretic Online Routing (CGOR) scheme, Game Theoretic Multi-Objective Routing (GMOR) scheme, Incentive-Based Ad-Hoc Network Routing (IANR) scheme, Coopetition Game-Based Multi-Path Routing (CGMR) scheme, and Trust-Based Incentive Cooperative Relay Routing (TICRR) scheme are explained in detail. In the CGOR scheme, adaptive online path setup and packet distribution algorithms are developed for wireless networks. The most important feature of the CGOR scheme is the integrated approach by employing a coordination paradigm to provide the energy efficiency and network stability during network operations. The GMOR scheme is a new game-theoretic routing scheme for sensor networks. The IANR scheme is designed as an adaptive online routing scheme by using an incentive-based model. In the IANR scheme, new path-setup, incentive-computing, and reservation algorithms are developed. For practical network operations, these developed algorithms are designed in a self-organizing, dynamically online, and distributed fashion to work together in a coordinated manner. The CGMR scheme is designed based on the coopetition game model and simulated annealing approach. In the CGMR scheme, wireless nodes are assumed as self-interested game players and make local decisions in a distributed manner. Therefore, routing packets are adaptively distributed through multiple paths in pursuit of the main goals such as load balancing and network reliability. For wireless networks, the TICRR scheme can take into account the measure of the probability of a relay node succeeding at a given relay service and maximize the network performance. By considering the current network condition, the TICRR scheme can select the most adaptable relay node and pay the incentive-price for relay service.

In chapter 10, power control schemes based on game theory are introduced; Evolutionary Game-Based Power Control (EGPC) scheme, Stackelberg Game-Based Power Control (SGPC) scheme, Dynamic Voltage Scaling (DVS) scheme, Weighted Voting-Based Power Control (WVPC) scheme, and Intervention Game-Based Multi-Objective Power Control (IGMPC) scheme are explained in detail. The

EGPC scheme is a new adaptive online power control scheme based on the evolutionary game theory. In this scheme, wireless devices are assumed to be self-regarding game players and make their decisions for the goal of maximizing their perceived payoffs. The SGPC scheme adopts the Stackelberg game model to design an adaptive power control algorithm. In the SGPC scheme, the traditional Stackelberg game is extended a dynamic iterative game model; players dynamically adapt their decisions based on the result of adaptive feedback process. In the DVS scheme, a new adaptive dynamic voltage-scaling algorithm is developed for QoS assurance and energy efficiency. Based on the repeated learning model, the developed algorithm dynamically schedules multimedia service requests to strike the appropriate performance balance between contradictory requirements. By using the concept of the weighted voting game, the WVPC scheme adaptively adjusts a transmit power level while ensuring relevant tradeoff between system efficiency and fairness. This power control paradigm can provide the ability to practically respond to current communication conditions and suitable for real network operations. The IGMPC scheme is developed for the femtocell network power control problem. In this scheme, the major issue is to provide the most proper combination of the efficiency and fairness issues. To deal with this multi-objective control problem, the IGMPC scheme employs the no-regret learning technique and intervention game model to design a power control scheme.

In chapter 11, game-based control schemes for resource allocation problems are explained; Nash Bargaining-Based Bandwidth Management (*NBBM*) scheme, Nash Bargaining-Based Voltage Scaling (*NBVS*) scheme, Kalai-Smorodinsky Bargaining-Based Bandwidth Adjustment (*KSBBA*) scheme, Negotiation Game-Based Cooperative Bandwidth Bargaining (*NGCBB*) scheme, Blotto Game-Based Strategic Resource Allocation (*BGSRA*) scheme, and Intervenient Stackelberg Game-Based Bandwidth Allocation (*ISGBA*) scheme are introduced. In the *NBBM* scheme, effective bandwidth management algorithms are designed for multimedia cellular networks. Based on the concept of Nash Bargaining Solution (NBS), the developed algorithms effectively allocate the bandwidth among multiple services while providing the required QoS. The *NBVS scheme* is developed as a new online multiprocessor power control scheme based on the NBS model, and would employ a dynamic online methodology for power management, which can improve adaptability under widely different and diversified multiprocessor system situations. The main design goal of the *NBVS* scheme is to simultaneously maximize energy efficiency while ensuring all task deadlines. The *KSBBA* scheme employed the Kalai-Smorodinsky Bargaining Solution (KSBS) for the development of an adaptive bandwidth adjustment algorithm. In addition, to effectively manage the bandwidth in virtual private networks, the developed control paradigm is realized in a dynamic online approach, which is practical for real network operations. By integrating the Nash and Kalai-Smorodinsky bargaining models, the *NGCBB* scheme adaptively controls the wireless bandwidth to maximize network efficiency. In the developed NBS and KSBS models, bargaining powers in the *NGCBB* scheme are decided according to the real-time negotiation process. It is a powerful method for resolving conflicts and enables the system to fairly and effectively control the bandwidth management problem. Blotto Game-Based Strategic Resource Allocation (*BGSRA*) scheme is developed for security problem. Blotto game constitutes a class of two-person zero-sum game in which the players are tasked to simultaneously distribute limited resources over several objects. For the efficient resource allocation, the *BGSRA* scheme employs the iterative bargaining approach to respond the current conditions. The *ISGBA* scheme derives a multi-objective decision criterion for each access point and develops a bargaining strategy selection algorithm for the dynamic bandwidth re-allocation. Based on the intervenient Stackelberg game model, the *ISGBA* scheme effectively formulates the competitive interaction situation between several access points for hierarchical wireless network systems.

In chapter 12, wireless bandwidth management schemes by using game models are introduced in detail. QoS-Aware Bandwidth Allocation (QoSBA) scheme, Adaptive Call Admission Control (ACAC) scheme, Mechanism Design-Based Online Bandwidth Allocation (MDOBA) scheme, Negotiation Bargaining Game-Based Bandwidth Management (NBGBM) scheme, and Dual-Level Bandwidth Management (DLBM) scheme are explained. The QoSBA scheme is developed as a new bandwidth allocation algorithm for multimedia networks. Based on the Modified Game Theory (MGT), the bandwidth is adaptively allocated to satisfy different QoS requirements. In addition, by using the Talmud allocation rule, a weight parameter is adjusted periodically to ensure the allocation fairness. Therefore, the system dynamically re-estimates the current network condition and iteratively adapts control decisions. The ACAC scheme is designed as an online call admission control scheme for the heterogeneous overlay network system. This scheme consists of network evaluation, selection and price computation algorithms. To effectively decide the service price, the methodology that the ACAC scheme adopted is the VCG mechanism; it can provide an excellent solution for the price computation problem. The main goal of the ACAC scheme is to maximize system efficiency while ensuring QoS prioritization. The MDOBA scheme is developed as a new adaptive online bandwidth allocation scheme for multimedia services. This scheme consists of bandwidth adaptation, price computation and CAC algorithms; these algorithms are sophisticatedly combined and mutually dependent on each other. This integrated approach gives excellent control flexibility under widely different and diversified network situations. The NBGBM scheme is developed for multi-hop cellular networks. By using the trust-based random arrival approach, the NBGBM scheme dynamically allocates the bandwidth in multi-hop relaying networks. The DLBM scheme is designed as a game-theoretic bandwidth management mechanism for the hierarchical multi-layer network system. The main goal of the DLBM scheme is to maximize bandwidth efficiency while providing service prioritization. Under various QoS constraints and dynamically changing network environments, it is almost impossible that a single control approach will achieve an optimal network performance. The DLBM scheme is designed as a dual-level structure, which consists of inter-network and intra-network bandwidth management algorithms.

In chapter 13, game-based control mechanisms for cognitive radio networks is introduced; Two-Way Matching Game-Based Bandwidth Sharing (TMGBS) scheme, Multi-Leader Multi-Follower Stackelberg (MMS) scheme, Reversed Stackelberg Bandwidth Sharing (RSBS) scheme, Trust-Based Radio Spectrum Sharing (TRSS) scheme, Repeated Bayesian-Based Spectrum Auction (RBSA) scheme, and Learning-Based Spectrum Sharing (LSS) scheme are explained in detail. The TMGBS scheme is a new adaptive cognitive radio bandwidth-sharing scheme based on the game theory. The main goal of the TMGBS scheme is to maximize the revenue of primary users while maximizing the bandwidth efficiency along with the satisfaction of the secondary users. To satisfy the design goal, the methodologies that the TMGBS scheme adopted are the two-sided matching game and modified game theory. The MMS scheme is a new multi-leader Stackelberg game-based spectrum-sharing scheme that solves the joint problem of licensed and unlicensed users in cognitive radio networks. To improve the spectrum utilization and users' satisfaction, control decisions are iteratively adjusted based on the feedback learning process. Therefore, the MMS scheme can capture the hierarchical interaction among players to get the desirable solution between two conflicting objectives – efficiency and fairness. The RSBS scheme is another hierarchical bandwidth-sharing scheme based on a reversed Stackelberg game model. Taking into account that both the base station and relay stations are selfish and rational, Stackelberg game is a powerful tool to model the bandwidth-sharing problem in multi-hop relaying cellular networks. The TRSS scheme is developed as a new spectrum-sharing scheme based on the game theory. This scheme is designed as a repeated Bayesian auction game. In the RBSA scheme, primary and secondary users are assumed to be self-regarding game players and make their decisions for the goal of maximizing their perceived payoffs. To adaptively decide their strategies, the basic concept of Bayesian inference technique is adopted. The LSS scheme is a new CR spectrum sharing algorithm by employing the dynamic coopetition game model. Coopetition game approach is an effective tool to describe CR sharing problems. The LSS scheme dynamically senses the spectrum based on the global game and efficiently re-allocates the available spectrum according to the trust-proportional bargaining approach.

In chapter 14, we consider the economic approach for network management; Stackelberg Game-Based Price Control (SGPC) scheme, Market Sharing Game-Based Bandwidth Management (MSGBM) scheme, Bargaining and Fictitious Play-Based Bandwidth Management (BFPBM) scheme, and Public Goods Game-Based File Sharing (PGGFS) scheme are investigated. The SGPC scheme is an adaptive online price control scheme based on the bi-level Stackelberg game model. In the SGPC scheme, the main challenge is to design a price control algorithm to use bandwidth as efficiently as possible. The MSGBM scheme develops a new bandwidth management algorithm for wireless network operations. In the MSGBM scheme, several access providers serve a set of users and users pay the price per bandwidth unit to the corresponding AP access. This interaction mechanism among independent access providers and users is modeled as the market sharing game. The BFPBM scheme effectively formulates the competitive interaction situation between several access providers and their users. The important feature of the BFPBM scheme is an ability to maintain bandwidth efficiency as high as possible by adaptively responding to current network system situations. In addition, the BFPBM scheme can provide a good tradeoff between the implementation complexity for the network management and optimized network performance. The PGGFS scheme is developed for P2P file sharing networks. To escape the social dilemma, the PGGFS scheme pays serious attention to trust evaluation, repeated interactions, and evolutionary learning techniques. In the PGGFS scheme, such techniques have been incorporated into the original public good game, and trust-based P2P mechanism is developed to induce all peers to share files as many as possible.

In chapter 15, we review the game based control approach for smart grid; Biform Game-Based Cognitive Radio Control (BGCRC) scheme and Coopetition Game-Based Grouping and Scheduling (CGGS) scheme are presented in detail. To support the fast-growing demand, the BGCRC scheme presents a biform game based cognitive radio communication algorithm, which is mainly motivated to use the unlicensed bandwidth while ensuring the need of explosive data traffic. The developed biform game approach is suitable to get a globally desirable network performance. The CGGS scheme is developed as a new smart grid management scheme. To maximize the overall system performance while satisfying the requirements of the individual appliances, this CGGS scheme consists of competitive grouping algorithm and cooperative scheduling algorithm. Therefore, this model is part competition and part cooperation.

In chapter 16, we investigate the game paradigm for wired networks; Evolutionary Minority Game-Based Congestion Control (EMGCC) scheme is explained in detail. The EMGCC scheme has been developed based on the evolutionary minority game model. In the EMGCC scheme, sender nodes (i.e., source nodes for packet transmissions) estimate the current traffic condition and adaptively select the best packet transmission strategy based on the real-time online monitoring. The main goal is to maximize network efficiency while ensuring QoS prioritization.

In chapter 17, recent game theory developments are discussed with reading lists and a few questions are considered looking towards the future of game theory. The development of game theory since the 1950s is given, together with some important open problems. The purpose of this chapter is to present a broad brush picture of the many areas of game theory and to predict the future research direction of game theory.

In summary, modern networks have become multifaceted, providing support for numerous bandwidth-hungry applications and a variety of devices, ranging from smart phones to tablet PCs to high-end servers. In addition, modern users expect the network to be available all the time, from any device, and to let them securely collaborate with coworkers. Game theory and convenient modeling have greatly facilitated the implementation of mathematical programming theory into the practice of commercial network design. This book systematically introduces the application of game theory in network design and surveys state-of-the-art game models for design, analysis, and management of networks, such as cellular, femtocell, mobile ad-hoc, overlay, sensor, and wireless local area networks. It provides a comprehensive technical guide covering introductory concepts, fundamental techniques, recent advances, and open issues in related topics.

This book can enable readers to grasp the fundamental concepts of game theory and their applications. Through the use of some state-of the-art control examples for different networks, we will illustrate the wide varieties of topics and their potential future design directions. This point is equally relevant and applicable in today's world of wireless network technology and design.

This book is intended primarily for use by network engineers, architects, or technicians who have a working knowledge of network protocols and technologies. In addition, this book will provide practical advice on applying the knowledge to internetwork design for graduate students in computer science, mathematics, and electrical engineering. Finally, this book is equally well-suited for self-study technical professionals since it discusses engineering issues in algorithm design as well as mathematical aspects.

Sungwook Kim
Sogang University, South Korea

Acknowledgment

I would like to thank many for their support. First and foremost, I am deeply grateful beyond my words to my academic advisor, Dr. Pramod K. Varshney, for his invaluable advice, criticism, faith, encouragement, and above all his thoughtfulness, which has made my work finally complete. He has given me academic guidance and has stood by me each and every time.

I can say that I have enjoyed my life. This is because of all the wonderful people I've been surrounded by. There are too many angels in my life that I need to give my thanks to, and I could not possibly give thanks to them all. Therefore, I would like to give my deepest and most sincere thanks to God, who kindly sent these angels to me.

My biggest thanks go to my parents, who always gave me their love, emotional support, and encouragement for as long as long as I can remember. They have been there throughout every challenge in my life. This book is dedicated to them. In addition, these acknowledgements would not be complete if I did not mention my grandparents. I hope they are looking down from somewhere with a smile. Words cannot truly express my deepest gratitude and appreciation to them. Definitely, they are remembered and accepted by me, now and forever.

Last but not the least, I cannot end without thanking my graduate students. They are the best. I am so incredibly grateful for each and every one of my students. I am forever grateful to have them in my life. I know they are there and I appreciate that more than they could ever understand.

Sungwook Kim
Sogang University, South Korea

Quotes and Testimonials

Find the truly original idea—that's the only way I will ever distinguish myself—it's the only way I'll ever...matter.

I've made the most important discovery of my life. It's only in the mysterious equation of love that any logical reasons can be found. I'm only here tonight because of you. You're the only reason I am...you are all my reasons.

A Beautiful Mind (2001)

Premier ne puis, second ne daigne, Mouton suis.

(First, I cannot be. Second, I do not condescend to be. Mouton, I am)

Premier je suis, Second je fus, Mouton ne change.

(First, I am. Second, I used to be. Mouton, I do not change)

Château Mouton Rothschild (1855, 1973)

In the land of research, you cannot walk by the light of someone else's lamp. You want to borrow mine. I would rather teach you how to make your own. Teaching only takes place when learning does. Learning only takes place when you teach something to yourself. The day you follow someone you cease to follow Truth. There was once a student who never became a mathematician because he blindly believed the answers he found at the back of his math textbook – and, ironically, the answers were correct. Please listen to every word no one was saying.

Anthony de Mello (1985)

Section 1
Fundamental Ideas of Game Theory

Chapter 1
Introduction

ABSTRACT

The situations to which game theory has actually been applied reflect its selective usefulness for problems and solutions of an individualistic and competitive nature, building in the values of the status quo. The main principal area of application has been economics. In economics, game theory has been used in studying competition for markets, advertising, planning under uncertainty, and so forth. Recently, game theory has also been applied to many other fields, such as law, ethics, sociology, biology, and of course, computer science. In all these applications, a close study of the formulation of the problem in the game theory perspective shows a strong inclination to work from existing values, to consider only currently contending parties and options, and in other ways, to exclude significant redefinitions of the problems at hand. This introductory chapter explores these and forms a basis for the rest of the book.

INTRODUCTION

Network Design is one of the most active research areas in computer science involving researchers from system architecture, networks, algorithm development, optimization technique, artificial intelligence and information theory. Generally, network design includes problems ranging from allocation of network resources, analysis and effects of competitive and/or cooperative agents, network protocols, network dynamics, performance optimization, to network traffic and topology control. In addition, many new network design paradigms such as sensor, ad hoc network management and smart grid networking add rich new flavors to existing problems. Usually, networks are a complicated mix of applications, protocols, device and link technologies, traffic flows, and routing algorithms. There may be tens of thousands of feasible configurations, each with different performance attributes and costs. Therefore, network design is challenging, requiring designers to balance user performance expectations with network-resource costs, capacities, capabilities, and use levels (Bragg, 2000).

Many systems that can be modeled using network design approach appear in various fields such as informatics, social science, economics, ecology, biology and engineering. If these systems can be modeled as complex network systems, a network design method that finds a desired network structure can become one of strong tools in large-scale system designs. With conventional network design methods, new network design

DOI: 10.4018/978-1-4666-6050-2.ch001

methods have been proposed (Mizuno, Okamoto, Koakutsu & Hirata 2012).

Optimization approach is one of the most important methods in network design. Therefore, a lot of research has been conducted to find an optimal solution for network control problems. In traditional optimization processes, one is quite often faced by a situation where more than one selfish agent is involved in decision making. Different agents might typically have different objectives. To get the optimal solution on the network design, multiple objective optimization techniques are necessary by taking into account complex interactions among network components. However, due to the model complexity among conflicting network performance criteria, it is practically unable to implement realistic network models. Recent results show a strong relation between network design and game theory. Game theory, an alternative name is interactive decision theory, is the study of mathematical models of conflict and cooperation between intelligent rational decision makers. It is a branch of applied mathematics as well as of applied science.

As the name of the theory suggests, game theory was first used to describe and model how human populations behave. Some scholars believe that they can actually predict how actual human populations will behave when confronted with situations analogous to the game being studied. Due to this reason, the essence of a game is the interdependence of player strategies. Therefore, game theory is thought as a science of strategy. It attempts to determine mathematically and logically the actions that *players* should take to secure the best outcomes for themselves in a wide array of *games* (Crossman, n.d.).

Usually, a game is a formal description of a strategic situation, and game theory is the study of decision-making where several players must make choices that potentially affect the interests of the other players. Game theory was originally an economic and mathematical theory that predicted

that human interaction had the characteristics of a game, including strategies, winners and losers, rewards and punishment, profits and cost, behavior of firms, markets, and consumers. The use of the game theory has since expanded in the social sciences and has been applied to political, sociological, and psychological behaviors as well. Recent advances in game theory have succeeded in describing and prescribing appropriate strategies in several situations of conflict and cooperation. But the theory is far from complete, and in many ways the design of successful strategy remains an art (Dixit, & Nalebuff, n.d.).

The basic ideas of game theory have appeared in various forms throughout history and in numerous sources, including the Bible, the Talmud, the writings of Charles Darwin, Brouwer's fixed-point theorem and so on. In game theory, the basic assumption is that the decision makers pursue some well defined objectives and take into account their knowledge or expectations of the other decision makers' behavior (Han, Niyato, Saad, Başar, & Hjørungnes 2011).

HISTORY OF GAME THEORY

Early discussions of games occurred long before the rise of modern, mathematical game theory. One reason why game is an exciting activity for humans is that it couples intellectual activity with direct competition; better thinking and learning generally results in winning more games. Thus, humans can test out and refine their intellectual skills by playing games against opponents, and evaluate their progress based on the results of the competition. During the first five centuries A.D., one problem discussed in the Babylonian Talmud is the so called marriage contract problem. Nowadays, it is recognized that the Talmud anticipates the modern theory of cooperative games ("Game theory," n.d.).

Game Theory in 19th Century

In 1713, James Waldegrave provided a minimax mixed strategy solution to a two-person version of the card game. Waldegrave's solution is a minimax mixed strategy equilibrium, but he made no extension of his result to other games, and expressed concern that a mixed strategy does not seem to be in the usual rules of play of games of chance (Walker, 2012). Although the practice of game theory dates back to Babylonian times or ancient Chinese history, the modern description of game theory is generally considered to have begun with the formal study of games was done by Antoine A. Cournot in 1838. He considered a duopoly and presented a solution that is a restricted version of the Nash equilibrium. In 1871, Charles Darwin gave his first game theoretic argument in evolutionary biology. Darwin argued that natural selection will act to equalize the sex ratio, which is the equilibrium. In 1881, Francis Y. Edgeworth proposed the contract curve as a solution to the problem of determining the outcome of trading between individuals. The concept of the core is a generalization of Edgeworth's contract curve ("Game theory," n.d.).

Game Theory in 1920s-1940s

In 1921-1927, Émile Borel proved a minimax theorem for two-person zero-sum matrix games only when the pay-off matrix was symmetric. Initially, he maintained that games with more possible strategies would not have minimax solutions, but by 1927, he considered this an open question as he had been unable to find a counter-example (Barran, M., n.d.). In 1928, John von Neumann demonstrated his minimax theory and provided a standard game method based on the Brouwer's fixed-point theorem. It stated that every two-person zero-sum game with finitely many pure strategies for each player is determined when mixed strategies are admitted. This variety of game has precisely one individually rational

payoff vector (Han, 2011). In 1930, the Danish mathematician F. Zeuthen proposed a solution to the bargaining problem. Later, J. Harsanyi showed that it is equivalent to Nash's bargaining solution (Harsanyi, & Selten, 1988). In 1937, John von Neumann was pursuing his topological work on the application of the fixed-point theorem, and discovered the existence of a connection between the minimax problem in game theory and the saddle point problem as an equilibrium in economic theory. In 1938, F. Zeuthen proved that the mathematical model had a winning strategy by using Brouwer's fixed point theorem. In 1934, German economist Stackelberg proposed a hierarchical strategic game model based on two kinds of different decision makers (Walker, 2012). However, game theory did not really exist as a unique field until Neumann published his book *Theory of Games and Economic Behavior*, with Oskar Morgenstern in 1944. This book provided an axiomatic theory of expected utility, which allowed mathematical statisticians and economists to treat decision-making under uncertainty ("Game theory," n.d.). This foundational work contains the method for finding mutually consistent solutions for two-person zero-sum games (Neumann & Morgenstern 1944).

Game Theory in 1950s-1960s

Game theory was developed extensively in the 1950s and 1960s. In 1950, Merrill M. Flood and Melvin Dresher discussed the prisoner's dilemma. During this time period, John Nash developed a criterion for mutual consistency of players' strategies, known as Nash equilibrium (Barran, M., n.d.). Nash equilibrium is a set of strategies such that no player has incentive to unilaterally change his action. This equilibrium is sufficiently general to allow for the analysis of non-cooperative games. Therefore, it has been a basic point of analysis since then. The publication of Nash's profoundly innovative articles in the early 1950s quickly refreshed the thinking of those few economists who had been seduced by game theory, and thereafter they directed their energies towards retrospective reconstructions. In 1951, George W. Brown described and discussed a simple iterative method for approximating solutions of discrete zero-sum games (Walker, 2012).

In the 1950s, the concepts of the core, the extensive form game, fictitious play, repeated games, matching games and the Shapley value were developed. The notion of the core as a general solution concept was developed by Lloyd Shapley and D. B. Gillies ("Game theory," n.d.). The core is the set of allocations that cannot be improved upon by any coalition. In 1953, L. Shapley characterized a solution concept that associates with each coalitional game. This solution is known as the Shapley Value. Along with the Shapley value, Lloyd Shapley developed the concept of stochastic game and potential game with Dov Monderer during 1950s. Around this same time, the first applications of game theory to philosophy and political science occurred. In 1954, one of the earliest applications of game theory to political science is the work of L. Shapley and M. Shubik. During 1954-55, differential games were developed by Rufus Isaacs. These games grew out of the problem of forming and solving military pursuit games. In 1955, R. B. Braithwaite proposed one of the first applications of game theory to philosophy and M. Shubik rediscovered in Cournot's work the premises of Nash's concept of equilibrium. In 1959, the notion of a strong equilibrium was introduced by R. J. Aumann and the relationship between Edgeworth's idea of the contract curve and the core was pointed out by M. Shubik (Aumann, & Maschler, 1995). Late 1950s, the first studies of repeated games were developed. At this time, the main result of Folk theorem appeared. The Folk theorem states that the equilibrium outcomes in an infinitely repeated game coincide with the feasible and strongly individually rational outcomes of the one-shot game on which it is based (Walker, 2012).

In 1961, William Vickrey introduced a new type of sealed-bid auction, where bidders submit written bids without knowing the bid of the other people in the auction, and in which the highest bidder wins, but the price paid is the second-highest bid (Vane, & Mulhearn, 2010). This auction format pointed out that bidders have a dominant strategy to bid their true values. In 1964, Carlton E. Lemke and J.T. Howson, Jr., described an algorithm for finding a Nash equilibrium in a bimatrix game. They also gave a constructive proof of the existence of an equilibrium point. In 1965, Reinhard Selten introduced his solution concept of subgame perfect equilibrium, which is an equilibrium such that players' strategies constitute a Nash equilibrium in every subgame of the original game (Harsanyi, 1988). In 1967, John Harsanyi developed the concepts of complete information and Bayesian games for the economic game model. This laid the theoretical groundwork for information economics that has become one of the major themes of economics and game theory (Han, 2011). In 1969, David Schmeidler introduced the concept of Nucleolus (Walker, 2012).

Game Theory in 1970s-1990s

In the 1970s, game theory was extensively applied in biology. In 1972, John Maynard Smith developed evolutionary game model and introduced the concept of an Evolutionarily Stable Strategy (ESS). Evolutionary game provides a dynamic framework for analyzing repeated interaction, and the ESS concept has since found increasing use within the economics and biology literature ("Evolutionary Game Theory," 2009). In 1973, Michael Spence proposed a signal game model to analyze job market signaling (Vane, 2010). One of the major uses of signal games both in economics and biology has been to determine under what conditions honest signaling can be an equilibrium of the game. Later, the signal game was extended as a screening game by David M. Kreps. In 1974, Robert Aumann introduced the concept of correlated equilibrium, which is a more general game solution than the well known Nash equilibrium (Aumann, 1995). In 1975, E. Kalai and M. Smorodinsky replaced Nash's independence of irrelevant alternatives axiom with a monotonicity axiom. The resulting solution is known as the Kalai-Smorodinsky solution. During the 1960s and 1970s, Leonid Hurwicz, Eric Maskin, and Roger Myerson had introduced and formalized the concept of incentive compatibility and developed a solution concept for a class of private information games by motivating players to disclose their private information (Altmana, Boulognea, El-Azouzia, Jiménezb & Wynterc 2006).

In 1982, David M. Kreps and Robert Wilson extended the idea of a subgame perfect equilibrium to subgames in the extensive form that began at information sets with imperfect information (Walker, 2012). They called this extended idea as sequential equilibria. In 1982, A. Rubinstein considered a non-cooperative approach to bargaining. He considered an alternating-offer game; offers are made sequentially until one is accepted. There is no bound on the number of offers that can be made but there is a cost to delay for each player. A. Rubinstein showed that the subgame perfect equilibrium is unique when each player's cost of time is given by some discount factor. In 1988, John C. Harsanyi and Reinhard Selten produced the first general theory of selecting between equilibria. They provided criteria for selecting one particular equilibrium point for any non-cooperative or cooperative game (Harsanyi, 1988). Game theory received special attention in 1994 with the awarding of the Nobel Prize in economics to J. Nash. Since then, many game theorists have won the Nobel Memorial Prize. At the end of the 1990s, game theory has been practically used in the design of auctions for allocating rights to the use of the electromagnetic spectrum bands to the mobile telecommunications industry (Walker, 2012). Today, game theory is a sort of umbrella or unified field theory for the rational side of social science, where social is interpreted broadly, to include human as well as non-human players (i.e., computers, animals, plants).

APPLIED AREAS OF GAME THEORY

Game theory is formally a branch of mathematics developed to deal with conflict-of-interest situations in social science. Although the origins of the theory can be traced to early mathematical articles in 1920s, the literature of the field has expanded enormously (Levine, n.d.). Initially, many applications of game theory are related to economics, but it has been applied to numerous fields ranging from political science, sociology, psychology, law, military science, moral philosophy, biology, information sciences to transportation engineering, and so on. Since the early 1990s, computer science and telecommunications have been added to this list.

Game Theory for Economics

Economics is the social science that analyzes the production, distribution, and consumption of goods and services. Game theory is the study of multi-person decision problems and a mathematically formalized theory of strategic interactions for modeling competing behaviors of rational agents. Such multi-person problems arise frequently in economics. Therefore, economics is one important field of game theory (Buck, n.d.). In the sixty years since the appearance of von Neumann and Morgenstern's book, game theory has been widely applied to problems in economics. Economists have suggested suitable game models of a particular economic situation, and presented various solution concepts. In economics, applications of game theory include a wide array such as auctions, bargaining, pricing, fair division, duopolies, oligopolies, mechanism design, etc (Han, 2011).

At the micro level of economics, models of trading processes (e.g., bargaining and auction models) involve game theory. Nowadays, it would be difficult to imagine a course in micro-economics that did not refer to game theory. At an intermediate level, labor and financial economics include game-theoretic models of the behavior of a firm in markets. At a high level of economics, international economics includes models in which the monetary authority and wage or price setters interact strategically to determine the effects of monetary policy (Gibbons, 1992).

In the development between game theory and economic theory, the role of the Hungarian mathematical genius, John von Neumann, appears more complex. An economic game theory perhaps preceded the mathematical theory elaborated by him. While he remains the undeniable intermediary between the mathematics of games and economics, it is necessary to recognize that he has contributed to eclipsing the old strategic approach to economic problems. At the end of the 1970s, the connections between game theory and economics entered a new phase. The game theory approach had progressively invaded the majority of sectors of economic analysis. Such was the case first of all with industrial economy, which was renewed by the contribution of games. Insurance economics, then monetary economics and financial economics and a part of international economics, all, one by one, were marked by this development. The economy of well-being and of justice have been affected, and more recently the economics of law. This particular evolution of game theory contradicts the prophecy of its principal founder. The relation between game theory and economic science is in the process of reversing itself. Economics is today no longer the domain of application for a mathematical theory. It has become the engine of development for a branch of knowledge. Indeed, a growing amount of cutting-edge research in game theory is the work of economists or of mathematicians who have converted to economics (Schmidt, 2002).

Game Theorists Who Have Received the Nobel Prize in Economics

Today, game theory has remains at the state-of-the-art of economic theory, with game theorists winning the Nobel Prize in Economics in 1994, 1996, 2001, 2005, 2007 and 2012. In 1994, J. Nash won the Nobel in 1994, along with game theorists John Harsanyi and Reinhard Selten. J. Nash established the mathematical principles of game theory, a branch of mathematics that examines the rivalries among competitors with mixed interests. Known as the Nash solution or the Nash equilibrium, his theory attempted to explain the dynamics of threat and action among competitors. Despite its practical limitations, the Nash solution was widely applied by business strategists. J. Harsanyi built on the work of Nash and enhanced Nash's equilibrium model by introducing the predictability of rivals' action based on the chance that they would choose one move or countermove over another (Walker, 2012). Harsanyi was also an ethics scholar who conducted formal investigations on appropriate behavior and correct social choices among competitors. Refining the research of Nash, R. Selten proposed theories that distinguished between reasonable and unreasonable decisions in predicting the outcome of games (Harsanyi, 1988). William Vickrey won the Nobel in 1996 for his pioneering work in incentives, asymmetric information, and auction theory, all crucial to the advance of effective strategy in a world of influence like chess, football, military strategy and business. In 2001, A. Michael Spence won the Nobel Prize for laying the foundations for the theory of markets with asymmetric information. Through his research on markets with asymmetric information, Spence developed the theory of signaling to show how better-informed individuals in the market communicate their information to the less-well-informed to avoid the problems associated with adverse selection (Vane, 2010). Later, it extended as a signaling game. Thomas Schelling and Robert Aumann won the 2005 Nobel for their game-theoretic work in conflict and cooperation, including contributions on credible commitments and repeated games. Aumann employed a mathematical approach to show that long-term social interaction could be analyzed using formal non-cooperative game theory. Through his methodologies and analyses of so-called infinitely repeated games, he identified the outcomes that could be sustained in long-term relations and demonstrated the prerequisites for cooperation in situations where there are many participants, infrequent interaction, or the potential for a break in relations and when participants' actions lack transparency (Aumann, 1995). Aumann also showed that peaceful cooperation is often an equilibrium solution in a repeated game even when the parties have strong short-term conflicting interests. Thus, cooperation is not necessarily dependent on goodwill or an outside arbiter (Aumann, 1995). Aumann named this observation the '*folk theorem*'. In 2007, Leonid Hurwicz, Eric Maskin and Roger Myerson won the Nobel prize for their work in mechanism design theory, a branch of game theory that extends the application of game theory to how different types of rules, or institutions, align individual incentives with overall social goals. Their work on allocation mechanisms has had a significant impact on the design of auctions, social welfare systems and many organizations (Myerson, 1997). Basically, mechanism design theory tries to simulate market conditions in such a way as to maximize gains for all parties. As buyers and sellers within a market rarely know one another's motives or ambitions, resources may be lost or misallocated because of information asymmetry. Myerson addressed this problem by proposing the revelation principle, wherein buyers are offered an incentive for truthfully reporting what they would pay for goods or services (Myerson, 1997). As described by Hurwicz, mechanism design theory addresses the gap in knowledge that exists between buyers and sellers. In ideal conditions, all parties have

equal information about the pricing of goods within markets (Hurwicz, & Reiter, 2008). In real world conditions, however, information asymmetry prevents buyers from knowing how much a seller should charge and limits the ability of sellers to determine how much a buyer will pay. The 'mechanism' of mechanism design is a specialized game in which participants submit messages to a central point and a rule determines the allocation of resources based on those messages. As a result of his study of mechanism design, Hurwicz concluded that the most efficient market system for both buyers and sellers is the double auction (Hurwicz, 2008). In addition, implementation theory introduced mechanisms to the market that would lead to optimal outcomes for all participants. This work had applications in the financial sector, in studies of voter behavior, and in business management (Breit, & Hirsch, 2009). Most recently, in 2012, the Nobel was awarded to Lloyd Shapley and Alvin Roth for their work using game theory for economic engineering. Shapley used cooperative game theory to study and compare different matching methods. A key part of Shapley's work was the deferred acceptance algorithm, which was devised to solve matching problems. A. Roth built on Shapley's theoretical work by showing empirically the conditions for the functioning of important markets in practice, and he demonstrated that stability is the key to understanding the success of particular market institutions (Roth, 2002).

Game Theory for Business Administration

Business administration is interchangeable with the performance or management of business operations, maybe including important decision making. Therefore, it is likely to include the efficient organization of people and other resources so as to direct activities toward common goals and objectives. In any business, interactions with customers, suppliers, other business partners, and competitors, as well as interactions across people and different organizations within the firm, play an integral role in any decision and its consequences. Due to globalization, now the entire world is the playground for many firms, increasing the complexity of these interactions. Given that each firm is part of a complex Web of interactions, any business decision or action taken by a firm impacts multiple entities that interact with or within that firm, and vice versa. Ignoring these interactions could lead to unexpected and potentially very undesirable outcomes (Erhun & Keskinocak, 2003).

As the interest of game theory grew, many researchers have focused on how game theory can help in a company's success in the competitive market place. The basic understanding of game theory is used to analyze a vast variety of interactions, ranging from individuals within firms competing in markets to nations engaged in international negotiations. Obviously, game theory can provide business models to look beyond their default view of people and companies they are working with. In business field, the most important practical application of game theory has been the study of crises in financial markets such as bank runs, currency crises, and bubbles. In addition, there are other relevant applications such as investments with payoff complementarities, firm competitions, revolutions and any other situation which displays strategic complementarity. Recently, a new hybrid game approach has been applied to business strategy. It is designed to formalize the notion of business strategy as making moves to try to shape the competitive environment in a favorable way (Colin, 2003, Brandenburger & Stuart 2007).

Principal-Agent Problem

In many business games, the actions of some players have direct consequences for other players. For example, the performance of a company, and in turn, the value to the shareholders, depends on the actions of the managers and workers that are part of the company. In recent years, there are some examples where top management engaged in misconduct to increase their own compensation while hurting both the shareholders and the workers. Since most shareholders are not directly involved in the operations of a company, it is important that compensation schemes align the interests of the workers and managers with those of the shareholders. This situation falls into the framework of *principal-agent* problems.

Principal-agent problem is a particular game-theoretic description of a situation. There is a player called a principal, and one or more other players called agents with utility functions that are in some sense different from the principal's. The principal can act more effectively through the agents than directly, and must construct incentive schemes to get them to behave at least partly according to the principal's interests. The actions of the agents may not be observable so it is not usually sufficient for the principal just to condition payment on the actions of the agents. In the *principal-agent* problem, the principal (i.e., shareholders) cannot directly control or monitor the actions of the agent (i.e., managers and workers), but can do so through incentives. Many business situations fall into the *principal-agent* framework, such as the relationships between auto manufacturers and dealers, prospective home buyers and real estate agents, franchisers and franchisees, and auctioneers and bidders. For *principal-agent* problems, game theory can improve strategic decision-making by providing valuable insights into the interactions of multiple self-interested agents and therefore it is increasingly being used in business and economics (Erhun & Keskinocak 2003).

Game Theory for Finance

Finance is the study of how people allocate their assets over time under conditions of certainty and uncertainty (Yasuda, 2010). A key point in finance, which affects decisions, is the time value of money, which states that a unit of currency today is worth more than the same unit of currency tomorrow. Finance aims to price assets based on their risk level, and expected rate of return. Therefore, finance is concerned with how the savings of investors are allocated through financial markets and intermediaries to firms, which use them to fund their activities. Usually, finance can be broadly divided into two fields. The first is *asset pricing*, which is concerned with the decisions of investors. The second is *corporate finance*, which is concerned with the decisions of firms. Traditional neoclassical economics did not attach much importance to either kind of finance. It was more concerned with the production, pricing and allocation of inputs and outputs and the operation of the markets for these. Therefore, models in traditional economics assumed certainty and in this context financial decisions are relatively straightforward. However, even with this simple methodology, important concepts such as the time value of money and discounting were developed. The inability of standard finance theories to provide satisfactory explanations for observed phenomena lead to a search for theories using new methodologies. This was particularly true in corporate finance where the existing models were so clearly unsatisfactory. Game theory has provided a methodology that has brought insights into many previously unexplained phenomena by allowing asymmetric information and strategic interaction to be incorporated into the analysis (Allen & Morris, 2002).

In *asset pricing*, the focus of Keynesian macroeconomics on uncertainly and the operation of financial markets led to the development of frameworks for analyzing risk. J. Keynes and J. Hicks took account of risk by adding a risk premium to the interest rate. However, there was no systematic theory underlying this risk premium. The key theoretical development was J. von Neumann and O. Morgenstern's axiomatic approach to choice under uncertainty. Their notion of expected utility, developed originally for

use in game theory, underlies the vast majority of theories of asset pricing. In *corporate finance*, the thorniest issue in finance has been what F. Black in 1976 termed '*the dividend puzzle*' (Black, 1976). Firms have historically paid out about a half of their earnings as dividends. Many of these dividends were received by investors in high tax brackets who, on the margin, paid substantial amounts of taxes on them. The puzzle has been to explain these observations. However, it was not until game-theoretic methods were applied that any progress was made in understanding this issue. S. Bhattacharya's model of dividends as a signal was one of the first models in finance to use game theory (Allen, 2002).

Principal-Agent Problem

In finance, capital structure refers to the way a corporation finances its assets through some combination of equity, debt, or hybrid securities. A firm's capital structure is then the composition or structure of its liabilities. In reality, capital structure may be highly complex and include dozens of sources. For capital structure, the first contributions in a game-theoretic vein were signaling models. In 1977, S. Ross develops a model where managers signal the prospects of the firm to the capital markets by choosing an appropriate level of debt (Ross, 1977). The reason this acts as a signal is that bankruptcy is costly. A high debt firm with good prospects will only incur these costs occasionally while a similarly levered firm with poor prospects will incur them often. A second contribution of game theory to understanding capital structure lies in the study of agency costs. In 1976, M. Jensen and W. Meckling pointed to two kinds of agency problems in corporations (Jensen, & Meckling, 1976). One is between equity holders and bondholders and the other is between equity holders and managers. The first arises because the owners of a levered firm have an incentive to take risks; they receive the surplus when returns are high but the bondholders bear the cost when default occurs. The second conflict arises when equity holders cannot fully control the actions of managers. This means that managers have an incentive to pursue their own interests rather than those of the equity holders (Allen, 2002).

Game Theory for Political Science

Political science is a social science discipline concerned with the study of the state, nation, government, and politics and policies of government. It deals extensively with the theory and practice of politics, and the analysis of political systems and political behavior, culture. In recent years, the usefulness of game theory in political science has been actively appreciated. Political applications of game theory are related to the political economy, public choice, war bargaining, positive political theory, voting systems, social choice theory, etc. Therefore, there is already a considerable body of literature using game theory or techniques closely related to game theory in application to political science ("Lecture notes," n.d.).

Initially, political scientists adapt contemporary game theory to political analysis. A notable example of game theory applied to political science is Hotel location model. In 1957, Anthony Downs applied the hotel firm location model to the political process in his book *An Economic Theory of Democracy* (Downs, 1957). Anthony Downs shows i) how the political candidates will converge to the ideology preferred by the median voter if voters are fully informed, and ii) why rational voters choose to remain ignorant while allowing candidate divergence. After the hotel location model, political scientists have focused on the non-cooperative game theory and its application to international relations, political economy, comparative politics, legislative voting rules and voting in mass elections. In each of these areas, researchers have developed game-theoretic models in which the players are often voters, states, special interest groups, and politicians. With the hotel location model, there are several topics in

political science to which the application of game theory is *prima facie* appealing. They are voting, the study of power, diplomacy, negotiation and bargaining behavior, coalition formation among political groups and logrolling (Zagare, 1986).

Voting and Strategic Choice

Much of the work on voting has left out the strategic aspects of voting and concentrated on the aggregation of individual preferences via the vote. The properties of different voting methods and different assumptions concerning the measurability and comparability of intensity of individual preferences have been considered. Thus majority voting, weighted majority voting, various rank ordering methods and rules for eliminating candidates and other schemes have been studied. A different but highly related approach to problems of political choice takes into account the strategic aspect of voting. Explicit assumptions must be made about not only what the individual knows about his own preferences but what he knows of the preferences of others. In most of the work it has either been explicitly assumed that individuals are informed of all preferences or the information conditions considered have not been fully specified. Studies of strategic voting may be divided into those using cooperative, non-cooperative or other solution concepts and can be further divided into those with a formal structure (e.g., political parties) assumed or those in which only individuals are considered in a setting with no institutional details specified explicitly. In 1969, a clear and concise application of the non-cooperative equilibrium solution to strategic voting has been made by R. Farquharson where he defines the conditions for sincere, straightforward or sophisticated voting (Farquharson, 1969). The theory of competition among political parties offers another important area of applications for the theory of games. Some starts have been made, as is reflected in the works of A. Downs, D. Chapman, B. Frey, M Shubik and others in 1950-60s. There are primarily based upon analogies between the economics of oligopolistic competition and non-cooperative party struggles. The tendency has been to apply some form of non-cooperative or mechanistic solution to the models. The classic work of R. A. Dahl describing political participation serves as a guide for those who wish to model different actors in political competition in 1961 (Shubik, 1973).

The study of game theoretic models of politics with large numbers of participants could be the case some light on the role of numbers in the political process and help to clarify some of the problems inherent in mass democracy. A small number of works containing formal mathematical models of voting processes where numbers of participants is a key variable already exist. They deal primarily with extensions of the voters' paradox of M. Condorcet or with simple game (Shubik, 1973).

Coalition Logrolling

J. S. Coleman, G. Tullock, R. Wilson and others have attempted to incorporate logrolling and the trading of votes into game theoretic models. In designing new legislatures, or attempting to obtain an a priori feeling for how the voting power of individuals might change with changes in the formal aspect of the voting structure. L. Shapley, M. Shubik, I. Mann and others have applied the value solution to obtain a measure of the importance of an individual. W. Riker, R.D. Luce, M. Leiserson and others have gone beyond simple voting to consider the nature of coalition formation. There are several basic difficulties in modeling which must be overcome in extensions of this variety. When W. Riker considers minimal winning coalitions, the more formally oriented game theorist might have difficulty in interlinking this quasi-dynamic discussion with the specific role played by minimal winning coalitions in simple games (Riker, 1962). At least, three cooperative solution concepts appear to be applicable to logrolling. They are the core, the value and the bargaining set. The existence of the core is undoubtedly a

necessary condition for the existence of a market for votes (Shubik, 1973).

Political Bargaining

In political science, most of the literature on bargaining that has made use of game theoretic concepts is concerned with party politics or with international negotiations. The work in political science has to some extent been influenced by the studies of bargaining in economics or by economists and game theorists extending various mixtures of economic analysis and game theoretic reasoning to political problems. Many of the problems faced in attempting to apply game theoretic reasoning to bargaining and negotiation are substantive. They involve the modeling of process. A useful bibliographic note on literature relevant to international negotiation is also supplied by F. Iklé (Iklé, 1964). In the book '*The Economics of Bargaining*', John Cross provides the static and process model of bargaining where stress is laid upon economic features such as the cost of the process. This approach is adaptable for the political scientist as well as the economist (Shubik, 1973).

In 1960, A. Rapoport stressed modeling problems in the application of game theoretic reasoning (Rapoport, 1960). T. C. Schelling provided many provocative simple games and analogies to international conflict situations. However there is a considerable danger in being misled if one tries to push analogies between extremely simple games and international bargaining too far. It is important to realize not only the power but the limitations of simple game models as a didactic device (Shubik, 1973).

Political Power

One of the key concerns of political science is the study of power. In the work on the various versions of a value solution the relationship between these solutions and the concept of power has been noted. The immediate game theoretic basis for the investigation of power is given in the writings of J. C. Harsanyi, J. Nash, R. Selten, L. Shapley and M. Shubik. A paradoxical aspect of value solutions is that they were primarily motivated by a concern for fairness and equitable division. The relationship between fair division and power comes in the way in which threats enter into a consideration of how to evaluate the no-bargain point may be determined by the power of the bargainers (Shubik, 1973). The fair division procedure is applied using this power-determined initial point as a basis for the settlement. The various value solutions are essentially static and undoubtedly fail to portray adequately the interplay of power and influence in a dynamic system. Nevertheless, they provided clear well-defined concepts which can be subjected to scrutiny and compared with the theories of power proposed by political scientists and other social scientists. Possibly one of the most comprehensive attempts to evaluate and reconcile the many approaches to the concept of power, including the game theoretic approaches, is '*The Descriptive Analysis of Power*' by J. Nagel (Nagel, 1975). With J. C. Harsanyi, this work would serve as sufficient guides to those who wish to pursue the investigation of the concept of power further (Shubik, 1973).

Game Theory for Biology

Biology is a natural science concerned with the study of life and living organisms, including their structure, function, growth, evolution, distribution, and taxonomy. In biology, game theory has been used to explain the evolutionism. Therefore, game theory has a prominent role in evolutionary biology, in particular in the ecological study of various phenomena ranging from conflict behavior to altruism. For example, 1:1 sex ratios are a result of evolutionary forces acting on individuals who could be seen as trying to maximize their number of grandchildren. Besides, the chicken game model has been used to analyze fighting behavior and territoriality. Recently, the signaling games and other communication games have been used to analyze the evolution of communication among animals ("Game theory," n.d.).

The best known game theory in biology is the evolutionary game theory. In 1973, Maynard Smith proposed the evolutionary game model (Smith & Price, 1973). His approach was less on equilibrium that corresponds to a notion of rationality, but rather on ones that would be maintained by evolutionary forces. Unlike traditional game models, the payoffs for evolutionary game are often interpreted as corresponding to fitness. Today, evolutionary game theory has been used to explain many seemingly incongruous phenomena in nature. In biological game theory, there is a prevailing methodology. This methodology involves developing a model of evolution and considering potential end points of evolution utilizing so called equilibrium concepts. Most common among these are the concept of a Nash equilibrium and an Evolutionarily Stable Strategy (ESS), which was introduced by M. Smith as a new solution concept. When an ecologist or an evolutionary biologist is confronted with an apparently maladaptive phenotype, they strive to answer two questions. First, why is this phenotype stable? Second, what led to the evolution of that behavior in the first place? The concept of Nash equilibrium and ESS is most clearly aimed at answering the first question. But it is also aimed at providing a partial answer to the second question. Biologists often claim that the equilibria they find are potential end points for an evolutionary process. Hence, the claim that a state is an equilibrium entails that the state is stable and also that it is reachable by evolution. However, the recent result from the game theoretic study in biology demonstrates that the equilibrium methodology alone is inadequate to answer the second major question, and that it has in fact been misleading. While the theoretical possibility of such problems has been known for some time, those pitfalls have been regarded as either obvious or unrealistic (Simon & Kevin, 2013).

Recently, David P. Barash synthesizes the newest ideas from biology to explore and explain the roots of human strategy. Based on the study of how individuals make decisions, he explores the give-and-take of spouses in determining an evening's plans, the behavior of investors in a market bubble, and the maneuvers of generals on a battlefield alongside the mating and fighting strategies of less rational animals. Ultimately, Barash's lively and clear examples shed light on what makes our decisions, and what we can glean from biological game theory and the natural world as we negotiate and compete every day (Barash, 2004).

Game Theory for Philosophy

Game theory has also challenged in philosophy. Philosophy is the study of general and fundamental problems, such as those connected with reality, existence, knowledge, values, reason, mind, and language. Philosophers have attempted to derive morality from self-interest. Since games like the Prisoner's dilemma present an apparent conflict between morality and self-interest, political philosophers try to develop a cooperation model from a general social contract view. They have also attempted to use evolutionary game theory in order to explain the emergence of human attitudes about morality and corresponding animal behaviors. Philosophers look at several games including the Prisoner's dilemma, Stag hunt, and the Nash bargaining game as providing an explanation for the emergence of attitudes about morality. The best-known application of game theory in philosophy is the standard interpretation of Hobbes's state of nature as a prisoner's dilemma (Hoekstra, 2003). A. Alexandra, B. Skyrms and D. Dodds argued that it should be the assurance game, the stag hunt game and a combination of the prisoner's dilemma and the assurance game, respectively (Bruin, 2005).

Game Theory for Epistemology

Epistemology is the branch of philosophy concerned with the nature and scope of knowledge and is also referred to as theory of knowledge. Probably the first to suggest applying game theory to epistemology is J. Kern in 1969. He analyzed the relation between the knower and the known as a strictly competitive two-person game. In 1979, J. Harsanyi analyzed the difference between act and rule utilitarianism in terms of the distinction between non-cooperative and cooperative game playing. In 1987, M. Blais discussed the role of trust in knowledge. The notorious epistemic puzzle of the *'surprise exam'* is modeled by E. Sober as a game of *'matching pennies'* in 1998. The next year, B. Zamora analyzed scientific revolutions and coalition formation in game theoretically (Bruin, 2005).

Game Theory for Ethics

Ethics, also known as moral philosophy, is a branch of philosophy that involves systematizing, defending and recommending concepts of right and wrong conduct ("Game Theory and Ethics," 2010). The earliest call to apply game theory in ethics is R. Braithwaite's 1954 lecture on a bargaining approach to distributive justice. Later, J. Smart and J. Mackie used simple game theoretic methods to shed light on utilitarianism. In 1977, E. Ullman-Margalit set apart game theoretic rationality and morality to prove that it is the function of morality to tame egoistic rationality (Ullman-Margalit, 1977). Recent contributions are P. Vanderschraaf on game theory in business ethics in 1999, S. Woodcock and J. Heath on the robustness of altruism as an evolutionary strategy in 2002, and B. Verbeek on the authority of moral norms in 2004 (Bruin, 2005).

It is plausible to suppose that morality is about meshing our own interests with those of others, sometimes consonant with ours and sometimes conflicting. Therefore, moral theorists must investigate rules, qualities, attitudes and emotions elicited by conduct, people and institutions. The particular rules, qualities, attitudes and emotions restrain us from thwarting the interests of others to better serve our own or which move us to advance mutual interests or to advance the interests of others at the expense of our own. Based on this situation, it is natural to expect that game theory might be useful in moral theorizing as a tool for the moral philosopher. However, in spite of a few promising forays by people who might be regarded as insiders to moral philosophy and several instructive suggestions by outsiders, this expectation has not materialized (Kuhn, 2004).

Game Theory for Computer Science

The nature of computing is changing because of success of Internet and the revolution in Information technology. The advancement in technologies has made it possible to commoditize the components such as network, computing, storage and software. In the new paradigm, there are multiple entities (hardware, software agents, protocols etc.) that work on behalf of different autonomous bodies, and provide services to other similar entities. These entities will work for their respective owners to achieve their individual goals, as opposed to obtaining a socially desirable system optimum. Often, such systems are not centrally planned, but evolve in a distributed fashion as a result of the interaction of entities; they can be modeled using concepts from game theory. Therefore, it is important to study traditional computer science concepts such as algorithm design, protocols, performance optimization under a game-theoretic model. Nowadays, game theory has come to play an increasingly important and vital role in the computer science field (Halpern, 2008).

Distributed computing is one computer science area and it is ripe for game theory. Distributed computing and game theory are interested in much the same problems - dealing with systems where there are many agents, facing uncertainty, and having possibly different goals. In practice, however, there has been a significant difference in emphasis in the two areas. In distributed computing, the focus has been on problems such as fault tolerance, asynchrony, scalability, and proving correctness of algorithms. In game theory, the focus has been on strategic concerns. Recently, there have been some working adding strategic concerns to standard problems in distributed computing as well as adding concerns of fault tolerance and asynchrony to standard problems in game theory. These researches introduced the basic concepts from game theory and discussed the solution and modeling of problems faced by computer scientists (Halpern, 2008). Also, a game-theoretic technique is adopted for proving lower bounds on the computational complexity of randomized online algorithms. Therefore, game theory can provide a theoretical basis to the area of resource auctions, peer-to-peer systems, and computer security and algorithmic mechanism design. Until now, computer scientists have used the game theory, i) to model interactive multi-agent systems, ii) to analyze complex systems with economic theory and, iii) to find effective solutions in games, and so on.

The most fundamental assumption in game theory is rationality and intelligence. Rational players are assumed to maximize their payoff and intelligent players are assumed to know everything. Therefore, players can make the same deductions about the situation. However, this assumption has been widely criticized. Experiments have shown that game players do not always act rationally and impossible to know everything. Fortunately, the players in computer science usually are devices programmed to operate in a certain way, thus the assumption of rational and intelligent behavior is more justified (Leino, 2003). There has been a great deal of work in both computer science and game theory on learning to play well in different settings. Therefore, one line of research in computer science has involved learning to play optimally in a reinforcement learning setting, where an agent interacts with an unknown environment (DaSilva & Srivastava 2004).

Game Theory for Telecommuications

With the deregulation of the telecommunication companies and the rapid growth of the Internet, the research area of telecommunication and networking has experienced a remarkable development. Internet has made it possible for many such geographically distributed autonomous entities to interact with each other and provide various services. In addition, modern telecommunication technique has to deal with large, heterogeneous networks in which a large number of autonomous agents interact. Game theory applies to a wide range of class relations to include both human and non-humans, like as intelligent network devices. In particular, the interactions among users or devices sharing a common network resource can be formally modeled as games. Traditional network management issues - routing, flow and congestion control, traffic pricing, load balancing, and quality of service provisioning, etc., - have been an active research field of game theoretic research. By using a game theoretic formulation, the overall network performance can be predicted (Han, 2011).

One reason that game theory is an appropriate tool in the setting of telecommunication networks is that game theory deals primarily with distributed optimization – individual users, who are selfish, make their own decisions instead of being controlled by a central authority. Many of the problems which must be solved in a communications system are known to be NP-hard; as a result solving these optimization problems centrally becomes computationally infeasible as network size increases. Because game theory fo-

cuses on distributed solutions to system problems, we expect systems designed with game-theoretic concerns in mind to be highly scalable. In addition, game theory typically assumes that all players seek to maximize their utility functions in a manner which is perfectly rational. When the players of a game become computerized agents, it is reasonable to assume that the device will be programmed to maximize the expected value of some utility function. Thus the strong rationality assumption seems more reasonable for network devices than for people. Therefore, game theory is better suited to solving communication problems - where the 'agents' are likely to be computerized network devices - than to solving human problems (MacKenzie & Wicker, 2001).

Game Theory for Linguistics

Linguistics is the scientific study of human language. Although linguistics is the scientific study of language, a number of other intellectual disciplines are relevant to language and intersect with it. A group of linguists use the term 'language' to refer to a communication system that developed to support cooperative activity and extend cooperative networks. Therefore, communication can be considered an extension of an existing game ("Game Theoretical Linguistics," n.d.). Since Lewis and Spence researches in 1969 and 1973, the strategic aspects of communication have intrigued game theorists, and there is a considerable body of literature on this topic. Most game theoretic studies of communication are not concerned with the specific properties of natural languages though. On the other hand, linguists have taken little notice of this line of research until the turn of the century, despite its obvious relevance. Within the last few years, this situation has changed somewhat (Jaeger, 2008). Various linguists of language interested in pragmatics or language evolution started to study and employ game theoretic techniques. Recently, several biologists use the evolutionary interpretation of game theory to study the evolution of communication in biological systems, including natural language. Therefore, a lively interdisciplinary community has emerged in recent years, which uses game theoretic techniques to study genuinely linguistic problems. However, the linguistic branch of game paradigm is still in its infancy, and a lot of the current discussion revolves about rather basic issues how linguistic concepts are to be mapped to game theoretic ones (Jaeger, 2008).

In 2000, A. Rubinstein (2000) published a monograph '*Economics and Language*' in which game theory is used on economics and language. Furthermore, the P. Parikh, R. van Rooy and many others had developed game theoretic models for various aspects of linguistic communication such as the distinction between the conventional meaning and the speaker's meaning. In 2003, De Jaegher related vagueness of linguistic utterances to correlated equilibria (Bruin, 2005).

Game Theory for Law

Nowadays, economists can tractably analyze complicated game models in which individual players are uncertain or uninformed. These advances have enabled economists to apply the new game theory to strategic aspects of everything from bankruptcy to plea bargaining and patent races. Law and economics take notice of these developments. Absolutely, the ideas from game theory and the economics of asymmetric information are applied to legal issues (Zaluski, n.d.). This approach is a highly useful approach to law. However, the advances of game theory have been slower to diffuse into legal reasoning than other economic contributions. One explanation for this slow diffusion is that new game theory techniques in a sense represent a research technology with high barriers to entry (Ayres, 1990). In 1998, D. Baird, R. Gertner and R. Picker published the book *Game Theory and the Law* (Baird, Gertner, & Picker, 1998). This book applies the

tools of game theory and information economics to advance the understanding of how laws work, and shows how such well-known games as the prisoner's dilemma, the battle of the sexes, beer-quiche and the Rubinstein bargaining game can illuminate many different kinds of legal problems. The authors show how game theory offers ways of thinking about problems in anti-discrimination, environmental, labor and many other areas of law (Baird, 1998).

Game Theory for Sociology

Sociology is the scientific study of human society and its origins, development, organizations, and institutions. It is a social science which uses various methods of empirical investigation and critical analysis to develop a body of knowledge about human social activity, structures, functions and thinking. Social interaction is a key concept in sociological thinking. If ego's payoffs depends on alters' choices, interactions are strategic. Game theory provides a precise, formal language to model situations of strategic interactions. While standard game theory builds on the concept of strictly rational actors, behavioral game theory modifies the restrictive assumptions by incorporating more realistic psychological motives in models of game theory. New developments, such as models of incomplete and asymmetric information, signaling models, the theory of repeated games, and evolutionary game theory enrich the applicability of game theory to sociological problems. For example, game theory led to new insights on the problems of social order and cooperation, contribution to collective goods, the emergence and stability of social norms, the problem of trust and commitment in social and economic transactions (Lafferty, 2001). Although game theory came into sporadic use in sociology since the 1960's, it has yet not become mainstream, not even in rational choice sociology. Therefore, game theory has not seen much practical application within sociology. Compared to economics, sociologists have been slow in discovering the possibilities that a formal mathematical approach to research problems can present. This situation is in stark contrast to the obvious potential of game theory and recent developments of modern game theory, behavioral game theory and experimental work for sociological research (Lafferty, 2001).

The current revival of game theory in sociology began in the mid-1980s. From the mid-1980s, some interesting game-related researches did take place among sociologists. This research was conducted by several different types of social scientists - by experimental social psychologists, sociologists, and political scientists. While in the 1950s there existed probably only a handful of sociologists who were able to understand technical game theory, the situation was quite different by the 1980s and even more so today. Sociologists of a new breed have emerged during the last few decades. They are fully capable of understanding recent game theory and using it for purposes of their own. However, to draw exclusively on mathematical game theory in the analysis is not that common among sociologists, and some other method is often used, such as simulation or experiments. Connected to this is the tendency among today's game-theoretical sociologists to have close ties to other fields of sociology, which demand a high technical capacity, such as rational choice sociology, social dilemma research, social exchange theory, or mathematical sociology. A few laboratory experiments involving game theory were carried out, and there was quite a bit of interest in using games as a general metaphor. In these experiments, the role of games in social life was studied, and attempts were made to use games as a device to develop sociological theory further (Swedberg, 2001).

REFERENCES

Allen, F., & Morris, S. (2002). Game Theory Models in Finance International Series. *Operations Research & Management Science*, *35*, 17–48.

Altmana, E., Boulognea, T., El-Azouzia, R., Jiménezb, T., & Wynterc, L. (2006). A survey on networking games in telecommunications. *Computers & Operations Research*, *33*, 286–311. doi:10.1016/j.cor.2004.06.005

Aumann, R. J., & Maschler, M. B. (1995). *Repeated Games With Incomplete Information*. Cambridge, MA: MIT Press.

Ayres, I. (1990). Playing Games with the Law. *Stanford Law Review*, *42*, 1291–1317. doi:10.2307/1228971

Baird, D. G., Gertner, R. H., & Picker, R. C. (1998). *Game Theory and the Law*. Cambridge, MA: Harvard University Press.

Barash, D. P. (2004). *The Survival Game*. New York: Times Books Henry Holt and Company.

Barran, M. (n.d.). *Game Theory: An Introductory Sketch*. Retrieved from http://scienceworld.wolfram.com/biography/Borel.html

Black, F. (1976). Studies in stock price volatility changes. In *Proceedings of Meeting of the Business and Economic Statistics Section,* (pp. 177-181). American Statistical Association.

Bragg, A. (2000). Which network design tool is right for you? *IT Professional*, *2*(5), 23–32. doi:10.1109/6294.877494

Brandenburger, A., & Stuart, H. (2007). Biform Games. *Management Science*, *53*, 537–549. doi:10.1287/mnsc.1060.0591

Breit, W., & Hirsch, B. T. (2009). *Lives Of The Laureates: Twenty-three Nobel Economists*. Cambridge, MA: The MIT Press.

Bruin, B. (2005). Game Theory in Philosophy. *Topoi*, *24*(2), 197–208. doi:10.1007/s11245-005-5055-3

Buck, A. J. (n.d.). *An Introduction to Game Theory with Economic Applications*. Retrieved from http://courses.temple.edu/economics/Game%20Outline/index02.html

Colin, C. F. (2003). *Behavioral Game Theory: Experiments in Strategic Interaction*. Princeton University Press.

Crossman, A. (n.d.). *Game Theory*. Retrieved from http://sociology.about.com/od/Sociological-Theory/a/Game-Theory.htm

DaSilva, L. A., & Srivastava, V. (2004). Node Participation in Ad-hoc and Peer-to-peer Networks: A Game-theoretic Formulation. In *Proceedings of Workshop on Games and Emergent Behavior in Distributed Computing Environments*. Birmingham, UK: Academic Press.

Dixit, A., & Nalebuff, B. (n.d.). *Game Theory, the concise encyclopedia of economics*. Retrieved from http://www.econlib.org/library/Enc/GameTheory.html

Downs, A. (1957). *An economic theory of democracy*. New York: Harper and Row.

Erhun, F., & Keskinocak, P. (2003). Game theory in Business application (Tech. rep.). Atlanta, GA: School of Industrial and system engineering, Georgia Inst. of Tech.

Evolutionary Game Theory. (2009). *The Stanford Encyclopedia of Philosophy*. Retrieved from http://plato.stanford.edu/entries/game-evolutionary/

Farquharson, R. (1969). *Theory of Voting*. New Haven, CT: Yale University Press.

Game Theoretical Linguistics. (n.d.). *From the Communication in Context*. Retrieved from http://www.cccom.ut.ee/?page_id=29

Game Theory and Ethics. (2010). Retrieved from http://plato.stanford.edu/entries/game-ethics/

Game Theory. (n.d.). Retrieved from http://en.wikipedia.org/wiki/Game_theory

Gibbons, R. (1992). *Game Theory for Applied Economists*. Princeton, NJ: Princeton University Press.

Halpern, J. Y. (2008). Computer science and game theory: A brief survey. In S. N. Durlauf, & L. E. Blume (Eds.), *Palgrave Dictionary of Economics*. Palgrave MacMillan. doi:10.1057/9780230226203.0287

Han, Z., Niyato, D., Saad, W., Başar, T., & Hjørungnes, A. (2011). *Game Theory in Wireless and Communication Networks*. Cambridge, UK: Cambridge University Press. doi:10.1017/CBO9780511895043

Harsanyi, J. C., & Selten, R. (1988). A General Theory Of Equilibrium Selection. In *Games*. Cambridge, MA: MIT Press.

Hoekstra, K. (2003). Hobbes on Law, Nature and Reason. *Journal of the History of Philosophy*, *41*(1), 111–120. doi:10.1353/hph.2002.0098

Hurwicz, L., & Reiter, S. (2008). *Designing Economic Mechanisms*. Cambridge, UK: Cambridge University Press.

Iklé, F. (1964). *How Nations Negotiate*. New York: Harper and Row.

Jaeger, G. (2008). Applications of Game Theory in Linguistics. *Language and Linguistics Compass*, *2/3*, 406–421. doi:10.1111/j.1749-818X.2008.00053.x

Jensen, M., & Meckling, W. (1976). Theory of the Firm: Managerial Behavior, Agency, Costs, and Ownership Structure. *Journal of Financial Economics*, 305–360. doi:10.1016/0304-405X(76)90026-X

Kuhn, S. T. (2004). Reflections on Ethics and Game Theory. *Synthese*, *141*(1), 1–44. doi:10.1023/B:SYNT.0000035846.91195.cb

Lafferty, R. (2001). *Practical applications of game theory in sociological research*. (Unpublished bachelor thesis). McGill University, Montreal, Canada.

Lecture Notes. (n.d.). Retrieved from http://www.gametheory.net/lectures/field.pl

Leino, J. (2003). *Applications of game theory in ad hoc networks*. (Unpublished master thesis). Helsinki University of Technology, Helsinki, Finland.

Levine, D. K. (n.d.). *What is Game Theory?* Retrieved from http://levine.sscnet.ucla.edu/general/whatis.htm

MacKenzie, A. B., & Wicker, S. B. (2001). Game theory in communications: motivation. *IEEE Globecom,* (2), 821-826.

McCain, R. A. (n.d.). *Émile Borel*. Retrieved from http://faculty.lebow.drexel.edu/McCainR/top/eco/game/nash.html

Mizuno, H., Okamoto, T., Koakutsu, S., & Hirata, H. (2012). A growing complex network design method with an adaptive multi-objective genetic algorithm and an inner link restructuring method. In *Proceedings of SICE Annual Conference (SICE)*, (pp. 1525–1531). SICE.

Myerson, R. B. (1997). *Game Theory: Analysis of Conflict*. Cambridge, MA: Harvard University Press.

Nagel, J. (1975). *Descriptive Analysis of Power*. New Haven, CT: Yale University Press.

Neumann, J. V., & Morgenstern, O. (1944). *Theory of games and economic behavior*. Princeton University Press.

Rapoport, A. (1960). *Fights, Games and Debates*. Ann Arbor, MI: The University of Michigan Press.

Riker, W. H. (1962). *The Theory of Political Coalitions*. New Haven, CT: Yale University Press.

Ross, S. A. (1977). The Determination of Financial Structure: The Incentive-Signalling Approach. *The Bell Journal of Economics*, *8*(1), 23–40. doi:10.2307/3003485

Roth, A. E. (2002). The Economist as Engineer: Game Theory, Experimentation, and Computation as Tools for Design Economics. *Econometrica, 70*(4), 1341-1378.

Schmidt, C. (Ed.). (2002). *Game Theory and Economic Analysis: A Quiet Revolution in Economics*. New York: Routledge. doi:10.4324/9780203167403

Shubik, M. (1973). *Game Theory and Political Science* (Cowles Foundation Discussion Paper No.351). Department of Economics, Yale University.

Simon, M. H., & Kevin, J. S. Z. (2013). Methodology in Biological Game Theory. *The British Journal for the Philosophy of Science*, 1–22. PMID:23526835

Smith, J. M., & Price, G. R. (1973). The logic of animal conflict. *Nature*, *246*(5427), 15–18. doi:10.1038/246015a0

Swedberg, R. (2001). Sociology and Game Theory: Contemporary and Historical Perspectives. *Theory and Society*, *30*(3), 301–335. doi:10.1023/A:1017532512350

Ullman-Margalit, E. (1977). *The Emergence of Norms*. Oxford, UK: Oxford University Press.

Vane, H. R., & Mulhearn, C. (2010). *James A. Mirrlees, William S. Vickrey, George A. Akerlof, A. Michael Spence and Joseph E. Stiglitz*. Edward Elgar Publishing.

Walker, P. (2012). *A Chronology of Game Theory*. Retrieved from http://www.econ.canterbury.ac.nz/personal_pages/paul_walker/gt/hist.htm

Yasuda, Y. (2010). *Game Theory in Finance*. Retrieved from http://yyasuda.blogspot.kr/2010/10/game-theory-in-finance.html

Zagare, F. C. (1986). Recent Advances in Game Theory and Political Science. In S. Long (Ed.), *Annual Review of Political Science*. Norwood, NJ: Ablex Publishing Corporation.

Zaluski, W. (n.d.). *On the Applications of Game Theory in Contract Law*. Retrieved from http://www.academia.edu/505649/On_the_Applications_of_Game_Theory_in_Contract_Law

KEY TERMS AND DEFINITIONS

Bargaining Problem: A problem of understanding how game players should cooperate when non-cooperation leads to Pareto-inefficient results. It is in essence an equilibrium selection problem; many games have multiple equilibria with varying payoffs for each player, forcing the players to negotiate on which equilibrium to target.

Equilibrium: A solution concept of a non-cooperative game involving two or more players, in which each player is assumed to know the equilibrium strategies of the other players, and no player has anything to gain by changing only their own strategy.

Evolutionarily Stable Strategy: A strategy which, if adopted by a population in a given environment, cannot be invaded by any alternative strategy that is initially rare. It is relevant in game theory, behavioural ecology, and evolutionary psychology.

Minimax Mixed Strategy: A decision rule used in decision theory, game theory, statistics and philosophy for minimizing the possible loss for a worst case (maximum loss) scenario. Alternatively, it can be thought of as maximizing the minimum gain (maximin or MaxMin).

Performance Optimization: The method about maximizing the performance. The motivation for such activity is called a performance problem, which can be real or anticipated.

Chapter 2
Basic Concepts for Game Theory

ABSTRACT

Game theory has been variously described as the science of strategy or that of conflict resolution. At its core, it has the characteristics of a mathematical construct: a clear set of concepts and assumptions, fundamental theorems, and applications to real world issues. The fact that the issues in question are mostly the domains of the social sciences, however, places game theory in a peculiar position compared to other mathematical and scientific disciplines. Following von Neumann and Morgenstern's book, it is customary to analyze what we call game situations by using parlor games—already existing ones or ones specially constructed for this very purpose—as analytical models. This chapter does this.

INTRODUCTION

The past decade has witnessed a huge explosion of interest in issues that intersect network design and game theory. In recent times, algorithmic game theory has been one of the most high-profile growth areas in theoretical computer science and telecommunication (Wooldridge, 2012). Game theory is the mathematical theory of interactions between self-interested agents. In particular, it focuses on decision making in settings where each player's decision can influence the outcomes of other players. In such settings, each player must consider how each other player will act in order to make an optimal choice. In game theory, 'game' means an abstract mathematical model of a multi-agent decision making setting (Wooldridge, 2012).

In game theory, a modeling situation is defined as a game to predict the outcome of complex interactions among entities. Usually, a normal game form ($\mathbb{G}$) can be formulated with three parameters: the players, a strategy or action space for each player (i.e., strategy set), and consequences of the actions (i.e., a set of payoffs). Mathematically, $\mathbb{G}$ can be defined as $\mathcal{N} \in \{\mathcal{N}, \{S_i\}_{i \in \mathcal{N}}, \{u_i\}_{i \in \mathcal{N}}\}$.

- $\mathcal{N}$ is the finite set of players.
- S_i is the set of strategies with player i.
- The utility function of player i (u_i) can be represented as the degree of satisfaction received by player i as the function of the strategy it chooses, s_i, and the action of other players:

DOI: 10.4018/978-1-4666-6050-2.ch002

$$s_{-i} = \left(s_1, \ldots, s_{i-1}, s_{i+1}, \ldots s_N\right).$$

Players are decision makers, who choose how they act. A player, such as a company, a nation, a wireless node, or even a biological species, may be independent and has to make specific actions that have mutual, possibly conflicting, consequences. Usually, players are assumed to be individually rational and act in a rational manner and try to ensure the best possible consequence according to their preferences. Strategy set is the collection of various actions available to the player. Each player has a number of possible actions and can choose an action to determine the resulting outcome of the game. Any kind of action of a player should be expressed with a suitable utility function, which maps every action to a real number. A payoff (or utility) function quantifies the satisfaction that a player can get from a particular action. Usually, utility of a player corresponds to the received payment minus the incurred cost. Based on the payoff, the outcome to the different players can be evaluated. Therefore, individual decision makers (i.e., players) try to find the best actions.

The most classic game theory example is the Prisoner's Dilemma ("Prisoner's dilemma," n.d.). The prisoner's dilemma is a canonical example of a game analyzed in game theory that shows why two individuals might not cooperate, even if it appears that it is in their best interests to do so. To put it simply, two prisoners are getting charged for a crime that they most likely did together, but the police aren't sure. So, they set up a deal where they question each suspect privately, and they can choose to cooperate (i.e., claim they did not commit the crime) or betray (i.e., admit to committing the crime). The punishments are as follows:

1. If one prisoner cooperates and the other betrays, the betrayer can be free while the cooperator must spend ten years in prison.
2. If both prisoners cooperate, the police don't want to risk wasting the lives of two innocent men, so give them each one year sentence.
3. If both prisoners betray, they will be punished for their crime with a three year sentence.

If we were to draw a matrix to represent the prisoners' payoffs, it would resemble Table 1.

If the other prisoner chooses to cooperate, betraying gives a better reward, and if the other prisoner chooses to betray then betraying also gives a better reward. Because betrayal always rewards more than cooperation, all purely rational self-interested prisoners would betray each other. Therefore, collaboration is dominated by betrayal in the classic version of the game. The interesting part of this result is that pursuing individual reward logically leads the prisoners to both betray, even though they would get a better reward if they both cooperated. In this situation, the only rational choice for a sentence-minimizing prisoner is to betray, since this gives it a better outcome, whatever the other does. Hence *both are worse off if both are rational than if both are irrational.* Specifically, each individual gets a lighter sentence

Table 1. Sample matrix for the prisoners' payoffs

	Prisoner B Stays Cooperates	**Prisoner B Betrays**
Prisoner A Stays Cooperates	Each serves 1 year	Prisoner A: 10 years Prisoner B: goes free
Prisoner A Betrays	Prisoner A: goes free Prisoner B: 10 years	Each serves 3 years

if both try to maximize their sentences than if both try to minimize them. Therefore, it is so-called 'prisoner's dilemma'.

Far from being mere curiosities, game-theoretic dilemmas occur throughout social life. Therefore, the concept of prisoner's dilemma is an interesting issue in the social sciences such as economics, politics and sociology, as well as to the biological sciences such as ethology and evolutionary biology (Howard, 1971). The arms races during Cold War period can be modeled as a Prisoner's Dilemma situation. Although the best strategy is for the Western and Eastern sides to disarm, the rational course for both sides is to arm. This is indeed what happened in real world, and both sides poured enormous resources in to military research and armament.

Initially, game theory assumes that games are represented in a flat form, as a matrix or tree. It also assumes that players have no resource limitations in terms of time or space, so that they can keep the entire game tree in memory, and can calculate all the possible consequences of each move. Given these assumptions, and as long as we could conceive an algorithm which played the game perfectly in finite time, the game would be effectively trivial. This means that the finite two-player perfect-information game (i.e., chess) is considered trivial to this field. However, when we take into account the resource limitations of the players, it is obvious that a player could never maintain the entire game tree (for a big game) in memory, nor consider all possible consequences of each action. Thus a player must consider possibilities and outcomes selectively, and make decisions based on less-than perfect information. As the player cannot in general see the exact influence of a move on the final goals of the game, it follows that her reasoning must be heuristic (Pell, 1993).

Learning can be defined as the capability of drawing intelligent decisions by self-adapting to the dynamics of the environment, taking into account the experience gained in past and present system states, and using long term benefit estimations. Learning is adamantly driven by the amount of information available at every game player. As a result, learning algorithmic game theory has become an increasingly important part of algorithmic research in recent years. In particular, machine learning has made continued progress in developing methods that can generalize from data, adapt to changing environments, and improve performance with experience, as well as progress in understanding fundamental underlying issues. There has recently been increasing interest in research at the intersection of game theory and learning algorithm. Such work is motivated by the observation that whilst these two fields have traditionally been viewed as disparate research areas, there is actually a great deal of commonality between them that can be exploited within both fields. By integrating over the distribution of opponent strategies rather than taking a simple empirical average, recent research work shows how insights from game theory can be used to derive a novel learning algorithms (Blum, 2008).

Most game-learning algorithms are designed to improve a program based on watching or playing against knowledgeable opponent players. Although it is certainly important to understand how a program (or player) could learn from good players, it is equally important to know how those good players became good in the first place. A much smaller proportion of learning work has considered how programs might become strong players while relying neither on active analysis nor on experience with experts. Most of these approaches can be considered as self-play, in which either a single player or a population of players evolves during competition on large numbers of contests. A related technique, which can also be viewed as a form of self-play, is that the basic playing program which learned to predict the expected-outcome of positions if played by random players. This was shown to be effective for constructing evaluation functions for some games (Pell, 1993).

To interpret game theory, descriptive and normative interpretations exist. These two interpretations present very different criteria for the question of whether game theory works (Wooldridge, 2012). Under a descriptive interpretation, we can view game theory as attempting to predict how game players will behave in strategic settings. Therefore, the descriptive interpretation suggests that we should look for whether game theory successfully predicts how people will make choices in settings that we can model as games. Some scholars believe that by finding the equilibria of games they can predict how actual human populations will behave when confronted with situations analogous to the game being studied. This descriptive interpretation of game theory has come under recent criticism. Game theorists assume players are *Homo economicus* and always act rationally to maximize their payoffs ("Homo economicus," n.d.). Moreover, they respond by comparing their assumptions to those used in physics. Thus while their assumptions do not always hold, they can treat game theory as a reasonable scientific ideal akin to the models used by physicists. However, real game players, e.g., human beings, often act either irrationally, or do not play equilibrium strategies. Therefore, the fundamental assumptions made by game theorists are often violated, and the question of how players reach an equilibrium remains open. Under a normative interpretation, we can view game theory as prescribing courses of action for players. That is, game theory tells players how they ought to act. Therefore, the normative interpretation suggests that we should examine whether we can obtain outcomes that are better than what we might otherwise have obtained (Wooldridge, 2012). Some scholars in the normative view see game theory not as a predictive tool for the behavior of human beings, but as a suggestion for how people ought to behave. Since a Nash equilibrium of a game constitutes one's best response to the actions of the other players, playing a strategy that is part of a Nash equilibrium seems appropriate. However,

this normative interpretation for game theory has also come under criticism. First, in some cases it is appropriate to play a non-equilibrium strategy if one expects others to play non-equilibrium strategies as well. Second, some cases, e.g., Prisoner's Dilemma, each game player pursuing his own self-interest leads all players to be worse off than if they had not pursued their own self-interests. Some scholars believe that this demonstrates the failure of game theory as a recommendation for behavior.

CLASSIFICATIONS OF GAMES

Games can be classified according to certain significant features and properties. Usually, games can be divided as two different groups based on various two-binary criteria; whether a game is a symmetric or not, or whether a game is a static game or not, or whether a game comprises perfect information or imperfect information, and so on. In this subsection, we study how to classify the games ("Game theory," n.d.).

Non-Cooperative Games vs. Cooperative Games

Typically, games can be divided into non-cooperative and cooperative games whether players are cooperative or non-cooperative. A game is non-cooperative if the players make decisions independently and are not able to form binding commitments. Therefore, players are in conflict and do not communicate or collaborate with each other. So, players try to ensure the best possible consequence according to the utility function. The prisoner's dilemma and the battle of the sexes are well known non-cooperative games.

Cooperative games, also called coalition games, are games in which players make binding commitments and find it beneficial to cooperate in the game. Therefore, legal systems or strict rules are required to adhere to players' promises.

In cooperative games, the joint actions of groups are analyzed, i.e. what is the outcome if a group of players cooperate. Therefore, the main interest in cooperative games is to fairly distribute the outcome to each player according to their contributions. In non-cooperative games this is not possible. Shapley value and Nash bargaining solution are well known cooperative games. Table 2 shows the main features of non-cooperative and cooperative games.

However, this two-binary classification has been questioned. Therefore, considerable efforts have been made to link the two type game models. Recently, hybrid games are proposed in a semi-cooperative manner. These games contain cooperative and non-cooperative elements. For instance, coalitions of players are formed in a cooperative game, but these play in a non-cooperative fashion.

Static Games vs. Dynamic Games

Static games are also called strategic, one-shot, single stage or simultaneous games. In static games, all players make decisions (or select a strategy) simultaneously, without knowledge of the strategies that are being chosen by other players. Even though the decisions may be made at different points in time, the game can be called a simultaneous game because each player has no information about the decisions of others. Static games are represented by the normal form and solved using the concept of a Nash equilibrium. Nash equilibrium is a solution concept of a non-cooperative game involving two or more players, in which each player is assumed to know the equilibrium strategies of the other players, and no player has anything to gain by changing only his own strategy unilaterally. If each player has chosen a strategy and no player can benefit by changing his or her strategy while the other players keep their strategies unchanged, then the current set of strategy choices and the corresponding payoffs constitute a Nash equilibrium (Osborne & Rubinstein, 1994).

Dynamic games, also called sequential, extensive or repeated games, define the possible orders of the events and players iteratively play a similar stage game. Unlike static games, players have at least some information about the strategies chosen on others and thus may contingent their play on earlier actions. This could not be perfect information about every action of earlier players. Therefore, the players observe the outcome

Table 2. Main features of non-cooperative and cooperative games

Game Model	Key Objective	Solution Concept	Type
Noncooperative game	Individual players act to maximize their own payoff.	Nash equilibrium Correlated equilibrium Bayesian Nash equilibrium Subgame Perfect Nash Equilibrium Evolutionary stable strategy Stackelberg equilibrium Wardrop Equilibrium Pareto Equilibrium -Equilibrium	Static game Dynamic game Repeated game Evolutionary game, Markovian game, Stackelberg game, Auction game Public goods game Contention game Intervention game Supermodular game Security game, etc.,
Cooperative game	Coalitions of players are formed and players have joint actions to gain mutual benefits	Nash bargaining solution Kalai-Smorodinsky Bargaining Solution Egalitarian Bargaining Solution Rubinstein Bargaining Solution	Coalitional game Bargaining game Matching game Voting game, etc.,

of the previous game round and make decisions for the next game round. Therefore, players can react adaptively to other players' decisions. For reasoning dynamic games, equilibrium concept for static games is insufficient. Therefore, a sub-game perfect equilibrium is adopted as a solution concept in extensive sequential dynamic games. If a strategy profile represents a Nash equilibrium in every sequence sub-game of the original game, it is defined as a sub-game perfect equilibrium, which is a refinement of a Nash equilibrium.

Dynamic games are also divided finite extensive games and infinite extensive games. Generally, dynamic games are finished in finite actions. Every finite dynamic game has a sub-game perfect equilibrium. It may be found by backward induction, which is an iterative process for solving finite extensive form. Some pure mathematical game models based on the set theory last for infinitely many actions. Since backward induction no more works on infinite games, logicians have proposed a tool, which they call '*coinduction*' to reason on infinite sequential games (Lescanne & Perrinel, 2012).

Discrete Games vs. Continuous Games

Some game models are concerned with finite, discrete games that have a finite number of players, strategies and outcomes. Therefore, game players choose from a finite set of pure strategies. These games are called discrete games. Most classical game models are discrete games. Discrete game concepts can be extended as continuous games. The continuous game allows games to include more general sets of pure strategies, which may be uncountably infinite continuous strategy set. Differential game and Cournot competition game are well-known continuous games. In differential games, the evolution of the players' state variables is governed by differential equations. By using the optimal control theory, optimal strategy is selected. Cournot game is used to describe an industry competition model in which companies compete on the amount of output they will produce.

Zero-Sum Games vs. Positive-Sum Games

According to player's payoff structures, games can be categorized into zero-sum and positive-sum (*or* non zero-sum) games. In particular, zero-sum games are a special case of constant-sum games. If the total sum of all players' benefits is always zero for every combination of strategies, these games are called as zero-sum games. It means that whatever gained by one player is lost by the other players. Therefore, zero-sum games are strictly competitive. Typical zero-sum games are gambling (i.e., Poker game) and most sporting events. All other games excluding zero-sum games are positive-sum games. Positive-sum games are non-strictly competitive, because such games generally have both competitive and cooperative elements. In positive-sum games, a gain by one player does not necessarily correspond with a loss by another player.

For a zero-sum game, an optimal solution can always be found. However, there is no universally accepted solution for positive-sum games. Since players in a positive-sum game have some complementary interests, there is no single optimal strategy that is preferable to all others. Many game models in network design are positive-sum games (Spangler, 2003).

n-Player Games vs. Population Games

The most common way for game classification is based on the number of game players (i.e., how many players in the game). Game is the formal model of an interactive situation. It typically involves several players. When a game has only 1 player, it is usually called as an individual decision problem with stochastic outcomes. In 1-player games, one player is faced with an optimization problem. It is equal to optimal decision process. Therefore, it can be viewed as optimal-control games. Usually, 1-player games can be divided as static 1-player games and dynamic 1-player games. Static 1-player games are formulized by using mathematical programming. Dynamic 1-player games are modeled based on the optimal control theory over a period of time. Differential games can be viewed as extensions of optimal-control theory. With two or more players, a problem becomes a theoretical game. The formal definition of a game specifies the players, their preferences, their information, the strategic actions available to them, and how these influence the outcome. Modern game theory began with the 2-player games (i.e., two-person zero-sum games). The normal strategic form of 2-player games is usually represented by a matrix which shows the players, strategies, and pay-offs. Games with an arbitrary, but finite, n ($n \geq 1$) number of players are often called n-player games.

Population games are considered to involve a population of players where strategy selections can change over time in response to the decisions made by all individual players in the population. Evolutionary game is a well-known population game (Sandholm, 2007).

Perfect Information Games vs. Imperfect Information Games

If each player knows every strategy of the other players that performed before that player at every point, this game is called a perfect information game. Therefore, the players are fully informed about each other player's strategy. Usually, extensive games can be games of perfect information. Card and chess games are well-known perfect information games. In addition, on the contrary, players in strategic games do not know exactly what strategies of other players took up to that point. In this case, players have to infer from their likely strategies. These games are called imperfect information games. Most game models studied in game theory are imperfect-information games. Furthermore, an imperfect information game model is a good framework in network design because the users of a network seldom know the exact actions of the other users (Leino, 2003).

Complete Information Games vs. Incomplete Information Games

Complete information game is a game if all factors of the game are common knowledge. Therefore, each player is aware of all other players and the set of strategies and payoffs for each player. Complete information game is a model of the theoretical pre-conditions of an efficient perfectly competitive market. In a sense, it is a requirement of the assumption also made in economic theory that market participants act rationally. All other games are games of incomplete information games. In an incomplete information game, at least one player is uncertain about another player's preferences. A sealed-bid auction is a well-known incomplete information game. A player knows his own valuation of the merchandise but does not know the valuations of the other bidders.

Perfect information game is often confused with complete information game, which is a similar concept. However, there is a tiny difference between the notions of complete information games and perfect information games. The notion of complete information is concerned with the information of the elements of the game, such as the strategy space, the possible payoffs, and so on. Therefore, complete information game requires that every player know the strategies and payoffs available to the other players but not necessarily the actions taken. However, the notion of perfect information is concerned with the information of the strategies taken by the other players or their sequence (Han, Niyato, Saad, Başar, & Hjørungnes, 2011).

Pure Strategy Games vs. Mixed Strategy Games

A pure strategy game provides a complete definition of how a player will play a game. In particular, it determines the strategy that a player will make for any game situation. Therefore, a player's strategy set is the set of pure strategies available to that player. In a mixed strategy game, a strategy may be random, or drawn from a probability distribution, which corresponds to how frequently each strategy is to be played. Therefore, there are infinitely many mixed strategies available to a player, even if their strategy set is finite. In particular, a mixed strategy game in which the player assigns a strictly positive probability to every pure strategy is called a *totally mixed strategy game.*

The prisoner's dilemma and the Stag hunt game are well-known pure strategy games. Rock-paper-scissors game is a good example of mixed strategy game. John Nash proved that there is an equilibrium for every finite pure strategy or mixed strategy game. If all players are playing pure strategies, pure strategy Nash equilibrium exists. If at least one player is playing a mixed strategy, there exists a mixed strategy Nash equilibrium ("Strategy," n.d.).

Unitary Games vs. Hybrid Games

Nowadays, a new viewpoint of game theory has been developed to understand complicated circumstances. Game designers try to mix two different type games and propose a new hybrid game model, which contains cooperative and non-cooperative features, simultaneously. All the traditional games excluding hybrid games can be called unitary games. Most traditional games are unitary games.

In hybrid games, players act competitively to maximize their profits. However, sometimes, the competition among players is transformed into a cooperative competition. Well-known hybrid game is biform game and co-opetition game (Brandenburger, & Stuart, 2007). Biform game is a hybrid non-cooperative and cooperative model to formalize the two-stage decision problem. Co-opetition game (co-opetition is a neologism coined to describe cooperative competition) is designed to provide an effective solution under cooperative and competitive situations. For example, co-opetition occurs when players interact with partial congruence of interests. They cooperate with each other to reach a higher payoff creation, and then, struggle to achieve better advantage in competitive manner.

Egalitarian Games vs. Hierarchical Games

Most classical games are designed based on the assumption that the players are symmetric, that is to say, when no single player dominates the decision process. However, there are other types of games wherein one of players has the ability to enforce his strategy on the other players. In these games, some hierarchy exists among players. Some players' decision priority is higher/lower than the others. Following the original work of H. von Stackelberg, the player who holds the higher priority and powerful position is called the leader, and the other players who rationally react to the leader's decision are called the followers.

Without loss of generality, all the games with symmetric players can be called egalitarian games. In egalitarian games, there are no hierarchical levels among players. On the other hand, some games including the hierarchy concept in decision making process are called hierarchical games. There can be multiple levels of hierarchy with many asymmetric players. Stackelberg games have been widely known as a good example of hierarchical games.

Symmetric Games vs. Asymmetric Games

A game is called a symmetric game if all players have the same strategy set, and the payoff to playing a given strategy depends only on the strategies being played, not on who plays them. Therefore, each player earns the same payoff when the player selects the same strategy against similar strategy of his competitors. In symmetric games, the identities of the players can be changed without changing the payoff to the strategies. Many well-known games are symmetric, for example, the prisoners' dilemma, the battle of the sexes, the stag hunt game and the chicken game. Symmetric games may naturally arise from models of automated-player interactions, since in these environments, the players may possess identical circumstances, capabilities, and perspectives by design (Cheng, Reeves, Vorobeychik, & Wellman, 2004). Asymmetric games are games where there are different strategy sets for players. The examples of asymmetric games are ultimatum game, Stackelberg game and the dictator game.

CLASSIFICATION OF GAME SOLUTIONS

Game theory puts forward a number of solution concepts that are typically intended to formulate some notion of rational choice in a game-theoretic setting. Therefore, solution concepts are thus at the heart of game theory (Wooldridge, 2012). A solution of a game is a set of the possible strategies and obtained when the players act rationally and intelligently. Generally, a solution is an outcome from which no player wants to deviate unilaterally. Solutions from each game model can be classified into different types according to their certain features and properties.

Equilibria are the most famous concept of solutions in non-cooperative games. If each player has chosen a strategy and no player can benefit by changing his or her strategy while the other players keep their strategies unchanged, the set of current strategy selections constitute a equilibrium. Bargaining solutions, core, Shapley value, nucleolus are well-known solutions for cooperative games. Bargaining solutions provide predictions about how the profit will be shared, or what division is fair, which may depend on the player utility functions. Various bargaining solutions have been proposed based on slightly different assumptions about what properties are desired. Core, Shapley value and nucleolus are solutions for coalitional cooperative games. The following subsection focuses on solutions in game models and explains the fundamental ideas.

Solutions for Non-Cooperative Games

Fundamental problem in game theory is determining how players reach their decisions. In particular, the question of how can players select their strategies is of ultimate importance. In recent years, there has been a proliferation of solutions for non-cooperative games. A typical research mainly focuses on the modeling an environment or strategic interaction, which is the relevant consequence of rational behaviors by all players. Equilibrium is a state that every player will select a utility-maximizing strategy given the strategies of every other player. This concept is very momentous and there are different types of equilibrium in non-cooperative games.

Nash Equilibrium

A Nash equilibrium, named after John Nash, is a well-know and classical solution concept in non-cooperative games. It is a set of strategies if each represents a best response to the other strategies. So, if all the players are playing the strategies in a Nash equilibrium, they have no unilateral incentive to deviate, since their strategy is the best they can do given what others are doing. A game in normal form may have either unique, multiple or no Nash equilibrium.

Formally, a Nash equilibrium of a strategic game $G = \{\mathcal{N}, \{S_i\}_{i \in \mathcal{N}}, \{u_i\}_{i \in \mathcal{N}}\}$, is defined as a vector of strategies $s^* = \left(s_1^*, \ldots, s_N^*\right) \in \mathbb{S}$ where $\mathbb{S} = S_1 \times S_2 \ldots \times S_n$ is the set of strategy profiles. Therefore, no unilateral deviation in strategy is profitable for any single player, that is

$$u_i\left(s_{-i}^*, s_i^*\right) > u_i\left(s_{-i}^*, s_i\right) \quad \text{for all} \quad s_i \in S_i \qquad (1)$$

where

$$s_{-i} = \left(s_1, \ldots, s_{i-1}, s_{i+1}, \ldots s_N\right)$$

is a vector of strategies, one for each player, except the player i.

Nash Equilibrium can be classified either a pure-strategy Nash Equilibrium or a mixed-strategy Nash Equilibrium. A pure strategy Nash equilibrium is a Nash equilibrium in which each player uses a pure strategy. If both players use the same strategy in the equilibrium, this kind of equilibrium is called a symmetric equilibrium. For example, the Nash equilibrium of the Prisoner's Dilemma game is a symmetric equilibrium, since both players use the same strategy (i.e., betray). Under mixed-strategy Nash Equilibrium, a pure strategy is chosen stochastically with a fixed frequency. Nash proved that every game with a finite number of players, who can dynamically choose from pure strategy set, has at least one mixed-strategy Nash equilibrium ("Nash equilibrium," n.d.).

For non-cooperative games, the strategy of a player at Nash equilibrium is the best response to the strategies of the other players. However, there are some disadvantages. First, the main weak point of Nash equilibrium is inefficiency. The solution of Nash equilibrium frequently does not coincide with a point that yield high utility values to all players. Therefore, the Nash equilibrium may sometimes appear non-rational in a perfect rational perspective. Second, there could be multiple Nash equilibria in a game, and if a player is restricted to adopting only pure strategies, the Nash equilibrium may not exist. Third, in the scenario of the Nash equilibrium, the players are assumed to be rational. That is, a player will always be able to maximize his payoff, which is consistent with his preferences among different alternative outcomes. This rationality of the player requires complete information and a well-defined and consistent set of strategies. However, in reality, this assumption rarely holds. Occasionally, game players make decisions irrationally due to the limited information about available strategies. Fourth, the idea of Nash equilibrium has mostly been developed in a static setting. Therefore, this approach cannot capture the adaptation of players to change their strategies and reach equilibrium over time. In addition, computing the mixed-strategy Nash equilibrium of a n-player game is generally very difficult. It requires arduous endeavors to solve multiple high-order polynomial equations (Wang, Han, & Liu, 2009).

Pareto Equilibrium

Pareto equilibrium is the concept of Nash equilibrium with efficiency. It is a set of strategies such that there is no other set of strategies where all players receive a higher payoff. Formally, a Pareto equilibrium of a strategic game $\{\mathcal{N}, \{s_i\}_{i \in \mathcal{N}}, \{u_i\}_{i \in \mathcal{N}}\}$ is a vector of strategies $s^* = \left(s_1^*, \ldots, s_N^*\right) \{s_i\}_{i \in \mathcal{N}}$, one for each player, such that there is no $s \in \{s_i\}_{i \in \mathcal{N}}$ that satisfies $u_i(s) > u_i(s^*)$ for all player $i \in \mathcal{N}$.

The idea of Pareto equilibrium is strongly related to the concept of Pareto optimality, which is explained later in the chapter.

Subgame Perfect Nash Equilibrium

A subgame perfect Nash equilibrium is an equilibrium such that players' strategies constitute a Nash equilibrium in every subgame of the original game. In game theory, a subgame is any part (a subset) of the base game. A subgame perfect Nash equilibrium may be found by backward induction technique, which is an iterative process for solving finite extensive sequential games. It proceeds by first considering the last time a decision might be made and choosing what to do in any situation at that time. Using this information, one can then determine what to do at the second-to-last time of decision. By iteratively repeating the backward induction technique, the best action for every possible situation can be obtained.

Sometimes, implausible Nash equilibria arise in games, such as incredible threats and promises. Such equilibria might be eliminated in perfect and complete information games by applying subgame perfect Nash equilibrium. However, it is not always possible to avail oneself of this solution concept in incomplete information games. Therefore, imperfect and incomplete information games, these implausible equilibria cannot always be eliminated.

Bayesian - Nash Equilibrium

In game theory, Bayesian game is an incomplete game with the probabilistic analysis, and a probability distribution is updated according to Bayes' rule. Following John C. Harsanyi's framework, Bayesian game is used to analyze imperfect information scenarios. In a non-Bayesian game, a strategy profile is a Nash equilibrium if every strategy in that profile is a best response to every other strategy in the profile; i.e., there is no strategy that a player could play that would yield a higher payoff, given all the strategies played by the other players. However, in a Bayesian game, rational

players are seeking to maximize their expected payoff, given their beliefs about the other players (Cox, 2006).

A Bayesian Nash equilibrium is defined as a strategy profile and beliefs specified for each player about the types of the other players. In dynamic games, this solution concept yields a lot of equilibria when no further restrictions are placed on players' beliefs. Especially, Bayesian Nash equilibrium results in some implausible equilibria, where players take turns sequentially rather than simultaneously. Due to this reason, Bayesian Nash equilibrium is thought as an incomplete tool to analyze dynamic games of incomplete information.

ε-Equilibrium

ε-equilibrium is a strategy profile that approximately satisfies the condition of Nash equilibrium (Han, 2011). When a player has chosen a strategy and it is impossible to gain more than ε in the expected payoff, the current set of strategies and the corresponding payoffs constitute a ε-equilibrium. That is formally formulated as

$$u_i\left(s_i^*, \boldsymbol{s}_{-i}^*\right) > u_i\left(s_i, \boldsymbol{s}_{-i}^*\right) - \mu,$$
$$\text{for all} \quad s_i \in S_i \tag{2}$$

ε-equilibrium is a near-Nash equilibrium, and ε is a real non-negative parameter. Every Nash Equilibrium is equivalent to a ε-equilibrium where ε = 0.

Correlated Equilibrium

In 1974, Robert Aumann introduced a solution concept - correlated equilibrium, which is more general than the Nash equilibrium. In the correlated equilibrium, each player chooses his strategy according to the player's observation and a strategy profile is chosen randomly according to a certain distribution. If no player would want to deviate from the recommended strategy while assuming the others don't deviate, the distribution is called a correlated equilibrium (Kunnumkal, 2004). To mathematically express, let $p(s_i, s_{-i})$ be the joint distribution of players to perform a specific strategy (s_i). If the strategy of the different players is independent, $p(s_i, s_{-i})$ is a product of each individual player's probability for different strategies. Given the recommended strategy (s_i), a correlated strategy $s = (s_i, s_{-i})$ is said to be a correlated equilibrium if we have as follows.

$$\sum_{s_{-i} \in S_{-i}} \begin{Bmatrix} p\left(s_i, \mathbf{s}_{-i}\right) \times U_i\left(s_i, \mathbf{s}_{-i}\right)\} \\ -\{p\left(s_i, \mathbf{s}_{-i}\right) \times U_i\left(s_i', \mathbf{s}_{-i}\right)\} \end{Bmatrix} \geq 0 \qquad (3)$$

where s_i, $s_i' \in S_i$, and $\mathbf{s}_{-i} \in S_{-i}$ for all players $i \in \mathcal{N}$. If the player i is to choose the recommendation strategy s_i, then choosing strategy s_i' instead of s_i cannot result in a higher expected payoff to the player i (Han2011).

Nash equilibrium corresponds to the special case of correlated equilibria. Therefore, Nash equilibrium is a point inside the correlated equilibria set. Usually, there are multiple correlated equilibrium. Therefore, which one is the most suitable should be very carefully considered in practical design (Wang, 2009). To satisfy this goal, the concept of *correlated optimal* is developed. A multi-strategy $\mathbf{s}^{all}$ is *correlated optimal* if it satisfies the following conditions.

$$\mathbf{s}^{all} = \arg\max_p \sum_{i \in N} E_p\left(U_i\right), \qquad (4)$$

$$\text{s.t.} \sum_{s_{-i} \in S_{-i}} \begin{Bmatrix} p\left(s_i, \mathbf{s}_{-i}\right) \\ \times U_i\left(s_i, \mathbf{s}_{-i}\right)\} \\ -\{p\left(s_i, \mathbf{s}_{-i}\right) \\ \times U_i\left(s_i', \mathbf{s}_{-i}\right) \end{Bmatrix} \geq 0.$$

$$\forall s_i, s_i' \in S_i,$$

and

$$\forall i \in N.$$

where $E_p\left(\cdot\right)$ is the expected average utility with p. The *correlated optimal* is the solution concept to achieve the highest social welfare. Even though the *correlated optimal* is a notion of efficiency, it does not necessarily result in a socially desirable distribution of resources: it makes no statement about equality, or the overall well-being of a society (Barr, 2012).

Wardrop Equilibrium

In 1952, John G. Wardrop developed the concept of Wardrop equilibrium in the context of road traffic. Initially, Wardrop considered the scenario of roads and a large number of vehicles traveling though the roads from an origin to a destination. The vehicles are interested in minimizing their travel time, which is dependent on each road's characteristics and the number of vehicles using it. This situation can be modeled by using a non-cooperative game, with the players being the vehicles attempting to find a shortest-path route while minimizing their travel time from origin to destination. Therefore, the main concept of Wardrop equilibrium can capture key features of a minimization problem among many selfish players and it is related to the idea of Nash equilibrium (Han, 2011), (Altmana, Boulognea, El-Azouzia, Jiménezb, & Wynterc, 2006).

In roads at the Wardrop equilibrium, two principles are assumed, i) all used path from a source to a destination have equal mean latencies, and ii) any unused path from a source to a destination has greater potential mean latency than that along the used paths. To formally express the Wardrop equilibrium, define 'class i' as all individual vehicles in belonging to population that have a given origin $s(i)$ and a given destination $d(i)$. Let u be the vector of strategies of all vehicles and S^i is the strategy set of vehicles in the class i. Therefore, S^i is identified with all the available paths in roads between $s(i)$ and $d(i)$. The path j's delay is defined as $D_j(u)$, $j \in S^i$. Then, letting $S_*^i \subset S^i$ be the subset of paths actually used by the vehicles in the class i, u^* is a Wardrop equilibrium if and only if it satisfies

$$D_j\left(u^*\right) = \min_{k \in S^i} D_k\left(u^*\right),$$
$$\cdots \ s.t., \ j \in S_*^i, \tag{5}$$

The Wardrop equilibrium has been applied to many problems in transportation and communication networks (Correa and Stier-Moses, 2010). However one drawback of Wardrop's user equilibrium is that it requires deterministic inputs of travel demand and supply. This assumption is not applicable in real world situations (Altmana, 2006).

Evolutionary Stable Strategy

Game theory developed to study the strategic interaction among rational self-regarding players. However, in the early 1970's, the theory underwent a transformation into evolutionary game theory. An important concept of evolutionary game theory is that of Evolutionarily Stable Strategy (*ESS*), which was defined and introduced by John Maynard Smith. Its aim is to investigate the effect of each individual behaving in a selfish manner, on a large population of such individuals, given that the best strategy to use for itself depends on the collective behavior of the population, which itself is composed of many of these same selfish individuals. Therefore, *ESS* is evolutionarily stable and cannot be invaded by any alternative strategy ("Evolutionarily Stable Strategies," n.d.). *ESS* solution can be obtained by repeating a symmetric game with comparing in an infinite population.

If all the players play strategy x and x is stable in the sense that a mutant playing with a different strategy y cannot successfully invade, then x is an *ESS*. More formally, x is an *ESS* if $U(x, z) > U(y, z)$ where the payoff for playing x against another playing z is greater than that for playing any other strategy y against z.

ESS is an equilibrium refinement of the Nash equilibrium and sometimes, it is associated with mixed strategy equilibriums. Equilibrium in *Hawk-Dove* game and in a biology oriented version of *Chicken* game is a very famous example of *ESS*. The main concept of *ESS* has been used widely in behavioural ecology, economics, anthropology, evolutionary psychology, philosophy, and political science (Krebs, & Davies, 1997). In addition, this approach also allows to increase our understanding of dynamical systems in biology and, more recently, in the social sciences with significant ramifications for philosophy.

Non-cooperative games constitute an important branch of game theory, and Nash equilibrium has been regarded as a general solution for non-cooperative games. Since the development of the Nash equilibrium concept, game theorists have proposed many related solution concepts, which refine the Nash equilibrium to overcome perceived flaws in the Nash concept. However, subsequent refinements and extensions of the Nash equilibrium concept share the main insight of Nash's concept. All equilibrium concepts analyze what choices will be made when each player takes into account the decision-making of others. Finally, we can draw the equilibria diagram for non-cooperative games. Figure 1 shows the relationship among different kinds of equilibria.

Solutions for Cooperative Games

Nowadays, cooperative games become a hot research topic and have received a generous concern. Cooperative games are games where groups of players (i.e., 'coalitions') may enforce cooperative behaviors. Therefore, players choose their

Figure 1. Equilibria for non-cooperative games

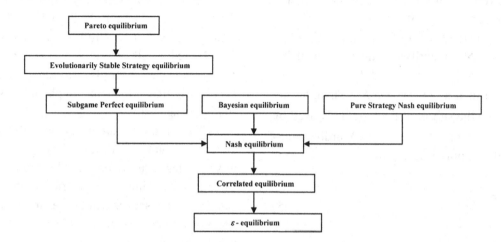

strategies through a consensus decision-making process. The key issue in cooperative games is how to divide the total payoffs of players. Many solution concepts have been proposed to answer this problem, each kind of which satisfies a certain rational behavior and reasonable principle. The aim of subsection is to study classical solutions for various cooperative games.

Pareto Optimality

Named after Italian economist Vilfredo Pareto, Pareto optimality (or Pareto efficiency) is a measure of efficiency. In Pareto optimality, no player can be made better off without hurting, or decreasing the payoffs of other players. To formally express the Pareto optimality ($v*$), let vector $v*$ is preferred to a vector v if each element of v is not strictly greater than the corresponding parameter of $v*$ and at least one parameter is strictly less: that is, $v_i \leq v_i^*$ for each element i and $v_j < v_j^*$ for some element j. It is expressed as $v \propto v^*$.

An outcome of a game is *Pareto dominated* if some other outcome would make at least one player better off without hurting any other player. A strategy change process can make at least one player better off without making any other player worse off, it is called a *Pareto improvement*.

Therefore, a solution is defined as Pareto optimal when no further *Pareto improvement* can be made ("Pareto Optimality," n.d.).

Weak Pareto optimality is also a solution concept, which nominally satisfies the same standard of Pareto optimal status. However, the conditions are weaker than Pareto optimal. A *weak Pareto optimal* is an allocation for which there are no possible alternative allocations whose realization would cause every individual to gain with the new allocation. In other words, a new allocation is only considered to be a Pareto improvement if it is strictly preferred by all individuals. Therefore, the set of Pareto optimal solutions is a subset of the set of *weak Pareto optimal* solutions, because a Pareto optimal solution satisfies the stronger requirement that there is no allocation that is strictly preferred by one individual player and weakly preferred by the rest players. When contrasted with *weak Pareto optimal*, a standard Pareto optimality may be referred to as a *strong Pareto optimal*.

The notion of Pareto optimal is very useful in economics and many other fields. However, the concept of Pareto optimality does not necessarily result in a socially desirable distribution of resources. Since there is no fairness consideration in Pareto optimality, some more refined fairness concept is required for the overall well-being society (Barr, 2012).

Core

Core is one of solution concepts for n-person cooperative games. Even the idea of the core already appeared in the work of Edgeworth in 1881, the modern definition was introduced by Donald B. Gillies in 1959. Core is the set of feasible allocations under which no subset (a *coalition*) has a value greater than the sum of its players' payoffs. Let the vector $\mathbf{x} = [\, x_1, ... \, x_i, ... \, x_n\,]$ be the received payoffs for players ($\mathbb{N} = \{1, 2, ..., n\}$). This payoff vector is *group rational* if $\sum_{i=1}^{n} x_i = \nu(\mathbb{N})$. In particular, the highest total payoff can be achieved by forming a coalition among all players. Also, the payoff vector is *individually rational* if $x_i \geq \nu(\{i\})$. It means that a player will not agree to receive payoff less than that the player could obtain without coalition. If the payoff vector $\mathbf{x}$ is both group rational and individually rational, it is defined as '*imputation*' like as.

$$\mathbf{x} = \left\{ \begin{array}{l} [x_1, ..., x_n] \mid \sum_{i \in \mathbb{N}} x_i = \nu(\mathbb{N}) \\ \text{and } x_i \geq \nu(\{i\}), \, \forall i \in \mathbb{N} \end{array} \right\} \quad (6)$$

An *imputation* $\mathbf{x}$ is unstable with coalition $\mathbb{S}$ ($\mathbb{S} \subset \mathbb{N}$) if $v(\mathbb{S}) > \sum_{i \in \mathbb{S}} x_i$. Specifically, if the imputation is unstable, there is at least one player who is unsatisfied. The core is defined as the set of imputations in which no coalition $\mathbb{S}$ has an incentive to reject the proposed payoff allocation, and to deviate from the grand coalition of all players while forming coalition $\mathbb{S}$ instead. Mathematically, core ($\mathcal{C}(\nu)$) is expressed as follows:

$$\mathcal{C}(\nu) = \left\{ \begin{array}{l} \mathbf{x} = [x_1, ..., x_n] \mid \sum_{i \in \mathbb{N}} x_i = \nu(\mathbb{N}) \\ \text{and} \sum_{i \in \mathbb{S}} x_i \geq \nu(\mathbb{S}), \, \forall \mathbb{S} \subset \mathbb{N} \end{array} \right\} \quad (7)$$

The core, sometimes it is called as a *cooperative Nash equilibrium*, is useful to obtain the stability condition of the coalitional cooperative game. However, it may contain several points and in some cases it could be empty. Therefore, the solution that provides the most preferable distribution strategy is required (Han, 2011).

To avoid the emptiness of core, L. Shapley and M. Shubik introduced the generalized concept for the core solution, named *strong ε-core*, in 1966 (Shapley, & Shubik, 1966). The *strong ε-core* for some number $\varepsilon \in \mathbb{R}$ is the set of payoff vectors

$$\mathcal{C}_\varepsilon(\nu) = \left\{ \begin{array}{l} \mathbf{x} = [x_1, ..., x_n] \mid \sum_{i \in \mathbb{N}} x_i = \nu(\mathbb{N}) \\ \text{and} \sum_{i \in \mathbb{S}} x_i \geq \nu(\mathbb{S}) - \varepsilon, \, \forall \mathbb{S} \subset \mathbb{N} \end{array} \right\} \quad (8)$$

The *strong ε-core* is the set of allocations where no coalition can improve its payoff by leaving the grand coalition, if it must pay the ε penalty for leaving. The value ε can be negative. In this case, the *strong ε-core* represents a bonus for leaving the grand coalition. Clearly, regardless of whether the core is empty, the *strong ε-core* will be nonempty for a large enough value of ε and empty for a small enough (possibly negative) value of ε (Shapley, 1966).

The *strong ε-core solution* can avoid the empty problem. However, the core can be quite large, so selecting a suitable core allocation can be difficult. Moreover, in many scenarios, the allocations that lie in the core can be unfair to one or more players (Han, 2011).

Shapley Value

In 1953, Lloyd Shapley proposed a new cooperative solution concept, Shapley Value. It assigns a unique distribution (among the players) of a total surplus generated by the coalition of all players. Shapley also proved that the Shapley Value can satisfy efficiency, symmetry and additivity. Main feature of Shapley Value is to provide a unique solution of a n-person cooperative game. For example, a coalition of players cooperates, and obtains a certain overall gain from that cooperation. Since some players may contribute more to the coalition than others, it is important to decide the final distribution of generated surplus among the players (Shapley value, n.d.). The Shapley value can provide one possible answer under the cooperative game situation.

To compute Shapley value, let us define the value function (v) over the real line like as $v : 2^N \to \mathbb{R}$ with $v(\varnothing) = 0$, and characterize unique mapping $\phi = [\phi_1..., \phi_i,..., \phi_n]$ that is the Shapley Value; ϕ_i is the payoff given to the player i by the Shapley Value ϕ. The Shapley Value is characterized by a collection of desirable properties or axioms described below (Han, 2011),(Cai, 2004).

1. **Efficiency:** It is in fact group rationality. Formally, $\sum_{i \in A} \phi_i(v) = v(\mathbb{A})$

2. **Symmetry:** When two players have the same contribution in a coalition, their assigned payoffs must be equal. In other words, if there exist the player i and j such that $v(\mathbb{S} \cup \{i\}) = v(\mathbb{S} \cup \{j\})$ and $i, j \notin \mathbb{S}$, then $\phi_i(v) = \phi_j(v)$

3. **Dummy:** It assigns no payoff to players that do not improve the value of any coalition. If there exists the player i such that $v(\mathbb{S}) = v(\mathbb{S} \cup \{i\})$ for $\mathbb{S}$ without i, then $\phi_i(v) = 0$. Therefore,

4. **Additivity:** If u and v are value functions, then $\phi(u + v) = \phi(u) + \phi(v)$. It links the value of different games u and v, and asserts that Shapley Value is a unique mapping over the space of all coalitional games.

Shapley showed that there exists a unique mapping, the Shapley value, from the space of all coalitional games to $\mathbb{R}^N$, that satisfies these four axioms (Han, 2011). Based on these properties, the Shapley Value can be obtained by considering the payoff depending on the order that player joins the coalition. In particular, the Shapley Value is the average payoff to a player if the players enter into the coalition in a completely random order. The Shapley Value $\phi = [\phi_1..., \phi_i,..., \phi_n]$ can be computed as follows:

$$\phi_i(v) = \sum_{\mathbb{S} \subset A, \; i \in A} \frac{(|\mathbb{S}| - 1)!(n - |\mathbb{S}|)!}{n!} \left(v(\mathbb{S}) - v(\mathbb{S} - \{i\})\right) \tag{9}$$

where $|\mathbb{S}|$ indicates the number of players in the set $\mathbb{S}$. $v(\mathbb{S})$ is the minimum payoff which the coalition S can guarantee its members (i.e., players), and $v(\mathbb{S} - \{i\})$ is the payoff secured by a coalition with the same members in $\mathbb{S}$ except the player i. In the Shapley Value, all the coalitions are regarded equal which means they have the same probability to appear. The first part of the formula can be interpreted as the probability of a coalition containing the player i with the size of $|\mathbb{S}|$. The second part is the payoff difference between the coalitions with and without the player i, which measures the contribution of the player i to the coalition. The bigger the difference, the more the player contributes to its coalition, then the more payoff he should earn (Han, 2011), (Cai, 2004).

The Nucleolus

In 1969, Schmeidler introduced the idea of *nucleolus*, which is a solution concept for cooperative games. The basic motivation of the nucleolus is to provide an allocation that minimizes the dissatisfaction of the players with the allocation they can receive in a given cooperative game. The nucleolus is quite an interesting concept, since it combines a number of fairness criteria with stability.

Usually, the model of cooperative game has two basic elements: the set of players and the payoff function. The set of players is expressed as $\mathcal{N} = \{1, 2, ..., n\}$. The meaning of payoff function (v) is a real function of set $\mathcal{N}$; any possible subset S of players (a coalition $\forall S \subset \mathcal{N}$) would produce the payoff $v(S)$. If coalition S and T are independent (i.e., $S \cap T = \varnothing$), then $v(S \cup T) \geq v(S) + v(T)$. In this cooperative game $(\mathcal{N}, v)$, there are two important issues, i) how the coalitions are formed amongst the players, and ii) how the payoff from a player is allocated. These two issues are strongly interrelated.

Instead of applying a general fairness axiom for finding a unique payoff allocation, the goal of nucleolus solution is to find a way to fairly allocate the payoff that is jointly created by players. Suppose $x = \{x_1, x_2, ..., x_n\}$ (i.e., $x \in \mathbb{R}^{\mathcal{N}}$) is the set of each player's payoff, $Y = \{y_1, y_2, ..., y_n\}$ is the set of the profit allocation imputation. As mentioned earlier, imputation is a payoff vector that is both individually rational and group-rational. The measure of dissatisfaction with an allocation x for a coalition $y \in Y$ is defined as the *excess value* like as $e(x, y) = v(y) - \sum_{j \in y} x_j$. If an allocation x can ensure that all *excess values* (or dissatisfaction indexes) are minimized, it is of particular interest as a solution for coalitional cooperative games. This is the main concept of *nucleolus* (Han, 2011), (SongHuai, Xinghua, Lu, & Hui, 2006).

Now, let $\psi(x)$ be the set of all *excess values* in a game ($\mathcal{N}, v$) arranged in non-increasing order. In other words, $\psi_i(x) \geq \psi_j(x)$, $\forall i < j$. Notice that x is in the core of v if it is an imputation and $\psi_1(x) \leq 0$. To define the *nucleolus*, we consider the lexicographic ordering of sets. For example, For two payoff sets u, w, it is said that $\psi(u)$ is lexicographically smaller than $\psi(w)$ if for some index c, we have $\psi_i(u) = \psi_i(w)$, $\forall i < c$ and $\psi_c(u) < \psi_c(w)$. The *nucleolus* of v is the lexicographically minimal imputation. Hence, the *nucleolus* minimizes the *excess vales* in a non-increasing order starting with the maximum *excess value*.

The *nucleolus* is group and individually rational (since it is an imputation), and unique in the game. If the core is not empty, the *nucleolus* is in the core. The process steps for computing the *nucleolus* are, i) to find the imputations that distribute the payoff of the grand coalition in such a way that the maximum *excess value* is minimized, ii) If this minimization has a unique solution, it is the *nucleolus*, iii) If not, searching for the imputations that minimize the second-largest *excess value*, iv) this process is repeated for all subsequent *excess values*, until a unique solution (i.e., the *nucleolus*) found. The applications of the *nucleolus* are numerous in cooperative game theory. One of the most prominent examples is the marriage contract problem that first appeared in the Babylonian Talmud (0-500 AD) (Han, 2011.

Even though the nucleolus is quite an interesting concept, and provides an optimal and fair solution to many applications, the main drawback is its computational complexity. Therefore, the applications that utilize the *nucleolus* remain scarce.

Nash Bargaining Solution

In 1950s, John Nash proposed a simple cooperative game model, which predicted an outcome of bargaining based only on information about each player's preferences. His bargaining game model is formulated by an expected utility function over the set of feasible agreements and the outcome which would result in case of disagreement.

Nash gave six axioms to provide the concept of efficiency and fairness for desirable bargaining solutions - *Individual rationality, feasibility, Symmetry, Pareto optimality, Independence of irrelevant alternatives* and *Invariance with respect to utility transformations*. If a solution can fulfill these six axioms, it is called as the Nash Bargaining Solution (NBS), which is a unique and fair Pareto optimal solution ("Bargaining problem," n.d.).

To formally express these axioms, we need to introduce some terminology. An *agreement point* is any strategy vector $(s_1, \ldots s_n) \in \mathbb{S}$ where $\mathbb{S}$ is the set of strategy profiles. It is a possible outcome of the bargaining process. A *disagreement point* is also a strategy that is expected to be the result of non-cooperative actions; it means a failure of the bargaining process. Each player i has its own utility function $(U_i(s_i))$ and it has also a minimum desired utility value ($U_i(s_i^0)$), which is the dis-agreement point. Assume $\mathbb{S}$ = { $\mathbb{S} = \left\{ (U_1(s_1), \ldots, U_n(s_n)) \right\} \subset \mathbb{R}^n$ is a feasible payoff set that is nonempty, convex, closed, and bounded. Let $d = (d_1, \ldots, d_n) = (U_1(s_i^0), \ldots, U_n(s_i^0)) \in \mathbb{R}^n$ be the disagreement point, and F be a function $F(\mathbf{S}, d) \to \mathbb{R}^n$. If the following Nash's six axioms are satisfied, $\mathbf{X}^* = (x_1^*, , x_i^*, , x_n^*) = F(\mathbf{S}, d)$ is said to be an NBS (Han, 2011), (Park & Schaar, 2007), (Han, Ji, & Liu, 2004).

1. **Individual Rationality:** NBS should be better off than the disagreement point. Therefore, no player is worse off than if the agreement fails. Formally, $x_i^* \geq d_i$ for all player i.

2. **Feasibility:** NBS is reasonable under the circumstances. That is, $\mathbf{X}^* \in \mathbb{S}$.

3. **Pareto Optimality:** NBS gives the maximum payoff to the players. Therefore, if there exists a solution $\mathbf{X}^* = (x_1^*, , x_i^*, , x_n^*)$, it shall be Pareto optimal.

4. **Invariance with Respect to Utility Transformations:** A utility function specifies a player's preferences. Therefore, different utility functions can be used to model the same preferences. However, the final outcome should not depend on which of these equivalent utility representations is used. In other words, for any linear scale transformation of the function ψ, $\psi\left(F(\mathbb{S}, d)\right) = F\left(\psi(\mathbb{S}), \psi(d)\right)$. This axiom is also called *Independence of Linear Transformations or scale covariance*.

5. **Independence of Irrelevant Alternatives:** The solution should be independent of ir-relevant alternatives. In other words, a reasonable outcome will be feasible after some payoff sets have been removed. If $\mathbf{X}^*$ is a bargaining solution for a bargaining set $\mathbb{S}$ then for any subset $\mathbb{S}'$ of $\mathbb{S}$ containing $\mathbf{X}^*$, $\mathbf{X}^*$ continues to be a bargaining solution. Formally, if $\mathbf{X}^* \in \mathbb{S}' \subset \mathbb{S}$ and $\mathbf{X}^* = F(\mathbb{S}, d)$, then $\mathbf{X}^* = F(\mathbb{S}', d)$.

6. **Symmetry:** Symmetry means that if the players' utilities are exactly the same, they should get symmetric payoffs (i.e., equal payoffs). Therefore, payoff should not dis-criminate between the identities of the play-ers, but only depend on utility functions. For example, if $\mathbb{S}$ is invariant under all exchanges of users, $F_i(\mathbb{S}, d) = F_j(\mathbb{S}, d)$ for all possible players i and j.

In the cooperative payoff region $\mathbb{S}$, all indi-vidually rational and Pareto optimal payoff pairs can be called the bargaining set; the NBS is located in the bargaining set. The axioms *Individual rationality*, *feasibility*, and *Pareto optimality* define the bargaining set. The other axioms are called axioms of fairness. The axiom *Invariance with respect to utility transformations* assures that the solution is invariant if affinely scaled. The axiom *Independence of irrelevant alternatives* states that if the bargaining solution of the larger set is found on a smaller domain, the solution is not affected by the domain size. The axiom *Symmetry* states that if two players have the same disagreement utility and the same set of feasible utility, then they will achieve the same NBS payoff (Han, 2011), (Park, & Schaar, 2007), (Han, Ji, & Liu, 2004).

The NBS is an effective tool to achieve a mutually desirable solution with a good balance between efficiency and fairness. However, NBS has focused on problems with convex feasible sets. This extreme assumption might be too strong; the convexity assumption has been questioned and caused some technical difficulties. Usually, the feasible set for real world control problems may be non-convex.

Kalai-Smorodinsky Bargaining Solution

In 1975, Ehud Kalai and Meir Smorodinsky introduced the fundamental solution concept of bargaining games. To get the desirable bargaining solution, they also gave six axioms - *Individual rationality*, *Feasibility*, *Symmetry*, *Pareto optimality*, *individual monotonicity* and *Invariance with respect to utility transformations*. In compare with NBS, the axiom *Independence of irrelevant alternatives* is substituted with the axiom *individual monotonicity*. A solution, which would satisfy these axioms, is called the *Kalai-Smorodinsky* Bargaining Solution (KSBS) (Han, 2011), (Park, & Schaar, 2007).

Individual monotonicity axiom means that the increasing of bargaining set size in a direction favorable to a specific player always benefits that

player. For example, let $(\mathbb{S},d)$ and $(\mathbb{S}',d)$ be two bargaining problems where $\mathbb{S}' \subset \mathbb{S}$. If the maximum achievable payoffs of all players are the same except the player i, the player i gains more payoff in $(\mathbb{S},d)$ than in $(\mathbb{S}',d)$ through the KSBS. Formally, if $\mathbb{S}' \subset \mathbb{S}$, $d=d'$ and $\max\limits_{\mathbf{X}\in\mathbb{S},\mathbf{X}\geq d} X_k = \max\limits_{\mathbf{X}'\in\mathbb{S}',\mathbf{X}'\geq d'} X_k'$ for all $k \in \{1, \ldots, N\} \backslash \{i\}$, then $F_i(\mathbb{S}',d) \geq F_i(\mathbb{S}',d)$ (Park, & Schaar, 2007).

Like as the NBS, the KSBS also provides a fair and optimal solution. In addition, KSBS can be used when the feasible payoff set is not convex. It is the main advantage of KSBS over the NBS. Due to this appealing property, the KSBS approach has been practically implemented in various resource management problems in economics and telecommunications (Davila, 2009).

Egalitarian Bargaining Solution

In 1977, E. Kalai and R. Myerson developed another interesting bargaining solution. It is the Egalitarian Bargaining Solution (EBS). Unlike other bargaining solutions, the egalitarian solution enjoys even stronger *monotonicity* requirements while satisfying independence conditions. Without using the Nash's axiom of *Invariance with respect to utility transformations*, the EBS attempts to grant equal gain to players. In other words, it is the point which maximizes the minimum payoff among players. This characterization can be extended to a large class of solutions including the α-proportional bargaining solution (Bossert, 1995).

Let $(\mathbb{S},d)$ be a two-person bargaining problem where $\mathbb{S} \subseteq \mathbb{R}^2$ is the feasible set of payoff vectors and $d \in \mathbb{R}^2$ is the disagreement point. The ideal point of a bargaining problem is simply defined by

$$F_i(\mathbb{S},d) = \max\left\{x_i | \mathbf{X} \in \mathbb{S}, \mathbf{X} \geq d\right\}, \qquad (10)$$
$$\text{s.t,} \quad \forall i = 1, 2.$$

The egalitarian bargaining solution is defined by letting the unique point $(x_1, x_2) = X \in \mathbb{S}$ such that

$$x_1 - d_1 = x_2 - d_2 \qquad (11)$$

A generalization of the egalitarian solution is the class of α-proportional (or weighted egalitarian) bargaining solution. It is also defined as the unique point $X \in \mathbb{S}$ such that

$$x_1 - d_1 = \alpha\left(x_2 - d_2\right) \qquad (12)$$

Clearly, α leads to the egalitarian bargaining solution.

The main feature of EBS is a *monotonicity* with respect to expansions of the feasible set. The *monotonicity* axiom imposes an *invariance* condition under decomposition of the bargaining process into several stages. Therefore, the *monotonicity* axiom can be replaced by step-by-step negotiation (Bossert, 1995). There are at least two advantages in the step-by-step negotiation. First, it makes it easier to implement a solution since the negotiation can be broken up into several stages. Second, the players do not have incentives to change the order of the negotiations. This process is likely to be observed in actual negotiations.

Rubinstein Bargaining Solution

In 1982, Israeli economist Ariel Rubinstein built up an alternating-offer bargain game based on the Stahl's limited negotiation model; it is known as a *Rubinstein-Stahl* bargaining process. This game model can provide a possible solution to the problem that two players are bargaining with the division of the benefits.

In Rubinstein-Stahl bargaining model, players have their own bargaining power (δ). The division proportion of the benefits can be obtained according to the bargaining power, which can be

computed at each player individually. A more bargaining power player benefits more from the bargaining. Players negotiate with each other by proposing offers alternately. After several rounds of negotiation, they finally reach an agreement as following (Rubinstein, 1982).

$$\left(x_1^*, x_2^*\right) = \begin{cases} \left(\dfrac{1-\delta_2}{1-\delta_1\delta_2}, \dfrac{\delta_2\left(1-\delta_1\right)}{1-\delta_1\delta_2}\right) \\ \text{if the player\_1 offers first} \\[2ex] \left(\dfrac{\delta_1\left(1-\delta_2\right)}{1-\delta_1\delta_2}, \dfrac{1-\delta_1}{1-\delta_1\delta_2}\right) \\ \text{if the player\_2 offers first} \end{cases}$$

$$(13)$$

$$\text{s.t.,} \left(x_1^*, x_2^*\right) \in \mathbf{R}^2 : x_1^* + x_2^* = 1, x_1^* \geq 0, x_2^* \geq 0$$

and

$$0 \leq \delta_1, \delta_2 \leq 1$$

It is obvious that $\dfrac{1-\delta_2}{1-\delta_1\delta_2} \geq \dfrac{\delta_2\left(1-\delta_1\right)}{1-\delta_1\delta_2}$ and $\dfrac{\delta_1\left(1-\delta_2\right)}{1-\delta_1\delta_2} \leq \dfrac{1-\delta_1}{1-\delta_1\delta_2}$. That is to say, there is a first-proposer advantage in the bargaining process. Traditionally, the bargaining power in the *Rubinstein-Stahl's* model is defined as follows.

$$\delta = e^{-\xi \times \Delta}, \quad \text{s.t.,} > 0 \qquad (14)$$

where $\triangle$ is the time period of negotiation round. Given the $\triangle$ is fixed (i.e., *unit_time*), δ is monotonic decreasing with the ξ. ξ is an instantaneous discount factor to adaptively adjust the bargaining power.

Especially, Rubinstein bargaining model provides a solution of a class of bargaining games that features alternating offers through an infinite time horizon. For a long time, the solution to this type of bargaining game was a mystery. Therefore, Rubinstein's solution is one of the most influential findings in cooperative game theory. Sometimes, it is considered as a non-cooperative implementation of the NBS, and is a solution for non-cooperative games. However, in this book, we treat it in the category of cooperative games.

For cooperative games, a solution concept is a vector that represents the allocation to each player. Researchers have proposed different solution concepts based on different views. Figure 2 shows the relationship among different kinds of solutions.

Figure 2. Solutions for cooperative games

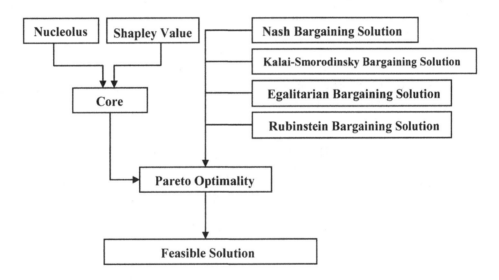

REFERENCES

Altmana, E., Boulognea, T., El-Azouzia, R., Jiménezb, T., & Wynterc, L. (2006). A survey on networking games in telecommunications. *Computers & Operations Research, 33,* 286–311. doi:10.1016/j.cor.2004.06.005

Bargaining Problem. (n.d.). Retrieved from http://www.answers.com/topic/bargaining-problem

Barr, N. (2012). *Economics of the Welfare State.* Oxford, UK: Oxford University Press.

Blum, A. (2008). *Online Learning, Regret Minimization, and Game Theory.* Retrieved from http://videolectures.net/mlss08au_blum_org/

Bossert, W., & Tan, G. (1995). An arbitration game and the egalitarian bargaining solution. *Social Choice and Welfare, 12,* 29–41. doi:10.1007/BF00182191

Brandenburger, A., & Stuart, H. (2007). Biform Games. *Management Science, 53,* 537–549. doi:10.1287/mnsc.1060.0591

Cai, J. (2004). Allocate fair payoff for cooperation in wireless ad hoc networks using Shapley Value. In *Proceedings of Parallel and Distributed Processing Symposium* (pp. 26-30). Academic Press.

Cheng, S. F., Reeves, D. M., Vorobeychik, Y., & Wellman, M. P. (2004). Notes on Equilibria in Symmetric Games. In *Proceedings of International Workshop on Game Theoretic and Decision Theoretic Agents,* (pp. 23-28). Academic Press.

Correa, J. R., & Stier-Moses, N. E. (2010). *Wardrop equilibria.* Retrieved from http://www.columbia.edu/~ns2224/papers/WEsurveyRev-2public.pdf

Cox, J. C. (2006). *Perfect Bayesian Equilibrium.* Retrieved from http://www.econport.org/content/handbook/gametheory/useful/equilibrium/perfect.html

Davila, J. (2009). *Kalai - Smorodinsky solution to bargaining problems.* Retrieved from http://cermsem.univ-paris1.fr/davila/teaching/BargTh/Bargaining%20slides%20-%202%20-%20Kalai-Smorodinsky.pdf

Evolutionarily Stable Strategies. (n.d.). Retrieved from http://ess.nbb.cornell.edu/ess.html

Game Theory. (n.d.). Retrieved from http://en.wikipedia.org/wiki/Game_theory

Han, Z., Ji, Z., & Liu, K. J. R. (2004). Low-complexity OFDMA channel allocation with Nash bargaining solution fairness. *IEEE Global Telecommunication Conf., 6,* 3726–3731.

Han, Z., Niyato, D., Saad, W., Başar, T., & Hjørungnes, A. (2011). *Game Theory in Wireless and Communication Networks.* Cambridge University Press. doi:10.1017/CBO9780511895043

Homo Economicus. (n.d.). Retrieved from http://rationalwiki.org/wiki/Homo_economicus

Howard, N. (1971). *Paradoxes of Rationality.* MIT Press.

Krebs, J. R., & Davies, N. B. (1997). *Behavioural Ecology: An Evolutionary Approach.* Wiley-Blackwell.

Kunnumkal, S. (2004). *Algorithmic Game Theory.* Retrieved from http://www.cs.cornell.edu/courses/cs684/2004sp/feb20.pdf

Leino, J. (2003). *Applications of game theory in ad hoc networks.* Academic Press.

Lescanne, P., & Perrinel, M. (2012). Backward coinduction, Nash equilibrium and the rationality of escalation. *Acta Informatica, 49*(3), 117–137. doi:10.1007/s00236-012-0153-3

Nash Equilibrium. (n.d.). Retrieved from http://economics.about.com/cs/economicsglossary/g/nashequilibrium.htm

Osborne, M. J., & Rubinstein, A. (1994). *A Course in Game Theory*. Cambridge, MA: MIT Press.

Pareto Optimality. (n.d.). Retrieved from http://www.economyprofessor.com/pareto-optimality-1906

Park, H. G., & Schaar, M. V. D. (2007). Bargaining Strategies for Networked Multimedia Resource Management. *IEEE Transactions on Signal Processing*, *55*(7), 3496–3511. doi:10.1109/TSP.2007.893755

Pell, B. D. (1993). *Strategy Generation and Evaluation for Meta-Game Playing*. (Ph.D dissertation). University of Cambridge, Cambridge, UK.

Prisoner's Dilemma. (n.d.). Retrieved from http://en.wikipedia.org/wiki/Prisoner's_dilemma

Rubinstein, A. (1982). Perfect equilibrium in a bargaining model. *Econometrica*, *50*, 97–109. doi:10.2307/1912531

Sandholm, W. H. (2007). *Evolutionary Game Theory*. Retrieved from http://www.ssc.wisc.edu/~whs/research/egt.pdf

Shapley, L. S., & Shubik, M. (1966). Quasicores in a monetary economy with non-convex preferences. *Econometrica*, *34*(4), 805–827. doi:10.2307/1910101

Shapley Value. (n.d.). Retrieved from http://www.answers.com/topic/shapley-value

SongHuai, D., Xinghua, Z., Lu, M., & Hui, X. (2006). A novel nucleolus-based loss allocation method in bilateral electricity markets. *IEEE Transactions on Power Systems*, *21*(1), 28–33. doi:10.1109/TPWRS.2005.860932

Spangler, B. (2003). *Positive-Sum, Zero-Sum, and Negative-Sum Situations*. Retrieved from http://www.beyondintractability.org/essay/sum

Strategy. (n.d.). Retrieved from http://en.wikipedia.org/wiki/Strategy_(game_theory)

Wang, B., Han, Z., & Liu, K. J. R. (2009). Peer-to-Peer File Sharing Game using Correlated Equilibrium. In *Proceedings of Annual Conference on Information Sciences and Systems*, (pp. 729-734). Academic Press.

Wooldridge, M. (2012). Does Game Theory Work? *IEEE Intelligent Systems*, *27*(6), 76–80. doi:10.1109/MIS.2012.108

KEY TERMS AND DEFINITIONS

Best Reply: A pure strategy for one player is a best reply to a given opponent's pure strategy if it yields his best possible payoff among all his available strategies, provided that his opponent sticks to the given strategy.

Game States: As a game proceeds, various states of the world it is describing can be achieved.

Payoff: A development of the game that the players value for itself according to their respective preferences.

Players: Independent decision-makers who influence the development of a game through their decisions.

Pure Strategies: A pure strategy for a player is a complete contingency plan (a game plan) that specifies in advance what he will do in any development of the game.

The Normal Form: The normal form of a game is a list of pure strategies for each player and the specification of an outcome (in utility terms) for each pair of pure strategies (one strategy per player).

Chapter 3
Game Models in Various Applications

ABSTRACT

Recently, game-theoretic models have become famous in many academic research areas. Therefore, many applications and extensions of the original game theoretic approach appear in many of the major science fields. Despite all the technical problems, the history of game theory suggests that it would be premature to abandon the tool, especially in the absence of a viable alternative. If anything, the development of game theory has been driven precisely by the realization of its limitations and attempts to overcome them. This chapter explores these ideas.

INTRODUCTION

In game theory, a lot of game models have been developed; each game has several features. Usually, games are broadly divided based on weather players make decisions independently or not. According to this criterion, game models can be broadly classified into two different groups; non-cooperative games and cooperative games. However, some special games contain the mixed features of non-cooperative and cooperative games.

The goal of this chapter is to explain the basic ideas for each game model, and give the readers some insights on how to model network design problems by means of game theory. In addition, the main concepts and properties for each model are illustrated. Therefore, readers can compare advantages and disadvantages of different game models.

NON-COOPERATIVE GAMES

In non-cooperative games, players make decisions independently and are unable to make any collaboration contracts with other players in the game. Therefore, a family of non-cooperative games is presented in which players do not cooperate and selfishly select a strategy that maximizes their own utility. Initially, traditional applications of game theory developed from these games. There are various kinds of non-cooperative games.

DOI: 10.4018/978-1-4666-6050-2.ch003

Static Game

If all players select their strategy simultaneously, without knowledge of the other players' strategies, these games are called static games. Sometimes, static games are also called strategic games, one-shot games, single stage games or simultaneous games. Traditionally, static games are represented by the normal form; if two players play a static game, it can be represented in a matrix format. Each element represents a pair of payoffs when a certain combination of strategies in used. Therefore, these games are called matrix games or coordination games.

One example of matrix games is the stag hunt game (Skyrms, 2004). In this game situation, two hunters go out on a hunt. Each can individually choose to hunt a stag or a hare. Each hunter must choose an action without knowing the choice of the other. If an individual hunts a stag, he must have the cooperation of his partner in order to succeed. An individual can get a hare by himself, but a hare is worth less than a stag. This is taken to be an important analogy for social cooperation. Therefore, the stag hunt game is used to describe a conflict between safety and social cooperation. Formally, the payoff matrix for the stag hunt is pictured in Table 1, where A (a) > B (b) ≥ D (d) > C (c).

A solution concept for static games is Nash equilibrium. In the stag hunt game, there are two Nash equilibria when both hunters hunt a stag and both hunters hunt a hare. Sometimes, like as the Prisoner's Dilemma, an equilibrium is not an efficient solution despite that players can get a Pareto efficient solution. Due to this reason,

Table 1. Sample matrix for the prisoners' payoffs

	Stag	**Hare**
Stag	A, a (e.g., 2,2)	C, b (e.g., 0,1)
Hare	B, c (e.g., 1,0)	D, d (e.g., 1,1)

many researchers focus on how to drive a game where players have a non-cooperative behavior to an optimal outcome.

Dynamic Game

Dynamic games are mathematical models of the interaction between different players who are controlling a dynamical situation. Players in a dynamic game have at least some information about the strategy chosen by the others and play a similar stage game dynamically (Han, Niyato, Saad, Başar, & Hjørungnes, 2011). Therefore, strategies of players influence the evolution over time. Based on the history of selected strategies, players select their strategies sequentially based on the mapping between the information available to the player and his strategy set. Unlike static games, the threats from other players can encourage cooperation without the need for communication among the players. Dynamic games are classified into three different classes - repeated games, sequential games and stochastic games.

Sequential Game

Sequential games constitute a major class of dynamic games in which players select their strategy following a certain predefined order. In a sequential game, a player can observe the strategies of other players who acted before him, and make a strategic choice accordingly. Therefore, each player can take alternate turns to make their selections, given information available on the selected strategies of the other players (Hossain, Niyato, & Han, 2009). In sequential games, the sequence of strategic selection made by the players strongly impacts the outcome of the game. If players cannot observe the actions of previous players, this game is a static game. Therefore, static game is a special case of sequential game.

According to the role of information, sequential games one can distinguish between perfect information sequential games and imperfect information sequential games. If a player observes the strategies of every other player who has gone before him, this game is a perfect information game. If some, but not all players observe prior strategies, while other players act simultaneously, the game is an imperfect information game (Hossain, 2009).

Sequential games are represented by the extensive form. In the *extensive form*, the game is represented as a tree, where the root of the tree is the start of the game. One level of the tree is referred as a *stage*. The nodes of a tree show the possible unfolding of the game, meaning that they represent the sequence relation of the moves of the players. This sequence of moves defines a *path* on the tree and is referred to as the *history h* of the game. Each node has a unique history and terminal nodes (i.e., leaf nodes) of the tree define a potential end of the game called *outcomes*. Extensive-form games can be used to describe sequential interactions more easily than strategic-form games (Hossain, 2009). To illustrate these concepts, the *sequential multiple access game* with perfect information is good example (Hossain, 2009), (Felegyhazi, & Hubaux, 2006). In this game, we assume that the two transmitters p_1 and p_2 are not perfectly synchronized, which means that p_1 always moves first (i.e., transmits or not) and p_2 observes the move of p_1 before making his own move. The strategy of player p_1 is to transmit (T) or to be quiet (Q). But the strategy of player p_2 has to define a move (T' or Q') given the previous move for player p_1. The payoffs are as specified in the tree. There are four outcomes represented by the four terminal nodes of the tree: (T, T'), (T, Q'), (Q, T') and (Q, Q'). The payoffs associated with each outcome respectively are assumed as follows (3,1), (1,2), (2,1) and (0,0) (Figure 1).

Sequential games are solved using the solution concept of subgame perfect equilibrium, which is a refinement of a Nash equilibrium for dynamic games. Therefore, players' strategies constitute a Nash equilibrium in every subgame of the original

Figure 1. Extensive form for the sequential multiple access game (Hossain, 2009)

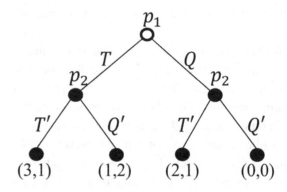

game. It may be found by backward induction, an iterative process for solving finite sequential games; working from the end of the game back to the root of the game tree involved having the player's best response in each layer. As a consequence of working backwards through a sequence of best responses, the subgame perfect equilibrium can be obtained (Han, 2011).

In the *sequential multiple access game*, if p_1 plays T, p_2 will play Q' to maximise his payoff and so p_1 will only receive 1. However, if p_1 plays Q, p_2 maximises his payoff by playing T' and p_1 receives 2. p_1 prefers 2 to 1. Therefore, p_1 will play Q and p_2 will play T'. This is the subgame perfect equilibrium.

Repeated Game

When a static non-cooperative strategic game is repeated over time, players iteratively interact by playing a similar stage game. This type of game is called as a repeated game. By repeating a game over time, the players may become aware of past behavior of the players and change their strategies accordingly. Therefore, a repeated game is an extensive form game which consists in some number of repetitions of some base game. Sequential games and repeated games are very similar, but there is a difference. In sequential games, players make decisions following a certain predefined order.

Beyond sequential games, a repeated game allows for a strategy to be contingent on past actions while allowing for reputation effects and retribution. It captures the idea that a player will have to take into account the impact of his current strategy on the future strategy of other players; this is called player's reputation. This approach can encourage cooperation.

Repeated games may be divided into finite or infinite games. Generally, infinitely repeated games can encourage cooperation. Since a player will play the game again with the same player, the threat of retaliation is real. Therefore, one essential part of infinitely repeated games is punishing players who deviate from this cooperative strategy. The punishment may be something like playing a strategy which leads to the reduced payoff to both players for the rest of the game.

For the T-period repeated game, at each period t, the actions during periods $1, ..., t-1$ are known to every player. Let β be the discount factor. The total discounted payoff for each player is computed by

$$\sum_{t=1}^{T} \beta^{t-1} U_k(t) \tag{1}$$

where $U_k(t)$ is the payoff to player k in the t'th game round. If $T = \infty$, the game is referred as the infinitely-repeated game (Han, 2011), (Han, Pandana, & Liu, 2005), (Owen, 2001). The average payoff ($\overline{U}$) to the player k is then given by:

$$\overline{U}_k (1 - \beta) \sum_{t=1}^{\infty} \beta^{t-1} U_k(t) \tag{2}$$

Note that for each player, maximizing total payoff is the same as maximizing average payoff. In (2), β is a discount factor. The valuation of the game diminishes with time depending on the discount factor β $(0 < \beta \leq 1)$. One way to inter-

pret the discount factor β is as an expression of traditional time preference. For example, if you received a dollar today you could deposit it in the bank and it would be worth $\$(1 + r)$ tomorrow, where r is the per-period rate of interest. You would be indifferent between a payment of $\$x^t$ today and $\$x^{t+\tau}$ received τ periods later only if the future values were equal: $(1 + r)x^t = x^{t+\tau}$. Comparing this indifference condition, we see that the two representations of inter-temporal preference are equivalent when $\beta = 1/(1+r)$. We can relate a player's discount factor β to player's *patience*. How much more does a player value a dollar today, at time t, than a dollar received $\tau > 0$ periods later? The relative value of the later dollar to the earlier is $\beta^{t+\tau} / \beta^t = \beta^\tau$. As $\beta \to 1, \beta^\tau \to 1$, so as the player's discount factor increases, the player values the later amount more and more nearly as much as the earlier payment. A person is more *patient*, the less she minds waiting for something valuable rather than receiving it immediately. So we interpret higher discount factors as higher levels of *patience* (Ratliff, 1996).

A history in a repeated game is a list $h^t = \left(s^0, s^1, ..., s^{t-1}\right)$ of what has previously occurred. Let H^t be the set of t-period histories. A strategy for player i is a sequence of maps $s_i^t : H^t \to S_i$. A mixed strategy σ_i is a sequence of maps $\sigma_i^t : H^t \to \Delta(S_i)$. A strategy profile is $\sigma = (\sigma_1, ..., \sigma_I)$.

Optimal method of playing a repeated game is not to repeatedly play a Nash strategy of the static game, but to cooperate and play a socially optimum strategy. There are many results in theorems which deal with how to achieve and maintain a socially optimal equilibrium in repeated games. These results are collectively called '*Folk Theorems*' (Han, 2005), (Owen, 2001).

Folk Theorem: Let $\left(\hat{\alpha}_1, ..., \hat{\alpha}_n\right)$ be the payoffs from a Nash equilibrium of game and let $\left(\alpha_1, ..., \alpha_n\right)$ be any feasible payoffs. There exists an equilibrium of the infinitely repeated game that attains $(\alpha_1,...,\alpha_n)$ as the average payoff for $\alpha_i > \hat{\alpha}_i, \forall i$, provided that β is sufficiently close to 1.

From Folk Theorem, we know that in an infinitely repeated game, any feasible outcome that gives each player better payoff than the Nash equilibrium can be obtained. Therefore, repeated game can be used to improve the performance of Nash equilibrium in one-shot interaction and repeated game strategies is considered as alternative methods to expand the set of equilibrium outcomes. By using the repeated game, the greedy players are forced to cooperate and have better payoffs. This is because the greedy player will get punishment from other players in the near future if he acts greedily. So, the hot issue of repeated games is defining a good rule to enforce the cooperation.

By using the repeated game, any feasible payoffs better than the Nash equilibrium can be obtained. The reason is that, with enough patience, a player's non-cooperative behavior will be punished by the future revenge from other cooperative players. In other words, a player's cooperation can be rewarded in the future by others' cooperation. Therefore, the key issue is how to define a good rule to achieve these better payoffs by enforcing cooperation among players. *tit-for-tat* and *cartel maintenance* are well-known rules for repeated games (Han, 2011), (Hossain, 2009), (Porter, 1983).

Tit-for-tat is a type of trigger strategy in which a player responds in one period with the same action his opponent used in the last period. The advantage of *tit-for-tat* is its implementation simplicity. However, there are two potential problems. First, the best response of a player is not the same action of the other opponent. Second, the information of other players' actions is hard to obtain (Han, 2011), (Hossain, 2009).

Cartel maintenance is one of the optimal design criteria (Porter, 1983). In the repeated game model, the basic idea of the *cartel maintenance* is

to provide enough threat to greedy players so as to prevent them from deviating from cooperation. If the cooperation is obtained, all players have better performances than those of non-cooperative plays. However, if any player deviates from cooperation while others still play cooperatively, this deviating player has a better payoff, while others have relatively worse payoffs. If no rule is employed, the cooperative players will also have incentives to deviate, and total payoff deteriorates due to the non-cooperation. Therefore, most repeated game models provide a punishment mechanism so that the current defecting gains of the selfish player will be outweighed by future punishment strategies from other players. For rational players, this threat of punishment prevents them from deviation, so the cooperation is enforced.

Based on the *Cartel maintenance*, the self-learning repeated game model was developed with parameter (V, T, N); T is a punishment time period, N is a number of predefined game rounds and V is a trigger threshold (Han, 2005). N is a constant, but T and V are variables and dynamically adjusted during the repeated game. At initial time, all players play game with the same strategy $\hat{s}$. The trigger threshold (V) is the payoff of the strategy $\hat{s}$. In each step, players play repeated game strategy.

If all players play cooperatively, every player will have some benefits. However, if any player deviates from cooperation by playing non-cooperatively and other players still play cooperatively, this player will have more benefits, while others suffer with lower benefits. In order to prevent players from deviation, the repeated game model provides a punishment mechanism. To implement punishment mechanism, player can observe the public information I_t (e.g. the outcome of the game) at time t. Here, it is assumed that a larger I_t stands for a higher cooperation level, resulting in higher performances for all players. In a punishment mechanism, the greedy player's short term benefit should be eliminated by the long term punishment. Based on the assumption of rational players, we can think that all players concern the long term payoff such as (2). Therefore, all players will have no incentive to deviate from cooperation. The self-learning repeated game model let distributed players learn the optimal strategy step by step, while within each step, the strategy of repeated game is applied to ensure the cooperation among players.

With increasing of T, the benefit of one time deviation will be eliminated out sooner or later. Therefore, the selfish players who deviate will have much lower payoff in the punishment period. So finally, no player wants to deviate and I_t is better than V. If the game status is stable in the cooperation during the nth game round ($n \in N$), the self-learning repeated game model assumes that the cooperation is enforced, and changes to the next step to improve the current cooperation. In the next step (i.e., $n+1^{th}$ game round), the algorithm tries to self-learn the optimal strategy by modifying the current strategy with the goal to optimize the payoff. Therefore, each player dynamically adjusts his strategy; different players may have different strategies. In the next game step, all players observe whether their payoffs become better or not. If not, the adjusted strategy is changed to the previous strategy. Otherwise, based on the adjusted strategies, the trigger threshold (V) is updated as the current average payoff $\left(V = \overline{I_t}\right)$, and the punishment time period (T) is adaptively adjusted. The T is designed to be long enough to let all defecting gains of the selfish players be outweighed by the punishment. Therefore, the players have no incentive to deviate from cooperation, since the players aim to maximize the long-run payoffs over time. With the new T value, a new repeated game is re-started. In the self-learning step, if the new sets of strategies are not good for all players, the original strategy $\left(\hat{s}\right)$ will be restored. If the new sets of strategies are good, the cooperation can be enforced by the future repeated game step. So the game will con-

verge to a stable status (Han, 2005). Practical algorithm is given as follows:

1. Player i plays the strategy $\left(\hat{s}\right)$ of the cooperation phase.
2. If the cooperation phase is played at time t and $I_t > V$, the player i plays the cooperation phase in the next time $t + 1$.
   a. Each player dynamically adjusts his strategy
   b. Based on the current I_t, strategies are decided and V and T are adaptively modified.
3. If the cooperation phase is played at time t and $I_t < V$ (i.e., someone deviates), the player i switches to a punishment phase during T time period.
   a. After the punishing T time period, players return to the cooperative phase in the next game round.
4. Self-learning repeated game is re-started until to reach the stable state.

The repeated game model uses the threat of punishment to maintain the cooperation for the current strategy and try to learn if there is a better strategy for cooperation. Even though repeated games have some advantages, there are shortcomings for practical implementation. In a repeated game, players perform monitoring and provide incentives in a distributed way. It is assumed that the game model involves a stable long-term relationship among players. However, many real world systems such as mobile and vehicular networks do not involve such stable long-term relationships. It can make the repeated game neither applicable nor useful. Moreover, repeated game strategies are constrained by the selfish behavior of players. In particular, equilibrium strategies must guarantee that players execute punishment and reward in the manner intended in their self-interest, which may require a complex structure of strategies (Park, & Scharr, 2011).

Stochastic Game

In the early 1950s, Lloyd Shapley introduced the concept of stochastic game, which is composed of a number of states. A stochastic game is a specialized dynamic game with probabilistic transitions between the different states of the game, and it can be generalized by using Markov decision process. Therefore, stochastic games generalize both Markov decision processes and repeated games, which correspond to the special case where there is only one state. Notice that a one-state stochastic game is equal to a repeated game, and a one-player stochastic game is equal to a Markov decision process (Han, 2011).

For example, at the beginning of each state, the game is in a particular state. In this state, the players select their actions and each player receives a payoff that depends on the current state and the chosen strategies. The game then moves to a new random state whose distribution depends on the previous state and the actions chosen by the players. Therefore, the stochastic game is played in a sequence of states. The procedure is repeated at the new state and the game continues for a finite or infinite number of states.

The formal definition of *n*-player stochastic game is as follows (Han, 2011): stochastic game consists of a finite, non-empty set of states *S*, a finite set $\mathcal{A}_i$ of strategies for the player *i*, a conditional probability distribution *p* on $S \times \left(\mathcal{A}_1 \times \mathcal{A}_2 \times ... \times \mathcal{A}_n \right)$, and payoff functions is defined based on the history space $\mathbb{H} = S \times \mathcal{A} \times S \times \mathcal{A} \cdots$, where $\mathcal{A} = \prod_{i=1}^{n} \mathcal{A}_i$. In particular, the game is called an *n*-player deterministic game if, for each state $s \in S$ and each strategy selection $\mathbf{a} = \left(a_1, a_2, ..., a_n \right)$, there is a unique state s' such that $p\left(s' \mid s, \mathbf{a} \right) = 1$.

If there is a finite number of players, the strategy sets, and the set of states are finite, then a stochastic game with a finite number of stages always has a

Nash equilibrium. For stochastic games, a Markov perfect equilibrium is another solution concept. It is a set of mixed strategies for each of the players, and a refinement of the concept of sub-game perfect Nash equilibrium to stochastic games. In a Markov perfect equilibrium, the strategies have the Markov property of memoryless, meaning that each player's mixed strategy can be conditioned only the state of the game. The state can only be decided according to the payoff-relevant information. Therefore, strategies that depend on signals, negotiation, or cooperation between the players are excluded. Finally, these strategies form a subgame perfect equilibrium of the stochastic game. Simply, Markov perfect equilibrium can be defined a subgame perfect equilibrium in which all players use Markov strategies (Maskin, & Tirole, 2001). Stochastic games have applications in industrial organization, macroeconomics, political economy, evolutionary biology and computer networks.

Markov game is an extension of game theory to Markov decision process like environments. In an Markov decision process, an optimal strategy is one that maximizes the expected sum of discounted reward and is *undominated*, meaning that there is no state from which any other strategy can achieve a better expected sum of discounted reward. For many Markov games, there is no strategy that is *undominated* because performance depends critically on the choice of opponent player. Therefore, the optimal stationary strategy is sometimes probabilistic, mapping states to discrete probability distributions over actions. A classic example is 'rock, paper, scissors game' in which any deterministic policy can be consistently defeated (Littman, 1994).

Jamming Game

Consider a two-player zero-sum game model in which there are only two players and they have diametrically opposed goals. This allows us to use a single utility function that one player tries to maximize and the other, called the *opponent*, tries to minimize. The solution of this game is based on the principal of securing the best of the worst for the player, the so called *minmax* strategy. It means that the player is required to maximize its gain against an opponent that plays at random. Assuming that $\mathbb{A}$ is the player's action set, and $\mathbb{O}$ is the opponent's action set, and $R(s, a, o)$ is denoted as an immediate reward to the player for taking action $a \in \mathbb{A}$ in state $s \in \mathbb{S}$ when its opponent takes action $o \in \mathbb{O}$. When $|\mathbb{O}| = 1$, this game becomes Markov decision process, and when $|\mathbb{S}| = 1$, this game becomes a matrix game (Littman, 1994).

Jamming game is a well-known non-cooperative zero-sum game. This game has been developed to explain the jamming problem in the wireless network MAC layer (Thamilarasu, & Sridhar, 2009), (Wang, Chatterjee, & Kwiat, 2010). Jamming problem can be modeled as 'selfish' transmitters try to maximize their own performance, while 'malicious' jamming nodes attempt to degrade the system performance. Formally, jamming problem is formulated as a game between two players $\{P_1, P_2\}$ - the jammer (P_1) and the monitor (P_2) with different objectives. Jammers are players who prevent and deny wireless channel access to regular users by jamming their communication. Monitors are players responsible for detecting the jamming attack. Jammers can be categorized as constant jammers (CJ), who continuously send out jamming signal into the channel, and reactive jammers (RJ), who send out jamming signal only if the channel

is active state. In a monitoring mechanism, there are also two different monitoring ways: continuously monitoring (M_c) and periodic monitoring (M_p). Continuous monitoring can always detect jamming but results in high energy consumption, and periodic monitoring consumes less energy, but with the potential risk of missing the attack. Table 2 shows the strategic form of jamming game is shown in where the strategy set as $S = S_1 \times S_2$; $S_1 = \{CJ, RJ\}$ for the jammer (P_1) and $S_2 = \{M_c, M_p\}$ for the monitor (P_2).

δ_g is the gain of detecting the attack. Let t be the monitoring duration for periodic monitor and θ be the attack duration for the reactive jammer. C_c and C_p are the costs for attack detection using continuous and periodic monitoring respectively. Similarly, α_g is the attacker gain for successfully launching an attack and C_j and $\hat{C}_j$ are the costs of attacking for the constant and reactive jammers.

Jamming games has a mixed-strategy Nash equilibrium with a mixed strategy for each player (Thamilarasu, 2009). To obtain the mixed-strategy Nash equilibrium, let p be the probability with which the monitor decides to continuously monitor the channel and $(1-p)$ be the probability of choosing periodic monitoring. Similarly, let q be the probability with which jammer decides to constantly jam the channel and $(1-q)$ be jammer's reactive jamming probability. The mixed equilibrium strategies obtained solving the equations are

Table 2. Sample matrix for Jamming game (Thamilarasu, 2009)

P2/P1	M_c	M_p
CJ	$\alpha_g - C_j, \delta_g - C_c$	$\alpha_g - C_j, t\left(\delta_g - C_p\right)$
RJ	$\theta\left(\alpha_g - \hat{C}_j\right), \delta_g - C_c$	$\theta\left(t\alpha_g - \hat{C}_j\right), t\left(\theta\delta_g - C_p\right)$

$$p^* = \frac{t\alpha_g - \hat{C}_g}{\alpha_g(1-t)}$$

and $\qquad\qquad\qquad\qquad\qquad\qquad$ (3)

$$q^* = \frac{\theta\delta_g - C_p}{\delta_g(1-\theta)}$$

$\{p^*, q^*\}$ pair constitutes an equilibrium solution to jamming game. As expected p^* and q^* are proportional to the cost of attacking and the cost of detecting respectively. From the equilibrium points, the probability of monitor using continuous strategy is dependent on the loss in detection or the attack gain. Also, when reactive jamming is more frequent, the cost of attacking is close to constant jamming and hence the best response for the monitor node is to choose continuous monitoring strategy. Similarly, it is observed that equilibrium point of jammer is proportional to monitor's detection gain. When the monitor has a high detection rate the probability of jammer using continuous monitoring decreases. It is interesting to note that the jammer's equilibrium strategy is dependent on the cost of periodic monitor. When the monitor deploys periodic monitoring frequently, the best response for the jammer is to constantly jam the channel to increase its attack success (Thamilarasu, 2009).

Potential Game

In 1973, Robert W. Rosenthal proposed the concept of potential game. A game is said to be a potential game if the incentive of all players to change their strategy can be expressed in one global function (i.e., the potential function). Generally, potential games can be categorized as ordinal potential games or exact potential games. In ordinal potential games, it must be possible to construct a single-dimensional potential function where the sign of the change in value is the same as the sign of the change in payoff of the deviating player. An ordinal potential game $P: S \rightarrow \mathbb{R}$ satisfies

$$\forall s_i' \in S_i, P(s_i', \mathbf{s}_{-i}) - P(s_i, \mathbf{s}_{-i}) > 0$$

if $\qquad\qquad\qquad\qquad\qquad\qquad$ (4)

$$u_i(s_i', \mathbf{s}_{-i}) - u_i(s_i, \mathbf{s}_{-i}) > 0$$

where S is the set of strategies. If the change caused by any player's unilateral action is exactly the same as the change in the potential function, this kind of game is called an exact potential game. A potential game becomes an exact potential game when:

$$\forall s_i' \in S_i, P(s_i', \mathbf{s}_{-i}) - P(s_i, \mathbf{s}_{-i}) =$$
$$u_i(s_i', \mathbf{s}_{-i}) - u_i(s_i, \mathbf{s}_{-i}) \qquad\qquad (5)$$

A global objective function P defined in (5) is called an exact potential function, where individual payoff change as a result of a unilateral player's action is exactly reflected in this global function (Mustika, Yamamoto, Murata, & Yoshida, 2010), (Liu, Ahmad, & Wu, 2009).

The existence of a potential function that reflects the change in the utility function of any unilateral deviating player is the characteristic of a potential game. If the potential of any strategy profile is finite, every sequence of improvement steps is finite. We can assume that Nash equilibrium is a local maximum (*or* minimum) point of the potential function, defined as a strategy profile where changing one coordinate cannot result in a greater potential function value. Therefore, any sequence of unilateral improvement steps converges to a pure strategy Nash equilibrium, which is also a local optimum point of a global objective given by the potential function.

To summarize, an important feature of a potential game is that potential game has been shown to always converge to a Nash equilibrium when the best response dynamics is performed. The best response dynamics is a dynamic process of updating strategies, in which a player chooses a strategy that maximizes its respective utility, given the current strategy of other players remain fixed (Maskin, 2010), (Liu, Ahmad, & Wu, 2009).

Best response dynamics ($s_i^{k+1}(s_{-i})$) of the player i to the strategy profile s_{-i} at time $k+1$ is a strategy that satisfies

$$s_i^{k+1}(s_{-i}) \in \arg\max_{s_i' \in S_i} u_i(s_i', s_{-i}^k) \qquad (6)$$

where $(s_i', s_{-i}^k) \in S_i$ denotes the action profile at time k. Therefore, the potential function is a useful tool to analyze equilibrium properties of games, since the incentives of all players are mapped into one function, and the set of pure Nash equilibrium can be found by locating the local optima of the potential function (Liu, 2009).

Congestion Game

Congestion games are a special case of potential games and first proposed by Robert W. Rosenthal in 1973. Rosenthal proved that any congestion game is a potential game. In 1996, Monderer and Shapley proved the converse; for any potential game, there is a congestion game with the same potential function.

In a congestion game, players and resources are defined, where the payoff of each player depends on the resources he chooses and the number of players choosing the same resource. A congestion game Γ is defined as a tuple { $\mathcal{N}$, $\mathcal{R}$, $\{S_i\}_{i \in \mathcal{N}}$, $\{c_r\}_{r \in \mathcal{R}}$ } where $\mathcal{N} = \{1,\ldots,n\}$ is the set of players, $\mathcal{R}$ is the set of resources, $s_i \subset 2^{\mathcal{R}}$ is the strategy space of player i, and $c_r: \mathcal{N} \to \mathcal{R}$ is a cost function associated with resource $r \in \mathcal{R}$. This function is related to the total number of players using resource r. $S = (s_1, \ldots, s_n)$ is a state of the game, in which the player i chooses strategy $s_1 \in S_i$. Players are assumed to act selfishly and aim at choosing strategies while minimizing their individual cost. The cost function c_f_i is a function of the strategy $s_1 \in S_i$ selected by the player i, with the current strategy profile of the other players, which is usually indicated with s_{-i}.

The cost function c_f_i is defined by $c\_f_i(s_i, s_{-i}) = \sum_{r \in s_i} c_r$. A player in this game aims to minimize its total cost which is the sum of costs over all resources that his strategy involves (Liu, Ahmad, & Wu, 2009).

Given any state S, an improvement step of the player i is a change of its strategy from s_i to s_i', such that the cost of the player i decreases. A classical result from Rosenthal work shows that sequences of improvement steps do not run into cycles, but reach a Nash equilibrium after a finite number of steps. This proposition is shown by a potential function argument. In particular, a potential function $\Phi(S): s_1 \times \ldots \times s_m \to R$ is defined as

$$\Phi(S) = \sum_{r \in \mathcal{R}} \sum_{i=1}^{n(r)} c_r(i) \qquad (7)$$

where $n(r)$ is the total number of players by using the resource r. Rosenthal's potential function can be shown to be ordinal, so congestion game is easily demonstrated to be a potential game. In fact, congestion game is a special case of potential game. Therefore, Nash equilibrium is the only fixed point of the dynamics defined by improvement steps. In the same way as the potential game, a pure Nash equilibrium is easily obtained in a congestion game through the sequence of improvement steps.

The market sharing game is a special case of congestion games (Goemans, Li, Mirrokni, & Thottan, 2006). In market sharing game, there is a set (N) of n players and a set (M) of m markets. Each market $i \in M$ has a sales volume (q_i), i.e., the market i's possible sales amount per unit time. Each market i has a price C_i corresponding to the price to sell something to players. Each player j has a total budget B_j. We are also given a bipartite graph $G = (M \cup N, E)$ in which an edge between the player j and the market i in $G ((j, i) \in E(G))$ means that the player j is interested in the market *i*. Each player should decide which subset of markets to purchase products. The player *j* can purchase something from a subset S_j of markets, if the sum of the prices C_i of the markets in S_j is less than or equal to B_j, i.e., $(\sum_{i \in S_j} C_i) \leq B_j$. The player *j* gets a payoff $R_i = q_i / n_i$ for purchasing products from the market *i*, where n_i is the number of players that purchase from the market *i*. Observe that the total payoff received by all players equal the total products of the being purchased in the markets (Goemans, 2006).

Formally, the market sharing game is defined as the tuple $(N, \{A_j\}, \{P_j(\cdot)\})$ where A_j is the set of strategies for the player *j*. With given the set of all the players' strategies, the utility function (P_j) for the player *j* is defined as $P_j : \prod_j A_j \to R$. In the market sharing game, feasible strategies are the set of markets that players can purchase something under the given budget constraint. The player *j*'s strategy is denoted by S_j. Therefore, S_j is a feasible strategy if $(\sum_{i \in S_j} C_i) \leq B_j$. Given the set ($S$) of strategies for all players, we can find the number of players n_i that purchases from the market *i*, and hence find the payoff of each market. The utility function of the player *j* is the sum of payoffs it gets from the markets he purchases, i.e., $P_j(S) = \sum_{i \in S_j} (q_i / n_i)$, where S_j is the set of markets that the player *j* purchases.

In the market sharing game, each player wants to maximize his own payoff. The social function is defined as the total amount of sales from the market, i.e., $\gamma(S) = \sum_i q_i$ for $S = (S_1, S_2, ..., S_n)$ and $i \in \bigcup_{j \in N} S_j$. Notice that this is also the sum of the utility functions of all players, i.e., $\gamma(S) = \sum_{j \in N} P_j(S)$. The strategy profile that maximizes the social function is called as *social optimum* and the value of this profile as *optimal social value*. It is obvious that, in a market sharing

game, given the set of strategies of other players, the best strategy of an player can be obtained by solving a knapsack problem where the value of market *i* is equal to q_i/n_i or $q_i/(n_i + 1)$ depending on whether the market *i* is currently selected by this player or not. The size of *i* in the knapsack instance is C_i, and the knapsack capacity is equal to B_j (Goemans, 2006).

The solution concept of market sharing game is also the Nash equilibrium. A strategy profile is a vector of strategies of all players: $S = (S_1, S_1, ..., S_n)$ and S is a pure strategy Nash equilibrium, if for any player *j*, given the strategies of all other players, the player *j* has no incentive to change its strategy S_j to any other subset to improve its payoff. As mentioned earlier, market sharing game is a kind of congestion game. Therefore, the best response dynamics can converges to pure Nash equilibria (Goemans, 2006).

Stackelberg Game

In 1934, German economist H. V. Stackelberg proposed a hierarchical strategic game model based on two kinds of different decision makers. Under a hierarchical decision making structure, one or more players declare and announce their strategies before the other players choose their strategies. In game theory terms, the declaring players are called as leaders while the players who react to the leaders are called as followers. Leaders are in position to enforce their own strategies on the followers.

Originally, Stackelberg game model was developed to explain the monopoly of industry; the leader is the incumbent monopoly of the industry and the follower is a new entrant. In this case, the leader has a commitment power and makes his decisions by considering the possible reactions of followers. The followers react dependently based on the decision of the leader while attempting to maximize their satisfaction. Therefore, leader and followers have their own hierarchy level, utility function and strategies; they are forced to act according to their hierarchy level. Stackelberg game model is mathematically formulated as follows.

$$\min_{x} F(x, y) \tag{8}$$

$$s.t., g(x, y) \leq 0,$$

$$y \in \arg\mathbf{min}\{f(x, y): h(x, y) \leq 0\},$$

where $F(x, y)$, $g(x, y)$ and x are called the higher level function, constraint and control parameter, respectively. They are used for the leader. The other function, constraint and parameter ($f(x, y)$, $h(x, y)$ and y) are defined for the follower.

The Stackelberg model can be solved to find the subgame perfect Nash equilibrium. It is the strategy profile that serves best each player, given the strategies of the other player and that entails every player playing in a Nash equilibrium in every subgame. In particular, Nash equilibrium solution concept in Stackelberg game is so-called Stackelberg equilibrium, which provides a reasonable hierarchical equilibrium solution concept when the roles of the players are asymmetric; one of the players has an ability to enforce his strategy on the other players. Usually, Stackelberg equilibrium is more efficient than the Nash equilibrium.

To formally express the Stacklberg equilibrium, let $\mathcal{G} = [\mathcal{K}, \{\mathcal{A}_k\}, U_k]$ represent a game where $\mathcal{K} = \{1, \cdots, K\}$ is the set of players, $\mathcal{A}_k$ is the set of actions available to user k, and U_k is the user k's payoff. The action a_k^* is a best response to actions $\boldsymbol{a}_{-k}$ and the set of user k's best response (*BR*) to $\boldsymbol{a}_{-k}$ is denoted as $BR_k(\boldsymbol{a}_{-k})$ if

$$U_k(BR_k(\boldsymbol{a}_{-k}), \boldsymbol{a}_{-k}) = U_k(a_k^*, \boldsymbol{a}_{-k}) \geq U_k(a_k, \boldsymbol{a}_{-k}),$$
$$\forall a_k \in \mathcal{A}_k \text{ and } k \in \mathcal{K} \tag{9}$$

With leader and follower, the action profile $\boldsymbol{a}$ is a Stacklberg equilibrium if leader maximizes his payoff subject to the constraint that follower chooses according to his best response function (Su, & Schaar, 2009). The leader begins the game by announcing its action. Then, the followers react to the leader's action. The Stackelberg equilibrium prescribes an optimal strategy for the leader if its followers always react by playing their Nash equilibrium strategies in the smaller subgame. For example, an action a_l^* is the Stackelberg equilibrium strategy for the leader if

$$U_l(a_l^*, BR_f(a_l^*)) \geq U_l(a_l, BR_f(a_l)), \forall a_l \in \mathcal{A}_l \tag{10}$$

where $BR_f(\cdot)$ is the follower's best response. Finally, Stackelberg equilibrium can be defined in the general case (Su, 2009). Let $NE(a_k)$ be the Nash equilibrium strategy of the remaining players if player k chooses to play a_k,

$$NE(a_k) = \boldsymbol{a}_{-k}, \forall a_i = BR_i(\boldsymbol{a}_{-i}), a_i \in \mathcal{A}_i \text{ and } i \neq k \tag{11}$$

The strategy profile $(a_k^*, NE(a_k^*))$ is a Stackelberg equilibrium with user k iff

$$U_k(a_k^*, NE(a_k^*)) \geq U_k(a_k, NE(a_k)), \forall a_k \in \mathcal{A}_k \tag{12}$$

Specifically, for the Stackelberg game, the equilibrium strategy can be derived by solving a bi-level programming. The concept of bi-level programming can be generalized allowing the analysis of an arbitrary number of levels and an arbitrary number of decision-makers. The decision makers at the upper level make their decisions first. Then, the decision makers at the lower level specify their decisions given the decisions made by the upper level. All of the divisions at the lower level react simultaneously to the preemptive decisions from the upper level. Bi-level programming problems can be analyzed using concepts from game theory. Within each level, the decision makers play an *n*-person positive sum game similar to those studied and solved by J. Nash. Between levels, the sequential decision process is an *n*-person leader-follower game similar to those studied and solved by von Stackelberg. Thus, the overall bi-level programming problem can be thought of as a Stackelberg game embedded with 'Nash-type' decision problems at each level. For this reason, bi-level programming problem is called a Nash-Stackelberg game (Yang, 2005).

Differential Game

In the 1950s and 1960s, Rufus P. Isaacs had developed a differential game for the modeling and analysis of conflict in the context of a dynamical system. The design idea of differential games is to extend static non-cooperative games into dynamic environments by adopting the optimal control theory. Therefore, differential games can be viewed as extensions of optimal-control theory. With conflicting goals, differential game is designed to solve optimal control problems. In differential games, the state of dynamic systems evolves over time under the influence of multiple inputs, and each input is under the control of a different player. Each player has a different objective function and each player attempts to control the state of the system so as to achieve his goal (Pierre, 2010).

The main components of differential games are the state variable, the control variable, the action set of each player, the objective functions of the players, the information structure and the relevant solution concept (Han, 2011). In a differential game, the state variable evolves over time, driven by the players' actions. The actions are generated by the strategies of the players, and defined for each player as mappings from the available information to the action set. A differential game is played over time $t \in [0, T]$, where

the time horizon of the game can be finite (i.e., $T < \infty$) or infinite (i.e., $T = \infty$) Let $\mathcal{N}$ denote the set of players, defined as $\mathcal{N} = \{1, \ldots, n\}$. The state vector for the game is described by the state variable $(x(t))$ at time t as follows.

$$\dot{x}(t) = F\big(x(t), a(t)\big) \tag{13}$$

where $a(t) = \big[a_1(t), \ldots, a_n(t)\big]^T$ is the collection of actions at time t where a_i is the player i's action $(i \in \mathcal{N})$.

Generally, the utility function in a differential game can be defined as the discounted value of the flow of instantaneous payoff over time (Han, 2011). Let $u_i(\cdot)$ denote the instantaneous utility function at time t for the player i. It is a function of the actions and state variables of all players. The cumulative payoff (J_i) of the player i is defined as the integral of instantaneous payoff over time, properly discounted, that is,

$$J_i\big(a_i, a_{-i}\big) = \int_0^T u_i\big(x(t), a_i(t), a_{-i}(t)\big) \times e^{-\beta t} dt, \tag{14}$$

where $a_{-i}(t)$ is the vector of actions of all players except the player i, and $\beta > 0$ is the discount factor. The objective of player i is to optimize this cumulative payoff by choosing an action $a_i(t)$ (i.e., $\max_{a_i(t)} J_i$).

A solution concept for differential games is also the Nash equilibrium. The derivation of Nash equilibrium involves the solution of n optimal control problems and maximization of the utility ($J_i(a_i, a_{-i})$). This process is carried out with respect to the action variable (a_i) of the player i. Since $a(t)$ is an action at time t that is generated by a control law $\gamma\big(x(t), t\big)$, the underlying optimization problem can be derived from (14).

$$\max_{\gamma_i} J_i\left(\gamma_i, \gamma_i^*\right) =$$

$$\int_0^T u_i\left(x(t), \gamma_i\left(x(t), t\right), \gamma_{-i}^*\left(x(t), t\right)\right) \times e^{-\gamma t} dt, \tag{15}$$

To solve this optimization problems optimal control theory is very useful. Optimal control theory technically adopts dynamic programming and the maximum principle as mathematical tools. Maximum principle can be derived from the principle of optimality, and dynamic programming is usually designed based on the principle of optimality. With this principle, an optimal process has the property that whatever the initial state and time are, all remaining decisions must also constitute an optimal solution. The core of dynamic programming, as applied to continuous-time optimal control, lies in a fundamental partial differential equation, called the Hamilton-Jacobi-Bellman (HJB) equation (Han, 2011), (Dockner, Jorgensen, Long, & Sorger, 2001). By using the dynamic programming and particularly the HJB equation, the optimization problem in (15) can be solved and the feedback Nash equilibrium solution $\left\{\gamma_1^*\left(x(t), t\right), ..., \gamma_n^*\left(x(t), t\right)\right\}$ is obtained.

Princess and Monster (PM) game is a pursuit-evasion game and was introduced as a kind of differential games. In 1965, Rufus Isaacs published the book '*Differential Games*' and presented a specific version of a search game under the name 'princess and monster' game. In the PM game, two players – monster and princess – are played in a region. The monster seeks out for the princess in a totally dark room, respectively any metric space Q with metric d_Q where nothing can be spotted apart from its boundary (Geupel, 2011). The monster, supposed highly intelligent, searches for the princess at a known speed. The princess is permitted full freedom of locomotion. They are each cognizant of its boundary, and the required time is the payoff.

Let $S = S(t)$ and $H = H(t)$ be continuous paths on Q that describe the movement of both players at which the speed of the monster is at most 1. Apart from that the monster and the princess can choose any starting point $S(0)$, respectively $H(0)$. Then the capture time, cost function or payoff T for S and H is

$$T = C(S, H) = \min\left\{t : S(t) = H(t)\right\} \tag{16}$$

As the monster wants to minimize T and the princess wants to maximize it, the game is called zero-sum. Therefore, T represents the gain of the princess and the loss of the monster (Geupel, 2011). The trajectories S and H are called pure strategies and their corresponding spaces are identified as follows: The pure strategy space $\mathcal{H}$ of the monster consists of all continuous paths $\mathcal{H} : [0, \infty] \mapsto Q$. Because of the limited speed of the princess, her pure strategy space $\mathcal{S}$ consists of all paths in $\mathcal{H}$ with Lipschitz constant 1; that is

$$\mathcal{S} = \left\{S : [0, \infty) \mapsto Q : d_Q\left(S(t), S(t')\right) \leq |t - t'|, \forall t, t' \geq 0\right\}$$

Due to the fact that none knows the chosen strategy of the opponent or just to assure oneself against the worst case, it is reasonable to choose the value of a strategy as the worst possible payoff for that strategy (Geupel, 2011), that is

$$V(S) =$$
$$\sup_{H \in \mathcal{H}} C(S, H) \forall S \in \mathcal{S} \text{ and } V(H) = \tag{17}$$
$$\inf_{S \in \mathcal{S}} C(S, H) \forall H \in \mathcal{H}$$

The pure value is the value of the game achieved only via pure strategies and is

$$V = \inf_{S \in \mathcal{S}} V(S) = \sup_{H \in \mathcal{H}} V(H) \tag{18}$$

Sometimes there is only a value that is arbitrary close to the pure value. But if the pure value exists, then there is for any $\varepsilon > 0$ a such called μ-optimal pure strategy whose value is worse only about ε. Or more exactly, if S_μ is an μ-optimal pure monster strategy and H_μ an μ-optimal pure princess strategy, then $V\left(S_\varepsilon\right) < \left(1 + \varepsilon\right) \times V$ and $V\left(H_\varepsilon\right) > \left(1 - \varepsilon\right) \times V$ holds. Thus V is the best guaranteed payoff for both players when they use both one fixed trajectory. But in general it doesn't suffice to use only pure strategies, because mostly there is no pure strategy that dominates all other pure strategies. So the monster and the princess have to make probabilistic choices among pure strategies which are called mixed strategies. Mathematically spoken, a mixed strategy for a player with pure strategy space $\mathcal{X}$ is the probability distribution over $\mathcal{X}$.

Let s be a density function of a mixed monster strategy and h be a density function of a mixed princess strategy depending on $\mathcal{S}$ and $\mathcal{H}$. Depending on $\mathcal{S} \times \mathcal{H}$, the expected capture time T^* can be defined as follows.

$$T^* = c\left(s,h\right) =$$
$$\sum_{(S,H)\in\mathcal{S}\times\mathcal{H}} x\left(S,H\right) \cdot C\left(S,H\right) = \qquad (19)$$
$$\int_{\mathcal{S}\times\mathcal{H}} x\left(S,H\right) \cdot C\left(S,H\right) d\left(S,H\right)$$

s.t., $x\left(S,H\right) = s\left(S\right) \cdot h\left(H\right) \forall S \in \mathcal{S}, \ \forall H \in \mathcal{H}.$

Anyway, the values of the mixed strategies and the value of the game can be easily transferred from the values declared in conjunction with pure strategies. $v\left(s\right) = \sup_h c\left(s,h\right)$ and $v\left(h\right) = \inf_s c\left(s,h\right)$ denote the value of a mixed monster strategy s, respectively of a mixed princess strategy h. Hence $v\left(s\right) \geq c\left(s,h\right) \geq v\left(h\right)$ for any s and for any h. If equality holds, the corresponding mixed strategies s and h are called optimal strategies while the coinciding values of both strategies form the value of the game v.

$$v = \inf_s v\left(s\right) = \sup_h v\left(h\right) \qquad (20)$$

In this case, there also exist for any ε so called ε-optimal strategies s_ε for the monster and h_ε for the princess, which satisfy

$$v\left(s_\varepsilon\right) \leq \left(1 + \varepsilon\right) \times v \text{ and } v\left(h_\varepsilon\right) \geq \left(1 - \varepsilon\right) \times v \qquad (21)$$

Bayesian Game

The game models – static, dynamic, potential, differential and Stackelberg games - were designed based on the governing assumption that all players have the complete information of the game, particularly on the players' strategies and utility functions. However, in many real world situations, the complete information of the game may be uncertain or may not be publicly available to other players. Therefore, it is difficult to know a priori the strategy of players. Due to this reason, complete information based non-cooperative game model does not seem to be practical, and cannot be directly applied for a real world (Ordoñez, 2006).

In 1967, John C. Harsanyi developed a highly innovative analysis of games of incomplete information and proposed a new game mode. In this game, a new concept 'type' of a player was introduced. The type is a probability distribution, which is used to express the belief about uncertain or unknown information of the game players. Type, which is independent and dynamically changed in game stages, determines the player's payoff function. Each player completely knows his own type, but not the types of other players. Therefore, the incompleteness of information means the uncertainty of the types and utility functions of other players. Such a Harsanyi's developed game is called Bayesian game because the probabilistic analysis of Bayes' inference rule is inherent in this game. Players have initial beliefs about the type of each player where a belief is a probability distribution over the possible types for a player. According to Bayes' inference rule, players can update their beliefs during the game process. Therefore, the belief that a player holds about another player's type might change on the basis of the strategies they have played. The main feature of Bayesian game is to relax the assumption that all information is completely known. This feasible approach can be used to predict the strategic behavior under incomplete information (Han, 2011), (Hossain, 2009).

In a Bayesian game, it is necessary to specify the strategy spaces, type spaces, payoff functions, and beliefs for every player. A strategy for a player is a complete plan of actions that covers every contingency that might arise for every type that player might be. A strategy must not only specify the actions of the player given the type that he is, but must also specify the actions that would be taken if he were of another type. Strategy spaces are defined accordingly. A type space for a player is just the set of all possible types of that player. The beliefs of a player describe the uncertainty of that player about the types of the other players. Each belief is the probability of the other players having particular types, given the type of the player with that belief, which is defined as *Prob(types of other players | type of this player)*. A payoff function is a two-place function of strategy profiles and types. If a player has a payoff function $u(x,t)$ and he has type t, the payoff received is $u(x^*, t)$, where x^* is the strategy profile played in the game (i.e. the vector of strategies played) (Han, 2011), (Hossain, 2009).

The formal definition of a Bayesian game is given as follows:

- Set of players $i \in \{1, 2, ..., n\}$ and action set available to player i is A_i, i.e., $a_i \in A_i$.
- Sets of possible types for all players T_i for $i \in \{1, 2, ..., n\}$, i.e., $t_i \in T_i$.
- Let $t = (t_1, ..., t_n)$, and $t_{-i} = (t_1, ..., t_{i-1}, t_{i+1}, ..., t_n)$.
- t is selected according to a joint probability distribution $p(t)$ on $T = T_1 \times \cdots \times T_n$.
- Strategy is defined as $s_i : T_i \to A_i$, and $s_i(t_i) \in A_i$ is the action that type t_i of player i takes. Payoff is define as $u_i(a_1, ..., a_n; t_1, ..., t_n)$.

The Bayesian game proceeds as follows: i) t is selected according to a joint probability distribution $p(t)$, ii) each player i observes realized type $\hat{t}_i$, iii) updates its beliefs: each player calculates with conditional probability of remaining types conditioned on $t_i = \hat{t}_i$, iv) denote distribution of t_{-i} conditioned on $\hat{t}_i$ by $p_i(t_{-i} | \hat{t}_i)$, v) finally, players take actions simultaneously.

Given strategy s_i, type t_i of player i plays action $s_i(t_i)$. With vector of type $t = (t_1, ..., t_n)$ and strategies $(s_1, ..., s_n)$, the realized action profile is $(s_i(t_i), ..., s_n(t_n))$. Player i of type $\hat{t}_i$ has beliefs about types of other players given by conditional probability distribution $p_i(t_{-i} | \hat{t}_i)$. The expected payoff of action s_i is

$$\sum_{t: t_i = \hat{t}_i} u_i\left(s_i, s_{-i}(t_{-i}), t\right) \times p_i\left(t_{-i} | \hat{t}_i\right) \qquad (22)$$

The action $s_i(\hat{t}_i)$ for player i is a best response to $s_{-i}(t_{-i})$ if and only if for all $s_i' \in A_i$,

$$\sum_{t: t_i = \hat{t}_i} u_i\left(s_i, s_{-i}(t_{-i}), t\right) \times p_i\left(t_{-i} | \hat{t}_i\right)$$
$$\geq \sum_{t: t_i = \hat{t}_i} u_i\left(s_i', s_{-i}(t_{-i}), t\right) \times p_i\left(t_{-i} | \hat{t}_i\right)$$

$$(23)$$

Each player's belief, which is the conditional probability distribution $p_i\left(\boldsymbol{t}_{-i}|\hat{t}_i\right)$, is updated periodically based on the Bayesian inference process. A Bayesian inference process is the process that the game player modifies his prior knowledge about the probability distribution according to the obtained information (Zeng, & Sycara, 1998). The Bayesian inference rule can be expressed as:

1. There exists a group of hypotheses H_1, H_2, ..., H_n relating to event e
2. e is the evidence, which corresponds to the obtained information that were not used in computing the prior probability.
    $P(H_i)$ is the prior probability, which is the probability of H_i before e is observed; $P(H_i) > 0$, where $H_i \bigcap H_j = \varnothing$, s.t., $i \neq j$.
3. $P\left(H_i / e\right)$ is the posterior probability, which is the probability of H_i after e is observed. This is the modified probability of a hypothesis given the observed evidence.
4. $P\left(e / H_i\right)$ is the conditional probability, and referred as the happening probability of e when H_i happens. It is also known as the likelihood, which indicates the compatibility of the evidence with the given hypothesis.
    a. Then the Bayesian inference rule formula can be defined as

$$P(H_i|e) = \frac{P\left(H_i\right) \times P(e|H_i)}{\sum_{k=1}^{n} P(e|H_k) \times P\left(H_k\right)} \qquad (24)$$

To enable readers to grasp the fundamental concepts of Bayesian inference, we introduce the buyer-supplier example (Zeng, & Sycara, 1998). In this example, there are two players – buyer and supplier. Buyer and supplier have their reservation price, RP_{buyer} and $RP_{supplier}$, respectively. A player's reservation price is the player's threshold of offer acceptability. Typically a reservation price is private to each player, and is different for each player. For example, a supplier's reservation price is the price such that the supplier player will not accept an offer below this price. A buyer's reservation price is the price such that the buyer will not accept an offer above this price. Both the buyer and the supplier will make concessions from their initial proposal. The buyer will increase his initial proposal, while the supplier will decrease his initial proposal. Eventually, a proposal will be acceptable to both.

It is obvious that although the buyer knows his own reservation price, the precise value of $RP_{supplier}$ is unknown to him. Nevertheless, the buyer is able to update his belief about $RP_{supplier}$ based on his interactions with the supplier and on his domain knowledge. As a result of inference process, the buyer is expected to gain more accurate expectation of the supplier's payoff structure and therefore make more advantageous offers. The buyer's partial belief about $RP_{supplier}$ can be represented by a set of hypotheses H_i, $i = 1, 2, ..., n$. For instance, H_1 can be '$RP_{supplier} = \$100$'; H_2 '$RP_{supplier} = \$90$'. A priori knowledge held by the buyer can be summarized as probabilistic evaluation over the set of hypotheses $\{H_i\}$ (e.g., $P(H_1) = 0.2$, $P(H_2) = 0.35,...$). The Bayesian inference occurs when the buyer receives new signals from the supplier. Along with domain-specific knowledge, these new signals enable the buyer to acquire new insights about $RP_{supplier}$ in the form of posterior subjective evaluation over H_i such as: 'Usually supplier will offer a price which is above their reservation price by 17%'. It can be represented by a set of conditional statements of similar form, one of which is shown as follows: $P(e_1|H_1) = 0.30$, where e_1 represents '$Offer_{supplier} = \$117$', and H_1 '$RP_{supplier} = \$100$'. Given the encoded domain knowledge in the form of conditional statements and the signal (e) in the form of offers made by the supplier, the buyer can use the standard Bayesian inference formula to revise his belief about $RP_{supplier}$ according to (24).

For simplicity, we suppose that the buyer knows that the supplier's reservation price is either \$100 or \$90. In other words, the buyer has only two hypotheses: H_1: '$RP_{supplier} = \$100$' and H_2: '$RP_{supplier} = \$90$'. At the beginning of the negotiation, the buyer does not have any other additional information. His a priori knowledge can be summarized as:

$P(H_1) = 0.5, P(H_2) = 0.5$. In addition, we suppose that the buyer is aware of 'Suppliers will typically offer a price which is above their reservation price by 17%', part of which is encoded as: $P(e_1|H_1) = 0.30$ and $P(e_1|H_2) = 0.05$, where e_1 denotes the event that the supplier asks \$117 for the goods under negotiation.

Now suppose that the supplier offers \$117. Given this signal and the domain knowledge, the buyer can calculate the posterior estimation of $RP_{supplier}$ as follows.

$$\begin{cases} P(H_1|e_1) = \dfrac{P(H_1) \times P(e_1|H_1)}{P(H_1) \times P(e_1|H_1) + P(H_2) \times P(e_1|H_2)} = 85.7\% \\ P(H_2|e_1) = \dfrac{P(H_2) \times P(e_1|H_2)}{P(H_2) \times P(e_1|H_1) + P(H_2) \times P(e_1|H_2)} = 14.3\% \end{cases}$$
$$(25)$$

Suppose that the buyer adopts a simple negotiation strategy: 'Propose a price which is equal to the estimated $RP_{supplier}$'. Prior to receiving the supplier's offer (\$117), the buyer would propose \$95 (the mean of the $RP_{supplier}$ subjective distribution). After receiving the offer from the supplier and updating his belief about $RP_{supplier}$, the buyer will propose \$98.57 instead. Since the new offer is calculated based on a more accurate estimation

of the supplier's utility structure, it might result in a potentially more beneficial final outcome for the buyer and may also help both sides reach the agreement more efficiently (Zeng, & Sycara, 1998).

The solution concept of the Bayesian game is the Bayesian Nash equilibrium; a strategy profile $(s_i(t_i),...,s_n(t_n))$ is a Bayesian Nash equilibrium if $s_i(t_i)$ is a best response to $s_{-i}(t_{-i}$ for all $t_i) \in T_i$ and for all players i. In other words, an action specified by the strategy of any given player has to be optimal, given strategies of all other players and beliefs of players (Hossain, 2009). In a Bayesian game, rational players are seeking to maximize their expected payoff, given their beliefs about the other players. A Bayesian Nash equilibrium is defined as a strategy profile and beliefs specified for each player about the types of the other players that maximizes the expected payoff for each player given their beliefs about the other players' types and given the strategies played by the other players. However, the solution concept of Bayesian Nash equilibrium yields an abundance of equilibria in dynamic games, when no further restrictions are placed on players' beliefs. This makes Bayesian Nash equilibrium an incomplete tool to analyze dynamic games of incomplete information (Hossain, 2009). To refine the implausible equilibria generated by the Bayesian Nash solution concept, the perfect Bayesian equilibrium solution was developed (Hossain, 2009). The main idea of perfect Bayesian equilibrium is to refine an abundance of Bayesian Nash equilibria in the same spirit in which subgame perfection equilibrium is to refine implausible Nash equilibria. The idea of perfect Bayesian equilibrium is profusely used to analyze the game theoretical models that are derived from a wide variety of economic situations. The common understanding is that a perfect Bayesian equilibrium must be sequentially rational given the beliefs of the players, which have to be computed using Bayes rule 'whenever possible'. Therefore, in the spirit of subgame perfection, the perfect Bayesian equilibrium demands that subsequent play must be optimal. This new equilibrium concept provides a minimal requirement that should be imposed on equilibrium concepts that are based on Bayesian rationality.

Evolutionary Game

In a traditional non-cooperative game, the players are assumed to be rational. This rationality of the player requires complete information of game. However, in reality, this assumption is rarely realistic. From experimental results in economics and the social sciences, people (i.e., game players) occasionally make decisions irrationally. Even though, the dynamics of the decision-making process can be modeled in extensive form, there is a limitation to capture the fact that a player can observe opponent players' behaviors, learn from this observation, and optimize the strategy selection according to the knowledge gained ("Evolutionary game theory," n.d.).

In 1974, Maynard Smith introduced the fundamental concept of an evolutionary game (Hofbauer, & Sigmund, 2003). It provides a dynamic framework for analyzing repeated interaction. At first, evolutionary game has been developed in biological sciences in order to explain the evolution of genetically determined social behavior. In this game, a population may consist of players genetically 'programmed' to play a certain strategy, and who reproduce proportionally to their payoffs. The payoffs depend on the strategies of the co-players; strategies with high payoff will spread within the entire populations of players. Other strategies which do poorly eventually die off (Hofbauer, & Sigmund, 2003), (Tao, & Wang, 1997). Therefore, evolutionary games do not require strong rationality. This approach is suitable for real world situations that involve human beings as players who may not act perfect rational behaviors. In evolutionary games, the dynamics of interactions among agents in the population can

be practically implemented. Therefore, strategy adaptation based on an evolutionary process can be obtained (Menasche, Figueiredo, & Silva, 2005), (Altman, El-Azouzi, Hayel, & Tembine, 2008).

The changing rate of the players' selection is defined as *Replicator Dynamics* (*RD*) (Hofbauer, 2003), (Menasche, 2005). When a player chooses a strategy, it can change the current game environment and triggers reactions by other players. After making further changes among players, this interaction mechanism gradually leads the game into a stable state. The *RD* describes the evolution in the proportion of each strategy to reach an equilibrium; a specific strategy evolves at a rate equal to the difference between the payoff of that strategy and the average payoff of the whole population (Altman, 2008). If the payoff of strategy i is small compared to other strategies, the selection probability for strategy i decreases in proportion to the expected payoff reduction. Therefore, the desirable strategy that will improve player's payoff is more likely to be selected. To maximize their expected payoffs, players iteratively change their current strategies and repeatedly interact with other players. When no individual player can improve his payoff by unilaterally changing his strategy, there is a stable set of strategies. In the jargon of evolutionary game theory, this set is referred to as the *evolutionarily stable strategies* (*ESS*) (Menasche, 2005). Under the *ESS*, the proportions of each strategy do not change in time and can be immune from being changed. It is relevant to the Darwinian evolution mechanism (Altman, 2008).

To represent the *RD* for the wireless network power control problem, let M be a number of possible strategies (i.e., power levels) and x_i is the selection probability for the strategy i. $\mathbb{X}$ is the M-dimensional vector $(x_1 \dots x_i \dots x_M)$ and $\dot{x}_i$ stands for the variation of $\dot{x}_i$, which is the *RD* for strategy i. $J(i, k)$ is denoted by the expected payoff for a player using strategy i when it encounters a player with strategy k, and $J(i, \mathbb{X})$ is the payoff for a player using strategy i when it encounters the rest of other players whose strategies are distributed in $\mathbb{X}$, which can be expressed like as $\sum_j (J(i,j) \times x_j)$ (Altman, 2008). Finally, the *RD* is defined as

$$\dot{x}_i = x_i \times \left(J\left(i,\ \mathbb{X}\right) - \sum_j x_j \times J\left(j,\ \mathbb{X}\right) \right)$$

$$= x_i \times \left(\sum_j x_j \times J\left(i,j\right) - \sum_j \sum_k x_j \times J\left(j,k\right) \times x_k \right)$$

(26)

The Nash equilibrium is the most common solution concept for non-cooperative games. To obtain this solution, classical game theory usually assumes players are capable of determining the Nash equilibrium that will be played. However, for some games, this assumption is too stringent because players have incomplete and inaccurate knowledge with bounded rationality. And, the decision-making process to reach an equilibrium becomes intractable with unreasonable complexity. Furthermore, multiple Nash equilibrium can co-exist. In contrast, evolutionary-game theory has been developed to model the behavior of biological agents (e.g., insects and animals). Hence, a strong rationality assumption is not required. Due to this reason, an evolutionary-game formulation will be suitable for scenarios that involve human beings as agents who may not display hyper-rational behavior. In addition, the solution of the evolutionary game (i.e., *ESS*) is designed based on an evolutionary process, which is dynamic in nature. Therefore, *ESS* can be obtained with reasonable complexity. Especially, *ESS* process can serve as a refinement to the Nash equilibrium when multiple Nash equilibria exist. As a new solution concept, *ESS* is also called evolutionary equilibrium.

Evolutionary game has proven itself to be invaluable in helping to explain many complex and challenging aspects of biology. It has been particularly helpful in establishing the basis of altruistic behaviors within the context of Darwinian competition process. Despite its origin and original purpose, the main idea of evolutionary game has emerged as an alternative perspective to classical game theory and become an interesting research field in economists, sociologists, anthropologists, and philosophers. In particular, evolutionary game model is especially suitable for problems which are non-linear, having large search space (for instance, NP hard problems), multi-dimensional and dynamic problems.

Supermodular Game

In 1978 and 1979, D. Topkis developed the notion of supermodular games. Supermodular games are a class of static non-cooperative games and characterized by 'strategic complementarities', which roughly means that when one player takes a higher action according to a defined order, the others want to do the same. In other words, supermodular games are characterized by increasing best responses (Khudabukhsh, 2006), (Milgrom, & Roberts, 1990).

For the formal definition of supermodular game, it is necessary to introduce the property of *increasing differences* (Han, 2011), (Moragrega, Closas, & Ibars, 2012). A function u_i has the *increasing difference* property in $\left(s_i, \mathbf{s}_{-i}\right)$, if

$$u_i\left(s_i', s_j'\right) - u_i\left(s_i, s_j'\right) \geq u_i\left(s', s_j\right) - u_i\left(s_i, s_j\right),$$

s.t., for all $s_i' \geq s_i$ and $s_j' \geq s_j$ (27)

It means that $u_i\left(s_i', s_j\right) - u_i\left(s_i, s_j\right)$ is increasing in s_j and $u_i\left(s_i, s_j'\right) - u_i\left(s_i, s_j\right)$ is increasing in s_i. A strategic form game $\Gamma = \left(\mathcal{N}, \left(s_i\right)_{i \in \mathcal{N}}, \left(u_i\right)_{i \in \mathcal{N}}\right)$ is a supermodular game if s_i is a compact subset of $\mathbb{R}$, u_i is continuous in all players strategies $\left(s_i\right)_{i \in \mathcal{N}}$, and u_i has *increasing differences* property in $\left(s_i, \mathbf{s}_{-i}\right)$.

In 1990, Milgrom and Roberts presented an interesting result related to the upper and lower bound of serially undominated strategy found in a supermodular game (Milgrom, 1990). The concept of upper and lower bounds is often helpful in finding the interesting region in the joint strategy space of the game. If $\overline{s}$ and $\underline{s}$ are respectively the highest and lowest pure strategy Nash equilibrium of a supermodular game, and U denotes the set of strategies that survive iterated deletion of strictly dominated strategies, then supremum for U (i.e., upper bound) = $\overline{s}$ and infimum for U (i.e., lower bound) = $\underline{s}$. If supermodular game has only one unique pure strategy Nash equilibrium, $\overline{s}$ and $\underline{s}$ will coincide and the set of strategies that survive iterated deletion of strictly dominated strategy will become identical; it is indicating that U will be a singleton and only the unique pure strategy Nash equilibrium will survive through the iterated removal of strictly dominated strategy. Since mixed strategy Nash equilibrium and correlated equilibrium are both subsets of U, all the solution concepts will give identical solution. This property is called *dominance solvability*. Usually, several refinements of Nash Equilibrium exist. The various iterative solution concepts also have their own versions of rationalized strategy. If a game is *dominance solvable*, all these alternatives produce the same unique result. Thus, *dominance solvability* is a desirable property for a game (Khudabukhsh, 2006).

To summarize, supermodular games have some desirable features. The set of strategies surviving iterated strict dominance has $\overline{s}$ and $\underline{s}$, and they are both Nash equilibria. Therefore, a pure-strategy Nash equilibrium exists, and the correlated equilibrium and the Nash equilibrium are the same. In addition, if a supermodular game has a unique Nash equilibrium, it is *dominance solvable* and the sequence of greedy best-response dynamics monotonically converges to an equilibrium. Therefore, each player has the same direction in other players' policies. In other words, the sequences of best response strategies are either all increase or all decrease (Han, 2011).

Supermodular games encompass many applied models, have nice comparative statics properties and behave well under various learning rules. In particular, supermodular games are analytically appealing since they have interesting properties regarding the existence of pure-strategy Nash equilibria and algorithms that can find these Nash equilibria.

Arms race game and investment game are the well-known examples of supermodular games (Khudabukhsh, 2006). In an arms race game, players are countries (N = {1, 2, 3, ..., n}) and engaged in an arms race. Each country $i (i \in N)$ selects its level of arms (x_i) and the utility function (u_i) has *increasing differences* property in (s_i, s_{i-1}). It means that the received payoff value of additional arms to any country i increases with the arms level of other countries. In other words, additional arms are considered to be more valuable when the military capability of one's adversaries are greater. During the Cold War, this game model was used to explain the nuclear armament between the United States, the Soviet Union, and their respective allies.

Investment game is another suitable example for supermodular games (Khudabukhsh, 2006). In this game, there are n companies $I_1, I_2, ..., I_n$ making investment $s_{i \in \{1,...,n\}} \in \{0,1\}$, and the payoffs are,

$$u_i\left(s_i, s_{i-1}\right) = \begin{cases} \pi\left(\sum_{j=1}^{j=n} s_j\right) when \ s_i \neq 0 \\ 0 \qquad\qquad when \ s_i = 0 \end{cases}$$

(28)

where π is increasing function in aggregate investment. Similarly, new technology adoption can also be viewed as a supermodular game. It becomes more profitable for a particular company to adopt a new technical standard when other companies are also doing the same.

Global Game

In 1993, Carlsson and van Damme originally defined the notion of global games. Global games are games of incomplete information where players receive possibly-correlated signals of the underlying state of real world. In global games, each player is assumed to be rational and knows the structure of other players' payoffs. The term global refers to the fact that, at each time, players can play any game selected from a subclass of all games, which adds an extra dimension to standard game-play. Therefore, global game is an ideal method for decentralized coordination amongst players. Many practical applications of global games have been developed in economics. The current work is the study of crises in financial markets such as bank runs, currency crises, and economic bubbles. In addition, investments with payoff complementarities, beauty contests, political riots and revolutions, and strategic-complementarity based economic situations are other relevant applications of global games (Dewatripont, Hansen, & Turnovsky, 2003). During 2000's, Vikram Krishnamurthy had developed various practical global game models, which were implemented in different communication networks (Carlsson, & Damme, 1993), (Krishnamurthy, 2009), (Krishnamurthy, 2008).

Usually, a game (G) can be described by its different payoff entries. At this time, a subgame ($g \in G$) can be defined; it can be drawn from some subclass of G. For players in such a situation, it is common knowledge that some game in G will be played but the players do not know which one. Initially, they have common prior beliefs represented by a probability distribution with support on some subclass of G. However, before choosing his action, each player gets additional (private) information in the form of a fuzzy observation of the actual game to be played. The resulting incomplete information game is called a global game. Formally, global game is described by the following steps:

1. A game (g) from G is selected.
2. Each player observes g with some noise.
3. Players choose actions simultaneously.
4. Payoffs are determined by g and the players' choices.

A simple way of modeling the above situation would be to let the players make observations directly in the G situation. Each player would then observe the payoffs of the actual game plus some error terms. However, an alternative formulation is used where the selected game (g) is observed indirectly through some parameter space which is mapped on G (Carlsson, 1993).

The typical bar problem is a well-known example of global games (Krishnamurthy, 2009), (Krishnamurthy, 2008). To model the bar problem as a global game, consider the following analogy comprising of a large number n of guests and k bars. Each guest receives noisy information about the quality of music playing at each bar. Each guest $i \in \{1,\ldots,n\}$ is in one of the bars $l \in \{1,\ldots,k\}$. Let γ_l denote the fraction of guests in the bar l. Let ψ_l denote the quality of music playing at the bar l. Each guest i obtains a noisy k-dimensional measurement vector $Y^{(i)}$ about the quality of music $\psi = (\psi_1,\ldots,\psi_k)$ playing at bars. Based on this noisy information $Y^{(i)}$, each guest needs to decide whether to stay in the current bar, or to leave the bar. When a guest selects the bar, he receives a payoff based on the music quality ($\varnothing$). If he goes from the bar l to the bar m, his payoff (U_{lm}) is defined as follows.

$$U_{lm} = \sum_{m \neq l} (\psi_m \times p_{lm}), \text{ s.t., } l,m \in \{1,\ldots,k\} \tag{29}$$

where p_{lm} denotes the probability that if a guest leaves the bar l, he will move to the other m bar ($m \neq l$). The payoff means that the expected quality of music he would receive from the other $k - 1$ bars. If a guest chooses to stay in the bar l, the payoff (U_{ll}) for him is given by.

$$U_{ll} = g_l(\psi_l) + f_l(\{\psi_l \times \gamma_l\} + \sum_{m \neq l} \{\gamma_m \times p_{ml} \times \xi_m\}),$$
$$\text{s.t., } l, m \in \{1, \dots, k\} \qquad (30)$$

where $S\alpha_l$ denotes the fraction of guests that decided to stay in the bar l, so that $(\alpha_l \times \gamma_l)$ is the fraction of all guests that decided to stay in the bar l. ξ_m is the probability that a guest leaves the bar m ($m \neq l$). As far as guests in the bar l are concerned, they have limited information about how guests in the other bars decide whether to stay or leave. This limited information is represented as the probability ξ_m and ($p_{ml} \times \xi_m$) denotes the probability that a guest leaves the bar m and goes to the bar l. Finally, $\sum_{m \neq l} (\gamma_m \times p_{ml} \times \xi_m)$ denotes the fraction of all guests that move to the bar l from the other $k - 1$ bars. In the payoff in (30), the first function $g_l(\emptyset_l)$ is an increasing function of $\emptyset_l$, which is obtained according to the quality of music. $g_l(\cdot)$ function implies that the better the music quality, the higher the payoff to the guest in staying at the bar l. The second function $f_l(\cdot)$ is defined by using the noisy information vector Y. Typically, the function $f_l(\cdot)$ is quasi-concave. For example, if too few guests are in the bar l, then $f_l(\cdot)$ is small due to lack of social interaction. Also if too many guests are in the bar, then $f_l(\cdot)$ is also small due to the crowded nature of the bar. By using mathematical techniques and eductive reasoning process, each guest can predict i) what proportion of guests will choose to remain in the bar l and ii) what proportion of new guests will arrive. Therefore, each guest can decide rationally whether to stay in his current bar or to leave to maximize his payoff. This mechanism can be modeled as a game, called a global game (Krishnamurthy, 2009), (Krishnamurthy, 2008).

Global game is an ideal method for decentralized coordination amongst agents and the above bar problem is an example of a global game. The bar problem example draws immediate parallels with the operation of large scale sensor networks. Especially, global games study interaction of a continuum of players who choose actions independently based on noisy observations of a common signal (Krishnamurthy, 2008). This is appropriate for sensor networks, which rely on imperfect information, and have limited coordination capabilities. V. Krishnamurthy had developed a global game model for sensor networks. In sensor networks, each sensor computes an estimate Y of the quality (or importance) of information X present in the data. Each sensor then decides whether to transmit or not to transmit its data to a base station. Let α denote the fraction of sensors that decide to transmit. If too few sensors transmit information, then the combined information from the sensors at the base station is not sufficiently accurate. If too many sensors transmit information, then network congestion results in wasted battery energy. The global game model can provide a solution how should the sensor decide in a decentralized manner whether or not to transmit to maximize its utility.

In a global game, each player observes a noisy signal indicating which of several possible games is being played, given that other players receive similar noisy signals. Since a player's utility depends on others' actions, the first step of global game is to predict the actions of other sensors. And then, each sensor acts as an independent player to optimize its operation. Sensors can operate in either an energy-efficient 'low-resolution' mode, or a more expensive 'high-resolution' mode. Therefore, sensors' strategy is mode selection, and the goal of each sensor is to determine a decision rule for mode selection based on a noisy environmental signal. Given the tight energy budget of current sensor networks, self-organization and self-configuration are particularly important for efficient operation. For mode selection, self-configuration allows sensor networks to efficiently extract information, by adjusting individual sensor behavior to form to their environment according to local conditions. Since environments evolve over time, and since centralized organization is costly in terms of communication and energy, self-configuration of sensors is the most feasible method for adapting sensors for this purpose (Krishnamurthy, 2008).

Each sensor can choose to collect information either in a low-resolution or high-resolution mode. Assume that a sensor only transmits data when in high-resolution mode. That is each sensor chooses action

$$u \in S = \{\text{'High\_resolution', 'Low\_resolution'}\} \tag{31}$$

For sensor diversity, multiple classes of sensors are considered, and each of the sensors can be classified into one of I possible classes, where I denotes a positive integer. Let $\mathcal{I} = \{1, 2, ..., I\}$ denote the set of possible sensor classes. Let r_J denote the proportion of sensors of class $J \in \mathcal{I}$. Therefore, $\sum_{J \in \mathcal{I}} r_J = 1$. Let α_J represent the proportion of sensors of class $J \in \mathcal{I}$ that are active, that is in high-resolution mode, at a given time. Define the activity vector profile like as

$$\alpha = (\alpha_1, ..., \alpha_I), \ \alpha_J \in [0,1] \text{ and } J \in \mathcal{I} \tag{32}$$

The proportion of all active sensors, which we denote as α is $\alpha = \sum_{J=1}^{I} r_J \times \alpha_J \in [0,1]$. Each sensor independently chooses action $u \in S$ based only on its measurement of actual environmental quality. Given the activity vector profile α, each

sensor i tries to maximize the expected payoff ($C^{(i)}(X, \alpha, u)$)

$$C^{(i)}(X, \alpha, u) =$$
$$\begin{cases} h_J(X, \alpha) = c_J(X) + f_J(\alpha), & \text{if } u = High\_Res \\ 0, & \text{if } u = Low\_Res \end{cases},$$
$$\text{s.t.}, \forall i \in J \tag{33}$$

where X is an environment quality vector obtained by each sensor. c_J represents the quality of information about in class J. Typically $c_J(X)$ is chosen as an increasing function of X. The higher the quality of the information, the more incentive a sensor has to transmit the information. $f_J(\alpha)$ is the reward earned by each sensor in class J when the proportion of active sensors is α. $f_J(\alpha)$ is defined as continuously differentiable with respect to each $\alpha_J, J \in \mathcal{I}$. In addition, for small α, there should be incentive to increase α, i.e., incentive for a sensor to turn on. However, for large α, too many sensors are active and cause inefficiency due to increased packet collisions. Therefore, for large α, there should be incentive for a sensor to turn off (Krishnamurthy, 2008).

For any sensor i, let $x^{(i)}$ and $u^{(i)}$ be a realization of environment quality observation ($x^{(i)} \in X$) and action ($u^{(i)} \in S$), respectively. Given its observation $x^{(i)}$, the goal of each sensor i is to select a strategy to optimize its payoff.

$$u^{(i)} = \max_{x^{(i)} \to S} E\left[C^{(i)}(X, \alpha, u) \right] \tag{34}$$

Recently, global game model also has been applied to decentralized spectrum access for cognitive radio networks. To meaningfully consider the possibility of spectrum access, global game can be adopted. In 2009, V. Krishnamurthy had developed a global game model for cognitive radio spectrum sensing problem (Krishnamurthy, 2009). Suppose that a system comprises N CRs and L channels with N_l denoting the number of

CRs in the channel $l \in \{1, ..., L\}$. At a given time instant, each CR measures the L dimensional vector $X = (X_1, ..., X_L)$, which is comprising of the quality of L channels. In the vector X, each component $X_{l \in \{1,...,L\}}$ models the bandwidth capacity of channel l. Let $r_l = N_l / N$ denote the fraction of CRs in a channel l (i.e., $r_l \in [0,1]$ and $\sum_{l=1}^{L} r_l = 1$). Based on the channel quality information X, each CR decides whether to stay in its current channel $l \in \{1, ..., L\}$ or to leave the channel. Let α_l denote the fraction of CRs that decide to stay in the channel l so that $r_l \times \alpha_l$ is the expected fraction of CRs that remain in the channel l.

If the CR leaves, a protocol chooses which channel its goes to next; the CR goes to channel m with probability p_{lm}; and $\sum_{m \neq l} X_m \times p_{lm}$ is the payoff, which is the expected quality of the channel he would receive from the other $L-1$ channels. p_{lm} denotes the probability that if a CR leaves l, it will move to another channel m ($l, m \in \{1, ..., L\}$). It measures the relative desirability of channel m compared to channel l.

If the CR chooses to stay in channel l, then it receives a payoff

$$X_l + f_l\left(\{\alpha_l \times r_l\} + \sum_{m \neq l} \{r_m \times p_{ml} \times \gamma_m\} \right).$$ X_l implies that the better the channel l quality, the higher the payoff in staying at the channel l. In the function $f(\cdot)$, $\sum_{m \neq l} \{r_m \times p_{ml} \times \gamma_m\}$ denotes the fraction of new CRs that move from the other $L-1$ channels to the channel l. If too few CRs are in the channel l, the resource of the channel is underutilized. If too many CRs are in the channel l, network congestion occurs. Therefore, $f(\cdot)$ should be chosen as a quasi-concave function and it is continuously differentiable with respect to each $\beta_l, l \in \{1, ..., L\}$. To decide

whether to stay or leave its current channel, each CR can be a game player and the interaction of all CRs can be modeled as a global game (Krishnamurthy, 2009). Each CR i in the channel l then chooses an action $u^{(i)} \in \{1,2\}$ = {stay, move}. The reward payoff by each CR i in the channel l is

$$\begin{cases} C_l(X, \alpha, u=1) = k_l \times X_l + f_l(\beta_l), \\ s.t., \beta_l = r_l \times \alpha_l + \sum_{m \neq l} r_m \times \gamma_m \times p_{ml} \\ C_l(X\alpha, u=2) = \sum_{m=1, m \neq l} k_{lm} \times p_{lm} \times X_m, \\ s.t., \sum_{m=1, m \neq l} p_{lm} = 1 \text{ and } p_{ll} = 0 \end{cases}$$

(35)

where k_l and k_{lm} denote user-defined positive constants to weigh the different components of the payoff. Recall α_l denotes the fraction of CRs that decide to remain in the channel l, ($l = 1, ..., L$) after receiving the measurement. From the perspective of the channel l, $\sum_{m \neq l} r_m \times \gamma_m \times p_{ml}$ denotes the expected fraction of new CRs that move to the channel l. Therefore, β_l ($0 \leq \beta_l \leq 1$) denotes the expected fraction of all CRs in the channel l after each CR has sensed its channel and made a decision as to whether to stay or move (Krishnamurthy, 2009). Each CR i in the channel l chooses its action $u \in \{1 \text{ (stay)}, 2 \text{ (leave)}\}$ to maximize its payoff.

$$u^{(i)} = \max_{x^{(i)} \to \{1(\text{stay}),2(\text{leave})\}} E\left[C^{(i)}(X, \alpha_l, u) \right]$$

(36)

The solution concept of global game is strategy equilibrium. V. Krishnamurthy showed that there are some Nash equilibria for sensor network global game and Bayesian Nash equilibria for global game for CR spectrum sensing problem (Krishnamurthy, 2009), (Krishnamurthy, 2008).

Signaling Game

In 1973, economist Michael Spence proposed a model to analyze job market signaling. Based on the Spence's model, David M. Kreps developed signaling game in 1987. A signaling game is a dynamic, Bayesian game with two players and describes a situation where one player has information the other player does not have. This situation of asymmetric information is very common in economics. Therefore, many applications of signaling games have been developed to solve economic problems ("Signaling Games," n.d.).

Game model for job market is good example for a signaling game (Spence, 1973). In this game, workers have a certain ability (high or low) that the employer does not know. The workers send a signal, which is their education level. The employers observe the workers' education, but have no idea about their ability. Only based on the workers' signals, the employers offer their wages (high or low). This model assumed that the level of education does not guarantee the high ability, and the cost of the education is higher for a low ability worker than for a high ability worker, who can have a chance to receive a scholarship or any other favors. The equilibrium concept is also relevant for signaling games. In the equilibrium state of signaling game, the benefits of education are only for high level ability workers, who are able to attain a specific level of education with the cost-effectiveness. In other words, workers with a high ability will get an education.

A traditional signaling game consists of two different type players - sender and receiver. The sender has a certain type from a type set Θ, whose typical element is θ ($\theta \in \Theta$). The type information is private to each sender and the receiver does not know the sender's type. According to the own type, the sender chooses a message m_s from his message set M ($m_s \in M$). Receiver observes m_s and chooses an action a_r from his action space A ($a_r \in A$). Receiver has prior beliefs about

sender's type before the start of the game. In other words, before observing the sender's message, the receiver believes that the probability ($p(\theta)$) that the sender is some type. Two players' payoffs dependent on, i) the sender's type, ii) the message chosen by the sender, and iii) the action chosen by the receiver (Gibbons, 1992), (Osborne, & Rubinstein, 1994). Sender's strategy (i.e., chooses a message) is a probability distribution $\sigma_s(\cdot|\theta)$ over message m_s for each type θ. To choose an action, a strategy for receiver is a probability distribution $\sigma_r(\cdot|m_s)$ over actions a_r for each message m_s. After both the players' interaction, the payoffs are awarded according to the message sent by the sender, the action taken by the receiver in response and the type θ of the sender (Patcha, & Park, 2006). When the receiver acts $\sigma_r(\cdot|m_s)$, the sender with type θ's payoff ($u_s(\sigma_s, \sigma_r, \theta)$) to $\sigma_s(\cdot|\theta)$ is defined as

$$u_s(\sigma_s, \sigma_r, \theta) = \sum_{m_s}\sum_{a_r}\sigma_s(m_s|\theta) \times \sigma_r(a_r|m_s) \times u_s(m_s, a_r, \theta)$$

(37)

where $u_s(m_s, a_r, \theta)$ is the sender's payoff to m_s. When the sender acts $\sigma_s(\cdot|\theta)$, the receiver's payoff ($u_r(\sigma_s, \sigma_r, \theta)$) with strategy $\sigma_r(\cdot|a_s)$ is defined as

$$u_r(\sigma_s, \sigma_r, \theta) = \sum_{\theta}p(\theta) \times \left\{\sum_{m_s}\sum_{a_r}\sigma_s(m_s|\theta) \times \sigma_r(a_r|m_s) \times u_r(m_s, a_r, \theta)\right\}$$

(38)

where $u_r(m_s, a_r, \theta)$ is the receiver's payoff to a_r. After players' interaction, receiver updates his beliefs about θ. A new posterior distribution $\mu(\cdot|m_s)$ over Θ is defined to reflect the result of the experiment. By using the Bayesian inference, $\mu(\cdot|m_s)$ is dynamically modified (Patcha, & Park, 2006). To summarize a signaling game, if

$\sigma_s(\cdot|\theta)$ denotes the sender's strategy, then receiver, who knows $\sigma_s(\cdot|\theta)$ and by observing m_s, use Bayes rule to update $p(\cdot)$ and $\mu(\cdot|m_s)$.

Perfect Bayesian equilibrium is relevant for a signaling game solution (Patcha, & Park, 2006). It is a refinement of Bayesian Nash equilibrium, which is an extension of Nash equilibrium to games of incomplete information. Perfect Bayesian equilibrium of signaling game is a strategy profile σ^* and posterior beliefs $\mu(\cdot|m_s)$ such that

for sender:

$$\forall\theta, \sigma_s^*(\cdot|\theta) \in \arg\max_{m_s} u_s\left(\alpha_s, \sigma_2^*, \theta\right),$$

for receiver :

$$\forall m_s, \sigma_r^*(\cdot|m_s) \in \arg\max_{a_r} \sum_{\theta} \mu(\theta|m_s) \times u_r\left(\sigma_s, \sigma_r, \theta\right),$$

and $\mu(\theta|m_s) = \dfrac{p(\theta) \times \sigma_s^*(m_s|\theta)}{\sum_{\theta' \in} p(\theta') \times \sigma_s^*(m_s|\theta')}$,

if $\sum_{\theta' \in \Theta} p(\theta') \times \sigma_s^*(m_s|\theta') > 0$

(39)

If $\sum_{\theta' \in \Theta} p(\theta') \times \sigma_s^*(m_s|\theta') = 0$, $\mu(\cdot|m_s)$ is any probability distribution on Θ.

A screening game is strongly related to a signaling game. Screening games can provide an effective solution for the principal-agent problem (Stiglitz, & Weiss, 1990). In the principal-agent situation, there are two players (i.e., agent and principal), who have different interests and asymmetric information. These players exchange information based in their actions. The difference between screening games and signaling games is that how information is exchanged. Instead choosing an action based on a signal, the receiver gives the proposal for a senders based on the type of the sender.

For instance, there is an employer (i.e., principal) and a worker (i.e., agent). The worker has a given skill level, and chooses the amount of effort he will exert. If the worker knows his ability, he can send a signal about his ability to the employer before being offered a wage. It is a scenario of signaling game. In the screening game, the employer offers a wage level first, and then the worker chooses a signal whether accepts or rejects a contract for a wage level. Since the offers may be contingent on the skill level of the worker, the worker is screened by the employer. This process is called screening and this interaction procedure can be modeled as screening game (Stiglitz, & Weiss, 1990).

Intervention Game

In 2010, Jaeok Park and Mihaela van der Schaar proposed a new game concept, called 'intervention game', based on the repeated game approach (Park, & Schaar, 2012). In traditional repeated game models, long-run frequent interaction is necessary, which usually requires an infinite horizon and sufficiently patient game players. However, in an intervention game model, an intervention device monitors the player's behavior and chooses an intervention action to directly interact with the players. This approach can deter misbehavior of a player by exerting punishment while loosening requirements for player's patience to get the solution (Park, 2011), (Park, 2012),

To provide a normal representation form of an intervention, consider a system where n players and an intervention device interact (Park, 2012). The set of players is finite and denoted by $\mathcal{N} = \{1,...,n\}$. The strategy space and a pure strategy of player i is denoted by $\mathbb{S}_i$ and s_i, respectively ($s_i \in \mathbb{S}_i$, for all $i \in \mathcal{N}$). The set of pure strategy profiles is denoted by $\mathbb{S} \triangleq \prod_{i \in \mathcal{N}} \mathbb{S}_i$.

A mixed strategy for player i is a probability distribution over $\mathbb{S}_i$ and it is denoted by $\beta_i \in \Delta(\mathbb{S}_i)$, where $\Delta(\mathbb{S}_i)$ is the set of all probability distributions over a set $\mathbb{S}_i$. A mixed strategy profile is represented by a vector

$$\beta = (\beta_1,...,\beta_N) \in \prod_{i \in \mathcal{N}} \Delta(\mathbb{S}_i).$$

The intervention device observes a signal (X), which is realized from the set (X) of all possible signals. Given a pure strategy profile $s = (s_1, \ldots, s_n)$, the probability distribution of signals ($\rho(s)$) is defined by a mapping $\rho : \mathbb{S} \to \Delta(\times)$ where $\rho(s) \in \Delta(X)$. When the signal set (X) is finite, the probability of a signal $\chi \in \chi$ is realized by $\rho(\mathrm{X} \mid s)$. After observing the realized signal, the intervention device takes its strategy, called an intervention strategy. It can be represented by a mapping $f : X \to \Delta(\mathbb{S}_0)$, which is called an *intervention rule* where s_0, β_0, and $\mathbb{S}_0$ are a pure strategy, a mixed strategy, and the set of pure strategies for the intervention device, respectively. With a signal χ, $f(\chi)$ (i.e., $f(\chi) \in \Delta(\mathbb{S}_0)$) is the mixed strategy. When $\mathbb{S}_0$ finite, the probability that the intervention device takes an strategy s_0 given a signal χ is denoted by $f(s_0 \mid \chi)$.

In the intervention game, a system manager determines the intervention rule used by the intervention device (Park, 2012). The manager can commit to an intervention rule by using a protocol embedded in the intervention device. Therefore, the payoffs of the players and the manager are determined by the strategies of the intervention device and the players and the realized signal. The payoff function of player $i \in \mathcal{N}$ is denoted by $u_i : \mathbb{S}_0 \times \mathbb{S} \times \chi \to \mathbb{R}$ and that of the manager by $u_0 : \mathbb{S}_0 \times \mathbb{S} \times \chi \to \mathbb{R}$. The pair (χ, ρ) and $\mathbb{S}_0$ are called the *monitoring technology* and *intervention capability* of the intervention device, respectively. Finally, the game played by the manager and the players is formulated as an *intervention game*, which is summarized by the data

$$\Gamma = \mathcal{N}_0, \left(\mathbb{S}_i\right)_{i \in \mathcal{N}_0}, \left(u_i\right)_{i \in \mathcal{N}_0}, \left(X, \rho\right), \mathcal{F} \qquad (40)$$

where $\mathcal{N}_0 \triangleq \mathcal{N} \cup \{0\}$ and the set of all possible intervention rules is denoted by $\mathcal{F}$. The sequence of events in an intervention game can be listed as follows.

- The manager chooses an intervention rule $f \in \mathcal{F}$.
- The players choose their strategies $\beta \in \prod_{i \in \mathcal{N}} \Delta(\mathbb{S}_i)$, knowing the intervention rule f chosen by the manager.
- A pure strategy profile s is realized following the probability distribution β, and a signal $\chi \in X$ is realized following the probability distribution $\rho(s)$.
- The intervention device chooses its strategy $s_0 \in \mathbb{S}_0$ following the probability distribution $f(\chi)$.

Intervention game can provide incentives successfully, and be applicable and useful in a system with a frequently changing population situation. The time-variant fluctuated situation is very common in many real world systems. In the intervention game, a central entity (i.e., the intervention device) performs monitoring and provides incentives, which can be programmed simply according to the design objective. However, in a large-scale system, the burden of monitoring and providing incentives can be too heavy for a single intervention device. In this case, multiple intervention devices that can communicate with each other can be developed (Park, 2011).

The traditional intervention game, which is designed based on the repeated game, can be transformed to a static intervention game. To develop this static game model, expected payoffs given an intervention rule and a pure strategy profile should be obtained. They can be computed by taking expectations with respect to signals and intervention strategies. The expected payoff function of player i is denoted by a function $v_i: \mathcal{F} \times \mathbb{S} \to \mathbb{R}$, while that of the manager is denoted by $v_0: \mathcal{F} \times \mathbb{S} \to \mathbb{R}$. If $\mathbb{S}_i$, for $i \in \mathcal{N}_0$, and X are all finite, an intervention game is also finite. In a finite intervention game, expected payoffs can be computed as

$$v_i(f,s) = \sum_{\chi \in X} \sum_{s_0 \in \mathbb{S}_0} u_i(s_0, s, \chi) \times f(s_0|\chi) \times \rho(\chi|s),$$
$$\text{s.t,} \quad i \in \mathcal{N}_0$$

(41)

Once the manager chooses an intervention rule f, the players play a static game, whose normal form representation is given by

$$\Gamma_f = \mathcal{N}, \left(\mathbb{S}_i\right)_{i \in \mathcal{N}_0}, \left(v_i(f,s)\right)_{i \in \mathcal{N}}$$

(42)

Intervention equilibrium is a solution concept of static intervention game (Park, 2011). Let $\mathcal{E}(f)$ is the set of strategy profiles sustained by f (i.e., $\mathcal{E}(f) \subset \prod_{i \in \mathcal{N}} \Delta(\mathbb{S}_i)$) and a pair (f, β) is attainable if $\beta \in \mathcal{E}(f)$. Formally,

$$\left(f^*, \beta^*\right) \in \mathcal{F} \times \prod_{i \in \mathcal{N}} \Delta(\mathbb{S}_i)$$

is an intervention equilibrium if $\beta^* \in \mathcal{E}(f^*)$ and $v_0(f^*, \beta^*) \geq v_0(f, \beta)$ for all (f, β). $f^* \in \mathcal{F}$ is an *optimal intervention rule* if there exists an optimal strategy profile $\beta^* \in \prod_{i \in \mathcal{N}} \Delta(\mathbb{S}_i)$ such that (f^*, β^*) is an intervention equilibrium. Therefore, an intervention equilibrium solves the following optimization problem.

$$\max_{(f,\hat{a})} v_0(f, \beta) \text{ s.t., } \beta \in \mathcal{E}(f)$$

(43)

The constraint $\beta \in \mathcal{E}(f)$ represents incentive constraints for the players, which require that the players choose the strategy profile $\hat{a}$ in their self-interest given the intervention rule f. Therefore, above optimization problem can be rewritten as follows.

$$\max_f \max_\beta v_0(f, \beta) \text{ s.t., } f \in \mathcal{F} \text{ and } \beta \in \mathcal{E}(f)$$

(44)

Then an intervention equilibrium can be considered as a subgame perfect equilibrium, with an implicit assumption that the manager can induce the players to choose the best Nash equilibrium for him in case of multiple Nash equilibria. In order to achieve an intervention equilibrium $\left(f^*, \beta^*\right)$, the manager announces the intervention rule f^* and recommends the strategy profile β^* to the players. Since $\beta^* \in \mathcal{E}(f^*)$, the players do not have an incentive to deviate unilaterally from β^* in the game Γ_{f^*}.

Intervention game is similar to the Stackelberg game. In an intervention game, the manager chooses an intervention rule before players take their actions. Therefore, the designer can be considered as a leader and players as followers. Intervention rule is a complete contingent plan for intervention actions with each possible signal about the actions of players. Thus, intervention games require more overhead for the leader than Stackelberg games. However, when the leader is only a manager who regulates players' payoffs, intervention games are more suitable for practical implementations than Stackelberg games. In intervention games, intervention actions can be adjusted to the observed behavior of players. So, intervention can be applied only when punishment is needed. On the contrary, Stackelberg games lack such adaptability (Park, 2011).

The intervention game can be extended to a scenario where the manager has incomplete information about agents. In the intervention game with incomplete information, the manager uses a procedure to induce players to reveal their private information as well as to take appropriate actions. For example, a procedure can be developed where players first send messages to the manager and then the manager chooses an intervention rule depending on the messages from players (Park, 2011).

Negotiation Game

Negotiation game is a dynamic process in which two or more players with different criteria, constraints, and preferences, jointly reach a mutually acceptable agreement on the terms of a transaction. In negotiation games, offers and counter offers are generated by lineal combinations of simple functions, called tactics. In the lineal combination, different weights allow the varying importance of the criteria to be modeled (Sierra, Faratin, & Jennings, 1997). To achieve flexibility in the negotiation game, the players may wish to change their ratings of the importance of the different criteria over time. The term '*strategy*' is denoted as the way in which a player changes the weights of the different tactics over time. Therefore, strategies combine tactics depending on the history of negotiations, and negotiation sequences influence one another by means of strategies (Zeng, 1998), (Sierra, 1997).

In 1982, H. Raiffa presented the basic model for bilateral negotiation (Raiffa, 1982). Let $i\left(i \in \left\{a,b\right\}\right)$ represent the negotiating players and $j\left(j \in \left\{1, \ldots ,n\right\}\right)$ the issues under negotiation. Let $x_j \in \left[min_j, max_j\right]$ be a value for the issue j. Between a delimited range, the value of each issue is determined. Each player has a scoring function $V_j^i : \left[min_j, max_j\right] \rightarrow \left[0,1\right]$ that gives the score player i assigns to a value of the issue j in the range of its acceptable values. For convenience, scores are kept in the interval [0, 1]. The next element of the model is the relative importance.

A player assigns the relative importance to each issue under negotiation. w_j^i is an importance of the issue j for the player i. The weights of both players (i.e., player a, b) are assumed to be normalized, i.e. $\sum_{1 \leq j \leq n} w_j^i = 1$, for all i in $\left\{a,b\right\}$. With these factors, it is now possible to define a player's scoring function for a *contract*:

$$V^i\left(\boldsymbol{x}\right) = \sum_{1 \leq j \leq n} w_j^i \times V_j^i\left(x_j\right), \text{s.t.}, \ \boldsymbol{x} = \left(x_1, \ldots ,x_n\right) \tag{45}$$

If both players use such an additive scoring function, it is possible to show how to compute the optimum value of $\boldsymbol{x}$ as an element on the efficient frontier of negotiation (Sierra, 1997), (Raiffa, 1982).

The Raiffa's bilateral negotiation model is valid for theoretic research areas. However, this model contains several implicit assumptions, which are inappropriate for practical implementations. First, to find the optimum value, the scoring functions have to be disclosed. This is, in general, inappropriate for competitive negotiation. Second, both players have to use the same additive scoring model. Third, there are pre-defined value regions for discussion. Therefore, players are necessary to define the limits of the scoring function. However, it is not always possible to find these common regions. Fourth, there are no notions of timing and resource issues in the negotiation (Sierra, Faratin, & Jennings, 1997).

In 1997, C. Sierra, et al, developed a practical negotiation game model (Sierra, Faratin, & Jennings, 1997). This model defines a range of strategies and tactics that players can employ to generate initial offers, evaluate proposals and offer counter proposals. In particular, Sierra's negotiation game model is based on computationally tractable assumptions and is demonstrated in the domain of business process management.

To formally express the Sierra's model, assume two players (i.e., player a, b) and let $x_{a \rightarrow b}^t$ be a vector of values proposed by the player a to the player b at time t, and $x^t_{a \to b}[j]$ be a value for the issue j. The range of values acceptable to the player a for the issue j will be represented as the interval $\left[min^a_j, \ max^a_j\right]$. A common global time is represented by a linearly ordered set of instants, namely *Time* (Sierra, 1997). A negotiation sequence between players a, b at time t noted $x^t_{a \leftrightarrow b}$ or $x^t_{b \leftrightarrow a}$, is any finite sequence of the form $\left\{x^{t_1}_{d_1 \to e_1}, \ x^{t_2}_{d_2 \to e_2}, ..., \ x^{t_n}_{d_n \to e_n}\right\}$ where:

1. The negotiation sequence contains only proposals between players a and b
2. Proposals are alternate between both players, i.e., $d_i, e_i \in \{a, b\}$, $e_i = d_{i+1}$ and $d_i \neq e_i$
3. If $k \leq l$ and $t_k \leq t_l$, it is ordered over time
4. $x^{t_i}_{d_i \to e_i}[j]$ (i.e., $x^{t_i}_{d_i \to e_i}[j] \in \left[min^{d_i}_j, \ max^{d_i}_j\right]$) is one of the particles $\{accept, reject\}$.

Index t_n represents an instant in the set *Time* such that $t_{n-1} \leq t_n$. We will say that a negotiation sequence is active if $x^{t_n}_{d_n \to e_n} \notin \{accept, reject\}$.

In the notation, there is a local time for each negotiation sequence (Sierra, 1997). The t_1 ($t_1 = 0$) is corresponds to the initial time value. When the player a receives an offer from the player b at time t, that is $x^t_{b \to a}$, he has to rate the offer using its scoring function. If the value of $V^a\left(x^t_{b \to a}\right)$ is greater than the value of the counter offer, then the player a accepts $x^t_{b \to a}$. Otherwise, the counter offer ($x^{t'}_{a \to b}$ with $t' > t$) is submitted at the time t'. The interpretation function I^a expresses this concept mechanism more formally; given the player a and its associated scoring function V^a, the interpretation by the player a at time t' is defined as:

$$I^a\left(t', x^t_{b \to a}\right) = \begin{cases} accept, & If\ V^a\left(x^t_{b \to a}\right) \geq V^a\left(x^{t'}_{a \to b}\right) \\ x^{t'}_{a \to b}, & otherwise \end{cases}$$

(46)

According to the offer $x^t_{b \to a}$ sent at time $t < t'$, $x^{t'}_{a \to b}$ is a *contract* that the player a would offer to the player b at the time of the interpretation. The result of $I^a\left(t', x^t_{b \to a}\right)$ is used to extend the current negotiation sequence between the players. Metaphorically, this interpretation also formulates the fact that a contract unacceptable today can be accepted tomorrow merely by the fact that time has passed.

In order to prepare a counter offer, $x^{t'}_{a \to b}$, the player a uses a set of tactics that generate new values for each variable in the negotiation set. Tactics are the set of functions that determine how to compute the value of a quantitative issue by considering a single criteria (Sierra, 1997). The set of values for the negotiation issue are then the range of the function, and the single criteria is its domain. Usually, the criteria are time, resources and previous offers and counter offers. Time-dependent tactic is the most common tactic for negotiation games. In this tactic, a player has a time deadline by which an agreement must be in place and is likely to concede more rapidly as the deadline approaches. Therefore, the predominant factor used to decide which value to offer next is the time (t). Time-dependent tactic consists of varying the acceptance value for the issue depending on the remaining negotiation time. This requires a constant t^a_{max} in the player a that represents an instant in the future by when the negotiation game must be completed. Initial offer is a point in the interval of values of the issue under negotiation. The value to be offered by the player a to the player b for issue j at time t ($0 \leq t \leq t^a_{max}$) is obtained as the following expression:

$$x_{a \to b}^{t}\left[j\right] = min_{j}^{a} + \left(1 - \pm_{j}^{a}\left(t\right)\right) \times \left(max_{j}^{a} - min_{j}^{a}\right)$$

$$(47)$$

The time-dependent $\alpha_{j}^{a}(t)$ function depends on time; it ensures that $0 \leq \alpha_{j}^{a}\left(t\right) \leq 1$, $\alpha_{j}^{a}\left(0\right) = 0$ and $\alpha_{j}^{a}\left(t_{max}^{a}\right) = 1$. At the initial time, the offer is the maximum value. When the time deadline is reached, the offer approximates the minimum value. Therefore, the offer always be between the value range. The time-dependent function ($\alpha_{j}^{a}(t)$) can be defined as follows (Sierra, 1997).

$$\alpha_{j}^{a}(t) = \begin{cases} k_{j}^{a} + (1 - k_{j}^{a})\left(\dfrac{\min(t, t_{\max})}{t_{\max}}\right)^{\frac{1}{\beta}} \\ \text{in case of polynomial function} \\ \exp\left[\left(1 - \dfrac{\min(t, t_{\max})}{t_{\max}}\right)^{\beta} \times \ln k_{j}^{a}\right] \\ \text{in case of exponential function} \end{cases}$$

$$(48)$$

where k_{j}^{a} is a constant to determine the value of issue j to be offered in the first proposal by player a, and the parameter β ($\beta \in \Re^{+}$) determines the convexity degree of the curve. The shape of the curve represents player's concession rate, which differentiates tactics in the negotiation. With a big value of β, the polynomial function concedes faster at the beginning than the exponential function, then they behave similarly. With a small value of β, the exponential function waits longer to start conceding than the polynomial function. Therefore, with each value of β, time-dependent functions represent an infinite number of possible tactics. The Sierra's game model for bilateral negotiation process can be extended as a multilateral negotiation game model for multiple players (Sierra, 1997).

In 1998, D. Zeng and K. Sycara introduced the bazaar game as a new negotiation model, which is designed to handle multi-player, multi-issue negotiation problems (Zeng, 1998). In particular, bazaar game model can represent negotiation context, and formulate the dynamics of negotiation, and support the learning capability of participating players. During the process of the bazaar game, the overall negotiation can be modeled as exchanging proposals and counter-proposals, as typically happens in human negotiations. Therefore, the bazaar game is a sequential decision making negotiation model that is capable of learning.

Most game-theoretic negotiation models assume that the player has infinite reasoning and computation capacity. Their assumption is highly improper for the players with bounded rationality. Usually, players don't have infinite reasoning capacity in negotiation process. Without the assumption of player's infinite smartness, the bazaar game adopts the player's learning mechanism. This approach differentiates the bazaar game from other negotiation game models (Zeng, 1998).

Formal definition of the bazaar game can be modeled by a 10-tuple like as

$$\mathcal{G} = \left\langle N, M, \Delta, A, H, Q, \ \Omega, \ P, C, E \right\rangle,$$

where N is the set of players, M is the set of issues in negotiation, Δ is a set of vectors whose elements describe each and every dimension of an agreement under negotiation (i.e., $\Delta \equiv \left\{\left(D_{j}\right)_{j \in M}\right\}$. A is a set composed of all the possible actions that can be taken by every member of the players set (i.e., $A \equiv \Delta \cup \left\{Accept, Quit\right\}$). Therefore, A is a set of possible agreements A_{i} for each player $i \in N$, $A_{i} \subset A$. H is sequences (finite or infinite) that satisfies the following properties:

1. The elements of each sequence are defined over A.
2. The empty sequence Φ is a member of H.

3. If $\left(a^k\right)_{k=1,\ldots,K} \in H$ and $L < K$ then $\left(a^k\right)_{k=1,\ldots,L} \in H$.

4. If
$$\left(a^k\right)_{k=1,\ldots,K} \in H$$
and
$$a^K \in \left\{Accept, Quit\right\}$$
then
$$a^k \notin \left\{Accept, Quit\right\}$$
when $k = 1,\ldots K\text{-}1$.

Each member of H is a *history*; each component of a history is an action taken by a player. A history $\left(a^k\right)_{k=1,\ldots,K}$ is terminal if there is no a_{K+1} such that $\left(a^k\right)_{k=1,\ldots,K}$. The set of terminal histories is denoted by Z. A function Q associates each non-terminal history $\left(h \in H \setminus Z\right)$ to a member of N, and determines the orderings of player responses. Ω is introduced to represent the players' knowledge and belief about the negotiation. For each non-terminal history h and each player $i \in N$, a subjective probability distribution $P_{h,i}$ defined over Ω. This distribution is a concise representation of the knowledge held by each player in each stage of negotiation. For each player $i \in N$, each non-terminal history h, and each action $a \in A_i$, there is an implementation cost $C_{i,h,a}$. E is the evaluation function for each player. For each terminal history $h = \left(a^k\right)_{k=1,\ldots,K}$ and each player $i \in N$, it is defined as $E^{(h,i)}\left(P_{h,i}\left(x\right),h\right)$ where $x \in \Omega$ and $h \in Z$.

Before negotiation starts, each player has a certain amount of knowledge about Ω, which may include the knowledge about the environment where the negotiation takes place, and may also include the prior knowledge about other players. Suppose the player i has been interacting with another player j for k times. In other words, the player i has sent the k offer or counteroffer to the

player j. Let us assume that neither *Accept* nor *Quit* has appeared in these offer and counteroffer. In the bazaar game, the following two pieces of information are available when the player i tries to figure out what to do next for his $k + 1$ offer:

1. Each and every history h that is a sequence of k actions is known to the player i. Denote this history $H_{i,k}$.

2. The set of subjective probability distribution over Ω, $P_{H_{i,k-1},i} \equiv \left\{P_{h,i} | h \in H_{i,k-1}\right\}$ is known to the player i.

The player takes the following steps to decide how to reply to the most recent action taken by other players:

Step 1: Update his subjective evaluation about the environment and other players using Bayesian rules. Given prior distribution $P_{H_{i,k-1},i}$, and newly incoming information $H_{i,k}$, calculate the posterior distribution $P_{H_{i,k},i}$.

Step 2: For $h \in H_{i,k}$, select the best action from A_i.

The bazaar game supports an open world model. Therefore, any change in the outside environment will have an impact on the player's subsequent decision making processes. This feature is highly desirable and is seldom found in other existing negotiation models. In addition, the bazaar game aims at modeling multi-issue negotiation processes. By incorporating multiple dimensions into the action space, the bazaar game is able to handle the complicated relationship of multiple issues. In most of existing negotiation game models, learning issues have been either simply ignored or oversimplified for theoretical convenience. In the bazaar game model, multi-player learning issue is addressed and conveniently supported by the iterative nature of sequential decision making and the explicit representation of beliefs about other players (Zeng, 1998). However, the bazaar game model requires heavy complicated computation overhead. Therefore, for real-time negotiation situation, it is hard to be practically implemented.

Minority Game

In 1997, Challet and Zhang proposed a game model called minority game to study the effects of bounded rationality (Kutsuna, & Fujita, 2011), (Shang, 2007). Minority game is a repeated game where players use a number of different strategies in order to join one of the two available groups, and those who belong to the minority group are rewarded. Classical minority game is designed for modeling the financial market made of bounded rational players with learning ability (Tanaka, & Tokuoka, 2006). The major function of those players is to decide one out of two possible actions, corresponding to buy or sell, and all players who have made the minority choice win the game. Let G be a set of an odd number of minority game players; all players synchronously repeat a round, and receive a profit when it becomes a winner of a round. In each round, each player selects one of two groups. Then, the minority of players with respect to the selected groups is determined as the winner of the round. Coarsely speaking, this kind of game model could be involved in a stock market where investors share information and make buy-or-sell decisions in order to gain profit. If the number of sellers of a particular stock is larger than the number of buyers, supply exceeds demand and one expects a decrease in the stock price. Then the buyers, being in minority, would win due to the low price levels. In the opposite case sellers would win, because excess demand would increase the price of the stock. In the long run, the price of the stock eventually settles down to its equilibrium value, i.e. supply and demand are close to each other and the public information has been efficiently utilized. The minority game

can be viewed as simulating the performances of competing individuals and the welfare of the society they compose. In particular, this approach is useful to analyze financial system since it can be seen as a simplified model of a market economy (Sysi-Aho, Saramäki, & Kaski, 2005).

Recently, minority game models are extended widely and can be a more useful model by adding a simple evolutionary-based learning procedure to reason game players. The Evolutionary Minority Game (EMG) is regarded as a paradigmatic model of the evolutionary version of minority game. It allows players dynamically to adapt their strategy according to their past experiences. The evolutionary learning, where underperforming results are discarded and new ones are generated for substitution, is well-known and effective method to solve a risk control problem. Therefore, players apply a very simple learning algorithm to discard bad strategies and create new ones. In the last few years, EMG has attracted considerable attentions and has been investigated extensively in many engineering fields (Tanaka, 2006).

In EMG, N players, where N is an odd number, repeatedly competing to be in a minority. At each time step, the players decide independently on one of two possible options, labeled 0 and 1. These players could be daily traders or rush-hour drivers, choosing 0 denotes choosing to buy a given asset or choosing to take route A, respectively, whereas choosing 1 denotes choosing to sell the asset or choosing to take route B. The winners are those in the minority group, i.e., the side with fewer agents. The only information available to players is the winning side of past m weeks, which is called the history. Therefore, there are a total of 2^m possible history bit-strings of length m. Each agent employs a set of strategies to forecast the outcome and a strategy is simply a lookup table that prescribes a binary output for all possible inputs, where the input is a history bit-string. Each player keeps track of the performance of his strategies and decide based on the most accurate one (Shang, & Wang, 2006).

For example, consider $m = 3$ and denoting $(xyz)w$ as the $m = 3$ bit string (xyz) and outcome t, an example memory would comprise $(000)1$, $(001)0$, $(010)0$, $(011)1$, $(100)0$, $(101)1$, $(110)0$, $(111)1$. Faced with a given bit string of length m, it might seem sensible for a player to simply choose the same option as that stored in the memory. The player will hence choose 1 following the next 111 sequence. However, if 0 turns out to be the winning group after (111), the entry $(111)1$ in the memory is replaced by $(111)0$. If all players act in this way, however, the system will be inefficient since all players will choose the same option and will lose. Therefore, each player has three individual parameters, namely selection probability (p), score and threshold. Following a given m-bit sequence, p is the probability that the player will choose the same action stored in the memory and $(1-p)$ is the chance that choose the opposite. Players who end up in the minority group are awarded a point whereas others loose one. If the score of a player drops below a threshold d, his p value is modified by taking a new value within a range R of the original one and his score is reset to zero (Shang, 2006).

While variations on the EMG with enhanced cooperation have been proposed and studied (Shang, 2006), (Quan, Wang, Hui, & Luo, 2003). Let $A(t)$ be the number of players choosing group 1 at time step t like as

$$A(t) = \sum_{i=1}^{N} x_i(t) \tag{49}$$

where $x_i(t)$ $(i = 1, \ldots, N)$ is an independent Bernoulli random variable that is 1 with probability $p_i(t)$ and zero with probability $(1 - p_i(t))$. Then, a measure of effectiveness can be defined as the variance of $A(t)$ over a time period T:

$$\sigma^2 = \frac{1}{T} \sum_{t=1}^{T} \left(A(t) - \overline{A} \right)^2,$$
$$\text{s.t.,} \quad \overline{A} = \frac{1}{T} \sum_{t=1}^{T} A(t) \tag{50}$$

where $\overline{A}$ is the mean of player choosing group 1. Therefore, the global cooperation among the players can be measured by σ^2. A smaller variance implies that the number of winners per turn is higher. The optimal value of variance σ^2 is 0.25, where the number of winning players reaches its optimal value $(N - 1)/2$ (Shang, 2006).

Contention Game

Game-theoretic approach has been applied extensively to study random access. Usually, random access is the ability to access an element at an arbitrary position in a sequence in equal time, independent of sequence size. The specific structure of random access game is derived from a control-theoretic viewpoint of contention control, and the utility functions are derived from the steady operating points of existing protocols or the desired operating points we want medium access control to achieve (Chen, Low, & Doyle, 2010). In 2007, L. Chen et al used game-theoretic model to capture the information and implementation constraints encountered in real networks. Thus a new game model was designed to guide distributed users to achieve system-wide performance objectives. This game-theoretic model, which is a multi-person non-cooperative game, is called as contention game or random access game for contention control (Chen, Low, & Doyle, 2007).

Consider a set N of wireless nodes in a wireless LAN with contention-based medium access. Assume that each node $i \in N$ attains a utility $u_i(p_i)$ when it accesses the channel with probability $p_i \in [\alpha_{\min}, \alpha_{\max}]$. That $u_i(\cdot)$ is assumed to be continuously differentiable, strictly concave, increasing, and with the curvatures bounded away from zero in $\left[\alpha_{\min}, \alpha_{\max}\right]$. Formally, contention game ($\mathcal{CG}$) is defined as follows (Chen, 2007).

$$\mathcal{CG} = \left\{ N, (S_i)_{i \in N}, (U_i)_{i \in N} \right\} \quad (51)$$

where N is a set of players (i.e., wireless nodes), player $i \in N$ strategy $S_i = \left\{ p_i | p_i \in \left[\alpha_{\min}, \alpha_{\max}\right] \right\}$ with $0 \leq \alpha_{\min} < \alpha_{\max} \leq 1$, and payoff function $U_i(\mathbf{p})$ is given by

$$U_i(\mathbf{p}) = u_i\left(p_i\right) - p_i \times q_i(\mathbf{p}), \text{ s.t., } q_i(\mathbf{p}) = 1 - \prod_{j \neq i}\left(1 - p_j\right) \quad (52)$$

where $q_i(\mathbf{p})$ is the conditional collision probability of node i. $p_i \times q_i$ is the collision probability experienced by node i and it can be seen as the cost resulting from collision. Therefore, if there is no collision, the throughput of node i is proportional to p_i. The main objective of contention game is to choose $\mathbf{p} = \left(p_1, p_2, ..., p_{|N|}\right)$ such that each node maximizes its payoff ($U_i(\mathbf{p})$); it is the net gain of utility from channel access, discounted by the cost due to collision. If all nodes in $\mathcal{CG}$ game have the same utility functions, the system is said to have homogeneous players. If the nodes have different utility functions, the system is said to have heterogeneous players. The system of heterogeneous players is to provide differentiated services to different wireless nodes. Since wireless nodes are not aware of channel access probabilities of others a priori, their interactions are modeled as a non-cooperative game (Chen, 007).

The solution concept of contention game is Nash equilibrium (Chen, 2010). Denote the strategy (channel access probability) selection for all nodes but i by $\mathbf{p}_{-i} = (p_1, p_2, ..., p_{i-1}, p_{i+1}, ..., p_{|N|})$, and write $\left(p_i, \mathbf{p}_{-i}\right)$ for the strategy profile $\left(p_1, p_2, ..., p_{i-1}, p_i, p_{i+1}, ..., p_{|N|}\right)$. A vector of access probability $\mathbf{p}^*$ is a Nash equilibrium if,

for all nodes $i \in N$, $U_i\left(p_i^*, \mathbf{p}_{-i}^*\right) \geq U_i(p_i, \mathbf{p}_{-i}^*)$ for all $p_i \in S_i$. L. Chen et al proved that there exists a Nash equilibrium for any $\mathcal{CG}$. The Nash equilibrium of $\mathcal{CG}$ include three meanings; i) the strategy of every node is the optimal response to the strategies of others, ii) the payoff of the optimal strategy is not less than that of the other strategies, iii) the system is in a relative steady state after all the nodes are at Nash equilibrium.

Dictator Game

The dictator game is a game model in experimental economics, similar to the ultimatum game (Henrich, Boyd, Bowles, Camerer, Fehr, & Gintis, 2004). In the ultimatum game, two players interact to decide how to divide a resource that is given to them. The first player proposes how to divide the resource between the two players, and the second player can either accept or reject this proposal. If the second player rejects, neither player receives anything. If the second player accepts, the resource is split according to the proposal; reciprocation is not an issue ("Dictator game," n.d.).

In the dictator game, the first player, 'the proposer', divides a resource. The second player, 'the responder', simply accepts the decision, which is made by the proposer. The responder has no strategic input into the outcome of the game. From the view of game theory, the dictator game is not formally a proper game model. Since the game's outcome only depends on the proposer's own actions, this situation is one of decision theory. However, despite this formal point, the dictator game is used in the game theory literature as an exceptional non-cooperative game. In economics, this game has been used to test the *homo economicus* model of individual behavior. Simply we can assume that if individuals were only concerned with their own economic well being, proposers would divide the entire resource to themselves and give nothing to the responder. However, experimental results have indicated that a proposer often divides the resource to the responders while reducing his profit (Bolton, Katok, & Zwick, 1998). In political science, other experiments have shown a relationship between political participation and dictator game while suggesting that it may be an externally valid indicator of concern for the well-being of others (Fowler, 2006).

The cooperative behavior game extends the dictator game one step (Cesarini, Dawes, Fowler, Johannesson, Lichtenstein, & Wallace, 2008). This game consists of two game players (i.e., dictator and partner) and a trust-level, which is an initial gift from the partner. The initial move is from the partner, who must decide how much of his initial endowment to trust with him (in the hopes of receiving some of it back). And then, the dictator unilaterally split the resource between himself and a partner. Normally, the partner is encouraged to give something to the dictator through a specification in the game's rules. The experiments rarely end in the subgame perfect Nash equilibrium of 'no trust'.

In 2007, R. Meshulam, S. Kraus, and B.J. Grosz proposed a new variant of the dictator game, which is called the Partner selection based Dictator game (PD game) (Meshulam, Kraus, & Grosz, 2007). The PD game is used to simulate repeated partner selection in an open multi-player setting environment. Based on the information source about potential partners' behaviors, the PD game focuses on scenarios in which players must choose partners to accomplish tasks. Therefore, there is a small group of potential partners. For the purpose of choosing good team members, the role of information exchange is important across a variety of application domains involving people, computer systems, or both as potential team members. The reputation system may augment individual information and thus help a player to select collaborators. In groups with dynamically changing membership, reputation systems are particularly helpful, even for small group sizes. Usually, the reputation system serves as a reposi-

tory of past experience, enabling a player who joins the environment to benefit indirectly from players who have already left.

The PD game introduces a repeated play and the need for choosing partners. It is the key element of small-group task scenarios. To express mathematically, the PD game involves a group of n players $N = \{P_1, P_1, \ldots P_n\}$ who play a game for a given number of rounds. At any time in the PD game, a subgroup (S) of the players (i.e., $S \subset N$, organized in a queue) are active players. The size of S is constant, $|S| = k$. Players leave and join this queue dynamically. After k rounds, one player is removed from S and another player, chosen randomly from N, is added to the end of the queue. Based on a distribution over the players in S, the probability that player at place i in S will leave is $\left(1 - p_l\right)^i \times p_l^{i+1}$, where p_l is a player-defined constant $(0 < p_l \leq 1)$. This distribution ensures that players positioned close to S's head are more likely to leave than players close to the tail (Meshulam, 2007).

In each round of the game, one active player is selected randomly to be the *chooser*. The chooser selects a partner to play one stage of the dictator game. This selected partner assumes the dictator role, deciding on a contribution c to a general pool, where c is a number of points between 0 and λ ($\lambda > 1$). The chooser must contribute the remaining points to reach a λ point contribution. The chooser and selected partner are given a reward of R points. The selected partner gains $R - c$ points and the chooser $R - (\lambda - c) = R + c - \lambda$ points in this round. The goal of each player is to maximize its own total reward.

The traditional dictator game is one of the simplest experimental economics or multi-agent system games that has a partner-feature and involves a trade-off between self- and other-utility. The PD game maintains this simplicity, but adds a special feature that can capture an essential characteristic of the repeated interaction situation while choosing specific players from the general group to be partners in the short-term (Meshulam, 2007).

Blotto Game

In 1921, French mathematician Émile Borel proposed the concept of Blotto game (Kovenocka, & Roberson, 2011), (Roberson, 2006). It is named after the fictional Colonel Blotto from Gross and Wagner's 1950 paper. In the Blotto game, the colonel was tasked with finding the optimum distribution of his soldiers over n battlefields knowing that: i) on each battlefield the party that has allocated the most soldiers will win, ii) both parties do not know how many soldiers the opposing party will allocate to each battlefield, and iii) both parties seek to maximize the number of battlefields they expect to win. Therefore, the Blotto game is the one-shot game in which players compete by simultaneously announcing distributions of force subject to their budget constraints (Partington, 2002). Originally, the Blotto game was developed as a two-person constant-sum game with complete information (Kovenocka, 2011), (Roberson, 2006). Since it was first proposed in 1921, most variations of the classic Blotto game remained unsolved. In 2006, B. Roberson characterized the set of equilibrium to most versions of the classic Blotto game (Roberson, 2006). Formally, the two-person Blotto game ($\mathcal{BG}$) is defined

$$\mathcal{BG} = \left\{ A, B, X_A, X_B, n \right\} \tag{53}$$

where A and B are players and n independent battlefields (Kovenocka, 2011). A has X_A units of force to distribute among the battlefields, and B has X_B units. Each player must distribute their forces without knowing the opponent's distribution. If A sends x_A^k units and B sends x_B^k units to the kth battlefield, the player who provides the higher level of force wins in the kth battlefield. The payoff for the whole game is the proportion of the wins on the individual battlefields. An equilibrium of this game is a pair of n-variate distributions. A distinguishing feature of the Blotto game is that an equilibrium is a pair of non-degenerate multi-dimensional mixed strategies (Kovenocka, 2011).

In 1938, Borel and Ville first solved the special case of $n = 3$ battlefields and symmetric resources. In 1950, Gross and Wagner extended it to any finite number of battlefields, and found equilibrium solutions. In 1958, Friedman published a partial characterization for n battlefields and asymmetric resources. Although many applications and extensions of Colonel Blotto were studied, there was a lull in significant developments until Roberson in 2006. Roberson established novel solutions and proved the uniqueness of Nash equilibrium payoffs for n battlefields and asymmetric resources. The Colonel Blotto game is a fundamental model for multidimensional strategic resource allocation, thereby widely applicable in fields from operations research, to advertising, to military and systems defense. One-dimension models, most frequently the all-pay auction, appears in economics to model political campaigns, lobbying, litigation, research and development races. Also, a redistributive politics model was developed by employing the Colonel Blotto game with asymmetric resources to simulate political candidates who simultaneously announce their fixed budget allocations and citizens who vote according to their higher utility (Modzelewski, Stein, & Yu, 2009).

In 2009, T. Adamo and A. Matros extended the original Blotto game into a stochastic n-player Blotto game (Adamo, & Matros, 2009). In that model, k players compete across a set of n battlefields with valuations that are common knowledge. These valuations may vary across battlefields, but each battlefield's valuation is the same for all players (Kovenocka, 2011). To mathematically express the n-person Blotto game, we assume that there are $k \in \mathcal{K}$ risk-neutral players. Each player k has her private budget X^k. We assume that each X^k is independently and identically distributed on the interval [0,1] according to the increasing distribution function F, where $F(0)=0$, $F(1)=1$. There are n prizes. The value of prize i is $W_i > 0$ for all players and $\sum_{i=1}^{n} W_i = 1$. Each player k has to allocate her budget X^k across all n prizes. All players submit their budget allocations and compete all n prizes simultaneously. We assume that player k wins prize i if

$$x_i^k > \max\left\{x_i^1, \ldots, x_i^{k-1}, x_i^{k+1}, \ldots, x_i^K\right\},$$

where x_i^j is the budget allocation of player j for prize i. Let $\mathfrak{B}$ denote the set of feasible allocations of player k; it is a n-dimensional vector $\left(x_1^k, \ldots, x_n^k\right)$,

$$\mathfrak{B} \equiv \left\{ \boldsymbol{\mathcal{X}} \in \mathbb{R}_+^n \mid \sum_{i=1}^{n} x_i^k \leq 1 \right\}$$

$$\text{s.t., } k \in \mathcal{K}, i \in \boldsymbol{\mathcal{X}} = \left\{1, \ldots, n\right\} \tag{54}$$

$$\text{and} \sum_{j=1}^{n} x_j^k = X^k$$

Player k obtains the following payoff $I_1^k W_1 + \ldots + I_n^k W_n$ where

$$I_i^k = \begin{cases} 1, & \text{if } x_i^k > \max\left\{x_i^1, \ldots, x_i^{k-1}, x_i^{k+1}, \ldots, x_i^K\right\} \\ \dfrac{1}{l} & \text{if } x_i^k = \max\left\{x_i^1, \ldots, x_i^K\right\} \\ & \text{and there are l such players} \\ 0, & \text{if } x_i^k < \max\left\{x_i^1, \ldots, x_i^{k-1}, x_i^{k+1}, \ldots, x_i^K\right\} \end{cases} \tag{55}$$

A strategy for a player k is a function $\beta^k = \left(\beta_1^k, \ldots, \beta_n^k\right) : [0,1] \rightarrow [0,1]^n$ which determines her budget allocation (Adamo, 2009). Of course, $\beta_1^k\left(x^k\right) + \ldots + \beta_n^k\left(x^k\right) \equiv x^k$ and $\hat{a}_i^k\left(x^k\right) \geq 0$ for any $k = 1,\ldots,K$ and $i = 1,\ldots,n$.

Recently, Cognitive Radio (CR) is initiated by the apparent lack of spectrum because of the current rigid spectrum management policies. This promising technology can potentially alleviate spectrum scarcity in wireless communications by allowing secondary users (SUs) to opportunistically access the spectrum that is licensed to primary users (PUs). The main task of CR networks is to ensure that the SUs can maximize spectrum utilization under the interference constraints of multiple PUs (Tan, Chuah, & Tan, 2011). In order to efficiently utilize the valuable spectrum, an efficient subcarrier allocation scheme is required for orthogonal frequency-division multiple access (OFDMA)-based CR networks. Besides, power allocation can be used in CR networks to control the interference from SUs to PUs. Hence, subcarrier allocation and power allocation are two synergistic techniques to achieve efficient spectrum utilization and guarantee protection for PUs. Apparently, the nature of Blotto game is similar to the environment of OFDMA-based CR networks in which SUs compete with each other to acquire a larger number of subcarriers with good channel conditions. Therefore it is suitable to model the subcarrier allocation and power allocation problems using Blotto games.

In 2011, C. Tan et al proposed a new Blotto game model for CR networks (Tan, 2011). To satisfy this goal, they developed subcarrier allocation and power allocation schemes based on Blotto games for both the uplink and downlink. In their work, they considered a more practical scenario by taking into account the correlation between adjacent subcarriers. Unlike the conventional auction method, they modeled the subcarrier allocation and power allocation problems into a multi-dimensional auction where SUs simultaneously compete for subcarriers using a limited budget. The bidding process in this auction can be characterized using a Blotto game and Nash equilibrium (NE) of the Blotto game could be used to solve the auction problem. Subject to the power, budget and interference constraints, the SUs need to wisely allocate their budget and power to win as many good subcarriers as possible. Two budget allocation and power allocation strategies are derived using a Lagrangian relaxation method and NE is shown to exist. They guided the proposed game model to achieve NE (Tan, 2011).

Hawk-Dove Game

In 1973, John Maynard Smith and George Price produced the basic concept of the Hawk-dove game. Hawk-dove game is an anti-coordination game, in which it is mutually beneficial for the players to play different strategies. Hawk-dove game is described as a struggle between 'birds' for a certain resource. The birds can either have an aggressive hawk-behavior, or a non-fighting dove-behavior. When two doves meet, they will equally share the resource with a small cost or without any costs for sharing, but when meeting a hawk, the dove leaves all of the resource to the hawk without a fight. However, two hawks will fight for the resource until one of them gets hurt so badly that it leaves the fight (Carlsson, & Johansson, 1997).

Hawk-dove game is also known as the chicken game or snowdrift game. In the chicken game, the name 'chicken' originates from the front-to-front car race where the first one to swerve from the collision course is a 'chicken'. Obviously, if they both cooperate, they will both avoid the crash and none of them will either be a winner or risk their lives. If one of them steers away, he will be chicken, but will survive, while the opponent will get all the honor. If they crash, the cost for both of them will be higher than the cost of being a chicken (Carlsson, 1997). The snowdrift game refers to an another situation. Imagine two drivers on their way home that are caught in a blizzard and trapped on either side of a snowdrift. Each driver has the option to get out and start shoveling or to remain in the cozy warmth of the car. If both start shoveling each has the benefit of getting home while sharing the labor costs. However, if only

one shovels, both drivers still get home but the lazy bum avoids the labor costs. Nevertheless and despite the shoveling, the benefit of getting home outweighs the awkward prospects of waiting for spring to melt the obstacle. From a game-theoretic point of view, hawk-dove, chicken and snowdrift games are identical. The different names stem from parallel development of the basic principles in different research areas (Osborne, 1994). There is a competition for a shared resource and the contestants can choose either conciliation or conflict. These games have been used to describe the mutual assured destruction of nuclear warfare, especially the sort of brinkmanship involved in the Cuban missile crisis.

Hawk-dove game model mainly studies the problems of strategy and balance which would help to ease the internal conflicts and competition among the same species and population. As the classical model of game theory, it has been widely applied in society. In the mode of the classic of hawk-dove game, there are two kinds of strategies to choose for players, one kind is hawk or attack strategy, the other is to adopt dove or peace strategy. The model is used to analysis the problem of competing for resource conflicts (Zhang, & He, 2012).

In Table 3, A and B represent game players. v represents the income after players play game for competing resources, and c represents cost, which is caused that players compete for resources. We define the probability of selecting hawk strategy is x, while the dove strategy is $y = 1 - x$, the payoff of player who selects hawk strategy is given by

$$UE_H = x \times (v - c) / 2 + y \times v \qquad (56)$$

Table 3. The payoff matrix of hawk and dove game

A\B	Hawk	Dove
Hawk	$v - c/2, v - c/2$	$v, 0$
Dove	$0, v$	$v/2, v/2$

The payoff of player who selects dove strategy is given by

$$UE_D = y \times v / 2 \qquad (57)$$

Considering perfect rationality, the Nash equilibrium depends on specific number of v and c. If $v > c$, whatever x is, we have $UE_H > UE_D$. Therefore, hawk strategy is dominant strategy, and Nash equilibrium consists of hawk-hawk strategies. However, it is not the Pareto optimal equilibrium, which is similar to Prisoner's Dilemma.

Let p (or q) be a probability when the player A (or B) chooses dove strategy, 1-p (or 1-q) be a probability when the player A chooses hawk strategy (Zhang, 2012). Let consider the expected payoff function of player A ($U_1(p,q)$) in the process of game as follows.

$$U_A(p,q) = (p, 1-p)\begin{bmatrix} \gamma & 0 \\ 0 & \zeta \end{bmatrix}\begin{bmatrix} q \\ 1-q \end{bmatrix} \qquad (58)$$

We assume that ζ is 1 and $\tilde{a}$ is 4. According to the analysis of payoff matrix of hawk and dove game, the formula (58) can be replaced by

$$U_A(p,q) = 5pq - q - p + 1 \qquad (59)$$

Taking formula (59) to extract the partial derivatives, then the first-order partial derivative is shown in formula (60).

$$\frac{\partial U_A(p,q)}{\partial p} = (5q - 1) = 0 \qquad (60)$$

Finally, mixed Nash equilibrium is obtained as (p^*, q^*) = (4/5, 1/5).

Public Goods Game

In economics, *Tragedy of the commons* is the well-known phenomenon, which is the depletion of a shared resource by individuals, acting independently and rationally according to each one's self-interest, despite their understanding that depleting the common resource is contrary to the group's long-term best interests. To avoid the *Tragedy of the Commons*, game theory plays a crucial role to encourage cooperation among selfish individuals ("Public goods game," n.d.). In 1954, P. A. Samuelson proposed a fundamental concept of Public Goods (PG) game (Samuelson, 1954). It is one of the core economic game models and has challenged societies throughout the changing times. As a generalization of the prisoner's dilemma, PG game has become a classic paradigm for studying collective dilemma and describing competitive interactions (Xu, & Fan, 2010), (Zhong, Chen, & Huang, 2008). Therefore, the problem of *Tragedy of the commons* can also be transformed as the modeling of PG game.

After introducing the basic concept of PG game, several public goods game models (e.g., iterative PG game, open PG game and PG game with punishment or reward) have been introduced (U, & Li, 2010), (Isaac, Walker, & Williams, 1994). Usually, PG games can be thought as a natural extension of the prisoner's dilemma to an arbitrary number of players. In the original PG game, the players in a competition group are randomly chosen from the whole population and the benefits of the struggle are allocated equally among all the participants irrespective of their contributions (Zhong, 2008). This approach leads to the disappearance of cooperators in the population and defection becomes the dominating strategy. In this sense, the rational equilibrium solution prescribed to '*homo economicus*' leads to economic stalemate. PG games are abundant in human and animal societies, and can be seen as basic examples of economic interactions (Hauert, De Monte, Hofbauer, & Sigmund, 2002).

Let consider a large population of players (N). Players can either contribute some fixed amount (c) or nothing at all. The return of the public good, i.e. the payoff to the players in the group, depends on the abundance of cooperators. If n_c denotes their number among the public goods players, the net payoff for cooperators ($\mathcal{P}_c$) and defectors $\left(\mathcal{P}_d\right)$ is given by

$$\mathcal{P}_c = \left(r \times c \times \frac{n_c}{N}\right) - c \text{ and } \mathcal{P}_d = r \times c \times \frac{n_c}{N}, \text{ s.t.,}$$
$$1 < r < N \tag{61}$$

where r denotes the interest rate on the common pool. The condition $1 < r < N$ states that each individual player is better off defecting than cooperating; selfish players will always avoid the cost of cooperation (c). Therefore, a collective of selfish players will never cooperate and defection is the dominating strategy (Hauert, 2002). If all players are better off cooperating than defecting, it deserves the name of PG game.

Situations of public goods games (i.e., conflict for the exploitation of common resources) are usually modelled as an N-person version of the prisoner's dilemma. Individuals can be cooperators or defectors; cooperators pay a cost for contributing to the public good, whereas defectors refrain from doing so; after all individuals are given the chance to contribute to the public good, the accumulated contribution is multiplied by an enhancement factor, and the total amount equally shared among all individuals (cooperators and defectors). As in the prisoner's dilemma, because an individual can always exploit the benefits of living in a group without contributing to the costs, defection is the dominant strategy (Archetti, 2009).

Volunteer's Dilemma Games

The volunteer's dilemma is an N-person public good game in which a public good is produced if

and only if at least one player volunteers to pay a cost. The basic model of volunteer's dilemma is the following: each of N individuals can choose to volunteer (Volunteer) or not (Ignore). A public good is produced if and only if at least one individual volunteers. Volunteering has a cost $c > 0$. Therefore, the individuals that volunteer have a payoff $1 - c$ and the ones that do not have a payoff 1. If nobody volunteers, the public good is not produced; everybody pays a cost $a > c$ (i.e., payoff $1 - a$). Therefore, each individual prefers that the public good is produced, but also prefers that it is someone else to volunteer (Archetti, 2009). If $N = 2$, the game with the two strategies Volunteer and Ignore has two asymmetric pure-strategy equilibria in which only one player volunteers, but they require coordination: it only works if the players decide in advance who is going to volunteer and when. The game has also a symmetric mixed-strategy equilibrium, which does not require coordination, in which $1 - c = \gamma \times (1 - a) + (1 - \gamma) \times 1$, where γ is the probability of ignoring (not volunteering). Therefore, at equilibrium $\gamma_{eq} = c/a$. The fitness of the pure strategy Volunteer (W_V) is $W_V = 1 - c$ and the fitness of the pure strategy Ignore (W_I) is

$$W_I = \gamma^{N-1}\left(1 - a\right) + \left(1 - \gamma^{N-1}\right).$$

The fitness of the mixed strategy is $W_{mix} = \gamma \times W_I + \left(1 - \gamma\right) \times W_V$. The mixed-strategy equilibrium (γ_{eq}) can be found by equating the fitness of the two pure strategies; $\gamma_{eq} = \left(c / a\right)^{1/(N-1)}$. This has interesting and counterintuitive consequences. First, and this is intuitive, the probability of ignoring increases with c and decreases with a. Second, the probability of ignoring increases with N (Archetti, 2009). The volunteer's dilemma can be applied to many cases in the social sciences.

Security Games

Network security is a complex and challenging problem. Hackers activities have significantly increased in cyber space, and have been causing damage by exploiting weaknesses in information infrastructure. The area of network defense mechanism design is receiving immense attention from the research community for more than two decades. However, the network security problem is far from completely solved. Recently, researchers have been exploring the applicability of game theoretic approaches to address cyber security problems and have proposed a handful of competing solutions (Liang, & Xiao, 2013), (Tambe, Jain, Pita, & Jiang, 2012), (Roy, Ellis, Shiva, Dasgupta, Shandilya, & Wu, 2010).

Game theoretic approaches have been introduced as a useful tool to handle these security problems. They offers promising perspectives, insights, and models to address the ever changing security threats in cyber space. Therefore, game theory is an increasingly important paradigm for modeling security domains. Security games, a special class of attacker-defender Stackelberg games, are at the heart of several major deployed decision support applications. In a security domain, a defender must perpetually defend a set of targets using a limited number of resources, whereas the attacker is able to surveil and learn the defender's strategy and attacks after careful planning. This fits precisely into the description of a Stackelberg game if the defender is mapped to the leader's role and the attacker is mapped to the follower's role. An action, or pure strategy, for the defender represents deploying a set of resources on patrols

or checkpoints. The pure strategy for an attacker represents an attack at a target. The strategy for the leader is a mixed strategy, a probability distribution over the pure strategies of the defender. Additionally, targets are also associated a set of payoff values that define the utilities for both the defender and the attacker in case of a successful or a failed attack (Tambe, 2012)

In a security game, a set of four payoffs is associated with each target. These four payoffs are the reward and penalty to both the defender and the attacker in case of a successful or an unsuccessful attack, and are sufficient to define the utilities for both players for all possible outcomes in the security domain. Table 4 shows an example security game with two targets, t_1 and t_2. In this example game, if the defender was protecting target t_1 and the attacker attacked t_1, the defender would get 2 units of reward whereas the attacker would receive -1 units (Tambe, 2012)

Security games make the assumption that it is always better for the defender to cover a target as compared to leaving it uncovered, whereas it is always better for the attacker to attack an uncovered target. Another feature of the security games is that the payoff of an outcome depends only on the target attacked, and whether or not it is covered by the defender. The payoffs do not depend on the remaining aspects of the defender allocation. Therefore, only the coverage probability of each target is required to compute the payoffs of the defender and the attacker (Tambe, 2012)

For the security games of interest, there is only one leader type (e.g., only one police force), although there can be multiple follower types (e.g., multiple attacker types). Each follower type

Table 4. Security game with two targets

Target	Defender		Attacker	
	Covered	Uncovered	Covered	Uncovered
t_1	2	0	-1	1
t_2	0	-2	-1	1

is represented using a different payoff matrix. The leader does not know the follower's type, but knows the probability distribution over them. Therefore, Stackelberg game model is adaptable to handle security problems with multiple types of players and own payoff values (Tambe, 2012). In particular, this leader-follower paradigm appears to fit many real-world security situations. A generic Stackelberg security game has two players; a defender which first decides how to use m identical resources to protect a set of targets T ($m<|T|$), and an attacker which observes the defender's strategy before choosing a target to attack. A defender's pure strategy is a subset of targets from T such that at most m targets from T are protected. An attacker's pure strategy is a target from T which will be attacked. A mixed strategy allows a player to play a probability distribution over pure strategies. From a mixed strategy of the defender, the overall coverage of each target can be computed. Formally, the defender's mixed strategy can be compactly represented as a coverage vector $\mathbf{c} = c_t$ where c_t is the probability that target t is covered. The attacker's mixed strategy $\mathbf{a} = a_t$ is a vector where a_t is the probability of attacking target t (An, Tambe, Ordóñez, Shieh, & Kiekintveld, 2011).

The payoffs for an agent depend on which target is attacked and how the target is covered. The defender's payoff for an uncovered attack is denoted as $U_d^u(t)$, and for a covered attack $U_d^c(t)$. Similarly, $U_a^u(t)$ and $U_a^c(t)$ are the attacker's payoffs. As a key property of security games, we can assume $\Delta_d(t) = U_d^c(t) - U_d^u(t) > 0$ and $\Delta_a(t) = U_a^u(t) - U_a^c(t) > 0$. Therefore, adding resources to cover a target hurts the attacker and helps the defender. For a strategy profile $\mathbf{c}, \mathbf{a}$, the expected payoffs for both agents are given by:

$$\begin{cases} U_d(\boldsymbol{c},\boldsymbol{a}) = \sum_{t \in T} at \times U_d(\boldsymbol{c},t), \text{ where } U_d(\boldsymbol{c},t) = \\ c_t \times U_d^c(t) + (1 - c_t) \times U_d^u(t) \\ U_a(\boldsymbol{c},\boldsymbol{a}) = \sum_{t \in T} a_t \times U_a(\boldsymbol{c},t) \\ \text{where } U_a(\boldsymbol{c},t) = c_t \times U_a^c(t) + (1 - c_t) \times U_a^u(t) \end{cases}$$

(62)

It follows that $U_d^u(t) \le U_d(\mathbf{c},\ t) \le U_d^c(t)$ and $U_a^c(t) \le U_a(\mathbf{c},\ t) \le U_a^u(t)$ for any target t. In an attacker-defender Stackelberg model, the defender chooses its strategy first, and the attacker chooses a strategy after observing the defender's choice. The attacker's response function is $(\mathbf{c}) : \mathbf{c} \to \mathbf{a}$ where the $g(\mathbf{c})$ is unique to every $\mathbf{c}$. The solution concept for Stackelberg security games is Strong Stackelberg Equilibrium (SSE). A pair of strategies $\mathbf{c}, g(\mathbf{c})$ form an SSE if they satisfy the following (An, 2011).

1. The defender plays a best-response: $U_d(\mathbf{c},g(\mathbf{c})) \ge U_d(\mathbf{c}',g(\mathbf{c}'))$ for any $\mathbf{c}'$.

2. The attacker plays a best-response: $g(\mathbf{c}) \in F_a(\mathbf{c})$ where $F_a(\mathbf{c}) = \operatorname*{argmax}_{\mathbf{a}} U_a(\mathbf{c},\ \mathbf{a})$ is the set of follower best-responses.

3. The attacker breaks ties optimally for the defender: $U_d(\mathbf{c},g(\mathbf{c})) \ge U_d(\mathbf{c},\ \mathbf{a}')$ for any $\mathbf{a}' \in F_a(\mathbf{c})$.

There always exists an optimal pure-strategy response for the attacker. Given the defender's strategy $\mathbf{c}$, the *attack set* $\Gamma(\mathbf{c}) = \operatorname*{argmax}_{t \in T} U_a(\mathbf{c},\ t)$ contains all targets that yield the maximum expected payoff for the attacker. Obviously, it follows that $U_a(\mathbf{c},\ \mathbf{a}) = U_a(\mathbf{c},\ t)$ for any $t \in \Gamma(\mathbf{c})$ (An, 2011). The Strong Stackelberg Equilibrium (SSE) assumes that the defender will choose an optimal mixed (randomized) strategy based on the assumption that the attacker will observe this strategy and choose an optimal response.

Multi-Objective Security Game

The burgeoning area of security games has focused on real-world domains where security agencies protect critical infrastructure from a diverse set of adaptive adversaries. There are security domains where the payoffs for preventing the different types of adversaries may take different forms, which are not readily comparable. Thus, it can be difficult to know how to weigh the different payoffs when deciding on a security strategy. To address the challenges of these domains, multi-objective security game has been proposed. This approach combines security games and multi-objective models (Brown, An, Kiekintveld, Ordóñez, & Tambe, 2012).

A multi-objective security game is a multi-player game between a defender and n attackers. The defender tries to prevent attacks by covering targets $T = \left\{ t_1, t_2, \ldots, t_{|T|} \right\}$ using m identical resources which can be distributed in a continuous fashion amongst the targets. The defender's strategy can be represented as a coverage vector $\mathbf{c} \in C$ where c_t is the amount of coverage for the target t. Usually, c_t represents the probability of the defender successfully preventing any attack on t.

$$C = \left\{ c_t \mid 0 \leq c_t \leq 1, \sum_{t \in T} c_t \leq m \right\}$$ is the defender's

strategy space. The attacker i's mixed strategy $\mathbf{a}_i = a_i^t$ is a vector where a_i^t is the probability of attacking t. U defines the payoff structure with U_i defining the payoff for the security game played between the defender and attacker i. $U_i^{c,d}(t)$ is the defender's utility if t is chosen by attacker i and is fully covered by a defender resource. If t is not covered, the defender's penalty is $U_i^{u,d}(t)$. The attacker's utility is denoted similarly by $U_i^{c,a}(t)$ and $U_i^{u,a}(t)$. A property of security

games is that $U_i^{c,d}(t) > U_i^{u,d}(t)$ and $U_i^{u,a}(t) > U_i^{c,a}(t)$. For a strategy profile $\mathbf{c}$, $\mathbf{a}_i$ for the game between the defender and attacker i, the expected utilities for both agents are given by:

$$\begin{aligned} U_i^d(\mathbf{c}, \mathbf{a}_i) &= \sum_{t \in T} a_i^t \times U_i^d(c_t, t), \\ U_i^a(\mathbf{c}, \mathbf{a}_i) &= \sum_{t \in T} a_t \times U_i^a(c_t, t) \end{aligned} \tag{63}$$

where

$U_i^d(c_t, t) = c_t \times U_i^{c,d}(t) + (1 - c_t) \times U_i^{u,d}(t)$ and
$U_i^a(c_t, t) = c_t \times U_i^{c,a}(t) + (1 - c_t) \times U_i^{u,d}(t)$ are
the payoff received by the defender and attacker i, respectively, if target t is attacked and is covered with c_t resources (Brown, 2012).

The solution concept of multi-objective security game is Strong Stackelberg Equilibrium, in which the defender selects an optimal strategy based on the assumption that the attacker will choose an optimal response, breaking ties in favor of the defender. When the defender uses the coverage vector $\mathbf{c}$ and attacker i attacks the best target while breaking ties in favor of the defender, $U_i^d(\mathbf{c})$ is denoted as the payoff received by the defender. With multiple attackers, the defender's utility (objective) space can be represented as a vector $U^d(\mathbf{c}) = U_i^d(\mathbf{c})$. Finally, the multi-objective security game in (Brown, 2012) defines a multi-objective optimization problem:

$$\max_{\mathbf{c} \in C} \left(U_1^d(\mathbf{c}), \ldots, U_n^d(\mathbf{c}) \right) \tag{64}$$

Solving such multi-objective optimization problems is a fundamentally different task. With multiple objectives functions, there exist tradeoffs between the different objectives such that increasing the value of one objective decreases the value of at least one other objective. Thus for multi-objective optimization, the traditional concept of optimality is replaced by Pareto optimality. Usually, a set of Pareto optimal (non-dominated) solutions refers to as the Pareto frontier. The Pareto frontier can be generated by solving a sequence of constrained single-objective optimization problems, where one objective is selected to be maximized while lower bounds are specified for the other objectives (Brown, 2012).

Anticipation Game

Cyber infrastructure is becoming very complex with interconnections of many systems and sub-systems which perform different level of services, and share valuable data and resources. This leads to extensive interactions which can yield to un-predictable vulnerabilities. As networks of hosts continue to grow, evaluating those vulnerabilities becomes very important. If an intruder compro-mises an important host machine, an intruder can possibly access other hosts on the subnet. Thus, a sophisticated attacker is more likely to go deeper into the network by hopping from one host to the other; bypassing firewalls, intrusion detection systems and other proactive defenses. Therefore, when evaluating the vulnerabilities on a large network infrastructure, one must not only be aware of the new vulnerabilities of each host, but also understand global vulnerabilities introduced through host interconnections in order to mitigate risks. In a network, each system is dependent on other systems and/or shares information based on the trust. Attackers typically exploit this trust by compromising various system weaknesses. Similarly, it is the responsibility of a defender or security administrator to keep the systems free from vulnerabilities and make them secure and trustworthy. Thus, this can be viewed as game playing between two players having opposite objectives in mind (Vejandla, Dasgupta, Kaushal, & Nino, 2010).

Security analysts often plot network intercon-nections in the form of flow graphs, and such graphs are very useful in understanding the global vulnerabilities of the network. An attack graph is a graph that typically illustrates all possible multi-stage, multi-host attack paths. During the past decade, various types of attack graphs have been proposed. They are very helpful in analyzing the security of a network. However, evaluating vulnerabilities entirely based on static intercon-nections is not enough, real time interaction among infrastructure components needs to be considered. In order to accommodate concurrent interactions and other factors, anticipation games were introduced (Vejandla, 2010).

In 2007, E. Bursztein developed a participation game for network security analysis (Bursztein & Mitchell, 2007). The anticipation game is an extension of attack graphs based on game theory. It is used to anticipate and analyze intruder and administrator concurrent interactions with the network. More specifically, an anticipation game is a simultaneous game played between a network attacker and a network defender on a game-board consisting of a dependency graph. The dependency graph defines which services exist on the network and how they are related. The moves of the game do not change this dependency graph, but they do change the attributes, such as the compromise attribute which is associated with the nodes to reflect players action (Bursztein, 2007).

An anticipation game is a timed game, the key difference between standard timed games and anticipation games is the dual-layer structure used in anticipation games. Its lower-layer is used to represent network information (Bursztein, 2009). Its upper-layer is used to model the network state evolution induced by players actions such as ex-ploiting a vulnerability. Therefore, anticipation games can be thought as a graph of graphs where the lower graph is the network state and the above graph describes the transition between one network state to another. The players of an anticipation games are called administrator and intruder and their actions are modeled by timed rules. They are called timed rules because a rule execution requires a certain amount of time to be executed. Each transition in the upper-layer represents the execution of one rule. In an anticipation game, a path is called a play. More formally a play is a sequence of action and states, such as

$$\rho : s_0 \times r_{0\times} s_1 \times r_1 . . . \text{where } \forall j : s_j \xrightarrow{r_j} s_{j+1,s_j}$$

and s_{j+1} are network states, and r_j is the rule used to make the transition (Bursztein, 2009).

In the anticipation game, each node of the graph represents a host in a network and describes its state. Usually, there are several other factors to be considered such as the player's concurrent interactions inside the network, cost, time etc. In order to accommodate these factors, the design of action strategies in anticipation games can be considered as a multi-objective optimization problem with conflicting objectives (such as cost, time and reward). To generate action strategies, several algorithms have been developed. Among these algorithms, the Non-dominated Sorting Genetic Algorithm (NSGA-II) and the Strength Pareto Evolutionary Algorithm (SPEA2), and Multi-Objective Evolutionary Algorithms (MOEA) have widely been studied and effectively used across a range of combinatorial optimization problems (Vejandla, 2010). An administrator and an intruder can select strategies based on the state of each node and perform actions to achieve their respective goals. Such an action may change the state of the node. Use of an anticipation game offers the following advantages: i) anticipation game allows modeling the concurrent interaction of the intruder and the administrator, ii) players' interactions can be described by timed decision rules, which consist of preconditions and post-conditions (Vejandla, 2010).

Classification of Non-Cooperative Game Models

All non-cooperative game theoretic approaches applied in network design problems require competitive players; the interactions among players may be modeled as games which may be described and solved using game theory. The subsection 3.1 has shown the classification of the non-cooperative game models for modeling players' interactions. These non-cooperative game models may be placed into two classes - complete information games and incomplete information games. Moreover, within complete information (*or* incomplete information) games, game model can be further grouped in terms of whether they are of perfect information or imperfect information. Table 5 shows a way of classifying the non-cooperative games in network managements.

COOPERATIVE GAMES

A cooperative game is a game where group of players, which is called as coalition, may enforce cooperative strategies. Therefore, players choose their strategies through a consensus decision-making process. Usually, non-cooperative game models study the strategic choices resulting from the interactions among competing players. In contrast, cooperative games provide analytical tools to study the behavior of rational players when they cooperate. In real life situations, cooperative game mechanisms are abundant (e.g. contract law).

Traditionally, cooperative games are divided two categories – coalitional games and bargaining games. Coalitional games describe the formation process for coalitions (i.e., cooperating groups of players) and prove that it is a very powerful tool for designing fair and efficient cooperation strategies. Bargaining games focus on the bargaining process among players who need to agree on

Table 5. Classification of non-cooperative game models

Non-Cooperative Games				
	Complete Information Games	Perfect Information Game	Static Games	The kind of game does not exist since all static games are of imperfect information
			Dynamic games	Strackelberg game: one leader who moves first and one follower.
		Imperfect information game	Static games	Two-player, zero-sum games
			Dynamic games	Stochastic, repeated games, Markov games
	Incomplete information games	Perfect information game	Static games	The kind of game does not exist since all static games are of imperfect information
			Dynamic games	Two player basic signaling games Two player Multi-stage Bayesin games - players have little information about the payoff function of each other. - Two-player fictitious play, and each player keeps updating the frequency of its opponents
		Imperfect information game	Static games	Two-player Bayesian game
			Dynamic games	Two-player Multi-stage Bayesin game - each player keeps updating its inference about the type of its opponent - the solution of the game is a series of optimal one-stage strategies based on the updated inference

the cooperation (Han, Niyato, Saad, Başar, & Hjørungnes, 2011).

Coalitional Games

There are two major research topics in coalitional games. The first topic involves partitioning a set of players into coalitions so that the sum of the rewards of all coalitions is maximized. The second topic involves how to divide the value of the coalition among agents. The theory of coalitional games provides a number of solution concepts, such as the core, the Shapley value, and the nucleolus.

Coalition Formation Game

Traditionally, forming effective coalitions is a major research challenge in multi-agent systems. In multi-agent systems, it is often benefit that agents form coalitions for achieving their goals. In game models, a coalition of players can also do things more efficiently than individual players can do. Therefore, for the effective modeling of

player cooperation, a coalition formation game has been developed (Han, 2011), (Vinyals, Bistaffa, Farinelli, & Rogers, 2012).

In many applications, coalition formation entails finding a coalitional structure that maximizes the total payoff (i.e., finding a Pareto-optimal payoff distribution for the players). Generally, coalition formation games are categorized as two types: static coalition formation game and dynamic coalition formation game. In the static coalition formation game, an external factor imposes a certain structure to form stable coalitions. Therefore, no player has an incentive to deviate. The main goal of static coalition-formation games is to study the properties of this structure, such as its stability. Formally, a static coalition formation game is defined by (N, v) which $N = \{p_1, \ldots, p_n\}$ is the set of players and v is a real-valued characteristic function such that $v(S) : 2^N \to \mathbb{R}$, s.t., $S \subset N$; a subset S is termed a coalition. Given a coalition game, a coalition structure $\mathcal{C} = \{S_1, \ldots, S_k\}$ is an exhaustive disjoint partition of the space of players into feasible coalitions and $v\left(\mathcal{C}\right) = \sum_{S \in \mathcal{C}} v\left(S\right)$. The coalition composed of all players is referred as a grand coalition (Han, 2011), (Vinyals, 2012), (Panah, & Khorsandi, 2011).

Compare to the static coalition-formation game, dynamic coalition-formation games constitute a richer framework. In static games, coalitions are already formed by an external factor. In dynamic coalition formation games, a challenging question is how to form a coalitional structure that is suitable to the studied game. In addition, the evolution of this structure is important. For example, if one or more players leave the game, the current coalition should be dynamically re-structured. Therefore, the main objectives of dynamic coalition-formation games are to analyze the formation of a coalitional structure through players' interaction, and to study the properties of this structure and its adaptability to environmental variations or externalities. By considering game dynamics, the properties from resulting coalitions and its adaptability to environment variable or externalities are important research issues (Han, 2011).

The coalition formation game can generally be considered to include three differentiated processes: *Coalitional Value Calculation, Coalition Structure Generation* and *Payoff Distribution*. In the *coalitional value calculation* process, players enumerate and evaluate all possible feasible coalitions that can be formed. With these values of feasible coalitions, the coalition structure ($\mathcal{C}^*$) with maximal value is identified in the *Coalition Structure Generation* process. Finally, *Payoff Distribution* process determines the payoff that each player in a coalition should obtain as a result of the actions taken by the coalition as a whole.

To implement a coalition formation algorithm, some definition and rules are necessary (Han, 2011). First of all, a collection of coalitions in the grand coalition $\mathcal{N}$, denoted $\mathcal{S}$, is defined as the set $\mathcal{S} = \left\{S_1, \ldots, S_k\right\}$ of mutually disjoint coali-

tions $S_i \subset \mathcal{N}$. In other words, a collection is arbitrary group of disjoint coalitions S_i of $\mathcal{N}$ not necessarily spanning all players of $\mathcal{N}$. If the collection spans all the players of $\mathcal{N}$ (i.e., $\mathcal{N} = \bigcup_{j=1}^{k} S_j$), this collection is simply a partition of $\mathcal{N}$. A *preference relation* $\rhd$ is an order defined for comparing two coalition collections $\xi = \left\{R_1, ..., R_l\right\}$ and $\mathcal{S} = \left\{S_1, \ldots, S_p\right\}$ that are partitions of the same subset $\mathcal{A} \subseteq \mathcal{N}$ (i.e., same players in ξ and $\mathcal{S}$). In this case, $\xi \rhd \mathcal{S}$ implies that the way $\hat{\imath}$ partitions $\mathcal{A}$ is preferred to the way $\mathcal{S}$ partitions $\mathcal{A}$. Based on the concept of *preference relation*, merge and split rules can be defined as follows (Han, 2011).

Merge Rule: Any set of coalitions $\left\{S_1, \ldots, S_k\right\}$ may be merged whenever the merged form is preferred by the players; i.e., where $\left\{\bigcup_{j=1}^{k} S_j\right\} \rhd \left\{S_1, \ldots, S_k\right\}$, therefore, $\left\{S_1, \ldots, S_k\right\} \rightarrow \left\{\bigcup_{j=1}^{k} S_j\right\}$.

Split Rule: Any coalition $\bigcup_{j=1}^{k} S_j$ may be split whenever a split form is preferred by the players; i.e., where $\left\{S_1, \ldots, S_k\right\} \rhd \left\{\bigcup_{j=1}^{k} S_j\right\}$, thus, $\left\{\bigcup_{j=1}^{k} S_j\right\} \rightarrow \left\{S_1, \ldots, S_k\right\}$.

The basic idea behind the merge-and-split rules is that given a set of players $\mathcal{N}$, any collection of disjoint coalitions $\left\{S_1, \ldots, S_k\right\}$, $S_k \subset \mathcal{N}$ can agree to merge into a single coalition $G = \bigcup_{i=1}^{k} S_i$, if this new coalition G is preferred by the players over the previous state. Similarly, a coalition S splits into smaller coalitions if the resulting collection $\left\{S_1, \ldots, S_k\right\}$ is preferred by the players over S. A decision to merge or split is reached only if it allows all involved players to maintain their payoffs with that of at least one user improving. Therefore, in a coalition formation algorithm based on the merge-and-split rules, players enter into a binding agreement to form a coalition through the merge operation if all players are able to improve their individual payoffs from the previous state. Similarly, players can only split this coalition if splitting does not decrease the payoff to any coalition member (Han, 2011).

Canonical Coalition Game

Canonical coalition games are a class of coalitional games. In such games, it is assumed that when forming a larger coalition is always beneficial to the players, who cannot do worse than by acting alone in non-cooperative manner. This property, called *superadditivity*, is defined as follows

$$v\left(S_1 \cup S_2\right) \geq v\left(S_1\right) + v\left(S_2\right),$$

s.t, $\forall S_1 \subset \mathcal{N}$, $S_2 \subset \mathcal{N}$ and $S_1 \cap S_2 = \varnothing$

(65)

Superadditivity implies that if coalition $S_1 \cup S_2$ forms, this new coalition can always give its members the better payoffs than they acted separately in the disjoint coalitions S_1 and S_2. Canonical games are defined based on the property of *superadditive*. Therefore, the players in canonical games always form the *grand coalition* $\mathcal{N}$ (i.e, the coalition of all the players) since the payoff received from $v\left(\mathcal{N}\right)$ is at least as large as the amount received by the players in any disjoint set of coalitions they could form. Due to this reason, the main goals of canonical games are, i) finding a payoff allocation that guarantees that no group of players has an incentive to leave the grand coalition (i.e., having a *stable* grand coali-

tion), and (ii) assessing the gains that the grand coalition can achieve as well as the fairness criteria that must be used for distributing these gains (i.e., having a *fair* grand coalition) To satisfy these two goals, a number of solution concepts - the core, the Shapley value, and the nucleolus - are presented. Among several cooperative canonical game solutions, the core is a strong solution concept for stability concepts, and the Shapley value is developed based on the fair distribution of total gains to the players, assuming that they all collaborate (Han, 2011).

A bankruptcy game is a well known example of canonical coalition games (Vassaki, Panagopoulos, & Constantinou, 2009). It is defined as $G\left(\mathcal{N}, v\right)$ where $\mathcal{N}$ represents the claimants of the bankruptcy situation and v is the characteristic function that associates to each coalition; its worth is defined as the part of the estate not claimed by its complement:

$$v\left(S\right) = \max(0, E - \sum_{i \in \mathcal{N} \setminus S} d_i), \forall S \subset \mathcal{N} \setminus \left\{\varnothing\right\}$$

and $E < \sum_{i \in N} d_i$

(66)

where $E \geq 0$ is an estate that has to be divided among the members of $\mathcal{N}$ (the claimants) and $\boldsymbol{d} \in R_+^{|\mathcal{N}|}$ is the claim vector (i.e., $d_i \in \boldsymbol{d}$). Equation (66) has been proven to be *supermodular* which means that the marginal payoff of increasing a player's strategy rises with the increase in other player strategies. A division rule is a function f that assigns a solution $f_i\left(E; d_i\right)$ for every $i \in N$ such that

$$0 \leq f_i\left(E; d_i\right) \leq d_i \text{ and}$$
$$\sum_{i=1}^{N} f_i\left(E; c\right) = E$$

(67)

These two restrictions imply that no claimant gets more than he claims or less than zero and that the total amount E is divided among the claimants. Let's consider a simple scenario to explain the solution of bankruptcy game. There are three claimants, $\mathcal{N} = \{A,B,C\}$, $E = 600$ and $d = \{400,300,171\}$. So, $G(\mathcal{N},v)$ is defined where $|\mathcal{N}| = 3$ and $v(\mathcal{N}) = 600$. Developing the characteristic functions as shown in Table 6.

Based on these values, we go through to the Shapley Value to compute the distribution. The Shapley Value is a very general method for equitable division (i.e., fairest allocation) of collectively gained profits among the several collaborative players. The basic criterion is to find the relative importance of every player regarding the cooperative activities. The formula given by Shapley is:

$$\phi_i(i) = \sum_{S \subset \mathcal{N}, \; i \in \mathcal{N}} \frac{(|S|-1)!(n-|S|)!}{n!} \times \left(i(S) - i(S \setminus \{i\})\right) \tag{68}$$

According to (68), a final solution for the bankruptcy game is (293, 193,114). It is a distribution vector for each claimant, and can be obtained as follows.

$$\phi_A(i) = \frac{0!2!}{3!}(129-0) + \frac{1!1!}{3!}(429-29) + \frac{1!1!}{3!}(300-0) + \frac{2!0!}{3!}(600-200) = 293$$

Table 6. Coalition structure

Coalition Type	Coalition Value
1-player coalition	$v(A) = $ max (0, 600- (300+171)) = 129
	$v(B) = $ max (0, 600- (400+171)) = 29
	$v(C) = $ max (0, 600- (400+300)) = 0
2-player coalition	$v(A,B) = $ max (0, 600- (171)) = 429
	$v(A,C) = $ max (0, 600- (300)) = 300
	$v(B,C) = $ max (0, 600- (400)) = 200
3-player coalition	$v(A,B,c) = $ max (0, 600- (0)) = 600

$$\phi_B\left(i\right) = \frac{0!2!}{3!}\left(29 - 0\right) +$$
$$\frac{1!1!}{3!}\left(429 - 129\right) +$$
$$\frac{1!1!}{3!}\left(200 - 0\right) + \frac{2!0!}{3!}\left(600 - 300\right) = 193$$

$$\phi_C\left(i\right) = \frac{0!2!}{3!}\left(0 - 0\right) +$$
$$\frac{1!1!}{3!}\left(300 - 129\right) + \frac{1!1!}{3!}\left(200 - 29\right) +$$
$$\frac{2!0!}{3!}\left(600 - 429\right) = 114$$

With the Shapley Value, various solution methods were developed for the bankruptcy game. A well-known division method is the Constrained Equal Award (*CEA*) method, which assigns the same sum to all players as long as it does not exceed each player's claim (Dagan, Serrano, & Volij, 1997). Specifically,

$$CEA_i\left(\boldsymbol{d}, E\right) = \min\left\{d_i, \lambda\right\} \tag{69}$$

where λ is chosen so that $\sum \min\left\{d_j, \lambda\right\} = E$, s.t., $j \in \mathcal{N}$. Another method proposed by O'Neill called the Random Arrival method (*RA*) is also employed as follows (O'Neill, 1982).

$$RA_i\left(\boldsymbol{d}, E\right) = \frac{1}{\mathcal{N}!} \sum_{\pi \in \prod^{\mathcal{N}}} \min\left\{d_i, \max\left\{E - \sum_{\substack{j \in N, \\ \pi(j) < \pi(i)}} d_j, \ 0\right\}\right\} \tag{70}$$

where $\prod^{\mathcal{N}}$ denote the class of permutation of $\mathcal{N}$. To maximize the network performance. The Talmud method, which was developed by R. Aumann and M. Maschler, is briefly presented as follows (Aumann, & Maschler, 1985).

$$\begin{vmatrix} T_i(\boldsymbol{d}, E) = \min\left\{\frac{d_i}{2}, \lambda\right\} \\ \text{If } \sum\left(\frac{d_i}{2}\right) \geq E, \text{ where } \lambda \text{ is chosen so that } \sum \min\left\{d_j, \lambda\right\} = E \\ T_i(\boldsymbol{d}, E) = d_i - \min\left\{\frac{d_i}{2}, \lambda\right\} \\ \text{If } \sum\left(\frac{d_i}{2}\right) \leq E \text{ where } \lambda \text{ is so that } \sum\left[d_{i-\min}\left\{\frac{d_i}{2}, \lambda\right\}\right] = E \end{vmatrix} \tag{71}$$

The most well-known solution concept for canonical coalitional games is the core. To provide an example of core solution, it is necessary to introduce some terminology (Vinyals, 2012), (Panah, 2011). A vector $\varphi = \left\{\varphi_1, \ldots, \varphi_n\right\}$ assigning some payoff to each player $p_i \in N$ is called an *allocation* and $\varphi\left(S\right) = \sum_{i \in S} \varphi_i$ for a coalition S. The payoff of player i (φ_i) can be obtained through a certain strategy selected by the player i. The core is the set of payoff allocations that guarantees that no players have an incentive to leave the current coalition in order to form another coalition. If $\varphi\left(S\right) = v\left(S\right)$ and $\varphi_i \geq v\left(\{i\}\right)$ for all S and all players (s.t., $S \in \mathcal{C}$ where $\mathcal{C}$ coalition structure), it means that all players and payoffs are individually rational and efficient, respectively. At this time, an allocation vector $\ddot{o}$ is called an *imputation* for a given $\mathcal{C}$. Therefore, an *imputation* is a payoff vector that is both individually rational and group rational.

A game outcome is a $\left(\mathcal{C}, \varphi\right)$ pair while assigning players to coalitions and allocating payoffs to players efficiently. The core is composed of all coalition structure, i.e., *imputation* tuples $\left(\mathcal{C}, \varphi\right)$, which determine stable allocations such that no feasible coalition has any incentive to deviate from the current coalitions. Formally, for a coalition game $\left(N, v\right)$, an allocation vector **x** is a core allocation if

$\mathbf{x} \in \mathbb{R}^N$ and if $\forall S \subset N, \nexists \mathbf{y} \in v\left(S\right)$,

s.t., $y_i \in \mathbf{y}$, $x_i \in \mathbf{x}$, and $y_i > x_i$ (72)

where S is a coalition that can achieve $\mathbf{x}$ by its own efforts and $\mathbf{y}$ is another allocation vector. For example, consider a game with three players, $\mathcal{N} = \left\{1, 2, 3\right\}$ (Han, 2011), (Vinyals, 2012), (Panah, 2011). The players, on their own, have no payoffs, hence v({1}) = v({2}) = v({3}) = 0. Any two-player coalition has a payoff like as v({1, 2}) = v({1, 3}) = v({2, 3}) = $\dfrac{2}{3}$. The grand coalition has a payoff v({1, 2, 3}) = 1. This case yields the core and shows what allocations stabilize the grand coalition. By manipulating $x_1 + x_2 + x_3 = v\left(\left\{1, 2, 3\right\}\right) = 1$, $x_1 \geq 0$, $x_2 \geq 0$, $x_1 \geq 0$, and

$$x_1 + x_2 \geq v\left(\left\{1, 2\right\}\right) = \frac{2}{3},$$

$$x_1 + x_3 \geq v\left(\left\{1, 3\right\}\right) = \frac{2}{3},,$$

$$x_2 + x_3 \geq v\left(\left\{2, 3\right\}\right) = \frac{2}{3}$$

the core of this game is found to be the unique vector

$$\mathbf{x} = \left[\frac{1}{3}\frac{1}{3}\frac{1}{3}\right],$$

which corresponds to an equal division of the total utility for the grand coalition among all three players.

Consider another example for core. Assume three players and let $\mathbf{r} = \left(r_1, r_2, r_3\right)$ be a vector representing the amount of resources allocated to the three players. The objective is to allocate the resources so that the total payoff of the coalition

Table 7. Coalition structure

Coalition	Coalition value
{∅}	0
{1}	10
{2}	10
{3}	20
{1,2}	50
{1,3}	40
{2,3}	70
{1,2,3}	100

is maximized, subjected to resource capacity constraints. We assume a coalition structure as shown in Table 7.

The imputations are the points $\left(r_1, r_2, r_3\right)$ such that $r_1 + r_2 + r_3 = 100$ and

$$r_1 \geq 10, \ r_2 \geq 10, \ r_3 \geq 20.$$

The set of the *imputations* for this coalition game is represented graphically as shown in Figure 2. It shows the core, which consists of all imputations in the trapezoidal area (Suliman, Pomalaza-Rez, Lehtomki, & Oppermann, 2004).

Matching Game

In 1962, David Gale and Lloyd Shapley derived an effective cooperative game model of finding a stable matching (Kimbrough, & Kuo, 2010). The Gale and Shapley presented model is very simple. A number of boys and girls have preferences for each other and would like to be matched. The question Gale and Shapley were especially interested in was whether there is a stable way to match each boy with a girl so that no unmatched pair can later find out that they can both do better by matching each other. To provide a stable matching solution, Gale and Shapley presented a deferred acceptance algorithm that achieves this objective. From labor markets to human courtship, the Gale and Shapley's model can create efficient pairing solutions; there are a number of application models for the Gale-Shapley solution. Below procedure describes the shows the algorithm of deferred acceptance algorithm (Algorithm 1), which is simple and easily understood.

The two-way matching game was developed for special matching problems. In a two-way matching game, players on each side have preferences over players on the other side, and have enough information to rank players on the other side. Therefore, player in one side tries to be matched to the other player in opposite side so as to satisfy both players as much as possible (Kimbrough, 2010).

In economics, exchange economy means a model of an economy with no production. Therefore, goods have already been produced, found, inherited, or endowed, and the only issue is how

Figure 2. The core of the three player cooperative game (Suliman, 2004)

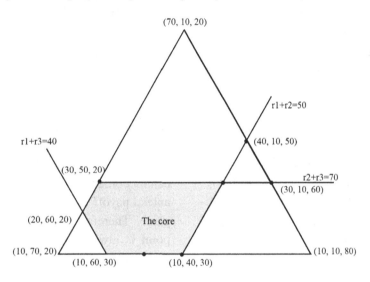

Algorithm 1. Deferred acceptance algorithm (Kimbrough, 2010)

Deferred acceptance algorithm for the simple marriage matching problem X proposes to Y
1: Assume: $\left|X\right| = \left|Y\right| = n$
2: Each $x \in X$ ranks each $y \in Y$, and each $y \in Y$ also ranks each $x \in X$.
3: *Matched* $\leftarrow \varnothing$, *unmatched* $\leftarrow \varnothing$.
4: For each *y*, *string.* $\mathbf{y} \leftarrow$ []
5: Each *x* proposes to its most-preferred *y*, appending *x* to ***string.y***.
6: Each *y* with *length* (***string.y***) >1 (i.e., with more than one proposal), retains in the string its most preferred member of the string, and removes the rest, adding them to *Unmatched*.
7: Do while *Unmatched* $= \varnothing$:
(a) Each $x \in$ *Unmatched* proposes to its most-preferred *y*, among the Ys that have not already rejected *x*, appending *x* to ***string.y***
(b) *Unmatched* $\leftarrow \varnothing$.
(c) Each *y* with *length* (***string.y***) > 1 (i.e., with more than one proposal), retains in the string its own most preferred member of the string, and removes the rest, adding them to *Unmatched*.
8: For each *x* remaining on some ***string.y***, (*x, y*) is added to *Matched*.
9: Stop. Each *x* is matched to a distinct *y*, who has *x* as the sole member of its string. This is recorded in *Matched*.

they should be distributed and consumed. The key issue in exchange economy is the efficiency or inefficiency of goods' allocations among consumers. The simplest exchange economy can be modeled like as: each agent comes to the market with one indivisible good and seeks to trade it for possibly more preferred ones that might be brought by other agents. Two-way matching game can provide an important answer to the question of exchange economy (Gillis, 1999). Gale and Shapley also showed that there exists a core allocation in the exchange economy, and presented a trading algorithm to achieve this objective. As a kind of cooperative game model, two-sided matching games dealt with widely in practice include pairing men with women, workers with employers, students with schools and so on (Kimbrough, 2010).

Bargaining Games

Bargaining games refer to situations where two or more players must reach agreement regarding how to distribute an object or resource amount. Conceptually, bargaining is precisely the opposite of the idealized 'perfect competition' among players. With the advent of game theory, attempts were made to develop theories of bargaining which would predict particular outcomes. A solution to the cooperative bargaining game model enables the game players to fairly and optimally determine their payoffs to make joint-agreements. Various solutions have been proposed based on slightly different assumptions about what properties are desired for the final agreement point.

Nash Bargaining Game

The bargaining solution proposed by J. Nash is Nash Bargaining Solution (NBS), which is the unique bargaining solution that satisfies six axioms

- *Individual rationality, feasibility, Symmetry, Pareto optimality, Independence of irrelevant alternatives* and *Invariance with respect to utility transformations*. The NBS is a function that assigns a non-empty set of feasible payoff vectors to a unique solution. Based on the traditional game theory, Nash bargaining solution can be formulated as follows. There are n players; player i has its own utility function (u_i). Assume $\mathbb{S} = \{(u_1, \ldots u_n)\} \subset \mathbb{R}^n$ is a joint-utility solution set that is nonempty, convex, closed, and bounded feasible utility set. In the $\mathbb{S}$, some solutions are characterized such that one player cannot increase his utility without decreasing the utility of any other players. This solution set is called as the Pareto optimal points/surface, which is payoff pairs in the cooperative trade-off area (Park, & Schaar, 2007). One agreement point u ($u \in \mathbb{S}$), which is an action vector in the Pareto surface, is a possible outcome of the bargaining process. A disagreement point (d) is an action vector $d = (d_1, \ldots d_n) \in \mathbb{S}$ that is expected to be the result if players cannot come to an agreement. It is at least guaranteed payoff for each player in the cooperative game. Therefore, the payoff at any agreement point is always higher or equal to the payoff achieved at the disagreement point. The pair ($\mathbb{S}$, d) defines the bargaining problem and following is the formal definition of bargaining solution.

$$\prod_i \left(u_i^* - d_i\right)^{\psi_i} = \max_{u_i \in \mathbb{S}} \prod_i \left(u_i - d_i\right)^{\psi i}, \quad (73)$$
where $u_i^* \in \mathbb{S}$ and $d_i \in d$

where ψ_i is the player i's bargaining power and $\sum_{i=1}^n \psi_i = 1$. Usually, the bargaining solution is strongly dependent on the bargaining powers. If different bargaining powers are used, the player with a higher bargaining power obtains a higher resource than the other players. In the game theory terminology, an outcome vector U^* ($u_i^* \in U^*$) is called the NBS. Therefore, in the multiple Pareto optimal solutions, the NBS decides the best one, which can give a unique and fair-efficient solution that fulfills the Nash axioms (Park, 2007).

Kalai-Smorodinsky Bargaining Game

Kalai-Smorodinsky Bargaining Solution (KSBS) is another bargaining solution. In contrast to NBS, the KSBS can be used when the feasible utility set is not convex. Therefore, the KSBS's main advantage is not requiring the convexity of the feasible utility set. It is a good point for practical implementations. Moreover, the KSBS provides different type of fairness as opposed to the NBS. Formally, the KSBS U^* (i.e., $U^* = \left(U_1^*, \ldots, U_n^*\right)$ where $U_i^* \in U^*$ is Pareto optimal) to n players satisfies

$$U^* = \mathbf{d} + \lambda_{\max} \times \left(U_{\max} - \mathbf{d}\right) \qquad (74)$$

where $\mathbf{S}$ is the feasible utility set and $\mathbf{d} = \left(d_1, \ldots, d_n\right)$ is the disagreement point; it represents payoffs when the game fails and the payoffs cannot be made. $U_{\max} = \left(U_{\max}^1, \ldots, U_{\max}^n\right) \geq \mathbf{d}$ is the ideal point for n players. Therefore, $U_{\max}^i$ is the player i's payoff (i.e., utility) when the total available resource is allocated. $\lambda_{\max}$ is the maximum λ value such that $\mathbf{d} + \lambda \times \left(U_{\max} - \mathbf{d}\right) \in \mathbf{S}$.

In Kalai-Smorodinsky game model, each player is a member of a team willing to compromise his own objective to gain a total optimal solution. By employing the KSBS approach, the team players cooperate with each other and make a collective decision. If an agreement among the

players cannot be reached, the payoff that the players will receive is given by the disagreement point $\mathbf{d} = \left(d_1, \ldots, d_n\right)$. To get the KSBS, the line (L) is defined based on the $\mathbf{d}$ as a starting point as follows.

$$L = \left\{U \mid \frac{U_1}{\omega_1 \times U_{\max}^1} = \ldots = \frac{U_n}{\omega_n \times U_{\max}^n}\right\},$$

$$\text{s.t.}, U_i > 0, \sum_{i=1}^{n} \omega_i = 1 \text{ and } \omega_i \geq 0 \qquad (75)$$

where ω_i ($0 < \omega_i < 1$) is the player i's bargaining power, which is the relative ability to exert influence over other players (Park, 2007). Geometrically, the KSBS is the intersection point ($U_1^*, \ldots, U_n^*$) between the bargaining set $\mathbf{S}$ and the line L. Since the KSBS is located in the $\mathbf{S}$ as well as in the line L in (75), the bargaining solution must satisfy

$$\frac{U_1^*}{\omega_1 \times U_1^{max}} = \ldots = \frac{U_n^*}{\omega_n \times U_n^{max}}, \text{ s.t}, (U_1^*, \ldots, U_n^*)$$
$$\in \mathbf{S} \qquad (76)$$

$U^* = (U_1^*, \ldots, U_n^*)$ is the KSBS, which exhibits important properties that can be used for effective resource allocation problems. Since all players incur the same utility penalty by participating in the cooperative game, the KSBS can be interpreted as an utility-based fair solution (Park, 2007).

Rubinstein Bargaining Games

Rubinstein bargaining model refers to a class of bargaining games that feature alternating offers through an infinite time horizon (Rubinstein, 1982). This model is considered as a new non-cooperative implementation of the NBS, and has been so influential because it constructs a simple and elegant model of bargaining in which agreement is reached immediately. The Rubinstein bargaining solution is useful not only in direct application, but as a component of more complex models of interactions in which players split a surplus at some point in the game they are playing.

To get the basic understanding of Rubinstein bargaining solution, let consider the scenario of two person division problem (Rasmusen, 2008). For example, Kim and Lee are splitting a pie of size 1. First, Kim makes an offer of a split of x_{Kim} for himself and $(1 - x_{Kim})$ for Lee. If Lee accepts, the game is over and the payoffs (π_{Kim} for Kim and π_{Lee} for Lee) are

$$\pi_{Kim} = x_{Kim} \text{ and } \pi_{Lee} = 1 - x_{Kim} \qquad (77)$$

If Lee rejects, a period of time passes, at the end of which Lee pays c_{Lee} and Kim pays c_{Kim}. Then, Lee makes an offer of a split of x_{Lee} for himself and $(1 - x_{Lee})$ for Kim. If Kim accepts, the game is over and the payoffs are

$$\pi_{Kim} = \delta_{Kim} \left[-c_{Kim} + \left(1 - x_{Lee}\right) \right]$$

and

$$\pi_{Lee} = \delta_{Lee} \left[-c_{Lee} + x_{Lee} \right] \qquad (78)$$

where δ is discount factor, and second-period payoffs are discounted by discount factors. If Kim rejects Lee's offer, another period of time elapses and she makes the next offer. The two players make alternating offers until agreement is reached, or forever if agreement is not reached.

In any subgame perfect equilibrium, Kim's first offer will be accepted immediately. In other words, the players would make more generous offers now that would equal any bigger payoffs without having to pay the bargaining costs. Denote Kim's equilibrium offer as x_A^* and Lee's equilibrium offer as x_{Lee}^*. We can assume that both players follow their equilibrium strategies. Therefore, in making Kim's offer, Kim realizes that if Lee could reject the Kim's offer, Lee will offer the next period proposal based on the x_{Lee}^*. it is $\delta_{Lee} \left[-c_{Lee} + x_{Lee}^* \right]$. By considering this scenario, Kim can make Lee willing to accept Kim's offer by making it generous enough to give Lee like as

$$1 - x_{Kim}^* = \delta_{Lee} \left[-c_{Lee} + x_{Lee}^* \right] \qquad (79)$$

In making Lee's offer, it is the same situation. Therefore Lee's offer is

$$1 - x_{Lee}^* = \delta_{Kim} \left[-c_{Kim} + x_{Kim}^* \right] \qquad (80)$$

According to (80), it can be derived as follows

$$1 = -\delta_{Lee} c_{Lee} + \delta_{Lee} x_{Lee}^* + x_{Kim}^* \rightarrow \quad \delta_{Lee} x_{Lee}^* = 1 + \delta_{Lee} c_{Lee} - x_{Kim}^* \qquad (81)$$

Therefore, x_{Lee}^* can be obtained

$$x_{Lee}^* = \frac{1 + \delta_{Lee} c_{Lee} - x_{Kim}^*}{\delta_{Lee}} \qquad (82)$$

In formula (82), x_{Lee}^*, can be substituted like as

$$1 - \frac{1 + \delta_{Lee} c_{Lee} - x_{Kim}^*}{\delta_{Lee}} = \delta_{Kim} \left[-c_{Kim} + x_{Kim}^* \right] \qquad (83)$$

And then, it can be derived as follows

$$\delta_{Lee} - 1 - \delta_{Lee} c_{Lee} + x^*_{Kim} = \delta_{Lee} \delta_{Kim} \left[-c_{Kim} + x^*_{Kim} \right]$$

$$\rightarrow$$

$$x^*_{Kim} = -\delta_{Lee} \delta_{Kim} c_{Kim} + \delta_{Lee} \delta_{Kim} x^*_{Kim} - \delta_{Lee} + 1 + \delta_{Lee} c_{Lee}$$

$$\rightarrow$$

$$x^*_{Kim} \left(1 - \delta_{Lee} \delta_{Kim} \right) = -\delta_{Lee} \delta_{Kim} c_{Kim} - \delta_{Lee} + 1 + \delta_{Lee} c_{Lee} \tag{84}$$

Therefore, x^*_{Kim} can be obtained

$$x^*_{Kim} = \frac{-\delta_{Lee} \delta_{Kim} c_{Kim} - \delta_{Lee} + 1 + \delta_{Lee} c_{Lee}}{1 - \delta_{Lee} \delta_{Kim}} \tag{85}$$

Finally, we get the Rubinstein solution if $c_{Kim} = c_{Lee} = 0$ and either $\delta_{Kim} \neq 1$ or $\delta_{Lee} \neq 1$:

$$x^*_{Kim} \left(c_{Kim} = c_{Lee} = 0 \right) = \frac{1 - \delta_{Lee}}{1 - \delta_{Lee} \delta_{Kim}} \tag{86}$$

Rubinstein solution for Lee's offer is exactly analogous.

For the case of three or more players engaged in bargaining, let's take a natural extension (e.g., n persons' bargaining) of the two-player Rubinstein solution model [3-2-23]. Initially a proposer is chosen, and he proposes a division of the pie: a vector $\mathbf{x} = \left\{ x_1, \ldots, x_n \right\} \in \mathbb{R}^n$ such that $\sum_i x_i \leq 1$ and $i \in N = \{ 1, \ldots, n \}$. Responders (i.e., the other players) say yes or no; if all accept, the proposed allocation is implemented and the game is over. Otherwise, one unit of time passes (which everyone discounts at the common rate β), and then the rejector makes a fresh proposal. A *stationary strategy* calls upon the player to take the same action always when it is his turn to propose or respond, provided that the ambient situation is the same (Ray, 2010).

Focus on responses. The player i will simply get payoff (z_i) as follows.

$$z_i \equiv 1 - \sum_{j \neq i} x_j \tag{87}$$

We assume that this is non-negative value and zero, otherwise. Turn to the player i's role as responder. By rejecting a proposal, the player i takes the initiative and gets his payoff tomorrow, valued today at βz_i. Therefore

$$x_i = \beta z_i = \beta \left(1 - \sum_{j \neq i} x_j \right) \tag{88}$$

Subtract βx_i from both sides; we then get

$$\left(1 - \beta \right) x_i = \beta \left(1 - X \right) \tag{89}$$

where X is just the sum of all the x_k's: $X = \sum_{k \in N} x_k$. Adding the above equation over all player i, we see that

$$\left(1 - \beta \right) X = n \times \beta \left(1 - X \right), \text{ s.t., } n = |N| \tag{90}$$

The formula (90) can be derived like as

$$X = \frac{n \times \beta}{1 + \left(n - 1 \right) \times \beta} \tag{91}$$

In the formula (89), X is replace by (91), then we see that

$$\left(1 - \beta \right) x_i = \frac{\beta \times \left(1 - \beta \right)}{1 + \left(n - 1 \right) \times \beta} \tag{92}$$

It can be derived like as

$$x_i = \frac{\beta}{1 + \left(n - 1\right) \times \beta} \qquad (93)$$

For every player i, this is what each responder gets. The proposer picks up the remainder, which is easily seen to be

$$\frac{1}{1 + \left(n - 1\right) \times \beta} \qquad (94)$$

All of this goes to equal division as $\beta \to 1$. Unfortunately, the beautiful uniqueness result for two-person Rubinstein bargaining no longer survives with n players (Ray, 2010).

Voting Game

Voting game is a new cooperative game model that incorporates elements from social choice theory. This game model can be used to analyze situations where voters would vote in favor of or against a decision. Until now, a lot of researches about voting games have been carried out in political science, economics, logic theory and distributed systems. Formally, a simple voting game (N, v) consists of players, who can be considered as voters, the possible strategies of the players, and utility functions of the strategies. In addition, voting game (N, v) is a cooperative game where $N = \left\{1, \ldots, n\right\}$ is a finite player set and $v : 2^N \to \left\{0,1\right\}$, such that $v\left(\varnothing\right) = 0$ and $v\left(S\right) \leq v\left(T\right)$ whenever $S \subset T$. It is based on the assumption that each player should decide whether he joins a coalition or not. A coalition is *winning* if $v\left(S\right) = 1$, and *losing* if $v\left(S\right) = 0$. With multiple voting games $v_1, \ldots, v_m$, a *m-majority voting game* is defined as (Algaba, & Bilbao, Garcia, & Lopez, 2003):

$$\left(v_1 \wedge \ldots \wedge v_m\right)\left(S\right) = \min\left\{v_t\left(S\right) : 1 \leq t \leq m\right\} \qquad (95)$$

A special subclass of voting games is the Weighted Voting Game (WVG). WVG is used in many voting schemes and has been applied in various political and economic organizations for structural or constitutional purposes. In WVGs, each player has a weight, and a coalition of players wins the game if its total weight exceeds a certain quota. Therefore, the weighted voting game model can formulate a decision-making process that is designed to give different amounts of influence to different members (Bachrach, Meir, Zuckerman, Rothe, & Rosenschein, 2009), (Zuckerman, Faliszewski, Bachrach, & Elkind, 2008). Mathematically, a WVG model is represented by the voting body $\left[q; \omega_1, \ldots \omega_n\right]$ where ω_i represents the voting weight of player i and q ($0 < \omega_i < q$) is the quota needed to win. All the weights and quota are positive real numbers. If $\mathcal{W}\left(\mathbb{S}\right) \geq q$ where $\mathcal{W}\left(\mathbb{S}\right) = \sum_{i \in \mathbb{S}} \omega_i$, a coalition $\mathbb{S}$ of players ($\mathbb{S} \subset N$) is *winner* and $v\left(\mathbb{S}\right) = 1$. Otherwise, it is *loser* and $v\left(\mathbb{S}\right) = 0$. Therefore, $v\left(\mathbb{S}\right) \in \left\{0,1\right\}$ for any $\mathbb{S}$ and if $\mathbb{S} \subset T \subset N$, then $v\left(\mathbb{S}\right) \leq v\left(T\right)$ (Bachrach, 2009), (Zuckerman, 2008). With multiple weighted voting games $v_1, \ldots, v_m$ where $v_t = \left[q^t; w_1^t, \ldots, w_n^t\right], 1 \leq t \leq m$, a *weighted m-majority voting game* is defined as follows (Algaba, 2003).

$$(v_1 \wedge \ldots \wedge v_m)S = \left\{ \begin{array}{l} 1, \text{ if } w^t(S) \geq q^t, 1 \leq t \leq m \text{ and } w^t(S) = \sum_{i \in S} w_i^t \\ 0, \text{ otherwise} \end{array} \right\} \qquad (96)$$

In voting games, a critical voter is a voter who, if he changed his vote from yes to no, would cause the measure to fail. Formally, the player i is critical in a coalition S when $v(S) = 1$ and $v(S \setminus i) \neq 1$. For each player $i \in N$, the number of coalitions in which the player i is critical in game (N, v) is denoted as $\varsigma_i(N, v)$. Based on the $\varsigma_i(N, v)$, Banzhaf index can be defined. The Banzhaf index, named after John F. Banzhaf III, is a power index defined by the probability of changing an outcome of a vote where voting rights are not necessarily equally divided among the voters (Aziz, Paterson, & Leecht, 2007), (Brams, & Affuso, 1976). To calculate the Banzhaf power index of a voter, all the winning coalitions are listed, and then count the critical voters. And then, a voter's power is measured as the fraction of all swing votes that he could cast. The Banzhaf index of player i in the WVG (N, v) is calculated as follows.

$$\beta_i = \frac{\eta_i(N, v)}{\sum_{i \in N} \eta_i(N, v)} \tag{97}$$

In the simple voting game (N, v), the probabilistic Banzhaf index (β_i') of the player i is equal to $\eta_i(N, v) / 2^{n-1}$ (Aziz, 2007). Nowadays, the Banzhaf power index is commonly used to measure voting power.

Election game is also a special case of voting games. Formally, election game model consists of two candidates $c = 1, 2$, and a finite voter set $N = \{1, ..., n\}$ with n self-interested voters that is common to both candidates. Let S be a nonempty set of possible strategies for the candidates, $S \subset \text{int}(\chi)$, $\chi \subset \mathbb{R}_+^n$, and each candidate picks a strategy $\psi_c \in S$. The strategy ψ_c is proposed by candidate c to the n voters. For the voter i ($i \in N$), the probability that the voter i votes for the candidate c is determined by a probabilistic voting function $V_i^c : S \times S \rightarrow [0,1]$. If the voter i

is faced with $(\psi_1, \psi_2) \in S \times S$ as the strategy pair chosen by two candidates, the payoff obtained by the voter i from either strategy can be evaluated according to $U_i(\psi_c)$ where $c = 1, 2$. Function $U(\psi_c)$ is defined based on each voter's preference (McFadden, 1974).

In an election game, the payoff function is allowed to have a stochastic component. In other words, if voters attempt to maximize their expected payoff, then both candidates are unsure of the exact voting choice that will be made by the voters. According to the voting function from qualitative choice theory (McFadden, 1974), the payoff function ($V_i^c(\psi_1, \psi_2)$) for the voter i is commonly represented as follows.

$$V_i^c(\psi_1, \psi_2) = \frac{f(\psi_c \mid i)}{f(\psi_c \mid i) + f(\psi_{k, k \neq c} \mid i)}$$
$$\text{s.t., } c = 1, 2 \tag{98}$$

where k is the c's complement, and $f(\psi_c \mid i)$ is a scaling function of the payoff for the voter i under candidate c's strategy ψ_c. In addition, $f(\psi_c \mid i)$ is also a continuously differentiable, positive, real-valued function. The expected margin of victory ($E\_V^c(\psi_1, \psi_2)$) for each candidate is the expected value for winning and it is defined as follows (Mukherjee, 2009), (Ledyard, 1984).

$$E\_V^c(\psi_1, \psi_2) = \sum_{i=1}^n \left[V_i^c(\psi_1, \psi_2) - V_i^k(\psi_1, \psi_2) \right] \times \frac{1}{n^2} \tag{99}$$

Each candidate tries to maximize his expected margin of victory, which is equivalent to maximizing his chances of winning the election when n is large.

Self-Modifying Protocol Games (*Nomic* Games)

Self-modifying protocol games, also called *Nomic* games have been developed as a kind of voting games. *Nomic* came from the Greek word νόμοζ (*nómos*), meaning 'law'. *Nomic* game is an abstract game of rule-making and legislation that recently gains popularity among a selected group of dedicated enthusiasts with access to international computer networks (Vreeswijk, 1995). The main concept of *Nomic* games is conceived and designed by Peter Suber, who presented it as a self-modifying game, based on reflexivity in law (Suber, 1990). P. Suber proposed the rules of *Nomic* game (Vreeswijk, 1995):

Rule 1: Players shall alternate in clockwise order, taking one whole turn apiece. Turns may not be skipped or passed, and parts of turns may not be omitted. All players begin with zero points.

Rule 2: One turn consists of two parts, in this order:
1. Proposing one rule change and having it voted on;
2. Throwing one die once and adding the number of its points on its face to one's score.

Rule 3: A rule change is adopted if and only if the vote is unanimous among the eligible voters.

The idea behind *Nomic* game is to change the rules of *Nomic* game. The game can be completely different at the end than it was at the start. The basic play is explained in rule 2: a player proposes a rule change, all the players vote on it, and if the vote succeeds, the change is immediately incorporated into the game. An interesting point is that rule 2 itself can be changed. If a player changes this rule successfully, then the way player play *Nomic* game changes, and the game proceeds from there. *Nomic* game is completely self-reflexive. Every rule of *Nomic* game can be changed. In principle, *Nomic* game can become any other

game. The importance of *Nomic* game for the theory of amendable protocols is that it offers an excellent 'playground', on which new ideas become prosperous (Vreeswijk, 1995).

The main features of *Nomic* games are flexibility, autonomy and continuity.

1. **Flexibility:** When players play by means of a modifiable rule, they are not committed to one particular type of interaction. Instead, they are enabled to adapt the rules of interaction partially to the circumstances under which they play.
2. **Autonomy:** Players that play via such protocols are capable to accommodate themselves to changing patterns of interaction, on their own initiative and without further player's intervention.
3. **Continuity:** With self-modifying rules, modifications are introduced and processed on the fly, without stopping, which is to the benefit of the continuity of the game.

Nomic games are commonly used in everyday life, especially, computer networks. In the near future, it is expected that computers will use communication protocols that allow them to change the protocol that they are using (Vreeswijk, 1995).

Classification of Cooperative Game Models

The two branches of game theory differ in how they formalize interdependence among the players. In the non-cooperative theory, a game is a detailed model of all the moves available to the players. By contrast, the cooperative theory abstracts away from this level of detail, and describes only the outcomes that result when the players come together in different combinations. Therefore, the non-cooperative theory might be better termed the procedural game theory, and the cooperative theory is called as the combinatorial game theory. This would indicate the real distinction between the two branches of the subject, namely that the first specifies various actions that are available to the players while the second describes the outcomes that result when the players come together in different combinations (Brandenburger, & Stuart, 2007).

The subsection 3.2 has shown the classification of the cooperative game models. These cooperative game models may be placed into subclasses - coalitional games, bargaining games, matching and voting games. Moreover, within coalitional games, game model can be further grouped in terms of coalition formation and canonical coalition games. Within bargaining games, game model can be further grouped in terms of Nash bargaining game, Kalai-Smorodinsky bargaining game, Egalitarian bargaining game and Rubinstein bargaining game. Table 8 shows a way of classifying the cooperative games in network managements.

SPECIAL DOMAINS OF GAME THEORY

Typically, games can be divided into non-cooperative games and cooperative games. However, an important subset of games cannot be classified into non-cooperative or cooperative games. In this book, these games are categorized as special games, which have special properties based on dif-

ferent kinds of approaches. Hybrid game contains mixed features of non-cooperative and cooperative games. This hybrid approach combines the advantages of non-cooperative and cooperative games to shape the real world environment in a favorable way. Auction game is an applied branch of game theory that deals with how people act in auction markets. There are a lot of different models for an auction. Each auction model has its own set of rules. Modified game theory is a multi-objective optimization algorithm. Even though many methods have been developed to achieve multi-objective solutions, one of the best known methods for generating a compromise solution is the cooperative game theory. However, cooperative game theory is hard to implement to get a solution in a multi-objective problem, which needs a two step optimization process. Modified game theory is a multi-objective optimization algorithm with the modification of the game theory. By combining the two optimization process, this approach can provide an effective solution in mathematical optimization problems involving more than one objective function to be optimized simultaneously. Reverse game theory (i.e., mechanism design and meta-games) is studying solution concepts for a class of private information games. In reverse game theory, major distinguishing feature is that a game designer chooses the game framework by considering the game's outcome. Meta-games are

Table 8. Classification of cooperative game models

Cooperative Games	Coalitional Games	Coalition Formation Game	Static Games	external factor imposes a certain structure to form stable coalitions	
			Dynamic Games	the current coalition can be dynamically re-structured	
		Canonical coalition game			Core
					Shapley Value
					Nucleolus
	Bargaining Games	Nash bargaining game		Accurately, Rubinstein game is designed based on the non-cooperative approach. Here, it is included cooperative category for convenience sake,	
		Kalai-S. bargaining game			
		Egalitarian bargaining game			
		Rubinstein bargaining game			
	Matching games		cooperative game model for finding a stable matching		
	Voting games		cooperative game model from social choice theory		

also games to reason about how to design games that produce desired outcomes. Therefore, meta-game can be thought of as inverse game model. In meta-games, the main issues are to develop the rules for games, and to maximize the utility value of the rule set developed. All of these special games are subfields of game theory. In this section, the main ideas of these special games are presented.

Hybrid Games

Hybrid games contain cooperative and non-cooperative elements. For instance, coalitions of players are formed in a cooperative game, but these players play in a non-cooperative fashion. Recently, biform game and coopetition game have been developed as a hybrid game.

Coopetition Games

In 1996, N. Barry and B. Adam had introduced a new concept of game model, called coopetition game, which combined the characteristics of non-cooperative and cooperative games. The term 'coopetition' is a neologism coined to describe cooperative competition. Therefore, coopetition is defined as the phenomenon that differs from competition or cooperation, and stresses two faces (i.e., cooperation and competition) of one relationship in the same situation. In coopetition games, every player, who strengthens their competitive advantages by cooperation, can achieve greater and reciprocal advantages. Due to this reason, an essential part in the coopetition game is the expression of individual decisions, which should cooperate while competing with each other game players (Sun, & Xu, 2005), (Guan, Yuan, & Zhang, 2008), (Bouncken, & Fredrich, 2011).

The formal definition of coopetition game ($\mathcal{G}$) is $\mathcal{G} = \left\langle N, \left(s_i\right), \left(uc_i\right), \mathcal{A}, \mathcal{Z} \right\rangle$ where N is the set of players $N = \left\{1, \ldots, n\right\}$ and s_i is the pure strategy space for each player i ($i \in N$). uc_i is

a payoff coefficient function for each player i. In coopetition games, uc_i is the standardization of a traditional payoff function (u_i). The standardization means to get the ratio between the payoff that a player can get at a certain strategy profile and the highest payoff that the player can gain. Therefore, $uc_i\left(s\right)$ denotes the satisfaction degree that the player i can obtain under strategy profiles $s = \left(s_1, \cdots, s_n\right)$. Denote $\mathcal{A}$ ($\mathcal{A} = s_1 \times \cdots \times s_n$) is the strategy space. A subset $\mathcal{Z}$ of $\mathcal{A}$ ($\mathcal{Z} \subset \mathcal{A}$) is called a *strategic extreme set*, if $s, w \in \mathcal{A}$ and $(\lambda \times s) + (1 - \lambda) \times w \in \mathcal{Z}$ (s.t., $0 \leq \lambda \leq 1$) imply $s, w \in \mathcal{Z}$. For any $s \in \mathcal{A}$, $M\left(s\right) = \{i' \in N \mid uc_{i'}\left(s\right) = \min_{i \in N} uc_i\left(s\right)\}$ is defined as the index set of s, which means the member of the players who obtain the lowest payoff coefficient function under profile s. A point s in $\mathcal{A}$ is called a *critical strategy* if there exists a strategic extreme set $\mathcal{Z}$ such that for $s \in \mathcal{A}$, $w \in \mathcal{Z}$ and $M\left(s\right) \subset M\left(w\right)$ imply $M\left(s\right) = M\left(w\right)$. In the other words, a *critical strategy* is a point with maximum index set in certain *strategic extreme set* (Brandenburger, & Stuart, 2007).

The solution concept of coopetitive games is coopetitive equilibrium. It is the one of the strategy profiles that much more players choose with higher satisfaction degrees, and is the counterbalance among players as well. According to the definition, the coopetitive equilibrium can be obtained like this; given the strategy profiles, each player finds the minimum payoff coefficients and selects a higher one among them (Brandenburger, 2007). Equilibrium (s^*) of coopetitive game $\mathcal{G}$ is some *critical strategy* $s^* \in \mathcal{A}$, and it is defined as follows.

$$s^* \arg\max_{s \in \mathcal{A}} \left\{ uc_{i \in M(s)}\left(s\right) \right\}$$

In cooperative situation, coalition without any conflict is supposed to construct. This coalition will maximizes its revenue and allocate it based on certain rules. Unfortunately, coalitions are usually destroyed because of players' self-concerned actions or some details that are ignored in the cooperative process. Coopetitive game model can avoid these conflicts. The self-concerned players can form stable coalition in competitive situation. At the same time, the coopetitive equilibria have advantages over those of non-cooperative games (Brandenburger, 2007).

Recently, coopetition game model has been extensively discussed in economics and management science. This model suggests that a judicious mixture of collaboration and competition is often advantageous in competitive environments. However, even though coopetition game model has received strong attentions, designing a coopetition game model for real-world problems is still difficult. There are many complicated restrictions, which are often self-contradictory and variable with the dynamic environment (Sun, 2005), (Guan, 2008), (Bouncken, 2011).

Biform Game

In 1996, A. Brandenburger and H. Stuart introduced the fundamental notion of the biform game to adaptively re-shape the competitive environment (Brandenburger, 2007). It is a hybrid non-cooperative and cooperative game model to formalize the two-stage decision problem. The first stage is the non-cooperative component of a biform game. Each player chooses a strategy to maximize his expected payoff while regarding a subsequent effect of the chosen strategies on the second stage. The second stage is the cooperative component to model the resulting competitive environment. In this stage, players form a coalition to generate a surplus, which is shared fairly and optimally. Therefore, an actual payoff is realized after the second-stage game. Recently, it has been proven that the biform game model is efficient when it

is applied to a business strategy (Brandenburger, 2007), (Stuart, 2005).

The general definition of n-player biform game is $\mathcal{B}$ ($N = \{1,...,n\}$; $S^1,...,S^n$; V; $\alpha^1,...,\alpha^n$; $\mathcal{P}(N)$). The set $N = \{1,...,n\}$ is the set of players. Each player $i \in N$ chooses a strategy s^i from the strategy set S^i. S^i is a finite strategy sets $S^1,...,S^n$ come from a general extensive-form game. $\mathcal{P}(N)$ denotes the power set of N, i.e., the set of all subsets of N. The number α^i ($0 \leq \alpha^i \leq 1$) is the player i's confidence index, which indicates how well the player i anticipates doing in the resulting cooperative games. V is a map from $S^1 \times \cdots \times S^n$ to the set of maps, and a map from $\mathcal{P}(N)$ to the reals, with $V(s^1,...,s^n)(\varnothing) = 0$ for every $s^1,...,s^n \in S^1 \times \cdots \times S^n$. Therefore, the resulting profile of strategies $s^1,...,s^n \in S^1 \times \cdots \times S^n$ defines a cooperative game with characteristic function $V(s^1,...,s^n) : \mathcal{P}(N) \to \mathbb{R}$. That is, for each $A \subset N, V(s^1,...,s^n)(A)$ is the value created by the subset A of players, given that the players chose the strategies $s^1,...,s^n$. If A is $\varnothing$, $V(s^1,...,s^n)(\varnothing) = 0$. The biform game model is a generalization of both the non-cooperative and cooperative game models. Therefore, there is a bijection between the subclass of n-player biform games and the class of n-player non-cooperative or cooperative games (Brandenburger, 2007).

Biform game adopts the following cooperative and non-cooperative steps:

Cooperative step:

C1: Compute the core of $V(s)$ with $s = \{s^1,...,s^n\}$ for each player $i \in N$.

C2: Calculate the projection of the core onto the i th coordinate axis.

C3: Calculate the $a^i : \left(1 - a^i\right)$ weighted average of the upper and lower endpoints of the projection.

Non-cooperative step:

N1: Obtain the every profile s of strategic choices.

N2: Assign to the player i a payoff equal to the selected strategy's weighted average as in **C3**).

N3: Find Nash equilibrium in a non-cooperative manner.

Given a profile s, the cooperative step is to restrict attention to core allocations in the resulting cooperative game $V(s)$. The implied range of payoffs to each player is calculated and each player i uses confidence index a^i to evaluate the given cooperative game $V(s)$. Therefore, a weighted average of the largest and smallest amounts of value is estimated and the player i can receive it as his payoff in the core. By using the confidence indices, a biform game can be transformed as a non-cooperative game. The solution (i.e., Nash equilibria) of this non-cooperative game may be obtained in standard non-cooperative game fashion by computing, iteratively eliminating dominated strategies, or some other method (Brandenburger, 2007)

Conceptually, biform game starts by obtaining the core solution in the first stage, and calculates the effect of competition among the players in the second stage. Therefore, in the first stage, strategic choices are made. However, there may be a range of values in the core, and some players face a residual bargaining problem, which is actively involved in confidence indices of players. In general, an optimistic player i will have a confidence index a^i close to 1, indicating that the player i anticipates capturing most of the value in the residual bargaining. A pessimistic player i will have the a^i close to zero, indicating that player i anticipates getting little of this residual value.

Therefore, the player's confidence index represents a view of the game. Based on these confidence indices, biform game can be remodeled as a non-cooperative game among the players and analysis of this game indicates which strategies will be chosen by the players (Brandenburger, 2007)

In 2007, Chatain and Zemsky developed a buyer-supplier relationship model as a biform game approach. First, suppliers make initial proposals and take organizational decisions. This stage is analyzed using a non-cooperative game theory approach. Then, suppliers negotiate with buyers. In this stage, a cooperative game theory is applied to characterize the outcome of bargaining among the player over how to distribute the total surplus. Each supplier's share of the total surplus is the product of its added value and its relative bargaining power (Hennet, & Mahjoub, 2010), (Chatain, & Zemsky, 2007).

In 2010, J. C. Hennet and S. Mahjou developed a quadratic production game as a biform game (Hennet, 2010). Their game is developed to explain a new supply chain model based on game theory. In particular, it has been observed that some networks of manufacturers have now organized themselves both internally, in a cooperative manner, by sharing their products and resources, and externally, as dominant non-cooperative actors relatively to their suppliers and customers. This two-level approach coins the concept of biform game and it is the leading trend of the profit sharing mechanism between manufacturers and retailers. In the quadratic production game, the manufacturing network is supposed to dominate the market, especially retailers. Therefore we can assume that the manufacturer's network acts as a Stackelberg leader and the retailer acts as a Stackelberg follower (Hennet, 2010). As a biform game, the quadratic production game combines a non-cooperative game (i.e., market game) with coopetition game (i.e., manufacture game). The market game is a non-cooperative game between a manufacturers' network and the market, and the manufacture game is a coopetition game within the manufacturing network.

For the market game model, consider a retailer selling on a market a set of products numbered $i = 1, \ldots, n$. In the market game between the retailer and the set of customers, the retailer plays first, by proposing a price vector $\boldsymbol{P} = \left(p_1 \ldots p_n \right)^T$ and the market reacts by buying a quantity that depends on this price. The supply-demand negotiation can be represented as an iterative process. The current price ($p_i(t)$) is the decision variable fixed by the retailer and the currently purchased quantity ($y_i(t)$) is the decision variable of the market. Let $\boldsymbol{Y}_i(t)$ and $\boldsymbol{P}_i(t)$ be the vectors of present and past quantities and prices purchased by customers at periods $t, t-1, t-2, \ldots t-h+1$, with the h system memory, supposed finite (Hennet, 2010). Generally, $\boldsymbol{Y}_i(t)$ is defined as follows.

$$y_i(t) = f_i\left(\boldsymbol{Y}_i(t-1), \boldsymbol{P}_i(t) \right) \qquad (101)$$

For each product $i = 1, \ldots, n$, the market game is supposed to reach a stable equilibrium for which the expected quantity (y_i) sold over a reference period. The expected quantity can be obtained through the demand curve as follows.

$$y_i = -\beta_i \times p_i + \varphi_i \qquad (102)$$

where β_i and φ_i are constant variables of the demand curve (Lariviere, & Porteus, 2001). Let $\boldsymbol{Y} = (y_1 \cdots y_n)^T$ be the output vector of products during a reference period. Usually, the retailer faces the inverse demand curve obtained from the optimality conditions of the market game (Lariviere, 2001). The products being assumed independent, the inverse demand curve for each product $i = 1, \ldots, n$ is

$$p_i = -\frac{1}{\beta_i} y_i + \frac{\varphi_i}{\beta_i} \text{ s.t., } \frac{1}{\beta_i} > 0 \qquad (103)$$

Since quantities and prices are non-negative, a necessary condition for equations (3-103) and p_i is defined as

$$p_i \leq p_i^{MAX} \text{ with } p_i^{MAX} = \frac{\varphi_i}{\beta_i} \qquad (104)$$

For each final product sold on the market, the retailer faces a stochastic demand. With the expected sold quantity ($y_{i,1 \leq i \leq n}$), the expected profit of the retailer over the reference period is

$$\prod{}^{R}(\boldsymbol{Y}) = \left(\boldsymbol{P} - \boldsymbol{W} \right)^T \times \boldsymbol{Y} \text{, s.t., } w_i \leq p_i \qquad (105)$$

where $\boldsymbol{P}$ (i.e., $p_i \in \boldsymbol{P}$) is the price vector and $\boldsymbol{W}$ (i.e., $w_i \in \boldsymbol{W}$) is the wholesale price vector. Now, we explain how to obtain $\boldsymbol{P}$ and $\boldsymbol{W}$. First, $\boldsymbol{P}$ is obtained from (103) in the form:

$$\boldsymbol{P} = -Diag\left(\frac{1}{\beta_i} \right) \times \boldsymbol{Y} + Diag\left(\frac{\varphi_i}{\beta_i} \right) \times 1 \qquad (106)$$

where $Diag\left(m_i \right)$ denotes a diagonal matrix with generic diagonal terms m_i, and $\boldsymbol{1}$ is the vector with all the components equal to 1, and the appropriate dimension (Hennet, 2010). The objective is to find the optimal vector $\boldsymbol{Y}^*$ that maximizes $\prod{}^{R}$, and $\prod{}^{R}$ can be re-written as follows.

$$\prod{}^{R}(\boldsymbol{Y}) = \left(-\boldsymbol{Y}^T \times Diag\left(\frac{1}{\beta_i} \right) \times \boldsymbol{Y} \right) + \left(1^T \times Diag\left(\frac{\varphi_i}{\beta_i} \right) \times \boldsymbol{Y} \right) - \left(\boldsymbol{W}^T \times \boldsymbol{Y} \right) \qquad (107)$$

The optimality condition takes the following form from (105)

$$\frac{\partial \prod^R}{\partial y_i} = -2\frac{1}{\beta_i}y_i + \frac{\varphi_i}{\beta_i} - w_i = 0 \qquad (108)$$

For each product, the optimal expected demand is

$$y_i = \frac{\varphi_i}{2} - \frac{\beta_i}{2}w_i \qquad (109)$$

According to (103) and (109), the proposed retail price is derived as follows.

$$p_i = \frac{\varphi_i}{2\hat{a}_i} + \frac{\beta_i}{2} \qquad (110)$$

Second, W is determined by the manufacturer's network and is related to the output vector Y. From (109), w_i is given by

$$w_i = \frac{\varphi_i}{\beta_i} - \frac{2}{\beta_i}y_i \qquad (111)$$

According to W, the retailer reacts by choosing the retail price to maximize his expected profit. From (105),(110) and (111), the retailer expected profit is given by

$$\prod^R\left(Y\right) = \sum_{i=1}^n \frac{y_i^2}{\beta_i} \qquad (112)$$

For the manufacturer game, consider a network of m firms represented by numbers in the set $\mathcal{N} = \left\{1, \ldots, m\right\}$. These firms are willing to cooperate to produce commodities and sell them in a market. The m manufacturers compete to be partners in a coalition $S \subseteq \mathcal{N}$. Each candidate enterprise is characterized by its production resources. Mathematically, each firm owns a vector

$\boldsymbol{B}^j = \left(B_{1,j}, \ldots\ldots, B_{r,j}\right)^T$, $j = 1 \ldots m$, of r types of resources. These resources can be used, directly or indirectly to produce the vector $\boldsymbol{Y} = \left(y_1, \ldots\ldots, y_m\right)^T$ of final products. The coalition incurs manufacturing costs $\boldsymbol{C} = \left(c_1, \ldots\ldots, c_m\right)^T$ per unit of each final product and sells the products at the wholesale price vector $\boldsymbol{W} = \left(w_1, \ldots\ldots, w_m\right)^T$ to the retailer who acts as an intermediate party between the manufacturers' network and the final consumers.

Under a wholesale price contracts, the coalition of manufacturers acts as the Stackelberg leader by fixing the wholesale price vector $\boldsymbol{W}$ as a take-it-or-leave-it proposal. As the follower, the retailer can only accept or reject the manufacturer's proposal. After the manufacturers network has set the vector ($\boldsymbol{W}$) of wholesale prices, the retailer determines $\boldsymbol{P}$ (or equivalently $\boldsymbol{Y}$) to maximize the his expected profit. Having anticipated the retailer's reaction function (106), the coalition determines $\boldsymbol{W}^*$ to maximize the expected profit. Therefore, the pair of optimal vectors $\left(\boldsymbol{W}^*, \boldsymbol{Y}^*\right)$ can be determined by the manufacturers' network (Hennet, 2010).

A coalition S is defined as a subset of the set $\mathcal{N}$ of m enterprises with characteristic vector $\boldsymbol{e}_s \in \{0,1\}^m$ such that:

$$\begin{cases} \left(e_s\right)_j = 1 \text{ if } j \in S \\ \left(e_s\right)_j = 0 \text{ if } j \notin S \end{cases} \qquad (113)$$

For the r types of resources considered $\left(k = 1, \ldots, r\right)$, let $\boldsymbol{B}_{k,j}$ be the amount of resource k available at enterprise j, $\boldsymbol{B} = \left(\boldsymbol{B}_{k,j}\right) \in \Re^{r \times m}$, and $A_{k,i}$ the amount of resource k necessary to produce one unit of product i, $\boldsymbol{A} = \left(A_{k,i}\right) \in \Re^{r \times m}$.

Resource capacity constraints for coalition S are thus written as $A \times Y \leq B \times e_S$

At the manufacture game stage, two different problems must be solved: the non-cooperative game problem of selecting the wholesale price vector W and the cooperative game problem of optimizing the production vector Y and the coalition characteristic vector e_S (Hennet, 2010).

W is computed by (111). With given W, the profit optimization can be formulated as follows:

$$\max_{Y, e_S} [(W - C)^T \times Y],$$
$$\text{s.t.,} \quad A \times Y \leq B \times e_S \ , \ Y \in \Re^m_+ \text{ and } e_S \in \{0,1\}^m$$
$$(114)$$

The manufacturing network, acting as the Stackelberg leader in the non-cooperative game with the retailer, anticipates the optimal reaction of the retailer by substituting equations (111) into the objective function of problem (114). Therefore, the profit optimization problem can be re-written as follows.

$$\max_{Y, e_S} \sum_{i=1}^n \left[\left(\frac{\varphi_i}{\beta_i} - c_i \right) y_i - \frac{2}{\beta_i} y_i^2 \right],$$

$$\text{s.t.,} A \times Y \leq B \times e_S, \ Y \in \Re^m_\alpha \text{ and } e_S \in \{0,1\}^m$$
$$(115)$$

Since the grand coalition generates the optimal profit (Hennet, 2010), we focus on the problem of profit allocation to the members of the grand coalition. The Shapley Value has been shown to possess the best properties in terms of balance and fairness. Therefore, the Shapley Value is adopted to allocate the expected profit among the manufacturer partners.

Finally, the quadratic production game can be executed through the following steps:

1. Set the optimal output vector Y computed by (115),

2. Set the wholesale price vector W computed by (111),

3. Set the market price vector P computed by (110),

4. Compute the Shapley value to allocate the profit for the manufacturer network.

Reverse Game Theory

Reverse game theory is a subfield in game theory to develop a solution concept of private information games. It is used to define a strategic situation to make a system exhibits good behaviors when independent agents pursue self-interested strategies (Anderegg, & Eidenbenz, 2003), (Shneidman, & Parkes, 2003), (Parkes, & Shneidman, 2004), (Dash, Parkes, & Jennings, 2003). In reverse game theory, the game designer is interested in the game's outcome and chooses the game structure. Such a game is called a 'game of mechanism design' or simply Mechanism Design (*MD*), and is usually solved by motivating players to disclose their private information.

MD considers a scenario where agents have private information and the mechanism designer desires to make a social choice depending on agents' private information. In order to elicit private information from agents, the designer uses a proper incentive mechanism. Since agents have no actions to choose strategy in mechanism design problems, there is no issue of motivating agents to take appropriate actions. Instead, the designer can fully control the social choice. In other words, the designer develops *MD* in order to provide incentives for agents to reveal private information truthfully, rather than incentives for agents to choose appropriate actions. Therefore, the *MD* is concerned with the design of game procedures (i.e., game rules and payoff functions) to implement an outcome with desirable properties in systems. Therefore, *MD* defines the strategic situation so that the system exhibits good behavior when self-interested agents pursue self-interested strategies (Anderegg, 2003), (Shneidman, 2003).

Traditional *MD* considers a setting with a set of agents N. Agents are assumed to be autonomous and economically rational; they select a best-response strategy to maximize their expected utility with other agents. Formally, a mechanism is a specification of possible agent strategies and a mapping from the set of played strategies to outcomes. Each agent has a specific type, which is private information only known to the agent, and describes how each agent values all possible outcomes. In the system, there is a set (ϑ) of possible outcomes $(s_1, \cdots, s_N)$, where s_i is the strategy of agent i. The ϑ is indicating which agents participate in the service activity. Agent i with type θ_i has a utility $u_i(\theta_i, o)$ for outcome o where $o \in \vartheta$. A strategy $s_i(\theta_i)$ defines the actions the agent i selects in the mechanism for all possible types θ_i; agent i chooses a strategy s_i to maximize its utility u_i. A mechanism $M = (\Sigma, f)$ comprises the set of possible actions (Σ) and mechanism rules (f). f selects actions and implements a particular outcome; $s_i(\theta_i) \in £$ and $f(\Theta) \in \vartheta$ where $\Theta = (\theta_1, \theta_2, \cdots, \theta_{|N|}) \in £^{|N|}$ (Dash, 2010), (Wang, & Schulzrinne, 2005), (Garg, Narahari, & Gujar, 2008), (Woodard, & Parkes, 2003).

Direct-revelation mechanisms are a special case of traditional mechanisms, in which agent-announced type, $\hat{\theta} \in \Theta$, is no longer necessarily truthful; $\hat{\theta}$ is written to emphasize that agents can misreport their true types. In some cases of *direct-revelation* mechanisms, each agent's dominant strategy is truth telling about its type. Therefore, whatever any other agent reports any type, agents can be truthful. This property is termed *strategyproof*, defined as follows.

$$u_i\big(f(\theta_i, \theta_{-i}); \theta_i\big) \geq u_i\big(f(\hat{\theta}_i, \theta_{-i}); \theta_i\big), \forall \theta_i, \forall \hat{\theta}_i \neq \theta_i, \forall \theta_{-i} \tag{116}$$

In the game theoretic sense, *strategyproof* means that honesty can cause an equilibrium status among game players. *Strategyproof* is particularly useful because an agent does not need to model the other agents' response. For a system and participants, it provides robustness and simplicity (Dash, 2003), (Wang, 2005), (Garg, 2008), (Woodard, 2003).

One of the major achievements of *MD* theory is the family of *direct-revelation* and *strategyproof* mechanisms, which are called Vickrey-Clarke-Groves (*VCG*) mechanism. The *VCG* mechanism has better computational properties than the original mechanism and provides a normative guide for the outcome and payments. When applying the *VCG* mechanism to complex *MD* problems, the optimal outcome can be obtained by the results of computationally tractable heuristic algorithms. In the *VCG* mechanism setting, agents have quasi-linear utility functions as follows (Parkes, 2004), (Dash, 2003), (Wang, 2005), (Garg, 2008), (Woodard, 2003), (Nisan, & Ronen, 2000).

$$u_i\big(k, p_i, \theta_i\big) = v_i\big(k, \theta_i\big) - p_i \tag{117}$$

where p_i is a monetary amount from the agent i and k is a feasible choice of the set of all possible choices. $v_i(k, \theta_i)$ defines the agent i's outcome of a choice k with its type θ_i. The *VCG* mechanism maximizes the total outcome of the system to the agents. Therefore, when the claim $\hat{\theta}_i$ is received from agent i, the *VCG* mechanism implements the choice k^* that maximizes $\sum_i v_i(k, \hat{\theta}_i)$; the choice rule ($k^*(\hat{\theta})$) and payment rule ($p_{vcg,i}(\hat{\theta})$) are defined as follows (Parkes, 2004), (Dash, 2003), (Wang, 2005), (Garg, 2008), (Woodard, 2003).

$$k^*\big(\hat{\theta}\big) = \mathrm{argmax}_{k \in \mathcal{K}} \sum_i v_i\big(k, \hat{\theta}_i\big) \text{ and}$$

$$p_{vcg,i}\big(\hat{\theta}\big) = v_i\big(k^*\big(\hat{\theta}\big), \hat{\theta}_i\big) - \big\{V_N - V_{N-i}\big\} \tag{118}$$

where V_N is the total reported outcome of $k*$ and V_{N-i} is the total reported outcome of the choice that would be implemented without agent i, i.e.

$$V_N = \max_{k \in \mathcal{K}} \sum_i v_i \left(k, \hat{\theta}_i \right)$$

and

$$V_{N-i} = \max_{k \in \mathcal{K}} \sum_{j \neq i} v_j \left(k, \hat{\theta}_j \right).$$

Auction Game

Auction game is an applied branch of economics and used as a tool to inform the design of real-world auctions. It deals with how people act in auction markets and researches the properties of auction markets. There are many possible game models for auctions. Typical issues of auction game are the efficiency of auction design, optimal and equilibrium bidding strategies, and revenue comparison. There are some types of auction that are used for the allocation of a single item (McAfee, & McMillan, 1987), (Schindler, 2003), (Klemperer, 1999, 2004), (Krishna, 2001):

1. **First-price sealed-bid auction:** Bidders place their bid in a sealed envelope and simultaneously hand them to the auctioneer. The envelopes are opened and the individual with the highest bid wins, paying a price equal to the exact amount that he or she bid.
2. **Second-price sealed-bid auction:** Bidders place their bid in a sealed envelope and simultaneously hand them to the auctioneer. The envelopes are opened and the individual with the highest bid wins, paying a price equal to the exact amount of the second highest bid. This auction is also called as Vickrey auction.
3. **English auctions:** The price is steadily raised by the auctioneer with bidders dropping out once the price becomes too high.

This continues until there remains only one bidder who wins the auction at the current price. This auction is also called as open ascending-bid auction.

4. **Japanese Auction:** It is a variation of the English auction. All bidders are considered in the auction with a continuously rising price. The only action that a bidder may take is to drop out of the auction. Once the bidder drops out of the auction, dropped bidder may not re-enter the auction. When the second-to-last bidder drops out of the auction, the auction stops immediately, and the last bidder to remain gets the object at that price. It is strategically equivalent to the generalized second-price auction, even though the second-price auction is a static game and the Japanese Auction is a dynamic game.
5. **Dutch auction:** The price starts at a level sufficiently high to deter all bidders and is progressively lowered until a bidder indicates that he is prepared to buy at the current price. This bidder wins the auction and pays the price at which he bid. This auction is also called as open descending-bid auction.

In auction games, the players are the buyers and the sellers. The strategy set of each player is a set of bid functions or reservation prices. Each bid function maps the buyer's value or seller's cost to a bid price. The payoff of each player is the expected profit of that player under a combination of strategies.

Auction games generally can be categorized private value games or common value games. In a private value model, each bidder assumes that each of the competing bidders obtains a random private value from a probability distribution. In a common value model, each bidder assumes that any other bidder obtains a random signal from a probability distribution common to all bidders. Usually, a private values model assumes that the values are independent across bidders, whereas a common value model assumes that the values are dependent up to the common parameters (McAfee, & McMillan, 1987), (Schindler, 2003), (Klemperer, 1999, 2004), (Krishna, 2001).

In 1961, William Vickrey proposed the Vickrey auction model, which is a type of sealed-bid auction, where bidders submit written bids without knowing the bid of the other people in the auction, and in which the highest bidder wins, but the price paid is the second-highest bid. A generalization of the Vickrey auction is known as the Vickrey–Clarke–Groves (*VCG*) mechanism. *VCG* mechanism has been derived from the Mechanism Design (*MD*) theory and can maintain the incentive to bid truthfully; it is the main feature of *VCG*. Traditional *VCG* mechanism consists of a specification of possible player strategies and the mapping of each strategy from a set of strategies to an outcome. Players are assumed to be autonomous and economically rational; they select a best-response strategy to maximize their expected utility with other players. In particular, the *VCG* mechanism has better computational properties than the original *MD* and provides a normative guide for outcomes and payments. (Anderegg, 2003), (Shneidman, 2003), (Parkes, 2004), (Dash, 2003), (Wang, 2005), (Garg, 2008), (Woodard, 2003).

The era of putting auction game to work began in 1993-94, with the design and operation of the radio spectrum auctions in the United States. Although the economic theory of auctions had its beginnings in the early 1960s, early research had little influence on practice. Since 1994, auction game theorists have designed spectrum sales for countries on six continents, power auctions in the US and Europe, and several smaller asset auctions. In 2000, the US National Science Foundation's 50th anniversary celebration featured the success of the US spectrum auctions to justify its support for fundamental research in subjects like game theory. By the end of 2001, just seven years after the first of the large modern auctions, the theo-

rists' designs had been used for worldwide sales totaling more than $100 billion (Milgrom, 2004).

Metagames

The basic model of traditional game theory supposes a number of players are rational and optimize their choices to get the most preferred outcome. This definition of rationality implies that rational players must be fine themselves at a so-called *equilibrium point* – a point where each is optimizing against the others' choices. Alarmingly, this model generates conceptual difficulties, called 'dilemmas'. Some game theorists required a modification of the assumption that people can or should be rational in the strict, game-theoretic sense. However, the mainstream reaction has been to formally ignore this request and continue to analyze game situations on the assumption of strict rationality. Reacting against this 'rationalist' tendency, new approach has been developed to resolve this unrealistic rationality requirement (Bots, & Hermans, 2003).

In 1960s, Nigel Howard developed metagame theory as a reconstruction of traditional game theory on a non-quantitative basis (Howard, 1971). Initially, a metagame is defined in mathematics as a descriptor for set interaction that governs subset interaction in certain cases. In metagames, players depart from the assumption of rationality, and take a strong interest in game analysis. Players should optimize given their *beliefs* about the others' choices, and *know* how the other would choose to react to such knowledge, and *know* each other's reactions to such reactions, and so on (Bots, 2003). In the metagame paradigm, we can design programs to take in the rules of unknown games and play those games without human assistance. Strong performance of metagames is evidence that the program, instead of the human player, has performed the analysis of each specific game. Playing metagame with increasingly general classes of games makes it possible to demonstrate correspondingly general problem-solving ability.

Nowadays, the metagaming is generally used to define any strategy, action or method used in a game. Therefore, the metagame approach involves framing a situation as a strategic game in which players try to realize their objectives by means of the options available to them. Due to this reason, another definition of metagame is inverse games, which refer to the *game-universe* outside of the game itself, and it is the use of out-of-game information to affect player's in-game decisions. For example, when certain persons are faced with conflict problems, the solution is often not easy to derive. Because an individual person will act in his best interest, it is not always possible to reach the best agreement for others involved in the conflict. In this case, the approach of metagame can provide a solution paradigm. Therefore, the metagame is also used to refer to a game with moves that consist of creating or modifying the rules of another game to maximize the payoff of the resulting rule set. So, players could play a metagame of optimizing the rules of games to maximize the satisfaction of play, and finally get the standard rules as an optimum. Instead of taking the concept of traditional fixed games, metagame theory allows players' preferences and perceived opportunities to vary as they redefine the game itself, as well as their positions in it. Therefore, the basic idea of metagame is related to mechanism design theory; it would be to create or make changes in the management rules to maximize its effectiveness or profitability. Simply, a specific military operation could be thought of as a metagame with the political ramifications of that operation on the war (Bots, 2003), (Howard, 1971), (Cao, & Li, 2009), (Mingers, & Rosenhead, 2001), (Mayer, & Veeneman, 1999).

The main components of metagames consist of players, options, outcomes, order of preference and metagame analysis. Players act in this conflict problem through a process called an option. One or several options exist for each player. Each option is not mutually exclusive. The player can take some of those options at the same time. The combina-

tion of options of each player describes a specific plan. In metagames, it is necessary to select the executable outcomes. Each player defines the order of preference among executable outcomes and gets a solution through the metagame analysis process. In particular, the practical application of metagame theory is based on the metagame analysis. Metagame analysis reflects on a problem in terms of decision issues, and players who may exert different options to gain control over these issues. Players try to realize their objectives by means of the options available to them. The subsequent metagame analysis gives insight in possible strategies and their outcome. Finally, it reveals what likely scenarios exist, and who has the power to control the course of events. Metagame analysis proceeds in three phases: analysis of options, scenario development, and scenario analysis (Cao, 2009), (Mingers, 2001), (Mayer, 1999).

1. Analysis of options: The first phase of analysis of options consists of the following four steps:
   a. Structure the problem by identifying the issues to be decided.
   b. Identify the players control the issues, either directly or indirectly.
   c. Ask how the players control the issues, resulting in an inventory of strategy options.
   d. Determine the dependencies between the strategy options.

   Full elaboration of these four steps provides a metagame model, which can then be analyzed in different ways. The possible outcomes of the game, based on the combination of options, are called *scenarios*.

2. Scenario development: If a game with n players s_1, ..., s_n who have O_i options ($i = 1$, ..., n), there are $O_1 \times ... \times O_n$ possible outcomes. Large numbers of players and options will obviously cause a combinatorial explosion, but the dependencies between options will reduce the number of scenarios, because

they rule out those containing logically or physically impossible combinations of options. When doing so, the analyst should take care to preserve these particular types of scenarios.

3. Scenario analysis: In this step, scenarios are actually analyzed by following four steps:

    a. Choose a particular scenario to analyze for stability. A scenario is stable if each player expects to do its part and expects others to do theirs.

    b. Identify all unilateral improvements for players and subsets of players from the particular scenario.

    c. Identify all sanctions that exist to deter the unilateral improvements. Steps 1) to 3) need to be repeated to analyze some additional scenarios. When a number of scenarios have been analyzed, one can proceed to the next step:

    d. Draw a strategic map that reveals how players can use their power to move from one scenario to another, and which moves are likely to occur in view of the players' preferences.

Metagame analysis is a process introduced to help resolve conflict problems in which the main focus is that of finding a stable state common to all players involved in the conflict. The state in which stability exists for all the players is the solution of the conflict problem (Cao, 2009). By playing a metagame analysis, players will learn in two different dimensions: the substantive-strategic dimension (understanding the problem) and the social dimension (understanding the other players' personalities).

The metagame should become a vehicle for learning for the players, much more than a tool for the analyst. Actually playing a metagame is also expected to enhance the emotional involvement of the players and their receptiveness for the 'lessons'

drawn from the game using the metagame analysis. To operate the metagame analysis, the concept of *'playable metagames'* has been developed (Bots, 2003). Developing a *playable metagame* requires that the metagame analysis has been performed with four factors: the selection of players, the social setting for their interaction, the rules of the game, and the debriefing.

1. The players enact the negotiations between the players. They should be consistent with the structure of the metagame, and yet allow players sufficient freedom to incorporate their own views.

2. The social setting can be configured in different ways, depending on the complexity of the game. In the simplest form, the players openly exchange their views.

3. The rules of the game must define how the game proceeds and when the game ends. The social setting and the rules of the game should enforce each other. Typically, the game will be organized in several rounds. Each round, players can interact under procedural rules, and at the end of a round they make their preferred option known to the game director. The interactive metagame ends when a subset of the players reaches agreement on a feasible scenario, or when a predefined number of rounds has been played.

4. The debriefing should stimulate the players to reflect on their initial perception of the situation, the sequence of events during the game, and the realism of the negotiations and the resulting scenario. Therefore, the debriefing should focus on player learning, rather than ex-post data collection by the analyst.

The solution concept of metagame is 'metaequilibria', which is points corresponding to equilibria in the metagame situations. When metagame has been completed, all players are taking the same position and can trust each other; a totally satisfactory type of solution becomes possible and is unanimously selected by all players. This is precisely the definition of the *core* of metagame. Metagame analysis is a practical, non-quantitative way of first exploring its *core* (Bots, 2003).

Modified Game Theory

Multi-objective optimization is an area of multiple criteria decision making, which is concerned with mathematical optimization problems involving more than one objective function to be optimized simultaneously. For multi-objective optimization problems, there does not exist a single best solution that simultaneously optimizes each objective. Therefore, researchers study multi-objective optimization problems from different viewpoints and, there exist different solution philosophies and goals when setting and solving them (Sunar, & Kahraman, 2001)

In game theory, each player is associated with an objective function so that player tries to maximize his profit at the expense of the profits of the other players. When adopting game theory into a multi-objective optimization problem, the profit of a player is viewed as a negative objective function relative to the profits of the other players, and the Pareto optimal solution is determined by solving the following problem (Sunar, 2001)

$$\min \quad f_c\left(c, X\right) = \sum_{i=1}^{r} c_i f_i\left(X\right), \qquad (119)$$

s.t., $c = \left[c_1 c_2 \cdots c_r\right]^T$, $0 \leq c_{i,1 \leq i \leq r} \leq 1$, and

$$\sum_{i=1}^{r} c_i = 1$$

For the purpose of comparing the relative efficiencies of the various multi-objective optimiza-

tion techniques, a supercriterion (S), also known as the bargaining model, is constructed as follows:

$$S = \prod_{i=1}^{r}\left[1 - f_{ni}\left(X\right)\right] \qquad (120)$$

where $f_{ni}\left(\cdot\right)$ is a normalized function and S will always have a value between 0 and 1. The supercriterion S gives an indication as to how far an objective function is from its worst value at any design. Thus the higher the value of S, the better the modeling and design in terms of a compromise solution (Sunar, 2001)

The minimization of the problem given by Eq. (119) and the maximization of the supercriterion S by Eq. (120) must be simultaneously accomplished in the game theory with c and X being optimization variables, which is numerically cumbersome. Due to the computational complexities involved with the original game theory, a modification to the method was suggested (Rao, & Freiheit, 1991). The solution given by the Modified Game Theory (*MGT*) is expected to be near the optimal solution obtained by the original game theory. The algorithm for the *MGT* is as follows (Sunar, 2001):

Step 1: Formulate the normalized supercretiron (S) according to (120).

Step 2: Formulate a Pareto optimal objective function (*FC*) in terms of the normalized objective functions. In this work, *FC* is formulated using the weighting method as

$$FC = \sum_{i=1}^{r} c_i f_{ni}\left(X\right), \qquad \text{s.t.,} \sum_{i=1}^{r} c_i = 1 \qquad (121)$$

Step 3: The new optimization problem is posed as

$$\min \quad \mathrm{F}\left(X\right) = FC - S_n \tag{122}$$

In the formular (122), *FC* is also formulated using the goal programming method as

$$FC = \left\{ \sum_{i=1}^{r} c_i \left[f_{ni}\left(\mathbf{X}\right) \right]^q \right\}^{1/q} \tag{123}$$

where $q \geq 2$. The generalized goal programming method proposed by Ignizio is adapted to nonlinear problems as follows (Ignizio, 1976):

$$\min \quad F\left(X\right) = \left\{ \sum_{i=1}^{r} c_i \left[d_i^+ + d_i^- \right] \right\}^{\frac{1}{q}} \tag{124}$$

s.t., $\quad q \geq 1 \quad$ and $\quad F_i\left(X\right) - d_i^+ + d_i^- = T_i$, $i \in \left\{1, 2, \ldots, r\right\}$

where d_i^+ and d_i^- are the under-achievement and over-achievement of the *i*th goal, respectively. T_i is the goal (or target) set by the designer for the *i*th objective function (Rao, Venkayya, & Khot, 1988). In this method, the designer sets goals to be attained for each objective and a measure of the deviations of the objective functions from their respective goals is minimized. Sometimes, the goal of the *i*th objective function is taken as its single optimum value, i.e., $T_i = F_i\left(\mathbf{X}_i^*\right)$. It is assumed that over-achievement of the goals is not possible and hence d_i^- need not be defined. Thus the problem stated in Eq. (124) finally becomes

$$\min \quad F\left(X\right) = \left\{ \sum_{i=1}^{r} c_i \left[F_i\left(X\right) - F_i\left(X_i^*\right) \right]^q \right\}^{1/q} \tag{125}$$

s.t., $q \geq 1$ and $F_i\left(X\right) - F_i\left(X_i^*\right) \geq 0$, $i \in \left\{1, 2, \ldots, r\right\}$

Generalized Game Theory

Classical game theory makes heroic and largely unrealistic assumptions about players: complete, shared, and valid knowledge of the game. Also, unrealistic assumptions are made about the abilities of players to compute the maximization of payoffs and about the consistency of their preferences. At the same time, a player is assumed as an egoist who tries to be a strategist, taking into account how other players might respond to him and whether or not his own action is the best response to the other players' expected actions. In addition, classical game theory assumes a social structure where the players are completely autonomous or independent from one another. However, players are not independent in social relationships (Burns, & Roszkowska, 2005), (Roszkowska, & Burns, 2002).

One development of classical game theory is Generalized Game Theory (GGT), which is an extension of game theory incorporating social theory concepts ("Generalized game theory," n.d.). Social theory concepts can be defined in a uniform way in terms of such rules and rule complexes; rule complex is a generalization of a set of rules. While critical of the classical game approach, GGT entails its extension and generalization through the formulation of the mathematical theory of rules and rule complexes (Burns, 2005). In GGT, games are conceptualized in a uniform and general way as rule complexes. Usually, the rules may be imprecise, possibly inconsistent, even dynamic and open to a greater or lesser extent to modification and transformation by the players. Based on the principle of rule revision and game restructuring, GGT has developed the theory of combining, revising, replacing, and transforming rules and rule complexes, and has modified the game model. Therefore, proponents of GGT have advocated the application of the theory to re-conceptualizing the individual and collective decision-making process. Further, the modeling of the players in GGT is especially open to the use of concepts such as incomplete information and bounded rationality. These types of games are referred to as *open games*, that is, games which are open to transformation. In particular, *open game* is in contrast to conceptualization of traditional games consisting of players who are autonomous payoff maximizers. Therefore, the players in *open games* may restructure and transform the game itself and the conditions of their actions and interactions. Some games which have specified, fixed players, fixed preference structures, fixed optimization procedures, and fixed action alternatives are called *closed games*. *Closed games* are most classical game theory models (Burns, 2005).

In GGT, players' knowledge may be only partial, possibly even invalid to varying degrees. It may also differ from player to player. At the same time, cognitive and computational capabilities of players are strictly bounded and may vary substantially. For each player, judgment mechanism for actions is also likely to vary due to the differences of players' roles and interests in the interaction situation. With incomplete and imperfect information, players' interactions and outcomes depend on their beliefs as well as estimates of one another's beliefs, values, and judgment qualities (Burns, 2005).

In the GGT approach, a well-specified game is a particular multi-player interaction structure in which the participating players have defined roles and role relationships. In general, players play a number of different roles and are involved in several social relationships and institutional domains. In GGT, the rule complex of a game guides and regulates the players in their actions and interactions (Burns, 2005).

Given an interaction situation S_t at time t, $G(t)$ is a GGT game where the participating players typically have defined roles and role relationships (Burns, 2005). Suppose that the player i is involved in a defined game $G(t)$. *ROLE* (i, t, G) denotes the player i's role complex in $G(t)$ at time moment $t \in$ T:

$$ROLE\ (i,\ t) \subset_g G(t),\ s.t.,\ t \in T \qquad (126)$$

The game $G(t)$ consists of a configuration of multiple players' roles with some general rules and rule complexes (R). The general game structure of $G(t)$ is realized as follows.

$$G(t) = [ROLE\ (1,\ t),\ ROLE\ (2,\ t),\ .\ .\ .,\ ROLE\ (k,\ t)\ ;\ R\ ],\ s.t.,\ k \in N \qquad (127)$$

where N is the set of GGT game players. A player's role is specified in GGT in terms of *MODEL* (i, t), *VALUE* (i, t), *ACT* (i, t), and J (i, t). The complex of beliefs (*MODEL* (i, t)) defines the situational reality, key interaction conditions, causal mechanisms, and possible scenarios of the interaction situation. The complex of values (*VALUE*(i, t)) includes values and norms relating to what is good or bad and what should and should not be done in the situation, respectively. *ACT* (i, t) is the repertoires of possible strategies, programs, and routines in the situation. J (i, t) is a judgment complex or function; it is utilized by the player i to organize the determination of decisions and actions in relation to other players in the situation S_t. The judgment complex consists of rules which enable the player i to come to conclusions about truth, validity, value, or choice of strategic actions in a given situation. In general, judgment is a core concept and a key aspect of player's decision making in GGT. Several types of judgments are distinguished in GGT, for instance, value judgments, factual judgments and action judgments, etc,. In the case of action judgment, the player seeks to take the course of action offered by the rules of the game which most closely fit the values held by the player (Burns, 2005).

Given an action repertoire *ACT* (i, t), the action determination judgment entails finding an action which is the best fit. The player chooses the action a^* that maximizes the goodness of fit between the anticipated consequences of actions and the consequences prescribed or indicated by the norm

(Burns, 2005). Formally, the player *i* selects the action a^* ($a^* \in ACT(i, t)$) for which

$$J(i, t(a^*)) = \max_{a_k}\left[J(i,t)(a_k) \right] \text{ for all } a_k \in ACT (i, t) \quad (128)$$

A general solution concept for GGT is a strategy or interaction order for the players. This should lead to a state that is acceptable by the all players, and is not necessarily a normative equilibrium, but represents the best result attainable under the circumstances. Solutions may be reached through a sequence of proposed alternatives; if the proposed solutions may be convergent, the players find the ultimately acceptable solution. E. Roszkowska and T. Burns showed that not every game has a common solution, and that divergent proposals may arise (Roszkowska, 2002). This may result in a no equilibrium being found, and stems from dropping the assumption for the existence of a Nash equilibrium when the game is finite or the game have complete information.

Classification of Special Game Models

The subsection 3.3 has shown the classification of the special game models. These special game models can not be included in two branches of game theory - non-cooperative or cooperative theory. These special game models may be placed into subclasses - hybrid games, reverse games, auction games, metagames, modified game and open games. Moreover, within hybrid games, game model can be further grouped in terms of coopetition game and biform game. The reverse game is commonly called as mechanism design. One of the major achievements of mechanism design is the Vickrey-Clarke-Groves (*VCG*) mechanism. Auction game is an applied branch of economics which deals with how people act in auction markets and researches the properties of auction markets. There are many possible models for real-world auctions. Metagames, modified game and open games are extended general game models. In this book, we classify these games into the subclass of special games (Table 9).

Table 9. Classification of special game models

Special games		Coopetition game	It combines the characteristics of non-cooperative and cooperative games.	
	Hybrid games	Biform game	It is a hybrid non-cooperative and cooperative game model to formalize the two-stage decision problem.	
	Reverse game	Mechanism Design	VCG mechanism	*Direct-revelation* and *strategyproof* mechanisms
			Game designer chooses the game structure	
	Auction game	It is an applied branch of economics and used as a tool to inform the design of real-world auctions.		
	Metagames	The game-universe outside of the game itself, and it is the use of out-of-game information to affect game decisions.		
	Modified game	It is a method for generating a compromise solution based on the concept of Pareto minimum solution.		
	Open game	Game model is generalized through the formulation of the mathematical theory of rules and rule complexes.		

REFERENCES

Adamo, T., & Matros, A. (2009). A Blotto game with incomplete information. *Economics Letters, 105*, 100–102. doi:10.1016/j.econlet.2009.06.025

Algaba, E., Bilbao, J., Garcia, J., & Lopez, J. (2003). Computing power indices in weighted multiple majority games. *Mathematical Social Sciences, 46*, 63–80. doi:10.1016/S0165-4896(02)00086-0

Altman, E., El-Azouzi, R., Hayel, Y., & Tembine, H. (2008). An Evolutionary Game approach for the design of congestion control protocols in wireless networks. In *Proceedings of Physicomnet Workshop*, (pp. 1-6). Academic Press.

An, B., Tambe, M., Ordóñez, F., Shieh, E. A., & Kiekintveld, C. (2011). Refinement of Strong Stackelberg Equilibria in Security Games. In *Proceedings of the Twenty-Fifth AAAI Conference on Artificial Intelligence*, (pp. 587-593). AAAI.

Anderegg, L., & Eidenbenz, S. (2003). Ad hoc-VCG: A truthful and cost-efficient routing protocol for mobile ad hoc networks with selfish agents. [ACM.]. *Proceedings of MobiCom, 03*, 245–259.

Archetti, M. (2009). Cooperation as a volunteer's dilemma and the strategy of conflict in public goods games. *Journal of Evolutionary Biology, 22*(11), 2192–2200. doi:10.1111/j.1420-9101.2009.01835.x PMID:19732256

Aumann, R., & Maschler, M. (1985). Game theoretic analysis of a bankruptcy problem from the Talmud. *Journal of Economic Theory, 36*, 195–213. doi:10.1016/0022-0531(85)90102-4

Aziz, H., Paterson, M., & Leecht, D. (2007). Efficient Algorithm for Designing Weighted Voting Games. [INMIC.]. *Proceedings of INMIC, 2007*, 1–6.

Bachrach, Y., Meir, R., Zuckerman, M., Rothe, J., & Rosenschein, J. S. (2009). The cost of stability in weighted voting games. In *Proceedings of AAMAS*, (pp. 1289-1290). AAMAS.

Bolton, G., Katok, E., & Zwick, R. (1998). Dictator game giving: Rules of fairness versus acts of kindness. *International Journal of Game Theory, 27*(2), 269–299. doi:10.1007/s001820050072

Bots, P. W. G., & Hermans, L. M. (2003). Developing 'playable metagames' for participatory stakeholder analysis. In *Proceedings of ISAGA* (pp. 25-29). ISAGA.

Bouncken, R. B., & Fredrich, V. (2011). Coopetition: Its successful management in the nexus of dependency and trust. In *Proceedings of PICMET*, (pp. 1-12). PICMET.

Brams, S. F., & Affuso, P. J. (1976). Power and size: A new paradox. *Theory and Decision, 7*, 29–56. doi:10.1007/BF00141101

Brandenburger, A., & Stuart, H. (2007). Biform Games. *Management Science, 53*, 537–549. doi:10.1287/mnsc.1060.0591

Brown, M., An, B., Kiekintveld, C., Ordóñez, F., & Tambe, M. (2012). Multi-Objective Optimization for Security Games. [AAMAS.]. *Proceedings of AAMAS, 12*, 863–870.

Burns, T. R., & Roszkowska, E. (2005). Generalized Game Theory: Assumptions, Principles, and Elaborations. *Studies in Logic, Grammar, and Rhetoric, 8*(21), 7–40.

Bursztein, E. (2009). Extending Anticipation Games with Location, Penalty and Timeline. *Lecture Notes in Computer Science, 5491*, 272–286. doi:10.1007/978-3-642-01465-9_18

Bursztein, E., & Mitchell, J. C. (2007). Using strategy objectives for network security analysis. [INSCRYPT.]. *Proceedings of Inscrypt, 09*, 337–349.

Cao, Y., & Li, R. (2009). Conflict Analysis between Tacit Knowledge Sharing and Its Exclusivity Based on Meta-game Theory. In *Proceedings of IEEC International Symposium on Information Engineering and Electronic Commerce*, (pp. 31-35). IEEC.

Carlsson, B., & Johansson, S. J. (1997). An Iterated Hawk-and-Dove Game. [LNCS]. *Proceedings of Agents and Multi-Agent Systems Formalisms, Methodologies, and Applications*, *1441*, 179–192. doi:10.1007/BFb0055028

Carlsson, H., & Damme, E. V. (1993). Global games and equilibrium selection. *Econometrica*, *61*(5), 989–1018. doi:10.2307/2951491

Cesarini, D., Dawes, C. T., Fowler, J. H., Johannesson, M., Lichtenstein, P., & Wallace, B. (2008). Heritability of cooperative behavior in the trust game. *Proceedings of the National Academy of Sciences of the United States of America*, *105*(10), 3721–3726. doi:10.1073/pnas.0710069105 PMID:18316737

Chatain, O., & Zemsky, P. (2007). The horizontal scope of the firm: organizational tradeoffs vs. buyer-supplier relationships. *Management Science*, *53*(4), 550–565. doi:10.1287/mnsc.1060.0680

Chen, L., Low, S. H., & Doyle, J. C. (2007). Contention control: A game-theoretic approach. In *Proceedings of IEEE Conference on Decision and Control*, (pp. 3428–3434). IEEE.

Chen, L., Low, S. H., & Doyle, J. C. (2010). Random Access Game and Medium Access Control Design. *IEEE/ACM Transactions on Networking*, *18*(4), 1303–1316. doi:10.1109/TNET.2010.2041066

Dagan, N., Serrano, R., & Volij, O. (1997). A non-cooperative view of consistent bankruptcy rules. *Games and Economic Behavior*, *18*, 55–72. doi:10.1006/game.1997.0526

Dash, R. K., Parkes, D. C., & Jennings, N. R. (2003). Computational Mechanism Design: A Call to Arms. *IEEE Intelligent Systems*, *18*(6), 40–47. doi:10.1109/MIS.2003.1249168

Dewatripont, M., Hansen, L. P., & Turnovsky, S. J. (2003). *Advances in Economics and Econometrics*. Cambridge, UK: Cambridge University Press.

Dictator Game. (n.d.). Retrieved from http://en.wikipedia.org/wiki/Dictator_game

Dockner, E., Jorgensen, S., Long, V. N., & Sorger, G. (2001). *Differential Games in Economics and Management Science*. Cambridge University Press.

Evolutionary Game Theory. (n.d.). Retrieved from http://en.wikipedia.org/wiki/Evolutionary_game_theory

Felegyhazi, M., &. Hubaux, J.-P. (2006). *Game Theory in Wireless Networks: A Tutorial* (EPFL Technical Report: LCA-REPORT-2006-002). Lausanne, Switzerland: Ecole Polytechnique F´ed´erale de Lausanne.

Fowler, J. H. (2006). Altruism and Turnout. *The Journal of Politics*, *68*(3), 674–683. doi:10.1111/j.1468-2508.2006.00453.x

Garg, D., Narahari, Y., & Gujar, S. (2008). Foundations of Mechanism Design: A Tutorial, Part 1: Key Concepts and Classical Results. *Sadhana*, *33*(2), 83–130. doi:10.1007/s12046-008-0008-3

Generalized Game Theory. (n.d.). Retrieved from http://en.wikipedia.org/wiki/Generalized_game_theory

Geupel, L. (2011). *The Princess and Monster Game on an Interval*. (Unpublished Bachelor's Thesis). Technische Universität, München, Germany.

Gibbons, R. (1992). *A Primer in Game Theory*. Prentice Hall.

Gillis, T. J. (1999). *Taxation and national destiny: a tax systems analysis and proposal*. Maximus Profectus.

Goemans, M. X., Li, L., Mirrokni, V. S., & Thottan, M. (2006). Market sharing games applied to content distribution in ad hoc networks. *IEEE Journal on Selected Areas in Communications*, *24*(5), 1020–1033. doi:10.1109/JSAC.2006.872884

Guan, Z., Yuan, D., & Zhang, H. (2008). Novel coopetition paradigm based on bargaining theory or collaborative multimedia resource management. In *Proceedings of IEEE PIMRC*, (pp. 1-5). IEEE.

Han, Z., Niyato, D., Saad, W., Başar, T., & Hjørungnes, A. (2011). *Game Theory in Wireless and Communication Networks*. Cambridge University Press. doi:10.1017/CBO9780511895043

Han, Z., Pandana, C., & Liu, K. J. R. (2005). A self-learning repeated game framework for optimizing packet forwarding networks. In *Proceedings of IEEE Wireless Communications and Networking Conference*, (pp. 2131–2136). IEEE.

Hauert, C., De Monte, S., Hofbauer, J., & Sigmund, K. (2002). Replicator dynamics in optional public goods games. *Journal of Theoretical Biology*, *218*, 187–194. doi:10.1006/jtbi.2002.3067 PMID:12381291

Hennet, J. C., & Mahjoub, S. (2010). Supply network formation as a biform game. In *Proceedings of Conference on Management and Control of Production Logistics*, (pp. 108-113). Academic Press.

Henrich, J., Boyd, R., Bowles, S., Camerer, C., Fehr, E., & Gintis, H. (2004). *Foundations of Human Sociality: Economic Experiments and Ethnographic Evidence from Fifteen Small-Scale Societies*. Oxford, UK: Oxford University Press. doi:10.1093/0199262055.001.0001

Hofbauer, J., & Sigmund, K. (2003). Evolutionary game dynamics. *Journal of Bulletin of the American Mathematical Society*, *40*, 479–519. doi:10.1090/S0273-0979-03-00988-1

Hossain, E., Niyato, D., & Han, Z. (2009). *Dynamic Spectrum Access and Management in Cognitive Radio Networks*. Cambridge University Press. doi:10.1017/CBO9780511609909

Howard, N. (1971). *Paradoxes of Rationality*. MIT Press.

Ibars, C., Navarro, M., & Giupponi, L. (2010). Distributed Demand Management in Smart Grid with a Congestion Game. In *Proceedings of First IEEE International Conference on Smart Grid Communications (SmartGridComm)*, (pp. 495-500). IEEE.

Ignizio, J. P. (1976). *Goal Programming and Extensions*. Lexington Books.

Isaac, R., Walker, J., & Williams, A. (1994). Group Size and the Voluntary Provision of Public Goods: Experimental Evidence Utilizing Large Groups. *Journal of Public Economics*, *54*(1), 1–36. doi:10.1016/0047-2727(94)90068-X

Khudabukhsh, A. R. (2006). *A Survey On Supermodular Games*. British Columbia, Canada: University of British Columbia.

Kimbrough, S., & Kuo, A. (2010). On heuristics for two-sided matching: revisiting the stable marriage problem as a multiobjective problem. In *Proceedings of the 12th annual conference on Genetic and evolutionary computation*, (pp. 1283-1290). Academic Press.

Klemperer, P. (1999). Auction theory: A guide to the literature. *Journal of Economic Surveys*, *13*(3), 227–286. doi:10.1111/1467-6419.00083

Klemperer, P. (2004). *Auctions: Theory and Practice*. Princeton University Press.

Kovenocka, D., & Roberson, B. (2011). A Blotto game with multi-dimensional incomplete information. *Economics Letters*, *113*(3), 273–275. doi:10.1016/j.econlet.2011.08.009

Krishna, V. (2001). *Auction theory*. New York: Elsevier.

Krishnamurthy, V. (2008). Decentralized Activation in Dense Sensor Networks via Global Games. *IEEE Transactions on Signal Processing*, *56*(10), 4936–4950. doi:10.1109/TSP.2008.926978

Krishnamurthy, V. (2009). Decentralized Spectrum Access Amongst Cognitive Radios - An Interacting Multivariate Global Game-Theoretic Approach. *IEEE Transactions on Signal Processing*, *57*(10), 3999–4013. doi:10.1109/TSP.2009.2022860

Kutsuna, H., & Fujita, S. (2011). A Fair and Efficient Congestion Avoidance Scheme Based on the Minority Game. *Journal of Information Processing Systems*, *7*(3), 531–542. doi:10.3745/JIPS.2011.7.3.531

Lariviere, M. A., & Porteus, E. L. (2001). Selling to the newsvendor: an analysis of price-only contracts. *Manufacturing & Service Operations Management*, *3*(4), 293–305. doi:10.1287/msom.3.4.293.9971

Ledyard, J. (1984). The pure theory of large two-candidate elections. *Public Choice*, *44*, 7–41. doi:10.1007/BF00124816

Liang, X., & Xiao, Y. (2013). Game Theory for Network Security. *IEEE Communications Surveys & Tutorials*, *15*(1), 472–486. doi:10.1109/SURV.2012.062612.00056

Littman, M. L. (1994). Markov games as a framework for multi-agent reinforcement learning. In *Proceedings of International Conference on Machine Learning*, (pp. 157-163). Academic Press.

Liu, M., Ahmad, S. H. A., & Wu, Y. (2009). Congestion Games with Resource Reuse and Applications in Spectrum Sharing. In *Proceedings of International Conference on Game Theory for Networks, (GameNets'09)*, (pp. 171-179). Academic Press.

Maskin, E., & Tirole, J. (2001). Markov Perfect Equilibrium. *Journal of Economic Theory*, *100*, 191–219. doi:10.1006/jeth.2000.2785

Mayer, I., & Veeneman, W. (1999). *Games in a world of infrastructures: Simulation-Games for Research, Learning, and Intervention*. Eburon Publishers.

McAfee, R. P., & McMillan, J. (1987). Auctions and Bidding. *Journal of Economic Literature*, *25*(2), 699–738.

McFadden, D. (1974). Conditional logit analysis of qualitative choice behavior. *Frontiers in Econometrics*, 105-142.

Menasche, D. S., Figueiredo, D. R., & Silva, E. S. (2005). An evolutionary game-theoretic approach to congestion control. *Performance Evaluation*, *62*(1-4), 295–312. doi:10.1016/j.peva.2005.07.028

Meshulam, R., Kraus, S., & Grosz, B. J. (2007). The Use of Reputation and Gossip in Small Cooperative Group Activities. In *Proceedings of International Conference on Intelligent Agent Technology*, (pp. 239-243). Academic Press.

Milgrom, P. (2004). *Putting Auction Theory to Work*. Cambridge University Press. doi:10.1017/CBO9780511813825

Milgrom, P., & Roberts, J. (1990). Rationalizability and Learning in Games with Strategic Complementarities. *Econometrica*, *58*, 1255–1278. doi:10.2307/2938316

Mingers, J., & Rosenhead, J. (2001). *Rational analysis for a problematic world revisited: problem structuring methods for complexity, uncertainty and conflict*. Wiley.

Modzelewski, K., Stein, J., & Yu, J. (2009). *An Experimental Study of Classic Colonel Blotto Games*. Cambridge, MA: MIT.

Moragrega, A., Closas, P., & Ibars, C. (2012). Supermodular game for energy efficient TOA-based positioning. In *Proceedings of IEEE International Workshop on Signal Processing Advances in Wireless Communications (SPAWC)*, (pp. 35-39). IEEE.

Mukherjee, A. (2009). Election Games for Resource Allocation in Multicarrier Multiuser Wireless Networks. In *Proceedings of IEEE MILCOM 2009*. IEEE.

Mustika, I. W., Yamamoto, K., Murata, H., & Yoshida, S. (2010). Spectrum Sharing with Interference Management for Distributed Cognitive Radio Networks: A Potential Game Approach. In *Proceedings of IEEE Vehicular Technology Conference (VTC 2010-Spring)*. IEEE.

Nisan, N., & Ronen, A. (2000). Computationally feasible VCG mechanisms. In *Proceedings of ACM Conference on Electronic Commerce*, (pp. 242-252). ACM.

O'Neill, B. (1982). A problem of rights arbitration from the Talmud. *Mathematical Social Sciences*, 2, 345–371. doi:10.1016/0165-4896(82)90029-4

Ordoñez, G. (2006). *Notes on Bayesian Gamesy*. Retrieved from http://www.sas.upenn.edu/~ordonez/pdfs/ECON%20201/NoteBAYES.pdf

Osborne, M. J., & Rubinstein, A. (1994). *A Course in Game Theory*. Cambridge, MA: MIT Press.

Owen, G. (2001). *Game theory*. Academic Press.

Panah, A. S., & Khorsandi, S. (2011). Overlay construction based on dynamic coalition formation game in P2P networks. In Proceedings of Signal Processing and Communication Systems (ICSPCS). ICSPCS.

Park, H. G., & Schaar, M. V. D. (2007a). Bargaining Strategies for Networked Multimedia Resource Management. *IEEE Transactions on Signal Processing*, 55(7), 3496–3511. doi:10.1109/TSP.2007.893755

Park, H. G., & Schaar, M. V. D. (2007b). Multi-User Multimedia Resource Management using Nash Bargaining Solution. [IEEE.]. *Proceedings of IEEE ICASSP*, 2007, 717–720.

Park, J. O., & Schaar, M. V. D. (2012). *The Theory of Intervention Games for Resource*. Academic Press.

Park, J. O., & Scharr, M. V. D. (2011). *A Note on the Intervention Framework*. Los Angeles: University of California.

Parkes, D. C., & Shneidman, J. (2004). Distributed Implementations of Vickrey-Clarke-Groves Mechanisms. In *Proceedings of the Third International Joint Conference on Autonomous Agents and MultiAgent Systems*, (pp. 261-268). Academic Press.

Patcha, A., & Park, J. M. (2006). A Game Theoretic Formulation for Intrusion Detection in Mobile Ad Hoc Networks. *I. J. Network Security*, 2(2), 131–137.

Pierre, C. (2010). *Introduction to differential games*. Retrieved from https://www.ceremade.dauphine.fr/~cardalia/CoursJeuxDiff.pdf

Porter, R. H. (1983). Optimal cartel trigger price strategies. *Journal of Economic Theory*, 29, 313–318. doi:10.1016/0022-0531(83)90050-9

Public Goods Game. (n.d.). Retrieved from http://en.wikipedia.org/wiki/Public_goods_game

Quan, H. J., Wang, B. H., Hui, P. M., & Luo, X. S. (2003). Self-segregation and enhanced cooperation in an evolving population through local information transmission. *Physica A: Statistical Mechanics and its Applications, Elsevier, 321*(1), 300-308.

Raiffa, H. (1982). *The Art and Science of Negotiation*. Harvard University Press.

Rao, S. S., & Freiheit, T. I. (1991). Modied Game Theory Approach to Multiobjective Optimization. *Journal of Mechanisms, Transmissions, and Automation in Design, 113*, 286–291.

Rao, S. S., Venkayya, V. B., & Khot, N. S. (1988). Optimization of Actively Controlled Structures Using Goal Programming Techniques. *International Journal for Numerical Methods in Engineering, 26*, 183–197. doi:10.1002/nme.1620260113

Rasmusen, E. B. (2008). *The Rubinstein Bargaining Model with Both Discounting and Fixed Per-Period Costs*. Indiana University.

Ratliff, J. (1996). *Infinitely, Repeated Games with Discounting: Game Theory Course Note*. Tucson, AZ: University of Arizona.

Ray, D. (2010). *Game Theory II- lecture notes*. London School of Economics.

Roberson, B. (2006). The Colonel Blotto game. *Economic Theory, 29*(1), 1–24. doi:10.1007/s00199-005-0071-5

Roszkowska, E., & Burns, T. R. (2002). *Fuzzy Judgment in Bargaining Games: Diverse Patterns of Price Determination and Transaction in Buyer-Seller Exchange*. Bielefeld, Germany: University of Bielefeld.

Roy, S., Ellis, C., Shiva, S., Dasgupta, D., Shandilya, V., & Wu, Q. (2010). A Survey of Game Theory as Applied to Network Security. In *Proceedings of IEEE HICSS*. IEEE.

Rubinstein, A. (1982). Perfect equilibrium in a bargaining model. *Econometrica, 50*, 97–109. doi:10.2307/1912531

Samuelson, P. A. (1954). The Pure Theory of Public Expenditure. *The Review of Economics and Statistics, 36*(4), 387–389. doi:10.2307/1925895

Schindler, J. (2003). *Late bidding on the Internet*. University of Vienna.

Shang, L., & Wang, X. F. (2006). Self-Organization of Evolutionary Minority Game on Scale-Free Networks. [ICNSC.]. *Proceedings of ICNSC, 06*, 1017–1021.

Shang, L. H. (2007). Self-organized Evolutionary Minority Game on Networks. In *Proceedings of IEEE International Conference on Control and Automation (ICCA 2007)*, (pp. 1885-1889). IEEE.

Shneidman, J., & Parkes, D. (2003). Rationality and self-interest in peer-to-peer networks. In *Proc. IPTPS'03*, (pp. 139-148). IPTPS.

Sierra, C., Faratin, P., & Jennings, N. R. (1997). A Service-Oriented Negotiation Model between Autonomous Agents. In *Proceedings of 8th European Workshop on Modeling Autonomous Agents in a Multi-Agent World (MAAMAW-97)*, (pp. 17-35). MAAMAW.

Signaling Games. (n.d.). Retrieved from http://faculty.arts.ubc.ca/pnorman/signalling.pdf

Skyrms, B. (2004). *The Stag Hunt and the Evolution of Social Structure*. Cambridge, UK: Cambridge University Press.

Spence, A. M. (1973). Job Market Signaling. *The Quarterly Journal of Economics, 87*(3), 355–374. doi:10.2307/1882010

Stiglitz, J., & Weiss, A. (1990). *Sorting out the Differences Between Screening and Signalling Models*. Oxford, UK: Oxford University Press.

Stuart, H. W. (2005). Biform Analysis of Inventory Competition. *Manufacturing & Service Operations Management, 7*(4), 347–359. doi:10.1287/msom.1050.0090

Su, Y., & Schaar, M. V. D. (2009). From competition to coopetition: Stackelberg equilibrium in multi-user power control games. [GameNets.]. *Proceedings of GameNets, 09,* 107–116.

Suber, P. (1990). *The Paradox of Self-Amendment, A Study of Logic, Law, Omnipotence, and Change.* Peter Lang Publishing.

Suliman, I. M., Pomalaza-Rez, C., Lehtomki, J., & Oppermann, I. (2004). Radio resource allocation in heterogeneous wireless networks using cooperative games. In *Proc. Nordic Radio Symposium.* Academic Press.

Sun, L., & Xu, X. (2005). Coopetitive game, equilibrium and their applications. In *Proceedings of AAIM,* (pp. 104-111). AAIM.

Sunar, M., & Kahraman, R. (2001). A Comparative Study of Multiobjective Optimization Methods in Structural Design. *Turkish Journal of Engineering & Environmental Sciences, 25,* 69–78.

Sysi-Aho, M., Saramäki, J., & Kaski, K. (2005). Invisible hand effect in an evolutionary minority game model. *Physica A, 347,* 639–652. doi:10.1016/j.physa.2004.08.029

Tambe, M., Jain, M., Pita, J. A., & Jiang, A. X. (2012). Game theory for security: Key algorithmic principles, deployed systems, lessons learned. In *Proceedings of Annual Allerton Conference* (pp. 1822-1829). Academic Press.

Tan, C. K., Chuah, T. C., & Tan, S. W. (2011). Fair subcarrier and power allocation for multiuser orthogonal frequency-division multiple access cognitive radio networks using a colonel blotto game. *IET Communications, 5*(11), 1607–1618. doi:10.1049/iet-com.2010.1021

Tanaka, Y. M., & Tokuoka, S. (2006). Minority Game as a Model for the Artificial Financial Markets. In *Proceedings of IEEE Congress on Evolutionary Computation (CEC 2006),* (pp. 2157-2162). IEEE.

Tao, Y., & Wang, Z. (1997). Effect of time delay and evolutionarily stable strategy. *Journal of Theoretical Biology, 187,* 111–116. doi:10.1006/jtbi.1997.0427 PMID:9236113

Thamilarasu, G., & Sridhar, R. (2009). Game Theoretic Modeling of Jamming Attacks in Ad hoc Networks. In *Proceedings of ICCCN 2009.* ICCCN.

U, M., & Li, Z. (2010). Public Goods Game Simulator with Reinforcement Learning Agents. In *Proceedings of ICMLA* (pp. 43-49). ICMLA.

Vassaki, S., Panagopoulos, A. D., & Constantinou, P. (2009). Bandwidth allocation in wireless access networks: Bankruptcy game vs cooperative game. In *Proceedings of ICUMT'09.* ICUMT.

Vejandla, P., Dasgupta, D., Kaushal, A., & Nino, F. (2010). Evolving Gaming Strategies for Attacker-Defender in a Simulated Network Environment. [IEEE.]. *Proceedings of IEEE SocialCom, 10,* 889–896.

Vinyals, M., Bistaffa, F., Farinelli, A., & Rogers, A. (2012). Stable coalition formation among energy consumers in the smart grid. In *Proceedings of AAMAS'2012.* AAMAS.

Vreeswijk, G. A. W. (1995). *Several experiments in elementary self-modifying protocol games, such as Nomic.* Maastricht University.

Wang, W. J., Chatterjee, M., & Kwiat, K. (2010). Attacker Detection Game in Wireless Networks with Channel Uncertainty. In *Proceedings of ICC'2010.* ICC.

Wang, X., & Schulzrinne, H. (2005). Incentive-Compatible Adaptation of Internet Real-Time Multimedia. *IEEE Journal on Selected Areas in Communications, 23*(2), 417–436. doi:10.1109/JSAC.2004.839399

Woodard, C. J., & Parkes, D. C. (2003). Strategy-proof mechanisms for ad hoc network formation. In *Proc. IPTPS'03.* IPTPS.

Xu, B., & Fan, L. (2010). Information disclosing and cooperation in public goods game with punishment. [ICISE.]. *Proceedings of ICISE, 2010*, 2896–2899.

Yang, M. H. (2005). *Nash-stackelberg equilibrium solutions for linear multidivisional multilevel programming problems.* (Doctoral Dissertation). State University of New York at Buffalo, Buffalo, NY.

Zeng, D., & Sycara, K. (1998). Bayesian Learning in Negotiation. *Int. J. Human-computer Studies, 48*, 125–141. doi:10.1006/ijhc.1997.0164

Zhang, S., & He, Y. P. (2012). The Analysis of Resource Conflicts Based on Hawk and Dove Game in Multi-projects Management. In *Proceedings of Fifth International Joint Conference on Computational Sciences and Optimization (CSO)*, (pp. 702–705). CSO.

Zhong, L. X., Chen, B. H., & Huang, C. Y. (2008). Networking Effects on Public Goods Game with Unequal Allocation. [ICNC.]. *Proceedings of ICNC, 08*, 217–221.

Zuckerman, M., Faliszewski, P., Bachrach, Y., & Elkind, E. (2008). Manipulating the Quota in Weighted Voting Games. In *Proceedings of Conference on Artificial Intelligence*, (pp. 13–17). Academic Press.

KEY TERMS AND DEFINITIONS

Asymmetric Game: A game where there are not identical strategy sets for players.

Cooperative Game: A game is cooperative if the players are able to form binding commitments. For instance, the legal system requires them to adhere to their promises.

Differential Game: The evolution of the players' state variables is governed by differential equations. The problem of finding an optimal strategy in a differential game is closely related to the optimal control theory.

Dynamic Game: A game where later players have some knowledge about earlier actions.

Hybrid Game: It contains cooperative and non-cooperative elements. For instance, coalitions of players are formed in a cooperative game, but these play in a non-cooperative fashion.

Metagames: Games that the play is the development of the rules for another game, the target or subject game. Metagames seek to maximize the utility value of the rule set developed. The theory of metagames is related to mechanism design theory.

Perfect Information Game: All players know the moves previously made by all other players. Thus, only sequential games can be games of perfect information because players in simultaneous games do not know the actions of the other players.

Simultaneous Game: A game where players move simultaneously, or if they do not move simultaneously, the later players are unaware of the earlier players' actions.

Symmetric Game: A game where the payoffs for playing a particular strategy depend only on the other strategies employed, not on who is playing them.

Section 2
Game Theoretic Applications for Network Management Issues

Chapter 4
Game Theory for Wireless Ad Hoc Networks

ABSTRACT

An ad hoc network typically refers to any set of networks where all devices have equal status on a network and are free to associate with any other ad hoc network device in link range. In particular, ad hoc network often refers to a mode of operation of IEEE 802.11 wireless networks. A wireless ad hoc network is a decentralized type of wireless network. The network is ad hoc because it does not rely on a pre-existing infrastructure, such as routers in wired networks or access points in managed (infrastructure) wireless networks. The decentralized nature of wireless ad hoc networks makes them suitable for a variety of applications where central nodes cannot be relied on and may improve the scalability of networks compared to wireless managed networks, though theoretical and practical limits to the overall capacity of such networks have been identified. This chapter explores this.

INTRODUCTION

Since John von Neumann and Oskar Morgenstern established their book in 1944, game theory can also be applied to many fields of science where decision makers have conflicting interests. Not surprisingly, game theory has also been applied to networking, in most cases to solve routing and resource allocation problems in a competitive environment. In particular, game theory allows us to investigate the existence, uniqueness and convergence to a steady state operating point when network devices perform independent adaptations. Therefore, it serves as a strong tool for a

rigorous analysis of distributed network protocols (Srivastava, Neel, MacKenzie, & Menon, 2005).

Nowadays, game theory was also applied to the wireless communication. Even if the research work were initially limited to conventional networks, the recent development of wireless networking motivated researches to seek for answers provided by game theory. A wireless ad hoc network is characterized by a distributed, dynamic, self-organizing architecture. Each node in the network is capable of independently adapting its operation based on the current environment according to predetermined algorithms and protocols. In a traditional game model, players are independent decision makers whose payoffs depend on other

DOI: 10.4018/978-1-4666-6050-2.ch004

players' actions. Nodes in an ad hoc network are characterized by the same feature. This similarity leads to a strong mapping between traditional game theory components and elements of an ad hoc network. In the game model for wireless ad hoc networking, players are nodes in the network, and strategy is action related to the functionality being studied. Utility function is performance metrics, for example, throughput, delay, target signal-to-noise ratio (Srivastava, 2005), (Felegyhazi, &. Hubaux, 2006).

These days, the old description of 7-layer network system model has been replaced by the new 5-layer network system model that was invented for the Internet. 5 layers are the physical, data link, network, transport and application layers. However, the mathematical analysis to the study of each layer in wireless ad hoc networks has met with limited success due to the complexity of mobility and traffic models, the dynamic topology, and the unpredictability of link quality that characterize such networks. Instead of the mathematical analysis, game theory is particularly attractive to analyze the performance of ad hoc networks. Therefore, game theory can be applied to the modeling of individual, independent decision makers at each wireless network layer (Srivastava, 2005). This chapter comprehensively surveys the existing researches on game theoretic approaches for the wireless communication networks; different types of game models are broadly reviewed. The aim of this chapter is to familiarize the readers with the state-of-the-art research on this topic and the different techniques for game theoretic modeling of wireless network systems.

PHYSICAL LAYER

Power control is a hot issue of the physical layer due to the potentially significant performance gains achieved when nodes limit their power level. In wireless communication systems, mobile terminals respond to the time varying nature of the channel by regulating their transmitter powers. Specifically, in a CDMA system, where signals of other terminals can be modeled as interfering noise signals, the major goal of this regulation is to achieve a certain signal to interference (SIR) ratio regardless of the channel conditions while minimizing the interference due to terminal transmit power level. Hence, there are two major reasons for a terminal to perform power control; the first one is the limit on the energy available to the mobile node, and the second reason is the increase in quality of service (QoS) by minimizing the interference (Mehta, & Kwak, 2009).

Distributed power control, which is adopted by a node, can be performed, that means, not only can the node adjust its power according to its own status, but also the distributed networking function can determine the proper power limit to optimize the performance of the whole network. From a physical layer perspective, performance is generally a function of the effective signal-to-interference-plus-noise ratio (SINR). When the nodes in a wireless network respond to changes in perceived SINR by adapting their signal, a physical layer interactive decision making process occurs. This signal adaptation can occur in the transmit power level.

Based on the game theory, several distributed power control models have been implemented in wireless networks (Srivastava, 2005). In the context of game theory, each node pursues a strategy that aims to maximize the utility by adjusting its transmitter power. In doing so, the action of one node influences the utilities of other nodes and causes them to adjust their powers. The distributed power control models are referred to as non-cooperative games because each node pursues a strategy based on locally available information. By contrast, a centralized power control model uses information about the state of all nodes to determine all the power levels. A centralized model corresponds to a cooperative game. The convergence of the distributed power control model corresponds to the existence of a

Nash equilibrium for the non-cooperative game, and the convergence of a centralized power control model corresponds to the Pareto efficiency (Goodman, & Mandayam, 1999). In other word, non-cooperative games provide a convenient framework for decentralization and distributed decision making in those applications, where as cooperative approaches of game theory have allowed to handle issues concerning fairness in power allocation. Most applications of game theory to power control consider mobile nodes as players of the same type and study strategic one-shot games with a fixed number of players (Tembine, Altman, ElAzouzi, & Sandholm, 2008).

Evolutionary Game in Physical Layer

In the past several years, evolutionary population game has been considered as an extension of the classical non-cooperative power control game. This game is played infinitely under some self-organizing process called 'hybrid dynamic' with many simultaneous local interactions. Each interaction concerns a random number of players (Tembine, 2008). The evolutionary game formalism identifies and studies two concepts: the Evolutionary Stable Strategy (ESS) and the Replicator Dynamics. If an ESS is reached, the proportions of each population do not change in time. In addition, at ESS, the populations are immune from being invaded by other small populations. This notion is stronger than Nash equilibrium in which it is only requested that a single user would not benefit by a change of its behavior. The ESS concept helps to understand mixed strategies in games with symmetric payoffs. A mixed strategy can be interpreted as a composition of the population. An ESS can be also interpreted as a Nash equilibrium of the one-shot game but a Nash equilibrium cannot be an ESS (Altman, El-Azouzi, Hayel, & Tembine, 2010). Evolutionary game theory considers a dynamic scenario where players are constantly interacting with others players and adapting their choices based on

the fitness they receive. A strategy having higher fitness than others tends to gain ground: this is formulated through rules describing the Replicator Dynamics of the sizes of populations of strategies. There are two advantages in doing so within the model of evolutionary games: i) it provides the stronger concept of equilibria, the ESS, and ii) it allows us to apply the generic convergence theory of replicator dynamics [(Altman, 2010).

Refereed Game in Physical Layer

An alternative power control game model is refereed game (MacKenzie, & Wicker, 2001). This game allows the base station to 'referee' the game by punishing users who attempt to cheat. If the base station acts as a 'referee', it is possible to achieve a solution which is a Pareto improvement over the Nash Equilibrium. Furthermore, it is possible to construct a model where actual power control decisions are still left to the discretion of individual users. In these cases, the base station's only power control function is to enforce the operating point chosen by the users (MacKenzie, 2001).

Repeated Game in Physical Layer

Another power control game model is a repeated game (MacKenzie, 2001). In this game, the players are assumed to be not myopic, but consider the impact of their current actions on future play. Usually, the game-theoretic analysis has assumed that the power control game is a one-shot game. In other words, users are myopic; their only concern is the current value of the utility function. These users are unable to consider the consequences of their actions on future iterations. In order to allow cooperation to develop between users, it is important to model the power control game as a repeated game. By modeling the situation as a repeated game, a user who cheats in the current time slot may be punished by the other users in future time slots. In addition, to modeling the situation as a repeated game, the power control game has an infinite horizon. As long as no user exceeds the desired received power, the system operates normally. If a user has exceeded the desired receive power, the rest of the users will punish the wayward user by increasing their powers to the Nash equilibrium of the one-shot game. Once adequate punishment has been dispensed, the system returns to normal. Finally, users who play this strategy are playing a subgame perfect equilibrium (MacKenzie, 2001).

Auction Game in Physical Layer

Recent advances in wireless decentralized and ad-hoc networking have led to an increasing attention on studying physical layer based security. The basic idea of physical layer security is to exploit the physical characteristics of the wireless channel to provide secure communications. The security is quantified by secrecy rate, which is defined as the maximum rate of reliable information from the source to the destination with no information obtained by the eavesdroppers. Auction theory, as a kind of game theory, was developed for the analysis from the perspective of incomplete information game. Nowadays, auction game models have been used in many applications for their simplicity, operability and fairness. In 2012, Tianyu Wang et al proposed a new sequential first-price auction and the Vickrey auction to allocate the relay power in a cognitive relay network (Wang, Song, Han, Cheng & Jiao, 2012). They considered an interference tolerant cognitive radio network in which a single primary user shares its frequency band with multiple pairs of secondary users and a one-way relay, with limited interference to the primary users. In this cognitive relay scenario, the total secrecy rate is intensively affected by the power allocation strategies of the relay. In other words, the transmit power of the relay needs efficient distribution for maximizing the sum secrecy rate of the secondary user pairs, meanwhile satisfying the interference constraint at the single primary user. To solve the relay power allocation

problem, they developed two multi-object auctions (i.e. the Vickrey auction) and the sequential first-price auction, and proved the existence of only equilibrium for each auction. It can be seen that the system secrecy rate curve of the Vickrey auction gradually coincides with that of the optimal allocation with increasing power units, while the sequential first-price auction reflects more fairness (Wang, 2012)

DATA LINK LAYER

In a multi-user wireless communication network, the transmitting nodes share the limited radio resources. Therefore, one critical issue is how the nodes share these resources to transmit data so that the optimal network performance can be achieved (Akkarajitsakul, Hossain, Niyato, & Kim, 2011). The medium access control problem, with many users contending for access to a shared communications medium, leads itself naturally to a game theoretic formulation. In these medium access control games, selfish users seek to maximize their utility by obtaining an unfair share of access to the channel (Srivastava, 2005). Various game models are considered under different scenarios, perspectives, or assumptions on transmitting nodes' behavior. The common aim of these models is to improve network performance such as throughput maximization, resource consumption minimization, and QoS guarantee.

Multiple access methods developed for wireless networks can be divided into five main groups, namely, Time-Division Multiple Access (TDMA), Frequency-Division Multiple Access (FDMA), and Code Division Multiple Access (CDMA), ALOHA, and Carrier Sense Multiple Access (CSMA)-based wireless networks. To develop multiple access methods, game theory has become a very useful mathematical tool to obtain solutions for resource allocation, channel assignment, power control, and cooperation enforcement among the nodes (Akkarajitsakul, 2011).

Figure 1. Basic concept of TDMA

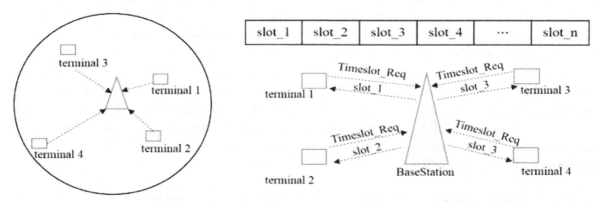

Game Models in TDMA

In TDMA, time is divided into fixed-length frames and each frame is divided into multiple time slots. Time slots are allocated to the nodes for data transmission. In TDMA, synchronization among the nodes is required to avoid interference (Figure 1).

In the channel access games for TDMA, nodes compete with each other to obtain time slots for their transmissions. Time slot allocation among the nodes is performed by using various game models. Game models can be formulated in which the nodes are able to choose transmission power in their allocated time slots. In TDMA access games nodes compete for time slots to achieve their objectives and meet QoS requirements. Noncooperative static game, auction game, dynamic game, and repeated game models can be applied for TDMA. To enforce cooperation among the nodes, a punishment and truth telling mechanism can be used (Akkarajitsakul, 2011).

In TDMA-based networks, one node could directly trade its own resource, e.g., data symbols and power for its cooperative partners relaying. Considering both the nodes are willing to cooperate in negotiating transactions and making the decisions, we can formulate the problem of fair resource sharing as a two-person bargaining game. In this game, each node is willing to seek cooperative relaying only if the channel capacity achieved through cooperation will not be lower than that achieved through noncooperation by utilizing the same amount of resource. In 2011, Guopeng Zhang et al proposed a new two-person cooperative game to perform the resource allocation for TDMA based commercial cooperative communication networks. In this game, one selfish node could trade its own resource (i.e., data symbols and power) for its cooperative partner's relaying directly. And both the nodes are willing to achieve an optimal channel capacity increase through cooperative relaying. They also proved that Nash bargaining solution based resource allocation is fair and Pareto optimal solution (Zhang, Yang, Liu, & Enjie, 2011).

Game Models in FDMA

In FDMA, radio frequency band is divided into multiple channels. The channels are allocated to the nodes for data transmission. In the channel access games for FDMA, most of the models consider how nodes (with single or multiple radio interfaces) choose channels for transmission (Figure 2).

In these game formulations, the number of radios, transmit rate, and power rate assigned to each channel correspond to nodes' actions. In FDMA, nodes compete for the available channels in the

Figure 2. Basic concept of FDMA

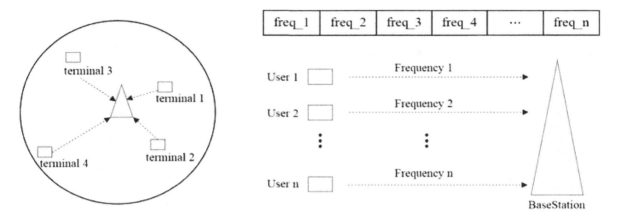

network. The solution in terms of equilibrium can be achieved for the complete and incomplete information cases. Non-cooperative static game, auction game, and cooperative game models can be used for FDMA (Akkarajitsakul, 2011).

Single-carrier frequency division multiple access (SC-FDMA) is suitable for the uplink transmission because of its low peak-to-average power ratio (PAPR) property compared to orthogonal frequency division multiple access (OFDMA). In SC-FDMA, the system capacity can be increased by allocating subcarriers to users who are in a good channel condition. However, if too many subcarriers are allocated to the single user in a good channel condition, the fairness among users degrades. The system capacity and fairness are in a tradeoff relation. To solve this tradeoff problem, the resource allocation based on Nash bargaining solution in the cooperative game theory has recently been studied. In 2012, Yusuke Sato et al proposed a reduced complexity suboptimal NBS based subcarrier allocation, which requires lower computational complexity while achieving the system capacity and fairness among users similar to the NBS (Sato, Ryusuke, Obara, & Adachi, 2012).

Game Models in CDMA

Future generations of broadband wireless mobile systems will aim to support a wide range of services and bit rates by employing a variety of techniques capable of achieving the highest possible spectrum efficiency. Code-division multiple access (CDMA) schemes have been considered as attractive multiple access schemes in both second-generation (2G) and third-generation (3G) wireless systems. In CDMA, multiple nodes can transmit data on the same channel simultaneously. The transmitted data by each node is encoded by using a unique spreading code. The spreading codes for the different users are orthogonal/near-orthogonal to each other. The receiver of each node can decode the original data correctly if the signal-to-interference-plus-noise ratio (SINR) is maintained above a threshold. In a CDMA system, each node is assigned with a different code to allow multiple users to be multiplexed over the same channel at the same time (Akkarajitsakul, 2011) (Figure 3).

Usually, signals of other users can be modeled as interfering noise signals, and the major goal of this system is to achieve a certain signal-to-

Figure 3. Basic concept of CDMA

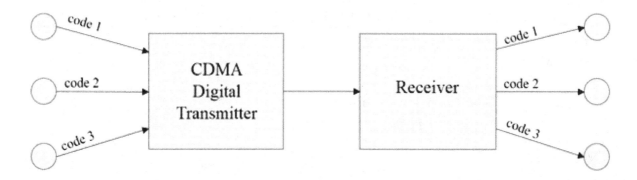

interference (SIR) ratio regardless of channel conditions while minimizing the interference due to user transmission power level. Hence, power control plays an even more crucial role in such systems. There are two major reasons for a user to exercise power control: the first one is the limit on the battery energy available to the mobile, and the second reason is the increase in capacity, which can be achieved by minimizing the interference. Power control in CDMA systems are in either open-loop or closed-loop form. In open-loop power control, the mobile regulates its transmitted power inversely proportional to the received power. In closed-loop power control, on the other hand, commands are transmitted to the mobile over the downlink to increase or decrease its uplink power (Alpcan, Basar, Srikant, & Altman, 2002). Recently, game theory has been used to study power control in CDMA networks and has been shown to be a very effective tool for examining this problem. Traditionally, in a CDMA system with self-interested nodes, the transmission power control can be modeled as complete and incomplete information non-cooperative games. In these games, each user needs to decide how much power to transmit over each carrier to maximize its overall utility. The utility function has been defined as the overall throughput divided by the total transmission power over all the carriers and has units of bits per joule. Also, cooperative game model for group-rational nodes can be used to achieve a Pareto optimal power control strategy (Akkarajitsakul, 2011).

Game Models in ALOHA

ALOHA protocol is the first random access protocol described in the literature for MAC layer. Despite of the bounty of works and efforts investigated in analyzing aloha-like protocols, Aloha is still an ideal tool to understand wireless behavior and users selfishness. In ALOHA, if a node has a packet to send, it will attempt to transmit the packet immediately. If the packet collides with packets from other nodes, the node will retransmit the packet later. The ALOHA protocol can be operated in a slotted fashion, in which case, time is divided into slots, and packet transmissions are aligned with the time slots.

When multiple users share a common channel and contend for access, a typical conflict problem arises. Recently, the selfish behavior of users in MAC protocols has been widely analyzed using game theory with all its powerful solution concepts. In most of the ALOHA-like game models, the nodes can choose either 'To transmit' or 'not to transmit' as their possible actions and the transmission powers of the nodes are assumed to be fixed. Then, the games have mixed strategy solutions. Non-cooperative game, cooperative game, evolutionary game, and Stackelberg game models can be used for ALOHA-like channel access. For the majority of the models, the solution is a threshold strategy. Along with channel access, power control and rate adaptation are also considered in the models. Some of the games can be shown to have solutions which are threshold strategies (Akkarajitsakul, 2011).

In 2008, Cho and Tobagi proposed two different types of Aloha games - cooperative and non-cooperative games. If mobile terminals cooperate to maximize a common objective of all mobile terminals, the game is called a cooperative Aloha game. On the other hand, mobile terminals may be selfish so that they are interested in maximizing their own payoffs instead of the common objective. This type of game is a non-cooperative Aloha game. The analysis results for these game models showed that the optimal strategies for cooperative games and Bayesian Nash Equilibria (BNEs) for non-cooperative games may have a specific form, a threshold strategy. They showed that a BNE for the non-cooperative game is always a threshold strategy along, and proved the existence and uniqueness of a BNE for the non-cooperative game (Cho, & Tobagi, 2008). In 2009, Sabir et al proposed a new non-cooperative hierarchical system based on the Stackelberg game concept. They considered a wireless system composed of one central receiver and several selfish transmitters communicating via the slotted aloha protocol. Each user tends to maximize his own throughput or minimize his expected delay of backlogged packets depending on his transmission probability and transmission probabilities of other users in the network. The main objective of this model is to improve the performance of slotted aloha-like protocols by introducing a hierarchy mechanism (Sabir, El-Azouzi, & Hayel, 2009). They showed that the performance, either in terms of throughput and delay of any player was improved compared to a system without hierarchy (i.e., Nash game).

Game Models in CSMA

CSMA is a probabilistic medium access method in which a node senses the status of the channel before attempting transmission. If the channel is idle, the node initiates a transmission attempt. If the transmission is unsuccessful due to a collision, the node waits for a packet retransmission interval and transmits again. Two of the improved variants of CSMA are CSMA with collision detection (CSMA/CD) and CSMA with collision avoidance (CSMA/CA). In CSMA/CD, assuming that a node is able to detect a collision, a transmission is terminated as soon as a collision is detected. The collision can be avoided by expanding the retransmission interval for the node to wait before a new transmission. If the channel is sensed busy before transmission, to decrease the probability of collisions on the channel, transmission is postponed for a random period of time (Figure 4).

In CSMA/CA games, the nodes in the network choose their backoff windows so that the equilibrium point can be achieved (Akkarajitsakul, 2011) (Figure 5).

Non-cooperative static game, non-cooperative dynamic game, and repeated game models have been proposed for modeling such CSMA environment in which users can select to transmit or to wait using a transmission probability. In cooperative games, each player has some knowledge about other players' actions and makes his decision accordingly. As this assumption is not always valid in wireless networks, it must be investigated that how the characteristics of wireless networks influence the decision making process of players and the resulting equilibria. The researches have shown that cooperative random access games can use radio resources more efficiently and fairly than non-cooperative ones. Thus to achieve an efficient and fair system with low collision, reception of control messages from other nodes seems necessary. It should be noted that message passing between nodes is based on cooperation assumption with the purpose of acquiring a system with a global goal. In addition, since the nodes can be selfish, a penalizing mechanism is required for the misbehaving nodes. Game theory mechanisms help to reward the generous users and punish the selfish users to obtain the global goal.

Figure 4. Basic concept of CSMA/CD

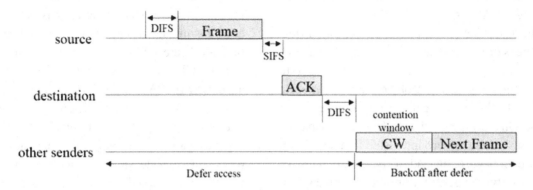

Figure 5. Basic concept of CSMA/CA

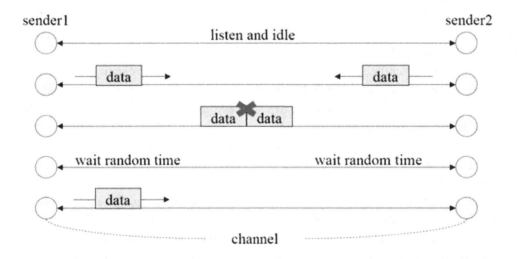

When nodes misbehave and try to monopolize the wireless channel, they are punished. Punishment mechanism has been presented to lead the system act around a Nash equilibrium that is also Pareto optimal (Ghazvini, Movahedinia, Jamshidi, & Moghim, 2010).

NETWORK LAYER

Functionalities of the network layer include the establishment and updating of routes and the forwarding of packets along those routes. Issues such as the presence of selfish nodes in a network, convergence of different routing techniques as the network changes, and the effects of different node behavior on routing, have been analyzed using game theory (Srivastava, 2005).

Forwarding Game in Network Layer

In wireless ad hoc routing games, players are usually the nodes themselves and the utility function is highly related to the energy consumption as well. In many cases, the term forwarding game is used to specify a game where the nodes decide whether to forward a packet for another node or not. In other words, forwarding game is designed to study how cooperation can be elicited from the nodes in a non-cooperative ad hoc network. Nowadays, a lot of forwarding game models have been presented in order to examine the cooperation level of such networks and identify their equilibria (Pavlidou, & Koltsidas, 2008). The packet-forwarding game belongs to the category of repeated non-cooperative games where the players play the game based on selfish considerations. When a node in ad hoc networks intends to send a packet to a destination node, it will need the help of other nodes to relay the packet if the destination node is located more than one hop away. A packet-forwarding game is often formed with a network consisting of a finite number of nodes operating in discrete time. The main operations a node can undertake are: i) initiating the transmission of its own packet, ii) relaying packets for other nodes, or iii) receiving packets from other nodes. Assuming that all the nodes are selfish and rational, a variety of strategies exist in the packet relaying operation. Since the nodes are mobile and usually have limited power supply, a major concern of each node is to preserve its battery power in order to stay operational for a longer period of time. Thus, expending one's own energy to relay packets for another node is considered unfavorable by a selfish and rational node in the absence of any incentive/punitive mechanism. In order to evaluate whether a node behaves cooperatively, its action when forwarding a packet needs to be observed by others. Most existing research work assumes that the nodes are capable of promiscuously listening to the transmissions of other nodes within its one-hop communication range. Therefore, the payoff of the packet-forwarding game will include the possible future gains from maintaining a reputation of being trustworthy through the altruistic act of relaying packets for other nodes (Urpi, Bonuccelli, & Giodano, 2003).

Bayesian Game in Network Layer

In order to extend the forwarding game models to form dynamic stage games with incomplete information, Nurmi (Nurmi, 2004) proposed a new dynamic Bayesian game. This game with discrete time approach demands that each node keeps track of all packets; they have sent in each time slot to each one of its neighbors. Again, each node has a belief about the other nodes' energy classes. A source uses the beliefs about the forwarders' energy classes to decide if it will send a packet. Similarly, a relay node uses its belief about the source's energy class to decide if it will forward the packet or not. However, these beliefs are not arbitrary; they are dependent on the packets sent by each node. What is interesting in this model is that the strategy of each node is not fixed or predetermined according to an algorithm, but it is a probability, whose distribution depends on the history of the game, the energy classes of the nodes and the actions of other nodes. The information collected by each node about the other nodes' status increases with time and the beliefs are updated using the Bayes' rule. The subgame perfect and perfect bayesian equilibria can be used to analyze the model under specific functions (Pavlidou, 2008).

Minimax Game in Network Layer

Minimax Games were proposed by using a different approach (Zakiuddina, Hawkins, & Moffat, 2005). This game is modeled as a zero sum game between two players – the set of routers and the network itself. In a minimax game, all nodes in the network constitute a single player (i.e., the set-of-routers) that runs the routing protocol or technique. This player's move consists in sending all the routing messages specified by the routing protocol. The second player (i.e., the network) changes the network topology by deciding which link between nodes will be up and active. The set-of-routers wins the game if all nodes maintain a correct view of the network when the game ends. On the other hand, the network wins if the nodes are mistaken about the network status and are unable to obtain the correct one. The game has an equilibrium when the min-max value of any player's payoff is equal to its max-min value. In a zero-sum game, the max-min value is defined as the maximum value that the maximizing player can get under the assumption that the minimizing player's objective is to minimize the payoff to the maximizing player (Pavlidou, 2008).

Bottleneck Game in Network Layer

An interesting view on routing modeling formulated a bottleneck game (Banner, & Orda, 2007). In conventional approaches to routing games, the performance is considered the sum of link cost functions. In bottleneck games, the bottleneck objectives are only characterized by the worst link. The target is to study the performance of a network where users route their traffic selfishly, aiming to optimize the performance of their bottlenecks. This gives rise to a non-cooperative game (Pavlidou, 2008). Bottleneck games emerge in many practical scenarios. One major framework is wireless networks, where each node has a limited battery so that the system objective is to maximize the minimum battery lifetime in the network while each user would route traffic so as to maximize the smallest battery lifetime along its routing topology. Traffic engineering is another major framework where bottleneck games are encountered. For example, in view of the limited size of transmission buffers, each of the users is interested in minimizing the utilization of its most utilized buffer in order to avoid deadlocks and reduce packet loss. Similarly, in congested networks, it is often desirable to minimize the utilization of the most utilized links so as to

move traffic away from congested hot spots to less utilized parts of the network. Other scenarios where bottleneck games appear can be found in frameworks where users attempt to enhance the ability to survive malicious attacks. Since such attacks are naturally aimed against the links (or nodes) that carry the largest amount of traffic, each user would be interested in minimizing the maximum amount of traffic that a link transfers in its routing topology (Banner, 2007).

Inter-Cluster Routing Game in Network Layer

Inter-cluster routing is formulated as a game theoretical model to study inter-cluster routing in sensor networks (Kannan, Ray, Kalidindi, & Iyengar, 2004). In this model, the effects of path length and path energy cost are considered at the same time. Although the shortest path is generally desirable, it is not the best option from the energy efficiency point of view. The inter-cluster routing game consists of a set of leader nodes (the cluster-heads) and sensor nodes. The players are the sensor nodes who should decide to forward a packet or not to another sensor mode. Based on the forwarding decisions of the sensor nodes, a path is formed for every source-destination pair of leader nodes (Pavlidou, 2008).

There are a lot of game theoretic models on the routing issue, which have been studied in wired and wireless networks. Usually, performance criteria of routing games are soundness, convergence and network overhead. Soundness is whether routers have a correct view of the network to make the correct routing decisions under frequent network changes. Convergence represents the length of time taken by the routers to have a correct view of the network topology as nodes move. Finally network overhead means the amount of data exchanged among routers to achieve convergence (Srivastava, 2005).

TRANSPORT LAYER

At the transport layer, game theoretic models have been developed to analyze the robustness of congestion control algorithms to the presence of selfish nodes in the network (Srivastava, 2005). Usually, the game formulated in the transport layer comprises nodes, which are capable of individually varying their congestion window with additive increase and multiplicative decrease parameters. The effect of such behavior in conjunction with buffer management policies implemented at the routers of wired networks has been studied for congestion control algorithms such as TCP-Reno, TCP-Tahoe and TCP-SACK. Most TCP protocols based on the game approach study on node selfish behaviors, especially evaluate the impact of greedy end-point behavior through a game-theoretic analysis of TCP. Each flow attempts to maximize the throughput, which is achieves by modifying its congestion control behavior (Feng, Zhang, Liu, Zhou, & Zhang, 2008).

Evolutionary Game in Transport Layer

Y. Zheng and Z. Feng presented an evolutionary game theoretic model for the resource competition among TCP flows in the Internet (Zheng, & Feng, 2001). In this evolutionary game model, TCP users select proper strategy and try to maximize their own payoff function in the resource competition game. Therefore, they compete for limited network resources. So, there is only one population of the players. The strategy set of TCP users in stage game is i) doubling congestion window (cwnd) per RTT in the slow-start phase, ii) cwnd increase one packet per RTT in congestion-avoidance phase, iii) cwnd decreases to one half of its current value. Evolutionary games involve strategic interaction over time. At any point in time, the strategic interaction is expressed as a stage game. Therefore, TCP users play the stage game when every ACK is received and every timeout is de-

tected. The stage game played by TCP users can be defined by a fitness or payoff function, which is the mean growth rate of cwnd. The dynamic adjustment process in TCP algorithm is: slow start, and then, cwnd is additively increased roughly every round trip time (RTT) until congestion is detected whereupon it is multiplicatively decreased. Congestion is detected by the loss of packets. The evolutionary game model in (Zheng, 2001). derived the relationship between the probability of packet loss and cwnd by using queueing theory and evolutionary game theory in a simple network topology (Zheng, 2001).

Minority Game in Transport Layer

In 2011, H. Kutsuna and S. Fujita proposed a new congestion control game model for high-speed communication networks, which attains a high communication throughput while keeping the fairness of the bandwidth assignment to the senders. The basic idea of this model is to adopt a minority game to realize a selective reduction of the transmission speed. More concretely, all senders play a game upon detecting congestion, and the transmission speed of each sender is reduced according to the results of the game. Minority game is a game that has recently attracted considerable attention in the field of complex systems, and it is known to have the remarkable property where the number of winners decreases to half of the number of players in spite of the selfish behavior of the players to increase its own profit. This approach significantly improves the throughput of AIMD while realizing a sufficiently fair reduction of the transmission speed (Kutsuna, & Fujita, 2011). This model can be extended for wireless ad hoc networks. However, when applying the congestion control algorithms developed for wired networks to wireless networks, it is necessary to consider the impact of the wireless medium on TCP. Due to mobility and packet losses caused by impairments of the wireless medium, link failures could inadvertently trigger a change in the congestion window. In the development of a TCP congestion control game, it will be necessary for a node to consider this effect before making its decision on setting the congestion control parameters (Srivastava, 2005).

APPLICATION LAYER

Based on the selfish behavior by nodes in wireless networks, incentive mechanisms are proposed to steer nodes towards constructive behavior. Emerging research in game theory applied to analyze the effectiveness of these incentive models (Srivastava, 2005). In such a model, a node is credited for cooperating with the other nodes towards a common network goal, and is debited when requesting service from others. One way of implementing the charge and reward model is by the introduction of *virtual currency*. In this method each node is rewarded with 'tokens' for providing service, which are used by the node for seeking services from others (Srivastava, 2005). References develop incentive compatible, cheat-proof mechanisms that apply the principles of mechanism design to enforce node collaboration for routing in ad hoc networks. In addition, different pricing models are often used to engineer an equilibrium that is desirable from the network's perspective.

Another technique for creating incentives is the form of reputation that each node gains through providing services to others. Each node builds a positive reputation for itself by cooperating with others and is tagged as 'good-behaving'. Otherwise, it is tagged as 'mis-behaving'. The nodes that gain a bad reputation are isolated from the network over time. Game theory has been used for the analysis of a reputation exchange mechanism. According to this mechanism, a node assigns reputation values to its neighbors based on its direct interactions with them and on indirect reputation information obtained from other nodes. This reputation mechanism is modeled as a complex node

strategy in a repeated game model. The analysis of this game approach helps to assess the robustness of the reputation model against different node strategies and derive conditions for cooperation (Srivastava, 2005). However, even though the bulk of work for incentive mechanism done in the past few years, it still is at a nascent stage.

Trust Game in Application Layer

Individual-level trust models are usually concerned with the computational methods used to evaluate the trustworthiness and reputation of a node based on the observed past behavior pattern. In these models, if a node of undesirable behavior is observed by another node, the observer will decrease the reputation of the node by adjusting the past evidence recorded. In a wireless communication system, the interaction among the nodes may have a degree of continuity. Therefore, dishonest behavior could result in losing utility from potential punishments imposed by other nodes or being isolated from the network. Thus, an effective system-level trust model should include punitive measures in their interaction protocols to deter selfish or malicious behaviors (Srivastava, 2005).

Nodes in wireless communications systems may be highly mobile. This characteristic poses unique challenges to enforcing the incentive/punitive measures in the system-level trust models. For a network with highly mobile nodes, the neighbors of a node may change frequently. This results in the nodes having a smaller number of interactions with a large number of different partners. Furthermore, nodes may dynamically leave or join different networks. An effective system-level trust model should include trust evidence dissemination mechanisms which ensure the prompt sharing of past observations of each node across networks. In non-cooperative ad hoc networks formed by energy constrained devices belonging to different users, it is rational for these devices to behave selfishly when others request their help to relay packets in order to prolong their operational lifetime. In 2003, Urpi et al., (Urpi, 2003) proved that in the absence of any punitive measures, the nodes in a non-cooperative ad hoc network will eventually settle in an equilibrium state in which each node can only communicate with its one-hop neighbors. Therefore, cooperation stimulation mechanisms are needed to keep a non-cooperative ad hoc network from converging to this undesirable equilibrium.

SUMMARY

This chapter provides a tutorial survey on game theoretic approaches for wireless ad hoc wireless networks. Emerging research in game theory applied to wireless networks shows much promise to help understand the complex interactions between nodes in this highly dynamic and distributed network environment. Usually, the employment of game theory in ad hoc networks has led to the application of games with imperfect monitoring. Therefore, game theory can offer an effective tool to model adaptations that may occur at different layers in wireless networks.

REFERENCES

Akkarajitsakul, K., Hossain, E., Niyato, D., & Kim, D. (2011). Game Theoretic Approaches for Multiple Access in Wireless Networks: A Survey. *IEEE Communications Surveys & Tutorials*, *13*(3), 372–395. doi:10.1109/SURV.2011.122310.000119

Alpcan, T., Basar, T., Srikant, R., & Altman, E. (2002). CDMA Uplink Power Control as a Noncooperative Game. *Wireless Networks*, *8*, 659–670. doi:10.1023/A:1020375225649

Altman, E., El-Azouzi, R., Hayel, Y., & Tembine, H. (2010). Evolutionary Games in Wireless Networks. *IEEE Transactions on Systems, Man, and Cybernetics*, *40*(3), 634–646. doi:10.1109/TSMCB.2009.2034631 PMID:19963703

Banner, R., & Orda, A. (2007). Bottleneck routing games in communication networks. *IEEE Journal on Selected Areas in Communications*, *25*, 1173–1179. doi:10.1109/JSAC.2007.070811

Cho, Y., & Tobagi, F. A. (2008). Cooperative and Non-Cooperative Aloha Games with Channel Capture Global Telecommunications Conference. In *Proceedings of IEEE GLOBECOM*. IEEE.

Felegyhazi, M., & Hubaux, J.-P. (2006). *Game Theory in Wireless Networks: A Tutorial* (EPFL Technical Report: LCA-REPORT-2006-002). Lausanne, Switzerland: Ecole Polytechnique F´ed´erale de Lausanne.

Feng, H., Zhang, S., Liu, C., Zhou, Q., & Zhang, M. (2008). TCP Veno Connection Game Model on Non-Cooperative Game Theory. In *Proceedings of IEEE WiCOM'08*. IEEE.

Ghazvini, M., Movahedinia, N., Jamshidi, K., & Moghim, N. (2010). Game Theory Applications in CSMA Methods. In *Proceedings of IEEE Communications Surveys & Tutorials*. IEEE.

Goodman, D., & Mandayam, N. (1999). Power control for wireless data. In *Proceedings of IEEE Mobile Multimedia Communications (MoMuC'99)*, (pp. 55-63). IEEE.

Kannan, R., Ray, L., Kalidindi, R., & Iyengar, S. (2004). Max-min length-energyconstrained routing in wireless sensor networks. In *Proc. 1st EWSN 2004*, (pp. 19–21, 234–249). EWSN.

Kutsuna, H., & Fujita, S. (2011). A Fair and Efficient Congestion Avoidance Scheme Based on the Minority Game. *Journal of Information Processing Systems*, *7*(3), 531–542. doi:10.3745/JIPS.2011.7.3.531

MacKenzie, A. B., & Wicker, S. B. (2001). Game theory in communications: motivation, explanation, and application to power control. [IEEE.]. *Proceedings of IEEE GLOBECOM*, *01*, 821–826.

Mehta, S., & Kwak, K. S. (2009). Game Theory and Cognitive Radio Based Wireless Networks. [KES-AMSTA.]. *Proceedings of KES-AMSTA, 09,* 803–812.

Nurmi, P. (2004). Modelling routing in wireless ad hoc networks with dynamic bayesian games. In *Proc. 1st SECON 2004,* (pp. 63–70). SECON.

Pavlidou, F. N., & Koltsidas, G. (2008). Game theory for routing modeling in communication networks — A survey. *Journal of Communications and Networks, 10*(3), 268–286. doi:10.1109/JCN.2008.6388348

Sabir, E., El-Azouzi, R., & Hayel, Y. (2009). A hierarchical slotted aloha game. In *Proceedings of International Conference on Game Theory for Networks,* (pp. 222-231). Academic Press.

Sato, Y., Ryusuke, M., Obara, T., & Adachi, F. (2012). Nash bargaining solution based subcarrier allocation for uplink SC-FDMA distributed antenna network. In *Proceedings of IEEE International Network Infrastructure and Digital Content,* (pp. 76-80). IEEE.

Srivastava, V., Neel, J., MacKenzie, A. B., & Menon, R. (2005). Using game theory to analyze wireless ad hoc networks. *IEEE Communications Surveys & Tutorials, 7*(4), 46–56. doi:10.1109/COMST.2005.1593279

Tembine, H., Altman, E., ElAzouzi, E. R., & Sandholm, W. H. (2008). Evolutionary game dynamics with migration for hybrid power control in wireless communications. In *Proceedings of IEEE CDC,* (pp. 4479-4484). IEEE.

Urpi, A., Bonuccelli, M., & Giodano, S. (2003). Modeling cooperation in mobile ad-hoc networks: A formal description of selfishness. In *Proc. Model. Optim. Mobile Ad Hoc Wireless Netw.* Academic Press.

Wang, T., Song, L., Han, Z., Cheng, X., & Jiao, B. (2012). Power Allocation using Vickrey Auction and Sequential First-Price Auction Games for Physical Layer Security in Cognitive Relay Networks. [IEEE.]. *Proceedings of the IEEE, ICC,* 1683–1687.

Zakiuddina, I., Hawkins, T., & Moffat, N. (2005). Towards a game theoretic understanding of ad-hoc routing. *Electronic Notes in Theoretical Computer Science, 11,* 67–92. doi:10.1016/j.entcs.2004.07.009

Zhang, G., Yang, K., Liu, P., & Enjie, D. (2011). Achieving User Cooperation Diversity in TDMA-Based Wireless Networks Using Cooperative Game Theory. *IEEE Communications Letters, 15*(2), 154–156. doi:10.1109/LCOMM.2011.122010.100629

Zheng, Y., & Feng, Z. (2001). Evolutionary game and resources competition in the Internet. In *Proceedings of SIBCOM,* (pp. 51-52). SIBCOM.

KEY TERMS AND DEFINITIONS

Ad Hoc Routing Protocol: A convention, or standard, that controls how nodes decide which way to route packets between computing devices in a mobile ad hoc network.

IEEE 802.11: A set of media access control (MAC) and physical layer (PHY) specifications for implementing wireless local area network (WLAN) computer communication in the 2.4, 3.6, 5 and 60 GHz frequency bands. They are created and maintained by the IEEE LAN/MAN Standards Committee (IEEE 802).

Mobile Ad Hoc Network (MANET): A self-configuring infra-structureless network of mobile devices connected by wireless; ad hoc is Latin and means 'for this purpose'.

Service Set: A set consisting of all the devices associated with a consumer or enterprise IEEE 802.11 wireless local area network (WLAN). The Service set can be local, independent, extended or mesh.

Wi-Fi Direct: A Wi-Fi standard that enables devices to connect easily with each other without requiring a wireless access point and to communicate at typical Wi-Fi speeds for everything from file transfer to Internet connectivity.

Chapter 5
Game Theory for Smart Grid

ABSTRACT

A smart grid is a modernized electrical grid that uses analog or digital information and communications technology to gather and act on information, such as information about the behaviors of suppliers and consumers, in an automated fashion to improve the efficiency, reliability, economics, and sustainability of the production and distribution of electricity. Therefore, smart grid is an evolved grid system that manages electricity demand in a sustainable, reliable, and economic manner, built on advanced infrastructure and tuned to facilitate the integration of all involved. Roll-out of smart grid technology also implies a fundamental re-engineering of the electricity services industry, although typical usage of the term is focused on the technical infrastructure. This chapter explores this idea.

INTRODUCTION

The traditional power grids are generally used to carry power from a few central generators to a large number of users or customers. In contrast, the Smart Grid (SG), regarded as the next generation power grid, uses two-way flows of electricity and information to create a widely distributed automated energy delivery network. By utilizing modern information technologies, the SG is capable of delivering power in more efficient ways and responding to wide ranging conditions and events. Broadly stated, the SG could respond to events that occur anywhere in the grid. Usually, the term *grid* is used for an electricity system that may support all or some of the following operations: electricity generation, electricity transmission, electricity distribution, electricity control, consumption, and adopt the corresponding strategies. And, the term *smart* in SG implies that the grid has the intelligence to realize advanced management objectives and functionalities. Most of such objectives are related to energy efficiency improvement, supply and demand balance, emission control, operation cost reduction, and utility maximization. Therefore, SG covers the entire spectrum of the energy system from the generation to the end points of consumption of the electricity (Fang, Misra, Xue, & Yang, 2012).

In this chapter, we provide a number of game theoretic approaches to solve a wide variety of problems in SG. The proliferation of advanced technologies and services in SG systems implies that disciplines such as game theory will naturally become a prominent tool in the design and analysis of SG. In particular, game theoretic approach

DOI: 10.4018/978-1-4666-6050-2.ch005

focuses on the design of micro-grid systems, demand-side management, and communications in order to support the distributed nature of the SG. In the past few years, distributed game approach is taken into account to improved scalability and efficiency of the game-based solutions (Fadlullah, Nozaki, Takeuchi, & Kato, 2011). The advantages of applying distributed game-theoretic techniques in any complex system such as the SG are accompanied by key technical challenges. Usually, non-cooperative games can be used to perform distributed demand-side management and real-time monitoring or to deploy and control micro-grids. On the other hand, economical factors such as markets and dynamic pricing are an essential part of the SG. In this respect, non-cooperative games provide several frameworks ranging from classical non-cooperative Nash games to advanced dynamic games, which enable to optimize and devise pricing strategies that adapt to the nature of the grid (Saad, Han, Poor, & Başar, 2012).

GAME MODELS FOR DEMAND SIDE MANAGEMENT

Controlling and influencing energy demand can reduce the overall peak load demand, reshape the demand profile, and increase the grid sustainability by reducing the overall cost and carbon emission levels. Therefore, demand side management is an important function in energy management of the future smart grid. Efficient demand side management can potentially avoid the construction of an under-utilized electrical infrastructure in terms of generation capacity, transmission lines and distribution networks (Figure 1). Most conventional demand-side management approaches for SG mainly focus on the interactions between a utility company and its customers (Fadlullah, 2011).

Recently, a lot of researches carried out to present an autonomous and distributed demand-side energy management system based on game theory. The essence of demand-side management revolves around the interactions between various entities with specific objectives which are reminiscent of the players' interactions in game theory. Since lowering peak demand and smoothing demand profile shaping reduces overall plant and capital cost requirements, the electric utility can use real-time pricing to convince some users to reduce their power demands, so that the total demand profile full of peaks can be shaped to a nicely smoothed demand profile. In fact, game theory provides a plethora of tools that can be applied for pricing and incentive mechanisms, scheduling of appliances, and efficient interconnection of heterogeneous nodes.

Figure 1. Demand side management

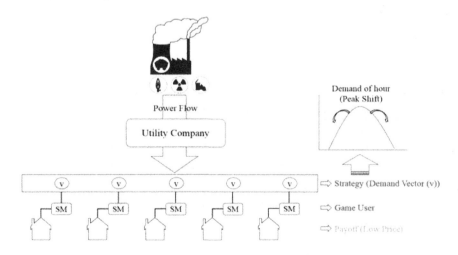

Scheduling Game for Demand-Side Management

In smart grids, an energy consumption scheduling game, which is a static non-cooperative game, is formulated in which the customers act as the players. The strategies of the players are the daily schedules of their household appliances and loads. The utility company can have appropriate pricing tariffs in order to differentiate the energy usage levels and durations. For a common scenario comprising a single utility company serving a number of customers, the global optimal performance in terms of minimizing the energy costs is achieved at the Nash equilibrium of the formulated energy consumption scheduling game. The players (i.e., customers) receive incentives to take part in the energy consumption scheduling game and to subscribe to this service. In the distributed demand-side energy management approach, each player applies his best response strategy to the current total load and tariffs of the SG (Fadlullah, 2011). The best response dynamics is an algorithm to find the Nash equilibrium. A best response algorithm mainly relies on a sequence of decisions in which each player chooses the strategy that maximizes its utility, given the current strategies of the other players. For the scheduling game, best response dynamics always converges to an equilibrium (Saad, 2012), (Mohsenian-Rad, Wong, Jatskevich, Schober, & Leon-Garcia, 2010).

Stackelberg Game for Demand-Side Management

Under multiple energy sources and the interactions among them, hierarchical games such as Stackelberg games are a good candidate to provide insights on the appliances' scheduling problem. This extension can lead to new challenges but also contributes to the deployment of smart demand-side management models that account for the aggregate user loads as well as the individual objectives of the users (Saad, 2012).

In 2013, Maharjan et al. proposed a Stackelberg game between utility companies and end-users to maximize the revenue of each utility company and the payoff of each user. The utility companies maximize their revenues by setting appropriate unit prices. The consumers choose power to buy from utility companies based on the unit prices. The payoff of each consumer depends on the prices set by all the sources. In turn, the price set by each utility company also depends on the prices of other utility companies. The utility companies play a non-cooperative game and the consumers find their optimal response to the utility companies' strategies. The interactions between the utility companies and the users are enabled by the bidirectional communications between them. Maharjan et al. derived analytical results for the Stackelberg equilibrium of the game and prove that a unique solution exists. They also developed a distributed algorithm which converges to the equilibrium with only local information available for both utility companies and end-users (Maharjan, Zhu, Zhang, Gjessing, & Basar, 2013).

Potential Game for Demand-Side Management

Using dynamic potential game theory, a novel game model was developed for the SG demand side management (Wu, Mohsenian-Rad, Huang, & Wang, 2011). This game model captures the self-interest of end users who participate in wind power integration over a substantial period of time. And then, the game model in (Wu, 2011) analyzes and coordinates the interactions among users to efficiently utilize the available renewable and conventional energy resources to minimize the total energy cost in the SG system. Further, it models the inter-temporal variations of the available wind power as a Markov chain based on field data. By applying backward induction, Nash equilibrium of the dynamic potential game is obtained. The closed-form expression was also developed to characterize the users' best strategies at the Nash equilibria of the formulated game model.

Differential Game for Demand-Side Management

Demand side management refers to the consumer side optimization so as to minimize the power cost as well as to reduce the burden for power grid. Consumers in the market maximize their utility by selecting an optimal demand response to the market price and their own need. The independent decision-making in a dynamic environment leads to a nonzero-sum differential game in which every user consumers to find an optimal demand policy to maximize its long term payoff. In 2012, Zhu et al. proposed a new differential game model for demand management in the smart grid. In this model, the system is comprised of two levels of problems. At the upper level, the demand response management device of each household purchases power from the market based on its demand and the price. At the lower level, the scheduler allocates its demanded power to multiple appliances. The decisions at each level are made by solving distributed optimization problems for each user or household. The distributed optimization at the upper level needs to take into account the price dynamics, which can be affected by the total demand of the users as well as the supply. Hence, the interdependence among the users leads to a dynamic game scenario that can be modeled by a N-person nonzero-sum differential game. The optimal power allocation within each household at the lower level, on the other hand, is decoupled from other users. Hence, the decisions at the lower level can be modeled by a static convex optimization model. They characterized the feedback Nash equilibrium of the game and obtained closed-form solutions for the homogeneous case (Zhu, Han, & Basar, 2012).

In conclusion, one of the key challenges of the future smart grid is designing demand-side management models that enable efficient management of the power supply and demand. Demand-side management schemes will always face technical challenges such as pricing, regulations, adaptive decision making, users' interactions, and dynamic operation. All of these issues are cornerstones to game theory, and, hence, this area is ripe for game theoretic techniques. In fact, demand-side management is perhaps the most natural setting for applying game theory due to the need of combining economical aspects such as pricing with strategic decision making by the various involved entities such as the suppliers and the consumers (Saad, 2012).

PRICING GAMES FOR SMART GRID LOAD BALANCING

In conventional energy market, the customers are expected to pay a fixed retail price for the consumed electricity. Generally, this retail pricing is changed based on the seasons or on a yearly basis. Therefore, flat pricing can lead to dead weight loss at off-peak times and excessive demand at the peak times that are not convenient for the utility provider. As a consequence, there may be short-term effects (small-scale blackouts) as well as long-term ones (excessive capacity build-up). Recently, non-cooperative price games have been proposed based on the class of atomic splittable flow games (Fadlullah, 2011). These price games demonstrated that consumer demand approaches to the Nash equilibrium operation points (Figure 2).

Stackelberg Game for Smart Grid Load Balancing

The smart grid must be also considered in order to realize a green cellular network. Since base stations are power hungry elements, absorbing them in the smart grid can significantly increase power efficiency. However, this important perspective has been ignored in the energy efficiency research on cellular networks. In 2012, a Stackelberg game

Figure 2. Pricing game for smart grid load balancing

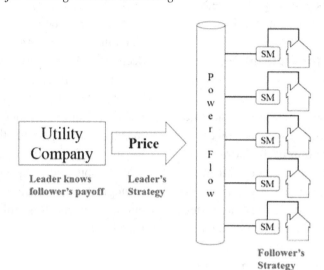

has been developed by Bu et al. for the decision problems of electricity price, energy-efficient power allocation and interference price. In this mode, multiple retailers provide the real-time electricity prices to the heterogeneous network due to market liberalization, and the macrocell base station and femtocell base stations adjust the amount of electricity by performing energy-efficient power allocation. As a three-level Stackelberg game, this approach models price decisions made by the electricity retailers, mitigates the interference effect, and guarantees QoS by using interference price. A backward induction method is used to analyze this Stackelberg game, since it can capture the sequential dependencies of the decisions in the stages of the game (Bu, & Yu, 2012).

Congestion Game for Smart Grid Load Balancing

From the SG system perspective, the overall objective is to smooth the electric demand curve and avoid overloading both the generating and distribution capacity of the grid. For the SG system, a network congestion game has been developed by modeling both demand and load using a directed

graph, in which the cost of a unit load over an edge depends on the total load over that edge (Fadlullah, 2011). Based on the capacity of the consumers, consumer' demands are managed in order to minimize a cost function or price. In the congestion game, the price levels are set for the demand vector of each player, and each player allocates demand as a response of other players' actions. In 2010, C. Ibars et al. demonstrated that congestion game can converge to a stable equilibrium point in a distributed manner (Ibars, Navarro, & Giupponi, 2010). They not only found the local optimum points of the Nash equilbria but also showed that it is possible to arrive at a global solution to the network problem by using the equivalence between the congestion and potential games (Fadlullah, 2011).

Matching Game for Smart Grid Load Balancing

In classical large-scale power systems, any energy mismatch between demand and generation is often assumed to be compensated. Therefore, it is of interest to have a mechanism which enables a distributed operation taking into account the individual constraints and objectives of each component. Most researches for traditional power systems deal either with managing the load (demand-side) or the energy source (supply-side). Smart grid can capture both the competition over the energy resources. To implement this mechanism, non-cooperative matching game approach can control both the loads and energy sources in a small-scale power system. For the strategic matching game between sources and loads in a SG system, the solution concept is also Nash equilibrium (Saad, 2012).

Population Game for Smart Grid Load Balancing

In the recent literature, large population games have been studied for the SG management (Zhu, & Basar, 2011). Based on the deterministic linear-quadratic differential game, the large population behavior was studied by taking the limit as a number of players go infinity, in the closed form solution of the game. Usually, a mean-field approach is used to study large population stochastic differential games by coupling a forward Fokker-Planck-Kolmogorov (FPK) equation together with a backward Hamilton-Jacobi-Bellman (HJB) equation. The population game model in (Zhu, 2011) was developed as a two-level multi-resolution game in which the inter-group interactions were analyzed using a mean-field approach, while the intra-group interactions were analyzed using a limiting approach. This approach can capture the macroscopic and microscopic interactions among a large population of players for SG demand response management.

DYNAMIC GAMES FOR SMART GRID

Many of the existing models for smart grid systems have focused on classical static non-cooperative games. However, it is of interest to investigate

dynamic game models both in cooperative and non-cooperative settings. The motivation for studying dynamic models stems from the pervasive presence of time-varying parameters in smart grids such as generation, demand, among others. Usually, dynamic game theory could be a cornerstone for capturing these parameters and designing better algorithms for improving the economical and technical aspects of future smart grids (Saad, 2012).

Sequential Games for Smart Grid

Perfect information dynamic games refer to the games having sequential move order and, in each round of the game, the player has the knowledge of the moves made by other players. In 2011, Aristidou et al. proposed a new dynamic sequential game model to provide a game formulation consisting of complete information so that each player's revenue function becomes common knowledge (Aristidou, Dimeas, & Hatziargyriou, 2011). In this model, there is an aggregator entity (i.e., electrical company) having the responsibility of satisfying the customers' energy demand. The aggregator is considered to be able to purchase energy from the primary power plant and also the distributed generation units of the smart grid. All the distributed generation units and the customers are considered to be equipped with smart meters which can receive signals from the aggregator. Therefore, the smart meters are assumed as players, and they play the game with the aggregator with the objective of maximizing their respective revenues. Therefore, multiple players interact with one another while striving to fulfill their goals (Fadlullah, 2011).

Hierarchical Game for Smart Grid

Another dynamic game was proposed for the SG management (Zhu, 2012). In this model, a two-layer optimization approach was established as a hierarchical model. At the lower level, for each player (i.e., household), different appliances are scheduled for energy consumption. At the upper level, dynamic game is used to capture the interaction among different players in their demand responses through the market price. This game model jointly considered the direct load control and demand management in response to market price. The market price was formulated by using the sticky price dynamics, so that the load requests from different players can influence the current price. Moreover, a stochastic random variable is added to the dynamics so as to characterize the price volatility. The independent decision-making in a dynamic environment leads to a non zero-sum dynamic game model in which every player seeks to find an optimal demand policy to maximize its long term payoff. The stage utility function of players is determined by the outcome of the optimal power allocation for scheduling their appliances. This two-level game model characterized the feedback Nash equilibrium of the game and obtained closed-form (Zhu, 2012).

Cooperative Game for Smart Grid

The future smart grid is envisioned to encompass a large number of micro-grids elements. The concept of a micro-grid is defined as a networked group of distributed energy sources such as solar panels or wind turbines located at the distribution network side. These sources can provide energy to small geographical areas. Whenever some micro-grids have an excess of power while others have a need for power, it might be beneficial for these micro-grids to exchange energy among each other instead of requesting it from the main grid. Energy exchange between nearby micro-grids can significantly reduce the amount of power. Thus, it is of interest to devise a model that enables such a local energy trade between micro-grid elements that are in need of energy (i.e., buyers) and micro-grids that have an excess of energy to transfer (i.e., sellers) (Saad, 2012) (Figure 3).

Nowadays, cooperative games are used to introduce a cooperative energy exchange mechanism in future grids. Usually, the micro-grids may want

Figure 3. Cooperative game for Smart Grid

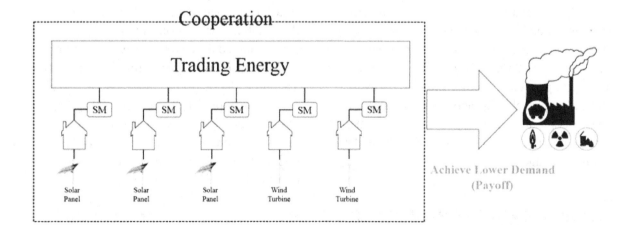

to form a cooperative group, (i.e., a coalition), which constitutes a local energy exchange market. Inside this coalition, the micro-grids can transfer power locally among each other thus reducing the power losses and improving the autonomy of the micro-grid network. Depending on their location and their power needs, the micro-grids have an incentive and a mutual benefit to cooperate so as to trade power locally within their given distribution network.

Auction Game for Smart Grid

To address how to match the sellers to the buyers while optimizing performance, there is one main game theoretic branch: auction theory (Saad, 2012). Auction theory is essentially an analytical framework used to study the interactions between a number of sellers and a number of buyers. The outcome of the auction is the price at which the trade takes place as well as the amount of good sold to each buyer. One suitable framework to model the matching between buyers and sellers could be through the use of a double auction. Nowadays, auction games are adopted to allocate load demands among customers while maximizing the social welfare in SG systems. Whether a micro-grid acts as a seller or a buyer is dependent on its current generation and demand state. In an auction game, buyers and sellers are players. The strategies of every player correspond to the price at which it is willing to buy/sell energy and the quantity that it wishes to sell/buy. The objective of each player is to determine the optimal quantity and price at which it wants to trade so as to optimize its objective function. Therefore, outcome of this auction determines the prices and quantities traded in the coalition (Saad, 2012). In 2011, Li et al. proposed a repeated Vickrey auction model to solve scheduling problem in smart grid. They showed that truthful bidding is a weakly dominant strategy for all customers in a one shot Vickrey auction. In addition, they also showed that if the utility introduce a positive reserve price, the

Vickrey auction becomes more robust to collusion by customers and the resulting unique Bayesian Nash equilibrium guarantees the basic profit of the utility (Li, Jayaweera, & Naseri, 2011).

ENERGY STORAGE MANAGEMENT IN SMART GRID

In smart grid, storage devices may be used to compensate for the variability of typical renewable electricity generation including wind, wave, and solar energy. If all the individual homes decide to store their electricity and charge their batteries at the same time, there will be a higher peak in demand in the electricity market. This would lead to potential power blackouts, infrastructure damage, and higher carbon emission to environment. To address these various issues involving storage agents in SG, multi-agent systems paradigm was proposed; multiple self-interested parties interact through smart meters. The paradigm provides a game-theoretic framework to study storage strategies that agents may adopt. Based on the normal electricity usage profile of all the customers in the considered SG, it is possible to compute the Nash equilibrium points, which describe when it is best for the agents to charge their batteries, use their stored electricity, or use electricity from the SG (Fadlullah, 2011) (Figure 4).

Scheduling Game for Energy Storage Management

The scheduling game in a SG system focuses on how the customers can schedule their appliances so as to minimize their billing charges. The underlying assumption was that the customers are acquiring energy so as to immediately use it for their appliances. However, in future SGs, energy storage is expected to be a key component in smart homes; it has a strong impact on demand-side management. For example, a customer may decide to store energy during off-peak hours and

Figure 4. Energy storage management in Smart Grid

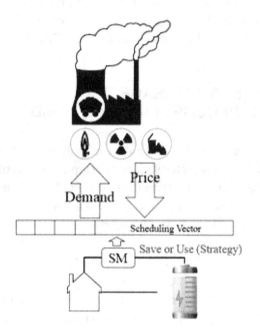

Game Theoretic Approach for Energy Storage Management

In 2013, Atzeni et al. proposed a new game model to control some kind of distributed energy storage devices (Atzeni, Ordóñez, Scutari, Palomar, & Fonollosa, 2013). Using a general energy pricing model, they tackled the grid optimization design from two different perspectives: a user-oriented optimization and a holistic-based design. In the former case, they optimized each user individually by formulating the grid optimization problem as a non-cooperative game, whose solution analysis was addressed building on the theory of variational inequalities. In the latter case, they focused instead on the joint optimization of the whole system, allowing some cooperation among the users. For both formulations, they devised distributed and iterative algorithms providing the optimal production/storage strategies of the users, along with their convergence properties. Both developed approaches allowed to compute the optimal strategies of the users in a distributed fashion and with limited information exchange between the central unit and the demand-side of the network. In addition, these two methods are valid for a general energy pricing model (Atzeni, 2013).

LEARNING BASED GAMES FOR SMART GRID

The future smart grid is envisioned as a large scale cyber-physical system encompassing advanced power, communications, control, and computing technologies. To accommodate these technologies, it will have to build on solid mathematical tools that can ensure an efficient and robust operation of such heterogeneous and large-scale cyber-physical systems. Clearly, game-theoretic approaches present a promising tool for the analysis of smart

use this stored energy to schedule its appliances, instead of obtaining this energy directly from the substation during peak hours. The introduction of smart home storage systems could significantly improve the energy-efficiency of the electricity market. In 2012, Saad proposed a new scheduling game to optimize the storage profile under a certain scheduled load (Saad, 2012). Through the agent-based learning strategies, it is demonstrated how the agents would be able to learn to purchase the most profitable storage capacity. Learning algorithm developed in this model does not rely solely on the day-ahead predictions, but adopts techniques from stochastic games to model the demand-side management problem with storage. Furthermore, through evolutionary game theoretic analysis, it is also revealed that prediction can be made on the portion of the population that would actually acquire storage capacity to maximize their savings (Saad, 2012).

grid systems. One of the most important solution concepts for game theory is equilibrium. To reach a desired equilibrium, an important aspect is to develop learning algorithms that enable the players. Essentially, a learning mechanism is an iterative process in which each iteration involves three key steps performed by every player; 1) observing the environment and current game state, 2) estimating the prospective utility, and 3) updating the strategy based on the observations (Saad, 2012). Recently, fictitious play, regret matching and several advanced learning algorithms have been studied for learning the equilibria of a game-theoretic model. Fictitious play refers to a family of iterative learning algorithms. At each iteration, each player is able to observe the actions of all other players and attempts to maximize its utility. Therefore, each player can subsequently select its optimal strategy, in a given iteration. It is shown that fictitious play always converges to a Nash equilibrium. Regret matching is a type of learning algorithm in which the players attempt to minimize their regret from using a certain action, i.e., the difference between the utility of always playing a certain action and the utility that they achieve by playing their current strategy. Reinforcement learning and stochastic learning algorithms are also used in various game-theoretic scenarios to find a desirable state of the system (Saad, 2012).

In classical game theoretic designs, one of the underlying assumptions is that the players are rational to optimize its individual utility. However, the underlying assumption of rationality is often unrealistic; one or more nodes might deviate from the intended play and make non-rational decisions. These inaccurate strategy choices can eventually lead to a non-convergence to the desired equilibrium and, impact the overall control system stability. To reach a certain equilibrium, the players must follow well-defined rules that enables them to observe the current game state and make a decision on their strategy choices. Therefore, learning is an integral part of game theory, and it lies at the heart of designing stable

and efficient models. In practical control systems such as the smart grid, individual nodes of the SG system interact with their strategies. When designing game-theoretic models for the smart grid, it is an important aspect to develop the learning mechanism, which enables the players to reach a certain desired game outcome design (Saad, 2012).

Evolutionary Game for Smart Grid

In 2012, Miorandi et al. proposed a new learning game model for SG systems (Miorandi, & De Pellegrini, 2012). This model relied extensively on concepts and tools from evolutionary games theory, and focused on distributed control mechanism that can be enforced by the operator through pricing algorithm. Between control agents serving different users, this model accounted for interactions among users. Agents can compare their actual electricity costs, and possibly decide to change their strategy to obtain an economical benefit. It derived the equilibrium points of the system in the form of Evolutionary Stable Strategies (Miorandi, 2012).

SUMMARY

Smart grid is a visionary user-centric system that will elevate the conventional power grid system to one which functions more cooperatively, responsively, and economically. In addition to the incumbent function of delivering electricity from suppliers to consumers, smart grid will also provide information and intelligence to the power grid to enable grid automation, active operation, and efficient demand response. Since game theory has a strong potential for the analysis of smart grid systems, game-theoretic approach presents a promising tool to address several emerging problems in SG systems. When game theory is applied to solve SG control problems, it is important whether the application is practically feasible or not. Therefore, in order to reap the benefits of game-theoretic designs, constant feedback between theory and practice is needed. For the future smart grid, game-theoretic design will have a strong role to play in the development and analysis of protocols (Saad, 2012).

REFERENCES

Aristidou, P., Dimeas, A., & Hatziargyriou, N. (2011). Microgrid Modelling and Analysis Using Game Theory Methods. *Lecture Notes of the Institute for Computer Sciences, Social Informatics, and Telecommunications Engineering, 54*(1), 12–19. doi:10.1007/978-3-642-19322-4_2

Atzeni, I., Ordóñez, L. G., Scutari, G., Palomar, D. P., & Fonollosa, J. R. (2013). Noncooperative and Cooperative Optimization of Distributed Energy Generation and Storage in the Demand-Side of the Smart Grid. *IEEE Transactions on Signal Processing, 61*(10), 2454–2472. doi:10.1109/TSP.2013.2248002

Bu, S., & Yu, F. R. (2012). Dynamic energy-efficient resource allocation in cognitive heterogeneous wireless networks with the smart grid. In *Proceedings of IEEE GLOBECOM*, (pp. 3032-3036). IEEE.

Fadlullah, Z. M., Nozaki, Y., Takeuchi, A., & Kato, N. (2011). A survey of game theoretic approaches in smart grid. In Proceedings of Wireless Communications and Signal Processing (WCSP). WCSP.

Fang, X., Misra, S., Xue, G., & Yang, D. (2012). The New and Improved Power Grid: A Survey. *IEEE Communications Surveys & Tutorials, 14*(4), 944–980. doi:10.1109/SURV.2011.101911.00087

Ibars, C., Navarro, M., & Giupponi, L. (2010). Distributed Demand Management in Smart Grid with a Congestion Game. In *Proceedings of IEEE SmartGridComm*. IEEE.

Li, D., Jayaweera, S. K., & Naseri, A. (2011). Auctioning game based Demand Response scheduling in smart grid. In *Proceedings of IEEE Online Conference on Green Communications*, (pp. 58-63). IEEE.

Maharjan, S., Zhu, Q., Zhang, Y., Gjessing, S., & Basar, T. (2013). Dependable Demand Response Management in the Smart Grid: A Stackelberg Game Approach. *IEEE Transactions on Smart Grid, 4*(1), 120–132. doi:10.1109/TSG.2012.2223766

Miorandi, D., & De Pellegrini, F. (2012). Demand-side management in smart grids: An evolutionary games perspective. In *Performance Evaluation Methodologies and Tools* (pp. 178–187). Academic Press. doi:10.4108/valuetools.2012.250351

Mohsenian-Rad, H., Wong, V. W. S., Jatskevich, J., Schober, R., & Leon-Garcia, A. (2010). Autonomous demand side management based on game-theoretic energy consumption scheduling for the future smart grid. *IEEE Trans. on Smart Grid, 1*(3), 320–331. doi:10.1109/TSG.2010.2089069

Saad, W., Han, Z., Poor, H. V., & Başar, T. (2012). Game-Theoretic Methods for the Smart Grid: An Overview of Microgrid Systems, Demand-Side Management, and Smart Grid Communications. *IEEE Signal Processing Magazine, 29*(5), 86–105. doi:10.1109/MSP.2012.2186410

Wu, C., Mohsenian-Rad, H., Huang, J., & Wang, A. Y. (2011). Demand side management for Wind Power Integration in microgrid using dynamic potential game theory. [IEEE.]. *Proceedings of IEEE GLOBECOM, 2011*, 1199–1204.

Zhu, Q., & Basar, T. (2011). A multi-resolution large population game framework for smart grid demand response management. In *Proceedings of International Conference on Control and Optimization (NetGCooP)*. NetGCooP.

Zhu, Q., Han, Z., & Basar, T. (2012). A differential game approach to distributed demand side management in smart grid. [IEEE.]. *Proceedings of the IEEE, ICC*, 3345–3350.

KEY TERMS AND DEFINITIONS

Grid Energy Storage: Methods used to store electricity on a large scale within an electrical power grid. Electrical energy is stored during times when production (from power plants) exceeds consumption and the stores are used at times when consumption exceeds production.

Open Smart Grid Protocol (OSGP): A family of specifications published by the European Telecommunications Standards Institute (ETSI) used in conjunction with the ISO/IEC 14908 control networking standard for smart grid applications.

Super Grid: A wide area transmission network that makes it possible to trade high volumes of electricity across great distances. It is sometimes also referred to as a *mega grid.*

Vehicle-to-Grid (V2G): A system in which plug-in electric vehicles, such as electric cars (BEVs) and plug-in hybrids (PHEVs), communicate with the power grid to sell demand response services by either delivering electricity into the grid or by throttling their charging rate.

Virtual Power Plant: A cluster of distributed generation installations, which are collectively run by a central control entity.

Wide Area Synchronous Grid: An electrical grid at a regional scale or greater that operates at a synchronized frequency and is electrically tied together during normal system conditions.

Chapter 6
Game Theory for Network Security

ABSTRACT

Network security consists of the provisions and policies adopted by a network administrator to prevent and monitor unauthorized access, misuse, modification, or denial of a computer network and network-accessible resources. It involves the authorization of access to data in a network, which is controlled by the network administrator. Usually, network security covers a variety of computer networks, both public and private, that are used in everyday jobs conducting transactions and communications among businesses, government agencies, and individuals. This chapter explores network security.

INTRODUCTION

Security is a critical concern around the world that arises in protecting our ports, airports, transportation or other critical national infrastructure from adversaries. Nowadays, security arises in problems ranging from physical to cyber physical systems. In particular, network security becomes a challenging topic, and the research community has been paying attention to the network security problem. However, the problems are far from being completely solved. For more than one decade, game theoretic approach has been recognized as a useful tool to handle network attacks (Liang, & Xiao, 2013), (Tambe, Jain, Pita, & Jiang, 2012), (Roy, Ellis, Shiva, Dasgupta, Shandilya, & Wu, 2010). In this chapter, we review the existing game-theory based solutions for network security problems (Figure 1).

DOI: 10.4018/978-1-4666-6050-2.ch006

NON-COOPERATIVE GAMES FOR NETWORK SECURITY

Most game theoretic approaches applied in network security require attack-defense; the interactions between attackers and defenders may be formulated as non-cooperative behaviors which may then be described and solved using game theory (Liang, 2013). Therefore, the most existing game-theoretic research as applied to network security falls under non-cooperative games. Non-cooperative game models including two subclasses, static games and dynamic games. Moreover, within static and dynamic subclasses, game model can be further grouped in terms of whether they are of complete information or whether they are of perfect information (Liang, 2013).

Figure 1. Game theory for network security

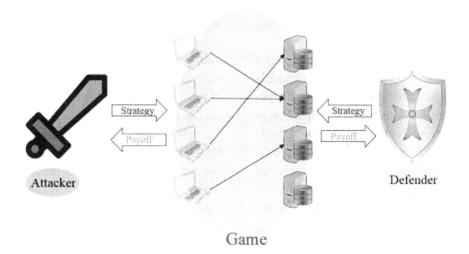

Game

Non-Cooperative Static Games

All static games are one-shot games of imperfect information. Therefore, static games with perfect information do not exist (Liang, 2013). According to the completeness of information, static games can be classified into two sub-classes - complete information static games and incomplete information static games. Complete information static games model the scenario of the interactions between attackers and defenders. The solution to complete information static games is the Nash equilibrium. When defenders could not always distinguish attackers from regular users, not only the interactions between attackers and defenders but also those between regular nodes and defenders should be considered. Therefore, the games are modeled as incomplete information static games, which could model the interactions not only between attackers and defenders, but also between regular nodes and defenders. In this game model, defenders keep an inference of the type (malicious or regular) of another node as its opponent. The solution to incomplete information static games is the Bayesian Nash equilibrium (Liang, 2013).

Static Games with Complete Imperfect Information

Complete imperfect information game is a game in which every player knows both the strategies and payoffs of all players in the game, but not necessarily the actions. In other words, this kind of game does not take into account the actions each player have already taken (Roy, 2010). Recently, some non-cooperative static games with complete imperfect information have been developed. Under information warfare scenario, attack-defense games are general-sum, two-player static games in which the action sets of the players are simply {attack, not attack} and {defend, not defend}. The payoff functions for the players capture the damage to the system and the costs to attack and to defend. The mixed strategy Nash equilibrium is obtained as the solution of game in the form of a combination consisting of the attacking probability and the defending probability (Liang, 2013). For investment efficient strategies in cyber security, attack-protect economic model was presented by using a computational approach to quantitative risk assessment. The main goal of this game model is how to protect the critical intellectual property in private and public sectors assuming the possibility of reverse engineering attacks (Carin, Cybenko, & Hughes, 2008).

With complete imperfect information, some multiple-player non-cooperative game models have been proposed to deal with the risk management for the multiple divisions in a security organization, or to optimally allocate their investments for the public protection and their self-insurances, or to analyze how the investment strategies of selfish users affect the security effectiveness in a network. The utility functions of the players are abstract and general enough to capture the interaction between the multiple players. As the solution concept of complete imperfect information games, the Nash Equilibrium is considered to be the optimal strategies for the network users (Liang, 2013).

Static Games with Incomplete Imperfect Information

Incomplete imperfect information games are those in which at least one player is unaware of the possible strategies and payoffs for at least one of the other players, and at least one player is not aware of the moves of at least one other player that have taken place. To handle these incomplete information games, Bayesian game approach is an adequate model. Nowadays, different kinds of Bayesian game models have been developed for the network attack-defense problem. In the case that the defender does not have enough information to verify a potential attacker, Liu et al. proposed a new Bayesian game, which models the interactions between a DDoS attacker and the network administrator (Liu, Zang, & Yu, 2005). This approach observed the ability to infer attacker intent, objectives, and strategies. This ability is important to effective risk assessment and harm prediction. Liu's game model specified the types of the potential attacker as {good, bad} and the utility functions of the defender and attacker, if

their actions and the type of the potential attacker are provided. The solution is an expected-utility maximizer (Liang, 2013). Another Bayesian game model in (Liu, Comaniciu, & Man, 2006) was proposed for a defender. The action set of the defender consists of '*monitor*' and '*not monitor*'. If its opponent is an attacker, then the opponent's action set consists of '*attack*' and '*not attack*'. However, if its opponent is a regular user, then the opponent's action set is composed of only '*not attack*'. Defender in a network updates its inference in the case that it is not able to verify whether its opponent is an attacker or a regular user. Even though this game model was designed as a multi-stage Bayesian Game, each stage of the game is a static Bayesian game. The solution concept of this game is Bayesian Nash equilibrium (Liang, 2013).

Non-Cooperative Dynamic Games

A game with more than one stage can be considered as a sequential structure of the decision making problems encountered by the players in a static game. This kind of game is referred to as dynamic game (Roy, 2010). While static game models in network security only consider one-short attack-defense interactions, in dynamic game models, a network security game is considered as a multiple stage process in each stage of which attackers and defenders play their actions in response to the history outputs of the game.

A dynamic game can be either of complete or incomplete information. Moreover, a dynamic game may involve perfect or imperfect information. In dynamic models of complete information, only the interactions between defenders and attackers are considered with an assumption that defenders are able to discriminate attackers from regular users. For network security scenarios in which the assumption above does not hold, researchers employ dynamic models of incomplete information. Dynamic games of perfect information such as the stackelberg game (Osborne, & Rubinstein,

1994) and the fictitious play (Nguyen, Alpcan, & Basar, 2009) indicates that in each stage of a game, parties (including defenders and attackers) play actions in turns and that when a party plays its action, it already knows the history actions of other parties and itself. In other dynamic games in which the parties either play actions at the same time in each stage of the game or take turns to play in each stage but have little information about the history actions in that stage when they play, researchers view the games as dynamic games of imperfect information (Liang, 2013).

Motivated by the above discussion, dynamic game models in network security consist of the following four subclasses: those of complete and perfect information, those of complete and imperfect information those of incomplete and perfect information and those of incomplete and imperfect information (Liang, 2013).

Dynamic Games with Complete Perfect Information

Dynamic complete perfect information game is a game in which each player is aware of the moves of all other players that have already taken place and every player knows both the strategies and pay-offs of all players in the game. Stackelberg game model has been adopted to implement dynamic games with complete and perfection information (Chen, & Leneutre, 2009), (Osborne, 1994). In Stackelberg games, models can be considered both the case in which the attacker moves first in the game and the defender follows and also the case in which they exchange roles. Each action in the players' action sets is specified as either attacking or defending each of the attack targets with a certain probability. The Stackelberg equilibrium for both cases is used to determine which role is better for each of the players (Liang, 2013).

Markov game and stochastic game also can be adopted to design a dynamic complete perfect information game. A new Markov game model was proposed for risk assessment of network in-

formation system considering the security status of both present and future (Xiaolin, Xiaobin, Yong, & Hongsheng, 2008). This game model identified that threats acting on vulnerability can induce risk and the risk will be larger and larger by threat spreading. On the other hand, the risk will be smaller and smaller by the system administrator's repairing the vulnerability. Essentially, the experiment involves a game of complete and perfect information with two players (Roy, 2010). Two-player zero-sum stochastic game model was also developed for an attacker and the network administrator (Nguyen, Alpcan, & Basar, 2009). This model assumed that the network consists of a set of interdependent nodes whose security assets and vulnerabilities are correlated. It utilized the concept of linear influence networks and modeled the interdependency among nodes by two weighted directed graphs, one signifying the relationship of security assets and the other denoting vulnerability correlation among the nodes (Roy, 2010).

Dynamic Games with Complete Imperfect Information

Usually, stochastic game approach has been widely used to implement dynamic complete imperfect games. Recently, a new two player zero-sum stochastic defense-attack game has been proposed between the attacker and defender (Sallhammar, Knapskog, & Helvik, 2005). In this game, the process of the state change can be modeled as a continuous-time Markov process with a transition rate matrix. Each entity in the matrix reflects the effect on the normal use of the system of the state change. The interaction between the attacker and the defender affects the transition rate matrix. It means that the transition rate matrix depends on the strategies that the attackers and defenders choose and the effects of normal use (Liang, 2013). Based on this idea, the defense-attack security game is modeled 1) identify the elements of the game, which are the states that are vulnerable to attack, 2) build action sets that capture the possible attack and defense methods for the two players; the action sets of the attacker and of the defender depend on the system state, 3) for every pair of actions for the defender and attacker, determine the probabilities of state transition from one game element to another, 4) determine the payoff function in each state element. From the payoff functions, the attack-defense game can only start at the vulnerable state. If the attacker chooses not to attack or the defender responds to the attack, the game ends. If the attack is successful and the state transitions to any other than the game elements, the game ends. If the attack is successful and the state transitions to any of the game elements, the game continues with a new play. The solution to this game is a Nash Equilibrium for each game element, but it is difficult to obtain the solution because the payoff functions are not defined explicitly (Liang, 2013).

Another stochastic game was proposed as a network attack-defense game (Lye, & Wing, 2005). This game can be viewed as plays in a sequence of time steps, where the system states in the time steps are random variables. In any time step, the players can take actions and they will gain a value for that time step based on the actions and the system state. At the next time step, the players can take actions, and so on. If the player holds the same strategy pair in each time step, the strategies are called stationary strategies. For a pair of players in a stage with stationary strategies, the return of each player is defined as the expected value of the weighted sum of its gains from the current time step and the following infinite number of time steps. The solution to this game is also Nash Equilibrium. In each state, it is a combination of the strategies of the players that maximize the returns (Liang, 2013).

Based on a stochastic game-theory model, Bommannavar et al. proposed a new dynamic learning game for the security risk management (Bommannavar, Alpan, & Bambos, 2011). In this model, the administrator of an organization with multiple nodes or assets selected optimal actions to diffuse the risks among the assets. The action sets of the administrator and of the attacker would consist of the possible defending probability distributions and the attacking probability distributions among the assets, respectively. The states of the system in the stochastic game were represented by the risk levels. A saddle point method was applied to determine the optimal strategy for the administrator. When the transition matrix is not known, the Q-learning method was employed to determine converging optimal strategies for the attacker and the administrator (Liang, 2013).

Dynamic Games with Incomplete Perfect Information

In the past few years, different kinds of games have been studied for dynamic incomplete perfect games. In 2006, continuous game model was adopted to model intrusion response as a resource allocation problem (Bloem, Alpcan, & Basar, 2006). In this game, a cost is associated with attacks and responses. The strategies are discretized both in time and intensity of actions, which eventually leads to a discretized model. The reaction functions uniquely minimize the strictly convex cost functions. After discretization, this model becomes a constrained integer optimization problem (Roy, 2010).

As an another approach, two-player basic signaling game has been developed to model intrusion detection in ad hoc wireless networks (Patcha, & Park, 2004). In this game model, a defender has incomplete information for determining the type of its opponent, which can be either an attacker or a regular node. The possible actions of the defender are to defend or not while its opponent can attack actively or act passively if the latter is an attacker. If the latter is a regular node, it can attack passively or act normally. The solution to this game is perfect Bayesian equilibrium.

In 2011, MAC level jamming attack game was developed as a two-player multi-stage Bayesian game in wireless network (Sagduyu, Berry, &

Ephremides, 2011). The type of each of the two nodes in the network was either a jamming attacker type or a selfish user type. The action set of each node was the possible transmission probabilities of that node. In this game, each node updated their actions at the end of each stage.

Dynamic Games with Incomplete Imperfect Information

As an incomplete and imperfect security game, Y. Liu proposed a two-player multi-stage Bayesian game (Liu, 2006). In this game model, players had incomplete information, and the solution concept to that game was a perfect Bayesian equilibrium. At each stage of the game, the players' optimal strategies for that stage were obtained based on their inferences of their opponents' types. At the end of a stage, each player updated its belief about the type of its opponent based on the current optimal strategies, the current belief of the type of its opponent, and the history of observed actions of its opponent.

As a repeated game with finite steps or infinite steps, the interaction of an attacker and the network administrator was modeled (Alpcan, & Baser, (2004). In this model, wireless sensor network was deployed to detect the attacks and the network system was considered as an imperfect

and 'fictitious' player similar to the 'nature' player in standard game theory. The Nash equilibrium strategies were computed assuming simple cost functions for the players (Roy, 2010).

Another repeated game model was developed to describe how to formulate the interaction between an attacker and a defender. As a repeated game, the attack-defense interaction was modeled with incomplete information. In this model, the utility of Nash and Bayesian equilibria were pointed out in representing the concepts to predict behavior. To get these solutions, appropriate linear algorithms were also developed (Liang, 2013), (Roy, 2010).

Non-Cooperative Evolutionary Games for Network Security

Conventional game theory is based on the fully rationality of player to analyze problems. The assumptions of fully rationality require the player having rational awareness, analytical reasoning ability, memory capacity, and accuracy requirements. However, since the player is unable to meet the high demands of such fully rationality in the real environment, the application of game theory is being limited in the real world. In contrast, evolutionary game theory requires the player with bounded rationality and dynamics of the game process. Bounded rationality assump-

Figure 2. Evolutionary game for network security

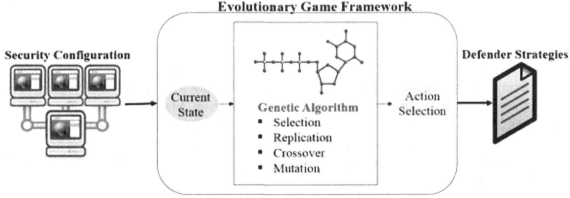

tion means that the player only knows a part of knowledge of the state of the game, such as the payoff, action strategies. The player cannot find the optimal strategy only according to a game. The player needs continual learning and imitation in the game, then the player finally finds the best strategy for himself (Figure 2) (Qiu, Chen, & Xu, 2010).

Nowadays, network security is of great importance for the mobile electronic commerce. Therefore, security investment is of vital significance for the mobile electronic commerce. In reality, the main body of the network security only has the bounded rationality, and the bounded rationality is just the assumption of evolutionary game theory. A new evolutionary game model was developed to analyze the security problem in the mobile electronic commerce chain (Sun, Kong, He, & You, 2008). In this model, penalty parameter was introduced to control the invest in information security. Based on the bounded rationality, this game model calculated replicator dynamics and analyzed evolutionary stable strategy to get the result. The result revealed that it was of great significance to reduce the investment cost of information security effectively. This approach provided a new thought to resolve information security problem in the mobile electronic commerce industry chain (Sun, 2008).

As an attack-defend model, another evolutionary game was proposed for wireless sensor networks (Qiu, 2010). Usually, sensor nodes have limited rationality of evolutionary learning ability. However, they can be active and dynamic to adjust their defensive strategies so as to achieve the most effective defense according to the attacker's different policies. The result of this game operation can verify the correctness of the theoretical analysis, feasibility and effectiveness of evolutionary game model (Qiu, 2010).

Based on information asymmetry between the protectors and attackers of cyber security, a new dynamic invest-attack game was developed based on the evolutionary game (Pan, & Xu, 2010).

Usually, development of cyber technology is in a state of tending to be perfect but impossible. Therefore, during the cyber security construction process, how to set proper security standard and investment quota in accordance with the important degree of its information is a universal problem of enterprises. If security overtakes demand, it is not only unnecessary, but also a waste of money. By considering this situation, the dynamic invest-attack game was developed as new game paradigm. Based on the evolutionary game approach, this game model was designed to balance the relationship among security, cost and efficiency in the process of cyber security management. And, it analyzed the motivation of decision making of players of both sides from microcosmic perspective (Pan, 2010).

Non-Cooperative Stackelberg Game for Network Security

Security is a critical concern around the world from physical to cyber physical systems. In all of these security problems, we have limited security resources which prevent full security coverage at all times; instead, limited security resources must be deployed intelligently taking into account differences in priorities of targets. Since Stackelberg game can appropriately model the strategic interaction between a defender and an attacker, it is well-suited to adversarial reasoning for security resource allocation and scheduling problems. Nowadays, security problems are increasingly studied using Stackelberg game (Tambe, 2012). Stackelberg game was first introduced to model leadership and commitment, and is now widely used to study security problems ranging from computer network security, missile defense systems, and terrorism. Models for arms inspections and border patrolling have also been modeled using inspection games, a related family of Stackelberg games. In the past several years, Bayesian Stackelberg games can be used to efficiently provide randomized patrolling or inspection strategies.

These models have led to some initial successes in this challenge problem arena, leading to advances over previous approaches in security scheduling and allocation (Tambe, 2012).

In a class of games known as Stackelberg games, one agent (i.e., leader) must commit to a strategy that can be observed by the other agent (i.e., follower) before the adversary chooses its own strategy. In Bayesian Stackelberg games, the leader is uncertain about the types of follower it may face. Such games are important in security domains. For example, a security agent, as a leader, must commit to a strategy of patrolling certain areas, and a robber, as a follower, has a chance to observe this strategy over time before choosing its own strategy of where to attack. Stackelberg games are commonly used to model attacker-defender scenarios in security domains, as well as in patrolling, and could potentially be used in many other situations such as network routing, pricing in transportation systems, setting up security checkpoints and other adversarial domains (Paruchuri, Pearce, Marecki, Tambe, Ordóñez, & Kraus, 2008).

In security games, the main goal of defender is to find the optimal mixed strategy while facing any of the attacker types. The attacker also learns the mixed strategy of the security agent and chooses a best-response for himself. Thus, the solution concept of security game is known as a Stackelberg equilibrium. However, this concept is a strong form of the Stackelberg equilibrium, which assumes that the follower will always break ties in favor of the leader in cases of indifference. So, the leader can always induce the favorable strong equilibrium by selecting a strategy arbitrarily close to the equilibrium that causes the follower to strictly prefer the desired strategy. A pair of strategies could form a Strong Stackelberg Equilibrium (SSE) if they satisfy follow three conditions; i) the defender plays a best-response, that is, the defender cannot get a higher payoff by choosing any other strategy, ii) the attacker play a best-response, that is, given a defender strategy, the attacker cannot get a higher payoff by attacking any other target, and iii) the attacker breaks ties in favor of the leader (Tambe, 2012), (An, Tambe, Ordóñez, Shieh, & Kiekintveld, 2011).

COOPERATIVE GAMES FOR NETWORK SECURITY

Cooperation between wireless network nodes is a promising technique for improving the physical layer security of wireless transmission in the presence of multiple eavesdroppers (Saad, Han, Basar, Debbah, & Hjørungnes, 2009). As a cooperative game, coalitional game with non-transferable utility was proposed to solve the physical layer security cooperation problem. In this game, a distributed algorithm for coalition formation was developed. Through this algorithm, the wireless users can autonomously cooperate and self-organize into disjoint independent coalitions while taking into account the security costs during information exchange (Saad, 2009).

Another cooperative game model was introduced for the security risk management between multiple divisions of a security organization (Saad, Alpcan, Basar, & Hjørungnes, 2010). In this game model, there are linear dependencies between the security resources in the divisions and between the vulnerabilities in those divisions. And then, one positive influence matrix and a negative influence matrix are introduced to represent the dependencies between the security resources and between the vulnerabilities in the divisions, respectively. To capture the positive effect of forming a coalition, any two divisions in the same coalition will have increased positive effect and reduced negative effect between them than they do without coalitions. In the cooperative game, two coalitions will form a new coalition if the price of forming a coalition per unit friction is below a threshold (Liang, 2013).

Nowadays, the problem of reducing the number of false positives generated by cooperative Intrusion Detection Systems (IDSs) in mobile ad hoc networks has been seriously considered (Figure 3).

Figure 3. Mobile ad hoc networks Intrusion Detection System (IDS)

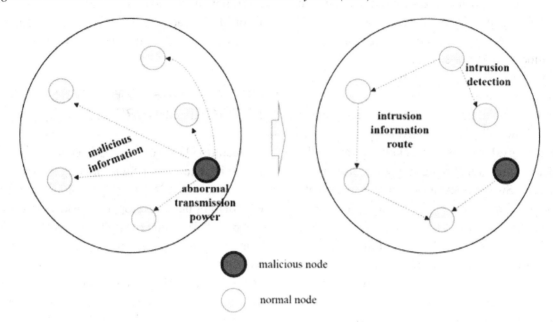

In 2007, Otrok et al. developed a new cooperative flexible model by using security classes where an IDS is able to operate in different modes at each security class (Otrok, Debbabi, Assi, & Bhattacharya, 2007). This model helps in minimizing false alarms and informing the prevention system accurately about the severity of an intrusion. In addition, Shapley value was used to formally express the cooperation among all the nodes. This game theoretic model assists in analyzing the contribution of each mobile node on each security class in order to decrease false positives taking into consideration the reputation of nodes (Otrok, 2007).

MULTI-OBJECTIVE OPTIMIZATION FOR SECURITY GAMES

Game theory is an increasingly important paradigm for modeling security domains which feature complex resource allocation. As a special class of attacker-defender games, security games are at the heart of several major deployed decision support applications. In these applications, the defender is trying to maximize a single objective. However, there are domains where the defender has to consider multiple objectives simultaneously. Given this diverse set of threats, selecting a security strategy is a significant challenge as no single strategy can minimize the threat for all attacker types. Thus, tradeoffs must be made and protecting more against one threat may increase the vulnerability to another threat (Brown, An, Kiekintveld, Ordóñez, & Tambe, 2012). Bayesian security games have been used to model domains where the defender is facing multiple attacker types. The threats posed by the different attacker types are weighted according to the relative likelihood of encountering that attacker type. There are three potential factors limiting the use of Bayesian security games: i) the defender may not have information on the probability distribution over attacker types, ii) it may be impossible or undesirable to directly compare and combine the defender rewards of different security games, and iii) only one solution is given, hiding the trade-offs between the objectives from the end user (Brown, 2012).

Recently, a new multi-objective security game has been developed by combining game theory and multi-objective optimization. In this game, the threats posed by the attacker types are treated as different objective functions which are not aggregated, thus eliminating the need for a probability distribution over attacker types. Unlike Bayesian security games which have a single optimal solution, multi-objective security game has a set of Pareto optimal solutions which is referred to as the Pareto frontier. By presenting the Pareto frontier to the end user, they are able to better understand the structure of their problem as well as the tradeoffs between different security strategies. As a result, end users are able to make a more informed decision on which strategy to enact (Brown, 2012).

Another multi-objective security game was proposed by using evolutionary approach (Vejandla, Dasgupta, Kaushal, & Nino, 2010). This work generated gaming strategies for the attacker-defender in cyber warfare, and extended anticipation games by introducing a multi-objective evolutionary algorithm to generate attacker-defender strategies. Given a network environment, attack graphs are defined in an anticipation game model to generate action strategies by analyzing vulnerabilities and security measures. A gaming strategy represents a sequence of decision rules that an attacker or the defender can employ to achieve player's desired goal. Based on the multi-objective evolutionary algorithm, the developed multi-objective security game implemented the anticipation game to generate action strategies. This model can be expand to model different kinds of attacks, such as DDoS attacks, buffer overflow, ping of death, etc. (Vejandla, 2010).

GAME THEORY FOR INFORMATION WARFARE

The term information warfare had its first recorded use in 1976 in an internal report by Thomas P. Rona of Boeing Corporation. However, information warfare did not become well known until it was discussed in the testimony of CIA Director John Deutch before the United States Senate Government Affairs Committee in 1996. While information warfare may appear to be restricted to government and military uses, the general public can have a quite different view. Because the term information warfare has specifically military connotations, the synonyms 'information assurance' and 'information operations' have more recently been introduced to emphasize the fact that the issues extend into the public and private civil sectors, like as financial, commercial and industrial fields. Other terms regularly used to refer to various aspects of information warfare include Hacker War, Net War, Cyber War, Cyber Terrorism, Software Warfare, and Digital Warfare. There have been many attempts to formulate a definition of information warfare. These have gradually developed to focus on the specific types of information based operations involved (Overill, 2001).

In 2002, Hamilton et al. outlined the areas of game theory which are relevant to information warfare (Hamilton, Miller, Ott, & Saydjari, 2002). Their work focused on a motivating example to illustrate the use of game theory in network security problems, and concluded with speculating about great possibilities in applying game theory to information warfare. They analyzed a few scenarios suggesting several potential courses of actions with predicted outcomes and what-if scenarios. In addition, they also identified the seven challenges in applying game theory to the domain of information warfare: 1) there is a limited database of relevant games played by real players, 2) both the attacker and the defender can launch multiple moves simultaneously, 3) players can take as long as they want to make moves, 4) the defender may not be able to correctly able to identify the end goal of the opponent, 5) at each step the flow of the game may change so that the known legal moves, both in number and kind, may change for each player, 6) the defender may find it hard to keep track of any possible change in the opponents resources and also his end goals, 7) it is hard to define precisely the timing for move and state updates. Absolutely, there is the potential for game theory to play a significant role in information warfare and to revolutionize the domain of information warfare. The combination of the ability to consider millions of possibilities, model attacker characteristics, and self-generate what-if scenarios seems too potent to ignore. However, even though the idea of applying game theory techniques to the domain of information warfare is extremely promising, it is by no means trivial. In particular, the domain of information warfare is significantly different from traditional game models. Therefore, there are numerous hurdles to overcome, and it creates a rich research environment for future work (Hamilton 2002).

SUMMARY

For the last decades, hacker activities have significantly increased in cyber space, and have been causing damage by exploiting weaknesses in information infrastructure. Considerable efforts are continuously being made by the research community to secure networks and associated devices. Recently, researchers have been exploring the applicability of game theoretic approaches to address cyber security problems and have proposed a handful of competing solutions. Game theory offers promising perspectives, insights, and models to address the ever changing security threats in cyber space.

The existing game theoretic approaches could be a pool of research directions on network security. However, there are some limitations of the existing game models. First, they lack scalability. Most of the game models for security games are two-player games. Therefore, for the problem scenarios with multiple attackers versus multiple

defenders, the security game should be modeled as a two-player game in which the whole of the attackers is treated as one player, as is the whole of defenders. Second, traditional static game models are not very realistic in most scenarios where the interactions between the attackers and the defenders are a series of events. Third, stochastic game models always assume that the defender and the attacker can detect the system state with no error. This assumption is not true in many realistic cases. Fourth, stochastic game models have shortcomings since they assume the states of the system are finite and zero-sum games. However, the states of the system seem to be continuous and a general-sum game model is more realistic for practical implementation (Liang, 2013). To overcome these limitations, possible future research directions for network security should include, 1) building game models involving three or more players for more network security application scenarios, 2) improving the existing stochastic game models by including an infinite state assumption to make the model more realistic, 3) studying the construction of payoff functions on network security game models. Improper payoff functions in a game model can reduce the effectiveness of the prediction of the attack-defense strategies (Liang, 2013).

This chapter provides a survey and classifications of existing game theoretic approaches to network security. This survey highlights important game theoretic approaches and their applications to network security. In spite of their limitations, game theoretic approaches for solving network security problems have shown that they are powerful tools. From this survey, readers can gain better understanding on the existing game theoretic approaches, and some insights on the further research directions on network security issues.

REFERENCES

Alpcan, T., & Baser, T. (2004). A game theoretic analysis of intrusion detection in access control systems. In *Proceedings of IEEE Conference on Decision and Control*, (pp. 1568-1573).

An, B., Tambe, M., Ordóñez, F., Shieh, E. A., & Kiekintveld, C. (2011). Refinement of Strong Stackelberg Equilibria in Security Games. In *Proceedings of the Twenty-Fifth AAAI Conference on Artificial Intelligence*, (pp. 587-593). AAAI.

Bloem, M., Alpcan, T., & Basar, T. (2006). Intrusion response as a resource allocation problem. In *Proceedings of IEEE Conference on Descision and Control*, (pp. 6283-6288). IEEE.

Bommannavar, P., Alpan, T., & Bambos, N. (2011). Security Risk Management via Dynamic Games with Learning. In *Proceedings of IEEE International Conference on Communications*. IEEE.

Brown, M., An, B., Kiekintveld, C., Ordóñez, F., & Tambe, M. (2012). Multi-Objective Optimization for Security Games. [AAMAS.]. *Proceedings of AAMAS*, *12*, 863–870.

Carin, L., Cybenko, G., & Hughes, J. (2008). Cyber security: The queries methodology. *IEEE Computer*, *41*(8), 20–26. doi:10.1109/MC.2008.295

Chen, L., & Leneutre, J. (2009). A game theoretical framework on intrusion detection in heterogeneous networks. *IEEE Trans. Inf. Forens. Security*, *4*(2), 165–178. doi:10.1109/TIFS.2009.2019154

Hamilton, S. N., Miller, W. L., Ott, A., & Saydjari, O. S. (2002). Challenges in applying game theory to the domain of information warfare. In *Proceedings of Information survivability workshop*. Academic Press.

Hamilton, S. N., Miller, W. L., Ott, A., & Saydjari, O. S. (2002). The role of game theory in information warfare. In *Proceedings of Information survivability workshop*. Academic Press.

Liang, X., & Xiao, Y. (2013). Game Theory for Network Security. *IEEE Communications Surveys & Tutorials*, *15*(1), 472–486. doi:10.1109/SURV.2012.062612.00056

Liu, P., Zang, W., & Yu, M. (2005). Incentive-based modeling and inference of attacker intent, objectives, and strategies. *ACM Transactions on Information and System Security*, *8*(1), 78–118. doi:10.1145/1053283.1053288

Liu, Y., Comaniciu, C., & Man, H. (2006). A Bayesian game approach for intrusion detection in wireless ad hoc networks. In *Game theory for communications and networks*. Academic Press. doi:10.1145/1190195.1190198

Lye, K., & Wing, J. (2005). Game strategies in network security. *International Journal of Information Security*, *4*(1-2), 71–86. doi:10.1007/s10207-004-0060-x

Nguyen, K. C., Alpcan, T., & Basar, T. (2009). Stochastic games for security in networks with interdependent nodes. In *Proceedings of GameNets* (pp. 697–703). GameNets. doi:10.1109/GAMENETS.2009.5137463

Nguyen, K. C., Alpcan, T., & Basar, T. (2009). Security games with incomplete information. In *Proceedings of IEEE ICC*. IEEE.

Osborne, M. J., & Rubinstein, A. (1994). *A Course in Game Theory*. MIT Press.

Otrok, H., Debbabi, M., Assi, C., & Bhattacharya, P. (2007). A Cooperative Approach for Analyzing Intrusions in Mobile Ad hoc Networks. In *Proceedings of ICDCSW'07*. ICDCSW.

Overill, R. E. (2001). Information warfare: battles in cyberspace. *Computing & Control Engineering Journal*, *12*(3), 125–128. doi:10.1049/cce:20010304

Pan, R., & Xu, C. (2010). Research on Decision of Cyber Security Investment Based on Evolutionary Game Model. In *Proceedings of Multimedia Information Networking and Security* (pp. 491–495). Academic Press. doi:10.1109/MINES.2010.110

Paruchuri, P., Pearce, J. P., Marecki, J., Tambe, M., Ordóñez, F., & Kraus, S. (2008). Paying games for security: An efficient exact algorithm for solving Bayesian Stackelberg games. [). AAMAS.]. *Proceedings of AAMAS, 2*, 895–902.

Patcha, A., & Park, D. J. (2004). A game theoretic approach to modeling intrusion detection in mobile ad hoc networks. In *Proceedings of IEEE workshop on Information Assurance and Security*, (pp. 280-284). IEEE.

Qiu, Y., Chen, Z., & Xu, L. (2010). Active Defense Model of Wireless Sensor Networks Based on Evolutionary Game Theory. In *Proceedings of Wireless Communications Networking and Mobile Computing*. Academic Press. doi:10.1109/WICOM.2010.5601100

Roy, S., Ellis, C., Shiva, S., Dasgupta, D., Shandilya, V., & Wu, Q. (2010). A Survey of Game Theory as Applied to Network Security. In *Proceedings of IEEE HICSS*. IEEE.

Saad, W., Alpcan, T., Basar, T., & Hjørungnes, A. (2010). Coalitional game theory for security risk management. In *Proceedings of Conf. on Internet Monitoring and Protection*, (pp. 35-40). Academic Press.

Saad, W., Han, Z., Basar, T., Debbah, M., & Hjørungnes, A. (2009). Physical layer security: Coalitional games for distributed cooperation. In *Proceedings of WiOPT*. WiOPT.

Sagduyu, Y., Berry, R., & Ephremides, A. (2011). Jamming games in wireless networks with incomplete information. *IEEE Communications Magazine, 49*(8), 112–118. doi:10.1109/MCOM.2011.5978424

Sallhammar, K., Knapskog, S., & Helvik, B. (2005). Using stochastic game theory to compute the expected behavior of attackers. In *Proceedings of International Symposium on Applications and the Internet Workshops (Saint2005)*, (pp. 102-105). Saint.

Sun, W., Kong, X., He, D., & You, X. (2008). Information security problem research based on game theory. In *Proceedings of International Symposium on Publication Electronic Commerce and Security*, (pp. 554-557). Academic Press.

Tambe, M., Jain, M., Pita, J. A., & Jiang, A. X. (2012). Game theory for security: Key algorithmic principles, deployed systems, lessons learned. In *Proceedings of Annual Allerton Conference*, (pp. 1822-1829). Academic Press.

Vejandla, P., Dasgupta, D., Kaushal, A., & Nino, F. (2010). Evolving Gaming Strategies for Attacker-Defender in a Simulated Network Environment. In *Proceedings of IEEE International Conference on Social Computing*, (pp. 889-896). IEEE.

Xiaolin, C., Xiaobin, T., Yong, Z., & Hongsheng, X. (2008). A Markov game theory-based risk assessment model for network information systems. In *Proceedings of International conference on computer science and software engineering*, (pp. 1057-1061). Academic Press.

KEY TERMS AND DEFINITIONS

Authentication: The act of confirming the truth of an attribute of a single piece of data (datum) or entity. In contrast with Identification which refers to the act of stating or otherwise indicating a claim purportedly attesting to a person or thing's identity, authentication is the process of actually confirming that identity.

Encryption: The process of encoding messages or information in such a way that only authorized parties can read it. Encryption doesn't prevent hacking but it reduces the likelihood that the hacker will be able to read the data that is encrypted.

Firewall: A software or hardware-based network security system that controls the incoming and outgoing network traffic by analyzing the data packets and determining whether they should be allowed through or not, based on applied rule set.

Physical Security: Security measures that are designed to deny unauthorized access to facilities, equipment and resources, and to protect personnel and property from damage or harm (such as espionage, theft, or terrorist attacks).

Chapter 7
Game Theory for Cognitive Radio Networks

ABSTRACT

A cognitive radio is an intelligent radio that can be programmed and configured dynamically. Its transceiver is designed to use the best wireless channels in its vicinity. Such a radio automatically detects available channels in the wireless spectrum, then accordingly changes its transmission or reception parameters to allow more concurrent wireless communications in a given spectrum band at one location. This process is a form of dynamic spectrum management. In recent years, the development of intelligent, adaptive wireless devices called cognitive radios, together with the introduction of secondary spectrum licensing, has led to a new paradigm in communications: cognitive networks. Cognitive networks are wireless networks that consist of several types of users: often a primary user and secondary users. These cognitive users employ their cognitive abilities to communicate without harming the primary users. The study of cognitive networks is relatively new and many questions are yet to be answered. This chapter furthers the study.

INTRODUCTION

With the rapid deployment of new wireless devices and applications, the last decade has witnessed a growing demand for wireless radio spectrum. However, current wireless networks are characterized by a static spectrum allocation policy where governmental agencies assign wireless spectrum to license holders on a long-term basis for large geographical regions. This fixed spectrum assignment policy becomes a bottleneck for more efficient spectrum utilization under which a great portion of the licensed spectrum is severely under-utilized. The inefficient usage of the limited spectrum resources urges the spectrum regulatory strategy to review their policy and start to seek for innovative communication technology that can exploit the wireless spectrum in a more intelligent and flexible way. Recently, dynamic spectrum access techniques were proposed to solve these spectrum inefficiency problems. The key enabling technology of dynamic spectrum access is Cognitive Radio (CR) technology, which provides the capability to share the wireless channel with licensed users in an opportunistic manner (Akyildiz, Lee, Vuran, & Mohanty, 2008).

DOI: 10.4018/978-1-4666-6050-2.ch007

Cognitive Radio (CR) networks will provide high bandwidth utilization to users via heterogeneous wireless architectures and dynamic spectrum access techniques. However, CR networks impose challenges due to the fluctuating nature of the available spectrum, as well as the diverse QoS requirements of various applications. Spectrum management functions can address these challenges for the realization of this new network paradigm (Akyildiz, 2008). Nowadays, game theory has been used in communication networks to model and analyze the interactive behaviors in a competitive area. Game theory is also a useful tool that can be used for radio spectrum management in a cognitive radio network. In the past several years, some of the game theoretic models were proposed for different CR control issues such as power control, call admission control, spectrum trading, spectrum competition, interference avoidance, spectrum sharing, and spectrum access (Akyildiz, 2008), (Zhang, & Yu, 2010).

Traditionally, a game is a model of interactive decision process, which includes at least two players. Each player is a decision making entity. In CR networks, the primary user (licensed users) and the secondary user (unlicensed users) are assumed both players. Their behaviors are rational and selfish. Each player has his action space and utility function, and the objective of game is to maximize his utility. Spectrum sharing is that the secondary users access the spectrum competitively and maximize its own income while the primary user is not interfered. This spectrum sharing process can be modeled as games. The game models for CR networks can be classified into three categories; non-cooperative, cooperative and economic spectrum sharing games.

NON-COOPERATIVE SPECTRUM SHARING GAMES

In this section, we discuss non-cooperative spectrum sharing games such as repeated game, potential game, supermodular game, and so on.

In a non-cooperative game with rational network users, each user only cares about his own benefit and chooses the optimal strategy that can maximize his payoff function (Figure 1). Such an outcome of the non-cooperative game is termed as Nash equilibrium, which is the most commonly used solution concept in game theory (Wang, Wu, & Liu, 2010).

Repeated Game for Cognitive Radio Networks

In order to model and analyze long-term interactions among players, the repeated game model is used where the game is played for multiple rounds. A repeated game is a special form of an extensive-form game in which each stage is a repetition of the same strategic-form game. The number of rounds may be finite or infinite, but usually the infinite case is more interesting. Because players care about not only the current payoff but also the future payoffs, and a player's current behavior can affect the other players' future behavior, cooperation and mutual trust among players can be established (Wang, Wu, & Liu, 2010). In order to improve the cooperation among secondary users, distributed spectrum access mechanisms based on the repeated game approach have been developed to achieve efficient and fair spectrum allocation (Li, Liu, & Zhang, 2010).

Repeated game is the combination of a series of subgame with the same structure. Since the participants can learn and summarize the results of subgame after several repeated game, repeated game extends the strategic space. In 2009, a repeated spectrum sharing game was proposed by using cheat-proof strategy (Zhang, & Yu, 2010). In this model, two cooperation rules with efficiency and fairness were considered. Under the constraints of these rules, the spectrum sharing problem is modeled as a repeated game where any deviation from cooperation will trigger the punishment. In addition, two cheat-proof strategies were also proposed to enforce that selfish users would report their true channel information. This

Figure 1. Non-cooperative spectrum sharing game

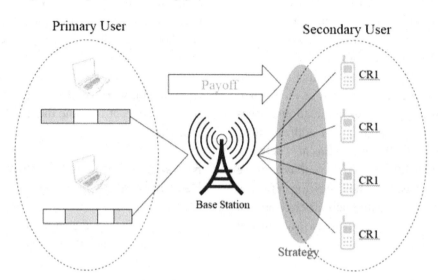

repeated game model can improve the effective of open spectrum sharing by reducing the interference among users. Finally, this approach can obtain the Nash equilibrium and achieve the optimization of spectrum sharing (Zhang, & Yu, 2010), (Zhang, & Yu, 2010).

Another repeated game model was developed for CR spectrum sharing process (Li, 2010). Usually, under the spectrum sharing scenario, multiple secondary systems coexist and interfere with each other. In this situation, large interference among secondary users will result in low spectrum efficiency since negotiation is infeasible for competitive secondary users from dissimilar secondary systems. Therefore, the usual assumption of spontaneous willingness to cooperate is unrealistic for secondary users. To stimulate cooperation among secondary users without negotiation, the repeated game model developed by Li (Li, 2010) was designed as a distributed spectrum access mechanism where only local information is available to use. Under the threat of punishment, selfish users were enforced to achieve cooperative spectrum opportunities. Therefore, unused licensed spectrum resources

are efficiently shared distributed among multiple primary and secondary users, and user interference is effectively suppressed by setting the optimal spectrum access probabilities (Li, 2010).

Potential Game for Cognitive Radio Networks

The Nash equilibrium gives the best strategy given that all the other players stick to their equilibrium strategy. When the system is implemented in a distributed manner, the question is how to find the Nash equilibrium, especially. One approach is to let players adjust their strategies iteratively based on accumulated observations as the game unfolds, and hopefully the process could converge to some equilibrium point. When the game has certain special structures, the iteration can converge and lead to the Nash equilibrium. Especially, if the game can be modeled as a potential game, convergence to the Nash equilibrium is guaranteed (Wang, Wu, & Liu, 2010).

Potential game is that kind of game which has special utility function called potential function. The function satisfies a differential that can be denoted by the change in value accrued by every unilaterally deviating player. In 2007, Xu et al. proposed a new potential game as a cooperative adaptive power control algorithm (Xu, Zhang, Zhou, & Liang, 2007). In this game, the utility function and potential function of ultra-wideband are introduced. Finally the procedure of power control is expressed as the process of maximum potential function for each active link to obtain adaptive power control in ultra-wideband networks. Through iterative and distributed algorithms, this model can verify that the Nash equilibrium of potential game is the extremum of their potential functions (Zhang, & Yu, 2010).

Based on the no-regret learning, another potential game has been proposed for cognitive radio networks (Hongshun, & Xiao, 2010). According to the advanced dynamic spectrum allocation algorithm, this potential game model in can have the best capacity performance while reducing the allocation cost. However, although the dynamic spectrum allocation algorithm based on potential game is effective approach for the spectrum allocation problem, how to reduce allocation cost in large-scale network or system adopting fast allocation algorithms is a considerable problem and must be solved (Hongshun, 2010).

For joint channel and power allocation in cognitive radio networks, a new potential game model was developed with local information (Canales, & Gállego, 2010). In order to characterize interference relationships among users, this game used simplified protocol model instead of the physical model. To obtain the maximum throughput in wireless networks, it is known to be hard to find the optima allocation solution. Since the problem is usually NP-hard, its analysis is typically tackled with heuristic algorithms. The obtained results by Canales were compared with a meta-heuristic genetic algorithm to show the correctness of the potential game based approach (Canales, 2010).

Supermodular Game for Cognitive Radio Networks

Dynamic spectrum access in cognitive radio networks has shown its great potential to solve the conflict between limited spectrum resources and increasing demand for wireless services. If user interference is effectively suppressed by setting the optimal spectrum access probabilities, unused licensed spectrum resources can be efficiently shared distributed among multiple primary users and secondary users (Li, 2010). Therefore, when various users share one radio spectrum channel in CR networks, co-channel interference must to be considered. As to the interference from secondary users, the primary user use the strategy to constraint the transmit power of primary user. In 2007, J. Li et al. proposed a new game model to control the distribution of power and channel for multi-users. First, this control problem was modeled as a non-cooperative game, and then then proved that it's a supermodular game. The main goal is to maximize the total system capacity of the network. The secondary users choose their power distribution in each channel according their payoff functions which considering both the capacity gain of themselves and the loss of the others. Supermodular game will converge to Nash equilibrium when every user could choose the strategy to maximize his utility function in every step. To make the supermodular game converge, a distributed scheduler can be applied to arrange the action of the secondary users to ensure only one user will choose his strategy in every step (Akyildiz, 2008), (Li, Chen, Li, & Ma, 2007).

Another supermodular game was developed to investigate the spectrum sharing in cognitive radio networks (Cheng, Yang, Fu, & Kwak, 2011). This model considered a Bertrand competition model, in which primary service providers compete to sell their spare spectrum and then to maximize their individual profits. In this work, the round-robin optimization algorithm was also developed to approximate the Nash equilibrium. Finally, the Bertrand competition was proven as a supermodular game.

Stackelberg Game for Cognitive Radio Networks

Spectrum trading process can be formulated as a microeconomic system with a sequence-independent game, where Nash equilibrium is expected to be the optimal solution among coequal participants. However, in practical cognitive radio networks, a primary User (PU) and a secondary User (SU) are not equal, since secondary users are considered as lower priority, and a basic requirement for secondary users is to avoid the interference to primary users in their vicinity. Therefore, such hierarchical and sequence-dependent gaming models merit further investigation in cognitive radio networks (Zhu, Suo, & Gao, 2010).

Stackelberg games are a class of games in game theory. In a standard Stackelberg game, one player acts as a leader and the rest as followers, and the main goal is to find an optimal strategy for the leader. In 2009, Li et al. investigated Stackelberg game model for the CR network resource allocation problem (Li, Wang, & Guizani, 2009). In this model, spectrum sharing was viewed as a spectrum trading process, i.e., spectrum pricing and purchasing, in which a market was formed by allowing the trading of spectrum between SUs and PUs. Spectrum trading gives SUs a chance to transmit and increases the total revenue of PUs at the same time. As the seller of spectrum, a PU first marks the price of a unit of spectrum according to the quality of spectrum and the demand from SUs. Then a SU decides on how much spectrum to buy after observing the price. These factors are incorporated into the utility functions of PUs and SUs. In reality, PUs that are often referred to as primary service providers may know more about

the market than SUs. In order to depict this information asymmetry, the spectrum trading process is modeled as a Stackelberg game, in which sellers actually control the outcome of the game since they know more. What PUs and SUs can gain when they enter the market is defined respectively by the profit and utility function. PUs mark the prices of spectrum aiming at maximizing their profits. SUs then decide on their demands of spectrum according to the marked price and channel quality. Since it can be assumed that PUs know the utility function of SUs, PUs are actually leaders and SUs are followers in this game. A leader selects a strategy first, and then the follower chooses its own according to the strategy it observes from the leader. These strategies can be obtained using backward induction which starts from the demand of followers and ends at the strategy of the leaders (Li, 2009). Finally, this Stackelberg model solved the pricing process of licensed users and got the Nash Equilibrium point.

Another Stackelberg game was developed based hierarchical framework to optimize the CR network performance (Xiao, Bi, & Niyato, 2010). By using a simple pricing function for licensed users, this model was implemented as a distributed algorithm to converge the Stackelberg equilibrium. In this Stackelberg game, SUs need to pay a certain price to PUs for using the licensed spectrum. For each SU, improving its performance and simultaneously decreasing the price paid to PUs is the main objective. PUs try to adjust the pricing function to control the number of SUs and avoid the licensed spectrum to be overcrowded. Apart from that, PUs should also choose the optimal price to maximize the revenue and to maintain the interference power lower than the highest tolerable level. More specifically, PUs can use the pricing function to 'scare away' the low performance SUs and only allow the high potential SUs to use the licensed spectrum. In addition, the pricing function of PUs also controls the transmit powers of SUs to maintain the power constraints even if SUs cannot know the interference temperature limit of PUs. If PUs can gradually decrease the prices, all SUs will automatically join the optimal sub-band without need to communicate with others or do the exhaustive search. This model proved that there is a unique Stackelberg Equilibrium (Xiao, 2010).

A reversed Stackelberg game for secure cooperative spectrum trading was proposed (Zhu, 2010). With cross-level metrics and hierarchical gaming structures, the PU can supervise whether the SU cooperates or not, and detect the compromised actions. The distinct features of this model are security and cooperation. Especially, cooperation is introduced between a PU and a SU where the latter one acts as a relay for the former one, and it is progressed under the cooperative contract where the relay work should meet the requirement of a certain quality of service (QoS) level, given a determined amount of spectrum shared by the primary user. Based on the hierarchical and sequence dependent architecture, it is more flexible for the PU to optimize the utility according to the SU's action. From this reversed Stackelberg game-based secure cooperative spectrum trading model, Stackelberg equilibrium is considered as a solution concept. It is considered as the cooperative contract between PUs and SUs, and therefore the robustness of spectrum trading market is greatly enhanced (Zhu, 2010).

Evolutionary Game for Cognitive Radio Networks

Evolutionary game theory provides an excellent means to address the strategic uncertainty that a player may face by exploring different actions, adaptively learning during the strategic interactions, and approaching the best response strategy under changing conditions and environments (Wang, Liu, & Clancy, 2010). For CR network spectrum sharing problems, some evolutionary game models have been developed. D. Niyato et al. modeled the dynamic market; multiple PUs

sell spectrum to multiple SUs (Niyato, Hossain, & Han, 2009). The goal is to make the income of the PUs and SUs' benefits be maximized. To satisfy this goal, the evolutionary game was used to model the SUs' behavior and a non-cooperative game was used to model the PUs' behavior. The PUs broadcast the spectrum resources for sale and the corresponding price to the SUs in a dedicated control channel. The SUs who want to buy the spectrum also send request information through this channel. In this market, the PUs compete with each other to sell the spectrum while SUs compete with each other to purchase the spectrum. The SUs are divided into several groups, each group member shares personal information, including his access to certain spectrum and payoff function and so on. SUs gradually change their access strategic choices by learning. This model was proven that the behavior of SUs would converge on the evolutionary equilibrium through an evolution process, and behavior of PUs would converge on the Nash equilibrium through an iterative algorithm for strategy adaptation (Niyato, 2009).

Another evolutionary game was developed to answer the question of "how to collaborate" in multiuser de-centralized cooperative spectrum sensing (Wang, 2010). This model derived the behavior dynamics and the evolutionarily stable strategy (ESS) of the SUs. It is proven that the dynamics converge to the ESS, which renders the possibility of a de-centralized implementation of the proposed sensing game. According to the dynamics, a distributed learning algorithm was also developed. In order to study the evolution of SUs' strategies and answer the question that how to cooperate in the evolutionary spectrum sensing game, SUs update their strategy profile with replicator dynamics equations, since a rational player should choose a strategy more often if that strategy brings a relatively higher payoff. Thus, the SUs could approach the ESS solely based on their own payoff observations (Wang, 2010).

COOPERATIVE SPECTRUM SHARING GAMES FOR COGNITIVE RADIO NETWORKS

Providing proper economic incentives is essential for the success of dynamic spectrum sharing. Cooperative spectrum sharing is one effective way to achieve this goal. In cooperative spectrum sharing, SUs relay traffics for PUs, in exchange for dedicated transmission time for the SUs' own communication needs. Initial study of cooperative spectrum sharing mechanisms assumed complete network information, i.e., PUs know SUs' channel conditions, resource constraints, and costs of transmission. This assumption is often too strong for practical networks (Duan, Gao, & Huang, 2011). Recently, the research for cooperative spectrum sharing havs been studied the cooperative spectrum sharing under incomplete information.

Bargaining Game for Cooperative Spectrum Sharing

Since network users must have an agreement (i.e., NBS) on how to fairly and efficiently share the available spectrum resources, bargaining game is an important type of cooperative spectrum sharing games. However, finding the NBS needs global information which is not always available. A distributed implementation model was proposed where users adapt their spectrum assignment to approximate the optimal assignment through bargaining within local groups (Cao, 2005). Although not explicitly stated, it actually falls into the category of the NBS, because the objective is to maximize the total logarithmic user throughput which is equivalent to maximizing the product of user payoffs (Wang, Wu, & Liu, 2010), (Cao, 2005). In this cooperative game model, neighboring players adjust spectrum band assignment for better system performance through one-to-one or one-to-many bargaining. In addition, a theoretic lower bound is derived to guide the bargaining

process. Suris et al. conducted a similar model, which iteratively updates the power allocation strategy using only local information (Suris, DaSilva, Han, & MacKenzie, 2007). In this game model, players allocate power to channels and their payoffs are the corresponding capacity. Given the assumption that players far away from each other have negligible interference, the global objective from a particular player's perspective is detached to two parts: i) the product of faraway players' payoffs, and ii) the product of neighboring players' payoffs. Because the player's power allocation strategy only affects the second term, maximizing the second term is equivalent to maximizing the global objective. Each player sequentially adjusts the strategy, and it was proved that the iterative process was convergent (Wang, Wu, & Liu, 2010). The concept of the NBS can also be applied to scenarios without explicit bargaining. In another cooperative game model, the NBS was employed to determine how to split payment among several users in a cognitive spectrum auction, where the auctioneer directly set the NBS as the price to each player, and they will be ready to accept because the NBS is an equilibrium (Wu, Wang, Liu, & Clancy, 2009). In this game model, the objective function was defined as the product of individual payoffs which is similar to the NBS, but additional constraints have been introduced to eliminate collusive behavior in the auction (Wang, 2010). Based on the local bargaining approach, Cao et al. proposed a cooperative game model for CR networks (Cao, & Zheng, 2005). This model can adapt network topology while significantly reducing computation overhead compared to that of the conventional topology-based optimization. Devices self-organize into bargaining groups, and members of each group coordinate to adjust their spectrum usage. Each node who wants to improve its spectrum usage negotiates one-to-one fairness bargaining with its neighbor nodes (Akyildiz, 2008), (Cao, 2005).

Coalitional Game for Cooperative Spectrum Sharing

Coalitional game is another important type of cooperative spectrum sharing games. It describes how a set of players can cooperate with others by forming cooperating groups and thus improve their payoff in a game. In a cognitive radio network, cooperation among rational users can generally improve the network performance due to the multiuser diversity and spatial diversity in a wireless environment (Figure 2). Thus, coalitional game theory has been used to study user cooperation and design optimal, fair, and efficient collaboration strategies (Wang, Wu, & Liu, 2010). In 2006, Mathur et al. designed a new coalitional game, which developed a spectrum sharing process through receiver cooperation (Mathur, Sankaranarayanan, & Mandayam, 2006). This game modeled the receiver cooperation in a Gaussian interference channel as a coalitional game with transferrable payoff, where the value of the game was defined as the sum-rate achieved by jointly decoding all users in the coalition. It was shown that the grand coalition that maximizes the sum-rate is stable, and the rate allocation to members of a coalition was solved by a bargaining game modeling. Receiver cooperation by forming a linear multiuser detector was modeled as a game without transferrable payoff, where the payoff of each player was the received SINR. At high SINR regime, the grand coalition was proved to be stable and sum-rate maximizing (Wang, Wu, & Liu, 2010). Another coalitional game was developed to model cooperative spectrum sensing among SUs as a coalition game without transferrable payoff (Saad, Han, Debbah, Hjørungnes, & Basar, 2009). In this game, a distributed algorithm was proposed for coalition formation through merge and split. It was shown that the SUs can self-organize into disjoint independent coalitions, and the detection probability was maximized while maintaining a certain false alarm level (Wang, Wu, & Liu, 2010).

Figure 2. Coalitional game for cooperative spectrum sharing

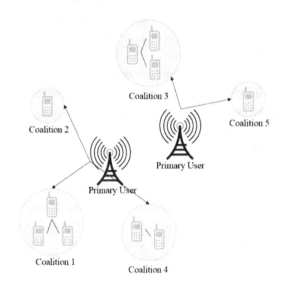

Cooperative Sensing Game for Spectrum Sharing

Spectrum sensing is one of the most important tasks for the operation of a cognitive radio network. But since communicating the sensing results periodically to other users consumes significant amount of energy, users tend to conserve energy by not sharing their results. This non-cooperation will lead to lesser clarity in spectrum occupancy map (Figure 3). Therefore, appropriate strategies are required to enforce cooperative sharing of the sensing results. In 2011, Kondareddy et al. proposed a new cross-layer game by exploiting the unique characteristics of cross-layer interaction in cognitive radios to sustain cooperative spectrum sensing (Kondareddy, & Agrawal, 2011). This game model was a combination of the spectrum sensing game in the physical layer and packet forwarding game in the network layer. Users punish those who do not share their sensing results by denying to cooperate in the network layer. The cross-layer game is modeled as a non-cooperative non zero-sum repeated game and a generous Tit-

For-Tat strategy is proposed to ensure cooperation even in the presence of collisions and spectrum mobility. They proved that the Nash Equilibrium of this strategy is mutual cooperation and that it is robust against attacks on spectrum sensing and sharing session (Kondareddy, 2011).

In 2010, Wang et al. formulated the cooperative spectrum sharing problem as a game between one PU and n SUs, where the PU selects a proper set of SUs to serve as the cooperative relays for its transmission (Wang, Gao, Gan, Wang, & Hossain, 2010). In return, the PU leases portion of channel access time to the selected secondary users for their own transmission. The PU's strategy is to select proper SUs and to determine the portion of channel access time left for SUs' transmission. An SU's strategy is to choose the power level used to help PU's transmission. In this game, the PU's utility function is related to its transmission rate, and an SU's utility function is not only related to its transmission rate but also the cost of power. The SU's access time is related to the effort it makes when it acts as cooperative relay, i.e., the power level it uses to help PU's transmission. Finally, they proved that there is a unique Nash equilibrium in the network, and we derive the strategies of PU and SUs in the Nash equilibrium (Wang, 2010).

Figure 3. Cooperative sensing game for spectrum sharing

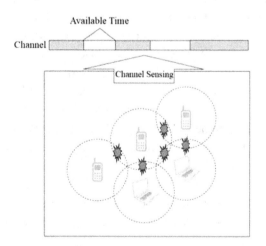

Another cooperative game model was developed to increase the agility of cognitive radio networks (Ganesan, & Li, 2005). This model can reduce the detection time and thus increase the overall agility. By employing different degrees of cooperation, this model has analyzed two approaches, i) non-cooperative, where each user detects the PU independently, but the first user to detect the PU informs the other cognitive users through a central controller, and ii) totally cooperative, where the users follow the *amplify-and-forward* cooperation protocol to reduce the detection time. This model has showed that cooperation between cognitive nodes increases the overall agility of the network (Ganesan, 2005).

ECONOMIC GAMES FOR COGNITIVE RADIO NETWORKS

As game theory studies interaction between rational and intelligent players, it can be applied to the economic world to deal with how people interact with each other in the market. The marriage of game theory and economic models yields interesting games and fruitful theoretic results in microeconomics and auction theory (Wang, Wu, & Liu, 2010). Nowadays, the application of game theory in economy has been applied into cognitive radio spectrum sharing process. Usually, economic models are suitable for the scenario of the secondary spectrum market where PUs are allowed to sell unused spectrum rights to SUs. PUs, as sellers, have the incentive to trade temporarily unused spectrum for monetary gains, while SUs, as buyers, may want to pay for spectrum resources for data transmissions. The deal is made through pricing, auctions, or other means. Economic games do not confine themselves to the scenario with explicit buyers and sellers, and the ideas behind can be extended to some cognitive radio scenarios other than secondary spectrum markets. As cognitive radio goes far beyond technology and its success will highly rely on the combination of technology, policy, and markets, it is of extreme importance to understand cognitive radio networks from the economic perspective and develop effective procedures (e.g., auction mechanisms) to regulate the spectrum market (Wang, Wu, & Liu, 2010).

Auction Game for Cognitive Radio Spectrum Sharing

Auction theory is an applied branch of game theory which analyzes interactions in auction markets and researches the game theoretic properties of auction markets. An auction, conducted by an auctioneer, is a process of buying and selling products by eliciting bids from potential buyers (i.e., bidders) and deciding the auction outcome based on the bids and auction rules. The rules of auction, or auction mechanisms, determine whom the goods are allocated to (i.e., the allocation rule) and how much price they have to pay (i.e., the payment rule). As efficient and important means

of resource allocation, auctions have quite a long history and have been widely used for a variety of objects, including antiques, real properties, bonds, spectrum resources, and so on. The spectrum allocation problem in cognitive radio networks can also be settled by auctions (Wang, Wu, & Liu, 2010) (Figure 4).

A novel auction game was developed for the spectrum trading by using microeconomics (Huang, Berry, & Honig, 2006). This model is similar to a share auction, or divisible auction, where a perfectly divisible good is split among bidders whose payments depend solely on the bids. A common form of bids in a share auction is for each user to submit his demand curve, i.e., the amount of goods a user desires as a function of the price. The auctioneer can compute a market clearing price based on the set of demand curves. In this game model, a user's demand curve for received power also depends on the demands of other users due to interference. And, this game

Figure 4. Auction game for cognitive radio spectrum sharing

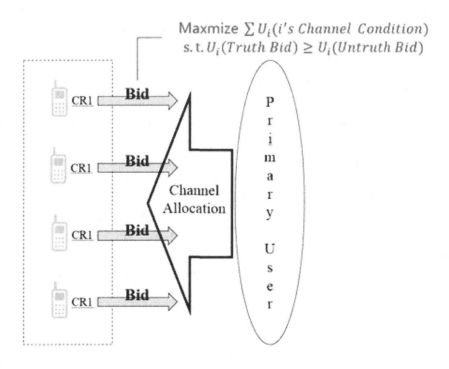

model formulated an iterative and distributed bid updating algorithm, which can converge globally to the Nash equilibrium of the auction (Huang, 2006). Another auction-based spectrum sharing model is a truthful and computationally efficient spectrum auction to support an eBay-like dynamic spectrum market (Zhou, Gandhi, Suri, & Zheng, 2008). This model is a single-sided spectrum auction only considering buyers. It allows wireless users to obtain and pay for the spectrum based on their demands. This auction model has been directly extended to the double auction mode (Zhou, & Zheng, 2009). It was developed to support truthful double spectrum auctions where multiple parties can trade spectrum based on their individual needs.

Under the condition that the auctioneer has complete information, winner determination and pricing mechanism have been implemented. In 2010, Xu et al. proposed a double auction game model for dynamic spectrum sharing (Xu, & Wang, 2010). This model allowed free spectrum bands trading between operators to improve the efficiency of the spectrum utilization. In addition, this approach investigated the practical wireless communication model by using the adaptive adjustable bidding/asking strategies. Another auction based non-cooperative game was characterized competitiveness among PUs and SUs (Mohammadian, & Abolhassani, 2010). This model presented a dynamic updating algorithm for the cost function of each PU, which aids PUs to achieve more demands from SUs in each stage of the dynamic spectrum sharing game. In 2011, Han et al. adopted the repeated auction model to maximize the tradeoff between the gain and cost in accessing spectrum bands (Han, Zheng, & Poor, 2011). To design a formulation with incomplete information, a nonparametric belief update algorithm was constructed based on the Dirichlet process.

Mechanism Design for Cognitive Radio Spectrum Sharing

In CR spectrum sharing problems, a fundamental question is to find the best way to allocate the available spectrum. This generalized allocation problem falls into the category of mechanism design, a field of game theory on a class of private information games. Mechanism design can be viewed a way to improve the efficiency of equilibrium by motivating players to compete honestly, so that the spectrum resources are allocated to players who value them most by means of transfers. Transfers must be collected and redistributed by a trusted entity. The distinguishing feature of mechanism design is that the game structure is designed by a game designer called a 'principal' who wants to choose a mechanism for his own interest. Like in an auction, the players, called the agents, hold some information that is not known by the others, and the principal asks the agents for some messages (i.e., the bids in an auction) to elicit the private information. Therefore, this is a game of incomplete information with each agent's private information, formally known as the type (Wang, Wu, & Liu, 2010).

In 2007, mechanism design has been applied to multimedia resource allocation problem in CR networks (Fattahi, Fu, Schaar, & Paganini, 2007). For the multimedia transmission, the utility function is defined as the expected distortion reduction resulting from using the channels. Since the system designer wants to maximize the system utility, mechanism based resource allocation is used to enforce users to represent their private parameters truthfully. Another mechanism design-based game model was developed to investigate dynamic spectrum access approaches in two scenarios: spectrum sharing in unlicensed bands and licensed bands (Wang, Wu, Ji, Liu, & Clancy, 2008). First, a self-enforcing truth-telling mechanism for unlicensed spectrum sharing was proposed based on repeated game modeling, in which the selfish users were motivated to share unlicensed spectrum, under the threat of punishment, and their cheating behavior was suppressed with the aid of a transfer function. The transfer function represents the payment that a user receives (or makes if it is negative) based on the private information. In this mechanism, it was shown that the users can get the highest utility only by announcing their true private information. Second, a collusion-resistant multistage dynamic spectrum pricing game for licensed spectrum sharing was proposed to optimize the overall spectrum efficiency and combat possible user collusion. Both approaches were demonstrated to alleviate the degradation of the system performance due to selfish users cheating (Wang, 2008). Another mechanism design based game model was proposed to investigate the design of a truthful auction for the case when a primary spectrum owner is willing to lease its idle spectral resources in sequential time periods (Sodagari, Attar, & Bilen, 2010). The secondary cognitive radios participate in the spectrum sharing auction by declaring to the primary their types, which consist of their arrival and departure time instances and valuations. This adapted methodology aims at reducing the collusion incentive among secondary users through the proper choice of the pricing policy and replacing second-price policy, such as in Vickrey–Clarke–Groves (VCG) auctions, by the critical value auction. In this model, auction is dynamic and is performed on-line, in contrast to static off-line schemes such as traditional VCG mechanism (Sodagari, 2010).

SECURITY GAMES FOR COGNITIVE RADIO NETWORKS

Due to the intrinsic feature of dynamic spectrum access, a cognitive radio network is very vulnerable to malicious attacks. First, in the opportunity-based spectrum access, secondary users do not own the spectrum band, and their access to that band cannot be protected from adversaries. Second, the spectrum availability is highly dynamic in nature, and the traditional security enhancing mechanisms are not directly applicable, since they only fit in a static spectrum environment. Third, some CR networks may work in a distributed fashion, which makes it more difficult to fight against malicious attacks than in a centralized system. Fourth, as cognitive radio networks benefit from technology evolution to be capable of utilizing spectrum adaptively and intelligently, the same technologies can also be exploited by malicious attackers to launch more complicated and unpredictable attacks with even greater damage. Therefore, ensuring security is critical issue for the wide deployment of CR networks (Wang, Wu, & Liu, 2010).

Game theory is a natural tool for the design of defense, since the interactions between the mutually distrustful parties can be modeled as a game model. For the last decades, different kinds of game models have been developed. As a dynamic game, stochastic game model can be used to help derive the optimal defense strategies that accommodate both the environment dynamics and the adaptive attacking strategy. For attacker tracking in multi-band networks, pursuit-evasion modeling can be used. If the attackers are viewed as mutants, evolutionary game theory can help legitimate users find stable equilibrium strategies that will overwhelm possible attacks. Coalitional games, graphical games, and network formation games can also help legitimate users form optimal partitions or networks to defend against multiple distributed attackers in a large area. These games are just a few examples that are potential solutions to security enhancement in cognitive radio networks. They can also be used to design dynamic spectrum allocation schemes in an environment without malicious attackers (Wang, Wu, & Liu, 2010).

Radio jamming is a Denial of Service (DoS) attack which targets at disrupting communications at the physical and link layers of a wireless network. By constantly injecting packets to a shared spectrum, a jamming attacker can prevent legitimate users from accessing an open spectrum band. Another type of jamming is to inject high interference power around the vicinity of a victim, so that the signal to noise ratio (SNR) deteriorates heavily and no data can be received correctly. In a cognitive radio network, malicious attackers can launch jamming attack to prevent efficient utilization of the spectrum opportunities. In 2011, Wang et al. investigated the security mechanism when secondary users are facing the jamming attack, and proposed a stochastic game model for anti-jamming defense (Wang, Wu, Liu, & Clancy, 2011). At each stage of the game, secondary users observed the spectrum availability, the channel quality, and the attackers' strategy from the status of jammed channels. According to this observation, secondary users will decide how many channels they should reserve for transmitting control and data messages and how to switch between the different channels. This stochastic game model can be generalized to model various defense mechanisms in other layers of a cognitive radio network, since it can well model the different dynamics due to the environment as well as the cognitive attackers (Wang, 2011).

SUMMARY

As the rapid development of wireless communication, the scarcity of spectrum becomes more and more prominent. Cognitive radio is proposed to overcome the problem of low spectrum utilization brought by static spectrum allocation. Game theory is an effective tool to model cognitive spectrum sharing. By using game theory, the spectrum sharing mechanism can achieve the higher utilization. In this chapter, we provide a comprehensive overview of spectrum sharing game models and classify state-of-the-art game theoretic research contributions on CR networks. For each category, we explain the fundamental concepts and proper-

ties, and provide a detailed discussion about the methodologies on how to apply game theory in spectrum sharing protocol design.

REFERENCES

Akyildiz, I. F., Lee, W., Vuran, M. C., & Mohanty, S. (2008). A survey on spectrum management in cognitive radio networks. *IEEE Communications Magazine*, *46*(4), 40–48. doi:10.1109/MCOM.2008.4481339

Canales, M., & Gállego, J. R. (2010). Potential game for joint channel and power allocation in cognitive radio networks. *Electronics Letters*, *46*(24), 1632–1634. doi:10.1049/el.2010.2627

Cao, L., & Zheng, H. (2005). Distributed Spectrum Allocation via Local Bargaining. In *Proceedings of IEEE SECON*, (pp. 475- 486). IEEE.

Cheng, H., Yang, Q., Fu, F., & Kwak, K. S. (2011). Spectrum sharing with smooth supermodular game in cognitive radio networks. In *Proceedings of Communications and Information Technologies* (pp. 543–547). Academic Press. doi:10.1109/ISCIT.2011.6092168

Duan, L., Gao, L., & Huang, J. (2011). Contract-based cooperative spectrum sharing. In *Proceedings of IEEE New Frontiers in Dynamic Spectrum Access Networks (DySPAN)*, (pp. 399-407). IEEE.

Fattahi, A., Fu, F., Schaar, M., & Paganini, F. (2007). Mechanism-based resource allocation for multimedia transmission over spectrum agile wireless networks. *IEEE Journal on Selected Areas in Communications*, *25*(3), 601–612. doi:10.1109/JSAC.2007.070410

Ganesan, G., & Li, Y. (2005). Cooperative spectrum sensing in cognitive radio networks. In *Proceedings of IEEE Int. Symp. on New Frontiers in Dynamic Spectrum Access Networks, DySPAN 2005*. IEEE.

Han, Z., Zheng, R., & Poor, H. V. (2011). Repeated Auctions with Bayesian Nonparametric Learning for Spectrum Access in Cognitive Radio Networks. *IEEE Transactions on Wireless Communications, 10*(3), 890–900. doi:10.1109/TWC.2011.010411.100838

Hongshun, Z., & Xiao, Y. (2010). Advanced Dynamic Spectrum Allocation Algorithm Based on Potential Game for Cognitive Radio. In *Proceedings of Information Engineering and Electronic Commerce*. Academic Press.

Huang, J., Berry, R., & Honig, M. L. (2006). Auction-based Spectrum Sharing. *ACM/Springer Mobile Networks and Apps., 405–18.*

Kondareddy, Y., & Agrawal, P. (2011). Enforcing Cooperative Spectrum Sensing in Cognitive Radio Networks. In *Proceedings of IEEE GLOBECOM*. IEEE.

Li, H., Liu, Y., & Zhang, D. (2010). Dynamic spectrum access for cognitive radio systems with repeated games. In *Proceedings of IEEE Wireless Communications, Networking and Information Security*, (pp. 59-62). IEEE.

Li, J., Chen, D., Li, W., & Ma, J. (2007). Multiuser Power and Channel Allocation Algorithm in Cognitive Radio. In *Proceedings of ICCP*. ICCP.

Li, Y., Wang, X., & Guizani, M. (2009). Resource Pricing with Primary Service Guarantees in Cognitive Radio Networks: A Stackelberg Game Approach. In *Proceedings of IEEE GLOBECOM*. IEEE.

Mathur, S., Sankaranarayanan, L., & Mandayam, N. (2006). Coalitional games in Gaussian interference channels. In *Proceedings of IEEE ISIT*, (pp. 2210–2214). IEEE.

Mohammadian, H. S., & Abolhassani, B. (2010). Auction-based spectrum sharing for multiple primary and secondary users in cognitive radio networks. In *Proceedings of IEEE Sarnoff Symposium*. IEEE.

Niyato, D., Hossain, E., & Han, Z. (2009). Dynamics of Multiple-Seller and Multiple-Buyer Spectrum Trading in Cognitive Radio Networks: A Game-Theoretic Modeling Approach. *IEEE Transactions on Mobile Computing, 8*(8), 1009–1022. doi:10.1109/TMC.2008.157

Saad, W., Han, Z., Debbah, M., Hjørungnes, A., & Basar, T. (2009). Coalitional games for distributed collaborative spectrum sensing in cognitive radio networks. In *Proceedings of IEEE INFOCOM* (pp. 2114–2122). IEEE. doi:10.1109/INFCOM.2009.5062135

Sodagari, S., Attar, A., & Bilen, S. G. (2010). Strategies to Achieve Truthful Spectrum Auctions for Cognitive Radio Networks Based on Mechanism Design. In *Proceedings of IEEE New Frontiers in Dynamic Spectrum*. IEEE.

Suris, J., DaSilva, L., Han, Z., & MacKenzie, A. (2007). Cooperative game theory fordistributed spectrum sharing. In *Proceedings of the IEEE International Conference on Communications*, (pp. 5282–5287). IEEE.

Wang, B., Liu, K., & Clancy, T. (2010). Evolutionary cooperative spectrum sensing game: how to collaborate? *IEEE Transactions on Communications, 58*(3), 890–900. doi:10.1109/TCOMM.2010.03.090084

Wang, B., Wu, Y., Ji, Z., Liu, K. J. R., & Clancy, T. C. (2008). Game theoretical mechanism design methods: suppressing cheating in cognitive radio networks. *IEEE Signal Processing Magazine, 25*(6), 74–84. doi:10.1109/MSP.2008.929552

Wang, B., Wu, Y., & Liu, K. J. R. (2010). Game theory for cognitive radio networks: An overview. *Computer Networks*, *54*, 2537–2561. doi:10.1016/j.comnet.2010.04.004

Wang, B., Wu, Y., Liu, K. J. R., & Clancy, T. C. (2011). An anti-jamming stochastic game for cognitive radio networks. *IEEE Journal on Selected Areas in Communications*, *29*(4), 877–889. doi:10.1109/JSAC.2011.110418

Wang, H., Gao, L., Gan, X., Wang, X., & Hossain, E. (2010). Cooperative Spectrum Sharing in Cognitive Radio Networks: A Game-Theoretic Approach. In *Proceedings of IEEE ICC*. IEEE.

Wu, Y., Wang, B., Liu, K. J. R., & Clancy, T. C. (2009). A scalable collusion-resistant multi-winner cognitive spectrum auction game. *IEEE Transactions on Communications*, *57*(12), 3805–3816. doi:10.1109/TCOMM.2009.12.080578

Wu, Y., Wang, B., Ray Liu, K. J., & Clancy, T. C. (2009). Repeated open spectrum sharing game with cheat-proof strategies. *IEEE Transactions on Wireless Communications*, 1922–1933.

Xiao, Y., Bi, G., & Niyato, D. (2010). Distributed optimization for cognitive radio networks using Stackelberg game. In *Proceedings of IEEE International Conference on Communication Systems*, (pp. 77-81). IEEE.

Xu, F., Zhang, L., Zhou, Z., & Liang, Q. (2007). Adaptive Power Control for Cooperative UWB Network Using Potential Game Theory. In *Proceedings of IEEE WCNC*, (pp. 1620-1624). IEEE.

Xu, W., & Wang, J. (2010). Double auction based spectrum sharing for wireless operators. In *Proceedings of IEEE International Symposium on Personal Indoor and Mobile Radio Communications (PIMRC)*, (pp. 2650–2654). IEEE.

Zhang, T., & Yu, X. (2010). Spectrum Sharing in Cognitive Radio Using Game Theory-A Survey. In *Proceedings of WiCOM*. WiCOM.

Zhou, X., Gandhi, S., Suri, S., & Zheng, H. (2008). eBay in the sky: strategy-proof wireless spectrum auctions. In *Proceedings of the ACM MobiCom Conference*, (pp. 2-13). ACM.

Zhou, X., & Zheng, H. (2009). TRUST: A General Framework for Truthful Double Spectrum Auctions. In Proceedings of IEEE Infocom, (pp. 999-1007). IEEE.

Zhu, Y., Suo, D., & Gao, Z. (2010). Secure Cooperative Spectrum Trading in Cognitive Radio Networks: A Reversed Stackelberg Approach. In *Proceedings of International Conference on Multimedia Communications*, (pp. 202-205). Academic Press.

KEY TERMS AND DEFINITIONS

Cross-Layer Optimization: An escape from the pure waterfall-like concept of the OSI communications model with virtually strict boundaries between layers. The cross layer approach transports feedback dynamically via the layer boundaries to enable the compensation by any control input to another layer but that layer directly affected by the detected deficiency.

Dynamic Spectrum Management: A set of techniques based on theoretical concepts in network information theory and game theory that is being researched and developed to improve the performance of a communication network as a whole.

Open Spectrum: A movement to get the Federal Communications Commission to provide more unlicensed, radio frequency spectrum that is available for use by all. Proponents of the '*commons model*' of open spectrum advocate a future where all the spectrum is shared, and in which people use Internet protocols to communicate with each other, and smart devices, which would find the most effective energy level, frequency, and mechanism.

Quality of Service (QoS): The overall performance of a telephony or computer network, particularly the performance seen by the users of the network.

Software-Defined Radio (SDR): A radio communication system where components that have been typically implemented in hardware are instead implemented by means of software on a personal computer or embedded system.

Spatial Multiplexing: A transmission technique in MIMO wireless communication to transmit independent and separately encoded data signals, so-called streams, from each of the multiple transmit antennas. Therefore, the space dimension is reused, or multiplexed, more than one time.

Chapter 8
Game Theory for Wireless Network Resource Management

ABSTRACT

Computer network bandwidth can be viewed as a limited resource. The users on the network compete for that resource. Their competition can be simulated using game theory models. No centralized regulation of network usage is possible because of the diverse ownership of network resources. Therefore, the problem is of ensuring the fair sharing of network resources. If a centralized system could be developed which would govern the use of the shared resources, each user would get an assigned network usage time or bandwidth, thereby limiting each person's usage of network resources to his or her fair share. As of yet, however, such a system remains an impossibility, making the situation of sharing network resources a competitive game between the users of the network and decreasing everyone's utility. This chapter explores this competitive game.

INTRODUCTION

Radio spectrum generally refers to radio channel (i.e., frequency band, time slot, channel access code) and transmission power. Usually, radio spectrum is a renewable resource that is finite in any instant of time but through its different dimensions of use: space, time, frequency and bandwidth, can be distributed to many users simultaneously. The process of distributing radio spectrum to users is radio resource management (Niyato, & Hossain, 2007). Nowadays, game theory can be used to design and analyze radio resource allocation protocols and corresponding network dynamics. In this chapter, we outline the game theory based radio resource management models.

DOI: 10.4018/978-1-4666-6050-2.ch008

GAME MODELS FOR WLAN RESOURCE MANAGEMENT

In 2004, Altman et al., proposed a non-cooperative game model for optimal random channel access in s Local Area Network (WLAN) (Altman, Borkar, & Kherani, 2004) (Figure 1). In this game model, the players are the nodes in the network, and the strategy of each player is the probability of a transmission attempt if there is a packet in the queue. The player's utility is defined as the payoff due to successful packet transmission. To achieve the Nash equilibrium of channel access, a distributed algorithm was proposed considering the constraint on battery power at the mobile node (Niyato, 2007). Another game model for WLANs

Figure 1. WLAN resource management

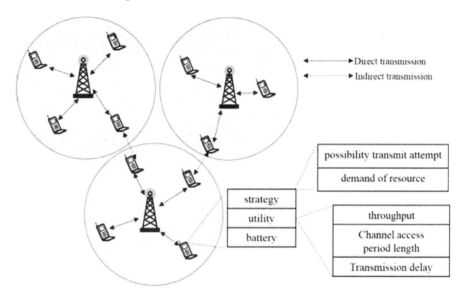

was proposed to support the QoS requirements (Berlemann, Hiertz, Walke, & Mangold, 2005). This game was designed as a radio resource sharing game among multiple wireless networks. In this game, the players are the different wireless networks, the strategy of each player corresponds to demand for resource allocation, and the payoff is obtained based on throughput, channel access period length, and transmission delay. Nash equilibrium is considered as the solution of the game in a bargaining domain (Niyato, 2007). For channel access in WLAN, another non-cooperative repeated game was formulated for CSMA/CA-based MAC protocol (Tan, & Guttag, 2005). The players of this game are the mobile nodes, and the strategy of each player is the data rate and average payload size. The payoff of each player is the achievable throughput. It was observed that the Nash equilibrium of this game cannot achieve the highest system throughput. However, by guaranteeing fair long-term channel access for each player, the total throughput achieved by all the nodes can be maximized (Niyato, 2007), (Tan, 2005).

Admission Control Game for WLAN

Recently, a variety of types of traffic must be accommodated in future WLAN environments. Therefore, a new distributed MAC function has been developed to support service differentiation (Kuo, Wu, & Chen, 2004). Besides, high speed WLAN environments are also expected to provide wireless Internet services in hot spots. Since there are usually multiple service providers competing for providing wireless network access in hot spots, mobile users are free to choose their own service providers. For a specific service provider, more flows are admitted to transmit in its coverage range, more revenue is gained. However, admitting many flows may make the wireless medium overloaded and degrade the QoS satisfactions of ongoing flows. Therefore, some mobile users may leave the current service provider and subscribe to wireless network access with another service provider. Under this competitive environment, an admission control game was formulated as a non zero-sum and non-cooperative game. As a solution, a Nash equilibrium was obtained (Kuo, 2004). Based on the game, a service provider not

Figure 2. WLAN admission control

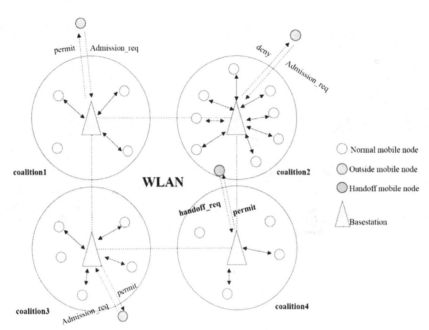

only fulfills most part QoS satisfactions of ongoing flows but also increases its own revenue (Figure 2).

Network Selection Game for WLAN

For the wireless network operation, a network selection and resource allocation game was developed (Malanchini, Cesana, & Gatti, 2012). Usually, wireless networks are often characterized by the interaction of different end users, communication technologies, and network operators. The game model by Malanchini analyzed the dynamics among these 'actors' by focusing on the processes of wireless network selection, where end users may choose among multiple available access networks to get connectivity, and resource allocation, where network operators may set their radio resources to provide connectivity. The interaction among end users was modeled as a non–cooperative congestion game where players (i.e., end users) selfishly selected the access network that minimized their perceived selection cost. In this model, a mathematical programming method was proposed to

find Nash equilibrium. The interaction among end users and network operators was assessed through a two-stage multi-leader/multi-follower game, where network operators (i.e., leaders) played in the first stage by properly setting the radio resources to maximize their users, and end users (i.e., followers) played in the second stage the aforementioned network selection game. The existence of exact and approximated sub-game perfect Nash equilibria of the two-stage game was thoroughly assessed (Malanchini, 2012).

GAME MODELS FOR CDMA NETWORK RESOURCE MANAGEMENT

Lately, extensive investigations have been carried out into the application of Code Division Multiple Access (CDMA) system, which can support wideband multimedia services at bit rates as high as 2 Mbps. The CDMA system employs spread-spectrum technology and a special coding scheme to allow multiple users to be multiplexed over the same physical channel. Therefore, CDMA system can achieve significant capacity gains and provide a number of radio resource management advantages not available in other multiple access systems. Game theory can be applied to the analysis of the CDMA control issues. With a formalized approach, many CDMA system interactive decision processes are currently addressed through game theory.

Admission Control Game for CDMA Networks

Call admission control (CAC) is one of the most important parts in radio resource management of CDMA networks, and it has an important effect on the quality of service. The most concern of traditional CAC strategies is to harmonize the blocking probability and dropping probability, so as to maximize the resource utility. With the development of radio network, not only resource utility is the emphasis of CAC but also fairness is becoming important. In the multimedia CDMA networks, if the high load stream traffic is admitted, it will over-use the resource greedily, which will cause the unfair use of the resource to other kinds of traffic.

In (Zhang, Fang, & Yuan, 2007), a new non-cooperative game for admission control for the CDMA system. In this game model, the accept probability of the new users was gained by using Cobb-Douglas utility function to construct a price function, then a Nash equilibrium point was obtained by using the accepting probability as the payoffs of a game. The fairness of resource utilization in different load situations was achieved by satisfying the concept of Nash equilibrium point.

In (Lin, Chatterjee, Das, & Basu, 2005), an integrated admission control and rate control method for CDMA wireless networks was modeled as a non-cooperative nonzero sum game between two players. The first player was a service provider whose strategy was to either accept or reject an incoming connection. The second player of this game was an incoming connection whose strategy was to either accept the offered service or churn to another service provider. The payoff of a service provider was obtained from the net revenue gained from the ongoing connections and the incoming connection. The payoff of an incoming connection was obtained from the utility due to assigned transmission rate and the penalty incurred if the connection chose to churn. Nash solution of a pure strategy was considered to determine whether an incoming connection can be accepted or not.

To control the CAC problems for the CDMA system, another game model was developed in (Virapanicharoen, & Benjapolakul, 2004). In this game, the problem of optimizing the call admission control thresholds in a multiservice CDMA networks to prioritize handoff calls over new calls was formulated. The players of this game were the service classes whose strategies were the corresponding thresholds for handoff calls, and the payoff for a player was the bandwidth utilization.

Network Selection Game for CDMA Networks

Due to the deregulation of the telecommunications industry, there is more than one service provider in any region. This gives the users the flexibility to switch their service provider if they are not satisfied with their service. In this perspective, another non-cooperative game for CDMA systems was designed for maximizing the utility of a carrier in a competitive market (Chatterjee, Haitao, Das, & Basu, 2003). This model formulated the power allocation problem between the carrier and the customers. For differentiated data services, three QoS classes have been considered where the higher class can always draw resources for the lower classes. A utility function was proposed which considered not only the revenue generated but also the risk probabilities of customers leaving the network. Utility was calculated at the time of a service admission request and the service was accepted if the new utility was more. In this game model, a desired solution is Nash equilibrium, which has the property that corresponds to utility-maximizing (Chatterjee, 2003).

Power Control Game for CDMA Networks

In 2011, Donmez et al., considered the uplink power control problem in a single-cell CDMA and proposed a *n*-person non-cooperative power control game (Donmez, 2011). In this game, each mobile user tried to maximize its own utility without any deal among the users. A utility function was defined for each user, which represented the user's choice with respect to the carrier-to-interference ratio (CIR) and the transmitter power. They proved that there exists an optimum operating point referred to as a Nash equilibrium that is unique (Donmez, 2011). Another non-cooperative game was formulated to develop a distributed power control algorithm for the CDMA system (Koskie, & Gajic, 2005). In this game, the players were the mobiles in a cell, and the strategy of each mobile was the transmission power. The payoff was determined based on signal-to-interference ratio, which determined the transmission quality. The transmission power of each mobile was obtained from the Nash equilibrium; it was obtained through an iterative algorithm (Niyato, 2007), (Koskie, 2005). In 2010, Musku et al., applied game theory to model the problem of joint transmission rate and power control for the uplink of a single cell CDMA system as a non-cooperative game (Musku, Chronopoulos, Popescu, & Stefanescu, 2010). The utility function used in this approach was defined by the ratio of throughput to the transmit power and its maximization implied optimal transmission rate and power. They showed the existence of Nash equilibria for the joint rate and power control game and formally stated the NRPG algorithm for joint rate and power control (Musku, 2010).

GAME MODELS FOR OFDM NETWORK RESOURCE MANAGEMENT

Recently, Orthogonal Frequency-Division Multiplexing (OFDM) is being considered as a modulation technique in networks; the spectrum of orthogonally modulated adjacent subcarriers can overlap, increasing transmission spectral efficiency. OFDM can distribute the data on several low data rate subcarriers (multi-carrier system) and serve connections with fine-granularity by the elastic allocation of low rate subcarriers according to the connection demands. Therefore, OFDM can enhance the performance of wireless transmission by transmitting data bits over multiple subcarriers.

Power Control Game for OFDM Networks

For OFDM-based wireless networks, a non-cooperative game was formulated to minimize transmission power while achieving the target rate requirement (Han, Ji, & Liu, 2004). In this game, the players were different users transmitting data over multiple sub-channels in a multi-cell OFDM network. The strategy was the transmission rate and power allocated to each sub-channel, and the payoff was calculated as the utility function based on transmission rate and power. To reach a Nash equilibrium, users performed the water-filling algorithm in a distributed way by using local information only (Han, 2004). Another non-cooperative power control game was developed for OFDM cellular systems (Gorji, Abolhassani, Honardar, Adibi, & Okhovat, 2010). In this game, power of each user was assumed as a resource and then solved power control problem based on the idea of the Nash Equilibrium. Based on game theory, a utility function was proposed that each user tried to maximize its own utility by adjusting the transmit power on every of its subcarriers. According to defined utility function, each user tried to maximize his transmitted data rate while minimizing allocated transmit power. This dynamic non-cooperative power control game can satisfy fairness among users at NE (Gorji, 2010). In 2006, Wang et al., formulated the multi-cell OFDM resource control problem as a non-cooperative power control game, and the properties of the Nash equilibrium was investigated (Wang, Xue, & Schulz, 2006). A specific utility function was defined considering the users' average utility per power, i.e., power unit based utility. All users rationally chose appropriate strategies to maximize their own utility in a distributed fashion. This game converged to the Nash equilibrium after several iterations. However, it was shown that the equilibrium solution was Pareto inefficient. To improve the OFDM system efficiency, this game model proposed a pricing policy to the user's transmit power by adding a penalty price. With the adoption of the price, the user's aggressive behavior was depressed and Pareto improvement was achieved (Wang, 2006).

Bargaining Game for OFDM Networks

Radio resource allocation is one of the key technologies in OFDM systems, where subcarriers and power are schedulable resources. In 2007, Zhang et al., solved the fair resource allocation problem based on the idea of the Nash bargaining solution, which not only provides the resource allocation of users that are Pareto optimal from the view of the whole system, but also are consistent with the fairness axioms of game theory (Zhang, Zeng, Feng, Zheng, & Ma, 2007). They developed a suboptimal solution of NBS via low-pass time window filter and first-order Taylor expansion, and then proposed an efficient and practical dynamic subcarriers allocation algorithm. In particular, based on the cooperative game theory, they focused on the effective and practical algorithm development for efficient and fair resource allocation in OFDM systems. Finally, it was confirmed that

the developed utility-based dynamic subcarriers allocation algorithm significantly enhanced the system performance and guaranteed utility fairness between users having different rate-sensitive applications (Zhang, 2007).

GAME MODELS FOR CELLULAR NETWORKS RESOURCE MANAGEMENT

Wireless network is an attractive technology provider to nomadic environment. Among several configuration of wireless network design, the cellular design is a notable one. Cellular network provides a high degree of spectrum reuse and efficient bandwidth management by allowing cell geometry repetitions along with frequency reuse feature. However, in cellular networks, bandwidth is still an extremely valuable and scarce resource. Therefore, all performance guarantees are conditional on currently available bandwidth capacity. In view of the remarkable growth in the number of users and the limited bandwidth, an efficient bandwidth management is very important and has been an active area of research over the last decade. Game theory has been used to study several radio resource management problems in cellular networks.

Dynamic Spectrum Access Game for Cellular Networks

A two-players non-zero sum game based on the Dynamic Spectrum Access (DSA) technique was presented for cellular operators (Kamal, Coupechoux, & Godlewski, 2009). DSA is a set of techniques based on theoretical concepts in network information theory and game theory that is being researched and developed to improve the network performance. Usually, two main axes of resource management - Joint Radio Resource Management (JRRM) and Dynamic Spectrum Access (DSA) - exist in the cellular context. In the RRM, one operator manages jointly his networks while making benefit of his own licensed bands. In the DSA (or called Inter-operator DSA), the competition and/or the cooperation aspects between different operators are explored. The game model developed by Kamal analyzed the interaction between cellular operators (i.e., players) with packet services by using inter-operator DSA algorithms (Kamal, 2009). An utility function for the operators that considered the users' bit rate, the blocking probability and the spectrum price was defined. In addition, a penalty function for the blocking probability control was developed. This game approach presented two system models: i) a centralized model was inspired by the Pareto optimality concept for the global welfare in terms of the operators rewards, and ii) a distributed model was inspired by the Nash equilibrium concept. In the second model, the convergence to Nash equilibrium was analyzed. Usually, a convergence period is needed to reach the unique equilibrium point, and there is a possibility of not converg-

ing to Nash equilibrium using the best-response algorithm (Kamal, 2009).

Cooperative Game for Cellular Networks

A novel cooperative bandwidth management game was proposed for multimedia cellular network resource management (Kim, 2011). Based on the well known cooperative game-theoretic concept of Nash bargaining, wireless bandwidth was controlled as efficiently as possible while ensuring quality-of-service (QoS) guarantees for higher-priority traffic services. To provide a reasonable compromise between efficiency and QoS provisioning, this game model was designed by employing two different algorithms; bandwidth reservation and migration algorithms. Based on the best compromise strategy, this approach can display desirable properties while maintaining the crucial notion of Nash bargaining solution, which can approximate the global system optimization (Figure 3).

Figure 3. Cellular network resource management

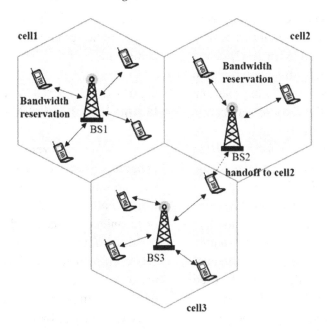

GAME MODELS FOR MULTI-HOP NETWORK RESOURCE MANAGEMENT

Cellular systems conventionally employ single hops between mobile units and the base station. Recently, edge-of-cell throughput is becoming a significant concern. A promising solution to the problem of improving coverage and throughput in cellular systems is the use of multi-hop relays. Under the guise of relay networks or cooperative diversity, there has been extensive research on multi-hop cellular networks. Many existing approaches to this problem have focused on competitive game-theory analysis (Jiang & Ward, 2011).

Cooperative Game for Multi-Hop Networks

A cooperative game based on the Kalai-Smorodinsky-Raiffa solution was proposed to study the behavior of nodes in multi-hop wireless networks (Jiang, 2011). This game assumed that the nodes were rational, selfish, but not malicious, independent agents. Thus, a node would cooperate only if it was able to benefit from such cooperation; otherwise it would compete with other nodes for more bandwidth. The incentive for cooperation was implicit: a node that did not cooperate would get less bandwidth. By assuming that the utility of a node is equal to its throughput, the fair bandwidth allocation in two-hop wireless networks can be computed (Jiang, 2011). Another game theory methodology was employed to solve the distribution of the radio resources for wireless multi-hop networks. This game theory approach can guarantee a fair and efficient channel sharing and maximizes the overall network performance (Roy, Wu, & Zawodniok, 2011). A new cooperative game model was developed for wireless multi-hop networks (Chen, Xu, & Li, 2010). By introducing the idea of cross-layer design and its cooperative mechanism, this game model combined the energy threshold in the physical layer and the channel ca-

pacity in the link layer. In addition, the cooperative bargaining game theory was applied to analyze the bargaining behavior of nodes in wireless multi-hop network. This cooperative game approach can efficiently improve the fairness and utility of the resource in the network (Chen, 2010).

Hierarchical Game for Multi-Hop Networks

In recent years, hierarchical multi-hop network architectures have emerged as an essential aspect of emerging communication networks. For instance, while cellular-based communication has been the leading architecture in the past decade, recent advances in wireless networking, such as the need for distributed multi-hop communication imposed a hierarchical architecture on many next generation wireless networks. In 2009, Saad et al., proposed a game theoretic approach to tackle the problem of the distributed formation of the hierarchical network architecture that connects the nodes in the uplink of a wireless multi-hop network (Saad, Zhu, Basar, Han, & Hjorungnes, 2009). They investigated the problem of the formation of this topology among a number of nodes and modeled the problem as a hierarchical network formation game. The developed game model divided the network into different hierarchy levels, whereby the nodes belonging to the same level engage in a non-cooperative Nash game. The nodes at the same level interact by selecting the mixed strategies that maximize their individual utilities, in terms of probability of successful multi-hop transmission, while taking into account the interference at every node in the communication path. As a solution to the game, they propose a novel equilibrium concept, the hierarchical Nash equilibrium, for a sequence of multi-stage Nash games, which can be found by backward induction analytically. For finding this equilibrium, they proposed a distributed myopic dynamics algorithm, based on fictitious play, in which each node computes the mixed strategies that maximize its utility which represents the probability of successful transmission over the multi-hop communication path in the presence of interference (Saad, 2009). Another hierarchical game for multi-hop networks was developed by Kwon et al., (Kwon, Lee, & Cioffi, 2009). In multi-hop networks, each node needs to send traffic via relay nodes, which behave independently while staying aware of energy constraints. To encourage a relay to forward the packets, this model formulated a Stackelberg game where two nodes sequentially bid their willingness weights to cooperate for their own benefits. Accordingly, all the nodes are encouraged to be cooperative only if a sender is cooperative and alternatively to be non-cooperative only if a sender is non-cooperative. This selective strategy changes the reputations of nodes depending on the amount of their bidding at each game and motivates them to maintain a good reputation so that all their respective packets can be treated well by other relays. As a solution, a Nash equilibrium was obtained (Kwon, 2009).

GAME MODELS FOR SENSOR NETWORK ENERGY MANAGEMENT

Sensor networks are dense wireless networks of small, low-cost sensors, which collect and disseminate environmental data. Wireless sensor networks facilitate monitoring and controlling of physical environments from remote locations with better accuracy. They have applications in a variety of fields such as environmental monitoring, military purposes and gathering sensing information in inhospitable locations. Sensor nodes have various energy and computational constraints because of their inexpensive nature and ad hoc method of deployment. Especially, restrictions in power resources need to be considered in order to improve the longevity of the nodes. Recently, game theoretic approaches to the power control problem have been applied in wireless networks. An important motivation for using a game theoretic

model in sensor networks is the fact that there is no central controller or infrastructure in sensor networks, and it's difficult for a node to have the knowledge of other nodes in such a dynamic changed environment (Figure 4).

Routing Game for Sensor Networks

In sensor networks, energy is the most scarce resource. To conserve energy, a node needs to consider whether a received packet should be forwarded or dropped. In 2006, Felegyhazi et al., proposed a new routing mechanism for sensor networks (Felegyhazi, Hubaux, & Buttyan, 2006). In this mechanism, the packet forwarding policy in a sensor node was formulated as a routing game and the Nash equilibrium was studied. The players in this game were the wireless nodes, and the strategy for each player was the level of cooperation to forward a received packet. The payoff for each node was computed from normalized throughput and the cost of forwarding packets. Different strategies (e.g., always defect, always cooperate, tit-for-tat) in a multistage game were studied analytically for different spatial distributions of the nodes and the topology of the network (Felegyhazi, 2006). Another routing game model has been developed for wireless sensor networks (Zhao, Zhang, & Zhang, 2008). Usually, the energy consumption can be reduced when nodes complete the topology control corporately and aggregate data coordinately. In this game model, the data transfer strategies considered the amount of data sent and forwarded by sensor nodes to reduce the energy consumption. By transferring data coordinately instead of transferring alone, some nodes formed a coalition based on the Markov-process. This approach can effectively reduce the energy consumption of wireless sensor networks (Zhao, 2008). Recently, a new routing game was developed by Lin et al., (Lin, & Wang, 2012). In this game model, energy fairness problem was considered for wireless sensor networks. However, the heterogeneous hostile operating conditions -

Figure 4. Sensor network energy management

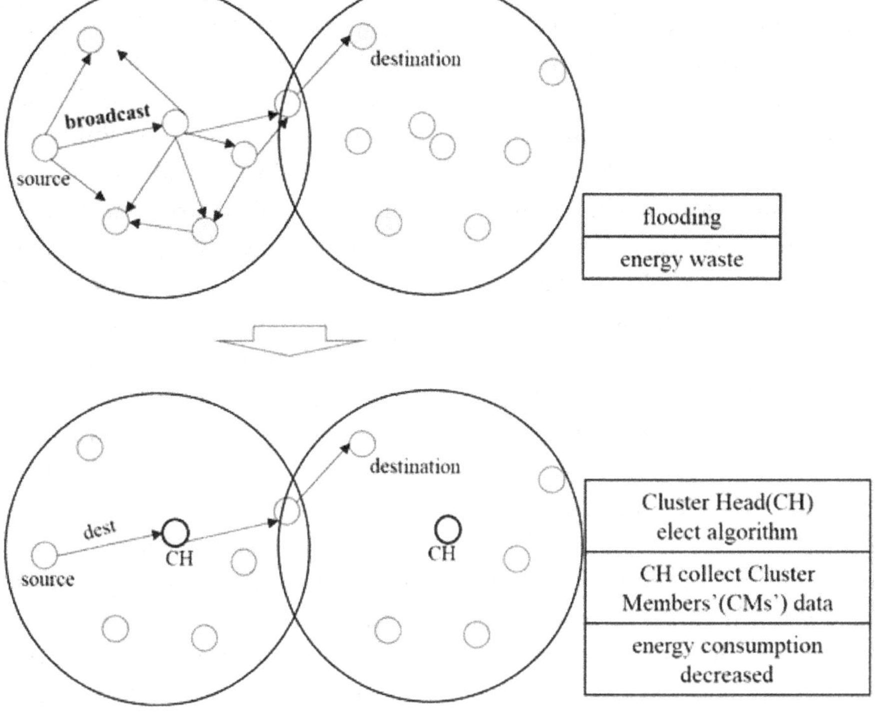

different transmission distances, varying fading environments and distinct remained energy levels - have made energy balancing a highly challenging design issue. To tackle this problem, the developed game was designed to model the packet transmission of sensor nodes. By properly designing the utility function, this game model got the Nash equilibrium while each node can optimize its own payoff. Therefore, the global objective (i.e., energy balancing) can be achieved. In addition, by imposing penalty mechanism on sensors to punish selfish behaviors, the delivery rate and delay constraints were also satisfied (Lin, 2012).

Security Game for Sensor Networks

Recently, some of the literatures using game theory approach for intrusion detection on wireless sensor networks were published. In 2006, Alpcan et al., discussed a two-player zero-sum Markov security game and analyzed through numerical

examples for various game parameters (Alpcan, & Basar, 2006). They considered a game model with limited observations in order to capture the interaction between the malicious attackers who try to gain unauthorized access to a networked system and the Intrusion Detection System (IDS) which allocates system resources to collect information for detection and decides on a response. By capturing the operation of a sensor network observing and reporting the attack information to the IDS as a finite-state Markov chain, they developed a stochastic and dynamic model. In this limited observation security game, players were played repeatedly over time reflecting the ongoing attacker-IDS interaction. This enables players to refine their own strategies by learning more about the system and their adversaries. Through the numerical analysis of an illustrative example, they studied the optimal mixed strategy solutions as well as evolution of player costs under various game parameters (Alpcan, 2006).

Srinivasan et al., described a game-theoretic algorithm based on Tit-For-Tat strategy, and designed to drive a system of nodes to Nash Equilibrium (NE) where each node achieves the best possible tradeoff between throughput and lifetime (Srinivasan, Nuggehalli, Chiasserini, & Rao, 2003). Assuming each node understands its maximum forwarding rate and maintains a history of experiences regarding the rate at which its forwarding requests are honored. But a node will reject a forwarding request beyond its maximum rate (outside healthy operating bounds) or if the node is forwarding more packets (as designed) than another node in the cluster. This latter condition allows a small amount of excess forwarding representing the generous portion of the algorithm (Srinivasan, 2003).

For prevention of denial of service (DoS) attacks in wireless sensor networks, a new game model was developed (Agah, Basu, & Das, 2005). In the developed game model, nodes prefer to participate in forwarding incoming packets and gaining reputation in the network. Nodes compete against each other, and the competition is based on auction theory. Therefore, an attack-defense problem was formulated as a non-cooperative nonzero-sum two-player game between an attacker and a wireless sensor network. This game achieved Nash equilibrium and thus leading to a defense strategy for the network (Agah, 2005).

GAME MODELS FOR 4G WIRELESS NETWORK RESOURCE MANAGEMENT

Wireless communication has revolutionized the way of our day-to-day communication and opened opportunities for many innovative applications in areas such as intelligent transportation system and multimedia entertainment system. While wireless technology has come a long way since its introduction, its adoption rate has increased significantly and new bandwidth hungry applica-

tions are evolving at the same time. Demand for a wireless technology that can support current and future emerging applications is on the rise, which has led to the introduction of 4G wireless standard and two major contenders for 4G standard include: the worldwide interoperability for microwave access (WiMAX) and the long term evolution advanced (LTE-A). Both of technologies target to deliver very high throughput with stringent quality of service, long range coverage and high spectral efficiency (Ahmad, & Habibi, 2012).

In particular, WiMAX and LTE-A technologies intend to provide broadband connectivity to both fixed and mobile users in a wireless metropolitan area network environment. To provide flexibility for different applications, the standard supports major deployment scenarios. However, although the physical and MAC layer signaling are well defined in the standard, radio resource management remains as an open issue. In 4G networks, game theory techniques can be applied for resource allocation problems to maximize the utility while satisfying the QoS requirements for the different connections (Niyato, 2007).

Cooperative Game for 4G Wireless Networks

In 2006, Niyato et al., proposed a new cooperative game model for bandwidth allocation in 4G heterogeneous wireless access networks (Niyato, & Hossain, 2006). In this model, the bandwidth allocation problem was formulated as a bankruptcy game, which is a special type of an *n*-person cooperative game. With a bankruptcy game, each network can cooperate to provide the requested bandwidth to a new connection. A coalition among the different wireless networks was formed to offer bandwidth to a new connection. In addition, the stability of the allocation was analyzed by using the concept of the core and the amount of allocated bandwidth to a connection in each network was obtained by using Shapley value. This is different from a non-cooperative approach in which each network is rational and selfish to maximize its own profit. In a non-cooperative environment, all networks compete with each other to achieve their objectives. More specifically, the difference between cooperative and non-cooperative approaches lies in the fact that the former is group oriented, whereas the latter is individual oriented. In a cooperative approach, groups of players seek fair resource allocation. On the other hand, in a non-cooperative approach, allocation is performed based on the individual's profit gained from the resource (Niyato, 2006),(Niyato, & Hossain, 2008).

Hierarchical Game for 4G Wireless Networks

For the resource management in 4G networks, a new hierarchical game model was developed (Niyato, 2008). This game model was designed as two-level approach and presented a game-theoretic model for bandwidth allocation and admission control in such a heterogeneous wireless access environment. First, a non-cooperative game was used to obtain the bandwidth allocations to a service area from the different access networks available in that service area (on a long-term basis). For this game, Nash equilibrium gave the optimal allocation which maximized the utilities of all the connections in the network. Second, a bargaining game was formulated to obtain the capacity reservation thresholds so that the connection-level QoS requirements can be satisfied for the different types of connections (on a long-term basis). Based on the obtained bandwidth allocation and the capacity reservation thresholds, vertical and horizontal handoff connections were prioritized over new connections, and an admission control strategy was used to limit the number of ongoing connections so that the QoS performances were maintained at the target level for the different types of connections. This game model provided a fair resource allocation in the different service areas while satisfying both the service providers' and the users' requirements. Also, it can adapt

to both long-term and short-term variations of network resources and traffic load conditions (Niyato, 2008).

Speed Game for 4G Wireless Networks

Existing resource management game models in 4G networks are not suitable for high speed mobile nodes, particularly when they move towards cell-edge region. Mobility at high vehicular speeds causes the multipath problem, which severely limits spectral efficiency and throughput when Inter-Cell Interference (ICI) and low signal to noise ratio are added. 4G standards like LTE–A and WiMAX are currently considering various options to address this problem of low cell-edge throughput. Usually, standard schemes that split radio resources among cell center and cell-edge band partly addresses the problem of ICI, but provides no real support for truly mobile nodes. A new game theoretic resource management approach was developed to intelligently support for mobile nodes (Ahmad, 2012). This model followed market based strategy where both cell center and cell-edge bands considered the demand supply status and participated in a game to increase the user utility and revenue index. The ultimate benefits of the proposed game model were lower connection dropping rates for mobile nodes and higher revenue return for the service providers (Ahmad, 2012).

Network Selection Game for 4G Wireless Networks

One of the main features of 4G networks will be heterogeneity in the wireless access environment in which a mobile can connect to multiple radio interfaces simultaneously. Therefore, network selection and efficient load balancing among different types of networks would be required to achieve high speed connectivity with seamless mobility. During the last years, the problem of network selection in wireless heterogeneous systems has attracted a lot of attention. Expecting that next generation mobile devices will allow connections to different types of networks, it is interesting to investigate the outcome of selfish behavior in that context. Game theory techniques can be used to adaptively select networks in a heterogeneous environment. For example, each network service provider can be modeled as a player of the game, and a strategy is the amount of offered bandwidth to a connection. The solution of the game can be obtained to maximize the network service providers' profit while satisfying the mobile users (Niyato, 2007). A new game model was presented for the network selection mechanism in 4G converged environments (Antoniou, & Pitsillides, 2008). This game was formulated between non-cooperative players, who were the access networks participating in the 4G environment. The players competed for a subset of service requests to admit in order to gain an amount of user-awarded value assigned to each service request by means of utility functions. Therefore, the motivation for the decision of each access network was user satisfaction. In this game, each access network maximized its payoff by admitting the services that indicated the higher preferences towards the specific access network (Antoniou, 2008). In 2009, another network selection game was proposed for 4G wireless networks (Niyato, & Hossain, 2009). This game was designed as an evolutionary game model to investigate the dynamics of network selection in heterogeneous wireless networks. In this game, users in different service areas competed for bandwidth from different wireless networks. A user selected the wireless access network based on its utility, which is a function of allocated bandwidth and price per connection. The dynamics of network selection was mathematically modeled by the replicator dynamics that described the adaptation in proportions of users choosing different networks. For dynamic evolutionary game-based network selection, population evolution and reinforcement

learning algorithms were also developed. The network-selection algorithm based on population evolution utilized information from all users in the same service area. On the other hand, in the reinforcement-learning-based algorithm, the users learned the performances and prices of different networks by interaction. Knowledge gained from learning was used to make the best decision for network selection. As a solution concept, the evolutionary equilibrium was obtained (Niyato, 2009)

SUMMARY

In this chapter, game theoretic issues for wireless network resource management are presented. We classify state-of-the-art research contributions on the network resource management and discuss the fundamental concepts and properties to explain on how to apply the game theory in resource sharing protocol design. This survey provides a tutorial overview on game theoretic approaches for network resource management with the most recent practical implementations. One of the future objectives is to study the scalability issues in large scale scenarios. Moreover, factors such as obstruction, mobility of nodes, and undesired, malicious and uncooperative user behavior will be investigated in terms of an impact on the network performance.

REFERENCES

Agah, A., Basu, K., & Das, S. K. (2005). Enforcing security for prevention of DoS attack in wireless sensor networks using economical modeling. In *Proceedings of IEEE International Conference on Mobile Ad hoc and Sensor Systems Conference*, (pp. 528-535). IEEE.

Ahmad, I., & Habibi, D. (2012). Resource Management in 4G Wireless Communications at Vehicular Speeds: A Game Theory Solution. In *Proceedings of IEEE VTC*. IEEE.

Alpcan, T., & Basar, T. (2006). An intrusion detection game with limited observations. In *Proceedings of International Symposium on Dynamic Games and Applications*. Academic Press.

Altman, E., Borkar, V. S., & Kherani, A. A. (2004). Optimal Random Access in Networks with Two-Way Traffic. In *Proceedings of IEEE PIMRC*, (pp. 609-613).

Antoniou, J., & Pitsillides, A. (2008). 4G Converged Environment: Modeling Network Selection as a Game. In *Proceedings of Mobile and Wireless Communications Summit*. Academic Press.

Berlemann, L., Hiertz, G. R., Walke, B. H., & Mangold, S. (2005). Radio Resource Sharing Games: Enabling QoS Support in Unlicensed Bands. *IEEE Network, 19*(4), 59–65. doi:10.1109/MNET.2005.1470684

Chatterjee, M., Haitao, L., Das, S. K., & Basu, K. (2003). A game theoretic approach for utility maximization in CDMA system. [IEEE.]. *Proceedings of the IEEE, ICC*, 412–416.

Chen, X., Xu, L., & Li, J. (2010). Bargaining Game and Cross-layer Design Based Optimization Strategy in Wireless Multi-hop Network. In *Proceedings of IEEE CIT*, (pp. 2570-2575). IEEE.

Donmez, N. (2011). A game-theoretic approach to efficient power control in CDMA data networks. In *Proceedings of IEEE INISTA*, (pp. 248-252). IEEE.

Felegyhazi, M., Hubaux, J., & Buttyan, L. (2006). Nash Equilibria of Packet Forwarding Strategies in Wireless Ad Hoc Networks. *IEEE Transactions on Mobile Computing, 5*(5), 463–476. doi:10.1109/TMC.2006.68

Gorji, A. E., Abolhassani, B., Honardar, K., Adibi, M., & Okhovat, M. (2010). Utility Fair Non-cooperative Game Approach for Resource Allocation in Multi-cell OFDM Systems. In *Proceedings of ICCMS*, (pp. 154-158). ICCMS.

Han, Z., Ji, Z., & Liu, K. J. R. (2004). Power Minimization for Multi-Cell OFDM Networks using Distributed Non-Cooperative Game Approach. In *Proceedings of IEEE GLOBECOM*, (pp. 3742-3747). IEEE.

Jiang, M., & Ward, P. A. S. (2011). A cooperative game-theory model for bandwidth allocation in multi-hop wireless networks. In *Proceedings of IEEE WiMob*, (pp. 222-229). IEEE.

Kamal, H., Coupechoux, M., & Godlewski, P. (2009). Inter-operator spectrum sharing for cellular networks using game theory. In *Proceedings of IEEE PIMRC*, (pp. 425-429). IEEE.

Kim, S. (2011). Cellular Network Bandwidth Management Scheme by using Nash Bargaining Solution. *IET Communications, 5*(3), 371–380. doi:10.1049/iet-com.2010.0309

Koskie, S., & Gajic, Z. (2005). A Nash Game Algorithm for SIR-based Power Control in 3G Wireless CDMA Networks. *IEEE/ACM Transactions on Networking, 13*(5), 1017–1026. doi:10.1109/TNET.2005.857068

Kuo, Y. L., Wu, E. H. K., & Chen, G. H. (2004). Noncooperative admission control for differentiated services in IEEE 802.11 WLANs. In *Proceedings of IEEE GLOBECOM*, (pp. 2981-2986). IEEE.

Kwon, H., Lee, H., & Cioffi, J. M. (2009). Cooperative Strategy by Stackelberg Games under Energy Constraint in Multi-Hop Relay Networks. In *Proceedings of IEEE GLOBECOM*. IEEE.

Lin, H., Chatterjee, M., Das, S. K., & Basu, K. (2005). ARC: An Integrated Admission and Rate Control Framework for Competitive Wireless CDMA Data Networks Using Noncooperative Games. *IEEE Transactions on Mobile Computing, 4*(3), 243–258. doi:10.1109/TMC.2005.35

Lin, X. H., & Wang, H. (2012). On using game theory to balance energy consumption in heterogeneous wireless sensor networks. In *Proceedings of IEEE Conference on Local Computer Networks*, (pp. 568-576). IEEE.

Malanchini, I., Cesana, M., & Gatti, N. (2012). Network Selection and Resource Allocation Games for Wireless Access Networks. *IEEE Transactions on Mobile Computing*, 1–14.

Musku, M. R., Chronopoulos, A. T., Popescu, D. C., & Stefanescu, A. (2010). A game-theoretic approach to joint rate and power control for uplink CDMA communications. *IEEE Transactions on Communications*, *58*(3), 923–932. doi:10.1109/TCOMM.2010.03.070205

Niyato, D., & Hossain, E. (2006). A Cooperative Game Framework for Bandwidth Allocation in 4G Heterogeneous Wireless Networks. [IEEE.]. *Proceedings of the IEEE, ICC*, 4357–4362.

Niyato, D., & Hossain, E. (2007). Radio resource management games in wireless networks: an approach to bandwidth allocation and admission control for polling service in IEEE 802.16. *IEEE Wireless Communications*, *14*(1), 27–35. doi:10.1109/MWC.2007.314548

Niyato, D., & Hossain, E. (2008). A noncooperative game-theoretic framework for radio resource management in 4G heterogeneous wireless access networks. *IEEE Transactions on Mobile Computing*, *7*(3), 332–345. doi:10.1109/TMC.2007.70727

Niyato, D., & Hossain, E. (2009). Dynamics of Network Selection in Heterogeneous Wireless Networks: An Evolutionary Game Approach. *IEEE Transactions on Vehicular Technology*, *58*(4), 2008–2017. doi:10.1109/TVT.2008.2004588

Roy, S., Wu, L., & Zawodniok, M. (2011). Spectrum management for wireless networks using adaptive control and game theory. In *Proceedings of IEEE WCNC*, (pp. 1062-1067). IEEE.

Saad, W., Zhu, Q., Basar, T., Han, Z., & Hjorungnes, A. (2009). Hierarchical Network Formation Games in the Uplink of Multi-Hop Wireless Networks. In *Proceedings of IEEE GLOBECOM*. IEEE.

Srinivasan, V., Nuggehalli, P., Chiasserini, C. F., & Rao, R. R. (2003). Cooperation in wireless ad hoc networks. In *Proceedings of IEEE INFOCOM* (pp. 808–817). IEEE.

Tan, G., & Guttag, J. (2005). The 802.11 MAC Protocol Leads to Inefficient Equilibria. In *Proc. IEEE INFOCOM*. IEEE.

Virapanicharoen, J., & Benjapolakul, W. (2004). Fair-Efficient Guard Bandwidth Coefficients Selection in Call Admission Control for Mobile Multimedia Communications using Game Theoretic Framework. [IEEE.]. *Proceedings of the IEEE, ICC*, 80–84.

Wang, L., Xue, Y., & Schulz, E. (2006). Resource Allocation in Multicell OFDM Systems Based on Noncooperative Game. In *Proceedings of IEEE PIMRC*. IEEE.

Zhang, H., Fang, X., & Yuan, Q. (2007). A Game Theory-based Fairness Call Admission Control Scheme for CDMA Systems. In *Proceedings of CHINACOM*, (pp. 1021-1025). CHINACOM.

Zhang, T., Zeng, Z., Feng, C., Zheng, J., & Ma, D. (2007). Utility Fair Resource Allocation Based on Game Theory in OFDM Systems. In *Proceedings of IEEE ICCCN*, (pp. 414-418). IEEE.

Zhao, L., Zhang, H., & Zhang, J. (2008). Using Incompletely Cooperative Game Theory in Wireless Sensor Networks. In *Proceedings of IEEE WCNC*, (pp. 1483-1488). IEEE.

KEY TERMS AND DEFINITIONS

Cellular Network: A wireless network distributed over land areas called cells, each served by at least one fixed-location transceiver, known as a cell site or base station. In a cellular network, each cell uses a different set of frequencies from neighboring cells, to avoid interference and provide guaranteed bandwidth within each cell.

Channel Capacity: The tightest upper bound on the rate of information that can be reliably transmitted over a communications channel. By the noisy-channel coding theorem, the channel capacity of a given channel is the limiting information rate that can be achieved with arbitrarily small error probability.

Code Division Multiple Access (CDMA): An example of multiple access, which is where several transmitters can send information simultaneously over a single communication channel. This allows several users to share a band of frequencies.

Media Access Control (MAC) Protocol: A sub-layer of the data link layer, which itself is layer 2. The MAC sub-layer provides addressing and channel access control mechanisms that make it possible for several terminals or network nodes to communicate within a multiple access network that incorporates a shared medium.

Radio Resource Management (RRM): The system level control of co-channel interference and other radio transmission characteristics in wireless communication systems. RRM involves strategies and algorithms for controlling parameters such as transmit power, user allocation, beamforming, data rates, handover criteria, modulation scheme, error coding scheme, etc. The objective is to utilize the limited radio-frequency spectrum resources and radio network infrastructure as efficiently as possible.

Spread-Spectrum Techniques: Methods by which a signal generated with a particular bandwidth is deliberately spread in the frequency domain, resulting in a signal with a wider bandwidth. These techniques are used for a variety of reasons, including the establishment of secure communications, increasing resistance to natural interference, noise and jamming, to prevent detection, and to limit power flux density.

Section 3
Advanced Game Paradigm Topics:
Case Studies in Network Design

Chapter 9
Game–Based Approach for Network Routing Applications

ABSTRACT

Traditionally, routing is the process of selecting best paths in a network. Recently, the term routing is much better described as simply forwarding. Routing is performed for many kinds of networks, including the telephone network, electronic data networks, and transportation networks. In a more narrow sense of the term, routing is often contrasted with bridging in its assumption that network addresses are structured and that similar addresses imply proximity within the network. Nowadays, routing has become the dominant form of addressing on the Internet, and bridging is still widely used within localized environments. This chapter explores routing.

COOPERATIVE GAME THEORETIC ONLINE ROUTING *(CGOR)* SCHEME

During wireless network operations, a widely used performance issue is energy efficiency. Along with the energy efficiency, another desirable property is load balancing. Recently, S. Kim proposed a new integrated routing scheme (Kim, 2010); it is composed of path setup and packet distribution algorithms. Due to the online self-adjustment technique, the path setup algorithm can adaptively estimate link costs and establish routing paths. Based on the *Shapley Value* approach, the developed packet distribution algorithm can provide a fair and efficient solution for the packet forwarding problem. Under widely different and diversified network situations, this collaborative approach can

offer a well-balanced network performance. The most important novelties of the *CGOR* scheme are its flexibility, adaptability and responsiveness to current traffic conditions.

Development Motivation

Recently, the explosive growth of new communication services and the widespread proliferation of multimedia data have necessitated the development for an efficient network management system. Traditionally, network management refers to the activities, methods, procedures, and tools that pertain to the operation, administration, maintenance, and provisioning of networked systems. Usually, network management is concerned with configuring resources in the network to support a

DOI: 10.4018/978-1-4666-6050-2.ch009

given service and to achieve greater internal efficiencies (Mahapatra, Anand, & Agrawal, 2006).

With the advance of wireless communication technology, low-cost and powerful wireless transceivers are widely used in mobile applications. Therefore, wireless/mobile networking is one of the strongest growth areas of communication technology today. For efficient wireless network operations, routing is very important; network performance is strongly related to routing algorithms. Therefore, much effort has been made trying to find adaptive network routing protocols (Zafar, Harle, Andonovic, & Khawaja, 2009).

To design an adaptive routing algorithm in wireless networks, several issues must be considered. Due to the limited energy supply of wireless device, energy is extremely valuable and scarce resource. Therefore, an efficient energy management strategy becomes a key factor in enhancing wireless network performance. Therefore, the main challenge in wireless networks is to use energy as efficiently as possible (Younis, Youssef, & Arisha, 2002). Another network management issue is load balancing. In computer science, load balancing is a technique to spread work between many computers, processes, hard disks or other resources in order to get optimal resource utilization and decrease computing time. In wireless networks, the meaning of load balancing is to ease out the heavy traffic load in a specific node or link by using multiple routing routes. With load balancing concept, routing packet can be evenly distributed in redundant communications links, which can prolong the network system lifetime from considering the load-sharing service (Huang, Ku, & Kung, 2009).

For efficient network management, control decisions must be dynamically adjustable to current situation. However, the future traffic patterns are generally not known. Furthermore, the fact that traffic patterns can vary dramatically over short periods of time makes the problem more challenging. Therefore, these decisions have to be made in real time, and without the knowledge

of future traffic requests at the decision time. Online algorithms are natural candidates for the design of efficient routing schemes in networks (Azar, 1998). An algorithm employing online computations is called an online algorithm. The term 'online computation problem' refers to decision problems where decisions must be made in real time based on past events without securing information about the future. In online computation, an algorithm must produce a sequence of decisions that will have an impact on the final quality of its overall performance. Formally, many online problems can be described as follows. An online algorithm $\mathcal{A}$ is presented with a request sequence $\sigma = \sigma(1), \sigma(2),..., \sigma(m)$. The algorithm $\mathcal{A}$ has to serve each request online, i.e., without knowledge of future requests. More precisely, when serving request $\sigma(t)$, $1 \leq t \leq m$, the algorithm does not know any request $\sigma(t')$ with $t' > t$. Serving requests incurs cost, and the goal is to serve the entire request sequence so that the total cost is as small as possible. This setting can also be regarded as a request-answer game (Azar, 1998).

Online algorithms are a natural topic of interest in many disciplines such as computer science, economics, and operations research. Online algorithms have been implicitly and explicitly studied for last several decades in the context of scheduling, optimization, data structures, and other computational topics. Many computational problems are intrinsically online in that they require immediate decisions to be made in real time. Paging in a virtual memory system is perhaps the most studied of such computational problems. Routing in communication networks is another obvious application. Decision making in the field of finance is another obvious area of interest (Azar, 1998).

Motivated by the above discussion, online algorithms (Kim, & Varshney, 2004) are natural candidates for the design of efficient routing schemes in wireless networks. Offline algorithms are unrealizable for the network management because it needs full knowledge of the future for an online problem. Based on the adaptive online approach, the design goal of the *CGOR* scheme is to satisfy energy efficiency and load balancing simultaneously. To satisfy this goal, the *CGOR* scheme provides a coordination paradigm by employing two different online algorithms; path setup and packet distribution algorithms. According to online measurements of current network conditions, the path setup algorithm establishes multiple routing paths. The packet distribution algorithm adaptively distributes routing packets through the established paths. Each algorithm in the *CGOR* scheme has different control strategies but works together toward an optimal network performance. By a sophisticated combination of these online algorithms, the *CGOR* scheme tries to approximate a well-balanced performance among conflicting requirements.

Game Model and Shapley Value

Game theory is a field of applied mathematics that provides an effective tool in modeling the interactions among independent decision makers. Usually, games can be divided into non-cooperative and cooperative games. In non-cooperative games, players are in conflict with each other; they do not communicate or collaborate. Their preferences can be expressed as a utility function; players try to ensure the best possible consequence according to the utility function (Leino, 2003). Cooperative games, also called coalition games, are games in which players make binding commitments and find it beneficial to cooperate in the game. In these games, the main interest is to fairly distribute the outcome to each player according to their contributions (Rextin, Irfan, Uzmi, 2004).

Especially, the operations contending for network resources rely on the cooperation of the each wireless terminal. In routing algorithm, data packets are forwarded by the cooperation of multiple nodes to reach the final destination. Therefore, the cooperation game models are attracting for wireless network managements; the core, bargaining

set, and *Shapley Value* are well-known solutions for cooperative games to decide the each player's profit (Cai, & Pooch, 2004).

The *CGOR* scheme is a new game theoretic routing scheme based on the *Shapley Value*. In the *CGOR* scheme, the basic concept of cooperative games is used as a design tool for a real network implementation. Therefore, the players are wireless devices programmed to operate in a certain way; each player follows mandated rules for the desired result of the whole system. The behavior decision mechanism based on the agreed protocols is more practical and justified for real network operations. By using a cooperative game technique, such as the *Shapley Value*, the *CGOR* scheme tries to approximate the optimal load balancing.

After a sequence of routing actions performed, the current network condition dynamically changes. Therefore, during the routing operations, each player should adapt his strategy to maximize the expected benefit. By using the online self-monitoring technique, the *CGOR* scheme can adaptively change current routing decisions. Therefore, the principle novelty of the online scheme is its feasibility, self-adaptability for network dynamics and effectiveness in providing a desirable solution in the real network operations.

Developed Algorithms in the *CGOR* Scheme

The *CGOR* scheme consists of two different online algorithms – path setup and packet distribution algorithms. To maximize energy efficiency, the path setup algorithm adaptively establishes routing paths. The packet distribution algorithm achieves an effective packet distribution by encouraging cooperative work; packet distribution means that routing packets are distributedly forwarded across two or more wireless links for load balancing. Based on the adaptive online approach, these algorithms cooperate with each other and work together toward an appropriate network performance.

Path Setup Algorithm

Usually, most of the wireless nodes are battery-powered. Therefore, energy consumption is a crucial issue; the less energy is spent, the longer the node remains operable. In wireless communications, energy consumption decreases proportional to the square of the propagation distance. For the energy efficient routing, data packets should be forwarded via short distance multi-hop links (Srivastava, Neel, MacKenzie, & Menon, 2005).

The path setup algorithm in the *CGOR* scheme establishes multi-hop paths to reach the final destination node. To configure energy efficient multi-hop routing paths, each wireless link is estimated in an adaptive online manner. In this scheme, an online value parameter (L_V) is defined for each link to estimate the degree of communication adaptability. In order to relatively handle dynamic network conditions, the L_V value from the node i to the node j is obtained as

$$L\_V_{ij} = \left[(1-\alpha) \times \left(\frac{d_{ij}}{D_M}\right)\right] + \left[\alpha \times \left(1 - \frac{E_j}{E_M}\right)\right] + \left[\beta \times \left(\frac{L_j}{ML}\right)\right]$$

(1)

where d_{ij} is distance from the node i to the node j, E_j is the remaining energy of the node j and L_j is the queue length of node j. E_M, D_M and ML are the initial energy, the maximum coverage range of each node, and the maximum queue length, respectively. Therefore, the d_{ij}, E_j and L_j are normalized by the D_M, E_M, and ML; the range is varied from 0 to 1.

The d_{ij} reflects the cost of the wireless communication; the closer a next node, the more attractive for routing due to the less communication cost. Distance estimation is based on measuring the received signal strength (RSSI) of the received messages, which is well known as Frii's transmission equation (Blumenthal, Reichenbach, & Timmermann, 2006). The E_j is the current residual energy of node j, which reflects the remaining lifetime of a wireless node. The nodes with more energy are favored for routing. The queue length (L) is defined as the amount of traffic buffering. Usually, it is used as a threshold to detect network congestion. If the input data rate exceeds the output data rate in a node, routing packets become congested; a queue length increases. Therefore, based on the queue length condition, it is possible to decide whether packet overflow occurs or not.

The α and β are control parameters to relatively estimate the current link situations. In this scheme, the energy state and the congestion situation are equally weighted. Due to the characteristics of wireless propagation, the energy consumption rate for wireless communications is strongly related to the inter-node distance. The parameter α controls the relative weights given to distance and remaining energy of corresponding node. Under diverse network environments, a fixed value of α cannot effectively adapt to the changing conditions. In this scheme, it is treated as an on-line decision problem and adaptively modify α value. When the remaining energy of the node i is high, this scheme can put more emphasis on the energy status of next node j, i.e., on ($1 - E_j/E_M$). In this case, a higher value of α is more suitable. When the remaining energy of the node i is not enough due to traffic overhead, the path selection should strongly depend on the energy dissipation for data transmission. In this case, a lower value of α is more suitable for the energy consumption rate, i.e., on d_{ij}/D_M; since the distance of two neighbor nodes directly affects the energy consumption rate. In the online algorithm, the value of α of the corresponding node i is dynamically adjusted based on the current rate of its remaining energy per initially assigned energy (E_i/E_M). Therefore, the system can be more responsive to current network conditions by the real-time network monitoring. The parameter β is an impact factor to evaluate the state of packet congestion. To avoid the detrimental packet loss effect, the congestion situation is fully considered to estimate L_V value; the β value is fixed as 1.

The L_V value can represent the normalized communication cost of each link. Therefore, based on the L_V value, the path setup algorithm in the *CGOR* scheme constructs adaptive multi-hop routing paths. Usually, the least communication cost path can be considered as a shortest path. Therefore, the path construction problem can be transformed into a problem to find the shortest path from a source to a destination node. A recent study suggested that the best approach for solving the shortest path problem is the Dijkstra's algorithm (Boukerche, Araujo, & Villas, 2006). In this scheme, the Dijkstra's algorithm is used to configure a multi-hop routing path.

During the operation of wireless networks, unexpected growth of traffic may develop in a specific link; it may create local traffic congestion. To alleviate this kind of traffic overload condition, the algorithm establishes multiple paths, and adaptively distributes routing packets through these paths.

To configure routing paths, each node calculates the L_V values for the locally connected links. Then, by using the Dijkstra's algorithm, the source node finds the least-cost path to reach the destination node. The next step is to find out alternative paths to ease out the heavy traffic load in a specific link. The routing algorithm attempts to configure the next least-cost path among the remaining nodes. This routing path formation process continues repeatedly until all the possible routing paths are established. Finally, the algorithm can construct multiple disjoint routing paths from the source node to the destination node. The main steps of the path setup algorithm are given next.

Step 1: At the initial time, the each node estimates the L_V values for the locally connected links according to 1).

Step 2: The d_{ij}, E_j and L_j values for node j are adaptively estimated based on the online manner.

Step 3: The α and β values of node j are dynamically assigned as the current rate of its remaining energy per initially assigned energy (E_i/E_M) and 1, respectively.

Step 4: Based on the L_V values, the source node finds the least-cost path to reach the destination node by using the Dijkstra's algorithm.

1. To start out, the source node assigns a path weight as zero.
2. The current node selects the least cost link to connect a neighbor node.
3. Add the link cost to the path weight if there is no less weighted path from the source node to the new selected node.
4. The selected node recursively searches the next node while minimizing the path weight.
5. Go to 4.2 and repeat the node-selection procedure until to reach the final designated node.
6. Finally, the most effective routing path can be established from the source node to the destination node.

Step 5: For load balancing, the routing algorithm attempts to configure the next least-cost path as an alternative path among the remaining nodes.

Step 6: This routing path process continues repeatedly until all the possible disjoint routing paths are established.

Packet Distribution Algorithm

In 1953, Lloyd Shapley proposed one method, *Shapley Value*, to obtain the solution of an *n*-player cooperative game (Niyato, & Hossain, 2006). The outcome is a payoff vector, which corresponds to the contribution of each player to the cooperative game. In this game, players cooperate in joint action for their own self-interest; a *coalition* $\mathbb{S}$ is defined as an alliance among players and the $\mathbb{S}$ is an element of *grand coalition* $\mathbb{A}$, $\mathbb{S} \subset \mathbb{A}$. The *grand coalition* means a universal set, which contains all *coalitions*. To compute the *Shapley Value*, it is necessary to define the *value function* $\phi_i(\nu)$ as the worth of player i in the game with a characteristic function ν. The function ν assigns a payoff value to each coalition. The *Shapley Value* $\phi = [\phi_1, ..., \phi_i, ..., \phi_n]$ can be computed as follows:

$$\phi_i(\nu) = \sum_{\mathbb{S} \subset A, \ i \in A} \frac{(|\mathbb{S}| - 1)!\,(n - |\mathbb{S}|)!}{n!} (\nu(\mathbb{S}) - v(\mathbb{S} - \{i\})) \tag{2}$$

where $|\mathbb{S}|$ indicates the number of players in the coalition $\mathbb{S}$. The $\nu(\mathbb{S})$ is the total expected gain from the coalition $\mathbb{S}$, and $\nu(\mathbb{S} - \{i\})$ is the gain secured by a coalition with the same players in $\mathbb{S}$ except i.

In this scheme, the routing strategy is to adaptively distribute routing packets to avoid traffic congestions. To provide a fair and efficient solution for the packet distribution problem, the *Shapley Value* method is used. In the *CGOR* scheme, the established paths are assumed as game players. Therefore, a coalition is formed by the combination of routing paths; if n paths are established in the path setup algorithm, it can be formulated as a n-person cooperative game. However, to keep the computation complexity under the control, the packet distribution algorithm should limit the total number of participating players. To effectively restrict the number of game players, an online path value (P_V) is defined, which is calculated as the sum of all L_V values in the path. Only a path that satisfies the following condition is qualified as a game participant.

$$P\_V_i \leq \eta \times (P\_V_{least}) \tag{3}$$

where P_V_{least} is the least P_V value among the established paths, P_V_i is the P_V value of the path i, and η is a control factor ($\eta > 1$) for an efficient coalition formation.

The game model can be expressed by a finite player set ($\mathbb{P}$) of the established paths, the amount of routing packets (M) per second and a capacity vector ($\mathbb{C}$) of the $\mathbb{P}$. To get an efficient network performance, player strategies should be decided in desirable ways. In the developed model, the routing service execution is protocoled as the profit for each player. Therefore, players try to offer bandwidth and energy as much as possible to gain the revenue from packet services.

Each established path would have different routing capacity. According to the P_V value, the path capacity can be estimated as follows.

$$C_i = \frac{\mu \times M}{\sum_{k \in P_i} L\_V_k} \tag{4}$$

where $c_i (c_i \in \mathbb{C})$ is the capacity of the path i and k is the link in path $P_i (P_i \in \mathbb{P})$. L_V_k is the L_V value of the link k and μ is a control factor to satisfy the condition of $\sum_{i \in P} c_i \geq M$. Generally, the packet distribution problem for n routing paths leads to the similar conflict situation as in the money division problem for n creditors. Therefore, the packet distribution algorithm is analogous to the bankruptcy game model (Niyato, 2006). The bankruptcy game assumes that a company becomes bankrupt and this company owes money to n creditors; the money is needed to be divided among these creditors. This conflicting situation also introduces an n player cooperative game where the players are seeking for the equilibrium point to divide the money.

In the packet distribution algorithm, the routing packets are adaptively distributed to each path. Based on the *Shapley Value* ϕ, the amount of packet distribution for each path is decided. By using the path capacity c_i, the characteristic function ν for the coalition $\mathbb{S}$ ($\nu(\mathbb{S})$) is defined based on the bankruptcy game model (Niyato, 2006).

$$\nu(\mathbb{S}) = \max(0, M - \sum_{i \notin \mathbb{S}} c_i) \tag{5}$$

where the function value of the empty coalition ($\nu(\phi)$) is assumed as 0. The important property of these characteristic functions is the super-additivity (Niyato, 2006); if $\mathbb{S}_1$ and $\mathbb{S}_2$ are disjoint coalitions, then $\nu(\mathbb{S}_1) + \nu(\mathbb{S}_2) \leq \nu(\mathbb{S}_1 \cup \mathbb{S}_2)$. Therefore, the grand coalition ($\mathbb{A}$) can guarantee more profit than any other coalitions. This property encourages each player to cooperate with others.

Based on the $\nu(\mathbb{S})$, the packet distribution algorithm can calculate the *Shapley Value* $\phi = [\phi_1, ..., \phi_i..., \phi_n]$ according to (2). The ϕ_i value represents the amount of the allocated packet in path i, which is not exceeding the path capacity c_i ($0 \leq \phi_i \leq c_i$, s.t $\sum_{i \in p} \phi_i = M$). Finally, the source node can distribute routing packets to each path based on the ϕ. The main steps of the packet distribution algorithm are given next.

Step 1: The source node becomes a coordinator based on the centralized approach and the established paths by the path setup algorithm are assumed as game players.

Step 2: To reduce computation complexity, only a path that satisfies the condition (3) is qualified as a game participant.

Step 3: Routing capacity of each established path can be estimated by using (4).

Step 4: Based on the routing capacity, the characteristic function ν for the coalition $\mathbb{S}$ ($\nu(\mathbb{S})$) is defined according to (5).

Step 5: Based on the $\nu(\mathbb{S})$, the packet distribution algorithm can calculate the *Shapley Value* $\phi = [\phi_1, ..., \phi_i..., \phi_n]$ by using (2).

Step 6: The source node can distribute routing packets to each path based on the ϕ; the ϕ_i value represents the amount of the allocated packet in path i.

The design goal of the *CGOR* scheme is trying to approximate the optimal network performance based on real-time measurement information. Under the dynamic changing network environments, the online approach can adaptively respond to the current network situations. In addition, to satisfy the energy efficiency and load balancing requirements, the algorithms act cooperatively with each other. Therefore, by the proper coordination and collaboration of two algorithms, control decisions are mutually dependent on each other to resolve conflicting performance criteria.

To implement the *CGOR* scheme, centralized and distributed control approaches are adopted. Each link cost is evaluated in a distributed way, which is practical for real network operations. For the path setup and packet distribution, the source node becomes a coordinator based on the centralized approach.

Recently, several routing schemes for wireless networks have been presented. The *QoS and Energy Aware Routing (QoS&E)* scheme (Mahapatra, 2006) is an energy and QoS aware routing protocol for real-time traffic. The *Adaptive Path-setup and Routing Protocol (APRP)* scheme (Akkaya & Younis, 2005) can find a least-cost, delay-constrained path based on the communication parameters such as energy reserve, transmission energy and error rate. Compared to these schemes, the proposed *CGOR* scheme attains better performance for wireless network managements. The simulation results shown in Figure 1 demonstrate that the performance comparison of the *CGOR* scheme with the *QoS&E* scheme and the *APRP* scheme.

Summary

In the *CGOR* scheme, adaptive online path setup and packet distribution algorithms are developed for wireless networks. To satisfy energy efficiency and load balancing requirements, the developed algorithms work together and act cooperatively with each other to enhance conflicting performance criteria. For energy efficiency, the path setup algorithm is designed in self-organizing and dynamic online fashion, which can improve adaptability for real wireless network operations. For load balancing, the methodology that the *CGOR* scheme adopt is the *Shapley Value*; it can provide a

Figure 1. Performance evaluations of the CGOR scheme

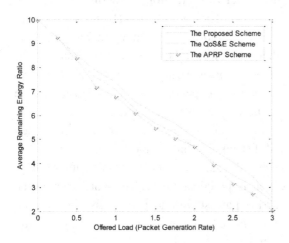

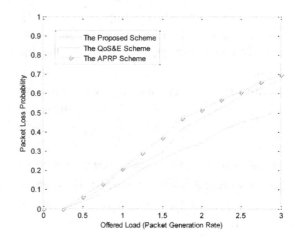

(a) Average Remaining Energy

(b) Packet loss probability

fair and efficient solution for the wireless network routing problem. The most important feature of the *CGOR* scheme is the integrated approach by employing a coordination paradigm.

GAME THEORETIC MULTI-OBJECTIVE ROUTING *(GMOR)* SCHEME

In wireless sensor networks, performance is strongly related to routing algorithms. However, unique characteristics of wireless communications make it difficult to design an efficient routing algorithm. Recently, S. Kim proposed a new routing scheme based on the game theoretic model (Kim, 2010b). By using the dynamic online approach, each sensor node can make routing decisions while ensuring good global properties. In addition, the developed routing paradigm is realized in a distributed way without central controller, which is practical for real network operations. The principle contributions of the *GMOR* scheme are its self-adaptability, scalability and responsiveness to current network situations.

Development Motivation

Nowadays, the sensor technology for small, low-cost and low-power nodes is one of the strongest growth areas in communication industry. Large numbers of sensors can be scattered randomly over a large area, where they will automatically sense and record local environmental conditions. Wireless Sensor Networks (WSNs) can be described as a collection of sensor nodes which co-ordinate to perform some specific actions (Rogers, David, & Jennings, 2005). Such WSNs are auto-organized networks for monitoring purposes, ranging from body health monitoring, battlefield surveillance, nuclear, biological and chemical detection, home automation to control applications. When making such networks operational, a key question is how to effectively manage the network resource, given the dynamic nature of the system and the limited knowledge of the network topology (Felemban, Lee, & Ekici, 2006).

Due to the limited energy supply of sensors, energy is an extremely valuable resource and directly influencing the network lifetime. In order to keep the network alive for a sufficiently long time, it is important to efficiently use the energy resource. Along with the energy efficiency, another significant issue is network reliability. If a node stops functioning due to run out of energy, the coverage of its node and routing paths via that node will be completely lost; it degrades the total network performance quite seriously. To avoid this disaster situation, the energy equilibrium among the nodes is a desirable feature. In WSNs, energy equilibrium refers to balance the remaining energy among sensor nodes (Bi, Li, & Sun, 2007). Therefore, a challenging task in WSNs is to design an efficient energy control algorithm while balancing the energy consumption among sensors.

For adaptive and efficient network operations, routing is very important; the network performance is strongly related to routing algorithms. In addition, the entire sensor network lifetime is determined by the battery of each individual sensor (Trivedi, Elangovan, Iyengar, & Balakrishnan, 2006). Therefore, all performance guarantees in WSNs are conditional on currently available energy and effective routing strategies. Until now, much effort has been made trying to find energy efficient routing algorithms, which can play a significant role in determining network performance. The *GMOR* scheme has focused on the basic concept of game theory to design a new sensor network routing algorithm. The design goal of routing algorithm is to take both energy efficiency and network stability during routing operations. To provide the most effective network performance, the competition and cooperation among sensors can be modeled as a game. The game theoretical perspective can offer many advantages to find an adaptable solution.

In general, due to heavy control and implementation overheads, centralized control approaches are impractical methods for large scale WSNs (Korad, & Sivalingam, 2006). Based on the physical distribution of the sensors and their limited localization ability, the need is increasing for network systems that operate a decentralized control mechanism (Iqbal, Gondal, & Dooley, 2006). Besides, for efficient network managements, control decisions must be dynamically

adjustable. Generally, these decisions have to be made in real time, and without the knowledge of future information at the decision time. Therefore, online algorithms are natural candidates for the efficient sensor network management. Under dynamically changing network environments, optimal offline algorithms are unrealizable. Based on these considerations, the *GMOR* scheme would employ distributed and dynamic online methodologies to develop a routing scheme.

Motivated by the above discussion, the *GMOR* scheme is developed as a new adaptive online routing scheme based on the game model. In the *GMOR* scheme, self-organized individual sensors make routing decisions with their view of the current network situation. Therefore, routing information is examined periodically to improve situation-awareness. In addition, to approximate an optimal network performance, local routing decisions should result in good global properties. To satisfy this goal, the *GMOR* scheme emphasizes autonomous actions according to pre-defined mathematical rules and flexible interaction strategies, which are effective and practical techniques for extracting knowledge to adapt current network changes (Wang, Martonosi, & Peh, L., 2006). Based on these adaptive online routing policies, each node can select the most proper routing path in an entirely distributed manner. The main novelties of the *GMOR* scheme are scalability for large sensor networks, self-adaptability for network dynamics, and effectiveness in providing a desirable solution in the real network operations.

Game Model for Wireless Sensor Networks

To represent a traditional game G, the game model components are given by $G = <N, \mathbb{S}, \{u_1, ..., u_n\}>$, where N is a number of players, $\mathbb{S}$ is a non-empty set of the strategies, and $u_i \in \{u_1, ..., u_n\}$ is the utility function of player i. Each player's satisfaction level can be translated into a quantifiable metric through a utility function. Therefore, a utility function is a measure of the satisfaction experienced by a player, which is as a result of a selected strategy. In the *GMOR* scheme, the developed utility function maps the user-level satisfaction to a real number, which represents the resulting payoff. The goal of each player is to maximize his own payoff by selecting a specific strategy where $\max_{S_i} : u_i(S_i) \to \Re, S_i \in \mathbb{S}$ (Srivastava, 2005).

In the *GMOR* scheme, sensor nodes are modeled as game players. To get an efficient path, players' competition and cooperation can be modeled as a routing game. Each player has the respective strategy set ($\mathbb{S} = \{\alpha_1, \alpha_2, \cdots, \alpha_m\}$), where | m | is the number of possible strategies. Traditionally, players act independently and self-interestedly. Therefore, a player seeks to choose the strategy to maximize his payoff. In the developed game model, each strategy represents a routing decision to select a next relay node, and the utility function measures the outcome of this decision.

The main goal of the *GMOR* scheme is to appropriately establish an effective routing path, which should ensure not only energy efficiency but also energy balance in sensor networks. To satisfy this purpose, multi-objective optimization techniques play a very important role. Over the past years, several studies dealing with this issue have been reported. Among various optimization techniques, the methodologies that the *GMOR* scheme adopted are Modified Game Theory (MGT) and ε-constraint methods. The MGT method is theoretically designed to reach a near Pareto optimal solution (Mehmet, & Ramazan, 2001). It can be practically applied without much deviation from the original game theory form. For the proactive path establishment, the MGT method is used to guarantee the energy efficiency; each node estimates each wireless link's status to decide routing decisions. The ε-constraint method optimizes one of the objective functions

while all the other objective functions are required to maintain the specified acceptable levels (Becerra, & Coello, 2006). Due to its simplicity, the ε-constraint method can be directly applied to real world network operations. For the reactive path re-configuration, the ε-constraint method is used by adopting multi-criteria into a utility function. Therefore, the established path can be changed adaptively to ensure the energy balance in dynamic network environments.

In the *GMOR* scheme, the MGT and ε-constraint techniques are sophisticatedly combined and mutually dependent on each other. Based on the real-time online monitoring, these two methods act cooperatively. Therefore, the integrated approach gives excellent adaptability and flexibility to satisfy the different performance requirements.

Online Utility Function for Routing Game

In wireless communications, energy consumption decreases proportional to the square of the propagation distance. Therefore, the short distance multi-hop transmission is suitable for energy efficient routing than a single long range transmission (Blumenthal, 2006). To configure the adaptive multi-hop routing path, one of major concerns is to design a utility function. The *GMOR* scheme defines two online functions (F_e and F_d) by using distance and remaining energy information. Based on the adaptive online manner, these functions can dynamically estimate the degree of communication adaptability for each link. For the link from the node i to the node j, the $F_e(j)$ and $F_d(i,j)$ are defined as

$$F_e(j) = \left(1 - \frac{e_j}{E_M}\right)$$

and

$$F_d\left(i,j\right) = \left(\frac{d_{ij}}{D_M}\right) \quad (6)$$

where e_j is the remaining energy of the node j and d_{ij} is the distance from the node i to the node j. E_M, D_M are the initial energy and the maximum coverage range of each sensor node, respectively. Therefore, the e_j and d_{ij} are normalized by the D_M and E_M; the range of F_e and F_d is varied from 0 to 1. The e value reflects the rest lifetime of a node; a node with more energy is favored for routing. The d value reflects the cost of the wireless communication; the nearest node is attractive for routing.

To get the proper combination of the F_e and F_d functions, the *GMOR* scheme uses the MGT method. In general, the MGT method may be concluded to provide the best compromise in the presence of different control functions (Mehmet, 2001). By practically applying the MGT, the F_e and F_d are transformed into a single objective function. To obtain this single function, the procedure is defined as follows. First, a normalized bargaining model (NBM_{ij}) for the link from the node i to the node j is constructed to compare the relative effectiveness.

$$NBM_{ij} = \prod_{k=1}^{2}\left[1 - f_k\left(j\right)\right], \text{ where } j \in N_i \quad (7)$$

where f_1 is F_e (j) and f_2 is F_d (i,j). N_i is the set of neighboring nodes of the node i. This bargaining model gives a normalized indication value ($0 \leq NBM_{ij} \leq 1$) as to how far a function is from its worst value. Therefore, the solution is optimized by maximizing the bargaining model. Second, a weighted average (WA_{ij}) for the link from the node i to the node j is formulated as follows.

$$WA_{ij} = \sum_{k=1}^{2}\gamma_k f_k\left(x\right), \text{ with } \sum_{k=1}^{2}\gamma_k = 1 \quad (8)$$

The parameter γ_k ($k = 1$ or 2) controls the relative weights given to remaining energy ($k = 1$) and distance ($k = 2$). Under diverse network environments, the fixed values for γ_k cannot effectively adapt to the changing conditions. The *GMOR* scheme treats it as an on-line decision problem and adaptively modifies γ_k value. When the remaining energy of the node i is high, the *GMOR* scheme can put more emphasis on the energy status of next node j, i.e., on ($1 - E_j /E_M$). In this case, a higher value of γ_1 is more suitable. When the remaining energy of the node i is not enough, the path selection should strongly depend on the energy dissipation for data transmission; the distance of two neighbor nodes directly affects the energy consumption rate. Therefore, the *GMOR* scheme can put more emphasis on d_{ij}/D_M. In this case, a higher value of γ_2 is more suitable.

In the *GMOR* scheme, by considering the mutual-interaction relationship, the γ_2 is defined as $1 - \gamma_1$, and the value of γ_1 is dynamically adjusted based on the current remaining energy rate of the corresponding node; e.g., the γ_1 value of the node i is e_i /E_M. Therefore, by using the real-time online monitoring, the system can be more responsive to current network conditions. Finally, according to (7) and (8), the multi-objective utility function (U_{mo}) of node i, which is used to decide a next relay node, is given by

$$U_{mo}\left(i\right) = \min_{j \in N_i}\left(WA_{ij} - NBM_{ij}\right) \quad (9)$$

Proactive Path Establishment

Within the sensor network, a single sink is responsible for regularly collecting data from each sensor node. Therefore, the routing topology might be tree structure; the root of a tree is the sink node, and the child nodes are sensors. At the initial time, the *GMOR* scheme proactively establishes routing paths for each node. First, the sink node broadcasts *route_setup* message. Within the power coverage area, message receiving sensors individually estimate the link cost according to (9) and, forward the *route_setup* message recursively to neighbor nodes. If a node has received multiple *route_setup* messages from the reachable neighbor nodes, this node adaptively select one of them to reach the sink node. For this routing decision, the *GMOR* scheme defines a cost parameter (C); it is computed as the sum of all link costs from the sink node to the current node. Therefore, each node tries to minimize the C value by adaptively selecting a relay node. If the sensor node i has received multiple messages, a relay node is decided as follows.

$$\text{relay node} = \arg\min_{h \in N_i} \left\{ h \mid C_h + \left(WA_{hi} - NBM_{hi} \right) \right\}$$
$$(10)$$

where the node h is one of message-sending neighbor nodes. Therefore, the current node i tries to select adaptively the node h as a relay node to reach the final sink node. The C value potentially incorporates more global network information; e.g., C_i is calculated by minimizing $C_h + (WA_{hi} - NBM_{hi})$. Therefore, individual node can make a local routing decision while ensuring good global performance. In an entirely distributed fashion, hop-by-hop path setup procedure is recursively repeated until all the remaining sensor nodes are connected. Finally, a tree-like routing topology is configured; each node keeps a path to reach the sink node.

Reactive Path Re-Configuration

The developed path establishment mechanism has been devoted to improve the energy efficiency. However, for reliable network operations, energy balancing should not be overlooked altogether. Therefore, energy equilibrium among nodes is a desirable feature and considered as another main metric. In the *GMOR* scheme, the major goal is to provide the most proper combination of the energy efficiency and network stability for routing operations. To satisfy this goal, the *GMOR* scheme applies the ε-constraint method to the function (10). To translate the selfish motives of nodes into desirable actions, an energy balancing condition is additionally given as a ε-constraint. In the *GMOR* scheme, the value of ε is the arithmetic mean of the child nodes' remaining energy. In order to adaptively estimate the ε value, each node continually measures the remaining energy amounts of its child-nodes; average of them is defined as the ε value. When a remaining energy falls below its own ε value, the path re-configuration mechanism is triggered. For the reactive routing decision, the function (10) is redefined as follows.

$$\text{relay node} = \arg\min_{h \in N_i} \left\{ h \mid C_h + \left(WA_{hi} - NBM_{hi} \right) \right\},$$

$$\text{where} \quad e_h > \varepsilon_h \qquad (11)$$

where ε_h is the ε value of the node h; the ε value is used as a threshold for energy balancing. When the e value of the node h (e_h) is lower than its own ε value (ε_h), the node h disconnects established links to its child nodes. The child node (i.e., node i) tries to find a new relay node according to (11). If there are no suitable nodes satisfying the ε-constraint condition, new relay nodes are selected by using (10). Based on this dynamic online approach, the *GMOR* scheme can evenly distribute the network load and balance the energy consumption among sensor nodes.

Online Game Model in the *GMOR* Scheme

The *GMOR* scheme is letting sensor nodes operate a routing task as players. When a player detects an event, he creates packets and sends them to the sink node. Usually, each player has multiple links to connect the neighbor players. In the game model, the selection of an outgoing link can be viewed as a strategy action taken by a player. According to the utility function (11), each player can find the best strategy in the routing game; packets are forwarded by the cooperation of multiple players. The path-setup algorithm adopts the novel loop-free a routing technique used in the well-known AODV algorithm. Therefore, all links in the path are tagged with destination sequence numbers, which guarantee that no routing loops can form even under extreme conditions.

After a sequence of routing actions performed, the current network condition dynamically changes. Therefore, during the routing operations, each player should adapt his strategy to maximize the expected benefit. By using the online self-monitoring technique, the reactive mechanism can adaptively change the current routing decision. In order to implement an online approach, the *GMOR* scheme partitions the time-axis into equal intervals of length *unit_time*. The value of *unit_time* is chosen based on the desired adjusting rate, which represents how closely the corresponding routing information reflects the changes in network environments.

Every *unit_time*, each player periodically re-evaluates the current strategy and gathers the remaining energy states from the child nodes. Through a distributed online fashion, this information is updated to make adaptive routing decisions. From the point of practical operations, the distributed approach can transfer the computational burden from a central node in the system to the distributed nodes. When individual players learn the better routing strategy, they dynamically change their current strategies. Considering this step-by-step interactive feedback process, the developed algorithm is designed as a repeated game. The main steps of the developed routing algorithm are given next.

Step 1: At the initial time, the sink node broadcasts the *route_setup* message to the neighbor nodes. The message receiving nodes estimate the cost (C) and recursively forwards the *route_setup* message with the estimated C value.

Step 2: If a sensor node has received multiple *route_setup* messages, the node selects one relay node according to (10). This proactive path setup procedure continues repeatedly until all the remaining nodes are connected.

Step 3: Based on the distributed online monitoring, the C and ε values are periodically updated in each individual node.

Step 4: When a sensor node detects an event, the node forwards data packets to one neighboring node; each node makes a locally optimal decision to select the next relay node. By using the globally integrated C value, these locally made decisions result in good global network performance.

Step 5: Based on the collection of hop-by-hop routing decisions, the data packet can progress to reach the sink node. The routing path is configured based on the proactive-reactive integrated approach.

Step 6: If the e value in a specific node falls below its own ε value, the path re-configuration mechanism is triggered. Reactively, the child nodes select a new relay node according to (11).

Step 7: Every *unit_time*, proceeds to step 3; each node can be self-monitoring constantly.

Recently, several control schemes for WSNs have been presented in research literature. The *Node Clustering in Wireless Sensor Networks* (*NCWSN*) scheme is an energy aware dual-path routing protocol for WSNs (Younis, Krunz & Ramasubramanian, 2006). The *NCWSN* scheme can improve the network performance by reducing the amount of energy spent and reacting to current network situations. The *Coordinated Routing Protocol for Sensor Network* (*CRPSN*) scheme is a grid-based coordinated routing protocol for sensor networks (Akl & Uttara, 2007). To distribute routing load over all the sensor nodes, the *CRPSN* scheme incorporates the load balancing concept in the routing protocol. Figure 2 demonstrates that

Figure 2. Performance evaluations of the GMOR scheme

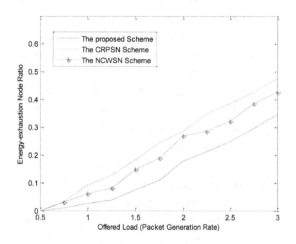

(a) Energy Exhausting Ratio

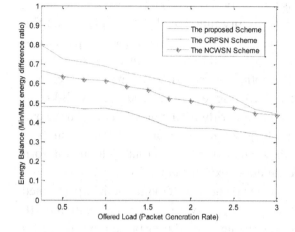

(b) Energy Balancing State in WSNs

the performance of the proposed *GMOR* scheme is generally superior to those of other existing schemes: the *NCWSN* scheme and the *CRPSN* scheme. Due to the adaptive online approach, the proposed *GMOR* scheme constantly monitors the current network conditions and can balance appropriate network performance.

Summary

Recently, game theory is increasingly finding use in many important applications, including wireless network managements. The *GMOR* scheme is a new game-theoretic routing scheme for WSNs. The main goal of the *GMOR* scheme is to provide the energy efficiency and network stability during network operations. In an entirely distributed online fashion, each individual node makes a local routing decision to find an efficient path. Under dynamic network environments, the established path can be dynamically re-configured to adapt network changes. This proactive-reactive integrated approach is the basic design concept of the routing game model.

INCENTIVE-BASED AD-HOC NETWORK ROUTING *(IANR)* SCHEME

Recently, mobile ad-hoc networks have received much attention on account of the proliferation of mobile devices and their potential applications. In ad-hoc networks, node cooperation can play a significant role in determining the network performance. However, methods for stimulating cooperation among nodes have not been investigated sufficiently. In 2012, S. Kim proposed a new Incentive-based Ad-hoc Network Routing *(IANR)* scheme for wireless ad-hoc networks (Kim, 2012). When the *IANR* scheme is used, nodes can cooperate with each other for a global goal. To maximize implementation practicality, the developed scheme is designed in an entirely distributed and online manner.

Development Motivation

With the advance of wireless communication technology, low-cost and powerful wireless transceivers are finding widespread use in mobile applications. Therefore, mobile ad-hoc networks (MANETs) have attracted significant interest in recent years and are considered as the technological counterpart of the ubiquitous computing concept (Kumar, Kambhatla, Hu, Lifson, & Xiao, 2008). For efficient MANET operations, routing is very important; network performance is strongly related to routing algorithms. Over the past few years, much effort has been devoted to design of adaptive MANET routing protocols. To develop a new routing algorithm, several factors need to be considered. For example, energy efficiency becomes a key objective during design on account of finite energy supplies (Yarvis, & Zorzi, 2008). In addition, next generation mobile networks are expected to support diverse multimedia applications; different multimedia services not only require different amounts of bandwidth but also have different Quality of Service (QoS) requirements. Therefore, QoS provisioning is another factor that needs to be considered in the design of MANET routing algorithms. However, a tradeoff is required to achieve both these objectives (Anderegg, & Eidenbenz, 2003).

The *IANR* scheme is a new routing scheme for MANETs. The developed scheme is designed to provide energy efficiency and QoS provisioning simultaneously. To find an optimum solution for these conflicting requirements, we need to study how each node's actions translate into an effective system-wide solution. For this purpose, the *IANR* scheme uses an incentive-based model because it can make a self-organizing MANET system effectively functional (Zhong, Chen, & Yang, 2003).

The *IANR* scheme is designed as an adaptive online routing scheme by using an incentive-based model. In MANETs, wireless nodes are assumed to be rational selfish agents. According to their local goals and information, self-organizing agents make local decisions to achieve their individual objectives. Therefore, the *IANR* scheme is developed to induce selfish agents to participate in routing; the incentive-based technique can align

the goals of selfish individual agents such as energy efficiency and QoS provisioning (Rogers, 2005).

Under various QoS constraints and dynamically changing wireless network environments, it is impossible for a single algorithm to provide globally desirable system-wide properties. To this end, it is necessary for various control algorithms to cooperate with each other. The developed routing scheme consists of path-setup, incentive-computing and reservation algorithms. The path-setup algorithm configures routing paths according to a specific requirement. The incentive-computing algorithm calculates each node's incentive according to the established path; it can stimulate cooperative actions in MANETs. To achieve the desired QoS, the reservation algorithm can reserve bandwidth for high priority traffic services. A sophisticated combination of these three algorithms ensures that the control decisions in each algorithm are mutually dependent on each other. Therefore, under dynamic network situations, the developed algorithms work together to satisfy contradictory requirements and ensure a well-balanced network performance for MANET systems. In addition, each node makes a routing decision in a distributed and online manner. From the viewpoint of practical operations, this scheme is suitable for real world network management.

Related Work

Recently, several routing schemes for ad-hoc networks have been presented in research literature. J. Y. Leu, et al., developed the *Multicast Power Greedy Clustering* (*MPGC*) scheme (Leu, Tsai, Chiang, & Huang, 2006), which is an adaptive power-aware and on-demand multicasting algorithm. The *MPGC* scheme uses greedy heuristic clustering, power aware multicasting and clustering maintenance techniques that maximize energy efficiency and prolong network lifetime.

To optimize the three QoS parameters i.e., delay, jitter and energy, R. Asokan, et.al proposed the *Swarm-based Distance Vector Routing* (*SDVR*) scheme (Asokan, Natarajan, & Nivetha, 2007). This scheme selects a minimum delay path with maximum residual energy at the nodes. In addition, QoS routes are selected using periodically obtained information, and by taking into consideration the jitter metric to keep the minimum and maximum delay values approximately equal to the average delay.

B. Sun and L. Li proposed the *Distributed QoS Multicast Routing* (*DQMRP*) scheme (Sun, & Li, 2006). This scheme is developed as a shared-tree QoS-based multicast routing protocol; the source nodes sends an explored frame to every neighboring node and the intermediate node transfers this received frame to all its neighbor nodes. The destination node chooses the path with minimum cost and sends an acknowledge-reply to the source nodes. During routing operations, the destination node sets aside all other feasible paths as backup paths.

The *Ant colony based Routing Algorithm* (*ARA*) scheme was proposed (Gunes, Sorges, & Bouazizi, 2002); in this scheme, swarm intelligence and ant-colony meta-heuristic techniques are used. This scheme consists of three phases: route discovery, route maintenance, and route failure handling. In the route discovery phase, new routes between nodes are discovered using forward and backward ants. Routes are maintained by subsequent data packets, i.e., as the data traverse the network, node pheromone values are modified to reinforce the routes.

G. Wang developed the logical *Hypercube-based Virtual Dynamic Backbone* (*HVDB*) scheme for an n-dimensional hypercube in a large-scale MANET (Wang, Cao, Zhang, Chan, & Wu, 2005). The *HVDB* scheme is a proactive, QoS-aware and hybrid multicast routing protocol. Owing to the regularity, symmetry properties, and small diameter of the hypercube, every node plays almost the same role. In addition, no single node is more loaded than any other node, and bottlenecks do not

exist unlike the case in tree-based architectures. In particular, the *HVDB* scheme can satisfy the new QoS requirements of - high availability and good load balancing - by using location information.

L. Barolli, et al., proposed the *Genetic Algorithm based Routing* (*GAR*) scheme for mobile ad hoc networks (Barolli, Koyama, Suganuma, & Shiratori, 2003). In the *GAR* scheme, only a small number of nodes are involved in route computation because a small population size is used. As a result, routing information is transmitted only for the nodes present in that population. Different routes are ranked by sorting; the first route is the best one, and the remaining routes are used as backup routes. Because a tree based genetic algorithm method is used in the *GAR* scheme, the delay and transmission success rate are considered as QoS parameters in this scheme.

The *incentive-based Repeated Routing* (*IRR*) scheme is an incentive-based routing model that captures the notion of repetition (Afergan, 2006). To provide a desirable solution, the *IRR* scheme examines certain fundamental properties to govern the behavior of autonomous agents. The *Distributed Routing Mechanism* (*DRM*) scheme is an adaptive and scalable routing scheme for wireless ad hoc networks. This scheme provides a cost-efficient routing mechanism for strategic agents. In addition, the *DRM* scheme is designed to maximize the benefit of each agent (Wu, & Shu, 2004).

Previous proposed routing schemes for MANETs have attracted much attention and given rise to unique challenges. However, these existing schemes have several shortcomings. Although a majority of previous work focused on specific performance metrics such as bandwidth, delay or energy efficiency, a trade off was required to satisfy conflicting network requirements. A major drawback of existing schemes is that they potentially lead to some inefficiency that restricts the achievement of their specific design goal. The second drawback is that they operate wireless networks through fixed system parameters. Under dynamic network environments, control algorithms using static thresholds can make potentially erroneous decisions. The third drawback is that these existing schemes cause extra overhead and require intractable computation to be performed.

Path Setup Algorithm in the *IANR* Scheme

In the *IANR* scheme, the main challenge is to achieve globally desirable goals such as energy efficiency and QoS provisioning. For this goal, the developed algorithms are incorporated in the *IANR* scheme. Based on the adaptive online approach, these algorithms act cooperatively to strike an appropriate network performance.

In wireless communications, energy consumption is a crucial issue; the less energy is spent, the longer the node remains operable. Usually, energy consumption decreases proportional to the square of the propagation distance (Kim, 2008). Therefore, for the energy efficient routing, data packets should be forwarded via short distance multi-hop links. In addition, some data in military, environmental and surveillance applications are valid only for a limited time duration. To ensure the real-time data delivery, the timeliness is considered as another main metric in routing algorithms.

In the *IANR* scheme, heterogeneous data can be categorized into two classes according to the required QoS: *class I* (real-time) traffic services and *class II* (non real-time) traffic services. *Class I* data traffic is highly delay sensitive. For example, video and audio data have real-time delivery requirements. However, file transfer, electronic mail, and remote terminal applications are rather tolerant of delays. Such flexible multimedia data type is called as *class II* traffic. Different multimedia services over networks not only require different amounts of bandwidth but also have different QoS requirements. A multimedia network should take into account the prioritization among different multimedia traffic services (Kim, & Varshney,

2005). Based on different data characteristics, the *IANR* scheme provides two different routing strategies; energy efficient strategy for *Class II* data service and QoS-aware routing strategy for *Class I* data service.

Energy Efficient Routing Strategy

To configure an energy efficient routing path, an online link parameter (D_EE) is defined; it estimates the degree of energy efficiency of each link. In order to relatively handle dynamic network conditions, the D_EE value from node i to node j is obtained as

$$D\_EE_{ij} = \left[(1-\alpha) \times \frac{d_{ij}}{D_M} \right] + \left[\alpha \times \left(1 - \frac{E_j}{E_M} \right) \right] \tag{12}$$

where d_{ij} is distance from node i to node j, E_j is remaining energy of node j. E_M and D_M are initial energy, and a maximum coverage range of each node, respectively. Therefore, d_{ij} and E_j are normalized by D_M and E_M; the range is varied from 0 to 1. d_{ij} reflects energy dissipation rate for wireless communications; the closer a next node, the more attractive for routing due to the less communication cost. E_j is a current residual energy of node j, which reflects a remaining lifetime of a wireless node. Usually, nodes with more energy are favored for routing. To estimate current link situations, the parameter α controls the relative weights given to distance and remaining energy of corresponding node. In the *IANR* scheme, the α control mechanism is the same approach in the *CGOR* scheme (Kim, 2010).

For *class II* data services, the developed path-setup algorithm establishes a multi-hop path from the viewpoint of energy efficiency. First, a source node broadcasts the *route_setup_II* message. Within the power coverage area, message receiving nodes individually estimate the energy cost according to (12). The *IANR* scheme defines an energy cost parameter (*EC*) for routing decisions; it is computed as the sum of all *D_EE* costs from source node to current node. Therefore, the *EC* value potentially incorporates more global network information. Each message receiving node updates routing information i.e., *EC* in the *route_setup_II* message and forwards it recursively to next neighbor nodes. If node *i* has received multiple messages from the reachable neighbor nodes, a relay node is adaptively decided to minimize the *EC* value as follows.

$$relay\_node = \arg\min_{j \in N_i}\left\{EC(j) + D\_EE_i(j)\right\} \tag{13}$$

where N_i is the set of neighbor node of node *i*, and *j* is a message-sending node in N_i. *EC(j)* is the *EC* value of node *j* and $D\_EE_i(j)$ is the *D_EE* value from node *i* to node *j*. In an entirely distributed fashion, this hop-by-hop path-setup procedure is recursively repeated until to reach destination node. Finally, destination node receives multiple *route_setup* messages. At this point, destination node selects the minimum *EC* cost path, which is the most energy efficient path. And then, destination node sends the *confirm* message backwards through selected route nodes. At last, source node has been informed the established routing path and the path set-up algorithm terminates

QoS-Aware Routing Strategy

To configure QoS-aware routing path, each wireless link is also estimated in an adaptive online manner. At this time, in contrast to the energy efficient routing strategy, an online link parameter (P_{loss}) is defined to represent packet loss probability. The P_{loss} value from node *i* to node *j* is obtained as

$$P_{loss\_ij} = \frac{L\_P_{ij}}{L\_P_{ij} + S\_P_{ij}} \tag{14}$$

where L_P_{ij}, S_P_{ij} are number of lost packets and number of successfully received packets from node *i* to node *j*, respectively. These parameter values are also estimated periodically, every *unit_time*. Based on the P_{loss} and deadline, the developed path-setup algorithm establishes a multi-hop path.

For routing decisions, total packet loss parameter (*PL*) and time delay parameter (*delay*) are defined; the *PL* is computed as a multiplication of packet loss probabilities and the *delay* is estimated as a summation of time delay from source node to current node. Therefore, the *PL* and *delay* parameters potentially incorporate more global network information from the viewpoint of QoS provisioning. When a node tries to send *class I* data, this node creates a *route_setup_I* message packet with a time deadline and *PL*; initially *PL* value is set as 1. And then, this message is forwarded to neighbor nodes. Each message receiving node individually estimates the P_{loss} value according to (14) and updates the *PL* value by simply multiplication of the estimated P_{loss}. Recursively, the *route_setup_I* message, which has the updated routing information i.e., *PL* and *delay*, is forwarded to neighbor nodes again. Next neighbor node also updates the *PL* value in the same manner. When a node has received multiple *route_setup_I* messages from reachable neighbor nodes, it adaptively selects one of them as a relay to configure a routing path. If node *i* has received multiple messages, a relay node is decided to minimize the *PL* while ensuring time deadline condition as follows.

$$relay\_node = \arg\min_{j \in N_i}\left\{PL(j) \times P_{loss\_i}(j)\right\},$$
$$\text{where } time\_limit - (delay_j + \eta_{ij}) \geq 0 \tag{15}$$

where $PL(j)$ is the PL value of node j and $P_{loss\_i}(j)$ is the P_{loss} value from node i to node j. $time\_limit$ is a requested time deadline for data transmission. $delay_j$ is the time delay from source node to node j and η_{ij} is the time delay from node i to node j. Based on this information, individual node can locally make routing decisions in a distributed manner while ensuring a desirable network performance. In the same manner as the energy efficient routing strategy, the path setup procedure is recursively repeated until to reach a destination node. Finally, it selects the minimum PL value path according to (15) and the source node has been informed the established routing path.

Incentive Computing Algorithm in the *IANR* Scheme

In wireless ad hoc networks, most routing algorithms are designed by relying on the assumption of node collaboration, according to which nodes are willing to act as relay nodes in a routing path. However, a node acting as a relay node has to sacrifice its energy and bandwidth. Selfish nodes have nothing to gain by conceding to forward a packet. Therefore, routing algorithms need to stimulate cooperative actions between network nodes in order to be effective (Anderegg, 2003).

In the *IANR* scheme, an incentive payment algorithm is developed to guide selfish nodes toward a socially optimal outcome. By paying the nodes appropriate incentives, the developed routing algorithm stimulates cooperation among nodes. The key concern during the development of this incentive-based algorithm is how much a relay node should be paid for data forwarding. Mechanism Design (*MD*) is used to define a strategic situation to make a system exhibits good behaviors when independent agents pursue self-interested strategies (Wang, & Schulzrinne, 2005), (Garg, Narahari, & Gujar, 2008). In the *IANR* scheme, the basic concept of *MD* is adopted to calculate the incentive payment for a relay node.

Traditional *MD* consists of a specification of possible agent strategies and the mapping of each strategy from a set of strategies to an outcome. Agents are assumed to be autonomous and economically rational; they select a best-response strategy to maximize their expected utility with other agents. The family of *direct-revelation* and *strategyproof* mechanisms has been derived from the *MD* theory and are referred to as Vickrey-Clarke-Groves (*VCG*) mechanism (Rextin, Irfan, & Uzmi, 2004), (Friedman, & Parkes, 2003). The *VCG* mechanism has better computational properties than the original *MD* and provides a normative guide for outcomes and payments. When applying the *VCG* mechanism to complex *MD* problems, a feasible outcome can be obtained from the results of computationally tractable heuristic algorithms (Dash, Parkes, & Jennings, 2003), (Nisan, & Ronen, 2000). Each agent in the *VCG* mechanism is of a specific type. According to its type, an agent selects a specific strategy, which defines the agent's actions. Generally, an agent type is represented by θ, (e.g., each agent i is of type θ_i).

The *VCG* mechanism is a special case among traditional mechanisms, in which the agent-announced type ($\hat{\theta}$) is no longer necessarily truthful; the symbol $\hat{\theta}$ indicates that agents can misreport their true types. Based on agent-announced types, the choice rule ($k^*(\hat{\theta})$) is defined as follows (Woodard, & Parkes, 2003).

$$k^*(\hat{\theta}) = \text{argmax}_{k \in \mathcal{K}} \sum_i v_i(k, \hat{\theta}_i) \qquad (16)$$

where k is a feasible choice of the set of all possible choices and $v_i(k, \hat{\theta}_i)$ defines the agent i's outcome of a choice k with its type $\hat{\theta}_i$; the *VCG* mechanism implements the choice $k*$ that maximizes $\sum_i v_i(k, \hat{\theta})$. Therefore, the *VCG* mechanism maximizes the total outcome of the system to the agents. Based on the $k^*\left(\hat{\theta}\right)$, the payment rule ($p_{vcg,i}(\hat{\theta})$) is defined as follows (Nisan, 2000), (Woodard, 2003).

$$p_{vcg,i}\left(\hat{\theta}\right) = v_i\left(k^*\left(\hat{\theta}\right),\hat{\theta}_i\right) - \left\{V_N - V_{N-i}\right\} \qquad (17)$$

where V_N is the total reported outcome of k^* and V_{N-i} is the total reported outcome of the choice that would be gotten without agent i, i.e.,

$$V_N = \max_{k\in K}\sum_i v_i\left(k,\hat{\theta}_i\right)$$

and

$$V_{N-i} = \max_{k\in K}\sum_{j\neq i} v_j\left(k,\hat{\theta}_j\right).$$

The *IANR* scheme modified the traditional static *VCG* mechanism and developed a new incentive computation algorithm to ensure good global performance. Under the assumption of selfish nodes, the developed algorithm is a variation of the *VCG* mechanism; it can estimate the incentive payment for a relay node in a distributed manner. During network routing operations, each node can choose its emission power to send data. At the same time, residual energy and packet loss probability also influence transmission cost. In the terminology of traditional incentive computation algorithms, private information such as power level, loss probability and residual energy determines each node's type. In the *IANR* scheme, by considering each node's type, the packet transmission cost for node i (Tc_i) is defined as follows.

$$Tc_i = \left[\sum_{k=1}^{3}\left(\omega_k \times f_k\right)\right] \times B_{packet},$$

where $f_1 = \dfrac{P_{emit}}{P_{max}}$, $f_2 = 1 - \dfrac{E_i}{E_M}$, $f_3 = P_{loss}$ $\qquad (18)$

where ω_k is a control parameter and B_{packet} is the packet size. P_{emit} and P_{loss} are the transmitting power and packet loss probability of the node i, respectively. P_{max} is the maximum power level.

As explained earlier the path-setup algorithm can establish a routing path by using (13) or (14). After establishing a path, each link's Tc can be estimated according to (18). Let $|PC|$ denote the total sum of all Tc values and $|PC_{-i}|$ denote the total sum of Tc values in the path that does not contain node i as a relay node. According to the transitory re-routing route, the $|PC_{-i}|$ value can be estimated. To make a detour around node i, node i's neighbor nodes are selected as alternative relay nodes in the same manner as in the path-setup algorithm. Finally, the incentive payment for relay node i (IP_i) is defined as follows.

$$IP_i = Tc_i - (|PC| - |PC_{-i}|) \qquad (19)$$

where $|PC| - |PC_{-i}|$ is the difference between the cost of path in which node i is included and that in which node i is not included. The term Tc_i corresponds to the data transmission cost incurred by node i. In comparison with the *VCG* model defined by (17), $v_i\left(k^*\left(\hat{\theta}\right),\hat{\theta}_i\right)$, V_N and V_{N-i} are replaced with Tc_i, $|PC|$ and $|PC_{-i}|$, respectively. Each relay node can estimate its own *IP* value and earn its fair incentive in a distributed fashion according to its individual contribution to data forwarding.

Traditional incentive computation algorithms focus on the idea that a single super-agent might unilaterally seek to manipulate an outcome. However, because of computation and communication overburdening, this central approach might be impractical for the system's overall operations. In the *IANR* scheme, a distributed online approach is developed to select an alternative relay node. Therefore, the developed algorithm in the *IANR* scheme can reduce model complexity during network routing operations.

Owing to the weakness of local decisions, the obtained solution may not be optimal result. For practical implementations in real network operations, the *IANR* scheme accepts this loss of optimality as the cost of the distributed online implementation. However, to overcome this limitation, local decisions can allow online renegotiation to become dynamically adjustable. By using the adaptive online technique, each node can adapt its behavior in the path-setup and incentive computing algorithms, and acts strategically to approximate an optimal network performance.

Reservation Algorithm in the *IANR* Scheme

Future wireless networks will support diverse multimedia applications. To provide QoS for higher priority applications, the system should guarantee a minimum amount of network resources for data communications. However, owing to dynamic topology and the property of shared wireless bandwidth, QoS provisioning for MANETs is a challenging task. Because of various QoS requests, bandwidth reservation algorithms are developed for ad-hoc networks. The key concept in the developed QoS control strategy is an economic approach for bandwidth reservation. Therefore, a source node must pay the price to take advantage of reservation services.

In the incentive computing algorithm, each relay node earns an incentive for its data forwarding service. In the *IANR* scheme, this incentive is defined as virtual money that can be used to achieve the desired QoS. Initially, no node has virtual money to pay for higher QoS services. By cooperation during data forwarding, all relay nodes independently set aside their earned virtual money, which is calculated using (19).

If a source node has enough virtual money, it explicitly sends signals to determine whether enough bandwidth is available at the relay nodes along the pre-established path. When bandwidth is available within QoS constraints, the source node can reserve the requested bandwidth for a new flow. Similar to the RSVP approach (Postigo-Boix, & Melús-Moreno, 2007), a reservation is made at every node during in the exploration and registration phases.

According to the total amount of communication data, the reservation payment is defined as $Tc_i \times P_n$, where P_n is the total number of transmitting packets. If a source node sends *class I* data using the reservation technique, the source node should consume its own virtual money. When the virtual money is exhausted or a reservation fails because of the lack of available bandwidth, the source node sends only data packets with a particular priority. Similar to the DiffServ approach, data packets are marked differently, i.e., as *class I* or *class II* services. In line with the preferential treatment method (Postigo-Boix, 2007), the network system aims to provide better QoS provisioning for *class I* data forwarding. Therefore, no service charge is expected from the source node for this purpose.

Game Model Procedure in the *IANR* Scheme

In the *IANR* scheme, the use of path-setup, incentive-computing and reservation algorithms is developed to satisfy the conflicting requirements of energy efficiency and QoS provisioning. According to the adaptive online approach, these algorithms are combined in a sophisticated manner into a holistic scheme, they act cooperatively and collaborate with each other. Under widely different MANET situations, this integrated scheme contributes to the overall goals of the systems. In addition, control decisions in each algorithm are made in an entirely distributed manner. Therefore, the *IANR* scheme offers excellent adaptability and flexibility for practical implementations. The main steps of the *IANR* scheme are given below.

Step 1: At the initial time, each node adaptively estimates d, E, α, L_P and S_P values based on the online manner.

Step 2: For data routing, a source node decides routing strategy according to data type (*class I* or *class II*).

Step 3: If data type is *class II*, each link cost is locally calculated according to (12) and path is configured using (13); proceeds to Step 5 for the next iteration.

Step 4: If data type is *class I*, each link cost is locally estimated according to (14) and path is configured using (15).

Step 5: For *class I* data services, a destination node selects the minimum *PL* value path. For *class II* data service, the minimum *EC* cost path is selected.

Step 6: In the selected path, each relay node estimates Tc_i, $|PC|$ and $|PC_{-i}|$ values using (18).

Step 7: According to (19), the incentive is computed; it is awarded to steer each relay node for cooperative routing. All relay nodes can put aside the incentive independently.

Step 8: For higher priority *class I* data services, a source node can reserve the bandwidth to guarantee QoS. The incentive in a source node is consumed by the service payment.

Step 9: If the incentive is exhausted or reservation fails, a source node only send data packets with given priority like as the DiffServ approach.

Figure 3 demonstrates that the performance of the proposed *IANR* scheme is generally superior to those of other existing schemes: the *IRR* scheme and the *DRM* scheme. Through the adaptive online approach, each algorithm in the *IANR* scheme constantly monitors the current traffic conditions and can balance network performance whereas other schemes cannot offer such an attractive network performance.

Summary

Recently, the design of effective routing algorithms in MANETs has been the subject of intense research. In the *IANR* scheme, new path-setup, incentive-computing and reservation algorithms are developed for MANETs. For practical network operations, these developed algorithms are designed in a self-organizing, dynamically online and distributed fashion, to work together in a coordinated manner. As a result, each wireless node is capable of independently adapting

Figure 3. Performance evaluations of the IANR scheme

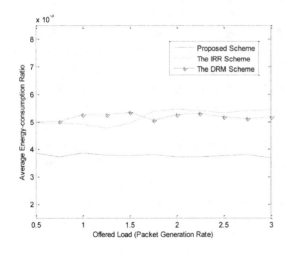

(a) Energy-consumption ratio

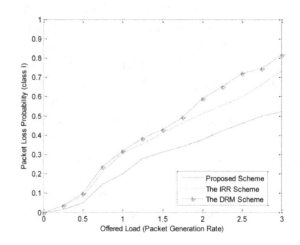

(b) Packet loss probability (class I data)

its actions and can quickly respond to real time network environment changes.

In the future, we expect the *IANR* scheme's methodology to be useful in developing new adaptive control algorithms for other research areas. Control decisions in inter-process communication, disk and memory management, file and I/O systems, CPU scheduling, and distributed operating system also need to be made before the entire input sequence is available. Therefore, the main concept employed in the *IANR* scheme, namely, the modified *VCG* mechanism approach based on real-time measurement information, is suitable not only for routing operations in multimedia MANETs but also for application requiring adaptive control algorithms.

COOPETITION GAME BASED MULTI-PATH ROUTING (*CGMR*) SCHEME FOR MOBILE AD-HOC NETWORKS

Mobile ad-hoc network represents a system of wireless mobile nodes that can freely and dynamically self-organize network topologies without any preexisting communication infrastructure. Due to characteristics like temporary topology and absence of centralized authority, routing is one of major issues in ad-hoc networks. Recently, S. Kim proposed a new Coopetition Game based Multi-path Routing (*CGMR*) scheme for mobile ad-hoc networks by employing both coopetition game model and simulated annealing approach. The combination mechanism of these two different approaches can achieve greater and reciprocal advantages in a hostile dynamic real world. Therefore, the *CGMR* scheme is a powerful method for finding an effective solution in the conflict mobile ad-hoc network routing problem.

Development Motivation

Due to the explosive growth of wireless communication technology, Mobile Ad-hoc NETworks (MANETs) are likely to be used in many practical applications, including personal area networks, home area networking, military environments, and search a rescue operations. MANETs are self-creating, self-organizing, and autonomous systems of mobile hosts connected by wireless links with no static infrastructure such as base station. When making such networks operational, a key question is how to effectively decide routing paths, given the dynamic nature of the system and the limited knowledge of the network topology. In recent times, a lot of attention has been attracted to design efficient routing protocols for efficient MANET operations (Deepalakshmi, & Radhakrishnan, 2009), (Qin, & Liu, 2009).

During the operation of MANETs, unexpected growth of traffic may develop in a specific routing path; it may create local traffic congestion. In order to alleviate this kind of traffic overload condition, load balancing strategy should be employed. In MANETs, the meaning of load balancing is to ease out the heavy traffic load in a specific path, which can ensure the balanced network resource assumption. To ensure the load balancing, multipath routing algorithms have been developed. Multi-path routing algorithm establishes multiple paths between a source and a destination node and spreads the traffic load along multiple routes. It can alleviate traffic congestion in a specific path. Therefore, multi-path routing algorithms can provide the route resilience while ensuring the reliability of data transmission (Klinkowski, Careglio, & Sole-Pareta, 2009), (Zafar, 2009).

The use of game theory has expanded to a wide variety of research areas and given the increased importance for decades. Recently, coopetition game model has been extensively discussed in economics and management science. This model suggested that a judicious mixture of competition and cooperation is often advantageous in competitive environments (Guan, Yuan, & Zhang, 2008), (Bouncken, & Fredrich, 2011). An essential part in the coopetition game is the expression of individual decisions by game players. To model autonomous interacting MANET nodes, the coopetition game process can be used to get an effective solution for routing problems (Sun, & Xu, 2005). With the game theory, meta-heuristic approach is widely recognized as a practical perspective to be implemented for real world network operations (Randall, McMahon, & Sugden, 2002). Traditionally, meta-heuristic algorithms try to improve a candidate solution iteratively with regard to a given measure of quality. Even though, this approach does not guarantee an optimal solution, it can be widely applied to various network control problems. Simulated annealing is a well-known probabilistic meta-heuristic algorithm for finding an effective solution (Bouleimen, & Lecocq, 2003), (Hussain, & Habib, 2009). To adaptively make a routing decision, the basic concept of simulated annealing approach can be adopted.

Motivated by the facts presented in the above discussion, the *CGMR* scheme is designed based on the coopetition game model and simulated annealing approach. In the *CGMR* scheme, wireless nodes are assumed as self-interested game players and make local decisions in a distributed manner. Therefore, routing packets are adaptively distributed through multiple paths in pursuit of the main goals such as load balancing and network reliability. Under diverse network environment changes, the *CGMR* scheme tries to approximate an optimal network performance. The important features of the *CGMR* scheme are i) interactive process to get an efficient network performance, ii) distributed approach for large-scale network operations, iii) ability to achieve load balancing for real network operations, and iv) feasibility for practical implementation.

Related Work

Recently, several routing schemes for MANETs have been presented. The *Proactive Congestion Reduction* (*PCR*) scheme focuses on adaptive routing strategies to help congestion reduction (Klinkowski, 2009). Based on a nonlinear optimization method for multi-path routings, the *PCR* scheme calculates a traffic splitting vector that determines a near-optimal traffic distribution over routing paths. The *Shortest Multipath Source* (*SMS*) scheme is one of the more generally accepted on-demand dynamic routing schemes that build multiple shortest partial disjoint paths (Zafar, 2009). The *SMS* scheme uses node-disjoint secondary paths to exploit fault tolerance, load balancing, and bandwidth aggregation.

Routing Algorithms in the *CGMR* Scheme

Multi-path routing algorithms are designed to split and transmit the traffic load through two or more different paths to a destination simultaneously. The *CGMR* scheme is developed as a new multi-path routing algorithm to balance the network load while ensuring efficient network performance.

Path Setup Algorithm

Usually, wireless link capacity continually varies because of the impacts from transmission power and interference, etc. Therefore, it is important to estimate the current link status by considering several control factors. To configure the adaptive multi-hop routing path, the algorithm in the *CGMR* scheme defines a link cost (*L_P*) for each link to estimate the degree of communication adaptability (Kim, 2010). In order to relatively handle dynamic network conditions, the *L_P* value from the node *i* to the node *j* is obtained as

$$L\_P_{ij} = \left[(1-\alpha) \times \left(\frac{d_{ij}}{D_M} \right) + \alpha \times \left(1 - \frac{E_j}{E_M} \right) \right] + \left[\omega \times \left(1 - E\_t_j \left(t_c \right) \right) \right] \quad (20)$$

where d_{ij} is distance from the node *i* to the node *j* and E_j is the remaining energy of the node *j*. E_M

and D_M are the initial energy and the maximum coverage range of each node. Therefore, the d_{ij} and E_j are normalized by the D_M and E_M; the range is varied from 0 to 1. The α is a control parameter to relatively estimate the current link situation. The d_{ij} reflects the cost of the wireless communication; the closer a next node, the more attractive for routing due to the less communication cost. The E_j is the current residual energy of node j, which reflects the remaining lifetime of a wireless node. The nodes with more energy are favored for routing. Due to the characteristics of wireless propagation, the energy consumption rate for wireless communications is strongly related to the inter-node distance. In the *CGMR* scheme, the α control mechanism is the same approach in the *CGOR* scheme (Kim, 2010).

$E\_t_j\left(t_c\right)$ is the entropy for the node j at the time (t_c). Usually, entropy is the uncertainty and a measure of the disorder in a system. It represents the topological change, which is a natural quantification of the effect of node mobility on MANET's connectivity service (An, Lee, & Kim, 2011). In the *CGMR* scheme, the basic concept of entropy is adopted for supporting and evaluating stable routing routes. For the mobile node j, the entropy $E\_t_j\left(t_c\right)$ is calculated as follows (An, 2011).

$$E_{tj}\left(t_c\right) = \frac{-\sum_{k \in F_j} P_k\left(t, \Delta_t\right) \times \log P_k\left(t, \Delta_t\right)}{\log C(F_j)},$$

$$\text{s.t.,} \quad P_k\left(t, \Delta_t\right) = \frac{a_{j,k}}{\sum_{i \in F_j} a_{j,i}} \tag{21}$$

where Δ_t is a time interval. F_j denotes the set of the neighboring nodes of node j, and $C(F_j)$ is the cardinality (degree) of set F_j. The *CGMR* scheme is interested in the stability of a part of a specific route. Therefore, F_j represents the two neighboring nodes of mobile node j over that route. $a_{j,i}$ represent a measure of the relative mobility among two nodes j and i like as

$$a_{j,i} = \frac{1}{I\_T} \times \sum_{l=1}^{I\_T} \left| v\left(j,i,t_l\right) \right|,$$
$$\text{s.t.,} \, v\left(j,i,t\right) = v\left(j,t\right) - v\left(i,t\right) \tag{22}$$

where $v\left(j,t\right)$ and $v\left(i,t\right)$ are the velocity vectors of node j and node i at time t, respectively. I_T is the number of discrete times t_l that mobility information can be calculated and disseminated to other neighboring nodes within time interval Δ_t. $v\left(j,i,t\right)$ is the relative velocity between nodes j and i at time t. Any change can be described as a change of variable values $a_{j,i}$ in the course of time t such as $a_{j,i}\left(t\right) \to a_{j,i}\left(t + \Delta_t\right)$. The entropy $E\_t_j\left(t_c\right)$ is normalized as $0 \le E\_t_j\left(t_c\right) \le 1$. If $E\_t_j\left(t_c\right)$ value is close to 1, the part of the route that represents the links of the path associated with an intermediate node j is stable. If $E\_t_j\left(t_c\right)$ value is close to 0, the local route is unstable (An, 2011). The parameter ω is an impact factor to evaluate the state of node mobility. To avoid the detrimental packet loss effect, the mobility situation is fully considered to estimate L_P value; the ω value is fixed as 1.

The L_P value can represent the normalized communication cost of each link. With the L_P value, the *CGMR* scheme defines the path cost (*PC*) parameter to calculate total routing path cost; *PC* is computed as the sum of all link costs from the source node to the current node. Based on the *PC* value, the routing algorithm in the *CGMR* scheme constructs adaptive multi-hop routing paths to reach the destination node. At the initial time for routing operations, the source node broadcasts its initial *PC* value (i.e., *PC* = 0). Within the power coverage area, message receiving relay nodes individually estimate the link cost according to (20) and estimate its *PC* value like as $PC + L\_P$. Some nodes can receive multiple *PC* values from reachable different neighbor nodes. For self-organizing and independent-effective controlling, each node keeps this information. For example, the node i can have received multiple *PC* values, i.e., PC_1, PC_k, PC_{N_i}, where PC_k is the receiving *PC* value of the message-sending neighbor node k ($1 \leq k \leq N_i$) and N_i is the number of total reachable neighbor nodes. In this case, the node i calculates its own PC_i value as follows.

$$PC_i = \arg \min_{k \in N_i} \left(PC_k + L\_P_{ik} \right) \qquad (23)$$

According to (23), the node i adaptively selects one neighbor node as a relay node while minimizing PC_i value, which is potentially incorporates more global network information. The estimated *PC* value is recursively forwarded to establish the routing path. This route formation process is repeated until that all available multi-paths from the source to the destination node are configured.

Simulated Annealing Routing Algorithm

Generally, multi-path routing algorithms face an essential challenge – how to distribute the volume of traffic to a specific path. In order to produce good solutions within a reasonable amount of computer time, the *CGMR* scheme does not seek the optimal allocation. Based on feedbacks of the real-time traffic measurements, it is designed in a simple but efficient meta-heuristic algorithm.

Simulated Annealing (SA) is a well known meta-heuristic method that has been applied successfully to combinatorial optimization problems (Randall, 2002). The term simulated annealing derives from the roughly analogous the natural phenomena of annealing of solids, which is accomplished by heating up a solid and allowing it to cold down slowly so that thermal equilibrium is maintained. Each step of the SA process replaces the current solution by a random 'nearby' solution, chosen with a probability that depends on the difference between the corresponding function values and on a global parameter T (called the temperature). The T is gradually decreased during the process to reach steady state or thermal equilibrium (Varadharajan, 2005), (Bouleimen, 2003).

In the algorithm of *CGMR* scheme, the SA approach is used to solving the multi-path routing problem. The basic concept of the developed algorithm is to proportionally load traffic on each route according to its adaptability. To transmit packets, each node selects a next relay node based on the *PC* information. From the point of view of the node i, selection probability of the neighbor node k (SP_k where $k \in N_i$) is defined as follows.

$$SP_k = \frac{TC_k}{\sum_{j=1}^{t} TC_j}, \text{ where } TC_k = 1$$
$$- \frac{\left(PC_j + L\_P_{ij} \right)}{\sum_{j=1}^{t} \left(PC_j + L\_P_{ij} \right)} \qquad (24)$$

Based on the *roulette-wheel* function (Zou, Mi, & Xu, 2006) of *SP* values, a next relay node is temporarily selected. For example, the probability of node k's selection is

$$SP_k \Big/ \sum_{j=1}^{t} SP_j,$$

where t is the total number of neighbor nodes. Therefore, the *CGMR* scheme can make the more adaptable nodes likely to be selected than the less adaptable nodes. In addition, to avoid a local optimal solution, the Boltzmann probability (*BP*) is adopted. The *BP* is defined as follows (Zou, 2006).

$$BP = \exp \left(- \frac{N_{pc} - C_{pc}}{T} \right) \qquad (25)$$

where N_{pc} is the *SP* value of new selected node and C_{pc} is the *SP* value of previously connected node; the difference between N_{pc} and C_{pc} (i.e., $N_{pc} - C_{pc}$) means the path adaptability alteration. *T* is a parameter to control the *BP* value. Metaphorically, it is the current 'temperature' of the system. Like as an annealing process, the *T* is decreased according to a cooling schedule. At the beginning of the annealing algorithm run, the initialization temperature is high enough so that possibility of accepting any decision changes whether it improves the solution or not. While time is ticking away, the *T* value decreases until the stopping condition is met. In the *CGMR* scheme, *T* value is set to the current ratio of the remaining packet amount to the total routing packet amount.

At the routing decision time, if the N_{pc} value is less than the C_{pc} value (i.e., $N_{pc} - C_{pc} < 0$), the new selected neighbor node replaces the current relay node. If the N_{pc} value is higher than the C_{pc} (i.e., $N_{pc} - C_{pc} > 0$), the new selected neighbor node is the worse choice than the current relay node. However, it might still be accepted as a new relay node to potentially avoid a local optima. In this case, a random number *X* is generated, where *X* is in the range of $\{0..1\}$. If the *X* is less than *BP* (i.e., $X < BP$), the new selected neighbor node replaces the current relay node. Otherwise, the current routing route is not changed. Based on the SA approach, individual nodes locally make routing decisions to select next relay nodes.

Coopetition Game for Routing Decision

When a node is selected as a next relay node, the selected node can make a decision whether to accept the packet relay request or not. For this decision procedure, the methodology that the *CGMR* scheme adopts is the game theory. Usually, game theory can be classified into two types according to the interaction of the players: non-cooperative game and cooperative game. In non-cooperative games, players are self-concerned

and make decision by themselves based on the strategy preferences. Therefore, non-cooperative equilibria are in general Pareto inefficient (Dirani, & Chahed, 2006). In cooperative situation, players make binding commitments and find it beneficial to cooperate in the game. To reach an agreement that gives mutual advantage, players bargain with each other. However, cooperative coalitions can be destroyed because of players' self-concerned actions that are ignored in the cooperative process (Sun, 2005). To avoid these conflicts, a new game paradigm is expected in the phenomenon that stresses two faces of cooperation and competition in the same situation.

In 1996, N. Barry and B. Adam had introduced a new concept of game model, called coopetition game, which combined the characteristics of non-cooperative and cooperative games. The coopetition game model is understood to achieve greater and reciprocal advantages for every player, who can strengthen their competitive advantages by cooperation. Even though coopetition game model has received strong attentions, designing a coopetition game model for real-world problems is still difficult. There are many complicated restrictions, which are often self-contradictory and variable with the dynamic environment (Guan, 2008), (Bouncken, 2011).

The *CGMR* scheme is design as a new ad-hoc network routing algorithm based on the coopetition paradigm, which consists of a judicious mixture of competition and cooperation. This strategy is an effective paradigm to solve complex routing problems in a dynamic network environment. Traditionally, routing problem can be modeled inherently as a non-deterministic approach. That means that network nodes always have the possibility of selecting alternative strategies and sequentially evaluate the current decision. In the *CGMR* scheme, all the node-pairs in the routing route make routing decisions in a non-deterministic manner; so packets are advanced distributively towards their destinations whenever possible.

For effective operations, the developed routing decision process is developed based on the cooperative negotiation mechanism, which employs competitive and cooperative techniques. Cooperative negotiation is traced back to a sequential negotiation between node-pairs. Each node focuses on strategy to maximize his payoff, but each node-pair also shares a common goal and makes a binding commitment according to the cooperative negotiation rules. Usually, negotiation process involves a number of steps including the exchange of common sequential offers and counter-offers, which are represented by linearly ordered proposals (Bian, & Luo, 2007), (Sun, Zhu, Li, & Zhou, 2007). In the developed process, $\omega^r_{i \to j}$ denotes the rth offering proposed by the node i to the node j as follows.

$\omega^r_{i \to j}$ = relay request from the node i to the node j, where $j \in N_i$ (26)

$\omega^{r+1}_{j \to i}$ denotes the counter offering proposed from the node j to the node i. Relay node j is selected based on the simulated annealing method. When the node j receives an offer ($\omega^r_{i \to j}$), the node j tries to maximize his own payoff by selecting a strategy where $\max_{S_i} : U_i(S_i) \to \Re, S_i \in$ {accept, reject}. For this decision, the negotiation function NF_j is formally expressed as follows.

$$NF_j\left(\omega^r_{i \to j}\right) =$$
$$\begin{cases} reject\ \omega^r_{i \to j}\ , if\ (U^{re}_j - U^{ac}_j) > 0\ and\ \xi^r_j > 0 \\ \\ accept\ \omega^r_{i \to j}\ , otherwise \end{cases}$$
$$(27)$$

$$U^{re}_j = e^{\left(\beta_j \times E^{re}_j\right)} - \frac{1}{\left(\gamma_j \times P^{re}_j\right) + 1},$$

s.t.,
$$U^{ac}_j = e^{\left(\beta_j \times E^{ac}_j\right)} - \frac{1}{\left(\gamma_j \times P^{ac}_j\right) + 1}$$ and $\xi^r_j =$

$$P^r_j - (\xi_j \times r)$$

where E^{ac}_j, P^{ac}_j (or E^{re}_j, P^{re}_j) are the node j's remaining energy and packet accept ratios, respectively, when the node j accepts (or rejects) the routing offer. ξ^r_j, P^r_j are the rth round negotiation power and packet accept ratio of the node j. β_j, γ_j are the node j's control factors for energy sensitivity and negotiation power preference, respectively.

The cooperation among players succeeds only when participating players are enthusiastically unified in pursuit of a common goal rather than individual objectives. To satisfy this goal, the *CGMR* scheme employs cooperative negotiation rules. First, the packet accept ratio (P) is defined as a negotiation power, which acts as an incentive to guides selfish nodes toward a socially optimal outcome. In wireless ad hoc networks, a node acting as a relay node has to sacrifice its energy and bandwidth. Selfish nodes have nothing to gain by conceding to forward a packet. Therefore, routing algorithm needs to stimulate cooperative actions between network nodes in order to be effective. Negotiation power can stimulate cooperation among nodes as an appropriate incentive. Second, discount factor ($\Delta \xi$) is defined to prevent infinite offering rounds. Each round, the value of ξ is decreased in steps equal to $\Delta \xi$. The *CGMR* scheme sets $\Delta \xi = R_j \times 0.2$.

If the offer ($\omega^r_{i \to j}$) is rejected, the node i selects again a new relay node j' ($j' \in N_i$) based on the simulated annealing algorithm. According to (24) and (25), the node i selects a new relay node (j') and proposes an offer ($\omega^{r+2}_{i \to j'}$). Every negotiation step, both players' negotiation power is reduced by discount factor. If no agreement is reached until the negotiation power of the power of node i becomes a negative value, the routing packet is dropped. Otherwise, if the negotiation power of the selected relay node is to become a negative value in advance, the relay node obligatorily accepts the routing offer. Therefore, in a given negotiation step, the negotiation process has been completed within a finite sequence of offers. In an entirely distributed fashion, this hop-by-hop path selection procedure is recursively repeated until the packet is reached to the destination node.

Game Model Procedure in the *CGMR* Scheme

The current business environment has led firms to cooperate and compete simultaneously. Therefore, cooperation and competition has become the current trend of business management and economic activities. The coopetition game combines collaboration and competition concepts; players cooperate in some areas and at the same time compete with each other. However, designing a coopetition game model is still difficult because there are time limitations and many complicated restrictions, which are often self-contradictory and variable with the dynamic environment (Bouncken, 2011).

The *CGMR* scheme develops a new coopetition game model for cooperation and competition co-existing MANET routing situations. Usually, classical game theory models often assume that all possible deals are available to players and no computation is required to find mutually acceptable solution. However, this traditional approach is not rational under the highly reconfigurable real world scenarios. In the *CGMR* scheme, routing is guided by employing a cooperative and competitive decision process. Therefore, self-interested ad-hoc nodes make routing decisions according to private preferences and cooperative negotiation rules, which are developed to instruct a node how to carry out offer and counter-offer, and gets a solution with high flexibility and adaptability in a hostile dynamic real world. To solve the dynamic and distributed routing problem, the main steps of the *CGMR* scheme are given next

Step 1: Each node dynamically estimates the d, E and α values based on the online manner.

Step 2: The L_P value is locally calculated according to (20).

Step 3: At the initial time for routing operations, the source node broadcasts the initial *PC* value to neighbor nodes. Each node calculates its *PC* value by using (23) and recursively forwards this information.

Step 4: Based on the *PC* value, route configuration process continues repeatedly until that all available multi-paths from the source to the destination node are configured.

Step 5: To transmit packets, each relay node temporarily selects a next relay node with the selection probability, which is estimated according to (24).

Step 6: If the N_{pc} value is less than the C_{pc} value (i.e., $N_{pc} - C_{pc} < 0$), the new selected neighbor node replaces the current relay node; proceeds to Step 8. Otherwise, go to Step 7.

Step 7: According to (25), the *BP* is estimated. If a generated random number (X) is less than the *BP* (i.e., $X < BP$), the new selected neighbor node replaces the current relay node. Otherwise, the established routing route is not changed.

Step 8: According to (26) and (27), the current node and the selected relay node negotiate with each other. If a relay node rejects the routing offer, the current node selects a new relay node according to (24) and (25). These behaviors are activated with selfish motives. Therefore, this procedure is the competitive part of the developed coopetition model.

Step 9: By employing cooperative negotiation rules, nodes in the negation process cooperate with each other and negotiation has been completed within a finite sequence of offers. Therefore, this procedure is the cooperative part of the developed coopetition model.

Step 10: In an entirely distributed fashion, this hop-by-hop path selection procedure is recursively repeated until the packet is reached to the destination node.

Step 11: Based on the real-time measurement, PC, ξ, T, E and P values are updated periodically for the adaptive routing.

Step 12: Individual node monitors the current network situation and makes a local routing decision iteratively.

The simulation results shown in Figure 4 demonstrate that the proposed *CGMR* scheme scheme generally exhibits better performance compared with the other existing schemes: the *PCR* scheme and the *SMS* scheme. Based on the adaptive simulated annealing and coopetition game model, the *CGMR* scheme constantly monitors the current traffic conditions and gets an efficient solution.

Summary

Recent advances in wireless technology and availability of mobile computing devices have generated a lot of interest in mobile ad-hoc networks. For these networks, the biggest challenge is to find routing paths to satisfy varying requirements. As a multi-path routing algorithm, the *CGMR* scheme is developed based on the coopetition game model and simulated annealing approach. For real network implementation, the *CGMR* scheme is designed in self-organizing, dynamic online, and interactive process. Therefore, each individual node has an ability to provide more adaptive control mechanism and makes a local routing decision to find an efficient path. Under dynamic network environments, the *CGMR* scheme can dynamically re-configure the established path to adapt network changes. In the future, the meta-heuristic approach can be extended to support delay sensitive data services. In addition, the basic concept of game-based adaptive online algorithms has become an interesting research topic in highly mobile ad-hoc networks.

TRUST BASED INCENTIVE COOPERATIVE RELAY ROUTING (*TICRR*) SCHEME FOR WIRELESS NETWORKS

Nowadays, cooperative communication has been proposed as an effective approach to enhance system performance in wireless networks. Recently,

Figure 4. Performance evaluations of the CGMR scheme

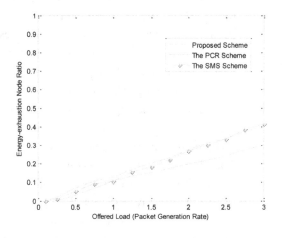

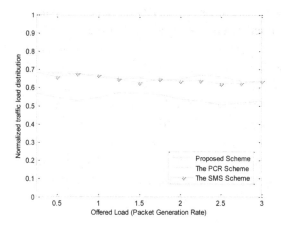

(a) Energy exhaustion ratio   (b) Normalized traffic load distribution

S. Kim proposed a new Trust based Incentive Cooperative Relay Routing (*TICRR*) scheme for wireless networks. Based on the trust based incentive mechanism, the *TICRR* scheme can take into account the measure of the probability of a relay node succeeding at a given relay service and maximize the network performance. By considering the current network condition, the *TICRR* scheme can select the most adaptable relay node and pay the incentive-price for relay service.

Development Motivation

Cooperative communication improves performance in wireless systems, but it requires some nodes to expend energy acting as relays. Since energy is scarce, wireless nodes refuse to cooperate in order to conserve resources. However, only when relay node expends extra energy on its behalf, network performance can increase. Due to this realistic constraint, cooperative communication has yet to see widespread use in practical wireless systems (Nokleby, & Aazhang, 2010). Therefore, it is necessary to design incentive-aware relay routing algorithms for stimulating cooperation among nodes. But despite the concerns, not much work has been done in this direction. The *TICRR* scheme addresses this problem by examining the trust based incentive mechanism. In the *TICRR* scheme, the attenuation window technique is adopted to estimate the trust value based on historical data (Xiang, 2013). Based on the individual trust value, the *TICRR* scheme selects an adaptive relay node and cooperative routing takes place with the help of the relay node, which is incentivized by the relay service price. To calculate the service price for a relay node, the basic concept of *Vickrey-Clarke-Groves* (*VCG*) mechanism (Kim, 2012a) is used. In the real-time online manner, the *TICRR* scheme's approach adaptably obtains the trust values and is able to select the relay node under dynamic changing wireless network environments; it is essential in order to maximize the network performance.

Recently, several cooperative communication schemes – the *Threshold based Cooperative Communication* (*TCC*) scheme (Viet-Anh, Pitaval, Blostein, Riihonen & Wichman, 2010) and the *Distributed Relay Routing* (*DRR*) scheme (Lei, Melodia, Batalama & Matyjas, 2010) - have been presented for wireless network systems. The *TCC* scheme (Viet-Anh, 2010) is a new approach to relay selection using a threshold-based transmission protocol for a wireless system. The *DRR* scheme (Lei, 2010) is a decentralized and localized algorithm for joint dynamic routing, relay assignment, and spectrum allocation in a distributed and dynamic environment.

Routing Algorithm in the *TICRR* Scheme

In the *TICRR* scheme, trust based *VCG* mechanism is used to design a new cooperative communication algorithm. Based on the trust value of each relay node, the most adaptable relay node is selected. To induce selfish relay nodes to participate cooperative communications, the relay service price is provided for the relay service. Finally, an effective solution can be obtained in the constantly changing environment.

Trust Evaluation for Relay Nodes

The *TICRR* scheme assumes a wireless network situation where there is a set (N) of potential relay nodes, $N = \{1,2..,i..,n\}$. Each relay node (i.e., $i \in N$) has a service value and privately-known relay cost of performing the service request τ. Let σ denote a particular relay service acceptance within the space of possible acceptances Ψ and τ^i represent that the node i allows to relay call service τ; $\sigma \in \Psi$ and $\Psi = \left\{\varnothing, \tau^1, \tau^2...\tau^n\right\}$ where $\varnothing$ denotes the case where the relay request is rejected. If $\Psi = \{\tau^i\}$, the relay node i participates the cooperative communication. The set of available power levels ($\mathbb{S}$) for each relay node is assumed as below.

$$\mathbb{S} = \{\Pi_{i \in N} p_i \mid p_i \in [p_{min}, p_{max}]\} \qquad (28)$$

where p_i is the power level of relay node i. The p_{min}, p_{max} are the pre-defined minimum and maximum power levels, respectively. Each relay node selects a power level from the $\mathbb{S}$, and estimates the expected value ($v_i(\tau)$) as follows.

$$v_i(\tau) = \left[W \times \log_2 \left(1 + \frac{\gamma_i(\mathbb{P})}{\Omega} \right) \right] / p_i$$

$$\text{s.t., } \gamma_i(\mathbb{P}) = \frac{p_i h_{ii}}{\vartheta_i + \sum_{j \neq i} p_j h_{ji}} \qquad (29)$$

where $\mathbb{P}$ is the power level vector for all nodes and W is the channel bandwidth of relay node i, and Ω ($\Omega \geq 1$) is the gap between uncoded M-QAM and the capacity, minus the coding gain (Kim, 2011). Usually, service value is defined as the number of information bits that are transmitted without error per unit-time. In wireless networks, it can be achieved with the SINR in the effective range. Therefore, to estimate the service value, the SINR should be obtained. The $\gamma_i(\mathbb{P})$ is a general formula for the relay i's SINR where ϑ_i is the background noise within the relay node i's bandwidth, h_{ji} is the path gain from the node j to the node i (Kim, 2011).

Under a dynamically changing network environment, there exists uncertainty about relay nodes successfully completing their assigned relay services. The *TICRR* scheme takes into account the trust value (T) of relay nodes. $T_i(t)$ is the relay node i's trust value at the time t. After the tth iteration, $T_i(t)$ is using the number of packets successfully serviced in the relay node i (α_t^i) divided by the total number of packets that have been sent from the source node to the relay node i ($\alpha_t^i + \beta_t^i$).

$$T_i(t) = \frac{\alpha_t^i}{\alpha_t^i + \beta_t^i} \qquad (30)$$

$T_i(t)$ is a general average function over the whole span of communication historical records. However, for a long-term period evaluation, the α_t^i and β_t^i will be accumulated and are growing into a very large value. In such case, a small amount of the recent malicious behaviours will be hard to be counted and thus has impact on the overall rating of trust. To solve this problem, attenuation window was introduced (Xiang, 2013). By considering more on the up-to-date records, the *TICRR* scheme can calculate the trust value ($T_i(t)$) while fade away the out-of-date records. Based on the attenuation window, the α_t^i and β_t^i values is obtained as below.

$$\alpha_t^i = \sum_{\lambda=k}^{n} e^{-\left(\frac{n+m-t(\lambda)}{c} \right)}$$

and $\qquad\qquad\qquad\qquad\qquad (31)$

$$\beta_t^i = \sum_{\lambda=j}^{m} e^{-\left(\frac{n+m-t(\lambda)}{c} \right)}$$

where the e is Euler's constant, and c is the coefficient to adjust the speed of decreasing in the results of α_t^i and β_t^i. The n and m are the total number of successfully serviced and non-successfully serviced packets, respectively. The k and j are the most out-of-date time for successfully serviced and non-successfully serviced packets, respectively. $t(\lambda)$ is the time t when λ occurs. For example, there are 3 successful service records regarding to the packet relaying but 2 non-successful service records, i.e. $n=3$ and $m=2$. Here the successful service time set are $t = \{1, 3, 5\}$ and non-successful service time set are $t = \{2, 4\}$. Thus the $k=1$ and $j=2$. As the time t is from ascending order that it reflects from oldest to latest in time sequence (Xiang, 2013). While t is growing bigger and bigger, the value of $(n+m-x)$ will become smaller and smaller, and finally $e^{-\left(\frac{n+m-t}{c}\right)}$ has a strong impact on the recent information. Moreover, the bigger value of coefficient c, the slower in speed of decreasing slopes of the value in $e^{-\left(\frac{n+m-t}{c}\right)}$ between 0 and 1. In such way, attenuation window can emphasize the most up-to-date records and fade away the out-of-date records by the speed controlled by the coefficient c.

Relay Selection and Relay Service Price Computation

The *TICRR* scheme adopts the basic concept of *T-VCG* mechanism to provide a normative guide for the payments of relay service (Kim, 2012a). Even more importantly, the *TICRR* scheme considers the trust value in computing the relay payment. With the estimated trust value, the expected payoff value of relay node, $\bar{\chi}\left(\tau, \sigma, \mathbb{T}\right)$, can be calculated as:

$$\bar{\chi}\left(\tau, \sigma, \mathbb{T}\right) = v_{\sigma}\left(\tau\right) \times T_{\sigma}\left(\tau\right), \text{ s.t., } \sigma \in \Psi \tag{32}$$

where $v_{\sigma}\left(\tau\right)$ is the expected value with relay task τ and $T_{\sigma}\left(\tau\right)$ is the trust value in the selected relay node σ, which performs the requested relay service τ. To implement the execution uncertainty by a given relay node, the network system needs to require relay nodes to report their trust value. $\mathbb{T} = T_{1}\left(\tau\right)...T_{\sigma}\left(\tau\right)...T_{n}\left(\tau\right)$ is the vector of trust values of all the relay nodes. In the *TICRR*

scheme, $\hat{\mathbb{T}}$ represents the vector of reported trust values $\hat{\mathbb{T}}_{1}\left(\tau\right),...,\hat{\mathbb{T}}_{n}\left(\tau\right)$; the superscripting the latter with '^' indicates that nodes can misreport their true types. With the expected payoff value, service execution cost is necessary to estimate the total profit. The cost function defines the instantaneous expense for the relaying service σ. It would be a linear function of the tower level, and given by $K \times \left(p_{\sigma}\right)^{q}$ where K and q are estimation parameters and p_{σ} is the power level for the σ service.

In the *TICRR* scheme, relay connections are adaptively controlled based on the accurate analysis of costs and payoffs to select the most suitable relay node. In more detail, the relay selection is determined as follows to maximize system efficiency.

$$S^{*}\left(\Psi, \hat{\mathbb{T}}\right) = arg \max_{\sigma \in \Psi}\left[\bar{\chi}\left(\tau, \sigma, \hat{\mathbb{T}}\right) - K \times \left(\hat{p}_{\sigma}\right)^{q}\right] \tag{33}$$

In the real world operation, $\mathbb{T}$ and p_{σ} can be misreported (i.e., $\hat{\mathbb{T}}$ and $\hat{p}_{\sigma}$). After selecting a relay node, the next step is to compute the relay price, which is an incentive to encourage relay communications. In the *TICRR* scheme, the relay service price is similar to that of the traditional *VCG* mechanism in that the marginal contribution of the selected relay node to the wireless network system; it is extracted by comparing the second best decision, excluding the selected relay node. Without the best relay node $S^{*}\left(\Psi, \hat{\mathbb{T}}\right)$, the second-best expected payoff for the relay service ($EU_{\sigma \in \Psi_{-S^{*}(\Psi,\hat{\mathbb{T}})}}\left(\Psi, \hat{\mathbb{T}}\right)$) is given by

$$EU_{\sigma \in \Psi_{-S^{*}(\Psi,\hat{\mathbb{T}})}}\left(\Psi, \hat{\mathbb{T}}\right) = \max_{\sigma \in \Psi_{-S^{*}(\Psi,\hat{\mathbb{T}})}}$$
$$\left[\bar{\chi}\left(\tau, \sigma, \hat{\mathbb{T}}\right) - K \times \left(\hat{p}_{\sigma}\right)^{q}\right] \tag{34}$$

where $\Psi_{-S^*\left(\Psi,\hat{\mathbb{T}}\right)}$ is the set of possible acceptances (Ψ) excluding the best relay node $S^*\left(\Psi,\hat{\mathbb{T}}\right)$. If the selected relay node ($S^*\left(\Psi,\hat{\mathbb{T}}\right)$) can success to provide relay service, the relay service price ($RSP_{S^*\left(\Psi,\hat{\mathbb{T}}\right)}$) is achieved based on the expected marginal contribution, which is the difference between the best and the second-best expected payoff.

$$RSP_{S^*\left(\Psi,\hat{\mathbb{T}}\right)} = \left[\bar{\chi}\left(\tau,\ S^*\left(\Psi,\hat{\mathbb{T}}\right),\hat{\mathbb{T}}\right) - K\times\left(\hat{p}_{S^*\left(\Psi,\hat{\mathbb{T}}\right)}\right)^q\right] - EU_{\sigma\in\Psi_{-S^*\left(\Psi,\hat{\mathbb{T}}\right)}}\left(\Psi,\hat{\mathbb{T}}\right)$$

Sometimes, the selected relay node (i.e., $S^*\left(\Psi,\hat{\mathbb{T}}\right)$) can fail to provide relay service. In this case, the $RSP_{S^*\left(\Psi,\hat{\mathbb{T}}\right)}$ is given by.

$$RSP_{S^*\left(\Psi,\hat{\mathbb{T}}\right)} = -EU_{\sigma\in\Psi_{-S^*\left(\Psi,\hat{\mathbb{T}}\right)}}\left(\Psi,\hat{\mathbb{T}}\right) \tag{36}$$

Finally, $RP_i\left(\hat{\mathbb{C}},\hat{\mathbb{P}},\sigma\right)$ can be obtained as follows by considering success and fail cases.

$$RSP_{S^*\left(\Psi,\hat{\mathbb{T}}\right)} = T_{S^*\left(\Psi,\hat{\mathbb{T}}\right)}\left(t\right)\times \left(\begin{array}{l}\left[\bar{\chi}\left(\tau,\ S^*\left(\Psi,\hat{\mathbb{T}}\right),\hat{\mathbb{T}}\right) - K\times\left(\hat{p}_{S^*\left(\Psi,\hat{\mathbb{T}}\right)}\right)^q\right] - \\ EU_{\sigma\in\Psi_{-S^*\left(\Psi,\hat{\mathbb{T}}\right)}}\left(\Psi,\hat{\mathbb{T}}\right)\end{array}\right)$$

$$+ \left(1 - T_{S^*\left(\Psi,\hat{\mathbb{T}}\right)}\left(t\right)\right)\times\left[-EU_{\sigma\in\Psi_{-S^*\left(\Psi,\hat{\mathbb{T}}\right)}}\left(\Psi,\hat{\mathbb{T}}\right)\right] \tag{37}$$

Summary

For next-generation wireless networks, cooperative communication is an emerging technology to overcome the current limitations of traditional wireless systems. The *TICRR* scheme has introduced a new trust-based incentive relay routing algorithm for wireless networks. Based on the trust based *VCG* mechanism, the *TICRR* scheme dynamically estimates relay nodes' trust levels and adaptively selects the most adaptable relay node for the data transmission.

REFERENCES

Afergan, M. (2006). Using Repeated Games to Design Incentive-Based Routing Systems. In *Proceedings of IEEE INFOCOM 2006*. IEEE. doi:10.1109/INFOCOM.2006.61

Akkaya, K., & Younis, M. (2005). An Energy-Aware QoS Routing Protocol for Wireless Sensor Networks. *Cluster Computing*, 8(2-3), 179–188. doi:10.1007/s10586-005-6183-7

Akl, R., & Uttara, S. (2007). Grid-based Coordinated Routing in Wireless Sensor Networks. In *Proceedings of IEEE Consumer Communications and Networking Conference*, (pp. 860-864). IEEE.

An, B. K., Lee, J. S., & Kim, N. S. (2011). An entropy based cooperative-aided routing protocol for mobile ad-hoc networks. In *Proceedings of IEEE ICUFN*, (pp. 31-36). IEEE.

Anderegg, L., & Eidenbenz, S. (2003). Ad hoc-vcg: A truthful and cost-efficient routing protocol for mobile ad hoc networks with selfish agents. In *Proceedings of MobiCom* (pp. 245–259). MobiCom. doi:10.1145/939010.939011

Asokan, R., Natarajan, A. M., & Nivetha, A. (2007). A Swarm-based Distance Vector Routing to Support Multiple Quality of Service (QoS) Metrics in Mobile Ad hoc Networks. *Journal of Computer Science*, *3*(9), 700–707. doi:10.3844/jcssp.2007.700.707

Azar, Y. (1998). *Online Algorithms - The State of the Art*. Springer.

Barolli, L., Koyama, A., Suganuma, T., & Shiratori, N. (2003). GAMAN: A GA based QoS routing method for mobile ad hoc networks. *Journal of Interconnection Networks*, *4*(3), 251–270. doi:10.1142/S0219265903000866

Becerra, R. L., & Coello, C. A. (2006). Solving Hard Multiobjective Optimization Problems Using ε-Constraint with Cultured Differential Evolution. *LNCS*, *4193*, 1611–3349.

Bi, Y., Li, N., & Sun, L. (2007). DAR: An energy-balanced data-gathering scheme for wireless sensor networks. *Computer Communications*, *30*(14-15), 2812–2825. doi:10.1016/j.comcom.2007.05.021

Bian, Z. A., & Luo, J. Z. (2007). A Cooperative Game Theory Based Coalitional Agent Negotiation Model in Network Service. *Lecture Notes in Computer Science*, *4402*, 447–458. doi:10.1007/978-3-540-72863-4_46

Blumenthal, J., Reichenbach, F., & Timmermann, D. (2006). Minimal Transmission Power vs. Signal Strength as Distance Estimation for Localization in Wireless Sensor Networks. In *Proceedings of IEEE SECON*, (pp. 761-766). IEEE.

Boukerche, A., Araujo, R. B., & Villas, L. (2006). A Wireless Actor and Sensor Networks QoS-Aware Routing Protocol for the Emergency Preparedness Class of Applications. In *Proceedings of Local Computer Networks* (pp. 832–839). IEEE. doi:10.1109/LCN.2006.322184

Bouleimen, K., & Lecocq, H. (2003). A new efficient simulated annealing algorithm for the resource-constrained project scheduling problem and its multiple mode version. *European Journal of Operational Research*, *149*(2), 268–281. doi:10.1016/S0377-2217(02)00761-0

Bouncken, R. B., & Fredrich, V. (2011). Coopetition: Its successful management in the nexus of dependency and trust. In *Proceedings of PICMET*. PICMET.

Cai, J., & Pooch, U. (2004). Allocate Fair Payoff for Cooperation in Wireless Ad Hoc Networks Using Shapley Value. In *Proceedings of PDPS*, (pp. 219-227). PDPS.

Dash, R., Parkes, D., & Jennings, N. (2003). Computational Mechanism Design: A Call to Arms. *IEEE Intelligent Systems*, *18*(6), 40–47. doi:10.1109/MIS.2003.1249168

Deepalakshmi, P., & Radhakrishnan, S. (2009). QoS Routing Algorithm for Mobile Ad Hoc Networks Using ACO. In *Proceedings of International Conference on Control, Automation, Communication and Energy Conservation*. Academic Press.

Dirani, M., & Chahed, T. (2006). Framework for Resource Allocation in Heterogeneous Wireless Networks Using Game Theory. In *Proceedings of EuroNGI Workshop*, (pp. 144-154). EuroNGI.

Felemban, E., Lee, C. G., & Ekici, E. (2006). MMSPEED: multipath Multi-SPEED protocol for QoS guarantee of reliability and. Timeliness in wireless sensor networks. *IEEE Transactions on Mobile Computing*, *5*(6), 738–754. doi:10.1109/TMC.2006.79

Friedman, E. J., & Parkes, D. D. (2003). Pricing WiFi at Starbucks: issues in online mechanism design. In *Proceedings of ACM Conference on Electronic Commerce*, (pp. 240-241). ACM.

Garg, D., Narahari, Y., & Gujar, S. (2008). Foundations of Mechanism Design: A Tutorial, Part 1: Key Concepts and Classical Results. *Sadhana. Indian Academy Proceedings in Engineering Sciences*, *33*(2), 83–130.

Guan, Z., Yuan, D., & Zhang, H. (2008). Novel coopetition paradigm based on bargaining theory or collaborative multimedia resource management. In *Proceedings of IEEE PIMRC'08*. IEEE.

Gunes, M., Sorges, U., & Bouazizi, I. (2002). ARA - The ant-colony based routing algorithm for MANETs. In *Proceedings of the International Conference on Parallel Processing Workshops*, (pp. 79-85). Academic Press.

Huang, C. M., Ku, H. H., & Kung, H. Y. (2009). Efficient power-consumption-based load-sharing topology control protocol for harsh environments in wireless sensor networks. *IET Communications*, *3*(5), 859–870. doi:10.1049/iet-com.2008.0217

Hussain, T., & Habib, S. J. (2009). Optimization of network clustering and hierarchy through simulated annealing. In *Proceedings of ACS/IEEE International Conference on Computer Systems and Applications*, (pp. 712-716). ACS/IEEE.

Iqbal, M., Gondal, I., & Dooley, L. (2006). An Energy-Aware Dynamic Clustering Algorithm for Load Balancing in Wireless Sensor Networks. *The Journal of Communication*, *1*(3), 10–19.

Kim, S. W. (2008). Energy Efficient Online Routing Algorithm for QoS-Sensitive Sensor Networks. *IEICE Transactions on Communications. E (Norwalk, Conn.)*, *91-B*(7), 2401–2404.

Kim, S. W. (2010a). Cooperative game theoretic online routing scheme for wireless network managements. *IET Communications*, *4*(17), 2074–2083. doi:10.1049/iet-com.2009.0686

Kim, S. W. (2010b). Game theoretic Multi-Objective Routing Scheme for Wireless Sensor Networks. *Ad Hoc & Sensor Wireless Networks*, *10*(4), 343–359.

Kim, S. W. (2011). Adaptive online power control scheme based on the evolutionary game theory. *IET Communications*, *5*(18), 2648–2655. doi:10.1049/iet-com.2011.0093

Kim, S. W. (2012a). Adaptive Call Admission Control Scheme for Heterogeneous Overlay Networks. *Journal of Communications and Networks*, *14*(4), 461–466. doi:10.1109/JCN.2012.6292253

Kim, S. W. (2012b). Adaptive Ad-hoc Network Routing Scheme by Using Incentive-based Model. *Ad Hoc & Sensor Wireless Networks*, *15*(2), 107–125.

Kim, S. W., & Varshney, P. K. (2004). An Integrated Adaptive Bandwidth Management Framework for QoS sensitive Multimedia Cellular Networks. *IEEE Transactions on Vehicular Technology*, *53*(3), 835–846. doi:10.1109/TVT.2004.825704

Kim, S. W., & Varshney, P. K. (2005). An Adaptive Bandwidth Allocation Algorithm for QoS guaranteed Multimedia Networks. *Computer Communications*, *28*(17), 1959–1969. doi:10.1016/j.comcom.2005.02.011

Klinkowski, M., Careglio, D., & Sole-Pareta, J. (2009). Reactive and proactive routing in labelled optical burst switching networks. *IET Communications*, *3*(3), 454–464. doi:10.1049/iet-com:20070498

Korad, U., & Sivalingam, K. M. (2006). Reliable data delivery in wireless sensor networks using distributed cluster monitoring. *International Journal of Sensor Networks*, *1*(1/2), 75–83. doi:10.1504/IJSNET.2006.010839

Kumar, S., Kambhatla, K., Hu, F., Lifson, M., & Xiao, Y. (2008). Ubiquitous Computing for Remote Cardiac Patient Monitoring: A Survey. *International Journal of Telemedicine and Applications*, (4): 1–19. doi:10.1155/2008/459185 PMID:18604301

Lei, D., Melodia, T., Batalama, S. N., & Matyjas, J. D. (2010). Distributed Routing, Relay Selection, and Spectrum Allocation in Cognitive and Cooperative Ad Hoc Networks. In *Proceedings of IEEE SECON*. IEEE.

Leino, J. (2003). *Applications of Game Theory in Ad Hoc Networks*. (Unpublished Master's Thesis). Helisnki University of Technology, Helisnki, Finland.

Leu, J. J. Y., Tsai, M. H., Chiang, T. C., & Huang, Y. M. (2006). Adaptive power aware clustering and multicasting protocol for mobile ad-hoc networks. In *Proceedings of Ubiquitous Intelligence and Computing* (pp. 331–340). Academic Press. doi:10.1007/11833529_34

Mahapatra, A., Anand, K., & Agrawal, D. P. (2006). QoS and Energy Aware Routing for Real Time Traffic in Wireless Sensor Networks. *Computer Communications*, *29*(4), 437–445. doi:10.1016/j.comcom.2004.12.028

Mehmet, S., & Ramazan, K. (2001). A Comparative Study of Multiobjective Optimization Methods in Structural Design. *Turkish Journal of Engineering and Environmental Sciences*, *25*(2), 69–78.

Nisan, N., & Ronen, A. (2000). Computationally feasible VCG mechanisms. In *Proceedings of ACM Conference on Electronic Commerce*, (pp. 242-252). ACM.

Niyato, D., & Hossain, E. (2006). A Cooperative Game Framework for Bandwidth Allocation in 4G Heterogeneous Wireless Networks. [IEEE.]. *Proceedings of the IEEE, ICC*, 4357–4362.

Nokleby, M., & Aazhang, B. (2010). User Cooperation for Energy-Efficient Cellular Communications. In *Proceedings of IEEE ICC'2010*. IEEE.

Parkes, D. C., Singh, S. P., & Yanovsky, D. (2004). Approximately efficient online mechanism design. In *Proceedings of Neural Information Processing Systems*. Academic Press.

Postigo-Boix, M., & Melús-Moreno, J. (2007). Performance evaluation of RSVP extensions for a guaranteed delivery scenario. *Computer Communications*, *30*(9), 2113–2121. doi:10.1016/j.comcom.2007.04.015

Qin, F., & Liu, Y. (2009). Multipath Routing for Mobile Ad Hoc Network. *Journal of Networks*, *4*(8), 771–778.

Randall, M., McMahon, G., & Sugden, S. (2002). A Simulated Annealing Approach to Communication Network Design. *Journal of Combinatorial Optimization*, *6*, 55–65. doi:10.1023/A:1013337324030

Rextin, A. T., Irfan, Z., & Uzmi, Z. A. (2004). Games Networks Play A Game Theoretic Approach to Networks. In *Proceedings of International Symposium on Parallel Architectures, Algorithms, and Networks*, (pp. 451-457). Academic Press.

Rogers, A., David, E., & Jennings, N. R. (2005). Self-organized routing for wireless microsensor networks. *IEEE Transactions on Systems, Man, and Cybernetics*, *35*(3), 349–359. doi:10.1109/TSMCA.2005.846382

Srivastava, V., Neel, J., MacKenzie, A. B., & Menon, R. (2005). Using game theory to analyze wireless ad hoc networks. *IEEE Communications Surveys & Tutorials, 7*(4), 46–56. doi:10.1109/COMST.2005.1593279

Sun, B., & Li, L. (2006). Distributed QoS multicast routing protocol in ad-hoc networks. *Journal of Systems Engineering and Electronics, 17*(3), 692–698. doi:10.1016/S1004-4132(06)60118-7

Sun, L., & Xu, X. (2005). Coopetitive game, equilibrium and their applications. In *Proceedings of International Conference on Algorithmic Applications in Management*, (pp. 104-111). Academic Press.

Sun, T., Zhu, Q., Li, S., & Zhou, M. (2007). Open, Dynamic and Continuous One-to-Many Negotiation System. In *Proceedings of BIC-TA 2007*, (pp. 87-93). BIC-TA.

Trivedi, N., Elangovan, G., Iyengar, S. S., & Balakrishnan, N. (2006). A Message-Efficient, Distributed Clustering Algorithm for Wireless Sensor and Actor Networks. In *Proceedings of IEEE International Conference on Multisensor Fusion and Integration for Intelligent Systems*, (pp. 53-58). IEEE.

Viet-Anh, L., Pitaval, R. A., Blostein, S., Riihonen, T., & Wichman, R. (2010). Green cooperative communication using threshold-based relay selection protocols. [ICGCS.]. *Proceedings of ICGCS, 2010*, 521–526.

Wang, G., Cao, J., Zhang, L., Chan, K. C. C., & Wu, J. (2005). A novel QoS multicast model in mobile ad-hoc networks. In *Proc. IEEE IPDPS*, (pp. 206-211). IEEE.

Wang, X., & Schulzrinne, H. (2005). Incentive-Compatible Adaptation of Internet Real-Time Multimedia. *IEEE Journal on Selected Areas in Communications, 23*(2), 417–436. doi:10.1109/JSAC.2004.839399

Wang, Y., Martonosi, M., & Peh, L. S. (2006). A supervised learning approach for routing optimizations in wireless sensor networks. In *Proceedings of International Symposium on Mobile Ad Hoc Networking & Computing*, (pp. 79–86). Academic Press.

Woodard, C. J., & Parkes, D. C. (2003). Strategy-proof mechanisms for ad hoc network formation. In *Proceedings of IEEE IPTPS*. IEEE.

Wu, M. Y., & Shu, W. (2004). RPP: a distributed routing mechanism for strategic wireless ad hoc networks. In *Proceedings of IEEE GLOBECOM*, (pp. 2885-2889). IEEE.

Xiang, M. (2013). *Trust-based energy aware geographical routing for smart grid communications networks*. (Master's Thesis). Auckland University of Technology.

Yarvis, M., & Zorzi, M. (2008). Ad hoc networks: Special issue on energy efficient design in wireless ad hoc and sensor networks. *Ad Hoc Networks, 6*(8), 1183–1184. doi:10.1016/j.adhoc.2007.11.005

Younis, M., Youssef, M., & Arisha, K. (2002). Energy-Aware Routing in Cluster-Based Sensor Networks. In *Proceedings of MASCOTS*, (pp. 129-136). MASCOTS.

Younis, O., Krunz, M., & Ramasubramanian, S. (2006). Node clustering in wireless sensor networks: recent developments and deployment challenges. *IEEE Network, 20*(3), 20–25. doi:10.1109/MNET.2006.1637928

Zafar, H., Harle, D., Andonovic, I., & Khawaja, Y. (2009). Performance evaluation of shortest multipath source routing scheme. *IET Communications, 3*(5), 700–713. doi:10.1049/iet-com.2008.0328

Zhong, S., Chen, J., & Yang, Y. (2003). Sprite: A Simple, Cheat-Proof, Credit-Based System for Mobile Ad-Hoc Networks. In Proceedings of IEEE INFOCOM, (pp. 1987–1997). IEEE.

Zou, Y., Mi, Z., & Xu, M. (2006). Dynamic Load Balancing Based on Roulette Wheel Selection. In *Proceedings of International Conference on Communications, Circuits and Systems*, (pp. 1732-1734). Academic Press.

KEY TERMS AND DEFINITIONS

Anycast Transmission: A network addressing and routing methodology in which datagrams from a single sender are routed to the topologically nearest node in a group of potential receivers, though it may be sent to several nodes, all identified by the same destination address.

Broadcasting Transmission: A method of transferring a message to all recipients simultaneously. It can be performed as a high level operation in a program, for example broadcasting Message Passing Interface, or it may be a low level networking operation, for example broadcasting on Ethernet.

Geocast Transmission: The delivery of information to a group of destinations in a network identified by their geographical locations. It is a specialized form of multicast addressing used by some routing protocols for mobile ad hoc networks.

Media Access Control Address (MAC Address): A unique identifier assigned to network interfaces for communications on the physical network segment. MAC addresses are used as a network address for most IEEE 802 network technologies, including Ethernet. Logically, MAC addresses are used in the media access control protocol sublayer of the OSI reference model.

Multicast Transmission: The delivery of a message or information to a group of destination computers simultaneously in a single transmission from the source. Copies are automatically created in other network elements, such as routers, but only when the topology of the network requires it.

Unicast Transmission: The sending of messages to a single network destination identified by a unique address.

Chapter 10
Power Control Schemes Based on Game Theory

ABSTRACT

Power control is the intelligent selection of transmitter power output in a communication system to achieve good performance within the system. The notion of good performance can depend on context and may include optimizing metrics such as link data rate, network capacity, geographic coverage and range, and life of the network and network devices. Power control algorithms are used in many contexts, including cellular networks, sensor networks, and wireless LANs. Typically, there is no simple answer to the problem of power control, and a good algorithm must strike a balance between the benefits and drawbacks associated with targeting a particular transmit power based on the performance criteria of most importance to the designer. This chapter discusses power control schemes.

EVOLUTIONARY GAME-BASED POWER CONTORL (*EGPC*) SCHEME

In view of the remarkable growth in the number of users and the limited network resource, an efficient network management is very important and has been an active area of research over the years. Especially, during wireless network operations, adaptive power control is an effective way to enhance the network performance. Recently, S. Kim proposed a new Evolutionary Game-based Power Control (*EGPC*) scheme based on the online approach (Kim, 2011). To converge a desirable network equilibrium, the developed scheme adaptively adjusts a transmit power level in a distributed online manner. For the efficient

network management, the online approach is dynamic and flexible that can adaptively respond to current network conditions.

Development Motivation

Recently, wireless/mobile networking is one of the strongest growth areas of communication technology. The explosive growth of new communication services and the widespread proliferation of multimedia data have necessitated the development for an efficient wireless network system. However, due to the limited energy supply, an efficient energy management becomes a key factor in enhancing network performance (Meshkati, Poor, Schwartz, & Balan, 2006). In

DOI: 10.4018/978-1-4666-6050-2.ch010

wireless networks, most of the wireless devices are battery-powered. Therefore, an adaptive power control strategy has been shown to be an effective way to maintain the energy efficiency in wireless devices. In addition, it can optimize the spatial reuse of wireless bandwidth by reducing the interference between wireless links. Therefore, the benefit of adaptive power control strategy is not just to increase battery life, but also to maximize the overall network performance (Feng, Mau, & Mandayam, 2004), (Holliday, Goldsmith, Glynn, & Bambos, 2004).

To understand the behavior of self-regarding applications or independent network users, a game model has some attractive features. However, due to some reasons, classical game theory cannot be directly applied to wireless network managements. First, players have very limited information. Therefore, it is usually impossible to delineate all conceivable strategies. Second, it is not easy to assign a payoff value to any given outcome, and also difficult to synchronize the activities of the different players. Third, due to the complexity of network situations, the mathematical modeling and numerical analysis have met with limited success (Xiao, Shan, & Ren, 2005).

In 1974, Maynard Smith introduced the fundamental concept of an evolutionary game theory. It has been developed in biological sciences in order to explain the evolution of genetically determined social behavior. In this theory, the payoffs depend on the actions of the co-players; strategies with high payoff will spread within the entire populations of players (Hofbauer, & Sigmund, 2003), (Tao, & Wang, 1997), (Menasche, Figueiredo, & Silva, 2005). Nowadays, the main idea of evolutionary game has emerged as an alternative perspective to classical game theory and become an interesting research field. It can be practically applied to wireless network managements without much deviation from its original form.

Usually, the performance in wireless networks is strongly related to power control algorithms. Power control decisions affect many aspects of

the network performance such as the signal QoS, interference and energy consumption (Ginde, Neel, & Buehrer, 2003), (Long, Zhang, Li, Yang, & Guan, 2007). The *EGPC* scheme is designed as a new power control algorithm by using the evolutionary game theory. Based on the evolutionary learning mechanism, the developed algorithm can constantly adapt each device's power level to get an appropriate performance balance between contradictory requirements.

The *EGPC* scheme is a new adaptive online power control scheme based on the evolutionary game theory. In the developed scheme, wireless devices are assumed to be self-regarding game players and make their decisions for the goal of maximizing their perceived payoffs. By using an adaptive online approach, each player's behavior might affect the behavior of other players. Therefore, control decisions are coupled with one another; the result of the each user's decisions is the input back to the other user's decision process. The dynamics of the interactive feedback mechanism can cause cascade interactions of players and players can make their decisions to quickly find the most profitable solution. Finally, it can lead the network system to an efficient equilibrium state.

Related Work

Recently, several power control schemes based on the game theory have been presented in research literature. The *Rate and Power Control (RPC)* scheme is a control algorithm based on game model for wireless communication (Yang, Li, & Li, 2009). This scheme introduced the classic form of non-cooperative power control model as a new framework. By considering the joint transmission rate and power control issues, the Nash equilibrium solution for either the transmit rate or the transmit power is achieved in the cognitive radio. In addition, a pricing function that relates to both transmit rate and power is introduced for improving the Pareto efficiency and fairness of the obtained Nash equilibrium solution.

The *Game based Power Control* (*GPC*) scheme can regulate the transmitter power to meet the different SINR requirements and enhance the total throughput effectively (Liu, Peng, Shao, Chen, & Wang, 2010). The *GPC* scheme adopted the game theory for power control modeling in cognitive radio system, and developed a new sigmoid efficiency function with non-liner pricing only related with user's SINR. In addition, non-cooperative power control game created by D. Goodman is applied for decentralized users. This approach is very suitable for cognitive radio system because of its regardless of the modulation of users' RAT.

The *Energy-Efficient Power Control* (*EEPC*) scheme is an effective power control algorithm for the uplink of relay-assisted DS/CDMA wireless networks. By using game-theoretic tools, the *EEPC* scheme has been designed as a non-cooperative power allocation game model. Numerical results are provided to show the existence and uniqueness of the Nash equilibrium (Zappone, Buzzi, & Jorswieck, 2011).

The *Interference Avoidance Power Control* (*IAPC*) scheme is a game model for spectrum leasing in cognitive radio. In this scheme, the primary users manage the leasing spectrum to get the interest and prevent undermining through set their interference cap and leasing price. And, the secondary users adjust the interference price so that the network can get the global optimum. The *IAPC* scheme solves the problems that the secondary users always are the optimum themselves not global optimum (Zhanjun, Chengchao, Yun, Huan, & Cong, 2010).

The *Cognitive Radio Power Control* (*CRPC*) scheme is a multi-antenna cognitive radio power control algorithm with the idea of game theory (Hou, Wang, & Hu, 2010). In this scheme, every user improves the transmitting power selfishly not considering other users, and other users choose the corresponding strategies. This interactive and repeated process is actually a kind of non-cooperative game; it will reach a balanced state that is called Nash equilibrium. The *CRPC* scheme

shows that the developed algorithm achieves the user transmitting power to make the global information transmission rate maximal after limited iterations, which proves the algorithm efficient.

The *Fair Power Control with Pricing* (*FPCP*) scheme investigated the fairness issue arising from resource allocation in wireless ad hoc networks (Tan, Sim, & Chuah, 2010). This scheme provided important insights on how the selfishness of autonomous nodes in ad hoc networks can lead to throughput unfairness especially in scenarios where users possess different power capabilities. The *FPCP* scheme is a payment-based power control algorithm using game theory where each user announces a set of price coefficients that reflects different compensations paid by other users for the interference they produce. This approach can converge to Nash equilibrium where at this point it is able to provide a fairer throughput share among users at the expense of a slight loss in total throughput.

The *Novel Distributed Power Control* (*NDPC*) scheme is a novel distributed power control game algorithm, focusing on cellular CDMA system (Chenglin, & Yan, 2009). By designing an effective cost function, the *NDPC* scheme can obtain faster convergence while maintaining higher average SIR. The *NDPC* scheme not only meets communication requirements of different users, but also achieves effective control of power. Therefore, the convergence rate of this scheme has greatly improved. However, the issue how to reduce the average power and improve average SIR while keeping faster convergence would not be solved.

In the *Uplink Power Control* (*UPC*) scheme, the game theory was applied to WiMAX uplink power control problems (Li, He, Zhang, & Huang, 2009). All co-channel users were game participants, and their uplink power was used as a strategy to achieve Nash equilibrium. In the *UPC* scheme, the utility function was build according to WiMAX wireless cellular systems. This approach can achieve the objective of ensuring uplink connection quality and suppressing co-channel interference.

Previous proposed schemes have been designed to control the power control problem in wireless networks. The interactions among users can be formally modeled as games. The outcome of these game models can be predicted by using a game theoretic formulation. However, these schemes are designed for specific network environments, and focus on theoretical analysis, i.e., the issue of existence and uniqueness of the Nash equilibrium. In addition, they rely on several assumptions that do not seem to be practical. Therefore, it is questionable whether these assumptions are satisfied under practical network operations.

Power Control Algorithms in the *EGPC* Scheme

In the *EGPC* scheme, evolutionary game theory is used to design a new adaptive online power control scheme. During the step-by-step game iteration, the *EGPC* scheme is adaptively responsive to the constantly changing network environment. Therefore, each user decides the transmit power level to efficiently control the co-channel interference problem. Finally, a fair-balanced solution can be obtained under diversified network situations.

Basic Assumption for Power Control Algorithm

Due to the interference interactions in wireless networks, power decisions made by one device will affect the performance of the other devices. Therefore, the main goal of power control problem is to decide how the co-channel link is shared among different devices while maximizing total network performance. In the developed game model, the co-channel link devices are defined as players. Each player attempts to maximize his throughput by increasing the transmission power. If the power level increases, the Signal-to-Interference plus Noise Ratio (SINR) level also increases, which will cause a lower bit error rate and higher throughput. However, the high SINR

is achieved at the expense of the increased co-channel interference and excessive battery consumption (Long, 2007), (Meshkati, 2006). Therefore, by considering this tradeoff, players adaptively select the most proper power level. In the *EGPC* scheme, the set of power control strategies ($\mathbb{S}$) is assumed as below.

$$\mathbb{S} = \{\Pi_{i \in N} p_i \mid p_i \in \left[p_{min}, p_{max} \right]\} \qquad (1)$$

where N is the number of users and p_i is the power level of player i. The p_{min}, p_{max} are the pre-defined minimum and maximum power levels, respectively. Each player selects a single strategy from the $\mathbb{S}$, and estimates the expected payoff through a utility function.

Usually, the main interest of each player is to maximize the amount of transmitted data with the lower energy consumption. However, as mentioned earlier, there is a fundamental tradeoff. To capture this conflicting relationship, a utility function is defined by considering the ratio of the throughput to transmit power (Long, 2007). In the developed game model, the utility function for player i (u_i) is defined as follows.

$$u_i \left(\mathbb{P} \right) = \frac{T_i \left(\mathbb{P} \right)}{p_i} \qquad (2)$$

where $\mathbb{P}$ is the transmit power vector ($p_1, ..., p_N$) for all users and $T_i \left(\mathbb{P} \right)$ is the throughput of player i. Usually, throughput is defined as the number of information bits that are transmitted without error per unit-time. In wireless networks, it can be achieved with the SINR in the effective range (Meshkati, 2006). Therefore, to estimate the throughput of each player, his SINR should be obtained first. A general formula for the player i's SINR ($\gamma_i \left(\mathbb{P} \right)$) is defined as follows (Long, 2007).

$$\gamma_i\left(\mathbb{P}\right) = \frac{p_i h_{ii}}{\sigma_i + \sum_{j \neq i} p_j h_{ji}} \qquad (3)$$

where σ_i is the background noise within the player's bandwidth, h_{ji} is the path gain from the transmitter of player j to the receiver of player i. The *EGPC* scheme follows the assumption of Long's paper (Long, 2007); device transmitters use variable-rate M-QAM, with a bounded probability of symbol error and trellis coding with a nominal coding gain. Therefore, the throughput of player i ($T_i\left(\mathbb{P}\right)$) can be expressed as

$$T_i\left(\mathbb{P}\right) = W \times \log_2\left(1 + \frac{\gamma_i\left(\mathbb{P}\right)}{\Omega}\right) \qquad (4)$$

where W is the channel bandwidth of player i, and Ω ($\Omega \geq 1$) is the gap between uncoded M-QAM and the capacity, minus the coding gain.

Usually, data signals have very low tolerance to errors. Therefore, if the SINR (γ) is below a target level (γ^*), it is unacceptable (payoff = 0). Based on this consideration, all the players try to maintain the minimum SINR value where $\gamma_i \geq \gamma_i^*, \forall i$. Finally, combining (2) with (4), the utility function for the player i is defined and parameterized as follows (Long, 2007).

$$u_i\left(p_i, \mathbb{P}_{-i}\right) = \begin{cases} \frac{1}{p_i} \times \left(W_i \times \log_2\left(1 + \gamma_i\left(\mathbb{P}\right) / \Omega\right)\right) & \text{if } \gamma_i\left(\mathbb{P}\right) \geq \gamma_i^* \\ 0 & \text{otherwise.} \end{cases} \qquad (5)$$

where $\mathbb{P}_{-i} = \left(p_1, p_2, \ldots p_{i-1}, p_{i+1}, \ldots p_n\right)$ is the transmit power vector without the player i's power level.

Evolutionary Game Process

The fundamental assumption of classical game theory is that players must be rational to determine their decisions. However, this assumption is obviously not satisfied under the real world network environment; experiments have shown that players do not always act rationally. The evolutionary game theory offers a more realistic model for players with bounded rationality (Hofbauer, 2003), (Tao, 1997). In this model, players learn how to select their strategies like as a tournament play where losing strategies are eliminated and winning strategies remain. Therefore, during the evolutionary game, players have a chance to reconsider the current strategy and react to maximize the expected payoff.

In the jargon of evolutionary game theory, the equilibrium strategies of players are called *Evolutionary Stable Strategies* (*ESS*) and the changing rate of the players' selection is defined as *Replicator Dynamics* (*RD*) (Hofbauer, 2003), (Tao, 1997). When a player chooses a strategy, it can change the current network environment and triggers reactions by other players. After making further changes among players, this interaction mechanism gradually leads the network system into a stable state. The *RD* describes the evolution in the proportion of each strategy to reach an equilibrium; a specific strategy evolves at a rate equal to the difference between the payoff of that strategy and the average payoff of the whole population (Altman, El-Azouzi, Hayel, & Tembine, 2008). If the payoff of strategy i is small compared to other strategies, the selection probability for strategy i decreases in proportion to the expected payoff reduction. Therefore, the desirable strategy that will improve player's payoff is more likely to be selected. To maximize their expected payoffs, players iteratively change their current strategies and repeatedly interact with other players. When no individual player can improve his payoff by unilaterally changing his strategy, this set of strategies is referred to as the *ESS* (Menasche, 2005). Under the *ESS*, the proportions of each strategy do not change in time and can be immune from being changed. It is relevant to the Darwinian evolution mechanism (Altman, 2008).

To represent the *RD* for the power control problem, let M be a number of possible power levels and x_i is the selection probability for the *i*th power level (strategy *i*). $\mathbb{X}$ is the M-dimensional vector ($x_1 \dots x_i \dots x_M$) and $\dot{x}_i$ stands for the variation of x_i, which is the *RD* for strategy *i*. $J(i, k)$ is denoted by the expected payoff for a player using strategy *i* when it encounters a player with strategy k, and $J(i, \mathbb{X})$ is the payoff for a player using strategy *i* when it encounters the rest of other players whose strategies are distributed in $\mathbb{X}$, which can be expressed like as $\sum_j (J(i,j) \times x_j)$. Finally, the *RD* is defined as

$$\dot{x}_i = x_i \times K \times \left(J\left(i, \mathbb{X}\right) - \sum_j x_j \times J\left(j, \mathbb{X}\right) \right)$$

$$= x_i \times K \times \left(\sum_j x_j \times J\left(i,j\right) - \sum_j \sum_k x_j \times J\left(j, k\right) \times x_k \right)$$

(6)

where K is a control factor, which can control the speed of convergence. Typically, K is defined as a fixed constant (Altman, 2008). In the *EGPC* scheme, the constant K is replaced by an online risk control function ($r\_c_{\pm}(x)$) to characterize the interaction manner of each player. This function is concerned with the behavior of decision makers who face a choice. To implement the $r\_c_{\pm}(x)$, the *EGPC* scheme would chose to use the constant absolute risk utility function of the expected utility theory (Byde, 2003). It is a well-known and effective method to solve a risk control

problem. By applying this theory, players can be broadly classified as either *risk-averse* or *risk-seeking* players. The risk preference of a player is determined by assuming function's twice-differentiability ($r\_c_{\pm}{}''(x)$); e.g., if $r\_c_{\pm}{}''(x) < 0$ (or $r_{c\pm}{}''(x) > 0$), a player is known as a *risk-averse* (or a *risk-seeking*) player (Byde, 2003). In the *EGPC* scheme, for the adaptive convergence to a stable network equilibrium, the risk control function for player *i* ($r\_c_{\pm}(x_i)$) is defined as follows.

$$r\_c_{\pm}\left(x_i\right) = \frac{1}{\alpha}\left(\mathrm{e}^{\pm x_i} - 1\right),$$

$$\text{where} \begin{cases} \alpha = -1 \, if \arg\max_i u_i\left(p_i, \mathbb{P}_{-i}\right) = \arg\max_i \dot{x}_i \\ \alpha = 1 \quad if \, otherwise \end{cases}$$

(7)

where x_i is ($J\left(i, \mathbb{X}\right) - \sum_j x_j \times J\left(j, \mathbb{X}\right)$) and $\dot{x}_i$ is the current estimated *RD* value for the player *i*. When a player currently has a higher probability to gain the better payoff (i.e., $\arg\max_i U_i\left(p_i, \mathbb{P}_{-i}\right)$ is same as $\arg\max_i \dot{x}_i$), he is most likely to be a *risk-averse* player; α is set to -1. Otherwise, a player will tend to be a *risk-seeking* player; α is set to 1. Based on this online fine-grained approach, the *EGPC* scheme can dynamically decide the α value to adapt the current network situation.

By using (6) and (7), each player maintains two variables, $J\left(i, \mathbb{X}\right)$ and $\dot{x}_i$, which are the basis for the next strategy decision. Under all possible network scenarios, players learn how to perform well by interacting with other players and dynamically adjust their power levels. Therefore, without any impractical rationality assumptions, players can modify their strategies in an effort to maximize their own goals.

Main Steps for Evolutionary Power Control Game

In general, traditional game models have focused on investigating *which* decisions are made or *what* decisions should be made. To implement these models, the most fundamental assumption is rationality; it is assumed that the players know everything about the game and they can make the same deductions about the situation. However, due to its unrealistic premise, this rationality assumption has been widely criticized. To overcome this drawback, the evolutionary game model investigates *how* decisions are made for control problems (Menasche, 2005).

In a single-cell CDMA system, there are a large number of co-channel wireless devices and devices (i.e., game players) adaptively select their power levels. Based on the feedback learning process, the *EGPC* scheme can capture how devices adapt their strategies to achieve the better benefit. This procedure is defined as an online power control algorithm. In the *EGPC* scheme, a selection probability for each strategy is dynamically changed based on the payoff ratio, which means the strategy evolution. Therefore, players examine their payoffs periodically in an entirely distributed fashion. If no player can benefit by changing his current selected strategy while the other players keep their strategies unchanged, all players find a satisfactory solution and do not change their strategies over a game processing time. This situation is defined as the system equilibrium.

At the end of each iteration, players evaluate their current *RD*. The *RD* of one player's strategy is used as the decision factor for the rest players, and the results of the other players' strategies are also used to make a player's decision for the next iteration. This interactive feedback process continues until the system equilibrium is obtained. Therefore, the game duration time is determined by the achievement of the network equilibrium. By considering this situation, the developed power control algorithm is formulated as a non-cooperative and repeated game. To evolve into a stable system equilibrium, it is a practical and suitable approach in real world network operations. The main steps of the developed power control algorithm are given next.

Step 1: At the initial iteration (n=0), the selection probability for each power level strategy is equally distributed. ($x_i(n) = 1/|\mathbb{P}|$, $\forall i$ where $|\mathbb{P}|$ is the number of strategies). This starting guess guarantees that each player enjoys the same benefit at the beginning of the game.

Step 2: Each player selects his own power level, $p_i \in \left[p_{min}, p_{max}\right]$ according to the current selection probability.

Step 3: In a distributed online manner, players re-estimate each strategy's selection probability according to the *RD*. The *n*th RD of the player *i* is obtained as follows.

$$\dot{x}_i(n+1) =$$

$$x_i(n) \times r\_c_{\pm} \left(\sum_j x_j(n) \times J(i,j) - \sum_j \sum_k x_j(n) \times J(j,k) \times x_k(n) \right)$$

(8)

where $r\_c_{\pm}(x)$ is the risk control function according to (7), and the α value is adaptively decided to exit from the evolutionary iteration loops as quickly as possible.

Step 4: When the change of *RD* is within a predefined minimum bound (ε), this change can be negligible. Otherwise, proceeds to Step 2 for the next iteration. This iterative feedback procedure continues until network system reaches to an efficient equilibrium state.

Step 5: If all players do not change their current strategy, they have converged to the *ESS*; proceed to Termination step.

Termination: Game processing time is over. Finally, the network equilibrium is achieved under widely diverse network environments.

The simulation results shown in Figure 1 demonstrate that the proposed *EGPC* scheme generally exhibits better performance compared with the other existing schemes: the *PCRG* scheme and the *ADPC* scheme. From simulation results, the *EGPC* scheme significantly outperforms the *PCRG* and *ADPC* schemes in terms of remaining energy ratio and network stability, etc.

Summary

During wireless network operations, an adaptive power control algorithm is a crucial issue and must be considered for the efficient network performance. By using an interactive learning process, wireless devices can adaptively adjust their power level to reach an effective network equilibrium. Due to the self-regarding feature, these control decisions are made by an entirely distributed fashion. In real world network operations, the distributed online approach is suitable for ultimate practical implementation. The principle contributions of the *EGPC* scheme are its adaptability, feasibility and effectiveness, which can produce an interesting fair-balanced solution for the wireless network power management problem. In the future, the research can be extended to include the implementation issues under noise interference. Wireless communications are disrupted by noise interference, shadowing by intervening objects such as hills, and attenuation by distance and by structures such as buildings. Therefore, practical implementation issues should be considered for real world operations.

STACKELBERG GAME-BASED POWER CONTORL (*SGPC*) SCHEME

In 2011, S. Kim proposed a new Stackelberg Game-based Power Control (*SGPC*) scheme (Kim, 2011b) to maximize the network throughput with fairness provisioning. Based on the Stackelberg game model, the *SGPC* scheme consists of two control mechanisms; user-level and system-level mechanisms. Control decisions in each mechanism act cooperatively and collaborate with each other to satisfy efficiency and fairness requirements.

Figure 1. Performance evaluations of the EGPC scheme

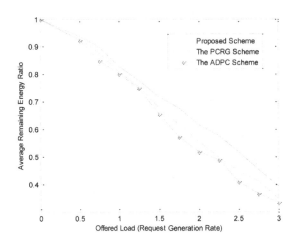

(a) Remaining Energy Ratio

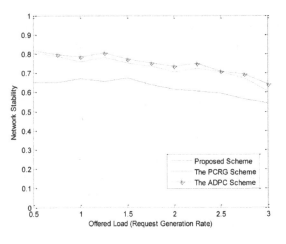

(b) Network Stability

Development Motivation

In wireless networks, the limited bandwidth has to be shared by several users. Therefore, efficient bandwidth management is very important for enhancing wireless network performance. In addition, fairness is another prominent issue for network managements. If the concept of fairness is not considered explicitly at the design stage of power control algorithms, different user requests can result in very unfair bandwidth allocations (Dianati, Shen, & Naik, 2005). However, fairness-oriented control approaches may lead to a system inefficiency, which degrades total network performance quite seriously (Dziong, & Mason, 1996).

In 1934, H. V. Stackelberg proposed a hierarchical game model based on two kinds of different decision makers; a leader and followers. One higher-level decision-maker, who is referred to as a leader, makes his decisions by considering the possible reactions of followers. Many lower-level decision-makers, who are referred to as followers, react dependently based on the decision of the leader while attempting to maximize their satisfaction (Wang, Han, & Liu, 2006).

The *SGPC* scheme adopts the Stackelberg game model to design an adaptive power control algorithm. Usually, based on the different objectives, power control algorithms can be classified as user-centric and system-centric methods (Feng, 2004). These two methods tend to result in qualitatively different network performance. From the viewpoint of the network operator, efficiency and fairness are critical performance metrics. Therefore, the system-centric method attempts to simultaneously optimize these conflicting objectives. From the viewpoint of users, a personal payoff is a very important factor; traditionally, users act independently and selfishly without considering the existence of other users. Therefore, the user-

centric method tries to maximize the interests of individual users. To get a good balance in network performance between the operator and users, it is necessary to effectively mediate these two control methods. To satisfy this goal, the Stackelberg game model may be concluded to be a proper model for the best compromise in the presence of conflicting objectives (Wang, 2006).

In the *SGPC* scheme, the traditional Stackelberg game is extended a dynamic iterative game model; players dynamically adapt their decisions based on the result of adaptive feedback process. In a realistic scenario, the network operator has more global network information; users make their reactions based on the network operator's decision. Therefore, in the developed model, the network operator plays the role of a leader and users become followers. It is suitable assumption for practical network operations. The *SGPC* scheme consists of two different mechanisms; system-level mechanism for the operator and user-level mechanism for users. In the system-level mechanism, network operator makes his decision compatible with the demand for the tradeoff between efficiency and fairness. The result of operator's decision is the input back to the user-level mechanism. In the user-level mechanism, users make their self-optimizing decisions in a distributed online manner. Based on the hierarchical interconnection of two mechanisms, control decisions can cause cascade interactions to reach an efficient network equilibrium.

Power Control Algorithm in the *SGPC* Scheme

Like as the *EGPC* scheme, the co-channel link devices are defined as players. In the user-level mechanism, the utility function for the player i is also defined as follows (Long, 2007).

$$u_i\left(p_i, \mathbb{P}_{-i}\right) =$$

$$\begin{cases} \dfrac{1}{p_i} \times \left(W \times \log_2\left(1 + \gamma_i\left(\mathbb{P}\right) / \Omega\right)\right) & \text{if } \gamma_i\left(\mathbb{P}\right) \geq \gamma_i^* \\ \qquad\qquad 0 & \text{otherwise.} \end{cases}$$

$$(9)$$

where $\mathbb{P}_{-i} = (p_1, p_2, \cdots p_{i-1}, p_{i+1}, \cdots p_n)$ is the transmit power vector without the player i's power level, and $\gamma_i(\mathbb{P})$ is the player i's SINR. The *SGPC* scheme follows the assumption of Long's paper (Long, 2007); Therefore, the throughput of player i ($T_i(\mathbb{P})$) can be expressed as

$$T_i\left(\mathbb{P}\right) = W \times \log_2\left(1 + \frac{\gamma_i\left(\mathbb{P}\right)}{\Omega}\right) \qquad (10)$$

where W is the bandwidth of each channel, and Ω ($\Omega \geq 1$) is the gap between uncoded M-QAM and the capacity, minus the coding gain (Long, 2007).

Generally, the network throughput is used as an indicator of network resource utilization. In the *SGPC* scheme, based on each user's transmitted data, total network throughput (T) is given by

$$T = \sum_{i=1}^{N} t_i \qquad (11)$$

where t_i is the personal throughput of user i. In the system-level mechanism, throughput maximization is one of main goals. However, throughput-oriented approaches do not provide any guarantees of fairness. Although the network might spend the same effort to serve different users, users with different channel qualities will enjoy different transmission rates that may be unfair from their point of view (Dianati, 2005). Therefore, fairness provisioning in multi-user network managements is another major goal to support a wide range of

multimedia services with diverse QoS requirements.

In the *SGPC* scheme, the concept of fairness is defined as a fair bandwidth allocation during network operations. It ensures the equitable transmission rate for different individual users (Dianati, 2005). To characterize this fairness notion, the *SGPC* scheme follows the Jain's fairness index (F_{index}), which has been frequently used to measure the fairness of network resource allocations.

$$F_{index} = \frac{\left(\sum_{i=1}^{N} \gamma_i\left(\mathbb{P}\right)\right)^2}{N \times \sum_{i=1}^{N}\left(\gamma_i\left(\mathbb{P}\right)\right)^2} \qquad (12)$$

The range of F_{index} is varied from 0 to 1. In the system-level mechanism, the major issue is to provide the most proper combination of the efficiency and fairness requirements. To deal with this multi-objective control problem, the *SGPC* scheme develop a multi-objective utility function based on the ε-constraint method (Becerra, & Coello, 2006). The developed utility function is expressed based on the function (9) and the F_{index} is used as a coefficient. In addition, the ε-constraint is given by a fairness condition. By using dynamic joint operations, the developed multi-objective utility function (*EF*) is formulated as follows.

$$EF = F_{index} \times \sum_{i=1}^{N}\left\{u_i\left(p_i, \mathbb{P}_{-i}\right)\right\} \text{ where}$$
$$p_i > \varepsilon_{min} \qquad (13)$$

where ε_{min} is the lower bound of transmission rate and P_i is the power level of user i. To guarantee the required QoS, each user should maintain the specified ε_{min} rate during communication services. However, under diverse network environments, a fixed ε_{min} value cannot effectively provide an appropriate performance balance between conflicting criteria. To approximate the equalized bandwidth sharing, the ε_{min} value should be increased; it can guarantee fairness. In contrast to the fairness, the bandwidth efficiency can be enhanced by decreasing the ε_{min} value. The *SGPC* scheme treats the ε_{min} modification as an on-line decision problem. To respond current network situations, the ε_{min} value is dynamically upgraded as follows.

$$\varepsilon_{k+1} = \begin{cases} \varepsilon^*, & if(EF_{k,i} \wedge \varepsilon_k) < (EF_{k,i} \wedge \varepsilon^*) \\ & \text{with } \varepsilon^* = \max(\varepsilon_k \times \left[1 + \frac{n_{upper}}{N}\right], \varepsilon_{min}) \\ \varepsilon_k, & \text{otherwise} \\ & \text{with } n_{upper} = \frac{1}{2} \times n_{upper} \end{cases}$$

(14)

where ε_k is the minimum transmission rate of kth iteration. N, n_{upper} are the total number of users and the number of users who currently satisfy the ε_k constraint, respectively. The ε_k value is adaptively adjusted based on the ratio of the n_{upper} to N, which represents the fairness status of current bandwidth allocations. If the new *EF* function payoff by using the updated ε^* is better than the current payoff by using the ε_k, the ε_k value is replaced by the ε^*. Otherwise, the variation of ε modification is down to one-half. It is similar to the sliding window protocol of TCP mechanism.

As the number of network users and bandwidth requests increase, network system might run out of bandwidth to accept new requested service; network congestion occurs. In order to adaptively handle the overloaded network environment, the operator also make a decision on how to efficiently provide appropriate grade of service level. At this time, it is necessary to degrade ε value, and then the already allocated bandwidth is reduced to the degraded ε value. When network is in a degraded operation mode, the ε modification process is as follows; it is executed in the inverse order of (14).

$$\varepsilon_{k+1} = \begin{cases} \varepsilon^*, & if(EF_{k,i} \wedge \varepsilon_k) < (EF_{k,i} \wedge \varepsilon^*) \\ & \text{with } \varepsilon^* = \max(\varepsilon_k \times \left[1 - \frac{n_{upper}}{N}\right], \varepsilon_{min}) \\ \varepsilon_k, & \text{otherwise} \\ & \text{with } n_{upper} = \frac{1}{2} \times n_{upper} \end{cases}$$

(15)

Based on the real-time network monitoring, the ε is adaptively adjusted. This adjustment process is iteratively repeated until the change of ε value is within a pre-defined minimum bound (Δ). By using the ε value as a threshold for transmission rates, the network operator can maintain the network efficiency while ensuring the network fairness. Therefore, the system-level mechanism can keep a good balance and find the best compromise solution for the multi-objective control problem.

To practically implement the dynamic network situation, the developed model is formulated as a repeated game; one player's behavior might affect the behavior of other players. During the step-by-step iteration, the system-level mechanism adjusts the ε value. Based on the online interactive manner, this fine-grained adjustment procedure is repeated until the best solution has been found for conflicting objectives.

Recently, several power control schemes for wireless networks have been presented. The *Adaptive and Distributed Power Control (ADPC)* scheme is a game-based power control algorithm to effectively schedule each user's power level (Long, 2007). This scheme can safely run in a fully selfish environment without any additional pricing and secure mechanism. The *Power Control with Repeated Game (PCRG)* scheme is a joint link adaptation and power control algorithm for wireless communications (Ginde, 2003). By using the game theory, this scheme results in correct control decisions and provides an acceptable level of interference to other co-channel links. The simulation results shown in Figure 2 demonstrate that the performance comparison of the proposed *SGPC* scheme with the *ADPC* scheme and the *PCRG* scheme.

Summary

During wireless network operations, utilizing the most appropriate power control strategy is a crucial issue and an effective way to enhance the network performance. The *SGPC* scheme is a new fair-efficient online power control algorithm based on the bi-level Stackelberg game model. Based on the dynamic online process, the *SGPC* scheme captures the hierarchical interactions and finds an effective power level to reach an efficient network equilibrium. By using socially desirable game rules, power control decisions are dynamically updated. Therefore, the developed game model can approximate the optimal solution between two conflicting objectives - efficiency and fairness.

DYNAMIC VOLTAGE SCALING *(DVS)* SCHEME

The past decade has seen a surge of research activities in the fields of mobile computing and wireless communication. In particular, recent technological advances have made portable devices, such as PDA, laptops, and wireless modems to be very compact and affordable. To effectively operate portable devices, energy efficiency and Quality of Service (QoS) provisioning are two primary concerns. Dynamic Voltage Scaling (DVS) is a common method for energy conservation for portable devices (Kim, 2011c). However, due to the amount of data that needs to be dynamically handled in varying time periods, it is difficult to apply conventional DVS techniques to QoS sensitive multimedia applications. In the *DVS* scheme, a new adaptive DVS algorithm is developed for QoS assurance and energy efficiency. Based on the repeated learning model, the developed algorithm dynamically schedules multimedia service requests to strike the appropriate performance balance between contradictory requirements.

Figure 2. Performance evaluations of the SGPC scheme

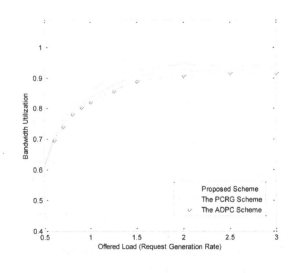

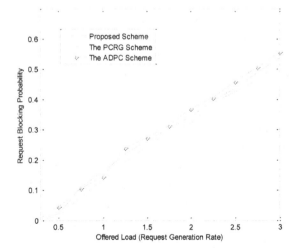

(a) Bandwidth Utilization   (b) Request Blocking Probability

Development Motivation

With the rapid increase in the number of portable device users, wireless networks have gained such wide popularity that new network infrastructure is continually introduced (Wang, Choi, & Kim, 2008). However, there are two fundamental aspects that make the operation problem challenging and interesting. The portable devices generally have limited energy sources. For this reason, there is a need to minimize the energy consumption of portable devices using energy conservation techniques. Recently, a large number of techniques have been developed to reduce the energy consumption of real-time network systems. One of the common energy conservation methods is Dynamic Voltage Scaling (DVS). DVS is a technique that offers adjustment of the voltage and the portable system's clock frequency depending on the task requirements during the execution time (Niu, & Quan, 2009). Usually, the clock frequency increases in proportion to the voltage while the energy consumed by the processors is proportional to a square of the voltage (Kim, 2009). Therefore, by lowering the voltage, the network system can improve energy efficiency.

Multimedia is a keyword in the evolving information age of the 21st century; it is becoming more popular among users to download multimedia data from the Internet. However, many multimedia services exhibit more complicated characteristics, generally called the Quality of Service (QoS) requirements. Nowadays, there has been increasing interest that incorporates DVS techniques to deal with QoS constraints. These approaches intend to enhance the QoS of the system and minimize the energy consumption in the context of power-aware scheduling (Niu, 2009). However, it is difficult to apply conventional DVS algorithms to multimedia application services because of variations of QoS requirements. In addition, the fundamental problem faced by DVS algorithms is the uncertainty regarding the future; tradition-

ally, the actual requirements of future services cannot be known in advance and it is impossible to predict them precisely.

Motivated by the above discussion, the *DVS* scheme is developed as a new adaptive DVS algorithm for wireless communications. The design goal is to enhance the QoS of the network system and to minimize the energy consumption simultaneously. To satisfy this goal, the methodology adopted in the *DVS* scheme is the repeated self-learning model. The dynamics of the interactive feedback learning mechanism can make control decisions to quickly find the most profitable solution.

Repeated Learning Based *DVS* Model

Recent proliferation of enabling technologies is causing an explosion in the number and type of multimedia services. In particular, real-time multimedia services are highly delay-sensitive. For example, video and audio services have real-time delivery requirements. Therefore, multimedia services need to guarantee their deadlines to ensure required QoS. The *DVS* scheme defines Ψ as the set of accepted service requests (*sr*) by the real-time network system, $\Psi = \{sr_1, sr_2, sr_3, sr_i, sr_n\}$, where n is the total number of accepted services, i.e., $n = \|\Psi\|$. During real world network operations, n is dynamically changed. The service request i is characterized by $\{a_i, d_i, t\_c_i\}$ where a_i is the arrival time, d_i is the deadline, and t_c_i is the total workload of service sr_i to be completed. Between its arrival time and the deadline, services are amenable to adaptation with variable processor speed, which is defined as a discrete voltage level with multiple grades of clock frequency in portable device. Each voltage level is characterized by different performance and energy consumption. At the current time (c_t), the processor speed $(S_p(c_t))$ is defined as the sum of assigned processor frequency level for each running service, which is given by

$$S_p(c_t) = \sum_{i=1}^{n} PS_i(c_t), \text{ where } sr_i \in \psi \text{ and } n = \|\psi\|$$

where $PS_i(c_t)$ denotes the processor frequency level for the service i at the current time.

Based on the physical law (Kim, 2009), adaptive voltage/frequency setting is useful for network energy efficiency; it is more energy efficient to slow down the processor power as much as possible.

Even though energy can be saved using DVS techniques, it is not adaptable to support QoS-imposed services. Usually, QoS requirements can be captured by metrics such as a deadline miss rate, which is closely related to the energy consumption (Niu, & Quan, 2006). To provide a reliable and energy efficient solution for multimedia applications, the developed algorithm should take into account QoS requirement and voltage/energy consumption at the same time.

To integrate energy efficiency and QoS level, one major concern is to design utility functions. In the *DVS* scheme, two utility functions (F_e and F_d) are defined by using current network information. Based on the adaptive online manner, these functions can dynamically estimate the degree of energy efficiency and QoS level as follows.

$$\begin{cases} F_e(v_c) = (\dfrac{v_c}{v_{max}})^2 \\ F_d(v_c, c_t) = (\sum_{i=1}^{n} \dfrac{R_i(c_t)}{fd_i - c_t}) / S_p(v_c) \end{cases} \quad (17)$$

where v_c, v_{max} are the current and maximum processor voltage level, respectively. $R_i(c_t)$, fd_i are the amount of remaining workload at the current time and the time deadline of the service i, respectively. $S_p(v_c)$ represents the processor frequency level (S_p) with the v_c. To get the proper combination of the F_e and F_d functions, they should

be transformed into a single objective function. To provide the best compromise in the presence of different control functions, the developed algorithm uses well-known *STEM* multi-objective optimization method (Mehmet, & Ramazan, 2001). Finally, the single object function is obtained as follows.

$$\min \left\{ \sum_{i=1}^{2} \left(w_i \left(f_i - f_i^* \right) \right)^p \right\}^{\frac{1}{p}}$$

$$\text{s.t. } w_i > 0, \sum_{i=1}^{2} w_i = 1 \quad (18)$$

where f_1 is $F_e(v_c)$ and f_2 is $F_d(v_c, c_t)$. In the developed model, f_1^* and f_2^* are 0, and p is set to 2. The w is control parameter for energy efficiency and QoS ensuring. Under diverse network environments, a fixed value of w cannot effectively adapt to the changing conditions. The *DVS* scheme treats it as an on-line decision problem and adaptively modifies w value. When the current $F_d(v_c, c_t)$ value is high, the developed algorithm can put more emphasis on the QoS ensuring. In this case, a higher value of w_2 is more suitable. Otherwise, the *DVS* scheme should strongly highlight the energy efficiency. In this case, a lower value of w_2 is more suitable for the energy consumption rate; since the QoS level ($F_d(v_c, c_t)$) directly affects the w values. In the developed algorithm, the value of w_2 is dynamically decided as the current $F_d(v_c, c_t)$ value, and w_1 is defined as $(1 - w_2)$.

In the *DVS* scheme, the repeated learning approach is applied to solve the multi-objective problem. Therefore, control decisions are made sequentially based on the repeated model. Usually, for T-period repeated model (Wang, Jij, & Liu, 2007), the total utility payoff is computed by

$$\sum_{t=c_t}^{T}\beta^{t-1}U_{mo}\left(v_c,t\right) \qquad (19)$$

where β is the discount factor and $U_{mo}(v_c,t)$ denotes the payoff with the v_c in period t. If $T=\infty$, the model is referred as the infinitely-repeated model. The average utility is then given by:

$$\bar{U}_{mo} = \left(1-\beta\right)\sum_{t=1}^{\infty}\beta^{t-1}U_{mo}\left(v_c,t\right) \qquad (20)$$

The developed self-learning algorithm is developed based on the infinitely repeated model; the basic idea is to learn the optimal network performance step by step. At every time period, the algorithm tries to self-learn the optimal voltage level by dynamically modifying v_c. With only current information, the network system can only observe the history of its own actions and the corresponding utility payoff. Therefore, the best way to approximate the optimal performance is to observe how it will affect its own utility payoff to change the v_c.

At the end of each time period, the network system evaluates the F_e and F_d function value. When the difference of these function values is larger than a pre-defined bound (δ), i.e., $|F_d\left(c_t,v_c\right)-F_e\left(v_c\right)|>\delta$, the developed algorithm is triggered; v_c is adjusted as follows.

$$v_{c+1} = v_c +\Delta,\ \text{where } \Delta = F_d\left(c_t,v_c\right)-F_e\left(v_c\right) \qquad (21)$$

Based on the new v_{c+1}, $\bar{U}_{mo}$ is estimated in the next time period. If the $\bar{U}_{mo}$ is less than the current $U_{mo}\left(v_c,c_t\right)$, the developed algorithm sets $\Delta = -(\Delta/2)$ and continue for the next adjustment processing. Otherwise, the new voltage level is adopted. This feedback self-learning procedure continues until the difference between $\bar{U}_{mo}$ and

the $U_{mo}\left(v_c,c_t\right)$ is within a pre-defined minimum bound (ε). During the step-by-step iteration, a fair-balanced solution can be obtained.

The developed algorithm does not require global objective functions unlike conventional optimization methods such as Lagrangian or dynamic programming. The *DVS* scheme does not focus on trying to get an optimal solution based on the traditional optimal solution itself, but instead, an adaptive online feedback model is developed. This approach can significantly reduce the computational complexity and overheads. It is practical and suitable for real implementation.

Recently, several dynamic voltage scaling schemes have been presented. The *Workload-Based Dynamic Voltage Scaling (WBDVS)* scheme proposed a less energy consumed DVS algorithm while maintaining the quality of service (Wang, 2008). In addition, this scheme dynamically determines frequency and voltage of processors to minimize data loss. The *Energy-aware Scheduling with QoS (ESQoS)* scheme is a DVS algorithm to reduce the energy consumption for real-time systems with QoS guarantee requirement (Niu, 2009). To ensure the schedulability for services, the *ESQoS* scheme determines the processor speed associated with each service. The simulation results shown in Figure 3 demonstrate that the proposed *DVS* scheme generally exhibits better performance compared with the other existing schemes: the *WBDVS* scheme and the *ESQoS* scheme. From simulation results, the *DVS* scheme significantly outperforms the *WBDVS* and *ESQoS* schemes in terms of remaining energy ratio and network stability, etc.

Summary

Wireless communication has a wide range of applications such as telecommunications, networking, device management as well as PC applications. To support various multimedia service, the development of energy efficient and QoS ensuring

Figure 3. Performance evaluations of the proposed DVS scheme

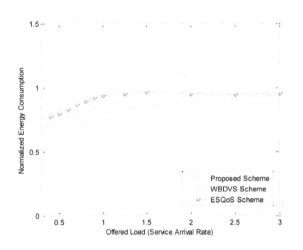
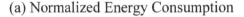
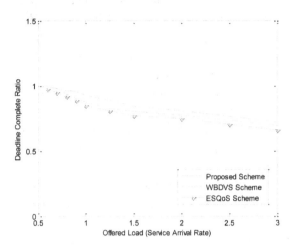

(a) Normalized Energy Consumption

(b) Deadline Complete Ratio

techniques is an important and active research field. The *DVS* scheme is a new DVS algorithm for multimedia communication services based on the repeated learning approach. The major goal is to maximize energy efficiency while ensuring service QoS. The main novelty of the *DVS* scheme is its adaptability, flexibility and responsiveness to current network conditions. This feature is highly desirable for real time network system management. For further research, the basic idea of self-learning DVS algorithm can be extended to develop new control algorithms in various ways.

WEIGHTED VOTING BASED POWER CONTROL (*WVPC*) SCHEME FOR FEMTOCELL NETWORKS

Future wireless networks are designed to cope with drastically increasing user demands. However, network resources reach the limits of their capacity to user requirements. Recently, femtocell networks have attracted much attention to enhance the efficiency of wireless resource usage. In 2013, S. Kim proposed a new Weighted Voting game based Power Control (*WVPC*) scheme for the femtocell network system (Kim, 2013). By using the

concept of the weighted voting game, the *WVPC* scheme adaptively adjusts a transmit power level while ensuring relevant tradeoff between system efficiency and fairness. This power control paradigm can provide the ability to practically respond to current communication conditions and suitable for real network operations.

Development Motivation

A promising approach for the efficient wireless bandwidth usage is through the cellular technology, which has greatly enhanced the network capability. In cellular networks, the capacity of a wireless link has increased by getting the transmitter and receiver closer to each other. Therefore, it is necessary to reduce cell sizes and transmit distance to improve cellular capacity (Chandrasekhar, Andrews, & Gatherer, 2008). The recent concept of femtocells offers an economically viable solution to achieving high cellular capacity and improved coverage. A femtocell is a small indoor area covered by a low-power access point, referred to as Femtocell Access Point (FAP). Usually, FAPs are situated around high user density hotspots to improve communication capacity. Therefore, the deployment of femtocell structure comprises a conventional cellular network plus embedded femtocell hotspots (Chowdhury, Bui, & Jang, 2011). The most important advantages of femtocell are very little upfront cost to offload huge traffic from the expensive cellular networks and the ability to achieve high data rate in some places where the macrocell can't provide signals with high quality. It is very meaningful in future wireless communication networks (Li, & Feng, 2011).

Key issues of femtocell operations are the design of effective power control protocols, which significantly influence the wireless network performance. In addition, the limited wireless bandwidth has to be shared fairly among several users. Fair resource assignment is another prominent factor for the femtocell management (Dianati, 2005), (Mo, & Walrand, 2000). Due to these reasons, the development of adaptive strategies for efficient power control and fair bandwidth assignment algorithms plays a critical role in determining overall network performance. However, it is a complex and difficult work under a dynamically changing network environment.

In recent years, algorithmic game theory has received a lot of attention in field of telecommunications. The reason for this interest is that game theory focuses on the research of intelligent game players, who can compete, cooperate and negotiate for their benefits. In telecommunication domains, network agents are selfish and built to maximize their payoffs without requiring human interventions. Therefore, it can be modeled by means of game theory (Bachrach, Meir, Zuckerman, Rothe, & Rosenschein, 2009). Cooperative game, also called coalition game, is a branch of game theory to deal with multi-person decision making situations. In a cooperative situation, the basic assumption is that players make binding commitments and find it beneficial to cooperate in the game. Therefore, the main interest is to fairly distribute the outcome to each player according to their contributions. Especially, the operations contending for network resources rely on the co-

operation of the each network agents. Therefore, cooperation game models are widely used for wireless network management algorithms.

Weighted voting game is a well-known cooperative game model and a lot of researches have been carried out in political science, economics, logic theory and distributed systems. In such games, each player has a weight, and a coalition of players wins the game if its total weight exceeds a certain quota. Therefore, the weighted voting game model can formulate a decision-making process that is designed to give different amounts of influence to different members (Bachrach, & Elkind, 2008). In femtocell networks, network agents must take a joint decision leading to a certain outcome, which may have a different impact on each of the agents. Therefore, voting based decision-making procedure is an attracting model for the femtocell network management (Zuckerman, Faliszewski, Bachrach, & Elkind, 2008).

Inspired by the preceding discussion, a new Weighted Voting game based Power Control (*WVPC*) scheme is developed. In the *WVPC* scheme, each mobile user is assigned a non-negative weight and makes a vote in favor of a specific femtocell base station. If the total weight of those voting is equal to or greater than the pre-defined value, that femtocell becomes to be a winner and can control its downlink power level. However, this efficient-oriented approach may lead to throughput unfairness. To avoid this unfairness problem, the *WVPC* scheme characterizes the concept of fairness, which is considered explicitly at the design stage of power control algorithm. Therefore, power and bandwidth in the winning femtocell are dynamically adjusted to provide a balanced solution. Based on the self-adaptability and real-time effectiveness, the main novelty of the *WVPC* scheme is the ability to ensure relevant tradeoff between efficiency and fairness.

Recently, two interesting femtocell power control schemes have been presented. The *Power Control in Overlay Femtocell (PCOF)* scheme can properly control the Quality of Service (QoS) in the femtocell users (Li, Qian, & Kataria, 2009). With feasibility conditions, new joint power control and dynamic channel re-allocation procedures are suggested such that the QoS of users was ensured all the time. In the *PCOF* scheme, the fundamental capacity limitation of spatial bandwidth sharing among a macrocell user and a femtocell user is identified. In addition, a downlink power control problem is formulated to address the co-channel interference, as well as provide QoS to both the macrocell user and the femtocell users. Therefore, the *PCOF* scheme is a joint power control, channel management and admission control procedure such that the priority of the macrocell users is always ensured. The *Game Theoretic Power Control (GTPC)* scheme was proposed as a power control algorithm by using a non-cooperative game model (Hong, Yun, & Cho, 2009). This scheme formulates a payoff function to provide fairness and minimize interference by considering loads of individual femtocells. In addition, the *GTPC* scheme proves that this payoff function can be appeared as a supermodular type. The *GTPC* scheme can be applied to the decentralized environment, and leads transmission power to reach a steady state condition, i.e. Nash Equilibrium. Through mathematical analysis and numerical results, the authors show that the *GTPC* scheme has several good characteristics.

Weighted Voting Game Based Selection Algorithm

In cooperative games with a finite set (N) of players, a function v is defined as $v : 2^N \rightarrow \mathbb{R}$, such that $(\varnothing) = 0$ and $v(M) \leq v(N)$ whenever $M \subseteq N$. It is based on the assumption that each player should decide whether he/she join a coalition or not. An important subclass of cooperation games is the Weighted Voting Game (WVG), which has been applied in various political and economic organizations for structural or constitutional purposes. A WVG is repre-

sented by the voting body $\left[q; \omega_1, \ldots \omega_n \right]$ where ω_i represents the voting weight of player i and q ($0 < \omega_i < q$) is the quota needed to win. All the weights and quota are positive real numbers. If $\mathcal{W}(\mathbb{S}) \geq q$ where $\mathcal{W}(\mathbb{S}) = \sum_{i \in \mathbb{S}} \omega_i$, a coalition $\mathbb{S}$ of players ($\mathbb{S} \subseteq N$) is *winner* and $v(\mathbb{S}) = 1$. Otherwise, it is *loser* and $v(\mathbb{S}) = 0$. Therefore, $v(\mathbb{S}) \in \{0,1\}$ for any $\mathbb{S}$ and if $\mathbb{S} \subseteq T \subseteq N$ then $v(\mathbb{S}) \leq v(T)$ (Bachrach, 2008), (Zuckerman, 2008).

The *WVPC* scheme develops a WVG model for users in femtocell networks. To design the WVG, the questions to be answered are what the weights and quota should be, how to calculate outcomes of a weighted vote, and finding the effective distribution of the resulting outcome from their joint action (Bachrach, 2008, 2009). Recently, voting game approaches have been well-studied. However, existing approaches only concerned and focused on theoretical modeling and mathematical analysis. Therefore, practical implementation issues are not yet well developed (Zuckerman, 2008). From a fundamental viewpoint, the *WVPC* scheme places more emphasis on the practical implementation in real world network operations.

In a dense traffic load area, a lot of FAPs are deployed within small coverage area. Therefore, users can receive many signals from the several neighbor FAPs. Under the multi-FAPs environment, each user is responsible for selecting a FAP to maximize its own payoff. Usually, the main interest of each user is to maximize the amount of transmitted data with the lower energy consumption. However, there is a fundamental tradeoff. To capture this conflicting relationship, a utility function is defined by considering the ratio of the throughput to transmit power (Meshkati, 2006), (Long, 2007). In the game model of the *WVPC* scheme, the utility function for the ith user with k^{th} FAP (U_i^k) is defined as follows.

$$U_i^k(\mathbb{P}) = \frac{T_i^k(\mathbb{P})}{u\_p_i}$$

s.t., $\_p_i \in \{u\_p_{min}, , , u\_p_{max}\}, 1 \leq i \leq n$

and

$$1 \leq k \leq m \tag{22}$$

where u_p_{min} and u_p_{max} are the pre-defined minimum and maximum uplink power levels. n, m are the number of macrocell users and FAPs, respectively. u_p_i is the uplink power level of ith user and $\mathbb{P}$ is the transmit uplink power vector. $T_i^k(\mathbb{P})$ is the throughput of ith user by using k^{th} FAP. Usually, throughput is defined as the number of information bits that are transmitted without error per unit-time. In wireless communications, it can be achieved with the SINR in the effective range. Therefore, to estimate the throughput of each user, his SINR should be obtained first. A general formula for the ith user's SINR from the kth FAP ($\gamma_i^k(\mathbb{P})$) is defined as follows (Meshkati, 2006), (Long, 2007).

$$\gamma_i^k(\mathbb{P}) = \frac{u\_p_k h_{ik}}{\sigma_i + \sum_{t \neq k} u\_p_t h_{it}}, \text{ s.t., } 1 \leq t \leq m \tag{23}$$

where σ_i is the background noise power, which is typically fixed value. h_{ik} (or h_{it}) refers to the ith user's path gain from the kth (or t^{th}) FAP. The *WVPC* scheme follows the assumption in of Long's paper (Long, 2007); users' device transmitters use variable-rate M-QAM, with a bounded probability of symbol error and trellis coding with a nominal coding gain. Therefore, the uplink throughput of the ith user from the kth FAP ($T_i^k(\mathbb{P})$) can be expressed as

$$T_i^k(\mathbb{P}) = W_i \times \log_2\left(1 + \frac{\gamma_i^k(\mathbb{P})}{\Omega}\right) \tag{24}$$

where W_i is the assigned channel bandwidth in the ith user, and Ω ($\Omega \geq 1$) is the gap between uncoded M-QAM and the capacity, minus the coding gain. By combining (22) with (24), the utility function for the ith user from the kth FAP is defined and parameterized as follows (Long, 2007).

$$U_i^k(u\_p_i, \mathbb{P}_{-i}) = \frac{1}{u\_p_i} \times \left[W_i \times \log_2\left(1 + \gamma_i^k(\mathbb{P})/\Omega\right)\right] \tag{25}$$

where $\mathbb{P}_{-i}$ is the uplink transmit power vector without the user i. In a distributed self-regarding fashion, each individual user in the femtocell network is independently interested in the sole goal of maximizing his utility function. Finally, the ith user's payoff is defined as follows.

$$U_i = \max_{\substack{u\_p_i \\ and\ k}} U_i^k(u\_p_i, \mathbb{P}_{-i}) =$$

$$\max_{\substack{u\_p_i \\ and\ k}} \frac{1}{u\_p_i} \times [W_i \times \log_2(1 + \gamma_i^k(\mathbb{P})/\Omega) \tag{26}$$

To maximize the network throughput, each user's received payoff based on the utility function is a critical factor. The *WVPC* scheme shall assume that each voter's weight is defined as his payoff ($\omega_i = U_i$) and the quota (Q) needed to win is defined as follows.

$$Q = \rho \times \sum_{i \in N} \omega_i, \text{ s.t., } \rho_{min} \leq \rho \leq 1 \tag{27}$$

where ρ is a decision factor for the quota. Under dynamically changing environments, a fixed value of ρ cannot effectively adapt to the current network condition. Therefore, the ρ value should be dynamically adjustable. In order to implement the ρ value adjustment, the *WVPC* scheme partitions the time-axis into equal intervals of length *unit_time*, and the parameter ρ can be dynamically decreased (*or* increased) by $\Delta \rho$. The value of ρ ($\rho_{min} \leq \rho \leq 1$) is multiples of $\Delta \rho$, and the *WVPC* scheme set $\Delta \rho = 0.1$. When a winner FAP is decided, the current ρ value is increased by $\Delta \rho$. If no FAP become to be winner during the predefined time period (T_P), the current ρ value is determined as $\rho = \min(\rho - \Delta \rho, \rho_{min})$.

Fairness Based Resource Control Algorithm

Fairness is a prominent issue for the network management. However, fairness-oriented control approaches may lead to a system inefficiency, which degrades total network performance quite seriously (Dianati, 2005). Therefore, the most proper combination of the efficiency and fairness requirements is the major issue. In the *WVPC* scheme, the fairness is defined as an equitable transmission rate for different individual users. To characterize the fairness notion, the *WVPC* scheme follows the Jain's fairness index (Dianati, 2005), which has been frequently used to measure the fairness of network resource allocations. The fairness among users in the winning coalition $\mathbb{S}$ ($F_{\mathbb{S}}$) is defined as follows.

$$F_{\mathbb{S}} = \frac{\left(\sum_{i \in \mathbb{S}} T_i \left(\mathbb{P} \right) \right)^2}{|\mathbb{S}| \times \sum_{i \in \mathbb{S}} \left(T_i \left(\mathbb{P} \right) \right)^2}, \text{ s.t., } \sum_{i \in \mathbb{S}} \omega_i \geq Q \tag{28}$$

The range of $F_{\mathbb{S}}$ is varied from 0 to 1. To improve the $F_{\mathbb{S}}$, the channel bandwidth for each user (W) is adjusted. For the fair-bandwidth allocation, the most common idea is max–min fairness concept (Mo, 2000). It aims at allocating as much as possible to poor users, while not un-

necessarily wasting resources. However, to achieve max–min fair rates, global information is needed. Therefore, this approach requires huge exchange of information (Mo, 2000). Based on the max–min fairness notion, the *WVPC* scheme developed a practical protocol to implement fair-based resource allocation in the winning coalition $\mathbb{S}$. The main goal of the *WVPC* scheme is to distribute bandwidth for each user's communication as evenly as possible, without unduly reducing system efficiency. First, the minimum bandwidth allocation amount (M_a) is estimated by the using fairness index ($F_{\mathbb{S}}$). And then, additional allocation amount (A_a) for each user is defined according to each throughput. The assigned bandwidth for the user i ($W_{i, i \in \mathbb{S}}$) is calculated as follows.

$$W_i = M\_a + A\_a_i, \text{ s.t.,}$$
$$M\_a = \left. \left(F_{\mathbb{S}} \times TW_{\mathbb{S}} \right) \middle/ n_{\mathbb{S}} \right. \tag{29}$$
$$A\_a_k = \eta \times \left[TW_{\mathbb{S}} - \left(F_{\mathbb{S}} \times TW_{\mathbb{S}} \right) \right] \text{ and } \eta = \left. \frac{1}{T_i \left(\mathbb{P} \right)} \middle/ \sum_{j=1}^{n_{\mathbb{S}}} \left(\frac{1}{T_j \left(\mathbb{P} \right)} \right) \right.$$

where $TW_{\mathbb{S}}$, $n_{\mathbb{S}}$ are total bandwidth amount and number of users in the coalition $\mathbb{S}$, respectively. A_a_i is an additional allocation for the user i and η is a control factors for the inverse weighted allocation. According to (29), the channel bandwidth adjustment continues until the all users' bandwidths in $\mathbb{S}$ are re-assigned.

Multi-Objective Utility Function for Efficiency and Fairness

In the *WVPC* scheme, the developed voting game model employs the double-decision rule in which two conditions must be satisfied in terms of efficiency and fairness. During the voting game, a coalition $\mathbb{S}$ is winning if $\sum_{i\in\mathbb{S}}\omega_i \geq Q$. And then, the winning FAP can select its downlink power level ($d\_p_\mathbb{S}$), which is adjusted within the pre-defined downlink power levels (i.e., $d\_p_\mathbb{S} \in \{d\_p_{min},,d\_p_{max}\}$). To decide the downlink power level, the *WVPC* scheme considers not only the system efficiency, but also the concept of fairness. To characterize the concept of efficiency, the efficiency index (E) is defined as follows.

$$E_\mathbb{S} = \frac{\sum_{i\in\mathbb{S}}U_i^d\left(d\_p_\mathbb{S}\right)}{|\mathbb{S}| \times \left(\max_i U_i^d\left(d\_p_\mathbb{S}\right)\right)}, \text{ s.t.,}$$

$$\sum_{i\in\mathbb{S}}\omega_i \geq Q \qquad (30)$$

where $U_i^d\left(d\_p_\mathbb{S}\right)$ is the user i's downlink utility with $d\_p_\mathbb{S}$ power level. To deal with this efficiency-fairness combination control problem, a multi-objective utility function (*M_EF*) is developed based on the weighted sum method. By using dynamic joint operations, the developed multi-objective utility function (*M_EF*) is formulated as follows.

$$M\_EF = \left[\beta \times E_\mathbb{S}\right] + \left[\left(1-\beta\right) \times F_\mathbb{S}\right], \text{ where } \beta$$

$$= \frac{\left(\sum_{i=1}^n T_i\left(\mathbb{P}\right)\right)^2}{n \times \sum_{i=1}^n \left(T_i\left(\mathbb{P}\right)\right)^2} \qquad (31)$$

where β controls the relative weights given to efficiency and fairness. By choosing a different weight value, the preference of the decision-maker is taken into account. Under diverse network environments, the *WVPC* scheme treats it as an on-line decision problem and adaptively modifies β value. When the fairness of all users in a macrocell is high, the *WVPC* scheme can put more emphasis on the system efficiency. In this case,

a higher value of β is more suitable. When the system fairness is low, the FAP's power control decision should strongly depend on the fairness. In this case, a lower value of β is more suitable for system fairness. In the online algorithm, the value of β is dynamically adjusted based on the total system fairness (i.e., F_N: the fairness index of all users in a macrocell). By the real-time network monitoring, the system can be more responsive to current network conditions. Finally, the winning FAP's downlink power level ($P_\mathbb{S}$) is decided as follows.

$$d\_P_\mathbb{S} = \max_{d\_P_\mathbb{S}}\left(M\_EF\right), \text{ s.t.,}$$

$$d\_P_{min} \leq d\_P_\mathbb{S} \leq d\_P_{max} \qquad (32)$$

$$= \max_{d\_P_\mathbb{S}}\left[\beta \times \frac{\sum_{i\in\mathbb{S}}U_i^d\left(d\_p_\mathbb{S}\right)}{|\mathbb{S}| \times \left(\max_i U_i^d\left(d\_p_\mathbb{S}\right)\right)}\right]$$

$$+ \left[\left(1-\beta\right) \times \frac{\left(\sum_{i\in\mathbb{S}}T_i\left(\mathbb{P}\right)\right)^2}{|\mathbb{S}| \times \sum_{i\in\mathbb{S}}\left(T_i\left(\mathbb{P}\right)\right)^2}\right]$$

The Main Steps of the *WVPC* Scheme

The main goal of the *WVPC* scheme is to ensure relevant tradeoff between efficiency and fairness. Even though the fairness-related solution concepts (e.g., the Shapley value) are well-studied, the computational complexity makes it practically unable to implement in the realistic network operation model. To maximize implementation practicality, the *WVPC* scheme would employ distributed and dynamic online game methodologies to develop a power control scheme. In general, due to heavy control and implementation overheads, centralized control approaches are impractical methods. But, a distributed mechanism can transfer the computational burden from a central system to the distributed nodes. In the algorithm of the *WVPC* scheme, users make their control decisions in a self-regarding distributed fashion. This distributed approach can dramatically reduce the computational complexity and overheads comparing to the traditional static centralized approach. Usually, the traditional optimal and centric algorithms have exponential time complexity. However, the *WVPC* scheme has polynomial time complexity for power control decisions. Therefore, the *WVPC* scheme can provide a good tradeoff between the practical implementation complexity and the optimized network performance.

In the algorithm of the *WVPC* scheme, the result of FAP's decision is the input back to users. At the end of each game's iteration, users dynamically re-estimate their decisions. This feedback-based repeated process can analyze strategic decisions and capture each user's behavior, which is defined as a power control algorithm. After a finite number of rounds, users' decisions can reach an efficient network solution. The main steps of the *WVPC* scheme are given next.

Step 1: At the initial game iteration, each mobile user dynamically selects the uplink power level(u_p) and the most adaptable FAP to maximize his payoff according to (26).

Step 2: If a FAP's weighted voting sum is larger than the current quota ($\sum_{i \in \mathbb{S}} \omega_i > Q$), this FAP becomes to be winner.

Step 3: For the coalition $\mathbb{S}$ of winning FAP, $F_\mathbb{S}$ and M_a are estimated based on (28) and (29), respectively.

Step 4: By using the bandwidth adjustment procedure, each user's channel bandwidth (W) in $\mathbb{S}$ is adjusted according to (29).

Step 5: According to (32), the winning FAP selects the best downlink power level to maximize the multi-objective payoff.

Step 6: The result of FAP's decision is the input back to users. At the end of each game's iteration, users iteratively adapt their decisions (i.e., uplink power level and FAP selection) to maximize their payoffs. This approach can analyze the current strategic decision in a distributed online manner.

Step 7: Every *unit_time*, the ρ and Q values are examined and adjusted periodically.

Step 8: By using the dynamics of feedback-based repeated process, FAPs and users can be interacting with one another and make their decisions in a way to reach an efficient network solution.

The simulation results shown in Figure 4 demonstrate that the proposed *WVPC* scheme scheme generally exhibits better performance compared with the other existing schemes: the *PCOF* and *GTPC* schemes. Based on the adaptive real-time monitoring, the *WVPC* scheme is flexible, adaptable and able to sense the dynamic changing network environment. This feature leads to a balance appropriate network performance while other *PCOF* and *GTPC* schemes cannot offer such an attractive network performance.

Summary

The femtocellular network is one of the most promising future network technologies to meet the demand of the tremendous increasing wireless capacity. During femtocell network operations, appropriate power control strategy is a crucial issue to enhance the network performance. The *WVPC* scheme is developed as a new fair-efficient power control scheme based on the WVG model. By using the dynamics of feedback loop, FAPs and users can be interacting with one another and adaptively make their decisions. Under rapidly changing network environments, the *WVPC* scheme is an effective way to reach a globally desirable network performance between two conflicting objectives -efficiency and fairness.

Figure 4. Performance evaluations of the WVPC scheme

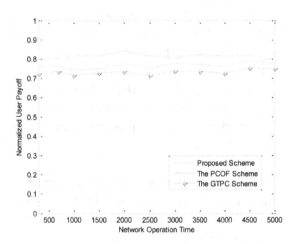

(a) Normalized User Payoff

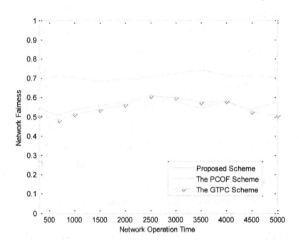

(b) Network Fairness

INTERVENTION GAME BASED MULTI-OBJECTIVE POWER CONTROL (*IGMPC*) SCHEME FOR FEMTOCELL NETWORKS

Future wireless networks are designed to cope with drastically increasing user demands. However, network resources reach the limits of their capacity to user requirements. Nowadays, femtocell has appeared as an effective solution to achieve better coverage for indoor users while improving the cellular network capacity. In femtocell networks, the most important issue is to design an efficient and fair power control protocol, which can significantly influences the network performance. Recently, S. Kim proposed a new Intervention Game based Multi-objective Power Control (*IGMPC*) scheme for femtocell networks based on the no-regret learning technique and intervention game model. The control paradigm in the *IGMPC* scheme can provide the ability to practically respond to current system conditions and suitable for real network operations. Under a dynamically changing network environment, the *IGMPC* scheme appropriately controls the power

level to balance network performance between efficiency and fairness.

Development Motivation

In spite of high network infrastructures, wireless bandwidth is a particularly scare resource. Therefore, new wireless technologies have been developed to support the remarkable growth in the number of users. A promising approach for the efficient wireless bandwidth usage is through the cellular technology, which has greatly enhanced the network capability. In cellular networks, the capacity of a wireless link has increased by getting the transmitter and receiver closer to each other. Therefore, it is necessary to reduce cell sizes and transmit distance to improve cellular capacity (Chandrasekhar, 2008), (Chowdhury, 2011).

To handle the growing demand of various traffic services, the emerging concept of femtocells offers an economically viable solution to achieving high cellular capacity and improved coverage. A femtocell is a small indoor area covered by a low-power access point, referred to as Femtocell Access Point (FAP). Usually, FAPs are situated around high user density hotspots to improve communication capacity. Therefore, the deployment of femtocell structure comprises a conventional cellular network plus embedded femtocell hotspots. The most important advantages of femtocell are very little upfront cost to offload huge traffic from the expensive cellular networks and the ability to achieve high data rate in some places where the macrocell can't provide signals with high quality. Therefore, femtocells provide cost-effective means of providing ubiquitous connectivity in future broadband wireless networks (Hong, 2009), (Lu, Sun, Wen, Su, & Ling, 2012).

In femtocell networks, the limited wireless bandwidth has to be shared fairly among several users. So, most of previous works for femtocell networks are focused on the bandwidth sharing and interference avoidance. However, fairness aspect is largely ignored by the recent research. To effectively operate the femtocell network, fair resource assignment is another prominent factor (Dianati, 2005), (Mo, 2000). But, multi-objective operation is a complex and difficult work under a dynamically changing network environment.

Network users should be able to learn from the environment and adapt the current network condition by making control decisions in real-time. Therefore, users who use learning techniques would acquire information from environment, build knowledge, and ultimately improve their performance. Until now, several learning algorithms have been developed to help users to learn from the dynamic network environment. No-regret learning algorithm is a well-known learning algorithm toward maximizing payoffs in non-deterministic settings. The efficacy of a no-regret algorithm is determined by comparing the performance of a set of alternative strategies. Generally, the no-regret algorithm can guarantee that the collective behavior converges to a coarse correlated equilibrium (Li, Shi, Liu, Yue, & Chen, 2010).

In 2010, Jaeok Park and Mihaela van der Schaar proposed a new game concept, called intervention game (Park, & Schaar, 2012). Based on the repeated game approach, this game model can highlight issues of cooperation and competition among individual users. In traditional repeated game models, long-run frequent interaction is necessary, which usually requires an infinite horizon and sufficiently patient game players. However, in an intervention game model, an intervention device monitors the player's behavior and chooses an intervention action to directly interact with the players. This approach can deter misbehavior of a player by exerting punishment while loosening requirements for player's patience to get the solution (Park, & Scharr, 2011). In particular, the intervention game can lead us to study the convergence behavior of certain learning algorithms. Therefore, the intervention game has recently received increasing attention as a tool to design and analyze distributed control algorithms.

Inspired by the preceding discussion, the *IGMPC* scheme is developed for the femtocell network power control problem. The major issue is to provide the most proper combination of the efficiency and fairness issues. To deal with this multi-objective control problem, the *IGMPC* scheme employs the no-regret learning technique and intervention game model to design a power control scheme. In the *IGMPC* scheme, each user dynamically selects a specific power level according to the no-regret learning algorithm. However, this no-regret learning approach may lead to throughput unfairness. To avoid this unfairness, the *IGMPC* scheme adopts the concept of intervention game, which considers the fairness at the design stage of game model. Based on the self-adaptability and real-time effectiveness, the main novelty of the *IGMPC* scheme is the ability to ensure relevant tradeoff between efficiency and fairness.

Related Work

Recently, several power control schemes - the *Game Theoretic Power Control* (*GTPC*) scheme (Hong, 2009) and the *Energy-Efficient Power*

Control (*EEPC*) scheme (Lu, 2012) - have been presented for femtocell networks. The *GTPC* scheme is a novel decentralized power control algorithm based on the game model. By considering fairness and loads of individual femtocells, the *GTPC* scheme sets up a payoff function to implement a game-based power control approach. The *EEPC* scheme presents a non-cooperative power control game for spectrum-sharing femtocell networks. To enhance energy efficiency, the *EEPC* scheme mitigates inter-tier interference for the uplink while achieving its target SINR.

Power Control Algorithms in the *IGMPC* Scheme

Key issue for effective femtocell operations is the development of adaptive strategies for efficient and fair power control solution. Based on the adaptive online iteration manner, the fine-grained power control algorithms in the *IGMPC* scheme are repeated until the best solution has been found for conflicting - efficiency and fairness - objectives.

No-Regret Learning Algorithm

Recently, there has been a significant impetus towards the deployment of femtocell solutions by several cellular providers, namely Sprint, Vodafone, Korea Telecom, SK Telecom, etc. During femtocell network operations, adaptive power control is a critical issue. In the *IGMPC* scheme, a new power control algorithm is developed to maximize each user's utility in a distributed manner. To satisfy this goal, the *IGMPC* scheme examines the applicability of no-regret learning technique, which has been proposed to improve the non-cooperative outcomes (Hart, & Mas-Colell, 2000). In the no-regret learning technique, the solution exhibits no regret and the probability of choosing a strategy is proportional to the 'regret' for not having chosen other strategies. Therefore, this procedure is not of the 'best-reply' variety or calibrated learning. Instead, all 'better' actions may

be chosen, with probabilities that are proportional to the apparent gains, as measured by the regrets. Therefore, there is always a positive probability of continuing to play this strategy and, moreover, changes from it occur only if there is reason to do so (Latifa, Gao, & Liu, 2012).

Based on the game theory, the *IGMPC* scheme considers a femtocell network where a FAP services the set ($\mathcal{N}$) of network users, who are game players (i.e., $\mathcal{N} = \{1, \ldots, n\}$). The strategy space of player i is denoted by $\mathbb{S}_i$, and an strategy for the player i is denoted by $s_i \in \mathbb{S}_i$., for all $i \in \mathcal{N}$. A strategy profile of the players other than the player i is written as $s_{-i} = \left(s_1, \ldots, s_{i-1}, s_{i+1}, \ldots, s_n\right)$. In the *IGMPC* scheme, the vector of strategies ($\mathbb{S}$), the utility function for the player i (U_i) and the throughput of player i ($T_i(\mathbb{S})$) are defined as the same approach in the *EGPC* scheme (Kim, 2011).

For every two different strategies j, $k \in \mathbb{S}$, suppose the player i were to replace the strategy j, every time it was played in the past, by the strategy k, the *IGMPC* scheme defines the regret of the player i for not playing k at time t as

$$R_i\left(j, k\right) = \max\left\{U_i\left(k, s_{-i}\right) - U_i\left(j, s_{-i}\right)], 0\right\},$$

$$\text{s.t., } \left(k, s_{-i}\right), \left(j, s_{-i}\right) \in \mathbb{S} \tag{33}$$

Originally, the regret-matching learning algorithm requires not only the current payoff information but also the total strategy history in the past. It's impractical assumption to adapt to current system conditions (Hart, 2000), (Latifa, 2012). Therefore, the *IGMPC* scheme modifies the traditional regret-matching learning algorithm. Realistically, users can know only the current payoff information. By considering this situation, the probability distribution for strategy selection

(Pr_{t+1}^i) used by the player i at time $t+1$ is defined as

$$\begin{cases} \mathrm{Pr}_{t+1}^i(k) = R_t^i(j,k) / {\sum_{l=1}^{ts} R_t^i(j,l)} & \text{for all } k \neq j, \\ \mathrm{Pr}_{t+1}^i(j) = 1 - \sum_{k \in \mathbb{S}_i : k \neq j} \mathrm{Pr}_{t+1}^i(k) \end{cases}$$

$$(34)$$

where ts is the total number of strategies (i.e., available power levels of a player). According to (34), players probabilistically adjust their power levels to respond current network situations. Therefore, players dynamically re-estimate and iteratively adapt their decisions to maximize their throughputs.

Intervention Game Model

During no-regret power control operations, system efficiency is a critical performance metric. However, this approach does not provide any guarantees of fairness among users. To get a fair-efficient solution, the *IGMPC* scheme adopts the intervention game model (Xiao, Park, & Schaar, 2012). Intervention game can be applicable and useful in a system with a frequently changing population situation. In the intervention game, a central entity (i.e., the intervention device) performs monitoring and acts explicitly, which can be programmed simply according to the design objective. During game operations, intervention actions can be adjusted to the observed behavior of players, and applied only when punishment is needed (Park, 2011).

To provide a normal representation form of an intervention game, the set of pure strategy profiles is denoted by $\mathbb{S} \triangleq \prod_{i \in \mathcal{N}} \mathbb{S}_i$. A mixed strategy for the player i is a probability distribution over $\mathbb{S}_i$ and it is denoted by $\beta_i \in \Delta(\mathbb{S}_i)$, where $\Delta(\mathbb{S}_i)$ is the set of all probability distributions over a set $\mathbb{S}_i$. Therefore, a mixed strategy

profile is represented by a vector $\beta = (\beta_1, \ldots, \beta_n) \in \prod_{i \in \mathcal{N}} \Delta(\mathbb{S}_i)$. The FAP observes a signal (χ) from players, which is realized from the set ($\mathcal{S}$) of all possible signals, takes its strategy, called an intervention strategy. It can be represented by a mapping $f : \mathcal{S} \to \Delta(\mathbb{S}_0)$, which is called an intervention rule where $\mathbb{S}_0$ is the set of pure strategies for the FAP.

To design an intervention game, the *IGMPC* scheme determines the intervention rule used by the FAP. The *IGMPC* scheme can define an intervention rule as a protocol embedded in the FAP. Therefore, the payoffs of the players are finally determined by the realized signal and the strategies of the FAP. The payoff function of player $i \in \mathcal{N}$ is denoted by $u_i : \mathbb{S}_0 \times \mathbb{S} \times \mathcal{S} \to \mathbb{R}$ and the payoffs of FAP by $u_0 : \mathbb{S}_0 \times \mathbb{S} \times \mathcal{S} \to \mathbb{R}$ where $\mathbb{S}_0$ is the set of intervention actions of FAP. In the *IGMPC* scheme, the traditional intervention game is extended to a scenario where the game designer (i.e., manager) has incomplete information about players. With incomplete information, the game designer develops a procedure to induce players to reveal their private information as well as to take appropriate actions. Therefore, each user selects his best strategy as a player and the FAP monitors the players' behaviors as an intervention device and chooses an adaptive intervention rule depending on the strategies from players.

In the *IGMPC* scheme, the FAP enforces players to transmit at desired power levels. Once the current power level vector of players (P_V) is determined, the FAP observes the P_V and chooses a strategy s_0 from $\mathbb{S}_0$. Hence, a strategy for the FAP can be represented by an intervention rule ($\mathcal{F}$) mapping $\mathcal{F}: \mathbb{S} \to \mathbb{S}_0$. Finally, the game ($\Gamma_{\mathcal{F}}$) played by the FAP and players is represented as an intervention game, which is formally given by

$$\Gamma_{\mathcal{F}} = \left\{ \mathcal{N}_0, \mathbb{S}_0, \left(\mathbb{S}_i \right)_{i \in \mathcal{N}_0}, \mathcal{F}, U_i^{\mathcal{F}} \left(s_0, s_i \right)_{i \in \mathcal{N}} \right\} \tag{35}$$

s.t., $\mathcal{N}_0 \triangleq \mathcal{N} \cup \{0\}$ and
$U_i^{\mathcal{F}} \left(s_0, s_i \right) : \mathbb{S}_0 \times \mathbb{S} \to \mathbb{R}$

According to $\mathcal{F}$, players are forced to ensure fairness. To characterize the fairness notion, the *IGMPC* scheme follows the Jain's fairness index (Dianati, 2005), which has been frequently used to measure the fairness of network resource allocations. The fairness among users is defined as follows.

$$F_{\mathcal{N}} = \frac{\left(\sum_{i \in \mathcal{N}} T_i \left(\mathbb{S} \right) \right)^2}{|\mathcal{N}| \times \sum_{i \in \mathcal{N}} \left(T_i \left(\mathbb{S} \right) \right)^2} \tag{36}$$

where $\mathbb{S} = \{ p_1, \ldots, p_n \}$ is the set of users' power level and $T_i \left(\mathbb{S} \right)$ is the throughput of user i. The range of $F_{\mathcal{N}}$ is varied from 0 to 1. To improve the $F_{\mathcal{N}}$, the power level of each user should be adjusted. In order to adaptively control the power level, the *IGMPC* scheme partitions the time-axis into equal intervals of length *unit_time* (i.e., a short time duration). Every *unit_time*, the current power levels are examined periodically by a real-time online approach.

In the *IGMPC* scheme, $\mathcal{F}$ is defined for the fairness issue in the femtocell network. To define $\mathcal{F}$, denote the upper level power ($\bar{p}$) as $\bar{p} = \sum_{i=1}^n p_i \times \left(1 + F_{\mathcal{N}}\right) / n$ where p_i, $\bar{p} > 0$. For fair-efficient online power control operation, $\mathcal{F}$ consists of three rules $\mathcal{F} = \{ f_1, f_2, f_3 \}$.

f_1: If $F_{\mathcal{N}} > 0.7$ (i.e., stable status), fair transmission rate is ensured for different individual users. Therefore, additional intervention is not necessary.

f_2: If $0.4 \leq F_{\mathcal{N}} \leq 0.7$ (i.e., monitoring status), intervention action is needed under a proper condition. First, if $p_{i,1 \leq i \leq n} > \bar{p}$, the FAP explicitly set the power level of user i as $\bar{p}$ ($p_i = \bar{p}$). Second, the multi-objective payoff (*MP*) for the femtocell system is obtained as $MP = F_{\mathcal{N}} \times \sum_{i \in \mathcal{N}} T_i \left(\mathbb{S} \right)$. If the previous *MP* is larger than a new obtained *MP*, the power level of user i is restored. It means that both efficiency and fairness are improved simultaneously, explicit intervention occurs.

f_3: If $F_{\mathcal{N}} < 0.4$ (i.e., insecure status), intervention action is necessary. Without the condition check, the FAP intervenes to provide fairness. First, if $p_{i,1 \leq i \leq n} > \bar{p}$, the FAP explicitly set the power level of user i as $\bar{p}$ ($p_i = \bar{p}$). Second, the FAP sets the power levels to maximize the α-fairness formulation as follows (Altman, Avrachenkov, & Garnaev, 2008).

$$\max_{\mathbb{P}} \quad \frac{1}{1 - \alpha} \times \sum_{i=1}^n \left(\left(T_i \left(\mathbb{S} \right) \right)^{1-\alpha} - 1 \right) \times \frac{1}{n},$$
$$\text{s.t.,} \quad \alpha = \frac{1}{F_{\mathcal{N}}} \tag{37}$$

In the α-fairness, the parameter α controls the relative weights given to efficiency and fairness. In particular, the case $\alpha \to \infty$ corresponds to the fairness maximization and the case $\alpha \to 1$ corresponds to the efficiency (i.e., total throughput) maximization.

By using the dynamics of feedback-based repeated process, the FAP periodically monitors the current femtocell network situation and adaptively intervenes to obtain a fair-efficient solution. Therefore, power levels of users are adjusted dynamically in the step-by-step interactive online manner.

The Main Steps of the *IGMPC* Scheme

In the *IGMPC* scheme, a new power control algorithm is developed for femtocell networks. The main goal of *IGMPC* scheme is to ensure relevant tradeoff between efficiency and fairness. To practically adapt the dynamic network situation, the *IGMPC* scheme employs the no-regret learning technique for efficiency and the intervention game model for fairness. Under the stable status, individual users select their power levels to maximize their efficiency. A selection probability for each strategy is dynamically changed based on the no-regret learning algorithm. Therefore, players examine their payoffs periodically in an entirely distributed fashion. Under the monitoring and insecure status, the FAP explicitly intervenes to obtain a fair-efficient solution. Based on the value of $F_{\mathcal{N}}$, the FAP selects the intervention rule $f_{i,1 \le i \le 3} \in \mathcal{F}$. The result of FAP's intervention is the input back to users. This feedback-based repeated process can analyze strategic decisions and capture each user's behavior, which is defined as a power control algorithm.

At the end of each game's iteration (i.e., *unit_time*), the FAP and users dynamically re-estimate and select their decisions. After a finite number of rounds, users' decisions can reach a fair-efficient network solution. If no user can benefit by changing his current selected strategy while the other users keep their strategies unchanged, all users find a satisfactory solution and do not change their strategies over a game processing time. This situation is defined as the system equilibrium. The main steps of the *IGMPC* scheme are given next.

Step 1: At the initial game iteration, users dynamically select their power level to maximize their payoff.

Step 2: The FAP estimate the degree of fairness ($F_{\mathcal{N}}$) by using (36).

Step 3: Based on the value of $F_{\mathcal{N}}$, the FAP select one rule ($f_{i,1 \le i \le 3} \in \mathcal{F}$) and intervenes to obtain a fair-efficient solution. The result of FAP's decision is the input back to users.

Step 4: By using (33) and (34), users iteratively re-estimate and adapt their power levels to maximize their payoffs. Also, the FAP periodically monitors the current network situation.

Step 5: In the step-by-step online manner, the FAP and users interact each other as an intervention device and game players. This interactive approach can analyze the current strategic decision in a distributed fashion.

Step 6: At the end of each game's iteration (i.e., *unit_time*), the FAP and users can dynamically adapt their decisions. It can control the tradeoff between efficiency and fairness.

Step 7: By using the dynamics of feedback-based repeated process, the femtocell network system maintains a fair-efficient status. If all users do not change their current strategies, they have converged to the system equilibrium.

Step 8: Constantly, the FAP and users are self-monitoring the current network situation. When a user drastically change his power level, it can re-trigger the power control algorithm; proceeds to Step 2 for the next iteration.

Recently, several power control schemes - the *Game Theoretic Power Control* (*GTPC*) scheme (Hong, 2009) and the *Energy-Efficient Power Control* (*EEPC*) scheme (Lu, 2012) - have been presented for femtocell networks. The *GTPC* scheme is a novel decentralized power control algorithm based on the game model. By considering fairness and loads of individual femtocells, the *GTPC* scheme sets up a payoff function to implement a game-based power control approach. The *EEPC* scheme presents a non-cooperative power control game for spectrum-sharing femtocell net-

Figure 5. Performance evaluations of the IGMPC scheme

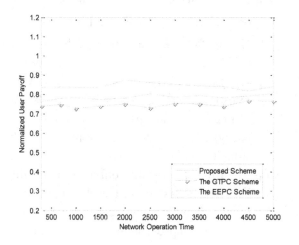

(a) Normalized payoff of users

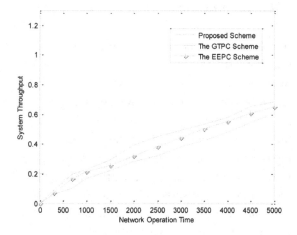

(b) System Throughput

works. To enhance energy efficiency, the *EEPC* scheme mitigates inter-tier interference for the uplink while achieving its target SINR. Figure 5 demonstrates that the performance of the proposed *IGMPC* scheme is generally superior to those of other existing schemes: the *GTPC* scheme and the *EEPC* scheme. Due to the inclusion of the adaptive feedback approach, the proposed *IGMPC* scheme constantly monitors the current network conditions and can strike an appropriate performance balance between conflicting requirements while other existing schemes cannot offer such an attractive performance.

Summary

For future 4G communication systems, femtocell networking is an emerging technology and can be extensively deployed with the aim of providing substantial improvements to cellular coverage and capacity. The *IGMPC* scheme has introduced a new femtocell network power control algorithm based on the no-regret learning technique and intervention game model. In the *IGMPC* scheme, power levels of users are adjusted dynamically in the step-by-step interactive online manner.

Simultaneously, the FAP periodically monitors the current network situation and intervenes to get a fair-efficient network performance. Therefore, based on the feedback learning process, the *IGMPC* scheme constantly monitors and adaptively handles the current femtocell network system to achieve the better benefit.

REFERENCES

Altman, E., Avrachenkov, K., & Garnaev, A. (2008). Generalized α-fair resource allocation in wireless networks. In *Proceedings of IEEE CDC*, (pp. 2414-2419). IEEE.

Altman, E., El-Azouzi, R., Hayel, Y., & Tembine, H. (2008). An Evolutionary Game approach for the design of congestion control protocols in wireless networks. In *Proceedings of Physicomnet workshop*. Academic Press.

Bachrach, Y., & Elkind, E. (2008). Divide and Conquer: False-Name Manipulations in Weighted Voting Games. In *Proceedings of International Conference on Autonomous Agents and Multiagent Systems*, (pp. 975-982). Academic Press.

Bachrach, Y., Meir, R., Zuckerman, M., Rothe, J., & Rosenschein, J. S. (2009). The cost of stability in weighted voting games. In *Proceedings of AAMAS*, (pp. 1289-1290). AAMAS.

Becerra, R. L., & Coello, C. A. (2006). Solving Hard Multiobjective Optimization Problems Using ε-Constraint with Cultured Differential Evolution. *LNCS, 4193*, 1611–3349.

Byde, A. (2003). Applying evolutionary game theory to auction mechanism design. In *Proceedings of IEEE International Conference on E-Commerce*, (pp. 347- 354). IEEE.

Chandrasekhar, V., Andrews, J., & Gatherer, A. (2008). Femtocell networks: a survey. *IEEE Communications Magazine, 46*(9), 59–67. doi:10.1109/MCOM.2008.4623708

Chenglin, Z., & Yan, G. (2009). A Novel Distributed Power Control Algorithm Based on Game Theory. In *Proceedings of International Conference on Wireless Communications, Networking and Mobile Computing*. Academic Press.

Chowdhury, M. Z., Bui, M. T., & Jang, Y. M. (2011). Neighbor cell list optimization for femtocell-to-femtocell handover in dense femtocellular networks. In *Proceedings of International Conference on Ubiquitous and Future Networks*, (pp. 241-245). Academic Press.

Dianati, M., Shen, X., & Naik, S. (2005). A New Fairness Index for Radio Resource Allocation in Wireless Networks. In *Proceedings of IEEE WCNC*, (pp. 712-715). IEEE.

Dziong, Z., & Mason, L. G. (1996). Fair-efficient call admission control policies for broadband networks-a game theoretic framework. *IEEE/ACM Transactions on Networking, 4*(1), 123–136. doi:10.1109/90.503768

Feng, N., Mau, S. C., & Mandayam, N. B. (2004). Pricing and power control for joint network-centric and user-centric radio resource management. *IEEE Transactions on Communications, 52*(9), 1547–1557. doi:10.1109/TCOMM.2004.833191

Ginde, S., Neel, J., & Buehrer, R. M. (2003). A game-theoretic analysis of joint link adaptation and distributed power control in GPRS. In *Proceedings of IEEE Vehicular Technology Conference*, (pp. 732-736). IEEE.

Hart, S., & Mas-Colell, A. (2000). A simple adaptive procedure leading to correlated equilibrium. *Econometrica, 68*(5), 1127–1150. doi:10.1111/1468-0262.00153

Hofbauer, J., & Sigmund, K. (2003). Evolutionary game dynamics. *Journal of Bulletin of the American Mathematical Society, 40*, 479–519. doi:10.1090/S0273-0979-03-00988-1

Holliday, T., Goldsmith, A. J., Glynn, P., & Bambos, N. (2004). Distributed. power and admission control for time varying wireless networks. In *Proceedings of IEEE GLOBECOM*, (pp. 768-774). IEEE.

Hong, E. J., Yun, S. Y., & Cho, D. H. (2009). Decentralized power control scheme in femtocell networks: A game theoretic approach. In *Proceedings of IEEE Personal, Indoor and Mobile Radio Communications*, (pp. 415-419). IEEE.

Hou, Y., Wang, Y., & Hu, B. (2010). Research on power control algorithm based on game theory in cognitive radio system. In *Proceedings of International Conference on Signal Processing Systems*, (pp. 614-618). Academic Press.

Kim, S. W. (2009). Adaptive online processor management algorithms for multimedia data communication with QoS sensitivity. *International Journal of Communication Systems, 22*(4), 469–482. doi:10.1002/dac.979

Kim, S. W. (2011a). An Adaptive Online Power Control Scheme based on the Evolutionary Game Theory. *IET Communications,5*(18), 2648–2655. doi:10.1049/iet-com.2011.0093

Kim, S. W. (2011b). Stackelberg Game-Based Power Control Scheme for Efficiency and Fairness Tradeoff. *IEICE Transactions, E94-B*(8), 2427-2430.

Kim, S. W. (2011c). QoS-Sensitive Dynamic Voltage Scaling Algorithm for Wireless Multimedia Services. *IEICE Transactions, E96-B*(1), 1745-1345.

Kim, S. W. (2013). Femtocell Network Power Control Scheme based on the Weighted Voting Game. *EURASIP Journal on Wireless Communications and Networking, 1*(44), 1–9.

Latifa, B., Gao, Z., & Liu, S. (2012). No-Regret learning for simultaneous power control and channel allocation in cognitive radio networks. In *Proceedings of IEEE ComComAp*, (pp. 267-271). IEEE.

Li, J., He, J., Zhang, Q., & Huang, S. (2009). A Game Theory Based WiMAX Uplink Power Control Algorithm. In *Proceedings of International Conference on Wireless Communications, Networking and Mobile Computing*. Academic Press.

Li, J., Shi, Z., Liu, W. Y., Yue, K., & Chen, R. J. (2010). No-Regret Learning for Cost Constrained Resource Selection Game. In *Proceedings of ICNC*, (pp. 2921-2925). ICNC.

Li, X., Qian, L., & Kataria, D. (2009). Downlink power control in co-channel macrocell femtocell overlay. In *Proceedings of Information Sciences and Systems* (pp. 383–388). Academic Press. doi:10.1109/CISS.2009.5054750

Li, Y., & Feng, Z. (2011). Enterprise femtocell network optimization based on neural network modeling. In *Proceedings of IEEE CCNC*, (pp. 1130-1131). IEEE.

Liu, Y., Peng, Q. C., Shao, H. Z., Chen, X. F., & Wang, L. (2010). Power control algorithm based on game theory in cognitive radio networks. In *Proceedings of International Conference on Apperceiving Computing and Intelligence Analysis,* (pp. 164-168). Academic Press.

Long, C., Zhang, Q., Li, B., Yang, H., & Guan, X. (2007). Non-Cooperative Power Control for Wireless Ad Hoc Networks with Repeated Games. *IEEE Journal on Selected Areas in Communications, 25*(6), 1101–1112. doi:10.1109/JSAC.2007.070805

Lu, Z., Sun, Y., Wen, X., Su, T., & Ling, D. (2012). An energy-efficient power control algorithm in femtocell networks. In *Proceedings of IEEE ICCSE*, (pp. 395-400). IEEE.

Mehmet, S., & Ramazan, K. (2001). A Comparative Study of Multiobjective Optimization Methods in Structural Design. *Turkish Journal of Engineering and Environmental Sciences, 25*(2), 69–78.

Menasche, D. S., Figueiredo, D. R., & Silva, E. S. (2005). An evolutionary game-theoretic approach to congestion control. *Performance Evaluation, 62*(1-4), 295–312. doi:10.1016/j.peva.2005.07.028

Meshkati, F., Poor, H. V., Schwartz, S. C., & Balan, R. V. (2006). Energy-efficient power and rate control with QoS constraints: a game-theoretic approach. In *Proceedings of IWCMC*, (pp. 1435-1440). IWCMC.

Mo, J., & Walrand, J. (2000). Fair end-to-end window-based congestion control. *IEEE/ACM Transactions on Networking, 8*(5), 556–567. doi:10.1109/90.879343

Niu, L., & Quan, G. (2006). Energy minimization for real-time systems with (m,k)-guarantee. *IEEE Transactions on VLSI Systems, 14*(7), 717–729. doi:10.1109/TVLSI.2006.878337

Niu, L., & Quan, G. (2009). Energy-Aware Scheduling for Practical Mode Real-Time Systems with QoS Guarantee. In *Proceedings of World Congress on Computer Science and Information Engineering,* (pp. 428 - 432). Academic Press.

Park, J. O., & Schaar, M. V. D. (2012). The Theory of Intervention Games for Resource Sharing in Wireless Communications. *IEEE Journal on Selected Areas in Communications, 30*(1), 165–175. doi:10.1109/JSAC.2012.120115

Park, J. O., & Scharr, M. V. D. (2011). *A Note on the Intervention Framework.* Los Angeles: University of California.

Tan, C. K., Sim, M. L., & Chuah, T. C. (2010). Fair power control for wireless ad hoc networks using game theory with pricing scheme. *IET Communications, 4*(3), 322–333. doi:10.1049/iet-com.2009.0225

Tao, Y., & Wang, Z. (1997). Effect of time delay and evolutionarily stable strategy. *Journal of Theoretical Biology, 187,* 111–116. doi:10.1006/jtbi.1997.0427 PMID:9236113

Wang, B., Han, Z., & Liu, K. J. R. (2006). Stackelberg game for distributed resource allocation over multiuser cooperative communication networks. In *Proceedings of IEEE Global Telecommunications Conference.* IEEE.

Wang, B., Jij, Z., & Liu, K. J. R. (2007). Self-Learning Repeated Game Framework for Distributed Primary-Prioritized Dynamic Spectrum Access. In *Proceedings of IEEE SECON,* (pp. 631 - 638). IEEE.

Wang, H., Choi, H., & Kim, J. (2008). Workload-Based Dynamic Voltage Scaling with the QoS for Streaming Video. In *Proceedings of IEEE International Symposium on Electronic Design, Test and Applications,* (pp. 236-239). IEEE.

Wang, H. M., Choi, H. S., & Kim, J. T. (2008). Workload-Based Dynamic Voltage Scaling with the QoS for Streaming Video. In *Proceedings of IEEE International Symposium on Electronic Design, Test and Applications,* (pp. 236 - 239). IEEE.

Xiao, Y., Park, J., & Schaar, M. V. D. (2012). Intervention in Power Control Games With Selfish Users. *IEEE Journal on Selected Areas in Communications, 6*(2), 165–179.

Xiao, Y., Shan, X., & Ren, Y. (2005). Game theory models for IEEE 802.11 DCF in wireless ad hoc networks. *IEEE Communications Magazine, 43*(3), 22–26. doi:10.1109/MCOM.2005.1404594

Yang, C., Li, J., & Li, W. (2009). Joint rate and power control based on game theory in cognitive radio networks. In *Proceedings of Fourth International Conference on Communications and Networking.* Academic Press.

Zappone, A., Buzzi, S., & Jorswieck, E. (2011). Energy-Efficient Power Control and Receiver Design in Relay-Assisted DS/CDMA Wireless Networks via Game Theory. In *Proceedings of IEEE Communications Letters.* IEEE.

Zhanjun, L., Chengchao, L., Yun, C., Huan, D., & Cong, R. (2010). An interference avoidance power control algorithm based on game theory. In *Proceedings of Second Pacific-Asia Conference on Circuits, Communications and System,* (pp. 414- 416). Academic Press.

Zuckerman, M., Faliszewski, P., Bachrach, Y., & Elkind, E. (2008). Manipulating the Quota in Weighted Voting Games. In *Proceedings of Conference on Artificial Intelligence,* (pp. 13–17). Academic Press.

KEY TERMS AND DEFINITIONS

Adjacent-Channel Interference (ACI): Interference caused by extraneous power from a signal in an adjacent channel. ACI may be caused by inadequate filtering, improper tuning or poor frequency control.

Bit Error Rate (BER): The number of bit errors divided by the total number of transferred bits during a studied time interval. BER is a unitless performance measure, often expressed as a percentage.

Code Rate: The proportion of the data-stream that is useful (non-redundant). That is, if the code rate is k/n, for every k bits of useful information, the coder generates totally n bits of data, of which n-k are redundant.

Interference: Anything which alters, modifies, or disrupts a signal as it travels along a channel between a source and a receiver. The term typically refers to the addition of unwanted signals to a useful signal.

Link Adaptation: A term used in wireless communications to denote the matching of the modulation, coding and other signal and protocol parameters to the conditions on the radio link.

Path Loss: The reduction in power density of an electromagnetic wave as it propagates through space. Path loss is a major component in the analysis and design of the link budget of a telecommunication system.

Chapter 11
Bargaining Solutions for Resource Allocation Problems

ABSTRACT

The first unified and systematic treatment of the modern theory of bargaining is presented together with many examples of how that theory is applied in a variety of bargaining situations. This chapter provides a masterful synthesis of the fundamental results and insights obtained from the wide-ranging and diverse bargaining theory literature. Furthermore, it develops new analyses and results, especially on the relative impacts of two or more forces on the bargaining outcome. Many topics—such as inside options, commitment tactics, and repeated bargaining situations—receive their most extensive treatment to date.

NASH BARGAINING BASED BANDWIDTH MANAGEMENT (*NBBM*) SCHEME

Bandwidth is an extremely valuable and scarce resource in wireless networks. Therefore, efficient bandwidth management plays an important role in determining network performance. For multimedia cellular networks, S. Kim proposed a new Nash Bargaining based Bandwidth Management (*NBBM*) scheme, which consists of adaptive bandwidth reservation and borrowing algorithms (Kim, 2011). Based on the well-known game theoretic concept of bargaining, wireless bandwidth is controlled as efficiently as possible while ensuring QoS guarantees for higher priority traffic services. Under dynamic network condition changes, control decisions in the developed algorithms are made adaptively to strike a well-balanced network performance.

DOI: 10.4018/978-1-4666-6050-2.ch011

Development Motivation

Nowadays, mobile networking technology needs to support an increasing range of services and the remarkable growth in the number of users. However, in spite of the emergence of high network infrastructures, wireless bandwidth is still an extremely valuable and scarce resource. Therefore, an efficient bandwidth management is very important and an active area of research over the last decade (Pati, 2007). A promising approach for the efficient wireless bandwidth usage is through the cellular concept. Cellular technology has greatly enhanced the network capability; the same bandwidth can be reused as much as possible by employing a collection of cells. This bandwidth reuse planning is an effective engineering task to improve the overall network performance (Kim, & Varshney, 2004).

Usually various multimedia data can be categorized into two classes according to the required QoS: *class I* (real-time) traffic services and *class II* (non real-time) traffic services. *Class I* data traffic is delay sensitive and *class II* data traffic is rather tolerant of delays. Based on different tolerance characteristics, *class I* data type has higher priority than *class II* data type. For next-generation multimedia cellular networks, the main challenge is to improve bandwidth efficiency while ensuring QoS for higher priority traffic services. To satisfy this goal, extensive research on bandwidth reservation and borrowing techniques has been carried out. Bandwidth reservation is a well-known strategy to enhance the network QoS. This strategy partitions available bandwidth and reserves some parts for higher priority services. To alleviate the traffic overload condition, bandwidth borrowing algorithms are developed. These algorithms migrate available bandwidth to approach perfect load balancing in cellular networks. The benefit of bandwidth reservation and borrowing strategies is to increase network QoS while maximizing the overall network performance (Kim, 2004).

Performance optimization is one of the most important issues in control problems. Until now, a lot of research dealing with performance optimization has been conducted. In 1950, John Nash introduced the fundamental notion of the Nash Bargaining Solution (NBS) to allocate the resource fairly and optimally. The NBS is a field of cooperative game theory and an effective tool to achieve a mutually desirable solution with a good balance between efficiency and fairness. In addition, the NBS does not require global objective functions unlike conventional optimization methods such as Lagrangian or dynamic programming (Park, & Schaar, 2007). Due to its many appealing properties, the basic concept of NBS has become an interesting research topic in a wider range of real life situations, such as economics, political science, sociology, psychology, biology, and so on.

In the *NBBM* scheme, effective bandwidth management algorithms are designed for multimedia cellular networks. Based on the concept of NBS, the developed algorithms effectively allocate the bandwidth among multiple services while providing the required QoS. Usually, the NBS has some attractive features to model the interactions among independent decision-makers and enforce collaborative behavior. However, due to some reasons, the classical NBS method cannot be directly applied to wireless network management. First, it is not amenable to complex non-convex problems; the utility space for the bandwidth allocation problem is not always convex (Suris, DaSilva, Han, & MacKenzie, 2007). Second, the traditional NBS was derived in the context of economics, so it is not appropriate for communication systems. Especially, a static one-shot game model is an impractical approach to justify realistic system operations. Third, due to the complexity of wireless network situations, mathematical modeling and numerical analysis have met with limited success.

The *NBBM* scheme was developed based on the NBS and would employ a dynamic online methodology for wireless network management, which can improve control adaptability and flexibility under widely different and diversified network situations. In the *NBBM* scheme, the traditional NBS method is modified to support dynamic network situations. By using the basic concept of NBS, the wireless bandwidth can be adaptively reserved and migrated to approximate the optimal network performance. The *NBBM* scheme consists of bandwidth reservation and borrowing algorithms. To strike an appropriate network performance, bandwidth reservation and borrowing strategies are incorporated in the *NBBM* scheme.

Nash Bargaining Solution

Traditionally, games can be divided into non-cooperative and cooperative games. In non-cooperative games, players are in conflict with each other and do not communicate or collaborate. Their preferences can be expressed as a utility function; players try to ensure the best possible consequence according to the utility function. Cooperative games, also called coalition games, are games in which players make binding commitments and find it beneficial to cooperate in the game. To reach an agreement that gives mutual advantage, players bargain with each other.

In cooperative games, the main interest is to fairly distribute the outcome to each player according to their contributions to make joint-agreements. Therefore, the cooperative game model is attracting for network resource management problems (Park, 2007), (Waslander, Inalhan, & Tomlin, 2004). The first cooperative game model was considered by John Nash for the case of a two-person game. Nash gave four axioms to provide the concept of efficiency and fairness - *Symmetry*, *Pareto optimality, Independence of irrelevant alternatives* and *Invariance with respect to utility transformations*. If the four axioms are satisfied, there exists a unique optimal solutio. This solution is called the Nash Bargaining Solution (NBS) (Park, & Schaar, 2007b), (Virapanicharoen, & Benjapolakul, 2004).

Based on the traditional game theory, the Nash bargaining solution can be formulated as follows. There are n players; player i has its own utility function (u_i). Assume $\mathbb{S} = \{(u_1, \dots u_n)\} \subset \mathbb{R}^n$ is a joint-utility solution set that is nonempty, convex, closed, and bounded feasible utility set. In the set $\mathbb{S}$, some solutions are characterized such that one player cannot increase his utility without decreasing the utility of any other players. This solution set is called as the Pareto optimal points/surface, which is payoff pairs in the cooperative trade-off area (Park, 2007, 2007b).

One agreement point u ($u \in \mathbb{S}$), which is an action vector in the Pareto surface, is a possible outcome of the bargaining process. A disagreement point (d) is an action vector $d = (d_1, \dots d_n) \in \mathbb{S}$ that is expected to be the result if players cannot reach an agreement. It is at least guaranteed for each user in the cooperative game. Therefore, the payoff at any agreement point is always

higher or equal to the payoff achieved at the disagreement point. The pair ($\mathbb{S}$, d) defines the bargaining problem; following is the formal definition of bargaining solution.

$$\prod_i (u_i^* - d_i) = \max_{u_i \in \mathbb{S}} \prod_i \left(u_i - d_i \right),$$

where $u_i^* \in \mathbb{S}$ and $d_i \in d$

(1)

In the game theory terminology, an outcome vector $< u_1^*, u_2^*, \,,, u_n^* >$ is called the NBS. Therefore, in the multiple Pareto optimal solutions, the NBS decides the best one, which can give a unique and fair-efficient solution that fulfills the Nash axioms (Park, 2007, 2007b).

Network Management Algorithms in the *NBBM* Scheme

Based on the Nash bargaining method, bandwidth reservation and borrowing algorithms in the *NBBM* scheme are designed as a cooperative game model and works together toward an optimal network performance.

Bandwidth Reservation Algorithm

Wireless cellular networks are comprised of a number of cells. Each cell is serviced by a base station (BS), which communicates with the users through wireless links. There is a node called the Mobile Switching Center (MSC) that works as a gateway to and from the wide area network. The MSC is responsible for a set of cells, called a cluster. Each cell in a cluster is assigned a different bandwidth.

The current trend in wireless cellular networks is to reduce the cell size to provide higher capacity and accommodate more users in a given area. When relatively small cell sizes are used, one of the main problems is that handoffs occur more frequently (Kim, 2004). In the handoff procedure, multimedia networks should support different bandwidth and

QoS requirements. From the user's perspective, abrupt interruption of a connected call is far more annoying than having a new call attempt blocked. To reduce the call dropping rate, some amount of bandwidth is reserved just for high-priority hand-off services. However, reservation strategy allows trading off between the desired QoS for handoff services and bandwidth utilization. Therefore, for the design of cellular network management, the critical issue is to determine adaptively the amount of reserved bandwidth while achieving high bandwidth utilization (Kim, 2004).

The NBS has some good features to understand the network control problems. Especially, due to the concept of fairness and efficiency, bandwidth management problems in the multimedia cellular networks have drawn a lot of interest in developing the NBS approach (Park, 2007, 2007b). In the *NBBM* scheme, an online bandwidth reservation algorithm is developed based on the NBS. For the adaptive online reservation, service requests are categorized into four different traffic groups. *Class I* handoff traffic services (*group I*), *class II* handoff traffic services (*group II*), *class I* new call traffic services (*group III*) and *class II* new call traffic services (*group IV*). According to the required QoS, *group I* traffic has higher priority over *groups II, III* and *IV*, and *group II* traffic has higher priority over *group III* and *IV*; *group III* traffic has higher priority over *group IV*. Based on the four traffic groups, the developed game model can be formulated as follows.

- **Players:** Traffic groups are assumed as players, which are denoted as P_1 (for *group I*), P_2 (for *group II*), P_3 (for *group III*) and P_4 (for *group IV*).

- **Strategies:** Four players (P_1, P_2, P_3 and P_4) have a finite number of strategies. The set of strategy for each player is the set of reserved bandwidth amounts. Let

$$S_{P1} = \{\alpha_1, \alpha_2, \cdots, \alpha_k\},$$

$$S_{P2} = \{\beta_1, \beta_2, \cdots, \beta_l\},$$

$$S_{P3} = \{\delta_1, \delta_2, \cdots, \delta_m\}$$

and

$$S_{P4} = \{\gamma_1, \gamma_2, \cdots, \gamma_n\}$$

be their respective strategy sets corresponding to the traffic types. The amounts of α, β, δ, and γ are dynamically defined based on game control rules.

- **Utility functions:** Each player has its own utility function, which represents the amount of satisfaction of a player toward the outcome of the game. The higher the value of the utility, the higher satisfaction of the player for that outcome. Recently, the concept of an utility function has been developed for the adaptive QoS model in wireless bandwidth management. To quantify players' satisfaction, the utility function for player i (UR_i) can be derived from (Niyato, & Hossain, 2008).

$$UR_i = \frac{1}{1 - \omega_i} \max\left(0, \left[1 - \omega_i \times \exp\left(Pr_i\right)\right]\right),$$

$$where \ i \in \{1, 2, 3, 4\} \qquad (2)$$

where Pr_i is the call dropping Fair-Efficient Guard Bandwidth probability ($i =1$ or 2) or blocking probability ($i =3$ or 4). ω_i ($0 < \omega_i < 1$) is a control parameter of the player i's utility function. In particular, the larger the value of ω_i, the more sensitive is the utility to the Pr_i. Due to the required QoS and traffic characteristics, ω_i value is defined as $\omega_4 < \omega_3 < \omega_2 < \omega_1$. Each base station can keep traffic history based on real time measurements. Based on the traffic information such as inter-arrival time, bandwidth capacity, channel size, call duration time, Pr_i can be estimated according to the Erlang's formula (Niyato, 2008) like as

$$Pr_i = \frac{E^m}{m!} \;/\; \sum_{c=0}^{m} \frac{E^c}{c!} \qquad (3)$$

where E is the total amount of offered traffic in Erlangs and m is the number of communication channels for the group i.

In the developed bargaining game, each player is a member of a team willing to compromise his own objective to gain a total optimal solution - in other words, a Pareto optimal solution. By employing the NBS approach, the team players cooperate with each other and make a collective decision. The total payoff (i.e., utility) for the players is given by $UR_{1,2,3,4} = \{(UR_1, UR_2, UR_3, UR_4)\}$. If an agreement among the players cannot be reached, the payoff that the players will receive is given by the disagreement point $UR_{1,2,3,4}^d = (UR_1^d, \; UR_2^d, \; UR_3^d, \; UR_4^d)$; it represents payoffs when the game fails and the bandwidth reservations cannot be made. The desirable best solution for an utility quartet ($UR_1^*, \; UR_2^*, \; UR_3^*, \; UR_4^*$) is obtained as follows.

$$\left(UR_1^*, \; UR_2^*, \; UR_3^*, \; UR_4^*\right) = \arg \max_{1 \le i \le 4} \prod_i \left(UR_i - UR_i^d\right)$$
$$(4)$$

However, the *NBBM* scheme does not focus on trying to get an optimal solution based on the traditional bargaining solution itself, but instead, an adaptive online feedback model is developed to approximate the optimized network performance. To provide the online flexibility, each BS reserves bandwidth for players (*group I, II, III* traffic services) in a distributed manner. Under dynamically changing network environments, the current amount of the reserved bandwidth should be dynamically adjustable. In the *NBBM* scheme, the reservation amount of each *group I*

(or *group II, group III*) is defined as α (or β, δ,), and the remaining bandwidth (γ) is assigned for *group IV* services.

To find the adaptive reservation amount, the following control rules are developed. The first rule, the amounts of α, β, δ, and γ can be adjusted based on the priority.

- To support the *group I* service, the BS tries to use the reserved bandwidth α. If the α is not sufficient, the α increases by the requested bandwidth while decreasing the γ. If the γ is also not sufficient, the δ is used. If the δ is also not available, the β is used.
- To support the *group II* service, the BS tries to use the reserved bandwidth β. If the β is not sufficient, the β increases while decreasing the γ. If the γ is not available, the δ is used.
- To support the *group III* service, the BS tries to use the reserved bandwidth δ. If the δ is not sufficient, the δ increases while decreasing the γ.
- The α, β, δ, and γ are dynamically adjusted based on the amount of requested bandwidth.

Even though the first rule is applied, a call dropping or blocking can occur. To ensure high bandwidth utilization, the second control rule is employed. When a service request can not get the requested bandwidth, the amounts of α, β, δ, and γ are modified according to the NBS in (4). However, the static NBS approach is not applicable. For real world network operations, the current optimal solution may not be an optimum result in the future. Therefore, the *NBBM* attempts to find the best solution adaptively in real time. To reduce computation complexity, the amount of bandwidth reallocation is specified in terms of basic bandwidth units (BBUs), where one BBU is the minimum amount (e.g., 512 Kbps) of partition modification. In addition, for practical implementations, the time interval is also defined as the *grace_period*. During the *grace_period*, the α, β, δ, and γ amounts are only re-adjusted based on the first rule. Therefore, after getting the best solution according to (4), *grace_period* is stared to reflect the currently obtained solution and to avoid ping-pong effect of control decisions.

Bandwidth Borrowing Algorithm

During the operation of cellular networks, unexpected growth of traffic may develop in a specific cell. When some cells have a traffic load that is substantially larger than the design load, it may create local traffic congestion. In order to cope with the problem of traffic overloads, load balancing concept can be employed. In wireless cellular networks, the common meaning of load balancing is to ease out the heavy traffic load by borrowing bandwidth from other cells. Therefore, this strategy is expected to be efficient when the traffic in the cellular network is non-uniform due to temporal and spatial fluctuations.

The main goal of the bandwidth borrowing algorithm is to provide appropriate load balancing over time. For the purpose of efficient load balancing, each cell is evaluated in terms of the amount of its unused bandwidth; it is defined as its *degree of availability* (B_A). The average value of B_A in a cluster is defined as the *average degree of availability* (B_A^{avg}) of a cluster, which is computed as the arithmetic mean B_A of each cell in the cluster.

$$B_A^{avg} =$$

$$\frac{\text{Sum of } degree\ of\ availability \left(B_A \right) \text{ of each cell in the cluster}}{\text{Number of cells in the cluster}}$$

(5)

In the *NBBM* scheme, the cells are categorized into two states based on the available bandwidth; S-cell and P-cell. If the adjustable bandwidth for reservation changes is less than the one BBU, this cell is defined as a P status cell (P-cell). When the current B_A of a cell is more than the B_A^{avg} in the corresponding cluster (i.e., $B_A > B_A^{avg}$), this cell is defined as a S-cell. In a P-cell, the traffic load is very heavy in that the total available bandwidth has reached a critical low point. When a cell becomes a P-cell, the bandwidth borrowing algorithm, residing in the MSC, is triggered to balance the amount of available bandwidth among cells. By taking into account the underlying dynamics of the wireless network, the bandwidth borrowing algorithm is developed to approximate the ideal NBS. To satisfy this goal, the developed game model can be formulated as follows.

- **Players:** Base stations (BSs) in each cluster are assumed as players.
- **Strategies:** Players have a finite number of strategies. The set of strategy for each player is the set of possible bandwidth migration amounts. Let $S\_S_{Pi} = \{\eta_1, \eta_2, \cdots, \eta_r\}$ be his respective strategy set corresponding to the player i.
- **Utility functions:** To quantify players' satisfaction, the following utility function is defined as follows.

$$UB_i = \frac{(k_1 \times \alpha_i) + (k_2 \times \beta_i) + (k_3 \times \delta_i) + (k_4 \times \gamma_i)}{B},$$

where $1 \leq i \leq n$ (6)

where n is the number of players (i.e., BSs) and B is the total bandwidth capacity of each cell. The amounts of $\alpha_i, \beta_i, \delta_i,$ and γ_i are the current reserved bandwidth of the ith BS. k_i is a control factor, which can reflect the priority of each reserved bandwidth. The total payoff for the players is given by $UB_{1..n} = \{(UB_1,,, UB_n)\}$. If an agreement among the players cannot be reached, the payoff that the players will receive is given by the disagreement point $UB_{1..n}^d = (UB_1^d,,, UB_n^d)$. It represents payoffs when the game fails and the bandwidth migration cannot be made.

In the *NBBM* scheme, bandwidth migration rules are employed for the adaptive management of load balancing. First, for the lower implementation complexity, the lendable bandwidth (B_A) in each cell is migrated based on a number of BBUs. Second, only S-status cells can be a lender cell. Third, the goal of load balancing algorithm is to minimize the maximum B_A in the current cluster. Based on these assumptions, the desirable solution ($UB^*_{1..n}$) is obtained as follows.

$$UB^*_{1..n} = \arg \max_{1 \leq i \leq n} \prod_i \left(UB_i - UB_i^d \right) \qquad (7)$$

To decide the bandwidth borrowing, the MSC computes B_A^{avg} and selects suitable lender cells (S-cells). From the cell having the maximum B_A, one BBU is sequentially borrowed and the outcome is estimated by using (7). Based on the migration rules, the bandwidth borrowing procedure continues until the best one is obtained from a set of possible solutions. When a lender cell has become a P-cell, the borrower cell returns the borrowed BBUs to the lender cell. In accordance with real time measurements of current network conditions, this online approach can provide almost perfect load balancing in the cellular network.

The Main Steps of the *NBBM* Scheme

Traditionally, NBS has focused on problems with convex feasible sets. However, this extreme assumption might be too strong; the convexity assumption has been questioned and caused some technical difficulties. Usually, the feasible set for online control problems can be non-convex (Denicolò, & Mariotti, 2000), (Conley, & Wilkie, 1996). In the *NBBM* scheme, the bargaining concept is extended to domains that include non-convex problems to develop online bandwidth management algorithms. To find the best solution for non-convex and complex optimization problems, the basic concept of the Nash

bargaining solution (NBS) and adaptive online algorithms are combined. The main objective of the *NBBM* scheme is to find an adaptive solution that can retain several of the desirable features of the Nash solution without convexity. Therefore, it is designed to practically approximate the NBS by taking a selection from the set of the Nash products;.

Unfortunately, the obtained solution may not be the NBS and impossible to satisfy all Nash's axioms; this loss of optimality is acceptable as the cost of real network operations. However, to lessen this limitation, control decisions are dynamically adjustable by using the adaptive online technique. Therefore, the NBS-based online scheme iteratively re-negotiates the current control decisions by considering of dynamic network changes. Therefore, the *NBBM* scheme can provide a good tradeoff between the implementation complexity for the real world network management and optimized network performance.

Based on the online feedback process, the *NBBM* scheme focuses on how each player can adapt his behavior and act strategically to approximate an optimal network performance. To implement this bargaining process, the *NBBM* scheme is formulated as a cooperative and multistage repeated game. The main steps of the bandwidth management algorithms are given next.

Step 1: Each BS reserves bandwidth in a distributed manner. At the initial time, the available bandwidth is equally divided for *group I*, *II*, *III* and *IV* traffic services. This starting guess guarantees that each player enjoys the same benefit at the beginning of the game.

Step 2: When the α is not sufficient to support the *group I* service request, the α increases by the requested bandwidth while decreasing the γ. If the γ is not available to satisfy this request, the δ is used. If the δ is not sufficient to satisfy this request, the β is used. If the β is also not available, go to Step 6

Step 3: When the β is not sufficient to support the *group II* service request, the β increases by the requested bandwidth while decreasing the γ. If the γ is not sufficient to satisfy this request, the δ is used. If the δ is also not available, go to Step 6

Step 4: When the δ is not sufficient to support the *group III* service request, the δ increases by the requested bandwidth while decreasing the γ. If the γ is not available, go to Step 6.

Step 5: When the γ is not sufficient to support the *group IV* service request, go to Step 6.

Step 6: If the current cell is a P-cell, go to Step 8. Otherwise, each reservation amount can be modified based on the NBS.

Step 7: Based on the current network condition, the best solution for bandwidth reservation can be obtained according to (4). To reduce computation complexity, the amount of α, β, δ, and γ is sequentially re-adjusted by the size of one BBU.

Step 8: For the load balancing, the MSC select suitable lender cells (S-cells). To lessen computation overhead, the bandwidth migration is also sequentially operated by the size of one BBU.

Step 9: Based on the migration rules, the bandwidth borrowing procedure continues until

the best solution for load balancing can be obtained according to (7).

Step 10: When a lender cell becomes a P-cell, the borrower cell returns the borrowed BBUs to the corresponding lender cell.

Recently, several bandwidth control schemes for multimedia cellular networks have been presented. The *Game-theoretic Call Admission Control (GCAC)* scheme provides a suitable solution model for fair and efficient call admission control problems (Virapanicharoen, 2004). To select fair-efficient threshold parameters for the asymmetrical traffic, cooperative game theoretic algorithms are proposed. The *GCAC* scheme can reduce the computational complexity while still providing a proper consideration of efficiency and fairness. The *Dynamic Multiple-threshold Bandwidth Reservation (DMBR)* scheme is capable of granting differential priorities to different traffic classes by dynamically adjusting bandwidth reservation thresholds (Chen, Li & Fang, 2005). The main contribution of the *DMBR* scheme is to adjust the admission control policy by taking into account some dynamic factors such as offered load. Figure 1 demonstrates that the performance of the proposed *NBBM* scheme is generally superior to those of other existing schemes: the *GCAC*

Figure 1. Performance evaluations of the NBBM scheme

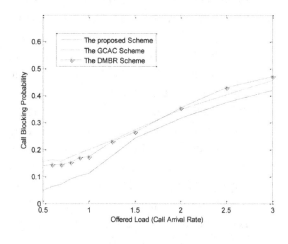

(a) Call Blocking Probability (CBP)

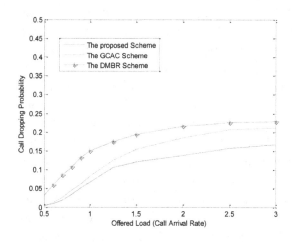

(b) Call Dropping Probability (CDP)

scheme and the *DMBR* scheme. By cooperation, coordination and collaboration of the reservation and borrowing algorithms, the proposed *NBBM* scheme can balance appropriate network performance while other schemes cannot offer such an attractive network performance.

Summary

Recently, multimedia applications are emerging, and they are deployed over bandwidth limited cellular networks. Therefore, efficient and flexible bandwidth management algorithms have attracted much attention and rapidly growing a critical issue. The *NBBM* scheme is presented based on the NBS. NBS method can help to solve the key control problems and be practicable to find the best one from a set of possible Pareto solutions for QoS sensitive multimedia networks. In addition, to provide a reasonable compromise between efficiency and QoS provisioning, the *NBBM* scheme is designed by employing two different online algorithms; bandwidth reservation and migration algorithms. Based on the best compromise strategy, the network system can display desirable properties while maintaining the crucial notion of NBS, which can approximate the global system optimization.

NASH BARGAINING BASED VOLTAGE SCALING (*NBVS*) SCHEME

In an effort to reduce energy consumption, research into adaptive power management in real-time systems has become widespread. Recently, S. Kim proposed a new Nash Bargaining based Voltage Scaling (*NBVS*) scheme for multiprocessor systems (Kim, 2011b). Based on the concept of the Nash bargaining solution, a processor's clock speed and supply voltage are dynamically adjusted to satisfy these conflicting performance metrics. In addition, the developed algorithm is implemented to react adaptively to the current system conditions by using an adaptive online approach.

Development Motivation

With the advanced technology of very large-scale integration (VLSI) circuit designs, modern embedded systems have evolved from a uniprocessor to a multiprocessor approach to enhance performance. Therefore, the use of multiprocessor systems is dramatically increasing and becoming the de-facto standard (Khan, & Ardil, 2009), (Mochocki, Hu, & Quan, 2002). In addition, applications in a multiprocessor system are consuming more energy due to the continuously increasing functionality. To support these energy-consuming task services, energy-aware multiprocessor system design has become a new frontier research field.

The dynamic voltage scaling (DVS) technique has been investigated extensively and several commercial DVS microprocessors have been developed (Mochocki, Hu, & Quan, 2007). A significant feature of DVS processors is in changing the operational voltage and frequency dynamically to adapt to current system conditions. Since power consumption has a quadratic dependency on the supply voltage, lowering the supply voltage is the most effective way to enhance system efficiency. However, many different applications, namely avionics, traffic control, automated factories, and military systems have specific requirements based on different characteristics, that is, execution cycles and a relative deadline; task services need to guarantee its deadline to ensure required quality of service (QoS). Therefore, DVS systems should consider the timing issue to meet deadline requirements. However, between energy efficiency and QoS provisioning, there is usually a tradeoff involved. To carefully balance among conflicting performance criteria, voltage scaling becomes a more challenging and complex control problem in real-world system operations (Mochocki, 2007), (Irani, Shukla, & Gupta, 2003).

The fundamental problem faced by control algorithms is to design a decision mechanism; an effective decision mechanism is a key factor for system performance. Game theory is a field of applied mathematics that provides an effective tool in modeling the interactions among independent decision makers In 1950, John Nash introduced a new model of cooperative game theory, that is, the Nash bargaining solution (NBS), to allocate resources fairly and optimally (Park, 2007), (Suris, 2007). The NBS can achieve a mutually desirable solution with a good balance between efficiency and fairness. In addition, the NBS does not require global objective functions, unlike conventional optimization methods, such as Lagrangian or dynamic programming. Based on these appealing properties, the basic concept of the NBS has found widespread use in many engineering fields. The *NBVS* scheme adopts the NBS model to design a real-time DVS control algorithm. However, for various reasons, the classical NBS method cannot be directly applied to the processor power management. First, the traditional NBS was derived in the context of economics, so it is not appropriate for dynamic multiprocessor systems. Second, a static one-shot game model is an impractical approach to justify realistic system operations. Third, it is technically unable to take into account complex interactions for multiple objectives. In addition, due to the model complexity, it is not amenable to mathematical modeling and numerical analysis.

The *NBVS* scheme is developed as a new online multiprocessor power control scheme based on the NBS model, and would employ a dynamic online methodology for power management, which can improve adaptability under widely different and diversified multiprocessor system situations. The main design goal of the *NBVS* scheme is to simultaneously maximize energy efficiency while ensuring all task deadlines.

Power Management Algorithm in the *NBVS* Scheme

Based on current system conditions, individual tasks are scheduled to globally optimize system performance. To get a satisfactory solution, processors adjust their power levels according to the NBS model and schedule tasks in an online interactive manner.

Basic System Model

Multiprocessor systems use two or more processors to execute tasks. Therefore, efficient task assignment to multiprocessors is one of the key issues for the effective system utilization. In the *NBVS* scheme, a new task scheduling algorithm is developed to adaptively spread workload among processors while ensuring energy efficiency for the total task processing.

As mentioned earlier, one promising power and energy reduction technique is voltage control. However, there is a power-delay tradeoff by controlling the supply voltage. For instance, under the Dhrystone 1.1 benchmark programs, an ARM7D processor can run at 33 MHz and 5 V as well as at 20 MHz and 3.3 V. The energy-performance measures at these two operation modes are 185 MIPS/watt and 579 MIPS/watt, and the MIPS measures are 30.6 and 19.1, respectively. Thus, if a system switches from 33 MHz and 5 V to 20 MHz and 3.3 V, there will be around (579–185)/579=68% reduction in energy consumption at an expense of (30.6–19.1)/19.1=60% increase of processing time (Burd, & Brodersen, 1996).

The *NBVS* scheme defines Ψ as the set of accepted service requests *sr* by the real-time system, $\Psi = \{sr_1, sr_2, sr_3, ..., sr_i, ..., sr_n\}$, where n is the total number of accepted services, that is, $n = \|\Psi\|$. During real-world system operations, n is dynamically changed. The service request i is characterized by $\{a_i, d_i, t\_c_i\}$ where a_i is the arrival time, d_i is the deadline, and t_c_i is the total workload of service sr_i to be completed.

In the DVS system, processors have different power states according to the set of voltage levels; each power state of a processor is characterized by a different speed (performance). Therefore, between its arrival time and the deadline, task services are amenable to adaptation with a variable processor speed, which is defined as a discrete voltage level with multiple grades of clock frequency. At the current time c_t, processor j's speed $S_{p\_j}(c_t)$ is defined as the sum of the assigned processor frequency level for each running service, which is given by

$$S_{p\_j}\left(c_t\right) = \sum_{i=1}^{n}\left\{PS_i\left(c_t\right) \times A\left(i,j\right)\right\}, \qquad (8)$$

where $A\left(i,j\right) = \begin{cases} 1 & if \, sr_i \, is \, accepted \, to \, the \, processor \, j, \\ 0 & otherwise, \end{cases}$

where n is the total number of requested tasks, and $PS_i(c_t)$ is the frequency level (speed) for the task i service at the current time.

When the offered system load is heavy, that is, the sum of the requested tasks exceeds the available processor capacity, an admission control algorithm needs to be employed. Based on the acceptance condition, the admission procedure makes a decision whether to accept a requested task or not.

Acceptance condition:

$$\max_{1<j<k}\left[\int_{c_t}^{d_t} MP_j\left(t\right)dt - \int_{c_t}^{d_t} S_{p\_j}\left(t\right)dt\right] \geq t\_c_i, \qquad (9)$$

where MP_j is the maximum speed (total processor computation capacity) of the processor j, and k is the total number of processors in the system. When a new task arrives, this task is accepted if the system meets the acceptance condition. Otherwise, the new requested task cannot be completely served within the deadline; the requested task is rejected.

Bargaining Model for Dynamic Voltage Scaling Algorithm

Based on physical law, energy is reduced in direct proportion to the processor power state; it is more energy efficient to slow down the processor power as much as possible. However, due to the required QoS, the time deadline should not be overlooked altogether. In the *NBVS* scheme, to approximate the optimal voltage, the developed multiprocessor power control algorithm is developed as a cooperative game model. Usually, the cooperative game approach is attractive for resource allocation and load balancing problems (Park, 2007), (Suris, 2007). The first cooperative game model was conceived by John Nash. Based on traditional game theory, Nash proposed the NBS, which can be formulated as follows: there are n players; player i has its own utility function (u_i). Assume $\mathbb{S} = \{(u_1,..., u_n)\} \subset \mathbb{R}^n$ is a joint-utility solution set that is a nonempty, convex, closed, and bounded feasible utility set. In set $\mathbb{S}$, some solutions are characterized such that one player cannot increase his utility without decreasing the utility of any other players. This solution set is called as the Pareto optimal points/surface, which are payoff pairs in the cooperative tradeoff area (Park, 2007).

One agreement point $\boldsymbol{u}$ ($\boldsymbol{u} \in \mathbb{S}$), which is an action vector in the Pareto surface, is a possible outcome of the bargaining process. A disagreement point $\boldsymbol{d}$ is an action vector $\boldsymbol{d} = (d_1, ..., d_n)$ $\in \mathbb{S}$ that is expected to be the result if players cannot reach agreement. This, at least, is guaranteed for each user in the cooperative game. Therefore, the payoff at any agreement point is always higher or equal to the payoff achieved at the disagreement point. The pair ($\mathbb{S}$, $\boldsymbol{d}$) defines the bargaining problem. The bargaining solution can formally be defined as

$$\prod_i \left(u_i^* - d_i\right) = \max_{u_i \in S} \prod_i \left(u_i - d_i\right),$$

where $u_i^* \in S$ and $d_i \in \boldsymbol{d}$. (10)

In game theory terminology, an outcome vector $u_1^*, u_2^*, \ldots, u_n^*$ is called the NBS. Therefore, in multiple Pareto optimal solutions, the NBS decides the best one, that is, the one which can give a unique and fair-efficient solution (Park, 2007).

The main advantage of using the NBS is that the overall management strategy allows use of lower level information, freeing itself from the need to execute complex algorithms. Especially, with the concept of fairness and efficiency, the NBS has some good features to develop control algorithms. The *NBVS* scheme is an adaptive voltage scaling algorithm based on the basic concept of the NBS. Based on multiprocessors, the developed game model can be formulated as follows.

- **Players:** Processors are assumed to be players.
- **Strategies:** Each player has a finite number of strategies. The strategy for each player is the voltage level; the DVS processor's voltage level is related to an associated processor speed.
- **Utility functions:** Each player has a utility function which represents the amount of satisfaction of a player toward the outcome of the game; the higher the value of the utility, the higher satisfaction of the player for that outcome. In the developed game model, the energy efficiency and timing requirement are considered simultaneously to quantify a player's satisfaction.

To provide a reliable and energy efficient solution for multimedia applications, the utility func-

tion should take into account QoS requirements and voltage/energy consumption at the same time. In the *NBVS* scheme, two utility functions F_e and F_d are defined by using current system information. Based on the adaptive online manner, these functions for the processor j can dynamically estimate the degree of energy efficiency and QoS level as

$$F_e\left(c_t\right) = \left(1 - \frac{S_{p\_j}\left(c_t\right)}{MP_j}\right)^2$$

and

$$F_d\left(c_t\right) = 1 - \left(\frac{1}{S_{p\_j}\left(c_t\right)} \times \sum_{i=1}^{n} \frac{R_i\left(c_t\right) \times A\left(i, j\right)}{fd_i - c_t}\right)$$

(11)

where $R_i(c_t)$ and fd_i are the amount of remaining workload at the current time and the time deadline of the service i, respectively.

To provide the best compromise of the F_e and F_d functions, the developed algorithm uses a well-known weighted-average multiobjective optimization method (Mehmet, & Ramazan, 2001). Finally, the utility function for player i (UF_i) is defined as

$$UF_i = \left[\left(1 - \gamma\right) \times F_e\left(v_c\right)\right] + \left[\gamma \times F_d\left(c_t\right)\right],$$ (12)

where the parameter γ controls the relative weights given to energy efficiency and the time deadline. Under diverse system environments, a fixed value for γ cannot effectively adapt. The *NBVS* scheme treats this as an online decision problem and adaptively modifies the γ value. When a new task request is rejected, the *NBVS* scheme can put more emphasis on the processor capacity, that is, on the F_d. In this case, a higher value of γ is more suitable. When all recent task requests are accepted, energy efficiency must be considered more seriously. Therefore, the *UF* should strongly depend on the F_e. In this case, a lower value of γ is more suitable. By considering the mutual-interaction relationship, the value of γ is dynamically adjusted based on the recent task blocking probability (TBP), which is the ratio of rejected tasks to the recently requested n tasks. Therefore, in the developed model, the current TBP value is assigned to the γ. By using this real-time online monitoring, the system can be more responsive to current system conditions.

Metaphorically speaking, each processor is a member of a team willing to compromise its own objective to gain a total optimal solution–in other words, a Pareto optimal solution. By employing the NBS model, the team players cooperate with each other and make a collective decision. If an agreement among the k players cannot be reached, the payoff that the players will receive is given by the disagreement point $UF^d = \left(UF_1^d, \ldots, UF_k^d \right)$, for example, 0 in the system. Finally, the desirable best solution, $UF^* = \left(UF_1^*, \ldots, UF_k^* \right)$ is given by

$$UF^* = \underset{1 \leq i \leq k}{\operatorname{argmax}} \prod_i \left(UF_i - UF_i^d \right). \qquad (13)$$

In the multiprocessor system, the task scheduler collectively controls a new task allocation for the best system performance. The developed algorithm transforms the task scheduling problem into the celebrated NBS model. According to (9), (12), and (13), a fair-efficient solution is obtained under widely different and diversified system situations.

Due to the adaptive online approach, the parameters in the NBVS scheme are flexible, adaptable, and able to sense dynamic changing current environments. Therefore, an important design principle underlying the developed algorithm is real-time decision making to solve the NBS model. It is essential in order to be close to the optimized system performance and can ensure efficient system performance.

The Main Steps of the *NBVS* Scheme

During task execution in multiprocessor systems, the system should adaptively schedule the requested workload. In order to dynamically schedule the accepted tasks in real-time, an adaptive online approach becomes more effective. In the *NBVS* scheme, the multiprocessor system constantly monitors current conditions and dynamically changes the control parameters. Therefore, the *NBVS* scheme can adjust adaptively past decision inaccuracies and repeatedly estimate the *UF* value for each processor. With only current information, the system can act to maximize the corresponding utility payoff. To approximate the optimized system performance, the main steps for the *NBVS* scheme are given next.

Step 1: When a new task request arrives, the task admission algorithm decides whether to accept this task or not according to (9).

Step 2: If a new task is rejected, go to step 5. Otherwise, this task is assigned a specific processor; proceed to step 3.

Step 3: Processors, which are satisfying the acceptance condition, estimate the F_e and F_d functions and get the *UF* based on the possible outcomes.

Step 4: An accepted task is assigned to a specific processor by using (13).

Step 5: When a running task is completed, the processor speed (frequency level) is re-adjusted to maximize the *UF* according to (12).

Step 6: To adaptively estimate the *UF*, the current system *TBP* value is assigned to the γ.

Step 7: The system is constantly self-monitoring the current system situation.

Recently, several DVS control schemes have been presented for the processor power management. The Energy Efficient Power Control (*EEPC*) scheme provides a suitable solution model for the power-aware control problem (Khan, 2009). For dynamic environments, the *EEPC* scheme also investigates resource allocation techniques to control real-time multiple tasks. The Transition-overhead Aware Voltage Scheduling (*TAVS*) scheme is designed to reduce the energy consumption of systems by considering transition time and energy overhead (Mochocki, 2007). Therefore, the *TAVS* scheme can effectively estimate the actual execution cycles and lead to better transition overhead management. Figure 2 demonstrates that the performance of the proposed *NBVS* scheme is generally superior to those of other existing schemes: the *EEPC* scheme and the *TAVS* scheme. From the simulation results, it can be seen that the proposed *NBVS* scheme based on the NBS model generally exhibits superior performance compared with the other existing schemes under light to heavy system load distributions.

Summary

The dynamic voltage scaling (DVS) technique plays a key role in real-time systems to reduce energy consumption. The *NBVS* scheme is a new DVS scheme for real-time multiprocessor systems.

Based on the NBS approach, the voltage-clock scaling problem is modeled as a cooperative game model. The novelty of the developed approach is its adaptability, flexibility, and responsiveness to current system conditions. This feature is highly desirable for real-time system management. Simulation results clearly indicate that the *NBVS* scheme provides well-balanced system performance among contradictory criteria, while other existing schemes cannot offer such an attractive system performance.

KALAI-SMORODINSKY BARGAINING BASED BANDWIDTH ADJUSTMENT (*KSBBA*) SCHEME

Virtual Private Network (VPN) is a cost effective method to provide integrated multimedia services. Usually heterogeneous multimedia data can be categorized into different types according to the required Quality of Service (QoS). Therefore, VPN should support the prioritization among different services. In order to support multiple types of services with different QoS requirements, efficient bandwidth management algorithms are

Figure 2. Performance evaluations of the NBVS scheme

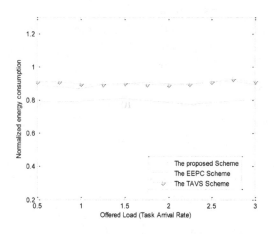

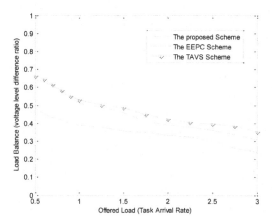

(a) Normalized energy consumption   (b) Load balancing in the multi-processor system

important issues. Recently, S. Kim proposed a new Kalai-Smorodinsky Bargaining based Bandwidth Adjustment (*KSBBA*) scheme (Kim, 2010). The *KSBBA* scheme employed the *Kalai-Smorodinsky* Bargaining Solution (KSBS) for the development of an adaptive bandwidth adjustment algorithm. In addition, to effectively manage the bandwidth in VPNs, the developed control paradigm is realized in a dynamic online approach, which is practical for real network operations.

Development Motivation

The current number of hosts in the Internet is approaching half billion. Such huge number is spread across many administrative domains, organized in a hierarchical structure, to cope with complexity and scale. Recently, corporations, organizations and facilities across the world are facing the problem of interconnecting their sub-networks. Within this scenario, Virtual Private Networks (VPNs) can package and ship user data from multiple access points to the corresponding destinations by using public networks such as Internet. Therefore, over the past years, a wide range of network architectures and technologies has been proposed to support the VPN services (Cui, & Bassiouni, 2003).

The functionality for services in VPNs should include the performance guarantee to users. Many of VPN users' applications not only require different amounts of bandwidth but also have different QoS requirements. Therefore, VPN should take into account the prioritization among different services (Rhee, Yoon, Choi, & Choi, 2001). To provide guaranteed QoS services, the network bandwidth should be shared appropriately to multiple users. For the implementation of bandwidth sharing mechanism, the bandwidth capacity should be dynamically shared into different application types and assigned to the organizations.

The bandwidth sharing among the participating service users is modeled as a bargaining problem. A solution to the bargaining problem enables the users to fairly and optimally determine their bandwidth allocation. There are two well-known bargaining solutions; the *Nash* bargaining solution (NBS) and the *Kalai-Smorodinsky* bargaining solution (KSBS) (Park, 2007). These solutions exhibit important properties that can be used for effective resource allocation. The NBS is a field of cooperative game theory and is an effective tool to achieve a mutually desirable solution with a good balance between efficiency and fairness. However, NBS has focused on problems with convex feasible sets. This extreme assumption might be too strong; the convexity assumption has been questioned and caused some technical difficulties. Usually, the feasible set for network control problems may be non-convex. In 1975, *Kalai* and *Smorodinsky* introduced the fundamental notion of the *Kalai-Smorodinsky* Bargaining Solution (KSBS) to allocate the resource fairly and optimally. KSBS can be used when the feasible utility set is not convex and does not require global objective functions unlike conventional optimization methods such as *Lagrangian* or dynamic programming. Due to its many appealing properties, the basic concept from KSBS has become an interesting research topic in network bandwidth management problems.

Motivated by the above discussion, the *KSBBA* scheme is designed as an effective online bandwidth adjustment algorithm for VPNs. By using the basic concept of KSBS model, the bandwidth can be adaptively adjusted to approximate the optimal network performance.

Bandwidth Adjustment Algorithm in the *KSBBA* Scheme

In cooperative games, the main interest is to fairly distribute the outcome to each player according to their contributions to make joint-agreements. Therefore, the cooperative game model is attractive for network resource management problems. To satisfy QoS requirements, the *KSBBA* scheme is proposed as an online bandwidth adjustment algorithm based on the KSBS model. KSBS gave four axioms to provide the concepts of efficiency and fairness - *Symmetry*, *Pareto optimality*, *Individual monotonicity* and *Invariance with respect to utility transformations*. If the four axioms are satisfied, there exists a unique optimal solution. This solution is called the *Kalai-Smorodinsky Bargaining Solution* (KSBS) (Park, 2007). To implement the adaptive bandwidth adjustment mechanism in VPNs, the *KSBBA* scheme is formulated as a game model:

- **Players:** Application data types are assumed as players, which are denoted as P_i (for type i), where $1 \leq i \leq n$. In the developed model, four different data types are assumed as players based on the required QoS.
- **Strategies:** Players have a finite number of strategies. The set of strategies for each player is the set of allocated bandwidth amounts. Let $S_i = \{\alpha_1, \alpha_2, \cdots, \alpha_k\}$ be the ith player's strategy set corresponding to its own traffic situations.
- **Utility functions:** Each player has its own utility function, which represents the amount of satisfaction of a player toward the outcome of the game. To quantify players' satisfaction, the utility function for player i (U_i) can be derived as follows.

$$U_i = \max\left(0, 1 - \exp\left(pr_i\right)\right) \quad (14)$$

where pr_i is the call blocking probability for player i. Based on the call arrival rate and holding time, pr_i can be obtained by using the well known Erlang's formula. Assume $\mathbf{S} = \{(U_1, \,,, U_n)\} \subset \mathbb{R}^n$ is a feasible utility set. The bargaining set $\mathbf{B}$ is the set of all individually rational, Pareto optimal payoff pairs in the cooperative payoff region $\mathbf{S}$. Therefore, in the solution set $\mathbf{B}$, one player cannot

increase his utility without decreasing the utility of any other players.

In the developed bargain ning game, each player is a member of a team willing to compromise his own objective to gain a total optimal solution. By employing the KSBS approach, the team players cooperate with each other and make a collective decision. If an agreement among the players cannot be reached, the payoff that the players will receive is given by the disagreement point $U_{1,,n}^d = (U_1^d ,,, U_n^d)$; it represents payoffs when the game fails and the bandwidth adjustment cannot be made. $U_{1,,n}^d$ can be the origin in the bandwidth allocation problem. Based on the $U_{1,,n}^d$ as a starting point, the line (L) is defined as follows.

$$L = \left\{ U \mid \frac{U_1}{\omega_1 \times U_1^{max}} = \ldots = \frac{U_n}{\omega_n \times U_n^{max}} \right\} \quad (15)$$

where $U_i > 0, \sum_{i=1}^n \omega_i = 1 \, and \, \omega_i \geq 0 \; for \, all \, i$

where U_i^{max} is the player i's payoff (i.e., utility) when the total available bandwidth is allocated. ω_i ($0 < \omega_i < 1$) is the player i's bargaining power, which is the relative ability to exert influence over other players. Usually, the bargaining solution is strongly dependent on the bargaining powers. If different bargaining powers are used, the user with a higher bargaining power obtains a higher QoS than the other players. Multimedia services have different required QoS over the same network. Therefore, the bargaining powers should be determined appropriately based on applications and network constraints. In the *KSBBA* scheme, determining the bargaining powers depends on a player's characteristics, i.e., $\omega_1 = 0.4$, $\omega_2 = 0.3$, $\omega_3 = 0.2$ and $\omega_4 = 0.1$. Therefore, the available bandwidth can be distributed to players based on the desired quality level for multimedia data. When two or more players have the same QoS requirement, they have identical bargaining power. In this case, the network bandwidth is shared equally to those players.

Geometrically, the KSBS is the intersection point (U_1^*,,, U_n^*) between the bargaining set **B** and the line *L*. Since the KSBS is located in the **B** as well as in the line *L* in (15), the bargaining solution must satisfy

$$\frac{U_1^*}{\omega_1 \times U_1^{max}} = \dots = \frac{U_n^*}{\omega_n \times U_n^{max}} \qquad (16)$$

The KSBS exhibits important properties that can be used for effective bandwidth adjustment. Since all players incur the same utility penalty by participating in the bandwidth management game, the KSBS can be interpreted as an utility-based fair bandwidth allocation.

Under dynamically changing network environments, the static KSBS is not applicable; the current optimal solution may not be an optimum result in the future. The *KSBBA* scheme does not focus on trying to get an optimal solution based on the traditional bargaining model itself, but instead, an adaptive feedback model is developed to approximate the optimized network performance. As network conditions change after bandwidth allocation, the developed model tries to find the best solution adaptively in the real-time online manner. To reduce the computation complexity, the amount of bandwidth adjustment is specified in terms of basic bandwidth units (BBUs), where one BBU is the minimum amount (e.g., 512 Kbps) of the bandwidth re-adjustment for optimal solution. Therefore, for practical implementations, the bandwidth allocation is sequentially negotiated by the size of one BBU.

To find the best solution for complex optimization problem, the *KSBBA* scheme combines the basic concept of the KSBS and adaptive online algorithm. The main objective of the

KSBBA scheme is to find an adaptive solution that can retain several of the desirable features of the *Kalai-Smorodinsky* solution. Based on the feedback process, the *KSBBA* scheme focuses on how each player can adapt his behavior and act strategically to approximate optimal network performance. To implement this bargaining process, the *KSBBA* scheme is formulated as a cooperative and multistage repeated game. The main steps of the developed bandwidth adjustment algorithm are given next.

Step 1: At the initial time, the available bandwidth is equally divided for four players (i.e, application data types). This starting guess guarantees that each player enjoys the same benefit at the beginning of the game.

Step 2: When a call blocking occurs, the currently allocated bandwidth is adjusted by one BBU to support this call service.

Step 3: One BBU from the allocated bandwidth for the other player is iteratively migrated.

Step 4: This bandwidth adjustment procedure continues to obtain a new KSBS according to (14), (15) and (16).

Step 5: A new bandwidth re-adjustment solution is achieved; game processing is temporary over.

Step 6: Under widely diverse network environments, the obtained solution is examined periodically - every specified time interval - to maintain the finest solution while avoiding ping-pong effect of control decisions.

Unfortunately, under various QoS constraints and a dynamically changing network traffic environment, the practically obtained solution may not be the exact KSBS; the *KSBBA* scheme accepts this loss of optimality as the cost of real network operations. However, to lessen this limitation, control decisions can be dynamically adjustable by using the adaptive online technique. By considering of dynamic network changes, the *KSBBA* scheme iteratively adjusts the bandwidth allocation.

When call requests are uniformly distributed over the network operation time, the developed algorithm can converge to the KSBS after a limited number of iterations. However, if the call request in the network is non-uniform due to temporal fluctuations, each player's utility value is changed dynamically. To approximate the optimized network performance, the interactive feedback process continues until the system would be stable. Therefore, the duration time of the developed algorithm is determined by the current network condition.

Summary

By constantly monitoring the current traffic conditions, the *KSBBA* scheme can balance appropriate network performance while other schemes cannot offer such an attractive network performance. In addition, the developed KSBS based bandwidth adjustment approach can provide a good tradeoff between implementation complexity and network performance. Based on the best compromise strategy, the network system can display desirable properties while maintaining the crucial notion of KSBS, which can approximate the global system optimization.

NEGOTIATION GAME BASED COOPERATIVE BANDWIDTH BARGAINING (*NGCBB*) SCHEME

Multi-hop Cellular Network (MCN) can preserve the advantages of traditional single-hop cellular networks and ad hoc relaying networks. In multi-hop network, efficient bandwidth management plays an important role in determining network performance. Recently, S. Kim proposed a new Negotiation Game based Cooperative Bandwidth Bargaining (*NGCBB*) scheme for MCNs (Kim, 2013). By integrating the *Nash* and *Kalai-Smorodinsky* bargaining models, the *NGCBB* scheme adaptively controls the wireless bandwidth to

maximize network efficiency. In the developed *Nash* and *Kalai-Smorodinsky* bargaining models, bargaining powers are decided according to the real-time negotiation process. It is a powerful method for resolving conflicts and enables the system to fairly and effectively control the bandwidth management problem.

Development Motivation

Recently, there has been increasing interest in integrating multi-hop relaying functionalities into cellular wireless networks. Multi-hop relaying can be used to assist communications to and from users at the cell edge or users experiencing deep fading in their home base station. This technology has greatly enhanced the network coverage and improved the overall network capacity. However, it requires effective control methods to improve bandwidth efficiency. When unexpected growth of traffic occurs in a specific relay station, wireless bandwidth should be dynamically migrated to approach a perfect load balancing. Therefore, an efficient bandwidth allocation algorithm is important to achieve maximum performance in MCNs (Le, & Hossain, 2007), (Park, & Jung, 2007).

A bargaining solution based on the cooperative game theory is an effective tool to achieve a mutually desirable solution between efficiency and fairness. Traditionally, the bargaining solution is obtained corresponding to the bargaining powers. Bargaining power is a concept related to the relative abilities of game players in a situation to exert influence over each other. To provide additional flexibility in choosing solution by taking into consideration the diversified network situation, it is necessary to admit differential bargaining powers. The *NGCBB* is a new bandwidth management scheme for multi-hop cellular networks. For the resource management problem, multiple bargaining solutions can be considered. The *Nash* Bargaining Solution (NBS) and the *Kalai-Smorodinsky* Bargaining Solution (KSBS) models can provide fairness and efficiency in the aspect of QoS; the efficiency is provided by the Pareto optimality requirement while fairness is achieved by satisfying the concept of equilibrium point. Therefore, the basic concept of NBS and KSBS was adopted to design the bandwidth management scheme. In addition, to adaptively adjust the bargaining powers, the *NGCBB* scheme presents a formal model of negotiation process. Negotiation is a dynamic process in which two or more negotiators with different preferences jointly reach a mutually acceptable agreement on the terms of a transaction (Bian, & Luo, 2007), (Sierra, Faratin, & Jennings, 1997). In the *NGCBB*, the purpose of the negotiation is to get an effective solution for bandwidth partitioning between different priority traffic services.

Bandwidth Allocation Algorithm in the *NGCBB* Scheme

Under diverse network conditions, the main challenge is to achieve the globally desirable goals such as bandwidth efficiency and QoS provisioning. To meet this objective, the *NGCBB* scheme is designed as a new bandwidth management scheme, which is composed of two different control algorithms; KSBS based bandwidth allocation algorithm and NBS based bandwidth partitioning algorithm. Based on the adaptive online approach, these algorithms are incorporated and act cooperatively to strike an appropriate performance.

KSBS Based Bandwidth Allocation Algorithm

By incorporating the flexibility of ad hoc networking, the MCN systems can increase system capacity, allow higher data rate services, and enlarge cell coverage; they are capable of achieving much higher throughput than current cellular systems. In MCNs, each cell is serviced by a base station (BS) and relay stations (RSs) are network elements deployed by BS for data delivery. The role of BS

is to allocate bandwidth for each RS to maximize network performance, and the role of RS is to adaptively partition the allocated bandwidth by estimating the current traffic situation.

During the operation of MCNs, unexpected growth of traffic may develop in a specific area. When some RSs have a traffic load that is substantially larger than the design load, it may create local traffic congestion. In order to cope with the problem of traffic overloads, load balancing concept can be employed. In the *NGCBB* scheme, the meaning of load balancing is to ease out the heavy traffic load by migrating bandwidth other stations. The KSBS has some good features to handle the bandwidth allocation problem for load balancing (Park, 2007). Therefore, the concept of KSBS can be applied to the bandwidth allocation algorithm to achieve an efficient and fair wireless bandwidth migration. In the developed KSBS model, RSs are assumed as game players and players have a finite number of strategies. The set of strategies for each player is the set of allocated bandwidth amounts. Each player (i.e., relay station) has its utility function, which represents the amount of satisfaction of a player toward the outcome of the game. To quantify players' satisfaction, the utility function for player i can be derived as follows.

$$U_i = \frac{A\_b(i)}{B(i)} \tag{17}$$

where $A\_b(i)$ and $B(i)$ are the currently using bandwidth and the total assigned bandwidth, respectively. To adaptively estimate the U_i value, the *NGCBB* scheme partitions the time-axis into equal intervals of length *unit_time*. In every *unit_time*, each RS monitors periodically its payoff (U) value and adjusts the available bandwidth dynamically in an online distributed manner. By employing the KSBS approach, the team players cooperate with each other and make a collective decision. The disagreement point $U_{1,n}^d = (U_1^d,$

..., U_n^d) can be the origin in the bandwidth allocation problem. Based on the $U_{1,n}^d$ as a starting point, the line (L) is defined as the same manner in the *KSBBA* scheme (Kim, 2010). Usually, the KSBS is strongly dependent on the bargaining powers (ω_i where $\sum_{i=1}^{n} \omega_i = 1$ and $0 < \omega_i < 1$). If different bargaining powers are used, the player with a higher bargaining power obtains a larger amount bandwidth than the other players. For the ω control procedure, the methodology that the *NGCBB* scheme adopted is the one-to-many negotiation mechanism. It can be treated as multiple, concurrent one-to-one bilateral negotiations; negotiation participants, i.e., game players, should not wait until having received offers from all its negotiation partners before generating counter-offers.

To implement a negotiation mechanism, the *NGCBB* scheme assume that negotiation process is divided into several rounds. Therefore, negotiation is a set of common sequential offers and counter-offers, which are represented by linearly ordered proposals (Sun, Zhu, Li, & Zhou, 2007). When the allocated bandwidth for a RS is fully used, the negotiation procedure is triggered. In the developed process, $\omega_{i \rightarrow BS}^1$ denotes the initial offering value proposed by the player i (i.e., i^{th} RS) to BS, and $\omega_{BS \rightarrow i}^2$ denotes the counter offering value proposed from the BS to the player i. In the *NGCBB* scheme, $\omega_{i \rightarrow BS}^1$ is estimated as follows.

$$\omega_{i \rightarrow BS}^1 = \omega_i^c + \text{"} \omega$$
$$\text{s.t.,} \quad \text{"} \omega = \text{"} \omega \times \nabla \delta^1 \tag{18}$$

where ω_i^c is the current bargaining power of the player i and $\Delta \omega$ is an increasing constant factor. $\nabla \delta^1$ ($0 \leq \nabla \delta^1 \leq 1$) is a discount factor for the initial offering (1th offering) ω value. $\nabla \delta^1$ is monotonic decreasing as negotiation goes by.

When the BS receives an offer ($\omega_{i \rightarrow BS}^1$) from the player i, the BS has to make a decision to accept this offer or not. If $\omega_{i \rightarrow BS}^1$ value is lesser than the value of the BS's counter-offer ($\omega_{BS \rightarrow i}^2$) value, the BS accepts the current offer ($\omega_{i \rightarrow BS}^1$). Otherwise, the counter-offer is submitted. The negotiation function NF^{BS} expresses this concept more formally:

$$NF^{BS}\left(1, \omega_{i \rightarrow BS}^1\right) =$$
$$\begin{cases} accept \, \omega_{i \rightarrow BS}^1 & , if \, \omega_{BS \rightarrow i}^2 \geq \omega_{i \rightarrow BS}^1 \\ \\ counter \, offer \, \omega_{BS \rightarrow i}^2 & , otherwise \end{cases} \tag{19}$$

In the *NGCBB* scheme, $\omega_{BS \rightarrow i}^2$ is obtained as follows.

$$\omega_{BS \rightarrow i}^2 = \omega_i^c + \left(\frac{U_i^c}{U_i^T} - \left(\frac{1}{n-1} \times \sum_{j=1, j \neq i}^{n-1} \frac{U_j^c}{U_j^T} \right) \right) \tag{20}$$

where U_j^T and U_j^c are the total allocated bandwidth and the currently using bandwidth for the player j, respectively. The result of $NF^{BS}\left(1, \omega_{i \rightarrow BS}^1\right)$ is used to extend the current negotiation process between the player i and BS; they negotiate with each other by proposing offers alternately. To prevent infinite offering rounds, negotiation process must have completed within a negotiation constraint. Finally, the developed negotiation process is defined as a finite sequence of the form $\left\{ \omega_{i \rightarrow BS}^1, \omega_{BS \rightarrow i}^2, \omega_{i \rightarrow BS}^3 \cdots, \omega_{BS \rightarrow i}^{max} \right\}$, where *max* is a constant that represents the maximum permitted rounds. If the negotiation does not reach an agreement within the negotiation constraint, $\omega_{BS \rightarrow i}^{max}$ value is forcibly set as a bargaining power for the player i.

Based on the obtained bargaining power, the developed algorithm dynamically adapts the amount of the expected allocated bandwidth. Therefore, the available bandwidth can be distributed to players adaptively. Geometrically, the KSBS is the intersection point (U_1^*, U_n^*) between the bargaining set **B** and the line *L*. Since the KSBS is located in the **B** as well as in the line *L*, the bargaining solution is obtained as the same manner in the the *KSBBA* scheme (Kim, 2010). In the *NGCBB* scheme, the developed bargaining model uses current information to provide more efficient control over network condition fluctuations. As network conditions change after bandwidth allocation, control parameters are decided in the real-time online manner and the developed model tries to find the best solution adaptively.

NBS Based Bandwidth Allocation Algorithm

When a user moves while a call is in progress, one of the main problems is handoff. From the user's perspective, abrupt interruption of a connected call is far more annoying than having a new call attempt blocked. If a connected call is terminated in the middle of service, user needs to restart everything to restore the disrupted service. Therefore, recently proposed bandwidth management schemes distinguish between new calls and hand-off calls, and give higher priority to hand-off calls in order to guarantee call's continuity; so the critical issue from QoS point of view is how to reduce the hand-off dropping probability.

To decrease the call-dropping rate while maintaining efficient bandwidth utilization, the wireless bandwidth should be shared dynamically. In the *NGCBB* scheme, a new NBS model was designed to solve the bandwidth partition problem. In the developed NBS model, two traffic classes are assumed as players. The set of strategies for each player is the set of allocated bandwidth amounts. Each player (i.e., traffic class) has its utility function. To represent each player's payoff, major concerns are QoS provisioning and band-

width efficiency. In the *NGCBB* scheme, two online functions (UF_1 and UF_2) were defined by using the current hand-off call dropping probability (D_P) and new call blocking probability (B_P). Based on the dynamic online manner, these utility functions for player *i* can be derived as follows.

$$UF_1 = \max\left(0, \left[1 - \exp\left(D\_P\right)\right]\right)$$

and

$$UF_2 = \max\left(0, \left[1 - \exp\left(B\_P\right)\right]\right) \quad (21)$$

Based on the traffic information such as inter-arrival time, bandwidth capacity, channel size, call duration time, D_P and D_P can be estimated according to the Erlang's formula (Niyato, 2008).

In each relay station, each player (i.e., *class I* traffic or *class II* traffic) is a member of a team willing to compromise his own objective to gain a total optimal solution - in other words, a Pareto optimal solution. By employing the NBS approach, the team players cooperate with each other and make a collective decision. The total payoff (i.e., utility) for two players is given by $TR_{1..2} = \{(UF_1, UF_2)\}$. If an agreement among the players cannot be reached, the payoff that the players will receive is given by the disagreement point $TR_{1..2}^d = (UF_1^d, UF_2^d)$; it represents payoffs when the game fails and the bandwidth allocation cannot be made (i.e., zero in the system). The desirable best solution for an utility quartet (UF_1^*, UF_2^*) is obtained as follows.

$$\left(UF_1^*, UF_2^*\right) = \arg\max_{1 \le i \le 2} \prod_i \left(UF_i - UF_i^d\right)^{\psi_i},$$
where $\psi_1 + \psi_2 = 1$

$$(22)$$

where ψ_1 is the bargaining powers of the player 1 (i.e., *class I* traffic) and ψ_2 is the bargaining powers of the player 2 (i.e., *class II* traffic). Based on the required QoS, players are asymmetric in their bargaining strengths. In the *NGCBB* scheme, the ψ value is dynamically adjustable to keep the QoS guarantee for higher priority services while ensuring bandwidth efficiency. When a handoff dropping occurs, ψ_1 value should be increased to satisfy the required QoS. Otherwise, the bandwidth is over allocated for higher priority services. Therefore, the over allocated bandwidth needs to be released for bandwidth efficiency.

By using a negotiation process as described above, players decide their ψ values in the same manner. However, due to the different traffic priority, the negotiation mechanism for ψ values provides two different processes. When a call dropping occurs, player 1 offers $\psi_{I \to II}^1$ to player 2, and $\psi_{II \to I}^2$ is the counter-offer. In the *NGCBB* scheme, $\psi_{I \to II}^1$ is estimated as follows.

$$\psi_{I \to II}^1 = \psi_1^c + \Delta\psi$$
$$\text{s.t.,} \quad \Delta\psi = \Delta\psi \times \nabla\delta^1 \qquad (23)$$

where $\Delta\psi$ is an increasing constant factor, and the discount factor ($\nabla\delta^1$) is monotonic decreasing in the same manner as used in (18). When player 2 receives an offer from player 1, the player 2 has to make a decision to accept this offer or not. If call blocking does not occur within the current *unit_time* ($B\_P = 0$), then the player 2 accepts the current offer ($\psi_{I \to II}^1$). Otherwise, the counter-offer is submitted. To implement this process, the negotiation function (N_F_{II}) is defined as follows.

$$N\_F_{II}\left(1, \psi_{I \to II}^1\right) =$$
$$\begin{cases} accept\,\psi_{I \to II}^1 & ,if\,B\_P = 0 \\ \\ counter\,offer\;\psi_{II \to I}^2 & ,otherwise \end{cases}$$
$$(24)$$

In the *NGCBB* scheme, $\psi_{II \to I}^2$ is obtained as follows.

$$\psi_{II \to I}^2 = \psi_{I \to II}^1 \times \left(1 - B\_P\right) \qquad (25)$$

where B_P is the call blocking probability at the current time. Therefore, it is dynamically changeable. Based on the result of $N\_F_{II}\left(1, \psi_{I \to II}^1\right)$, players negotiate with each other by proposing offers alternately. After the maximum constraint round of negotiation, players finally reach an agreement or not. If the negotiation process does not reach an agreement, players' control powers are forcibly set based on the last offer of the player 1, i.e., $\psi_1 = \psi_{I \to II}^{max}$ and $\psi_2 = 1 - \psi_1$; this decision is made by considering the traffic priority.

When a call blocking occurs, player 2 offers $\psi_{II \to I}^1$ to player 1, and $\psi_{I \to II}^2$ is the counter-offer. In the *NGCBB* scheme, $\psi_{II \to I}^1$ is estimated as follows.

$$\psi_{II \to I}^1 = \psi_2^c + \Delta\psi$$
$$s.t., \quad \Delta\psi = \Delta\psi \times \nabla\delta^1 \qquad (26)$$

When player 1 receives an offer from player 2, the player 1 has to make a decision to accept this offer or not. If $\psi_{II \to I}^1$ value is lesser than the value of the player 1's counter-offer ($\psi_{I \to II}^2$) value, then the player 1 accepts the current offer ($\psi_{II \to I}^1$). Otherwise, the counter-offer is submitted. The negotiation function (N_F_I) expresses this process as follows.

$$N\_F_I\left(1, \psi_{II \to I}^1\right) =$$
$$\begin{cases} accept\,\psi_{II \to I}^1 & ,if\,\psi_{I \to II}^2 \geq \psi_{II \to I}^1 \\ \\ counter\,offer\;\psi_{I \to II}^2 & ,otherwise \end{cases}$$
$$(27)$$

In the developed model, $\psi_{II \to I}^2$ is obtained as follows.

$$\psi_{I \to II}^2 = \psi_{II \to I}^1 \times \left(\frac{U_I^T - U_I^c}{U_I^T} \right) \tag{28}$$

where U_I^T and U_I^c are the total allocated bandwidth and the currently using bandwidth for the player 1, respectively. If players fail to reach an agreement, players' control powers are decided based on the last offer value of the player 1.

The Main Steps of the *NGCBB* Scheme

In the *NGCBB* scheme, a new bandwidth management scheme is developed based on the *Nash* and *Kalai-Smorodinsky* bargaining solutions. Especially, the *NGCBB* scheme does not focus on trying to get an optimal solution based on the traditional bargaining model itself. Under dynamically changing network environments, the traditional static approach is not applicable; the current optimal solution may not be an optimum result in the future. Therefore, the *NGCBB* scheme is designed based on the adaptive negotiation process to approximate the optimized network performance. By using the real-time online approach, payoffs are dynamically estimated and players iteratively modify their bargaining powers to achieve the better network performance. Based on the adjusted bargaining power, the *NGCBB* scheme dynamically adapts the amount of the expected bandwidth to provide a suitable balance between the desired QoS and high bandwidth utilization.

Step 1: At the initial time, the available bandwidth and bargaining power are equally divided for each relay station. In addition, allocated bandwidth is equally partitioned for each traffic services. This starting guess guarantees that each relay station and different priority

services can enjoy the same benefit at the beginning of the game.

Step 2: In every *unit_time*, relay stations monitor their utility functions by using (17); the base station collets this information to estimate $\sum_j U_j$.

Step 3: The bandwidth re-allocation procedure continues to obtain a new KSBS. To lessen computation overhead, the bandwidth is sequentially re-allocated by the size of one BBU.

Step 4: Under widely diverse network environments, the obtained solution is examined periodically to maintain the finest solution. By using (19) and (20), players dynamically adjust their ω values based on the negotiation process.

Step 5: After bandwidth re-allocation for relay stations, the allocated bandwidth is shared for different priority services by using NBS model. According to (22), bandwidth is partitioned adaptively between traffic *class I* and *class II*.

Step 6: By using (23)-(28), ψ values are re-adjusted adaptively, which are used to re-partition the available bandwidth in each RS.

Step 7: Under widely diverse network environments, base station and each relay station are self-monitoring constantly for the next iterative processing; go to Step 2. Therefore, the obtained solution is examined periodically to maintain the finest solution.

Recently, several bandwidth management schemes for multi-hop cellular networks have been presented. The Range Extension with Fixed Relays Networks (*REFRN*) scheme can significantly increase the network coverage by the employment of digital fixed relays (Huining, Yanikomeroglu, Falconer, & Periyalwar, 2004). In the *REFRN* scheme, a novel channel assignment method is developed to prevent potential capacity loss without any penalty in capacity. The Resource Allocation in Cellular Multi-hop Networks (*RACMN*) scheme presents effective scheduling algorithms for multi-hop network model (Newton, Thompson, & Naden, 2008). By employing the combination of round robin or equal throughput scheduling methods, the actual benefit of this scheme is to spatially reuse the wireless bandwidth for the network efficiency.

Figure 3 demonstrates that the performance of the proposed *NGCBB* scheme is generally superior to those of other existing schemes: the *REFRN* scheme and the *RACMN* scheme. From the simulation results, it can be seen that the proposed *NGCBB* scheme, in general, performs better than the other existing schemes under diversified network traffic condition changes.

Summary

In the *NGCBB* scheme, the bargaining concept is extended to develop an effective bandwidth management scheme. Based on the KSBS and NBS methodologies, the main objective of developed algorithms is to effectively allocate and share the wireless bandwidth. By constantly monitoring the current network condition, the developed bargaining models in the *NGCBB* scheme iteratively renegotiate the bargaining powers to approximate an optimal solution. Therefore, network system can obtain higher bandwidth efficiency while ensuring QoS for higher priority traffic services. In addition, the *NGCBB* scheme approach can provide a good tradeoff between the implementation complexity and the optimized network performance.

BLOTTO GAME BASED STRATEGIC RESOURCE ALLCATION (*BGSRA*) SCHEME

Security is a key concern around the world, particularly given the threat of terrorism. However, limited security resources prevent full security coverage at all times. Therefore, these limited resources must be deployed intelligently taking into account differences in priorities of targets requiring security coverage. Game theory is well-suited to adversarial reasoning for security

Figure 3. Performance evaluations of the NGCBB scheme

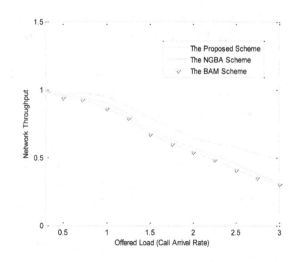

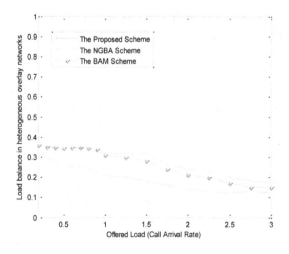

(a) Normalized Network Throughput   (b) Load balance in overlay networks

resource allocation and scheduling problems. Recently, S. Kim proposed a new Blotto Game based Strategic Resource Allocation (*BGSRA*) scheme for security problem. Blotto game constitutes a class of two-person zero-sum game in which the players are tasked to simultaneously distribute limited resources over several objects. For the efficient resource allocation, the *BGSRA* scheme employs the iterative bargaining approach to respond the current conditions.

Development Motivation

Security is a complex and challenging problem ranging from physical to cyber physical systems. Providing security for transportation systems, computer networks, and other critical infrastructure is a large and growing problem. However, security resources (e.g., police officers, canine units, or checkpoints) are limited. Therefore, these limited resources must be dynamically allocated to protect against a wide variety of potential threats. Traditional solution methods handle multiple security problems by enumerating all possible combinations of resource assignments. This approach grows combinatorially in the number of resources, which makes it computationally infeasible to solve large problems (Kiekintveld & Tambe, 2009), (Korzhyk, Conitzer & Parr 2011).

To efficiently allocate security resources, game theory is increasingly ranging from computer network security to terrorism. It is an important paradigm for modeling security domains which feature complex resource allocation. Most game theoretic approaches applied in security problems require attack-defense; the interactions between attackers and defenders may be formulated as non-cooperative behaviors which may then be described and solved using game theory. In 1921, French mathematician Émile Borel proposed the concept of Blotto game. This game is a two-person constant-sum game in which each player has

limited resources to distribute onto n independent battlefields without knowledge of the opponent's actions. The player who allocates a higher number of resources on battlefield i ($1 \leq i \leq n$) wins that battlefield and its associated payoff. Both players seek to maximize the expected number of battlefields won (Wittman, 2011). The Blotto game is a fundamental model for multidimensional strategic resource allocation, thereby widely applicable in fields from operations research, to advertising, to military and systems defense.

In the *BGSRA* scheme, a new strategic resource allocation algorithm is designed for security problems. In this scheme, a two-person (i.e., attacker and defender) constant-sum Blotto game model is adopted to formulate a security problem. Additionally, the key idea of an iterative bargaining approach is used for solving general Blotto games. Under dynamic changing situations, the *BGSRA* scheme can get globally desirable properties such as adaptability, feasibility and effectiveness for realistic system operations.

Recently, several strategic security resource allocation schemes have been presented for complex security control systems. The Intrusion Response as a Resource Allocation (*IRRA*) scheme in (Bloem, Alpcan & Basar 2006) is an algorithm for effective scarce resource allocation for responding to attacks. This scheme modeled the interaction between a malicious attacker and the intrusion detection system as a non-cooperative non-zero sum game. The Multi-Objective Genetic Security (*MOGS*) scheme in (Viduto, Maple, Huang & Bochenkov, 2012) developed a model of quantitative risk analysis to support effective decision making. This scheme determined the preferred trade-off between investment cost and resulting risk. The main novelty of the *MOGS* scheme is to demonstrate a decision support strategy when a selection of security countermeasures to be performed considering reduced risk and cost.

Security Resource Allocation Algorithms in the *BGSRA* Scheme

Algorithms for computing game-theoretic solutions have recently found several real-world applications to security, including the strategic allocation of checkpoints and canine units. Usually, security games are generally non zero-sum two-player games between a defender, who allocates defensive resources to targets (or subsets of targets), and an attacker, who chooses which target to attack. The attacked target determines both players' payoffs. If the target is defended by defender's resources, the defender's payoff increases while decreasing the attacker's payoff (Korzhyk, 2011). This leads to a key question of which game-theoretic model should be used to solve the security problem.

The Blotto game is one of the classic games of game theory. Two generals are competing in a battle over a certain number of battlefields. Each general has to decide how to divide his available troops amongst the fields. On each field, the side that deployed the most troops wins the battle. The general who divides his troops most effectively and wins the most battles wins the game. The Blotto game has far-reaching implications wherever multi-front division of resources is involved, including business, logistics, and political campaigns (Wittman, 2011).

To mathematically express the Blotto game for security problems, the *BGSRA* scheme assumes that an attacker (A) and a defender (D) have their private resources (X^A and X^D), and there are n battlefields. A and D have to allocate their X^A and X^D across all n battlefields, and compete all n battlefields simultaneously. D wins the battlefield i ($1 \leq i \leq n$) if $x_i^D > x_i^A$, where x_i^D (*or* x_i^A) is the resource allocation of D (*or* A) for the battlefield i. Let $\mathbb{S}^A$ and $\mathbb{S}^D$ denote the set of feasible resource allocations of A and B, respectively; they are n-dimensional vectors

$\left(x_1^A, \ldots, x_n^A \right)$ and $(x_1^D, \ldots, x_n^D)$. The payoff function (P_D) for D is defined as

$$P_D(\mathbb{S}^A, \mathbb{S}^D) = \sum_{i=1}^n f_i(x_i^A, x_i^D),$$

$$s.t., f_i(x_i^A, x_i^D) = \begin{cases} 1n\alpha, & \text{if } x_i^D > x_i^A \\ 1n\,{}^{\alpha_i}\!/_2, & \text{if } x_i^D = x_i^A \\ 0, & \text{if } x_i^D < x_i^A \end{cases} \quad (29)$$

where α_i is a weighted factor for the i battlefield. It is defined based on the relative importance of ith security issue. In the *BGSRA* scheme, there are n payoff functions ($f_i\left(x_i^A, x_i^D\right)$, where $1 \leq i \leq n$) for n battlefields. According to (29), $P_D\left(\mathbb{S}^A, \mathbb{S}^D\right)$ can be rewritten as follows.

$$P_D\left(\mathbb{S}^A, \mathbb{S}^D\right) = \ln(g_1 \times .. \times g_i \times .. \times g_n) = \ln\left(\prod_{i=1}^n g_i\right),$$

$$s.t., g_i \in \left\{ \alpha_i, {}^{\alpha_i}\!/_2, 1 \right\}$$

$$(30)$$

In the *BGSRA* scheme, all possible D's payoff pairs ($f_1\left(x_1^A, x_1^D\right), \ldots, f_n\left(x_n^A, x_n^D\right)$) that n payoffs jointly achieve form a feasible payoff set $\mathbb{S}^A$. In game theory, each player seeks to maximize his payoff function. To effectively obtain a solution, John Nash proposed a solution concept, called Nash Bargaining Solution (NBS), which is formulated by expected payoff functions over the set of feasible agreements and the outcome which would result in case of disagreement. NBS is an effective tool to achieve a mutually desirable solution by allocating the resource optimally. In addition, it does not require global objective functions unlike conventional optimization methods such as Lagrangian or dynamic programming. Due to its many appealing properties, the basic concept of NBS has become an interesting research topic in a wider range of real life situations.

In the *BGSRA* scheme, the defender (*D*) also tries to maximize $P_D\left(\mathbb{S}^A, \mathbb{S}^D\right)$ based on the NBS approach. Therefore, the main goal of *D* can be expressed as follows.

$$\mathbf{max} \ P_D\left(\mathbb{S}^A, \mathbb{S}^D\right) \cong \max_{g_i \in \mathbb{S}} \prod_{1 \le i \le n} g_i \cong \max_{g_i \in \mathbb{S}} \prod_{1 \le i \le n} \left(g_i - d_i\right),$$
where $d_{i,1\le i \le n} \in \boldsymbol{d}$

(31)

where $\boldsymbol{d}$ is a disagreement vector $\boldsymbol{d} = (d_1, .. \ d_n)$ $\in \mathbb{S}^D$ and a disagreement point $d_{i,1 \le i \le n}$ represents a minimum payoff of each battlefield. Therefore, $\boldsymbol{d}$ is a set of least guaranteed payoffs for a defender.

Usually, the NBS is conventionally found based on the exhaustive search, i.e., all feasible payoff pairs in $\mathbb{S}$ are examined. But, the exhaustive search becomes significantly inefficient when the amount of resources and the number of battlefields increase. In addition, the solution should be obtained in real time for security problems. Therefore, it is challenging to compute an optimal NBS solution due to the exponential computation complexity (Kim, Park & Frossard 2012). Another weak point of traditional NBS is that it requires complete information; game players are assumed to know everything in order to maximize their payoffs. However, in reality, this assumption rarely holds. Occasionally, game players make decisions irrationally due to the limited information about available strategies. In order to overcome these problems, the *BGSRA* scheme decomposes the feasible payoff set into smaller sub-feasible payoff sets, and then find the Nash Bargaining Solution (NBS) by iteratively applying the NBS approach in each sub-feasible payoff sets. This iterative approach can significantly reduce the computation complexity compared to a conventional method, where a defender bargains over the whole feasible payoff set to find the NBS

(Kim, Park & Frossard 2012). In addition, a defender (*D*) in the *BGSRA* scheme can make decisions based on less-than perfect information and learn the current system situation to approximate an optimal solution. Learning can be defined as the capability of drawing intelligent decisions by self-adapting to the dynamics of the environment, taking into account the experience gained in past and present system states, and using long term benefit estimations. Therefore, the important novelties of the *BGSRA* scheme are self-adaptability for system dynamics and effectiveness for real world operations.

Based on the feedback learning process, the *BGSRA* scheme can capture a defender adapt his strategy to achieve the better payoff. This procedure is defined as a strategic security resource allocation algorithm. Based on the feasible payoff set ($\mathbb{S}^D$) of all possible *D*'s payoff pairs, the *i*th sub-feasible payoff set $\mathbb{S}_i^D$ can be similarly defined as

$$\mathbb{S}_i^D = \left\{ \begin{array}{l} \left(g_1(x_1^D), \ldots, g_n\left(x_n^D\right)\right) \in \mathbb{R}_+^n \\ \left| \sum_{k=1}^n x_k^D \le X^D \text{ and } P_D^{i-1}\left(\mathbb{S}_{i-1}^A, \mathbb{S}_{i-1}^D\right) \le P_D^i\left(\mathbb{S}_i^A, \mathbb{S}_i^D\right) \right. \end{array} \right\}$$

(32)

where X^D is the *D*'s available security resource and x_k^D is the resource allocated to the *k*th battlefield. $\mathbb{R}_+^n$ denotes a set of non-negative real number.

The iterative sub-NBS algorithm begins by considering the first sub-feasible payoff set $\mathbb{S}_1^D$. At the initial iteration (i = 1), the security resource is equally distributed. $\mathbb{S}_1^D$ is considered as the disagreement vector for the next sub-NBS ($\mathbb{S}_2^D$). Correspondingly, the *i*th sub-NBS ($\mathbb{S}_i^D$) is computed by considering the (*i* − 1)th sub-NBS ($\mathbb{S}_{i-1}^D$). At the *i*th iteration, a defender selects his strategy ($\mathbb{S}_i^D$) based on the $\mathbb{S}_{i-1}^A$. Therefore, the attacker's strategy ($\mathbb{S}^A$) is used as the decision factor of the defender for the next iteration. This interactive feedback process continues iteratively in a step-by-step manner. It may be the only realistic approach to solve complex and dynamically changing security problems.

In the *BGSRA* scheme, resource allocation rules are employed to get the next sub-NBS. First, select the *D*'s lost battlefields (e.g., $f_{i,1 \leq i \leq n}\left(x_i^A, x_i^D\right) = 0$) at the current iteration. Second, the selected battlefields are decreasingly sorted according to their weighted factors (α). Third, the allocated resources in the selected battlefields are dynamically reallocated. The battlefield of the highest α value (e.g., $\alpha_{i,1 \leq i \leq n}$) obtains the security resource as follows.

$$x_i^D = \frac{\alpha_i}{\sum_{j \in \mathbb{F}} \alpha_j} \times T_R \times \psi \qquad (33)$$

where $\mathbb{F}$ is the set of selected battlefields and T_R is the total allocated resource in $\mathbb{F}$. ψ is a constant factor to adjust the allocating resource amount. In the *BGSRA* scheme, $\psi > 1$. Therefore, the lower α value battlefields can not get the security resource. Fourth, if the estimated $P_D\left(\mathbb{S}^A, \mathbb{S}^D\right)$ is less than the previous $P_D\left(\mathbb{S}^A, \mathbb{S}^D\right)$, ψ value is increased in steps equal to Δ. Finally, a new $P_D\left(\mathbb{S}^A, \mathbb{S}^D\right)$ is obtained or maintains the status quo. When the increase of $P_D\left(\mathbb{S}^A, \mathbb{S}^D\right)$ is within a pre-defined minimum bound (ε) and $\mathbb{S}^A$ is not changed, the *BGSRA* scheme assumes that the security control system reaches to an efficient stable state; the game process is temporarily stop. If $\mathbb{S}^A$ is changed, the resource allocation algorithm is re-triggered, and back to the initial step to obtain a new NBS.

Summary

For the last decades, hacker activities have significantly increased in cyber space, and have been causing damage by exploiting weaknesses in information infrastructure. Recently, researchers have been exploring the applicability of game theoretic approaches to address security problems and have proposed a handful of competing solutions. In the *BGSRA* scheme, the Blotto game concept is extended to address the ever changing security threats. Based on the iterative NBS methodology, the main objective of *BGSRA* scheme is to effectively allocate the security resources. By constantly monitoring the current system condition, the *BGSRA* scheme iteratively re-negotiates the current strategy to approximate an optimal solution. The developed Blotto game approach is not only better for the security resource allocation problem, but also it can capture situations in economics, politics, law, biology, and sports.

INTERVENIENT STACKELBERG GAME BASED BANDWIDTH ALLOCATION (*ISGBA*) SCHEME

Recently, S. Kim proposed an Intervenient Stackelberg Game based Bandwidth Allocation (*ISGBA*) scheme for hierarchical wireless network systems. The *ISGBA* scheme derives a multi-objective decision criterion for each access point, and develops a bargaining strategy selection algorithm for the dynamic bandwidth re-allocation. Based on the intervenient Stackelberg game model, the *ISGBA* scheme effectively formulates the competitive interaction situation between several access points.

Development Motivation

Nowadays, bandwidth demand is growing exponentially due to the increased new applications. However, wireless bandwidth is a naturally limited and scarce resource. Therefore, efficient bandwidth management plays a critical role in determining network performance. In wireless network systems, there are a number of interacting intelligent agents. Each agent makes behavioral choices in the context of a dynamic environment that is formed by the collective actions. To understand the behavior of self-regarding agents, game theory has some attractive features (Kim, 2011). Game theory is a field of applied mathematics that provides an effective tool in modeling the interactions among independent agents. However, classical game theory makes the assumption that game players are perfectly rational. This supposition is too strong to implement in the real world game player. For the practical game operation, players should be modeled with bounded rationality (Kim, 2011), (Garroppo, Giordano, and Iacono, 2009).

Based on the facts presented above, the *ISGBA* scheme is developed as a new bandwidth allocation scheme based on the feedback-based game theory. By adopting the intervenient Stackelberg game model, the *ISGBA* scheme is designed as an iterative online process approach. In each iteration, network agents observe the current network environment, estimate the prospective utility, and update the strategy based on the observations. Under incomplete information situations, this feedback-based online approach can be used to make a logical, quantitative decision. The important feature of the *ISGBA* scheme is an ability to maintain system efficiency as high as possible by adaptively responding to current network situations.

Recently, several network resource management schemes – the *Per-link Threshold based Bandwidth Allocation* (*PTBA*) scheme (Jeong and Kim, 2013) and the *Energy-efficient Dynamic Load Distribution* (*EDLD*) scheme (Oh, Lee and Choi, 2013) - have been presented for wireless network systems. The *PTBA* scheme investigates optimal switching technique between coordinated APs. In this scheme, the per-link information between an AP and the user is assumed available

at a time and is compared with a predetermined threshold to determine either switching or staying. The *EDLD* scheme is developed as a novel dynamic energy-efficient load distribution algorithm for heterogeneous wireless networks. For an effective load distribution, the *EDLD* scheme is designed based on the simple greedy load distribution algorithm, which is inspired by the mathematical background of the Lagrangian algorithm.

Multi-Objective Decision Criterion

In a wireless network system, there are multiple Channel Providers (CPs) and Access Providers (APs). The CP allocates the available bandwidth to APs and each AP leases the bandwidth among End Users (EUs) who registered that AP. In this paper, the *ISGBA* scheme formalizes the bandwidth management algorithm abstractly in terms of an intervenient Stackelberg game model. In our game model, there are a single CP, n APs ($\{AP_1, AP_i, AP_n\}, n \in \mathcal{N}$) and m EUs. From the viewpoint of CP, the effective bandwidth allocation among APs is a very important factor in order to obtain fair-efficient network performance. To satisfy this goal, one of major concerns is to design a utility function for each AP. In this paper, the *ISGBA* scheme defines two online functions (F_b and F_u) by using call blocking probability and bandwidth utilization information. Based on the adaptive online manner, these functions can dynamically estimate the current statue of APs. For the AP i, the $F_b(i)$ and $F_u(i)$ are defined as

$$F_b(i) = \min\left(1, \left[\omega_i \times \exp\left(Pr_i\right)\right]\right) \text{ and}$$

$$F_u(i) = \left(1 - \frac{B_c(i)}{B(i)}\right) \tag{34}$$

where Pr_i is the call blocking probability and ω_i ($0 < \omega_i < 1$) is a control parameter of the sensitivity to the Pr_i. $B(i)$ is the total amount of allocated bandwidth and $B_c(i)$ is the currently used bandwidth in the AP i. To get the proper combination of the F_b and F_u functions, the *ISGBA* scheme uses the Modified Game Theory (MGT) method. In general, the MGT method may be concluded to provide the best compromise in the presence of different control functions (Kim, 2010b). By practically applying the MGT, the F_b and F_u are transformed into a single objective function. To obtain this single function, the procedure is defined as follows. First, a normalized bargaining model (*NBM(i)*) for the AP i is constructed to compare the relative effectiveness.

$$NBM\left(i\right) = \prod_{k=1}^{2}\left[1 - f_k\left(i\right)\right],$$

where $f_1\left(i\right) = F_b\left(i\right)$ and $f_2\left(i\right) = F_u\left(i\right)$ (35)

This bargaining model gives a normalized indication value ($0 \leq NBM(i) \leq 1$) as to how far a function is from its worst value. Therefore, the solution is optimized by maximizing the bargaining model (Kim, 2010b). Second, a weighted average ($WA\left(i\right)$) for the AP i is formulated as follows.

$$WA\left(i\right) = \sum_{k=1}^{2}\gamma_k f_k\left(x\right), \text{ with } \sum_{k=1}^{2}\gamma_k = 1$$

(36)

The parameter γ_k ($k = 1$ or 2) controls the relative weights given to the blocking probability ($k = 1$) and bandwidth utilization ($k = 2$). Under diverse network environments, the fixed values for γ_k cannot effectively adapt to the changing conditions. The *ISGBA* scheme treats it as an online decision problem and adaptively modifies γ_k value. When the blocking probability of the AP i is high, the *ISGBA* scheme can put more emphasis on the function $f_1\left(i\right)$. In this case, a higher value of γ_1 is more suitable. Otherwise, the *WA* $\left(i\right)$ should strongly depend on the bandwidth

utilization. In this case, a higher value of γ_2 is more suitable. In the *ISGBA* scheme , the value of γ_1 is dynamically adjusted based on the current call blocking probability of the corresponding AP; e.g., the γ_1 value of the AP i is Pr_i and the γ_2 is defined as 1- γ_1. Therefore, by using the real-time online monitoring, the system can be more responsive to current network conditions. According to (35) and (36), the multi-objective utility function ($U_{mo}\left(i\right)$) of the AP i is given by

$$U_{mo}\left(i\right) = \left(WA\left(i\right) - NBM\left(i\right)\right)$$ (37)

Based on each AP's U_{mo}, the *ISGBA* scheme can estimate the outcome differentials among APs. Finally, Outcome Differential Level (*ODL*) among APs is obtained as follows.

$$ODL = \max_{i,j \in \mathcal{N}} \left(\left| U_{mo}\left(i\right) - U_{mo}\left(j\right) \right| \right)$$ (38)

Adaptable Bargaining Strategy Selection Method

During wireless network operations, the role of CP is to allocate bandwidth for each AP. To get a fair-efficient bandwidth allocation, the *ISGBA* scheme develops a new bandwidth re-allocation algorithm based on the intervenient Stackelberg game model; it can be applicable and useful in a system with a frequently changing situation. In the algorithm of the *ISGBA* scheme, the CP (i.e., an intervenient leader) monitors APs (i.e., followers) and acts explicitly, which can be programmed simply according to the bandwidth re-allocation rule (). Based on the effective bargaining strategies, consists of four rules = { f_1, f_2, f_3, f_4 }.

f_1 : **Nash Bargaining Solution (NBS):** The main feature of NBS is to achieve a mutually desirable solution with a good balance between efficiency and fairness. NBS is obtained as follows.

$$NBS = \arg \max_A \prod_{i \in \mathcal{N}} \left(NBM\left(i\right)^A \right) \quad (39)$$

The solution set of all possible combinations of bandwidth allocation represents the game feasible set A.

f_2 : **Kalai-Smorodinsky Bargaining Solution (KSBS):** The main feature of KSBS is that the increasing of bargaining set size in a direction favorable to a specific player always benefits that player. Therefore, self-interested AP also can be satisfied. In KSBS, the ideal payoff ($NBM\left(i\right)_{max}$) for each AP is the maximum effectiveness in the ideal situation. KSBS is obtained as a weighted max-min solution (Garroppo, 2009).

$$KSBS = \arg\max_A \left\{ \min_{i \in \mathcal{N}} \left(\frac{NBM\left(i\right)^A}{NBM\left(i\right)_{max}} \right) \right\} \quad (40)$$

f_3 : **Utilitarian Bargaining Solution (UBS):** This bargaining solution does not consider fairness issues among APs. In the point view of efficiency, only the sum of APs' effectiveness is maximized. This solution can be formulated as the following (Garroppo, 2009):

$$UBS = \arg\max_A \sum_{i \in \mathcal{N}} NBM\left(i\right)^A \quad (41)$$

f_4 : **Egalitarian Bargaining Solution (EBS):** This bargaining solution follows the max-min effectiveness concept (Garroppo, 2009):

$$EBS = \arg\max_A \left\{ \min_{i \in \mathcal{N}} NBM\left(i\right)^A \right\} \quad (42)$$

At the initial time, the available bandwidth is equally divided for APs. This starting guess guarantees that each AP enjoys the same benefit at the beginning of the game. After initialization period, the CP periodically observes the current AP situations and adaptively selects a bandwidth re-allocation rule to obtain a fair-efficient solution. In the algorithm of the *ISGBA* scheme, rule mapping conditions are employed for the adaptive bargaining strategy selection;

1. If the average B_c (B_{ave}) of APs is less than the predefined bandwidth utilization (B_p), f_3 is selected to improve the system effectiveness.
2. If ($B_{ave} > B_p$) and ($ODL < 0.2$), f_4 is selected to equally share the benefits.
3. If ($B_{ave} > B_p$) and ($0.2 \le ODL \le 0.7$), f_1 is selected to fairly share the mutual benefits accruing from cooperation.
4. If ($B_{ave} > B_p$) and ($0.7 \le ODL \le 1$), f_2 is selected to obtain a benefit-based fair solution.

By using this dynamics of feedback process, the allocated bandwidth is periodically adjusted. In the step-by-step interactive online manner, a fair-efficient solution is eventually obtained.

Summary

For next-generation wireless networks, dynamic bandwidth allocation algorithm is significant to improve network performance. The *ISGBA* scheme has introduced a new feedback-based adaptive bandwidth re-allocation algorithm. Based on the intervenient Stackelberg game model, the *ISGBA* scheme iteratively estimates the current network situations and adaptively re-allocates the available bandwidth for APs.

REFERENCES

Bian, Z. A., & Luo, J. Z. (2007). A Cooperative Game Theory Based Coalitional Agent Negotiation Model in Network Service. *Lecture Notes in Computer Science, 4402*, 447–458. doi:10.1007/978-3-540-72863-4_46

Bloem, M., Alpcan, T., & Basar, T. (2006). Intrusion Response as a Resource Allocation Problem. In *Proceedings of IEEE Conference on Decision and Control*, (pp. 6283-6288). IEEE.

Burd, T. D., & Brodersen, R. W. (1996). Processor Design for Portable Systems. *The Journal of VLSI Signal Processing, 13*, 203–221. doi:10.1007/BF01130406

Chen, X., Li, B., & Fang, Y. (2005). A Dynamic Multiple-Threshold Bandwidth Reservation (DMTBR) Scheme for QoS Provisioning in Multimedia Wireless Networks. *IEEE Transactions on Wireless Communications, 4*(2), 583–592. doi:10.1109/TWC.2004.843053

Conley, J. P., & Wilkie, S. (1996). An Extension of the Nash Bargaining Solution to Nonconvex Problems. *Games and Economic Behavior, 13*(1), 26–38. doi:10.1006/game.1996.0023

Cui, W., & Bassiouni, M. A. (2003). Virtual private network bandwidth management with traffic prediction. *Computer Networks, 42*(6), 765–778. doi:10.1016/S1389-1286(03)00217-2

Denicolò, V., & Mariotti, M. (2000). Nash Bargaining Theory, Nonconvex Problems and Social Welfare Ordering. *Theory and Decision, 48*(4), 351–358. doi:10.1023/A:1005278100070

Garroppo, R. G., Giordano, S., & Iacono, D. (2009). Radio-Aware Scheduler for WiMAX Systems Based on Time-Utility Function and Game Theory. In *Proceedings of IEEE GLOBECOM 2009*. IEEE.

Huining, H., Yanikomeroglu, H., Falconer, D. D., & Periyalwar, S. (2004). Range extension without capacity penalty in cellular networks with digital fixed relays. In *Proceedings of IEEE GLOBECOM*, (pp. 3053–3057). IEEE.

Irani, S., Shukla, S., & Gupta, R. (2003). Online Strategies for Dynamic Power Management in Systems with Multiple Power-Saving States. *ACM Trans. Embedded Computing Syst., 2*(3), 325–346. doi:10.1145/860176.860180

Jeong, D. K., & Kim, D. (2013). Optimal access point switching with per-link threshold under nonhomogeneous bandwidth allocation. In Proceedings of Information and Communication Technology (ICoICT), (pp. 187-191). ICoICT.

Khan, S. U., & Ardil, C. (2009). Energy Efficient Resource Allocation in Distributed Computing Systems. In Proceedings of Distributed, High-Performance and Grid Computing, (pp. 667-673). Academic Press.

Kiekintveld, C., & Tambe, M. (2009). Computing optimal randomized resource allocations for massive security games. [AAMAS.]. *Proceedings of AAMAS, 09*, 689–696.

Kim, E., Park, H., & Frossard, P. (2012). Low complexity iterative multimedia resource allocation based on game theoretic approach. In *Proceedings of IEEE ISCAS*, (pp. 1099-1102). IEEE.

Kim, S. W. (2010). Dynamic Online Bandwidth Adjustment Scheme Based on Kalai-Smorodinsky Bargaining Solution. *IEICE Trans. on Communications, E93.B*(7), 1935-1938.

Kim, S. W. (2011). Cellular Network Bandwidth Management Scheme by using Nash Bargaining Solution. *IET Communications, 5*(3), 371–380. doi:10.1049/iet-com.2010.0309

Kim, S. W. (2011). Adaptive Online Voltage Scaling Scheme based on the Nash Bargaining Solution. *ETRI Journal*, *33*(3), 407–414. doi:10.4218/etrij.11.0110.0417

Kim, S. W. (2013). Multi-hop Network Bandwidth Management Scheme based on Cooperrative Bargaining Models. *Wireless Personal Communications*. doi:10.1007/s11277-013-1199-4

Kim, S. W., & Varshney, P. K. (2004). An Integrated Adaptive Bandwidth Management Framework for QoS sensitive Multimedia Cellular Networks. *IEEE Transactions on Vehicular Technology*, *53*(3), 835–846. doi:10.1109/TVT.2004.825704

Korzhyk, D., Conitzer, V., & Parr, R. (2011). Security Games with Multiple Attacker Resources. [IJCAI.]. *Proceedings of IJCAI*, *11*, 273–279.

Le, L., & Hossain, E. (2007). Multihop Cellular Networks: Potential Gains, Research Challenges, and a Resource Allocation Framework. *IEEE Communications Magazine*, *45*(9), 66–73. doi:10.1109/MCOM.2007.4342859

Mehmet, S., & Ramazan, K. (2001). A Comparative Study of Multiobjective Optimization Methods in Structural Design. *Turkish Journal of Engineering and Environmental Sciences*, *25*(2), 69–78.

Mochocki, B., Hu, X. S., & Quan, G. (2002). A Realistic Variable Voltage Scheduling Model for Real-Time Applications. In *Proceedings of Computer Aided Design* (pp. 726–731). Academic Press. doi:10.1109/ICCAD.2002.1167612

Mochocki, B., Hu, X. S., & Quan, G. (2007). Transition-Overhead-Aware Voltage Scheduling for Fixed-Priority Real-Time Systems. *ACM Transactions on Design Automation of Electronic Systems*, *12*(2), 1–12. doi:10.1145/1230800.1230803

Newton, M., Thompson, J. S., & Naden, J. M. (2008). Wireless systems Resource allocation in the downlink of cellular multi-hop networks. *European Transactions on Telecommunications*, *19*(3), 299–314. doi:10.1002/ett.1264

Niyato, D., & Hossain, E. (2008). A noncooperative game-theoretic framework for radio resource management in 4G heterogeneous wireless access networks. *IEEE Transactions on Mobile Computing*, *7*(3), 332–345. doi:10.1109/TMC.2007.70727

Oh, H., Lee, J., & Choi, J. (2013). Energy-efficient dynamic load distribution for heterogeneous access networks. In *Proceedings of ICT Convergence (ICTC)*, (pp. 18-23). ICTC.

Park, H. G., & Schaar, M. V. D. (2007a). Bargaining Strategies for Networked Multimedia Resource Management. *IEEE Transactions on Signal Processing*, *55*(7), 3496–3511. doi:10.1109/TSP.2007.893755

Park, H. G., & Schaar, M. V. D. (2007b). Multi-User Multimedia Resource Management using Nash Bargaining Solution. In *Proceedings of IEEE ICASSP*, (pp. 717-720). IEEE.

Park, Y. S., & Jung, E. S. (2007). Resource-Aware Routing Algorithms for Multi-hop Cellular Networks. In *Proceedings of International Conference on Multimedia and Ubiquitous Engineering*, (pp. 1164-1167). Academic Press.

Pati, H. K. (2007). A distributed adaptive guard channel reservation scheme for cellular networks. *International Journal of Communication Systems*, *20*(9), 1037–1058. doi:10.1002/dac.857

Rhee, S. H., Yoon, J. W., Choi, H. J., & Choi, I. S. (2001). Dynamic Capacity Resizing of Virtual Backbone Network. In *Proceedings of the First International Conference on Networking*, (pp. 698-708). Academic Press.

Sierra, C., Faratin, P., & Jennings, N. R. (1997). A Service-Oriented Negotiation Model between Autonomous Agents. In *Proceedings of European Workshop on Modeling Autonomous Agents in a Multi-Agent World*, (pp. 17-35). Academic Press.

Sun, T., Zhu, Q., Li, S., & Zhou, M. (2007). Open, Dynamic and Continuous One-to-Many Negotiation System. In *Proceedings of BIC-TA*, (pp. 87-93). BIC-TA.

Suris, J., DaSilva, L., Han, Z., & MacKenzie, A. (2007). Cooperative game theory for distributed spectrum sharing. [IEEE.]. *Proceedings of the IEEE, ICC*, 5282–5287.

Viduto, V., Maple, C., Huang, W., & Bochenkov, A. (2012). A multi-objective genetic algorithm for minimising network security risk and cost. In *Proceedings of IEEE HPCS,* (pp. 462-467). IEEE.

Virapanicharoen, J., & Benjapolakul, W. (2004). Fair-Efficient Guard Bandwidth Coefficients Selection in Call Admission Control for Mobile Multimedia Communications using Game Theoretic Framework. [IEEE.]. *Proceedings of the IEEE, ICC*, 80–84.

Waslander, S. L., Inalhan, G., & Tomlin, C. J. (2004). *Decentralized Optimization via Nash Bargaining*. Kluwer Academic Press.

Wittman, M. D. (2011). *Solving the Blotto Game: A Computational Approach*. MIT.

KEY TERMS AND DEFINITIONS

Consensus Decision-Making: A group decision making process that seeks the consent of all participants. Consensus may be defined professionally as an acceptable resolution, one that can be supported, even if not the favorite of each individual. Consensus decision-making is thus concerned with the process of deliberating and finalizing a decision, and the social and political effects of using this process.

Coordination Game: Coordination game is a formalization of the idea of a coordination problem, which is widespread in the social sciences, including economics, meaning situations in which all parties can realize mutual gains, but only by making mutually consistent decisions.

Correlated Equilibrium: A solution concept that is more general than the well known Nash equilibrium. The idea is that each player chooses his/her action according to his/her observation of the value of the same public signal. A strategy assigns an action to every possible observation a player can make. If no player would want to deviate from the recommended strategy (assuming the others don't deviate), the distribution is called a correlated equilibrium.

Focal Point: A solution that people will tend to use in the absence of communication, because it seems natural, special, or relevant to them.

Pareto Optimality: A state of allocation of resources in which it is impossible to make any one individual better off without making at least one individual worse off. The concept has applications in academic fields such as economics and engineering.

Status Quo: A Latin term meaning the existing state of affairs. To maintain the status quo is to keep the things the way they presently are.

Chapter 12
Bandwidth Management Algorithms by Using Game Models

ABSTRACT

In spite of the emergence of high network infrastructures, bandwidth is still an extremely valuable and scarce resource. Therefore, all performance guarantees in communication networks are conditional on currently available bandwidth capacity. In view of the remarkable growth in the number of users and the limited bandwidth, an efficient bandwidth management is very important and has been an active area of research over the last decade. Bandwidth management is the process of measuring and controlling the communications (traffic, packets) on a network link to avoid filling the link to capacity or overfilling the link, which would result in network congestion and poor performance of the network. The objective of these mechanisms is to maximize the overall network performance. This chapter discusses bandwidth management.

QOS-AWARE BANDWIDTH ALLCATION (*QSBA*) SCHEME

Bandwidth is an extremely valuable and scarce resource in multimedia networks. Therefore, efficient bandwidth management is necessary in order to provide high Quality of Service (QoS) to users. Recently, S. Kim proposed a new QoS-aware Bandwidth Allocation (*QSBA*) scheme for the efficient use of available bandwidth (Kim, 2010). By using the multi-objective optimization technique and Talmud allocation rule, the bandwidth is adaptively controlled to maximize network efficiency while ensuring QoS provision-

ing. In addition, the *QSBA* scheme adopts the online feedback strategy to dynamically respond to current network conditions.

Development Motivation

In recent years, the explosive growth of new services and the rapid and widespread proliferation of multimedia data have necessitated the development of an efficient network management system. The network system is expected to provide diversified traffic services and enhance network performance simultaneously. Usually heterogeneous multimedia data can be categorized into

DOI: 10.4018/978-1-4666-6050-2.ch012

two classes according to the required Quality of Service (QoS): class I (real-time) services and class II (non-real-time) services. Different multimedia services over networks not only require different amounts of bandwidth but also have different QoS requirements (Yang, Ou, Guild, & Chen, 2009).

During network operations, the limited bandwidth has to be shared by several users. Therefore, fairness is another prominent issue for the network management. If the concept of fairness is not considered explicitly at the design stage of bandwidth allocation algorithm, different allocation requests can result in very unfair bandwidth allocations. However, fairness-oriented allocation methods may lead to a system inefficiency, which degrades total network performance quite seriously.

The *QSBA* scheme is developed as a new bandwidth allocation algorithm for multimedia networks. To approximate an optimal network performance, the developed algorithm has focused on the basic concept of online decision process. Based on the Modified Game Theory (MGT) (Mehmet, & Ramazan, 2001), the bandwidth is adaptively allocated to satisfy different QoS requirements. In addition, by using the Talmud allocation rule (Li, & Cui, 2009), a weight parameter is adjusted periodically to ensure the allocation fairness. Therefore, the system dynamically re-estimates the current network condition and iteratively adapts control decisions. Under dynamically changing network environments, this online strategy can find the best solution for conflicting objectives.

Network Control Algorithms in the *QSBA* Scheme

Recent advances in network technologies have made it possible to provide heterogeneous multimedia services. However, multimedia service makes the problem more complex, since each service requires different bandwidth allocation and has different characteristics according to the required QoS. Class I data services require real-time deliveries. Therefore, the system should guarantee a fixed amount of bandwidth allocation. However, class II data services are more flexible; they need only to guarantee their time deadlines. Therefore, between the start time and the deadline, class II services are amenable to adaptation with variable bandwidth allocation. The *QSBA* scheme defines Ψ as the set of accepted service requests (*sr*) by the network, $\Psi = \{ sr_1, sr_2, sr_3, _{,,,} sr_{i,,} sr_n \}$, where *n* is the total number of running services, i.e., $n = \| \Psi \|$. During real world system operations, *n* is dynamically changed. The class II service request *i* is characterized by $\{ a_i, d_i, t\_c_i \}$ where a_i is the arrival time, d_i is the deadline, and t_c_i is the total workload of service sr_i to be completed. However, the class I service request *j* is characterized only by $\{ b_j \}$ where b_j is the requested bandwidth during the operation of service.

To estimate QoS provisioning for each service, the *QSBA* scheme defines two QoS functions (F_{class_I} and F_{class_II}). By using the adaptive online manner, the F_{class_I} and F_{class_II} evaluate the QoS for class I and class II services, respectively. In order to implement these functions, the *QSBA* scheme partition the time-axis into equal intervals of length *unit_time*. In the developed algorithm, a control parameter is adjusted periodically, every *unit_time*, in order to maintain well-balanced network performance considering conflicting QoS criteria. At the current time (c_t), the F_{class_I} and F_{class_II} are given by

$$\begin{bmatrix} F_{class_I}(ct) = 1 - \left[\sum_{k \in U_1} (b_k \times A(k)) \middle/ \sum_{k \in U_1} b_k \right] \\ F_{class\_II}(ct) = D - M_{II} \middle/ \sum_{k \in U_{II}} (A(k)) \end{bmatrix}$$

(1)

where

$$A(k) = \begin{cases} 1, & if\ request\ k\ is\ allocated\ (b_k)\ or\ accepted\ (t\_c_k) \\ 0, & otherwise \end{cases}$$

where U_I (or U_{II}) is the set of all requested class I (or class II) services in the current *unit_time*. D_M_{II} is the expected number of deadline miss services in U_{II}. Based on the currently allocated class II service bandwidth and the earliest deadline first scheduling, the D_M_{II} can be estimated.

To get the proper combination of the F_{class_I} and F_{class_II} functions, the *QSBA* scheme uses the MGT method. In general, the MGT method may be concluded to provide the best compromise in the presence of different control functions (Mehmet, 2001). By practically applying the MGT, the F_{class_I} and F_{class_II} are transformed into a single objective function. To obtain this single function, the procedure is defined as follows. First, a normalized bargaining model (*NBM*) is constructed to compare the relative effectiveness.

$$NBM = \prod_{k=1}^{2}\left(1 - f_k\left(c_t\right)\right)$$

where $f_1(c_t) = F_{class\_I}$ *and* $f_2(ct) = F_{class\_II}$

(2)

This bargaining model gives a normalized indication value ($0 \leq NBM \leq 1$) as to how far a function is from its worst value. Therefore, the solution is optimized by maximizing the bargaining model. Second, a weighted average (*WA*) for online functions is formulated as follows.

$$WA = \sum_{k=1}^{2} \gamma_k f_k\left(c_t\right), \text{ with } \sum_{k=1}^{2} \gamma_k = 1$$

(3)

Finally, according to (2) and (3), the multi-objective utility function (U_{mo}) is given by

$$U_{mo} = \min_{BT\_I + BT\_II = TB}\left(WA - NBM\right)$$

(4)

The parameter γ_k ($k = 1$ or 2) in (3) controls the relative weights given to class I QoS provi-

sioning ($k = 1$) and class II QoS provisioning ($k = 2$). In the *QSBA* scheme, Talmud rule is adopted to dynamically decide the γ value; Talmud rule was originally proposed in the Talmud over 3,000 years ago to fairly solve the estate division problem (Li, 2009).

Talmud Rule for the Bandwidth Allocation

1. If $(B_I/2 + B_{II}/2) \geq TB$, then $B_{T\_I} = \min\{ B_I/2, \lambda\}$ and $B_{T\_II} = \min\{ B_{II}/2, \lambda\}$, where λ is chosen so that $B_{T\_I} + B_{T\_II} = TB$.

2. If $(B_I/2 + B_{II}/2) < TB$, then $B_{T\_I} = B_I - \min\{ B_I/2, \lambda\}$ and $B_{T\_II} = B_{II} - \min\{ B_{II}/2, \lambda\}$, where λ is chosen so that $B_{T\_I} + B_{T\_II} = TB$.

where B_I is $\sum_{i \in U_I} b_i$ and B_{II} is

$$\sum_{j \in U_{II}} \left(\frac{t - c_j}{d_j - a_j}\right).$$

Based on the B_{T_I} and B_{T_II}, the *QSBA* scheme can adaptively adjust the γ value, i.e., $\gamma_1 = B_{T\_I} / TB$ and $\gamma_2 = 1 - \gamma_1$.

In the multimedia network system, service scheduler collectively controls bandwidth allocation for the best system performance. According to (1),(2) and (3), an efficient solution is obtained under widely different and diversified system situations. Based on the step-by-step interactive feedback process, the main steps of the *QSBA* scheme are given next.

Step 1: At the initial time, the network system has enough bandwidth to support servicers. The requested bandwidth is allocated from the unused bandwidth; proceeds to step 5.

Step 2: When the available bandwidth is not sufficient to ensure service, the developed bandwidth allocation algorithm is triggered.

Step 3: At the time when the running service is terminated, the allocated bandwidth is released. According to (1),(2) and (3), the released bandwidth is assigned to the B_I or B_{II} bandwidth pools in order to satisfying the formula (4).

Step 4: Every *unit_time*, the weight parameter γ is dynamically adjusted based on the Talmud rule.

Step 5: The network system is self-monitoring constantly and tries to allocate available bandwidth for incoming service requests. If the bandwidth allocation fails, then the new service request is rejected.

Recently, several bandwidth allocation algorithms have been presented. The *Quality-Added Dynamic Bandwidth Allocation (QADBA)* scheme is a dynamic bandwidth allocation scheme to provide end-to-end differentiated service of diverse QoS requirements (Yang, 2009). By taking into consideration the specific features of networks, the *QADBA* scheme can support class-of-service fairness. The *QoS-adaptive Bandwidth Allocation (QoSBA)* scheme is also an adaptive bandwidth allocation scheme based on the real-time measurement analysis (Wang, 2009). In order to ensure the QoS in networks, the *QoSBA* scheme makes use of the measurement report frames and normalized QoS level to maximize the weight sum of QoS. The *QADBA* and *QoSBA* schemes also provide accurate bandwidth allocation mechanisms in order to optimize network performance. Figure 1 demonstrates that the performance of the proposed *QSBA* scheme is generally superior to those of other existing schemes: the *QADBA* scheme and the *QoSBA* scheme.

Summary

In the *QSBA* scheme, the major goal is to maximize network performance while ensuring conflicting QoS criteria. The main novelty of the *QSBA* scheme is its adaptability, flexibility and responsiveness to current system conditions. This feature is highly desirable for real time network management.

Figure 1. Performance evaluations of the QSBA scheme

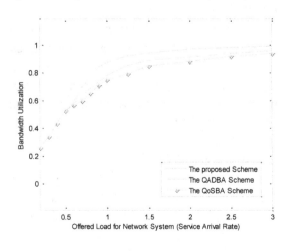

(a) Bandwidth Utilization

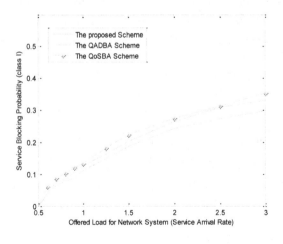

(b) Service blocking probability

ADAPTIVE CALL ADMISSION CONTROL (*ACAC*) SCHEME FOR HETEROGENEOUS OVERLAY NETWORKS

Future heterogeneous overlay network system must be able to support ubiquitous access across multiple wireless networks. To coordinate these diverse network environments, one challenging task is a call admission decision among different types of networks. Recently, S. Kim proposed a new Adaptive Call Admission Control (*ACAC*) scheme to provide QoS provisioning while ensuring system efficiency (Kim, 2012). Based on the interplay between network structure and dynamics, the *ACAC* scheme estimates the network's QoS level and adaptively adjusts the service price with the aim of maximizing the network performance. According to the real-time online approach, the *ACAC* scheme can dynamically adapt to the current network conditions.

Development Motivation

Recently, user requirements are growing faster than ever and the limitations of the current wireless network systems have forced to take a next step for the more advanced and efficient technologies. The future network system is expected to provide a comprehensive IP solution where multimedia services can be delivered to the user on an 'Anytime, Anywhere' basis with a satisfactory high data rate, premium quality and high security. To satisfy this goal, multi-layer networks are a collection of infrared, radio wireless LAN, cellular and satellite networks as an overlaid structure (Khan, Qadeer, Ansari, & Waheed, 2009). Therefore, there is a significant need to integrate all disparate wireless technologies; this convergence poses many challenges, which should be solved before the deployment of a real overlay network (Niyato, & Hossain, 2008).

Network Quality of Service (QoS) refers to the ability of the network to handle traffic services while satisfying the need of certain applications. Different applications not only require different amounts of bandwidth, but also have different QoS requirements. For example, real-time applications can tolerate some degree of traffic loss while non real-time applications cannot. However, real-time applications are delay sensitive and non real-time applications are rather tolerant of delays. Factors of network QoS evaluation are availability (uptime), bandwidth (throughput), latency (delay), and error rate, etc. For the effective future network operation, the main challenge is to provide QoS ensuring for various traffic services (Kim, & Varshney, 2004).

For the integration of heterogeneous wireless networks, the most important issue is call admission control. In the overlay networks, call admission process means the decision what is the best network for call services (Wang, Katz, & Giese, 1999). To adaptively make these decisions, the overlay system dynamically collects each network current conditions and selects the best reachable network. Another important part of network operations is a pricing strategy; adaptive pricing strategies can maximize the network revenue. Due to this reason, developing an effective call admission and price computation algorithms have been an active area of research over the last decade (Chen, Zhou, Chai, Tang, & Zhao, 2010), (Friedman, & Parkes, 2003).

During the 1960s and 1970s, *William Vickrey*, *Edward H. Clarke*, and *Theodore Groves* had developed an elegant auction mechanism referred to as *Vickrey-Clarke-Groves* (*VCG*) mechanism (Dash, Parkes, & Jennings, 2003), (Garg, Narahari, & Gujar, 2008). It is a type of sealed-bid auction where multiple items are up for bid, and each bidder submits a different value for each item. The goal of the *VCG* mechanism is to define rules and payoff functions to reach a desired outcome, which is called social optimum. Therefore, the *VCG* mechanism can be thought of as inverse game theory – where game theory reasons about how agents will play a game, the *VCG* mechanism reasons about how to design games that produce desired outcomes (Parkes, Singh, & Yanovsky, 2004). Many applications of the *VCG* mechanism are related to economics, but it is also a powerful tool to model a wider range of real life situations.

For the efficient network management, call admission decisions must be dynamically adjustable. However, the future service requests are generally not known. These decisions have to be made in real time, and without the knowledge of future information at the decision time. Therefore, online algorithms are natural candidates for the design of efficient control schemes in real world network operations. Besides, under dynamically changing network environments, traditional static control strategies are not acceptable. Based on these considerations, the *ACAC* scheme would employ a dynamic online methodology, which can improve control adaptability and flexibility under widely different and diversified network situations.

Motivated by the above discussion, the *ACAC* scheme is designed as an online call admission control scheme for the heterogeneous overlay network system. The *ACAC* scheme consists of network evaluation, selection and price computation algorithms. When users try to connect the network system, the network evaluation algorithm estimates each network's QoS level based on the real-time online approach. The selection algorithm selects the best adaptable wireless network from the all reachable wireless networks. After selecting a network, the price computation algorithm calculates the service charge. To effectively decide the service price, the methodology that the *ACAC* scheme adopted is the *VCG* mechanism; it can provide an excellent solution for the price computation problem. The main goal of the *ACAC* scheme is to maximize system efficiency while ensuring QoS prioritization. Under various QoS constraints and dynamically changing environments, the *ACAC* scheme can get a globally desirable network performance.

The novelty of the *ACAC* scheme is adaptive responsibility to current network based on the real-time online approach. Therefore, the *ACAC* scheme

can maximize network performance under widely different and diversified traffic load situations.

Bandwidth Management Algorithm in the *ACAC* Scheme

The developed algorithms in the *ACAC* scheme dynamically collect the current information of each network, and make control decisions for the heterogeneous overlay network system. To reach a desirable system performance, the developed approach can be concluded to be an effective solution.

Metrics for QoS Level in Overlay Network System

The multi-layer network system is composed by several wireless networks. These heterogeneous networks coexist to form hierarchical network system and have overlapping areas of coverage to provide services, where each has its own characteristics in terms of capacity, bandwidth, latency, and technology (Luo, Ji, & Li, 2009). Therefore, an important challenge for overlay networks is to coordinate the different types of networks. The general architecture of hierarchical wireless network system is shown in Figure 2 The higher the level of overlay, the larger the coverage area it has, and the lower bandwidths and longer delays per service it offers (Wang, 1999).

Every application has its own QoS requirements and different networks also provide different QoS level. To obtain the best balance between performance and network resource usage, call requests should be accepted to the most suitable network. Traditionally, call admission mechanism is defined to limit the number of call connections for the better network performance. In the *ACAC* scheme, it is designated as a strategy to select the best network based on user preference and different service type issues.

Due to the widespread deployment of overlapping wireless networks, determining the best network is a challenging task. For this decision,

Figure 2. Multitier overlay network structure

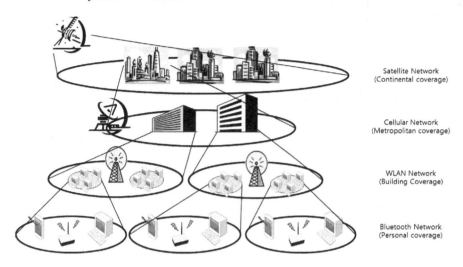

each network estimates itself according to the QoS factors, such as bandwidth utilization, packet error rate, latency, and so on. Usually, network QoS can be characterized in four ways; 1) services will perform better when higher bandwidth is available, 2) packet error rate won't degrade much the performance for video streaming or voice conversation service, but this is not the case in Email or FTP applications, 3) real-time services will need low latency network while non-real-time services will not be so sensitive to latency, 4) the user may want to stay in the network with lowest power consumption to get longer battery life (Niyato, & Hossain, 2006). By considering these QoS factors, the *ACAC* scheme defines an online function to quantify the QoS level (Q_L_i) of the network *i* as follows.

$$Q\_L_i = \prod_{i=1}^{4}\left(1 - f_i\right)^{\lambda_i} \qquad (5)$$

s.t., $f_1 = B_i\Big/B_M$, $f_2 = E_i\Big/E_M$, $f_3 = P_i\Big/P_M$, $f_4 = L_i\Big/L_M$

and $\sum_{i=1}^{4}\lambda_i = 1$

where B_i , E_i , P_i and L_i are the current bandwidth usage ratio, packet error rate, power consumption

and latency, respectively. B_M , E_M , P_M and L_M are the maximum bandwidth usage ratio, maximum packet error rate, maximum power consumption and maximum latency, respectively. Therefore f_i value is normalized ($0 \le f_i \le 1$); normalization is needed to ensure that the sum of the values in different units is meaningful. The variable λ is the weight factor and it's assigned according to each factor's importance. Users may specify and modify the importance of each parameter λ_i at run-time. For example, when the mobile host's battery is running out (*or* the emergent call service), P_i (*or* L_i) factors should be considered seriously. If a network has greater QoS measures to fulfill the QoS requirements of the call request, then the evaluation values calculated by using (5) would be higher.

During network operations, new call requests arrive in real time. At this time, call admission decisions are made from the network system. For this decision, the developed network evaluation algorithm estimates available networks based on its corresponding Q_L value. Based on the real-time online approach, this value is collected to monitor the current information of each network. Therefore, the developed algorithm can response to the constantly changing network environment.

Network Selection Algorithm for Overlay Network System

A primary goal of call admission control scheme is to make it possible to balance the traffic load across heterogeneous networks with comparable QoS performance. To satisfy this goal, each network estimates its QoS level. At the time of call connection, the control system gets reachable networks to support the request service and evaluates those networks' QoS level. Based on the quantification of reachable networks, the developed selection algorithm provides an overall call admission strategy to actively select the most suitable network.

The *Vickrey-Clarke-Groves* (*VCG*) mechanism, which has *direct-revelation* and *strategyproof* properties, had been developed how to manage control problems that involve multiple self-interested agents. The goal of the *VCG* mechanism is to define rules and payoff functions to reach a desired outcome, which is called social optimum (Dash, 2003),(Garg, 2008). However, an important underpinning assumption of the *VCG* mechanism is that an agent always successfully completes every assigned task. Sometimes, the agent may not be successful in completing their assigned tasks (Ramchurn, Mezzetti, Giovannucci, Rodriguez, Dash, & Jennings, 2009). Recently, *Ramchurn et al.,* developed the trust-based *VCG* (*T-VCG*) mechanism in the presence of execution uncertainty. They considered the reputation of a service performer within the system, in addition to its self-report (Ramchurn, 2009). The *ACAC* scheme adopted the *T-VCG* mechanism to effectively solve the network selection and price computation problems.

There is a set of overlay networks, $N = \{1,2..,i..,n\}$. Each network (i.e., $i \in N$) has a privately-known service cost ($c_i(\tau)$) and value ($v_i(\tau)$) of performing the service request τ. Let σ denote a particular call acceptance within the space of possible acceptances Ψ and τ^i represent that network i gets call service τ; $\sigma \in \Psi$ and $\Psi = \{\varnothing, \tau^1, \tau^2 ... \tau^n\}$ where $\varnothing$ denotes the case where the call request is rejected (Ramchurn, 2009). If $\Psi = \{\tau^i\}$, the cost and value of Ψ ($c_i(\Psi)$ and $v_i(\Psi)$) are $c_i(\tau)$ and $v_i(\tau)$, respectively. Otherwise, $c_i(\Psi) = v_i(\tau) = 0$. Finally, let $r_i(\Psi)$ be the payment by the user to network i based on its call acceptance in Ψ.

Usually, real-time traffic (*class I*) services require strict end-to-end performance guarantees and they are designed to be transmitted at a fixed bandwidth during the lifetime of the call. Therefore, they have step utility functions. However, non real-time traffic (*class II*) services are rather tolerant of delays and can gracefully adjust their transmission rates. Therefore, they have concave utility functions, which provide multiple QoS levels based on the dynamic bandwidth allocation. According to the different data types, the call τ's utility value per bit in the network i ($v_i(\tau)$) can be defined as follows (Dharwadkar, Siegel, & Chong, 2000).

$$\begin{cases} v_i(\tau) = \begin{cases} 1 \times Q\_L_i, & \text{when } b_\tau \geq mb_\tau \\ 0, & \text{when } b_\tau < mb_\tau \end{cases} \text{ where } \tau \in classI \\ v_i(\tau) = \dfrac{1 - e^{-\beta_\tau \times (b_\tau - mb_\tau)}}{1 - e^{-\beta_\tau \times (Mb_\tau - mb_\tau)}} \times Q\_L_i \text{ where } \tau \in classII \end{cases}$$

where b_τ is the currently allocated bandwidth (*bps*) of the call τ. Mb_τ, mb_τ are the maximum and minimum bandwidth requests of the call τ, respectively. According to (5), the QoS level of the network i (Q_L_i) is obtained. For the *class II* data type, the value β is chosen based on the average slope of the linear utility function of the request. To reflect the difference of quantitative QoS requirements, the β can quantify the adaptability of an application (Dharwadkar, 2000). In the network i, service cost per bit ($c_i(\tau)$) is defined according to (6).

$c_i\left(\tau\right) = v_i\left(\tau\right) \times p_i$, where

$$\begin{cases} p_i = 1 & if\ i \in class\ I \\ p_i = 0.8 & if\ i \in class\ II \end{cases} \quad (7)$$

where p_i is the price per bit of the call i. The *VCG* mechanism is a special case among traditional mechanisms; agents may not wish to report their true costs if reporting these falsely leads to a preferable outcome for them. The *ACAC* scheme will therefore distinguish between the actual cost ($c\left(\tau\right)$) and the reported cost ($\hat{c}\left(\tau\right)$), which is no longer necessarily truthful. The superscripting the latter with '^' indicates that agents can misreport their true types (Ramchurn, 2009).

Under various QoS constraints and a dynamically changing network traffic environment, there exists uncertainty about agents successfully completing their assigned services. In the *ACAC* scheme, the Possibility of Success (*PoS*) of new call service is taken into account. $PoS_i\left(\tau\right)$ is the *PoS* of the network i with the service τ; it is commonly observed from the online monitoring. In order to estimate the *PoS*, the *ACAC* scheme partitions the time-axis into equal intervals of length *unit_time*. Every *unit_time*, the call completion probability of each network is examined periodically. To handle traffic fluctuations in wireless networks, the *ACAC* scheme estimates *PoS* value based on the *PoS* history and recent *PoS* changes in each network. The developed algorithm adjusts the *PoS* value of call service τ ($PoS\left(\tau\right)$) as a weighted average of two quantities as follows.

$$PoS\left(\tau\right) = [(1-\gamma) \times PoS_{ave}] + [\gamma \times PoS_c] \quad (8)$$

where PoS_{ave} is the total average *PoS* value at the current time (t_c) and PoS_c is the *PoS* value during the time interval [t_c - *unit_time*,]. The parameter γ controls the relative weights given to recent and past network histories in online decision. Under diverse traffic environments, a fixed value of γ cannot effectively adapt to the changing network conditions. Therefore, the developed algorithm dynamically modifies γ at the end of each *unit_time* period. When the current bandwidth usage ratio (BUR_c) is high, *PoS* value should strongly depend on the recent network condition, i.e., on. PoS_c. In this case, a higher value of γ is more suitable. If the BUR_c is low, the *ACAC* scheme can put more emphasis on traffic history, i.e., on PoS_{ave}. In this case, a lower value of γ is more suitable. In the *ACAC* scheme, the *ACAC* scheme treats the γ value decision as an on-line decision problem; the value of γ is adjusted adaptively based on the BUR_c of each network. Therefore, each network dynamically adjusts the value of γ to make the system more responsive to current traffic conditions.

The developed price computation algorithm can estimate the service price that take into account the execution uncertainty. With the *PoS* of the call service, the expected value of overlay system, $\bar{v}_{os}\left(\Psi, \mathbb{P}\right)$, can be calculated as:

$$\bar{v}_{os}\left(\sigma, \mathbb{P}\right) = v_{os}\left(\sigma\right) \times PoS_\sigma\left(\tau\right),\ \text{s.t.,}\ \sigma \in \Psi \quad (9)$$

where $PoS_\sigma\left(\tau\right)$ is the *PoS* value in the selected network, which performs the requested call service (i.e., $\sigma \in \Psi$).

$$\mathbb{P} = PoS_1\left(\tau\right)...PoS_i\left(\tau\right)...PoS_n\left(\tau\right)$$

is the vector of *PoS* values of all the networks. To implement the execution uncertainty by a given network, the overlay system needs to require networks to report their *PoS* with the service execution cost ($\hat{c}$). $\mathbb{P}$ represents the vector of reported *PoS* values $P\hat{o}S_1\left(\tau\right),...,P\hat{o}S_n\left(\tau\right)$ (Ramchurn, 2009).

For the call service request, the *ACAC* scheme selects the most suitable network to achieve system efficiency; call connections are adaptively controlled based on the accurate analysis of cost and benefits of each access networks. In more detail, the network selection for a call admission decision is determined as follows (Ramchurn, 2009).

$$\mathcal{A}^*\left(\hat{\mathbb{C}},\hat{\mathbb{P}}\right) = arg\max_{\sigma\in\Psi}\left[\overline{v}_{os}\left(\sigma,\hat{\mathbb{P}}\right) - \sum_{i\in N}\hat{c}_i\left(\sigma\right)\right]$$
(10)

Price Computation Algorithm for Overlay Network System

After selecting a network, the price computation algorithm is triggered. The developed price computation algorithm adopts the basic concept of *T-VCG* mechanism to provide a normative guide for the payments of call service. Even more importantly, the *ACAC* scheme considers the *PoS* in computing the service payment. This price is realistic in real-world network operations where networks can, and often do, fail in their call services. In the traditional *VCG* mechanism, each agent is of a specific type. According to its type, an agent selects a specific strategy, which defines the agent's actions. Generally, an agent type is represented by θ, (e.g., each agent i is of type θ_i) (Dash, 2003),(Parkes, 2004). As mentioned earlier, agent-announced type ($\hat{\theta}$) in the *VCG* mechanism is no longer necessarily truthful; the symbol $\hat{\theta}$ indicates that agents can misreport their true types. Based on agent-announced types, the payment rule ($p_{vcg,i}(\theta)$) is defined as follows.

$$p_{vcg,i}\left(\hat{\theta}\right) = v_i\left(k^*\left(\hat{\theta}\right),\hat{\theta}_i\right) - \left\{V_N - V_{N-i}\right\}, \text{ s.t.,}$$
$$k^*\left(\hat{\theta}\right) = \text{argmax}_{k\in\mathcal{K}}\sum_i v_i\left(k,\hat{\theta}_i\right)$$
(11)

where k is a feasible choice of the set of all possible choices and $v_i\left(k,\hat{\theta}_i\right)$ defines the agent i's outcome of a choice k with its type $\hat{\theta}_i$. V_N is the total reported outcome of k^* and V_{N-i} is the total reported outcome of the choice that would be gotten without agent i, i.e.,

$$V_N = \max_{k\in\mathcal{K}}\sum_i v_i\left(k,\hat{\theta}_i\right)$$

and

$$V_{N-i} = \max_{k\in\mathcal{K}}\sum_{j\neq i} v_j\left(k,\hat{\theta}_j\right)$$

(Dash, 2003), (Garg, 2008), (Parkes, 2004).

In the *ACAC* scheme, the service price is similar to that of the traditional *VCG* mechanism in that the marginal contribution of the selected network to the overlay system is extracted by comparing the second best decision, excluding the selected network. The difference is the expected marginal contribution. Therefore, the service price ($SP_i\left(\hat{\mathbb{C}},\hat{\mathbb{P}},\sigma\right)$) of the network i is achieved as follows (Ramchurn, 2009):

$$SP_i\left(\hat{\mathbb{C}},\hat{\mathbb{P}},\sigma\right) =$$
$$\begin{cases} v_{os}(\mathcal{A}^*(\hat{\mathbb{C}},\hat{\mathbb{P}})) - \max_{\theta\in\Psi_{-i}}(\overline{v}_{os}(\theta,\hat{\mathbb{P}}) - \sum_{j\in N\backslash i}\hat{c}_j(\theta), \\ \text{if the assigned service is successfully completed} \\ -\max_{\theta\in\Psi_{-i}}(\overline{v}_{os}(\theta,\hat{\mathbb{P}}) - \sum_{j\in N\backslash i}\hat{c}_j(\theta) \end{cases}$$
(12)

where Ψ_{-i} is the set of possible acceptances (Ψ) excluding the network i. In comparison with the *VCG* model defined by (11), $v_i\left(k^*\left(\hat{\theta}\right),\hat{\theta}_i\right), V_N$ and V_{N-i} are replaced with $v_{os}\left(\mathcal{A}^*\left(\hat{\mathbb{C}},\hat{\mathbb{P}}\right)\right), \overline{v}_{os}\left(\theta,\hat{\mathbb{P}}\right)$ and $\sum_{j\in N\backslash i}\hat{c}_j\left(\theta\right)$, respectively. Finally, $SP_i\left(\hat{\mathbb{C}},\hat{\mathbb{P}},\sigma\right)$ is obtained as follows (Ramchurn, 2009).

$$
\begin{aligned}
SP_i\left(\hat{\mathbb{C}},\hat{\mathbb{P}},\sigma\right) &= PoS_i\left(\tau\right)\left[v_{os}\left(\mathcal{A}^*\left(\hat{\mathbb{C}},\hat{\mathbb{P}}\right)\right) - \max_{\theta\in\Psi_{-i}}\left(\overline{v}_{os}\left(\theta,\hat{\mathbb{P}}\right) - \sum_{j\in N\backslash i}\hat{c}_j\left(\theta\right)\right)\right] \\
&\quad + \left(1 - PoS_i\left(\tau\right)\right)\left[-\max_{\theta\in\Psi_{-i}}\left(\overline{v}_{os}\left(\theta,\hat{\mathbb{P}}\right) - \sum_{j\in N\backslash i}\hat{c}_j\left(\theta\right)\right)\right] \\
&= \overline{v}_{os}\left(\mathcal{A}^*\left(\hat{\mathbb{C}},\hat{\mathbb{P}}\right)\right) - \max_{\theta\in\Psi_{-i}}\left(\overline{v}_{os}\left(\theta,\hat{\mathbb{P}}\right) - \sum_{j\in N\backslash i}\hat{c}_j\left(\theta\right)\right)
\end{aligned}
$$

The Main Steps of the *ACAC* Scheme

In the *ACAC* scheme, the network evaluation, selection and price computation algorithms are developed. Under dynamically changing network environments, these algorithms are sophisticatedly combined into the holistic scheme and act cooperatively and collaborate with each other. In addition, control decisions are made dynamically in a real-time online manner, which is practical approach to be implemented for real network operations. Therefore, the *ACAC* scheme dynamically adapts the current network condition and can effectively approximate an optimal network performance. The main steps of the *ACAC* scheme are given next.

Step 1: In each network, the QoS factors (i.e., *B*, *E*, *P*, *L*) and control parameters (i.e., γ, $PoS\left(\tau\right)$) are adaptively estimated in a distributed online manner.

Step 2: The overlay system continuously collects the current QoS information from the all reachable wireless networks. According to (5), the *ACAC* scheme quantifies the QoS level of each network.

Step 3: When a new call request arrives, each network's service value ($v\left(\tau\right)$) and cost ($c\left(\tau\right)$) of performing the service request τ can be estimated by using (6) and (7).

Step 4: Every *unit_time*, the value of γ is adjusted adaptively based on the BUR_c. Based on this value, each network calculates its $PoS\left(\tau\right)$ according to (8).

Step 5: With the *PoS* of the call service, the expected value of overlay system, $\overline{v}_{os}\left(\Psi,\mathbb{P}\right)$, can be calculated by using (9).

Step 6: Based on the $\overline{v}_{os}\left(\Psi,\mathbb{P}\right)$ value, the most suitable network for a call service is determined by using (10)

Step 7: After the network selection, the price computation algorithm is triggered. If the network i is selected, the service price ($SP_i\left(\hat{\mathbb{C}},\hat{\mathbb{P}},\sigma\right)$) is achieved by using (13).

Step 8: Under widely diverse network environments, each network is self-monitoring constantly to estimate itself; proceed to Step 1.

Recently, several call admission control schemes have been presented for heterogeneous multi-layer networks. The Noncooperative Game-theoretic Bandwidth Allocation (*NGBA*) scheme is a novel call control algorithm for maximizing the user performance-price-ratio (Chen, 2010). In the *NGBA* scheme, the relationship between competitive SPs and users is modeled as a noncooperative game. Therefore, the Nash equilibrium solutions corresponding to the best response price offered by SP is obtained. The Bandwidth Allocation Mechanism (*BAM*) scheme is a mechanism for the allocation of the bandwidth of overlay networks (Dramitinos, 2009). In particular, the *BAM* scheme is an incentive-compatible, efficient,

Figure 3. Performance evaluations of the ACAC scheme

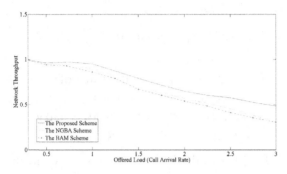

(a) Normalized network throughput   (b) Load balance in overlay networks

auction-based mechanism based on the repeated game. This scheme addressed the problem of deciding on which user flows to admit and how the bandwidth to be allocated while attaining efficiency. Figure 3 demonstrates that the performance of the proposed *ACAC* scheme is generally superior to those of other existing schemes: the *NGBA* scheme and the *BAM* scheme.

Summary

In the heterogeneous overlay networks, call admission and price computation problem is an important issue for effective network operations. The *ACAC* scheme is a new call admission control scheme for heterogeneous multi-layer networks. The main goal of the *ACAC* scheme is to maximize network performance while providing service QoS. To satisfy this goal, the *ACAC* scheme consists of network evaluation, selection and price computation algorithms. According to the *T_VCG* mechanism, the *ACAC* scheme dynamically select the best network for call service and effectively estimate the service price. For practical network operations, these developed algorithms are designed in an adaptive online fashion, and work together in a coordinated manner. Therefore, the *ACAC* scheme can quickly respond to real time network environment changes, and be suitable for ultimate practical implementation. The principle

contributions of the *ACAC* scheme are its adaptability, feasibility and effectiveness.

MECHANISM DESIGN BASED ONLINE BANDWIDTH ALLOCATION (*MDOBA*) SCHEME

During wireless multimedia network operations, user cooperation can play a significant role in determining system performance. However, until now, how to stimulate cooperation among users is not well addressed. In 2012, S. Kim proposed a new Mechanism Design based Online Bandwidth Allocation (*MDOBA*) scheme (Kim, 2012). The *MDOBA* scheme consists of bandwidth adaptation, call admission control and pricing computation algorithms to strike an appropriate network performance. These algorithms are designed based on the adaptive online manner and work together to maximize bandwidth efficiency economically.

Development Motivation

In recent years, the requirements placed on wireless networks have increased dramatically. However, in spite of the emergence of high network infrastructures, wireless bandwidth is still an extremely valuable and scarce resource. Therefore, all performance guarantees in wireless networks are conditional on currently available bandwidth capacity. In view of the remarkable growth in the number of users and the limited bandwidth, an efficient bandwidth management is very important and has been an active area of research over the last decade.

Multimedia is a keyword in the evolving information age of the 21st century. Recent proliferation of enabling communication technologies is causing an explosion in the number of multimedia services. Different multimedia services have different priorities, bandwidth requirements and delay tolerance; they not only require different amounts of bandwidth but also have different Quality of Service (QoS) requirements. Therefore, efficient bandwidth control while ensuring QoS guarantees for multimedia services is becoming a critical issue in wireless networks. However, there is a trade off between the ability to satisfy QoS requirements and bandwidth efficiency (Chen, & Su, 2007).

Until now, several network control strategies have been developed for multimedia services. Bandwidth adaptation technique is a well-known method to control more bandwidth consuming multimedia services. Under overloaded network environments, this adaptation technique can dynamically adjust the allocated bandwidth while maximizing the network performance. Another effective method for the bandwidth management is a pricing strategy. Usually, users are price sensitive (Paschalidis, & Tsitsiklis, 2000). Therefore, the network can send signals to users through price and effectively influence their behaviors to fit the current available bandwidth (Hou, Yang, & Papavassiliou, 2002). With the adaptation and pricing methods, Call Admission Control (CAC) is also an effective strategy to maximize the network revenue. In wireless networks, the CAC strategy controls the number of call connections while modifying users' demands to provide the desired QoS (Yee, Choong, Low, Tan, & Chien, 2007).

Develops from traditional game theory, Mechanism Design (MD) can give the agents incentives to act and interact in particular ways (Dash, 2003). The goal of MD is to define rules and payoff functions to reach a desired outcome, which is called social optimum. Therefore, MD can be thought of as inverse game theory – where game theory reasons about how agents will play a game, MD reasons about how to design games that produce desired outcomes (Anderegg, & Eidenbenz, 2003), (Shneidman, & Parkes, 2003). Many applications of MD are related to economics, but it is also a powerful tool to model a wider range of real life situations.

Classic mechanism design considers a static situation in which a one-time decision is made and all agents are assumed to be patient enough to wait for the decision. However, in real world network operations, control decisions must be made sequentially without the knowledge of future information (Parkes, 2004). Motivated by the above discussion, the *MDOBA* scheme is developed as a new adaptive online bandwidth allocation scheme for multimedia services. In the *MDOBA* scheme, network users are assumed to be rational selfish agents. Based on their goals and information, these self-organizing agents make decisions in pursuit of their individual objectives (Friedman, 2003). In the *MDOBA* scheme, online mechanism design concept is applied to stimulate cooperation actions among users. Under various QoS constraints and dynamically changing environments, the *MDOBA* scheme can get a globally desirable network performance. To satisfy the conflicting requirements, the *MDOBA* scheme consists of bandwidth adaptation, price computation and CAC algorithms; these algorithms are sophisticatedly combined and mutually dependent on each other. This integrated approach gives excellent control flexibility under widely different and diversified network situations.

As ubiquitous network access has spurred the growth of multimedia applications, it has raised the necessary of next generation future network. Therefore, it is believed that future networks are being designed to support congestion control and various QoS ensuring. The *MDOBA* scheme can provide the QoS provisioning for higher priority services, and alleviate the network congestion. Without question, it is a highly desirable feature for future network operations.

Recently, several bandwidth allocation schemes for wireless networks have been presented in research literature. The Traffic Forecasting and Dynamic Bandwidth Provisioning (*TFDBP*) scheme in (Krithikaivasan, Zeng, Deka, & Medhi, 2007) is a dynamic bandwidth provisioning algorithm. Based on the periodically measured traffic data, this scheme presents a probability-hop forecasting algorithm using the confidence-bounds of the mean forecast value from the conditional forecast distribution. The *TFDBP* scheme is developed to allow trade off between the under-provisioning and the utilization, while addressing the overhead cost of updating bandwidth. The *Adaptive Bandwidth Allocation with Flexible QoS* (*ABAFQ*) scheme in (Persone, & Campagna, 2009) provides adaptive bandwidth allocation and admission control techniques to maintain the excellent network performance. Based on two different classes of requests, the *ABAFQ* scheme can keep the requests at the highest possible level within the negotiated QoS. Especially, this scheme provided the upgrade-and-degrade (u-d) mechanism to give high quality while maintaining the performance of each class. When an arrival call occurs during a congestion period, a degradation mechanism is initiated to free bandwidth to admit the new arrival call. When a departure call occurs, an upgrade mechanism is initiated to increase the actual level of quality if possible. Beyond the traditional metrics such as the blocking and dropping probabilities for each class, the authors proposed threshold metrics to evaluate the cost of the u-d mechanism and the QoS level provided. In addition, to deal with the integrated services characteristics, the *ABAFQ* scheme allows the inclusion of different classes and each request of a given class can be served

according to different service levels. However, system parameters, which are used to evaluate the cost of the u-d mechanism and the QoS level, are fixed values. Under dynamic network environments, this static approach is inappropriate to operate real world network systems. In addition, the *ABAFQ* scheme did not consider economic aspects to increase bandwidth usability.

The *Conservative and Adaptive Quality of Service* (*CAQoS*) scheme in (Yee, 2007) performs call admissions while achieving the efficient bandwidth utilization by using a designated provisioning model. Unlike most conventional schemes which gradually scale-down the bandwidth rates of ongoing connections to accommodate new connection/handoff requests, the *CAQoS* scheme introduces an early scaling-down of bandwidth for the QoS provisioning. The objectives of this scheme are to minimize the need for frequent bandwidth reallocation and to achieve lower call blocking and handoff dropping rates while maximizing the overall bandwidth utilization. In the *CAQoS* scheme, the bandwidth partition in a cell is divided into four regions, namely the used, available, conserved, and reserved segments. The used bandwidth is the bandwidth currently used by the ongoing connections. The available bandwidth is the bandwidth to be used for new connection. The conserved bandwidth is actually the total bandwidth extracted from some/all ongoing connections. The reserved bandwidth contains the bandwidth that is reserved for future handoff connections. Whenever the network is overloaded, only new calls with real-time priority will be admitted while ongoing lower priority calls (non real-time) would receive a degraded bandwidth rate or be forced to terminate. With an early scale-down bandwidth feature of the *CAQoS* scheme, there is a high probability that new calls will be directly admitted, this lowers the need to perform bandwidth reallocation.

Bandwidth Allocation Algorithms in the *MDOBA* Scheme

The *MDOBA* scheme combines bandwidth adaptation and pricing methods to provide an overall call admission strategy. Based on the adaptive online approach, the allocated bandwidth and price can be dynamically adjustable. Therefore, call connections are adaptively controlled to response constantly changing network environments.

Bandwidth Adaptation Algorithm

Bandwidth adaptation is becoming a very attractive method to cope with the network resource fluctuations. In order to ensure the efficient network performance, this technique dynamically allocates bandwidth to different call services. To implement the bandwidth adaptation process, QoS should be defined to determine the degree of users' satisfaction (Hou, 2002), (Anderegg, 2003). The *MDOBA* scheme adopted the concept of utility function in microeconomics to quantify the user's perceived QoS. Based on the collective effect of service performance, a utility function maps its bandwidth allocation to the user satisfaction, which represents the 'level of satisfaction' of an application. The shape of utility functions varies according to the characteristic of each application (Garg, 2008).

According to the different data types, the value of call i's utility function (u_f) is defined as the same approach in the *ACAC* scheme (Kim, 2012). There are two kinds of bandwidth adaptation; for degrade and upgrade mechanisms. Under overloaded network conditions, the degrade policy applies at the time of a new call request. If the allocated bandwidth to connected calls is larger than the minimum requirement, it can be reduced. The upgrade policy applies at the time of a call completion. The released bandwidth by a complete call can be allocated to the existing degraded call connections in order to restore the

reduced bandwidth. With multiple grades of service quality, allocated bandwidths for ongoing call connections can be dynamically adjusted while maximizing the network performance.

Call Admission Control Algorithm

The wireless bandwidth is limited and freely shared by all network users. Therefore, if independent and selfish users demand the bandwidth to maximize their satisfactions, not all the requests can be completely served. Even though the bandwidth adaptation algorithm dynamically adjusts the wireless bandwidth, the heavy traffic load situation can cause a new call blocking. At this time, Call Admission Control (CAC) needs to be started to limit the number of call connections for the better network performance (Chen, 2007).

When a new request is not accepted, this request terminates or may try again in the near future. Usually, re-try calls have intense aspirations for the network service over first-try calls. Therefore, the *MDOBA* scheme gives a higher price to re-try calls; the call with higher price would be easily accepted according to the price strategy. In the *MDOBA* scheme, the role of pricing is investigated as an additional dimension of the call admission process. Each service price (sp) is defined based on three attributes; allocated bandwidth amount, price level and utility function as follows.

$$sp_i(b_i) = \left(u\_f_i(b_i) + p\_l_i \right) \times p_i \times b_i,$$

$$\text{where } \begin{cases} p_i = 1.2 \ \ if \ i \in class \ I \\ p_i = 0.8 \ \ if \ i \in class \ II \end{cases} \quad (14)$$

where b_i, p_l_i are the allocated bandwidth (bps) and the price level of the call i, respectively. The p_i is the normal price per bit of the call i; it is a fixed value for each data type. In the *MDOBA* scheme, p_l_i is defined as a discrete value, which increases sequentially in steps equal to ΔP_l based on the number of re-trials.

During network operations, new call requests arrive in real time. If there is available bandwidth to assign a requested call, the new call is accepted. Otherwise, the allocated bandwidth for existing *class II* calls can be reduced to accept the new request. If the released bandwidth by adaptation technique is sufficient to support the new service request, it is accepted. Otherwise, call admission decisions are made based on the extra charge in the price strategy and call preemption technique.

Price Computation Algorithm

Mechanism design (*MD*) is used to define a strategic situation to make a system exhibits good behaviors when independent agents pursue self-interested strategies (Wang, & Schulzrinne, 2005), (Garg, 2008). In the *MDOBA* scheme, the basic concept of *MD* is adopted to calculate the Extra-charge (*Ec*) for the call service under heavy traffic load situations. To alleviate the traffic congestion, the *Ec* is provided as a negative incentive in the current network.

The *VCG* mechanism is a special case of traditional *MD*, in which the agent-announced type ($\hat{\theta}$) is no longer necessarily truthful; the symbol $\hat{\theta}$ indicates that agents can misreport their true types. Based on agent-announced types, the choice rule ($k^*\left(\hat{\theta}\right)$) and the payment rule ($p_{vcg,i}(\hat{\theta})$) is defined as the same manner in the *IANR* scheme (Kim, 2012). follows (Woodard, & Parkes, 2003).

In the *MDOBA* scheme, a new price computation algorithm is developed. For the efficient bandwidth management, the developed approach adopts the *VCG* mechanism concept. When a network congestion occurs (i.e., the new call request cannot be accepted due to the lack of available bandwidth), the price computation algorithm is triggered to impose an extra price charge. Usually, higher bandwidth price encourages users to give up their services. Therefore, by imposing extra

cost, the *MDOBA* scheme can specify which call connection is to be preempted. However, if all the users of existing call services willingly pay the extra cost, a new call request is rejected.

To practically estimate an Extra-charge (*Ec*) of call connections, the *MDOBA* scheme modified the traditional static *VCG* mechanism. For the design of price computation algorithm, users are assumed to have different utility functions for their call services and sequentially make online decisions to maximize their payoff. In the terminology of the *MD*, a utility function is called as each user's type. Under heavy traffic load situations, the *MDOBA* scheme begins to impose an *Ec* to control the traffic congestion problem. Let k denote a particular set of call services within the space ($\mathbb{N}$) of all possible sets for the call acceptance. Let τ and ψ denote a existing call (i.e., $\tau \in {}^o$) and a new call request, respectively. The main goal of the *MDOBA* scheme is to maximize the network revenue (*NR*). To satisfy this goal, the extra charge for τ service (Ec_τ) is defined as follows.

$$Ec_\tau = \begin{cases} NR_{-\tau,\psi} - NR \ , \ if \ NR < NR_{-\tau,\psi} \\ \\ 0 \qquad , \ otherwise \end{cases}$$

(15)

$$s.t., NR_{-\tau,\psi} = \underset{{}^o \in \mathbb{N}_{-\tau}}{\arg\max}$$
$$\left([\sum_{i \in {}^o, i \neq \tau} c\_sp_i\left(\overline{b}_i\right)] + c\_sp_\psi\left(\overline{b}_\psi\right) \right)$$
and
$$\left([\sum_{i \in {}^o, i \neq \tau} \overline{b}_i] + \overline{b}_\psi \right) \leq B$$

where $\overline{b}_i$ is the degraded bandwidth of the call i and B is the total available bandwidth of network system. $NR_{-\tau,\psi}$ is an expected *NR*, which includes the new request call (ψ) while preempting the ongoing call τ. Therefore, ($NR_{-\tau,\psi} - NR$) is the difference between the revenue in which the existing call τ service is replaced by the new requested call (ψ). If NR is less than the $NR_{-\tau,\psi}$, the extra cost (Ec_τ) is used as a negative incentive, which could have strong influence on the behavior of the call τ's user. Finally, the total service cost (Tsc_τ) for the call τ's service is given by.

$$Tsc_\tau = \begin{cases} sp_\tau\left(\overline{b}_\tau\right) + Ec_\tau & , \ if \ NR < NR_{-\tau,\psi} \\ \\ sp_\tau\left(\overline{b}_\tau\right) & , \ otherwise \end{cases}$$

(16)

If the user of call τ would not agree to pay the new price (Tsc_τ), the call τ service is preempted to accept the new call request (ψ).

The Main Steps of the *MDOBA* Scheme

In the *MDOBA* scheme, the bandwidth adaptation, CAC and pricing computation algorithms are proposed to implement adaptive bandwidth allocations. Under widely different traffic load intensities, these algorithms are sophisticatedly combined into the holistic scheme and act cooperatively and collaborate with each other. In addition, control decisions are made dynamically in an adaptive online manner, which is practical approach to be implemented for real network operations. Therefore, the *MDOBA* scheme can effectively approximate an optimal network performance. The main steps of the *MDOBA* scheme are given next.

Step 1: When there is enough bandwidth, a call request is provided by the maximum bandwidth allocation.

Step 2: Due to the user's intense aspiration, the *MDOBA* scheme gives a higher price to retry calls. Based on the number of re-trials, the price level (P_l) increases sequentially in steps equal to ΔP_l.

Step 3: Under overloaded network situations (i.e., the network system has not sufficient bandwidth to support new service requests), the bandwidth adaptation algorithm is triggered to the existing *class II* call connections.

Step 4: If the released bandwidth by adaptation technique is sufficient to support the new service request, it is accepted; proceeds to Step 6.

Step 5: According to (15) and (16), the new *Tsc* is calculated. If the existing user would not agree to pay the new *Tsc*, the running call is preempted to accept the new call request. Otherwise, the new call request is rejected.

Step 6: When an ongoing call is completed, the allocated bandwidth is re-allocated to the existing degraded call connections in order to restore the reduced bandwidth.

Step 7: Based on the real time online manner, the network system continuously monitors the current network conditions.

Figure 4 demonstrates that the performance of the proposed *MDOBA* scheme is generally superior to those of other existing schemes: the *ABAFQ* scheme and the *CAQoS* scheme. These results verify the considerable performance improvement that can be achieved by the integration of bandwidth adaptation, call admission and price control processes in wireless networks.

Summary

In the *MDOBA* scheme, a variation of the *VCG* mechanism is developed, which outlines an extension of the mechanism design model for wireless multimedia services. To respond to the network environment changes, each user is capable of independently adapting its actions. Based on the

Figure 4. Performance evaluations of the MDOBA scheme

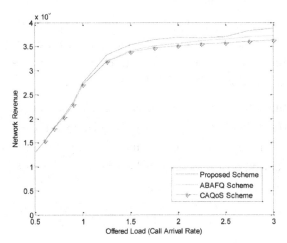

(a) Call Blocking Probability (CBP)　　　　　(b) Network Revenue

online *VCG* mechanism, the *MDOBA* scheme stimulates cooperative decisions from the network users and guide selfish users to achieve a globally desirable network performance. In addition, for practical network operations, the *MDOBA* scheme is designed in dynamic online fashion, and work together by employing a coordination paradigm. Therefore, the *MDOBA* scheme can provide a good tradeoff among conflicting requirements.

NEGOTIATION BARGAINING GAME BASED BANDWIDTH MANAGEMENT (NBGBM) SCHEME FOR MULTI-HOP RELAYING NETWORKS

Nowadays, Multi-hop Relaying Network (MRN) has gained wide acceptance as a next step towards future radio networks. MRN can extend the service area as well as improve the performance of wireless networks. To exploit the multi-hop relaying operation, an important issue is how to properly control wireless bandwidth. Recently, S. Kim proposed a new Negotiation Bargaining Game based Bandwidth Management (*NBGBM*) scheme for MRNs. By integrating the random arrival rule

and Nash bargaining model, the *NBGBM* scheme adaptively controls the wireless bandwidth to maximize network efficiency. In the *NBGBM* scheme, trust value and bargaining powers are decided according to the Bayesian inference and real-time negotiation process, respectively. This approach can make the network system be close to the optimized network performance.

Development Motivation

Multi-hop Relaying Networks (MRN) use relay stations (RS) to extend or enhance the coverage of a base station (BS) in a cellular network. The BS is attached to a wired backhaul, and RSs use wireless transmission to connect to the BS and to the end-users, while direct BS and end-users connection is also possible. Traditionally, multi-hop relaying technique has been studied in the context of ad hoc wireless networks as a means of enabling the network operation without any infrastructure. In a past few years, this approach has been widely considered as a supplementary technology to increase the cell coverage and enhance the throughput of next generation wireless systems. However, due to the requirement for extra wireless bandwidth for relaying hops, and the sensitivity to the quality of relaying routes, MRNs require a well-designed bandwidth allocation strategy in order to secure performance gains (Le, & Hossain, 2007), (Park, & Jung, 2007).

Recent advances in wireless communication technologies have made it possible to provide heterogeneous traffic services. However, various traffic services make the problem more complex, since each call requires different bandwidth assignment and has a different priority according to the required Quality-of-Service (QoS). Usually, service requests are categorized into two different classes; handoff traffic services (*class I*) and new call traffic services (*class II*). According to the required QoS, *class I* traffic has higher priority over *class II* traffic. To share bandwidth among traffic services with different QoS requirements, available bandwidth is divided into distinct parts corresponding to particular traffic classes. This bandwidth partitioning strategy plays an important role in determining network performance.

In game theory, the bankruptcy problem is a distribution problem involving the allocation of a given amount of a perfectly divisible resource among a group of players. The focus is on the case where the amount is insufficient to satisfy all their demands. There are several division methods. Especially, random arrival rule is a well-known method for the resource distribution problem (Chun, & Lee, 2007). In addition, a bargaining solution based on the cooperative game theory is another effective tool to achieve a mutually desirable solution between efficiency and fairness. Traditionally, the bargaining solution is obtained corresponding to the bargaining powers. Bargaining power is a concept related to the relative abilities of game players in a situation to exert influence over each other. To provide additional flexibility in choosing solution by taking into consideration the diversified network situation, it is necessary to admit differential bargaining powers (Park, & Schaar, 2007), (Kimura, Yamamoto, Murata, & Yoshida, 2008). Random arrival rule and bargain-

ing solution can provide predictions about how the limited resource it will be shared, or what division is fair, which may depend on the player utility functions. Based on these considerations, a cooperative game methodology is employed for multi-hop cellular network management, which can improve control adaptability and flexibility under widely different and diversified network situations.

Motivated by the above discussion, the *NBGBM* scheme is developed for multi-hop cellular networks. By using the trust-based random arrival approach, the *NBGBM* scheme dynamically allocates the bandwidth in MRN. To support different QoS traffic services, the allocated bandwidth should be partitioned. To solve this partition problem, the *NBGBM* scheme adopts the basic concept of Nash Bargaining Solution (NBS). Usually, the NBS has some attractive features to model the interactions among independent decision-makers and enforce collaborative behavior. In particular, it can provide fairness and efficiency in the aspect of QoS. The bargaining solution is strongly dependent on the bargaining powers. If different bargaining powers are used, the players with a higher bargaining power obtains a higher resource than the other players. To adaptively adjust the bargaining powers, the *NBGBM* scheme presents a formal model of negotiation process. Negotiation is a dynamic process in which two or more negotiators with different preferences jointly reach a mutually acceptable agreement on the terms of a transaction (Sierra, Faratin, & Jennings, 1997). In the *NBGBM* scheme, the purpose of the negotiation is to get an effective solution for the bandwidth partitioning between different priority traffic services.

Survey About Game Theory Based Bandwidth Management Approach

Recently, several schemes for wireless networks have been presented in research literature. The *Game-theoretic Call Admission Control* (*GCAC*) scheme provides a suitable solution model for fair and efficient call admission control problems (Virapanicharoen, & Benjapolakul, 2005). To select fair-efficient threshold parameters for the asymmetrical traffic, cooperative game theoretic algorithms are proposed. The *GCAC* scheme can reduce the computational complexity while still providing a proper consideration of efficiency and fairness. The *Dynamic Multiple-threshold Bandwidth Reservation (DMBR)* scheme is capable of granting differential priorities to different traffic classes by dynamically adjusting bandwidth reservation thresholds (Chen, Li, & Fang, 2005). The main contribution of the *DMBR* scheme is to adjust the admission control policy by taking into account some dynamic factors such as offered load. S. Kim proposed adaptive bandwidth reservation and borrowing algorithms for multimedia cellular networks (Kim, 2011). Based on the well-known game theoretic concept of bargaining, wireless bandwidth is controlled as efficiently as possible while ensuring QoS guarantees for higher priority traffic services.

The *Pricing and Power Control for Bandwidth (PPCB)* scheme allocates bandwidth between conflicting users and network provider as a non-cooperative game model (Feng, Mau, Mandayam, 2004). It is shown that the proposed strategy in the *PPCB* scheme results in a unique Nash equilibrium, and there exists a unique bandwidth price that maximized the revenue of the network. The *Real-time Incentive Compatible Adaptation (RICA)* scheme dynamically decides the price based on a reasonable user utility function (Wang, 2005). Users adapt their sending rates and QoS requests in response to changes in service prices. Therefore, it can achieve significant gains in network availability, revenue, and user-perceived benefit. The *Power Control with Repeated Game (PCRG)* scheme is a joint link adaptation and power control algorithm for wireless communications (Ginde, Neel, & Buehrer, 2003). By using the game theory, this scheme results in correct power control decisions and pro-

vides an acceptable level of interference to other co-channel links. The *Adaptive and Distributed Power Control (ADPC)* scheme is a game-based power control algorithm to effectively schedule each user's power level (Long, Zhang, Li, Yang, & Guan, 2007). This scheme can safely run in a fully selfish environment without any additional pricing and secure mechanism.

Utility-based Multi-service Bandwidth Allocation (*UMBA*) scheme is a bandwidth allocation approach for multiple services (Luo, 2009). In the *UMBA* scheme, a utility function is introduced to estimate the effect of network performance and the bandwidth offered by different wireless access networks is normalized by using their corresponding capacities. Based on the concept of network utility, the *UMBA* scheme allocates bandwidth flexibly depending on the utility fairness. The Game-Theoretic Bandwidth Allocation (*GTBA*) scheme is an efficient bandwidth allocation algorithm based on the game-model approach (Niyato, 2008). The *GTBA* scheme is designed to support users, who can connect to different wireless access networks. Based on the allocated bandwidth, call control mechanism is used to maintain the QoS performance for the different types of services.

The *Demand-Matching Spectrum Sharing (DMSS)* scheme is a non-cooperative game model for CR bandwidth sharing problems (Liu, Shen, Song, & Wang, 2009). This scheme enables each unlicensed user to access appropriate bandwidth by using the *Nelder-Mead* direct search method. In addition, matching factors between the user demand and the bandwidth characteristics are built up and the *Nash* equilibrium is achieved by adopting demand matching factor. The *Dynamic Bandwidth Selection Game (DBSG)* scheme is designed as a game theoretic framework to evaluate bandwidth management functionalities in CR networks (Malanchini, Cesana, Gatti, 2009). In the *DBSG* scheme, different quality measures are considered to select the best bandwidth opportunity under the tight constraint.

The Noncooperative Game-theoretic Bandwidth Allocation (*NGBA*) scheme is a novel call control algorithm for maximizing the user performance-price-ratio (Chen, 2010). In the *NGBA* scheme, the relationship between competitive SPs and users is modeled as a non-cooperative game. Therefore, the Nash equilibrium solutions corresponding to the best response price offered by SP is obtained. The Bandwidth Allocation Mechanism (*BAM*) scheme is a mechanism for the allocation of the bandwidth of 4G networks (Dramitinos, & Lassous, 2009). In particular, the *BAM* scheme is an incentive-compatible, efficient, auction-based mechanism based on the repeated game. This scheme addressed the problem of deciding on which user flows to admit and how the bandwidth of the integrated access of a 4G network should be allocated to the competing user services while attaining efficiency.

The *Range Extension with Fixed Relays Networks (REFRN)* scheme can significantly increase the network coverage by the employment of digital fixed relays (Huining, Yanikomeroglu, Falconer, & Periyalwar, 2004). In the *REFRN* scheme, a novel channel assignment method is developed to prevent potential capacity loss without any penalty in capacity. The *Resource Allocation in Cellular Multi-hop Networks (RACMN)* scheme presents effective scheduling algorithms for multi-hop network model (Newton, Thompson, & Naden, 2008). By employing the combination of round robin or equal throughput scheduling methods, the actual benefit of this scheme is to spatially reuse the wireless bandwidth for the network efficiency. The *Novel Resource Allocation with Relay Technology (NRART)* scheme is wireless frequency allocation algorithm for the multi-hop cellular network (Wen, & Wu, 2012). By using the resource sharing pool, the *NRART* scheme supports the dynamic frequency resource allocation to enhance the system spectral efficiency. The *Genetic Algorithm based Dynamic Resource Allocation (GADRA)* scheme purposes a way to op-

timize the multi-hop cellular network (Ayyadurai, Moessner, & Tafazolli, 2011). According to the genetic algorithm, the *GADRA* scheme adaptively resizes the cell coverage limit and dynamically allocates resources based on active user demands. The changing traffic demands require dynamic network reconfiguration to maintain proportional fairness in achieving the throughput.

Previous proposed schemes have been designed based on the game theory to control the wireless bandwidth in multimedia networks. The interactions among users sharing the wireless bandwidth can be formally modeled as games. The outcome of these games can be predicted by using a game theoretic formulation. The existing schemes try to design game theoretic solutions for specific bandwidth allocation applications.

Bandwidth Management Algorithms in the *NBGBM* Scheme

For the effective bandwidth allocation, the *NBGBM* scheme evaluates the trust value according to the Bayesian inference. And then, the available bandwidth is allocated by using the trust-based random arrival rule. For the adaptive bandwidth partitioning, Nash bargaining approach is adopted to support different QoS traffic services. To adjust the bargaining powers, the *NBGBM* scheme designs a negotiation process. Based on the adaptive online approach, these algorithms are incorporated and act cooperatively to strike an appropriate performance.

Bayesian Approach for Trust Evaluation

By incorporating the flexibility of ad hoc networking, the MRN systems can increase system capacity, allow higher data rate services, and enlarge cell coverage; they are capable of achieving much higher throughput than current cellular systems. In MRNs, each cell is serviced by a base station

(BS) and relay stations (RSs) are network elements deployed by the BS for data delivery. The role of the BS is to allocate bandwidth for each RS and supervises whether the RSs cooperates or not for the performance of the whole system. To support QoS ensuring, the role of RSs is to adaptively partition the allocated bandwidth by estimating the current traffic situation (Le, 2007). This situation leads us to develop an adaptive trust based bandwidth allocation algorithm. Based on the RSs' trust levels, the BS can give advantages in bandwidth allocation for cooperative RS's. To estimate these trust levels, the *NBGBM* scheme adopts the principle from Bayesian inference. In 1967, John Harsanyi introduced the Bayesian inference model under incomplete information. This approach relaxes the assumption that all information is completely known to predict the outcome of the uncertainty. Therefore, the concept of Bayesian inference model can be used to provide solutions to predict the future trust values based on the historical data (Zouridaki, Mark, Hejmo, & Thomas, 2005), (Changiz, Halabian, Yu, Lambadaris, & Tang, 2010).

In a single cell of MRN, the *NBGBM* scheme can assume that there are one BS and a set $N = \{1,..,n\}$ of RSs. For effective bandwidth allocation, the BS should distinguish between trustworthy and unreliable RSs. Therefore, the BS estimates the RS's trust value (T), which is evaluated based on the RS's behavior. The *NBGBM* scheme assumes that the T is a random variable taking values on the interval [0,1] and represents a notion of trust level associated with a given RS. If a RS behaves reliably, it does successfully relay the data packets. Therefore, the T value for each RS is calculated based on its success rate and failure rate of packet relay-transmissions (Zouridaki, 2005), (Changiz, 2010). For the T value calculation, the *NBGBM* scheme uses the Bayesian inference method. It is well-suited for stochastic problems. To model the Bayesian inference, some parameters should be defined. When the BS monitors the behavior of ith RS as an actor, a prob-

ability p_i is defined to estimate the ith RS's faithful behavior; p_i represents the packet delivery success ratio. Since p_i value can be drawn independently from the observation, p_i value for next time period is unknown. This uncertainty can be solved by assuming that p_i is drawn according to a prior distribution that is updated as new observations become available. As is commonly done (Zouridaki, 2005), (Changiz, 2010), the *NBGBM* scheme uses a Binomial distribution for this prior distribution. With parameters p_i and $q_i = 1 - p_i$, Binomial distribution suitably shows how confidence grows when the number of observations grows. Iteratively, the BS updates this prior distribution by performing observations, i.e., counting the number of packets entering the ith RS and the number of successfully serviced packets by that RS. In the *NBGBM* scheme, there are n different RSs. Therefore, each BS maintains n different distributions for each RS.

During the tth time period, suppose that the *NBGBM* scheme observes the total number of packets (N_i^t) that have been sent from the BS to the ith RS and let M_i^t be the number of packets successfully serviced by the ith RS. Also assume that the random variable p_i is derived from a prior distribution $f_{t-1}(p_i)$ (Zouridaki, 2005), (Changiz, 2010). Based on the N_i^t, M_i^t and $f_{t-1}(p_i)$ values, the BS can derive the posterior distribution of random variable p_i via Bayes' rule as follows.

$$f_t(p_i) = \frac{P(M_i^t = m_i^t | p_i, N_i^t = n_i^t) f_{t-1}(p_i)}{\int_0^1 P(M_i^t = m_i^t | p_i, N_i^t = n_i^t) f_{t-1}(p_i) dp_i}$$
(17)

where $P(M_i^t = m_i^t | p_i, N_i^t = n_i^t)$ is called the likelihood function (Zouridaki, 2005), (Changiz,

2010), and has followed a Binomial distribution like as.

$$P\left(M_i^t = m_i^t | p_i, N_i^t = n_i^t\right) =$$
$$\binom{n_i^t}{m_i^t} \left(p_i\right)^{m_i^t} \left(q_i\right)^{n_i^t - m_i^t}, \qquad (18)$$
$$\text{s.t.}, q_i = 1 - p_i$$

Binomial distribution and Beta distribution are a conjugate pair and Beta distribution can easily derive the distribution function of p_i. It means that the posterior distribution $f_t\left(p_i\right)$ follows a Beta distribution with parameters α and β (Zouridaki, 2005), (Changiz, 2010). However, at the beginning (iteration $t = 0$), the *NBGBM* scheme haw no information about distribution of p_i. Therefore, the *NBGBM* scheme assumes that $f_0\left(p_i\right)$ follows a uniform distribution over the interval $\left[0,1\right]$, i.e.,

$$f_0\left(p_i\right) = U\left(0,1\right) = Beta\left(1,1\right),$$
$$\text{s.t.}, Beta\left(\alpha,\beta\right) = \frac{\left(p_i\right)^{\left(\alpha-1\right)} \left(q_i\right)^{\left(\beta-1\right)}}{\int_0^1 \left(p_i\right)^{\left(\alpha-1\right)} \left(q_i\right)^{\left(\beta-1\right)} dp_i}$$
$$\qquad (19)$$

In other words, given that $M_i^t = m_i^t$ and $N_i^t = n_i^t$ parameters, $f_t\left(p_i\right)$ follows a $Beta\left(\alpha_t, \beta_t\right)$ distribution, and α_t and β_t parameters are defined recursively like as:

$$\alpha_t = \alpha_{t-1} + m_i^t \text{ and } \beta_t = \beta_{t-1} + n_i^t - m_i^t, \text{ s.t.,}$$
$$\alpha_0 = 1 \text{ and } \beta_0 = 1 \qquad (20)$$

Finally, $f_t\left(p_i\right)$ can be obtained as follows.

$$f_t\left(p_i\right) = Beta\left(\alpha_{t-1} + m_i^t, \beta_{t-1} + n_i^t - m_i^t\right),$$
$$\text{where } t \geq 0$$
$$\qquad (21)$$

Without any need to calculate (17), the *NB-GBM* scheme can construct a recursive formula to update the prior distribution function $f_t\left(p_i\right)$ according to (19) and (21). From the viewpoint of the BS, the ith RS's trust value after the tth iteration ($T_i\left(t\right)$) is defined as the expected value of p_i with respect to the corresponding distribution function $f_t\left(p_i\right)$ (Zouridaki, 2005), (Changiz, 2010); it is equal to the mean value of the $Beta\left(\alpha_t, \beta_t\right)$ as follows.

$$T_i\left(t\right) = \frac{\alpha_t}{\alpha_t + \beta_t} \qquad (22)$$

Each RS has a certain bandwidth request and the BS attempts to distribute the bandwidth to individual RSs in a fair manner. The *NBGBM* scheme defines that B is the total amount of bandwidth and c_i is the bandwidth request of ith RS. Based on the RSs' trust values ($T_i\left(t\right)$, s.t., $1 \leq i \leq n$), the *NBGBM* scheme designs a new dynamic and adaptive bandwidth allocation algorithm. To efficiently use the scarce bandwidth resource, the *NBGBM* scheme adopts the main concept of O'Neill's Random Arrival Rule (RAR) (Chun, 2007). RAR is based on the first-come first-serve principle. However, to remove the unfairness associated with a particular order, the RAR takes the arithmetic average over all orders of request arrivals.

In the developed algorithm in the *NBGBM* scheme, bandwidth allocation depends on the order in which RSs arrive; the *NBGBM* scheme assumes that all orders of RS arrivals are equally possible. When RSs are arriving one after the other, they are fully compensated until available bandwidth runs out. If the available bandwidth is insufficient to satisfy all demands of RSs (i.e., $\sum_{i \in N} c_i > B$), the developed algorithm is triggered. In this case, a formal definition of bandwidth allocation for the ith RS at $(t+1)^{th}$ iteration ($BA_i(t+1)$) is formulated as follows.

$$BA_i(t+1) =$$

$$\frac{1}{N!} \sum_{\pi \in \Pi^N} \min \left\{ (T_i(t) \times c_i), \max \left\{ B - \sum_{\substack{j \in N, \\ \pi(j) < \pi(i)}} (T_j(t) \times c_j), 0 \right\} \right\}$$

where Π^N denote the class of permutation of N. To maximize the network performance, the allocated bandwidth amount of each RS should be adapted dynamically according to (23). In order to implement this online approach, the NBGBM scheme partitions the time-axis into equal intervals of length *unit_time* (i.e., a short time duration). Every *unit_time*, the BS periodically re-evaluates the current network situation and adaptively reallocates bandwidth among RSs. Therefore, during network operations, the BS subsequently changes the current bandwidth allocation in the step-by-step interactive online manner.

NBS Based Bandwidth Allocation Algorithm

When a user moves while a call is in progress, one of the main problems is handoff. From the user's perspective, abrupt interruption of a connected call is far more annoying than having a new call attempt blocked. If a connected call is terminated in the middle of service, user needs to restart everything to restore the disrupted service. Therefore, recently proposed bandwidth management schemes distinguish between new calls and hand-off calls, and give higher priority to hand-off calls in order to guarantee call's continuity; so the critical issue from QoS point of view is how to reduce the hand-off dropping probability.

To decrease the call-dropping rate while maintaining efficient bandwidth utilization, the wireless bandwidth in each BS and RS should be partitioned dynamically. The NBGBM scheme designs a new NBS model to solve the bandwidth partition problem. In the developed NBS model, two traffic classes are assumed as players. The set of strategies for each player is the set of allocated bandwidth amounts. Each player (i.e., traffic class) has its utility function. To represent each player's payoff, major concerns are QoS provisioning and bandwidth efficiency. The NBGBM scheme defines two online functions (UF_1 and UF_2) by using the current hand-off call dropping probability (D_P) and new call blocking probability (B_P). Based on the dynamic online manner, these utility functions for the player i can be derived as follows.

$$UF_1 = \max \left(0, \left[1 - \exp \left(D\_P \right) \right] \right) \text{ and}$$

$$UF_2 = \max \left(0, \left[1 - \exp \left(B\_P \right) \right] \right) \quad (24)$$

Based on the traffic information such as inter-arrival time, bandwidth capacity, channel size, call duration time, D_P and D_P can be estimated according to the Erlang's formula (Niyato, 2008).

In each relay station, each player (i.e., *class I* traffic or *class II* traffic) is a member of a team willing to compromise his own objective to gain a total optimal solution - in other words, a Pareto optimal solution. By employing the NBS approach, the team players cooperate with each other and make a collective decision. The total payoff (i.e., utility) for two players is given by $TR_{1..2} = \{(UF_1, UF_2)\}$. If an agreement among the players cannot be reached, the payoff that the players will receive is given by the disagreement point $TR_{1..2}^d = (UF_1^d, UF_2^d)$; it represents payoffs when the game fails and the bandwidth allocation cannot be made (i.e., zero in the system). The desirable best solution for an utility quartet (UF_1^*, UF_2^*) is obtained as follows.

$$\left(UF_1^*, UF_2^*\right) = \arg\max_{UF_i} \prod_{1 \le i \le 2} \left(UF_i - UF_i^d\right)^{\psi_i},$$

where $\psi_1 + \psi_2 = 1$

$$\tag{25}$$

where ψ_1 is the bargaining powers of the player 1 (i.e., *class I* traffic) and ψ_2 is the bargaining powers of the player 2 (i.e., *class II* traffic). Based on the required QoS, players are asymmetric in their bargaining strengths. In the *NBGBM* scheme, the ψ value is dynamically adjustable to keep the QoS guarantee for higher priority services while ensuring bandwidth efficiency. When a handoff dropping occurs, ψ_1 value should be increased to satisfy the required QoS. Otherwise, if the bandwidth is over allocated for higher priority services, the over allocated bandwidth needs to be released for bandwidth efficiency.

Due to the different traffic priority, the negotiation mechanism for ψ values provides two different processes. When a call dropping occurs, the player 1 offers $\psi_{I \to II}^1$ to the player 2, and $\psi_{II \to I}^2$ is the counter-offer. In the *NBGBM* scheme, $\psi_{I \to II}^1$ is estimated as follows.

$$\psi_{I \to II}^1 = \psi_1^c + \Delta\psi_1 \tag{26}$$

where ψ_1^c and $\Delta\psi_1$ are the current bargaining power and an increasing constant factor for the player 1. Each negotiation round, ψ_1^c is the fixed value, but $\Delta\psi_1$ value gradually decreases by the discount factor ($\nabla\delta^1$, i.e., $\Delta\psi_1 = \Delta\psi_1 - \nabla\delta^1$). When the player 2 receives an offer from the player 1, the player 2 has to make a decision to accept this offer or not. If call blocking does not occur within the current *unit_time*, then the player 2 accepts the current offer ($\psi_{I \to II}^1$). Otherwise, the counter-offer is submitted. To implement this process, the negotiation function (N_F_{II}) is defined as follows.

$$N\_F_{II}\left(1, \psi_{I \to II}^1\right) = \begin{cases} accept \ \psi_{I \to II}^1, if \ B\_P_c = 0 \\[2ex] counter \ offer \ \psi_{II \to I}^2, otherwise \end{cases}$$

$$\tag{27}$$

where B_P_c is the call blocking probability at the current *unit_time*. Therefore, B_P_c is dynamically changeable according to the current network condition. In the *NBGBM* scheme, $\psi_{II \to I}^2$ is obtained as follows.

$$\psi_{II \to I}^2 = \psi_{I \to II}^1 \times \frac{1}{\sqrt{\left(\varphi \times \left(1 - B\_P_c\right)\right)^2 + \left[\left(1 - \varphi\right) \times \left(\dfrac{U_{II}^T - U_{II}^c}{U_{II}^T}\right)\right]^2}}$$

$$\tag{28}$$

where φ is a control parameter to relatively estimate the current network situation for *class II* traffic service. U_{II}^T and U_{II}^c are the total allocated bandwidth and the currently using bandwidth for the *class II* traffic, respectively. Based on the result of $N\_F_{II}\left(1, \psi_{I \to II}^1\right)$, the next step of negotiation is decided. When $\psi_{II \to I}^2$ is offered by the player 2, the player 1 estimates a new count offer ($\psi_{I \to II}^3$) according to (26). Due to the discount factor, $\psi_{I \to II}^3$ is a little bit decreased as compared with the previous offer ($\psi_{I \to II}^1$). Recursively, players negotiate with each other by proposing counter-offers alternately. After the maximum constraint round of negotiation, players finally reach an agreement or not. To prevent infinite offering rounds, negotiation process must have completed within a negotiation constraint. Finally, the developed negotiation process is defined as a finite sequence of the form $\left\{\psi^1, \psi^2, \ldots, \psi^{max}\right\}$, where *max* is a constant that represents the maximum permitted rounds. If the negotiation process does not reach an agreement within *max* rounds, players' control powers are forcibly set based on the last offer of the player 1, i.e., $\psi_1 = \psi_{I \to II}^{max}$ and $\psi_2 = 1 - \psi_1$; this decision is made by considering the traffic priority.

When a call blocking occurs, the player 2 offers $\psi_{II \to I}^1$ to the player 1, and $\psi_{I \to II}^2$ is the counter-offer. In the *NBGBM* scheme, $\psi_{II \to I}^1$ is estimated as follows.

$$\psi_{I \to II}^1 = \psi_1^c + \Delta\psi_1$$

where ψ_2^c and $\Delta\psi_2$ are the current bargaining power and an increasing constant factor for the player 2. Each negotiation round, ψ_2^c is the fixed value, but $\Delta\psi_2$ value gradually decreases by the discount factor ($\nabla\delta^2$ i.e., $\Delta\psi_2 = \Delta\psi_2 - \nabla\delta^2$). When the player 1 receives an offer from the player 2, the player 1 has to make a decision to accept this offer or not. If $\psi_{II \to I}^1$ value is lesser than the value of the player 1's counter-offer ($\psi_{I \to II}^2$) value, then the player 1 accepts the current offer ($\psi_{II \to I}^1$). Otherwise, the counter-offer is submitted. The negotiation function (N_F_I) expresses this process as follows.

$$N\_F_I\left(1, \psi_{II \to I}^1\right) = \begin{cases} accept\ \psi_{II \to I}^1 & , if\ \psi_{I \to II}^2 \geq \psi_{II \to I}^1 \\ counter\ offer\ \psi_{I \to II}^2 & , otherwise \end{cases}$$

(30)

In the *NBGBM* scheme, $\psi_{I \to II}^2$ is obtained as follows.

$$\psi_{I \to II}^2 = \psi_{II \to I}^1 \times \frac{}{\sqrt{\left(\varphi \times \left(1 - D\_P_c\right)\right)^2 + \left(\left(1 - \varphi\right) \times \left(\frac{U_I^T - U_I^c}{U_I^T}\right)\right)^2}}$$

where U_I^T and U_I^c are the total allocated bandwidth and the currently using bandwidth for the *class I*

traffic, respectively. Therefore, the offer $\psi_{I \to II}^2$ depends on the current network situation for *class I* traffic service. If players fail to reach an agreement within *max* rounds, players' control powers are decided based on the last offer value of the player 1 (Box 1).

The Main Steps of the NBGBM Scheme

In the *NBGBM* scheme, new bandwidth management algorithms are developed based on the trust value based random arrival rule and Nash bargaining solution. These developed algorithms are sophisticatedly combined into the holistic scheme and act cooperatively and collaborate with each other. Under dynamically changing network environments, the traditional static approach is not applicable; the current optimal solution may not be an optimum result in the future. Therefore, control decisions should be made dynamically to effectively approximate an optimal network performance. By using the real-time online approach, the *NBGBM* scheme dynamically estimates the current network condition and adaptively adapts the amount of the allocated bandwidth to provide a suitable balance between the desired QoS and high bandwidth utilization. The main steps of the *NBGBM* scheme are given next.

Step 1: At the initial time, the available bandwidth and bargaining power are equally divided for each relay station. In addition, allocated bandwidth is equally partitioned for each traffic services. This starting guess guarantees that each relay station and different priority services can enjoy the same benefit at the beginning of the game.

Step 2: In every *unit_time*, the BS monitors each RS's behavior and estimates the RS's trust value (T) by using (22).

Step 3: If the available bandwidth is insufficient to satisfy all demands of RSs (i.e., $\sum_{i \in N} c_i >$

Box 1. Negotiation algorithm for bargaining power decision.

```
/* One negotiation round (e.g., offer or counter-offer) occurs once in each unit_time. Therefore, within
the time constraint (maximum number of rounds × unit_time), the negotiation process is periodically
performed and completed. */
```

WHEN a call dropping occurs
{
the player 1 (*class I* traffic) estimates $\psi^1_{I \to II}$ according to (26) and offers $\psi^1_{I \to II}$ to the player 2.
the player 2 responses based on (27)
IF call blocking does not occur within the current *unit_time*
{ the player 2 accepts the current offer ($\psi^1_{I \to II}$)
BREAK; }
ELSE
{ the player 2 proposes the counter-offer according to (28)
IF the player 1 accepts the counter-offer ($\psi^2_{II \to I}$) **THEN**
BREAK;
ELSE
{
WHILE offering round is within *max*
{ players negotiate with each other by proposing offers alternately
IF the negotiation process reaches an agreement
 BREAK;
 }
Finally, $\psi_1 = \psi^{max}_{I \to II}$ and $\psi_2 = 1 - \psi_1$, **BREAK;** }
}
    }
}
WHEN a call blocking occurs
{
the player 2 (*class II* traffic) estimates $\psi^1_{II \to I}$ according to (29) and offers $\psi^1_{II \to I}$ to the player 1.
the player 1 responses based on (30)
IF the player 1 accepts the offer ($\psi^1_{II \to I}$) **THEN**
BREAK;
ELSE
{
WHILE offering round is within *max*
{ players negotiate with each other by proposing offers alternately
IF the negotiation process reaches an agreement
 BREAK;
 }
Finally, $\psi_1 = \psi^{max}_{I \to II}$ and $\psi_2 = 1 - \psi_1$, **BREAK;**
}
}
```
```

B), the allocated bandwidth amount of each RS should be dynamically adapted according to (23).

Step 4: After bandwidth re-allocation for relay stations, the allocated bandwidth is shared for different priority services by using NBS model. By using (26)-(31), ψ values are re-adjusted adaptively, which are used to re-partition the available bandwidth in each RS.

Step 5: According to (25), bandwidth is partitioned between traffic *class I* and *class II*.

Step 6: Under widely diverse network environments, base station and each relay station are self-monitoring constantly for the next iterative processing; go to Step 2. Therefore, the obtained solution is examined periodically to maintain the finest solution.

The simulation results shown in Figure 5 demonstrate that the performance comparison of the *NBGBM* scheme with the *REFRN* scheme, the *RACMN* scheme, the *NRART* scheme and the *GADRA* scheme. Compared with the existing schemes, the proposed *NBGBM* scheme can increase network efficiency and QoS under diversified network traffic condition changes.

Summary

For next-generation wireless networks, multi-hop relay networking is an emerging technology to overcome the current limitations of traditional cellular systems. The *NBGBM* scheme is developed for MRNs based on the random arrival rule and NBS methodologies. The *NBGBM* scheme iteratively re-estimates the RSs' trust levels and adaptively allocates the available bandwidth to each RS. The allocated bandwidth is dynamically shared. By constantly monitoring the current network condition, the developed bargaining model iteratively re-negotiates the bargaining powers to approximate an optimal solution. Therefore, network system can obtain higher bandwidth efficiency while ensuring QoS for higher priority traffic services. Future work will include relay station positioning, frequency reuse for relays and usage of cooperative diversity techniques in MRNs.

Figure 5. Performance evaluations of the NBGBM scheme

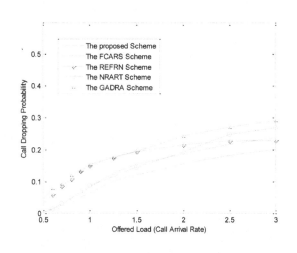

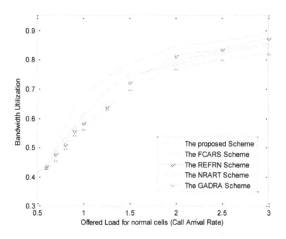

(a) Call Dropping Probability

(b) Bandwidth utilization

DUAL-LEVEL BANDWIDTH MANAGEMENT (*DLBM*) SCHEME FOR OVERLAY NETWORKS

Given the overlaying structure and heterogeneous 4G network characteristics, the interworking between heterogeneous wireless networks is one promising approach. To exploit the hierarchical multi-layer network operation, an important issue is how to properly control bandwidth. Recently, S. Kim proposed a new bandwidth management scheme by employing the dual-level game model. For the adaptive bandwidth allocation, an inter-network algorithm is designed based on the non-cooperative game model. To support different priority services, an intra-network algorithm is developed according to the bargaining game model. Under diverse network condition changes, this dual-level game approach is essential to provide a suitable tradeoff between the desired QoS and high bandwidth utilization.

Development Motivation

Recently, wireless/mobile networking is one of the strongest growth areas of communication technology. Based on the anywhere and anytime service concept, users want to enjoy mobility, seamless access and high quality of service in an all-IP network. To satisfy this goal, wireless networks facilitate Internetworking between various existing heterogeneous wireless networks. Therefore, current trends show that many different wireless networks coexist to provide wireless access (Niyato, 2008), (Luo, 2009). A common structure used in existing heterogeneous wireless networks is a multi-layer network scheme consisting of macro-cell, micro-cell and pico-cell networks. These three different networks often have overlapping areas of coverage and form multitier architecture. Based on the hierarchical interdependence among different networks, the multi-layer network system is envisaged to be the network structure to achieve

a high network performance and broad coverage (Niyato, 2006), (Song, Zhuang, & Cheng, 2007).

To understand the behavior of self-regarding networks or independent users, a game model has some attractive features. Non-cooperative game is a kind of game model. In non-cooperative games, players are in conflict with each other and do not communicate or collaborate. Their preferences can be expressed as a utility function; each player seeks to choose a strategy that maximizes its own utility. Therefore, a family of non-cooperative games is presented as the actions of the single players and Nash equilibrium point is considered as a solution concept. Bargaining games are games in which players make binding commitments and find it beneficial to cooperate in the game. To reach an agreement that gives mutual advantages, players bargain with each other. In bargaining games, the joint actions of players are analyzed; the interest is in what kind of bargains form. In recent years, bandwidth management by using non-cooperative and bargaining game models is one of the strongest research areas (Park, & Schaar, 2007), (Suris, DaSilva, Han, & MacKenzie, 2007).

Motivated by the above discussion, the *DLBM* scheme is designed as a game-theoretic bandwidth management mechanism for the hierarchical multi-layer network system. The main goal of the *DLBM* scheme is to maximize bandwidth efficiency while providing service prioritization. Under various QoS constraints and dynamically changing network environments, it is almost impossible that a single control approach will achieve an optimal network performance. The *DLBM* scheme is designed as a dual-level structure, which consists of inter-network and intra-network bandwidth management algorithms. The inter-network algorithm allocates the limited available bandwidth to each layer network based on the non-cooperative game model. Under competitive network environment, the non-cooperative game approach can effectively allocate the bandwidth for different service areas. In each layer network, the intra-network algorithm partitions the allocated bandwidth to support different priority traffic services. According to the *Rubinstein-Stahl* bargaining model (Zhao, & Zhao, 2002), (Pan, & Fang, 2008), (Xie, Zhou, Hao, Ai, & Song, 2010), the wireless bandwidth can be shared adaptively, which is essential to provide a suitable tradeoff between the desired QoS and high bandwidth utilization.

Recently, several bandwidth allocation schemes have been presented for hierarchical multi-layer networks. The Utility-based Multi-service Bandwidth Allocation (*UMBA*) scheme is a bandwidth allocation approach for multiple services (Luo, 2009). In the *UMBA* scheme, a utility function is introduced to estimate the effect of network performance and the bandwidth offered by different wireless access networks is normalized by using their corresponding capacities. Based on the concept of network utility, the *UMBA* scheme allocates bandwidth flexibly depending on the utility fairness. The Game-Theoretic Bandwidth Allocation (*GTBA*) scheme is an efficient bandwidth allocation algorithm based on the game-model approach (Niyato, & Hossain, 2008). The *GTBA* scheme is designed to support users, who can connect to different wireless access networks. Based on the allocated bandwidth, call control mechanism is used to maintain the QoS performance for the different types of services.

Bandwidth Allocation Algorithm in the *DLBM* Scheme

Based on the dual-level game model, the *DLBM* scheme can provide a globally desirable system performance while ensuring QoS for the higher priority traffic service.

Inter-Network Bandwidth Allocation Algorithm

The *DLBM* scheme considers a multi-tier hierarchical wireless network system. A key concept of multi-tier wireless networking is the unification of

several heterogeneous networks of varying coverage into a single logical network that provides the best of all coverage (Lohi, Weerakoon, & Aghvami, 1999). Typically, a geographic region is subdivided into three areas; global, local and hotspot areas. Each area is served by macro-cell network, micro-cell network and pico-cell network, respectively. These heterogeneous networks coexist to form hierarchical network system and have overlapping areas of coverage to provide services (Ning, Zhu, Li, & Wu, 2006). The general architecture of hierarchical wireless network system is shown in Figure 6

In order to satisfy increasing demand for traffic services, one of the most important control issues is bandwidth allocation. To efficiently allocate the limited wireless bandwidth to overlaying different networks, a well-known methodology is the non-cooperative game theory. Based on the game theory notations, the developed game model can be formulated as follows.

- **Players:** Networks are assumed as players, which are denoted as P_1 (for macro-cell network) and P_2 (for micro-cell network).
- **Strategies:** Two players (P_1 and P_2) have strategies. The set of strategy for each player is the possible amounts of bandwidth allocation.
- **Utility functions:** Each player has its own utility function, which represents the amount of satisfaction of a player toward the outcome of the game. The higher the value of the utility, the higher satisfaction of the player for that outcome. To quantify players' satisfaction, the utility function for player i (U_i) is derived as follows (Niyato, & Hossain, 2008).

$$U_i = \omega_i \times \log\left(\alpha \times b_i\right) \tag{32}$$

where b_i is the amount of currently allocated bandwidth for the player i. ω_i is a control parameter indicating of the scale of the U_i and α is constant indicating the shape of the U_i.

The design goal of inter-network algorithm is to allocate available bandwidth to a particular network while maximizing network performance. The inter-network algorithm in the *DLBM* scheme is developed based on the *GTBA* scheme (Niyato, & Hossain, 2008). Therefore, a non-cooperative game model is formulated and the Nash equilibrium is obtained as the solution. The Nash equilibrium is a strategy set of all players' strategies with the property that each player has chosen a strategy and no player can benefit by changing his strategy while the other players keep their strategies unchanged (Niyato, & Hossain, 2008).

In the developed algorithm, the allocated bandwidth amount for the macro-cell network (P_1) is defined as B_{Ma}, for the micro-cell network (P_2) is defined as B_{mi}, and for the pico-cell network is defined as B_{pi}; $B_{Ma} + B_{mi} + B_{pi} = T\_B$ where T_B is the total amount of available bandwidth for hierarchical network system. Let M_b_{Ma} denote the allocated bandwidth by the P_1 to the macro-cell area excluding the micro-cell and pico-cell areas (area ψ in Figure 6), and M_b_{mi} denote the allocated bandwidth by the P_1 to the micro-cell area excluding the pico-cell area (area σ in Figure 6), and M_b_{pi} denote the allocated bandwidth offered by the P_1 to the pico-cell area (area φ in Figure 6) where $M\_b_{Ma} + M\_b_{mi} + M\_b_{pi} = B_{Ma}$. Note that m_b_{mi} denote the allocated bandwidth offered by the P_2 to the area σ, and let m_b_{pi} denote the allocated bandwidth by the P_2 to the area φ where $m\_b_{mi} + m\_b_{pi} = B_{mi}$ (Niyato, & Hossain, 2008).

Figure 6. Multitier cellular structure

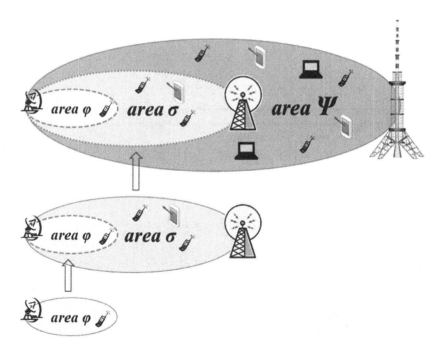

In the developed game model, the strategies for the macro-cell network (P_1) are M_b_{mi} and M_b_{pi}. The payoff for the P_1 is the utility (U_{macro}) gained from the allocated bandwidth to all service areas (ψ, σ and φ). Specifically, the U_{macro} for the P_1 is given in Box 2 by Niyato (Niyato, & Hossain, 2008) where N_{Ma}, N_{mi} and N_{pi} are the number of ongoing users in ψ, σ and φ areas, respectively. ω_{Ma_m}, ω_{mi_m} and ω_{pi_m} parameters control the relative weights given to each service area (i.e., ψ, σ, φ). Under diverse traffic environments, a fixed value of ω cannot effectively adapt to the changing network conditions. To adaptively decide the ω values, the time-axis is partitioned into equal intervals of length *unit_time*. Every *unit_time*, macro-cell network system monitors periodically its bandwidth utilization (BU) for each area. In the *DLBM* scheme, network utilization is the ratio of current network traffic to the maximum traffic that the system can handle. Through monitoring the BU, the macro-cell network system can adjust the weight parameter (ω) for the area ψ (ω_{Ma_m}), the area σ (ω_{mi_m}) and the area φ (ω_{pi_m}) as follows:

$$\omega_{Ma\_m} = \frac{BU_{Ma}}{BU_T}, \quad \omega_{mi\_m} = \frac{BU_{mi}}{BU_T} \quad \text{and} \quad \omega_{pi\_m} = \frac{BU_{pi}}{BU_T}$$

(34)

s.t., $BU_T = BU_{Ma} + BU_{mi} + BU_{pi}$

In the developed game model, the strategy for the micro-cell network (P_2) is m_b_{mi}. The payoff for the P_2 is the utility (U_{micro}) gained from the allocated bandwidth to service areas σ and φ. The U_{micro} for the P_2 is given in Box 3 by Niyato (Niyato, & Hossain, 2008).

Nash equilibrium, in which no player has anything to gain by changing only his own strategy unilaterally, is a solution concept of a non-cooperative game. The set of strategies $\left(M\_b_{mi}^*, M\_b_{pi}^*, m\_b_{mi}^* \right)$ is a Nash equilibrium (Niyato, & Hossain, 2008) if

$$U_{macro}\left(M\_b_{mi}^*, M\_b_{pi}^*, m\_b_{mi}^* \right) \geq$$
$$U_{macro}\left(M\_b_{mi}, M\_b_{pi}, m\_b_{mi}^* \right) \quad \forall M\_b_{mi}, M\_b_{pi}$$

(36)

Box 2.

$$U_{macro}\left(M\_b_{mi}, M\_b_{pi}, m\_b_{mi} \right)$$
$$= \left[\left(\omega_{Ma\_m} \times N_{Ma} \times log\left(\alpha \times \frac{B_{Ma} - \left(M\_b_{mi} + M\_b_{pi} \right)}{N_{Ma}} \right) \right) \right.$$
$$+ \left[\left(\omega_{mi\_m} \times N_{mi} \times log\left(\alpha \times \frac{M\_b_{mi}}{N_{mi}} \right) - \omega_{mi\_m} \times N_{mi} \times log(\alpha \times \frac{m\_b_{mi}}{N_{mi}}) \right) \right.$$
$$+ \left(\omega_{pi\_m} \times N_{pi} \times log\left(\alpha \times \frac{B_{mi} + B_{pi} - m\_b_{mi+} M\_b_{pi}}{N_{pi}} \right) - \omega_{pi\_m} \times N_{pi} \right.$$
$$\times log\left(\alpha \times \frac{B_{mi} + B_{pi} - m\_b_{mi}}{N_{pi}} \right) \right]$$

(33)

Box 3.

$$U_{micro}\left(M\_b_{mi}, M\_b_{pi}, m\_b_{mi}\right) = \left[\left(\omega_{mi} \times N_{mi} \times log\left(\alpha \times \frac{m_{b_{mi}} + M_{bmi}}{N_{mi}}\right) - \omega_{mi} \times N_{mi} \times log\left(\alpha \times \frac{M\_b_{mi}}{N_{mi}}\right)\right)$$

$$+ \left(\omega_{pi} \times N_{pi} \times log\left(\alpha \times \frac{B_{mi} + B_{pi} - m\_b_{mi} + M\_b_{pi}}{N_{pi}}\right) - \omega_{pi} \times N_{pi}\right.$$

$$\left.\left.\times log\left(\alpha \times \frac{B_{pi} + M\_b_{pi}}{N_{pi}}\right)\right)\right]$$

$$(35)$$

$$U_{micro}\left(M\_b_{mi}^*, M\_b_{pi}^*, m\_b_{mi}^*\right) \geq$$
$$U_{micro}\left(M\_b_{mi}^*, M\_b_{pi}^*, m\_b_{mi}\right) \quad \forall m\_b_{mi}$$
$$(37)$$

To determine the Nash equilibrium, the *DLBM* scheme should find out the best response functions for both P_1 and P_2 players. The best response of the P_1, given that the P_2 chooses strategy (m_b_{mi}'), is obtained by finding strategy M_b_{mi} and M_b_{pi} that maximizes the U_{macro} function of the P_1 (Niyato, & Hossain, 2008).

$$\left(M\_b_{mi}^*, M\_b_{pi}^*\right) =$$
$$\arg \max_{M\_b_{mi}, M\_b_{pi}} U_{macro}\left(M\_b_{mi}, M\_b_{pi}, m\_b_{mi}'\right)$$
$$(38)$$

The best response of the P_2, given that the P_1 chooses strategy $\left(M\_b_{mi}', M\_b_{pi}'\right)$, is expressed as follows (Niyato, & Hossain, 2008):

$$\left(m\_b_{mi}^*\right) = \arg\max_{m\_b_{mi}} U_{micro}\left(M\_b_{mi}', M\_b_{pi}', m\_b_{mi}\right)$$
$$(39)$$

To get the best response for the P_1, the *DLBM* scheme partially differentiates U_{macro} with respect

to M_b_{mi} and M_b_{pi} assuming that m_b_{mi} is constant (Niyato, & Hossain, 2008).

$$\frac{\partial U_{macro}\left(M\_b_{mi}, M\_b_{pi}, m\_b_{mi}\right)}{\partial M\_b_{mi}} = 0 \Rightarrow$$

$$\frac{\omega_{Ma} \times N_{Ma}}{B_{Ma} - M\_b_{mi} - M\_b_{pi}} = \frac{\omega_{mi} \times N_{mi}}{m\_b_{mi} + M\_b_{mi}}$$
$$(40)$$

$$\frac{\partial U_{macro}\left(M\_b_{mi}, M\_b_{pi}, m\_b_{mi}\right)}{\partial M\_b_{pi}} = 0 \Rightarrow$$

$$\frac{\omega_{Ma} \times N_{Ma}}{B_{Ma} - M\_b_{mi} - M\_b_{pi}} = \frac{\omega_{pi} \times N_{pi}}{B_{mi} + B_{pi} - m\_b_{mi} + M\_b_{pi}}$$
$$(41)$$

To get the best response for the P_2, the *DLBM* scheme partially differentiates U_{micro} with respect to m_b_{mi} assuming that M_b_{mi} and M_b_{pi} are constants (Niyato, & Hossain, 2008).

$$\frac{\partial U_{micro}\left(M\_b_{mi}, M\_b_{pi}, m\_b_{mi}\right)}{\partial m\_b_{mi}} = 0 \Rightarrow$$

$$\frac{\omega_{mi} \times N_{mi}}{m\_b_{mi} + M\_b_{mi}} = \frac{\omega_{pi} \times N_{pi}}{B_{mi} + B_{pi} - m\_b_{mi} + M\_b_{pi}} \tag{42}$$

By solving the above equations (40)-(42), the *DLBM* scheme can obtain the Nash equilibrium (Niyato, & Hossain, 2008). Theorem 1 shows that the Nash equilibrium solution from the inter-network bandwidth allocation game is optimal; it can maximize the total network utility.

Theorem 1: *Nash equilibrium solution for the inter-network bandwidth allocation game is optimal solution for the hierarchical network system* (Niyato, & Hossain, 2008)

Proof: In the hierarchical network system, the total utility for the entire service region can be obtained from the function shown in Box 4.

To maximize the system's total utility (U_{tot}), a solution should be formulated as follows (Niyato, & Hossain, 2008):

Maximize :

$$U_{tot}\left(M\_b_{Ma}, M\_b_{mi}, M\_b_{pi}, m\_b_{mi}, m\_b_{pi} \right) \tag{44}$$

s.t., $M\_b_{Ma} + M\_b_{mi} + M\_b_{pi} = B_{Ma}$ and $m\_b_{mi} + m\_b_{pi} = B_{mi}$

To obtain the optimal solution, the *DLBM* scheme partially differentiates (43) with respect to each of the decision variables (Niyato, & Hossain, 2008).

$$\frac{\partial U_{tot}}{\partial M\_b_{mi}} = 0 \Rightarrow \frac{\omega_{Ma} \times N_{Ma}}{B_{Ma} - M\_b_{mi} - M\_b_{pi}} = \frac{\omega_{mi} \times N_{mi}}{M\_b_{mi} + m\_b_{mi}} \tag{45}$$

$$\frac{\partial U_{tot}}{\partial M\_b_{pi}} = 0 \Rightarrow \frac{\omega_{Ma} \times N_{Ma}}{B_{Ma} - M\_b_{mi} - M\_b_{pi}} = \frac{\omega_{pi} \times N_{pi}}{M\_b_{pi} + m\_b_{pi} + B_{pi}} \tag{46}$$

$$\frac{\partial U_{tot}}{\partial m\_b_{mi}} = 0 \Rightarrow \frac{\omega_{mi} \times N_{mi}}{m\_b_{mi} + M\_b_{mi}} = \frac{\omega_{pi} \times N_{pi}}{M\_b_{pi} + m\_b_{pi} + B_{pi}} \tag{47}$$

Box 4.

$$U_{tot}(M\_b_{Ma}, M\_b_{mi}, M\_b_{pi}, m\_b_{mi}, m\_b_{pi}$$
$$= \left[\omega_{Ma} \times N_{Ma} \times \log\left(\alpha \times \frac{B_{Ma} - M\_b_{mi} - M\_b_{pi}}{N_{Ma}} \right) + \omega_{mi} \times N_{mi} \right.$$
$$\times \log\left(\alpha \times \frac{M\_b_{mi} + m\_b_{mi}}{N_{mi}} \right) + \omega_{pi} \times N_{pi}$$
$$\left. \times \log\left(\alpha \times \frac{M\_b_{pi} + m\_b_{pi} + B_{pi}}{N_{pi}} \right) \right] \tag{43}$$

where M_b_{Ma} and m_b_{mi} can be easily obtained from the constraints in (44). Then, the optimal values of $M\_b_{Ma}, M\_b_{mi}, M\_b_{pi}, m\_b_{mi}$ and m_b_{pi} are the same as $M\_b^*_{Ma}, M\_b^*_{mi}, M\_b^*_{pi}, m\_b^*_{mi}$ and $m\_b^*_{pi}$, respectively. Therefore, Nash equilibrium solution from the inter-network bandwidth allocation game is an optimal solution (Niyato, & Hossain, 2008)

Intra-Network Bandwidth Allocation Algorithm

During network operations, the limited bandwidth has to be shared by different priority services. To support different QoS requirements, network system should take into account the service prioritization. For the implementation of bandwidth sharing protocol, the bandwidth capacity should be dynamically partitioned into different priority services.

A solution to the bargaining game model enables the game players to fairly and optimally determine their payoffs to make joint-agreements (Park, & Schaar, 2007), (Suris, 2007). Therefore, the bargaining model is attractive for the bandwidth partitioning problem. In the *DLBM* scheme, a bargaining game model is formulated to solve the bandwidth partitioning problem. In order to design an effective bargaining model, we can seek help from Economics. In 1982, Israeli economist *Ariel Rubinstein* built up an alternating-offer bargain model based on the Stahl's limited negotiation model; it is known as a *Rubinstein-Stahl* bargaining process. This model can provide a possible solution to the problem that two players are bargaining with the division of the benefits (Zhao, 2002), (Pan, 2008).

In *Rubinstein-Stahl* model, players have their own bargaining power (δ). The division proportion of the benefits can be obtained according to the bargaining power, which can be computed at each player individually. A more bargaining power player benefits more from the bargaining. They negotiate with each other by proposing offers

alternately. After several rounds of negotiation, players finally reach an agreement as following (Zhao, 2002), (Pan, 2008).

$$\left(x_1^*, x_2^*\right) = \begin{cases} \left(\dfrac{1-\delta_2}{1-\delta_1\delta_2}, \dfrac{\delta_2(1-\delta_1)}{1-\delta_1\delta_2}\right) & \text{if the player\_1 offers first} \\ \left(\dfrac{\delta_1(1-\delta_2)}{1-\delta_1\delta_2}, \dfrac{1-\delta_1}{1-\delta_1\delta_2}\right) & \text{if the player\_2 offers first} \end{cases}$$

(48)

s.t., $\left(x_1^*, x_2^*\right) \in \mathbf{R}^2 : x_1^* + x_2^* = 1, x_1^* \geq 0, x_2^* \geq 0$ and $0 \leq \delta_1, \delta_s \leq 1$

It is obvious that

$$\frac{1-\delta_2}{1-\delta_1\delta_2} \geq \frac{\delta_2\left(1-\delta_1\right)}{1-\delta_1\delta_2}$$

and

$$\frac{\delta_1\left(1-\delta_2\right)}{1-\delta_1\delta_2} \leq \frac{1-\delta_1}{1-\delta_1\delta_2}.$$

That is to say, there is a first-proposer advantage in the bargaining process. Traditionally, the bargaining power in the *Rubinstein-Stahl's* model is defined as follows (Pan, 2008).

$$\delta = e^{-\xi \times \Delta}, \text{ s.t., } \xi > 0 \tag{49}$$

where Δ is the time period of negotiation round. Given the Δ is fixed (i.e., *unit_time*), δ is monotonic decreasing with ξ. In the developed model, ξ is an instantaneous discount factor to adaptively adjust the bargaining power.

The *DLBM* scheme develops an intra-network bandwidth partitioning algorithm for each layer network. To support different priority traffic services, the intra-network algorithm partitions the allocated bandwidth. In the developed algorithm, the bandwidth partitioning problem is formulated according to the *Rubinstein-Stahl* bargaining model. Based on the different priority, traffic groups are assumed as players, which are denoted as the *player_1* (i.e., class I traffic services) and *player_2* (i.e., class II traffic services). The *Rubinstein-Stahl* bargaining model can provide an effective solution to partition the available bandwidth, which describes both class I and class II traffic services how to share the bandwidth through bargaining. A solution is got at a pair (x_1^*, x_2^*), where x_1^* and x_2^* are the amount of bandwidth for the *player_1* and *player_2*, respectively.

In the scenario of the *Rubinstein-Stahl* model, each player has different discount factor. To provide more efficient control over network condition fluctuations, these factors should be adjusted dynamically under various network situations. In the bargaining model of the *DLBM* scheme, the information of call blocking probability is used to dynamically modify ξ values. When the current class I traffic load is heavy, the network does not has sufficient bandwidth to support class I services. Thus, call service requests are likely to be rejected and blocking probability increases. In this case, a lower value of the *player_1*'s discount factor (ξ_I) is more suitable. If the reverse has been the case (i.e., current class II traffic load is heavy), a lower value of the *player_2*'s discount factor (ξ_I) is suitable. According to the traffic priority, the *DLBM* scheme gives preference to the *player_1*. At the end of each *unit_time* period, each player dynamically adjusts the value of ξ to make the system more responsive to current network conditions. The determination condition is given below.

$$\begin{cases} \xi_I = \xi_I - \varepsilon_I \times \xi_I \text{ and } \xi_{II} = 1 - \xi_I, \text{ if } \varepsilon_I > 0 \text{ and } \varepsilon_{II} \geq 0 \\ \xi_{II} = \xi_{II} - \varepsilon_{II} \times \xi_{II} \text{ and } \xi_I = 1 - \xi_{II}, \text{ If } \varepsilon_I = 0 \text{ and } \varepsilon_{II} > 0 \\ \xi_I = \xi_I \text{ and } \xi_{II} = \xi_{II}, \text{ otherwise} \end{cases}$$

where ε_I and ε_{II} are the class I and call II call blocking probabilities during the current *unit_time*. As network situations change after bandwidth partitioning, each player adaptively adjusts their discount factors (ξ_I and ξ_{II}) to finds the best solution. Therefore, the available bandwidth can be dynamically re-distributed to different priority traffic services.

The Main Steps of the *DLBM* Scheme

Under dynamically changing network environments, the *DLBM* scheme is designed as a dual-level game model; it consists of inter-network and intra-network bandwidth management algorithms. Based on the current network conditions, the *DLBM* scheme dynamically adapts the amount of the allocated bandwidth for the hierarchical network system. In each layer network (i.e., macro-cell network, micro-cell network and pico-cell network), the allocated bandwidth is adaptively partitioned for different priority traffic services. The major objective of the *DLBM* scheme is to maximize the network performance while providing a suitable tradeoff between the desired QoS and high bandwidth utilization. Based on the real-time feedback process, each network can adapt its behavior and act strategically to achieve the major design goal. The main steps of the *DLBM* scheme are given next.

Step 1: At the initial time, the available bandwidth is assigned based on the ratio of the coverage area for hierarchical overlay networks. And then, the allocated bandwidth in each layer network is equally divided for different priority traffic services. This starting guess guarantees that each network enjoys the same benefit at the beginning of the game.

Step 2: Every *unit_time*, each network estimates its utility function (U) according to (32)-(35), and reports its current payoff to the central system.

Step 3: Based on the allocated bandwidth, each network partitions the allocated bandwidth; one part is used for the class I traffic services and the other is used for the class II traffic services.

Step 4: When its own partition is saturated due to bandwidth scarcity, the intra-network bandwidth management algorithm is triggered. The saturated part player, who is a lower-level game player, offers first to move the partition boundary by using (50).

Step 5: According to (48), the available bandwidth is adaptively re-partitioned.

Step 6: After the bandwidth re-distribution, network system periodically examines the obtained solution to maintain the finest solution. By using (49) and (50), δ, ε, ξ_I and ξ_{II} values are estimated at the end of every *unit_time*.

Step 7: When the allocated bandwidth in a specific network is not available to support the new call service, the inter-network bandwidth management algorithm is triggered. The upper-level game player (i.e., the congested network) requests the bandwidth re-allocation to the central system.

Step 8: For each layer network, the central system controller decides the amount of bandwidth re-allocation by using (38),(39),(40),(41) and (42).

Step 9: Under widely diverse network environments, the system controller and each network are self-monitoring constantly for the next iterative feedback processing; proceed to Step 2.

Summary

With the incidence of a variety of heterogeneous multi-layer networks, bandwidth management problem is an important issue for effective network operations. The *DLBM* scheme is developed based on the dual-level game model. The main goal of the *DLBM* scheme is to maximize network performance while providing service prioritization. To satisfy this goal, the *DLBM* scheme consists of inter-network and intra-network bandwidth management algorithms. According to the non-cooperative game model, the inter-network algorithm allocates the bandwidth to each layer network. Based on the *Rubinstein-Stahl* bargaining model, the intra-network algorithm partitions the allocated bandwidth to provide a suitable tradeoff between the desired QoS and high bandwidth utilization.

REFERENCES

Anderegg, L., & Eidenbenz, S. (2003). Ad hoc-vcg: A truthful and cost-efficient routing protocol for mobile ad hoc networks with selfish agents. In *Proceedings of MobiCom* (pp. 245–259). ACM. doi:10.1145/939010.939011

Ayyadurai, V., Moessner, K., & Tafazolli, R. (2011). Multihop cellular network optimization using genetic algorithms. In *Proceedings of IEEE Network and Service Management*. IEEE.

Changiz, R., Halabian, H., Yu, F. R., Lambadaris, I., & Tang, H. (2010). Trust Management in Wireless Mobile Networks with Cooperative Communications. In *Proceedings of EUC 2010*, (pp. 498-503). EUC.

Chen, Q. B., Zhou, W. G., Chai, R., Tang, L., & Zhao, Y. L. (2010). A noncooperative game-theoretic vertical handoff in 4G heterogeneous wireless networks. In *Proceedings of International Conference on Communications and Networking*. Academic Press.

Chen, X., Li, B., & Fang, Y. (2005). A Dynamic Multiple-Threshold Bandwidth Reservation (DMTBR) Scheme for QoS Provisioning in Multimedia Wireless Networks. *IEEE Transactions on Wireless Communications*, 4(2), 583–592. doi:10.1109/TWC.2004.843053

Chen, Y. M., & Su, C. L. (2007). Meeting QoS Requirements of Mobile Computing by Dual-Level Congestion Control. In *Proceedings of GPC*, (pp. 241-251). GPC.

Chun, Y. S., & Lee, J. H. (2007). On the convergence of the random arrival rule in large claims problems. *International Journal of Game Theory*, *36*(2), 259–273. doi:10.1007/s00182-007-0075-4

Dash, R., Parkes, D., & Jennings, N. (2003). Computational Mechanism Design: A Call to Arms. *IEEE Intelligent Systems*, *18*(6), 40–47. doi:10.1109/MIS.2003.1249168

Dharwadkar, P., Siegel, H. J., & Chong, E. K. P. (2000). *A Study of Dynamic Bandwidth Allocation with Preemption and Degradation for Prioritized Requests*. Purdue University, School of Electrical and Computer Engineering, Technical Report No. TR-ECE 00-9.

Dramitinos, M., & Lassous, I. G. (2009). A bandwidth allocation mechanism for 4G. In *Proceedings of European Wireless Technology Conference*, (pp. 96-99). Academic Press.

Feng, N., Mau, S. C., & Mandayam, N. B. (2004). Pricing and power control for joint network-centric and user-centric radio resource management. *IEEE Transactions on Communications*, *52*(9), 1547–1557. doi:10.1109/TCOMM.2004.833191

Friedman, E. J., & Parkes, D. D. (2003). Pricing WiFi at Starbucks: issues in online mechanism design. In *Proceedings of ACM Conference on Electronic Commerce*, (pp. 240-241). ACM.

Garg, D., Narahari, Y., & Gujar, S. (2008). Foundations of Mechanism Design: A Tutorial, Part 1: Key Concepts and Classical Results. *Sadhana. Indian Academy Proceedings in Engineering Sciences*, *33*(2), 83–130.

Ginde, S., Neel, J., & Buehrer, R. M. (2003). A game-theoretic analysis of joint link adaptation and distributed power control in GPRS. In *Proceedings of IEEE Vehicular Technology Conference*, (pp. 732-736). IEEE.

Hou, J., Yang, J., & Papavassiliou, S. (2002). Integration of pricing with call admission control to meet qos requirements in cellular networks. *IEEE Transactions on Parallel and Distributed Systems*, *13*, 898–909. doi:10.1109/TPDS.2002.1036064

Huining, H., Yanikomeroglu, H., Falconer, D. D., & Periyalwar, S. (2004). Range extension without capacity penalty in cellular networks with digital fixed relays. In *Proceedings of IEEE GLOBECOM*, (pp. 3053-3057). IEEE.

Khan, A. H., Qadeer, M. A., Ansari, J. A., & Waheed, S. (2009). 4G as a Next Generation Wireless Network. In *Proceedings of Future Computer and Communication* (pp. 334–338). Academic Press. doi:10.1109/ICFCC.2009.108

Kim, S. W. (2010). QoS-Aware Bandwidth Allocation Algorithm for Multimedia Service Networks. *IEICE Transactions on Communications. E (Norwalk, Conn.)*, *94-B*(3), 810–812.

Kim, S. W. (2011). Cellular Network Bandwidth Management Scheme by using Nash Bargaining Solution. *IET Communications*, *5*(3), 371–380. doi:10.1049/iet-com.2010.0309

Kim, S. W. (2012). Adaptive call admission control scheme for heterogeneous overlay networks. *Journal of Communications and Networks*, *14*(4), 461–466. doi:10.1109/JCN.2012.6292253

Kim, S. W. (2012). An Online Bandwidth Allocation Scheme Based on Mechanism Design Model. *IEICE Transactions*, *96-B*(1), 321–324.

Kim, S. W., & Varshney, P. K. (2004). An Integrated Adaptive Bandwidth Management Framework for QoS sensitive Multimedia Cellular Networks. *IEEE Transactions on Vehicular Technology, 53*(3), 835–846. doi:10.1109/TVT.2004.825704

Kimura, K., Yamamoto, K., Murata, H., & Yoshida, S. (2008). Fair channel and route selection algorithm using Nash bargaining solutions in multi-hop radio networks. In *Proceedings of IEEE International Workhop on Wireless Distributed Networks*. IEEE.

Krithikaivasan, B., Zeng, Y., Deka, K., & Medhi, D. (2007). ARCH-Based Traffic Forecasting and Dynamic Bandwidth Provisioning for Periodically Measured Nonstationary Traffic. *IEEE/ACM Transactions on Networking, 15*(3), 683–696. doi:10.1109/TNET.2007.893217

Le, L., & Hossain, E. (2007). Multihop Cellular Networks: Potential Gains, Research Challenges, and a Resource Allocation Framework. *IEEE Communications Magazine, 45*(9), 66–73. doi:10.1109/MCOM.2007.4342859

Li, X., & Cui, J. (2009). Real-time water resources allocation: methodology and mechanism. In *Proceedings of IEEM*, (pp. 1637-1641). IEEM.

Liu, J., Shen, L., Song, T., & Wang, X. (2009). Demand-matching spectrum sharing game for non-cooperative cognitive radio network. In *Proceedings of International Conference on Wireless Communications & Signal Processing*. Academic Press.

Lohi, M., Weerakoon, D., & Aghvami, A. H. (1999). Trends in multi-layer cellular system design and handover design. In *Proceedings of IEEE Wireless Communications and Networking Conference*, (pp. 898 - 902). IEEE.

Long, C., Zhang, Q., Li, B., Yang, H., & Guan, X. (2007). Non-Cooperative Power Control for Wireless Ad Hoc Networks with Repeated Games. *IEEE Journal on Selected Areas in Communications, 25*(6), 1101–1112. doi:10.1109/JSAC.2007.070805

Luo, C., Ji, H., & Li, Y. (2009). Utility-Based Multi-Service Bandwidth Allocation in the 4G Heterogeneous Wireless Access Networks. In *Proceedings of IEEE WCNC*. IEEE.

Malanchini, I., Cesana, M., & Gatti, N. (2009). On Spectrum Selection Games in Cognitive Radio Networks. In *Proceedings of IEEE GLOBECOM*. IEEE.

Mehmet, S., & Ramazan, K. (2001). A Comparative Study of Multiobjective Optimization Methods in Structural Design. *Turkish Journal of Engineering and Environmental Sciences, 25*(2), 69–78.

Newton, M., Thompson, J. S., & Naden, J. M. (2008). Wireless systems Resource allocation in the downlink of cellular multi-hop networks. *European Transactions on Telecommunications, 19*(3), 299–314. doi:10.1002/ett.1264

Ning, G., Zhu, G., Li, Q., & Wu, R. (2006). Dynamic Load Balancing Based on Sojourn Time in Multitier Cellular Systems. In *Proceedings of IEEE Vehicular Technology Conference*, (pp. 111-116). IEEE.

Nisan, N., & Ronen, A. (2000). Computationally feasible VCG mechanisms. In *Proceedings of ACM Conference on Electronic Commerce*, (pp. 242-252). ACM.

Niyato, D., & Hossain, E. (2006). WLC04-5: Bandwidth Allocation in 4G Heterogeneous Wireless Access Networks: A Noncooperative Game Theoretical Approach. In *Proceedings of IEEE GLOBECOM*. IEEE.

Niyato, D., & Hossain, E. (2008). A noncooperative game-theoretic framework for radio resource management in 4G heterogeneous wireless access networks. *IEEE Transactions on Mobile Computing, 7*(3), 332–345. doi:10.1109/TMC.2007.70727

Pan, M., & Fang, Y. (2008). Bargaining based pairwise cooperative spectrum sensing for Cognitive Radio networks. In *Proceedings of IEEE MILCOM*. IEEE.

Park, H. G., & Schaar, M. V. D. (2007). Bargaining Strategies for Networked Multimedia Resource Management. *IEEE Transactions on Signal Processing, 55*(7), 3496–3511. doi:10.1109/TSP.2007.893755

Park, Y. S., & Jung, E. S. (2007). Resource-Aware Routing Algorithms for Multi-hop Cellular Networks. In *Proceedings of International Conference on Multimedia and Ubiquitous Engineering*, (pp. 1164-1167). Academic Press.

Parkes, D. C., Singh, S. P., & Yanovsky, D. (2004). Approximately efficient online mechanism design. In *Proceedings of Conference on Neural Information Processing Systems*. Academic Press.

Paschalidis, I. C., & Tsitsiklis, J. N. (2000). Congestion-dependent pricing of network services. *IEEE/ACM Transactions on Networking, 8*(2), 171–184. doi:10.1109/90.842140

Persone, V. N., & Campagna, E. (2009). Adaptive bandwidth allocation and admission control for wireless integrated service networks with flexible QoS. In *Proceedings of International Conference on Simulation Tools and Techniques*, (pp. 85-95). Academic Press.

Ramchurn, S. D., Mezzetti, C., Giovannucci, A., Rodriguez, J. A., Dash, R. K., & Jennings, N. R. (2009). Trust-Based Mechanisms for Robust and Efficient Task Allocation in the Presence of Execution Uncertainty. *Journal of Artificial Intelligence Research, 35*(1), 119–159.

Shneidman, J., & Parkes, D. (2003). Rationality and self-interest in peer-to-peer networks. In *Proceedings of IPTPS*, (pp. 139-148). IPTPS.

Sierra, C., Faratin, P., & Jennings, N. R. (1997). A Service-Oriented Negotiation Model between Autonomous Agents. In *Proceedings of European Workshop on Modeling Autonomous Agents in a Multi-Agent World*, (pp. 17-35). Academic Press.

Song, W., Zhuang, W., & Cheng, Y. (2007). Load balancing for cellular/WLAN integrated networks. *IEEE Network, 21*(1), 27–34. doi:10.1109/MNET.2007.314535

Suris, J., DaSilva, L., Han, Z., & MacKenzie, A. (2007). Cooperative game theory for distributed spectrum sharing. In *Proceedings of the IEEE International Conference on Communications*, (pp. 5282–5287). IEEE.

Virapanicharoen, J., & Benjapolakul, W. (2005). Fair-Efficient Guard Bandwidth Coefficients Selection in Call Admission Control for Mobile Multimedia Communications Using Framework of Game Theory. *IEICE Transactions on Communications. E (Norwalk, Conn.), 88-A*(7), 1869–1880.

Wang, H., Wang, F., Ke, Z., & Guo, Z. (2009). QoS-Adaptive Bandwidth Allocation Scheme Based on Measurement Report Real-Time Analysis. [WiCom.]. *Proceedings of WiCom, 09*, 4278–4281.

Wang, H. J., Katz, R. H., & Giese, J. (1999). Policy-enabled handoffs across heterogeneous wireless networks. In *Proceedings of IEEE Workshop on Mobile Computing Systems and Applications*, (pp. 51-60). IEEE.

Wang, X., & Schulzrinne, H. (2005). Incentive-Compatible Adaptation of Internet Real-Time Multimedia. *IEEE Journal on Selected Areas in Communications, 23*(2), 417–436. doi:10.1109/JSAC.2004.839399

Wen, S., & Wu, H. (2012). A Novel Resource Allocation Scheme for Station Area. In *Proceedings of IEEE Wireless Communications, Networking and Mobile Computing*. IEEE.

Woodard, C. J., & Parkes, D. C. (2003). Strategy-proof mechanisms for ad hoc network formation. In *Proceedings of IPTPS*. IPTPS.

Xie, B., Zhou, W., Hao, C., Ai, X., & Song, J. (2010). A Novel Bargaining Based Relay Selection and Power Allocation Scheme for Distributed Cooperative Communication Networks. In *Proceedings of IEEE VTC*. IEEE.

Yang, K., Ou, S., Guild, K., & Chen, H. H. (2009). Convergence of ethernet PON and IEEE 802.16 broadband access networks and its QoS-aware dynamic bandwidth allocation scheme. *IEEE JSAC, 27*(2), 101–116.

Yee, Y. C., Choong, K. N., Low, A. L. Y., Tan, S. W., & Chien, S. F. (2007). A conservative approach to adaptive call admission control for QoS provisioning in multimedia wireless networks. *Computer Communications Archive, 30*(2), 249–260. doi:10.1016/j.comcom.2006.08.025

Zhao, Y., & Zhao, H. (2002). Study on negotiation strategy. In *Proceedings of International Conference On Power System Technology*, (pp. 1335-1338). Academic Press.

Zouridaki, C., Mark, B. L., Hejmo, M., & Thomas, R. K. (2005). A Quantitative Trust Establishment Framework for Reliable Data Packet Delivery in MANETs. In *Proceedings of ACM SASN*. ACM.

KEY TERMS AND DEFINITIONS

Network Congestion: When a link or node is carrying so much data that its quality of service deteriorates. Typical effects include queueing delay, packet loss or the blocking of new connections. A consequence of these latter two is that an incremental increase in offered load leads either only to a small increase in network throughput, or to an actual reduction in network throughput.

Network Management: The activities, methods, procedures, and tools that pertain to the operation, administration, maintenance, and provisioning of networked systems. Network management is essential to command and control practices and is generally carried out of a network operations center.

Network Traffic Measurement: The process of measuring the amount and type of traffic on a particular network. This is especially important with regard to effective bandwidth management.

Performance Management: Activities which ensure that goals are consistently being met in an effective and efficient manner. Performance management can focus on the performance of an organization, a department, employee, or even the processes to build a product of service, as well as many other areas.

Resource Reservation Protocol (RSVP): A transport layer protocol designed to reserve resources across a network for an integrated services internet. RSVP operates over an IPv4 or IPv6 internet layer and provides receiver-initiated setup of resource reservations for multicast or unicast data flows with scaling and robustness.

Chapter 13
Game–Based Control Mechanisms for Cognitive Radio Networks

ABSTRACT

Comprehensive control mechanism in cognitive radio networks is an important research topic within the scope of empowering cognitive radio functionality in beyond-4G mobile networks. Providing control mechanism for secondary users without interference with primary users is an ambitious task, which requires innovative management architecture designs and routing solutions. Operational challenges such as opportunistic spectrum access, solving problems related to spectrum and network heterogeneities, and requests for the provisioning of Quality-of-Service to different applications must be resolved. As part of a novel management architecture, the control mechanism advances a new approach for cognitive radio networks. We explore this in this chapter.

TWO-WAY MATCHING GAME BASED BANDWIDTH SHARING (TMGBS) SCHEME

Bandwidth is an extremely valuable and scarce resource, and may become congested to accommodate diverse services in wireless communications. To enhance the efficiency of bandwidth usage, the concept of cognitive radio has emerged as a new design paradigm. Recently, S. Kim proposed a new Two-way Matching Game based Bandwidth Sharing (*TMGBS*) scheme for cognitive radio networks (Kim, 2013). Under dynamically changing network environments, the *TMGBS* scheme

formulates the bandwidth sharing problem as a two-way matching game model. In addition, modified game theory is adopted to reach a near Pareto optimal solution while avoiding bandwidth inefficiency. This approach can make the system more responsive to the current network situation.

Development Motivation

Recently, multimedia wireless applications are growing so rapidly that bandwidth scarcity has become a bottleneck of wireless communication development. Therefore, efficient bandwidth management becomes a key factor in enhancing

DOI: 10.4018/978-1-4666-6050-2.ch013

network performance. However, during traditional network operations, bandwidth is statically allocated to licensed users and regulated via a fixed assignment policy and; this static allocation approach is not efficient. Currently, it has been observed that allocated bandwidth bands are largely unused in any time and location; these are referred to as bandwidth holes (Niyato & Hossain, 2007), (Niyato & Hossain, 2008). To maximize bandwidth efficiency, bandwidth holes can be shared opportunistically while efficiently avoiding interference.

Cognitive Radio (CR) is a paradigm for wireless communications in which a wireless node changes its transmission or reception parameters to communicate efficiently with licensed or unlicensed users. By detecting unoccupied bandwidth holes in the radio spectrum environment, the CR technique can allow unlicensed users to use bandwidth holes as long as they cause no intolerable interference to licensed users. Therefore, CR has been developed as an emerging technique for the dynamic bandwidth sharing. Based on this technique, the bandwidth utilization and users' satisfaction can be enhanced dramatically (Liu, Shen, Song, & Wang, 2009). Under dynamically changing environments, licensed and unlicensed users have to coordinate with each other in order to obtain the best solution for all. The benefits of cooperation can be achieved through negotiation among the CR users. Therefore, the CR users have to bargain with each other to achieve a fair and efficient solution. It motivates the development of adaptive bandwidth sharing algorithms based on the cooperative bargaining model (Niyato, 2008).

The *TMGBS* scheme is a new adaptive CR bandwidth sharing scheme based on the game theory. The main goal of the *TMGBS* scheme is to maximize the revenue of primary users while maximizing the bandwidth efficiency along with the satisfaction of the secondary users. To satisfy the design goal, the methodologies that the *TMGBS* scheme adopted are the two-sided matching game (Kimbrough, & Kuo, 2010), (Malanchini, Cesana,

Gatti, 2009) and modified game theory (Mehmet, & Ramazan, 2001), (Kim, 2010). The proposed approach can model the dynamic behavior of each user and adapt their actions adaptively. Usually, most previous work in the area of cognitive radio emphasized the technical aspect of bandwidth sharing like as bandwidth sensing technique or dynamic access protocol (Niyato, 2008). However, the *TMGBS* scheme focuses on the economic aspect of bandwidth sharing; it refers to the bargaining process of selling-and-buying bandwidth in a CR environment.

To develop a two-sided matching game, two sets of individual players are given and asked to form pairs consisting of one member from each set; a player from one side can be matched only with a player from the other side. Matching can be regarded as stable only if it left no pair of players on opposite sides who were not matched to each other but would both prefer to be. A special property of two-sided matching game is that stable matching always exists (Li, Xu, Liu, Wang, & Han, 2010). In the *TMGBS* scheme, the bandwidth sharing problem in CR networks is designed as a two-sided matching model; licensed and unlicensed users are defined as primary and secondary users, respectively. One side set only consists of primary users, who offer the amount of sharing bandwidth to maximize their revenues. The other side set consists of secondary users, who can purchase bandwidth to improve their QoS satisfactions. Primary and secondary users are assumed to be self-regarding game players and select their strategies to maximize their perceived payoffs. Based on the dynamic bandwidth sharing strategy, the bandwidth utilization and users' satisfaction can be enhanced dramatically (Niyato, 2008).

To satisfy both primary and secondary users' purposes, multi-objective optimization techniques play a very important role. Over the past years, several studies dealing with this issue have been reported. Among various optimization techniques, the Modified Game Theory (MGT) is a well-known method to reach a near Pareto optimal solution; it is theoretically designed and practically applied without much deviation from the original game theory form (Mehmet, 2001), (Kim, 2010). In the *TMGBS* scheme, the MGT method is used to implement dynamic user behaviors in CR systems. Therefore, based on the two-sided matching model and MGT technique, the *TMGBS* scheme can provide an effective matching-pair solution for the bandwidth sharing problem. Finally, it is proved that the developed two-sided matching game is a potential game. Potential games have nice properties, such as uniqueness of equilibrium and convergence of heuristic algorithms to the equilibrium (Marden, Arslan, & Shamma, 2009), (Park & Schaar, 2007). According to the theoretical analysis, the developed two-sided matching game has at least one Nash equilibrium. During game processing, each player can improve deviate to a better strategy. Under the finite improvement property, the game process eventually ends, obviously in a Nash equilibrium.

Bandwidth Sharing Algorithm in the *TMGBS* Scheme

To understand the behavior of independent users, a game model has attractive features. For CR operations, the *TMGBS* scheme is designed by using a two-way matching game and modified game theory. The dynamics of game process can cause cascade interactions of players while improving bandwidth utilization and user's satisfaction.

Matching Game Model

In 1962, David Gale and Lloyd Shapley derived an effective model of finding a stable matching. From labor *DBSG* markets to human courtship, the Gale and Shapley's model can create efficient pairing solutions; there are a number of application models for the Gale-Shapley solution. The two-way matching game was developed for special matching problems. In a two-way matching game, players on each side have preferences over players on the other side, and have enough information to rank players on the other side. Therefore, player in one side tries to be matched to the other player in opposite side so as to satisfy both players as much as possible (Kimbrough, 2010), (Malanchini, 2009). As a kind of cooperative game model, two-sided matching games dealt with widely in practice include pairing men with women, workers with employers, students with schools and so on (Niyato, 2007).

Usually, a large portion of the assigned wireless bandwidth is used sporadically, and considerable amount of the bandwidth is detected out of use both in space and time. This situation leads to underutilization of a significant amount of bandwidth. Therefore, to make full use of the idle bandwidth, the Cognitive Radio (CR) technique has been proposed (Heo, Shin, Nam, Lee, Park, & Cho, 2008). The main feature of CR networks is the capability to share the wireless channel with licensed users in an opportunistic manner. In the CR network system, two types of users are considered; primary users (i.e. licensed user) and secondary users (i.e. unlicensed user). A primary user has exclusive access to designated bandwidth while a secondary user is allowed to temporally occupy the idle bandwidth which primary user does not use. If primary users come back to use their designated bandwidths, the secondary users should release the momentary-using bandwidth and try to find other idle bandwidths (Heo, 2008).

For CR networks, the *TMGBS* scheme is developed as a new bandwidth sharing scheme based on the two-way matching model. When the bandwidths of primary users (PUs) are not fully utilized, PUs have an opportunity to sell their spare bandwidth for the revenue maximization. Secondary users (SUs) want to buy bandwidth to improve their QoS satisfactions (Li, 2010). To implement the dynamics of bandwidth sharing process, a presumption is that one side set consists of PUs and the other side set consists of SUs. PUs and SUs have own interests and capacities to act on them. In the *TMGBS* scheme, matches among multiple-sellers and multiple-buyers are operated to achieve the desired network system objective.

The *TMGBS* scheme focuses on the economic aspect of bandwidth sharing. In economics, exchanges can be performed directly between goods and services or using a medium of exchange (Niyato, 2008). However, in CR networks, bandwidth sharing can be performed based on the exchange between bandwidth and money. From the economic viewpoint, supply function of bandwidth owners determines the amount of selling bandwidth; bandwidth selling can generate the additional revenue for PUs. Similarly, demand function of bandwidth leaseholders determines the amount of purchasing bandwidth; bandwidth purchasing can enhance the satisfaction of SUs. Supply function is derived from the payoff gained by the primary service and the revenue received from selling bandwidth to the secondary services (Niyato, 2007). In the *TMGBS* scheme, the profit function (P_U) of the primary user i is defined as follows.

$$P\_U_i = \left[\alpha_i \times u\left(B_i\right)\right] + \left[\left(1 - \alpha_i\right) \times \left(P_i \times Q_i\right)\right],$$

$$\text{s.t., } u\left(B_i\right) = \ln\left(W_i - Q_i\right) \tag{1}$$

where B_i, P_i are the actually allocated bandwidth for user i's primary services and the price charged for the bandwidth selling, respectively. $u(B_i)$ is the QoS satisfaction function of user i. W_i is the total bandwidth amount for user i, and Q_i is the selling bandwidth amount to the secondary user, i.e., $B_i = W_i - Q_i$. The parameter α_i controls the relative weights given to QoS satisfaction ($u(B_i)$) and revenue ($P_i \times Q_i$). Under diverse network environments, each user has different preference between QoS satisfaction and revenue. Therefore, α value should be dynamically adjustable for each primary user.

To gain the highest profit, this P_U function is partially differentiated with respect to Q_i (Niyato, 2007). Based on the price P_i, the *TMGBS* scheme can estimate how much bandwidth of the primary user i is shared with the secondary user. The maximum profit of primary user i can be expressed as follows:

$$\frac{\partial P\_U_i}{\partial Q_i} = 0 = \frac{-\alpha_i}{W_i - Q_i} + \left(1 - \alpha_i\right) \times P_i \tag{2}$$

It is obtained that P_U function is partially differentiated with respect to Q_i. For the demand function of secondary user, the profit function (S_U) of the secondary user j is defined as follows.

$$S\_U_j = \left[\beta_j \times u\left(Q_j\right)\right] - \left[\left(1 - \beta_j\right) \times \left(P_j \times Q_j\right)\right],$$

$$\text{s.t., } u\left(Q_j\right) = \ln\left(Q_i\right) \tag{3}$$

where Q_j is the amount of user j's purchasing bandwidth. The parameter β_j also controls the relative weights like as α_i. Based on a preference diversity between QoS satisfaction and budget, β value also should be dynamically adjustable for each secondary user. To gain the maximum profit, this S_U function is partially differentiated with respect to Q_j (Niyato, 2007). Finally, the *TMGBS* scheme has the supply function (S_i) of primary user i and the demand function (D_j) of secondary user j are defined as follows.

$$S_i = Q_i = W_i - \left[\frac{\alpha_i}{1 - \alpha_i} \times \frac{1}{P_i}\right]$$

and

$$D_j = Q_j = \left[\frac{\beta_j}{1 - \beta_j} \times \frac{1}{P_j} \right] \tag{4}$$

Differentiation is a method to compute the rate at which a dependent output changes with respect to the change in the independent input. After differentiation, supply and demand functions are obtained.

Modified Game Theory for Multi-Objective Optimization

Players have their own expectations. PU player i ($i \in \mathcal{M} = \{m_1,..., m_g\}$, where g is the total number of PUs) has two bargaining terms; the selling bandwidth amount (S_i) and expected revenue ($P_i \times Q_i$). At the same time, SU player j ($j \in \mathbb{N}$ $= \{n_1,..., n_f\}$, where f is the total number of SUs) has two bargaining terms; the demanding bandwidth amount (D_j) and budget ($P_j \times Q_j$).

To decide the effective matching pairs, one of major concerns is to design matching functions. The *TMGBS* scheme defines two functions (F_{d_s} and F_p) based on individual users' preferences; the F_{d_s} (i,j) and F_p (i,j) are defined as follows.

$$F_{d\_s}\left(i, j\right) = \left[\left\| \frac{F_{i1} - f_{j1}}{\max\left(F_{i1}, f_{j1}\right)} \right\|^2 \right]^{\frac{1}{2}}$$

and

$$F_p\left(i, j\right) = \left[\left\| \frac{F_{i2} - f_{j2}}{\max\left(F_{i2}, f_{j2}\right)} \right\|^2 \right]^{\frac{1}{2}} \tag{5}$$

where F_{i1}, F_{i2} are the primary user i's S_i and P_iQ_i ($i \in \mathcal{M}$), respectively. f_{j1}, f_{j2} are the secondary user j's D_j and $P_j \times Q_j$ ($j \in \mathbb{N}$), respec-

tively. Therefore, the F_{d_s} and F_p are normalized; the range is varied from 0 to 1. Usually, object functions are designed according to the concept of relative distance. In the *TMGBS* scheme, F_{d_s} (i,j) and F_p (i,j) are developed based on the Tchebychev method; It has the advantage of being able to solve multi-objective optimization problem (Mehmet, 2001).

In the *TMGBS* scheme, the MGT method is used to get the proper combination of the F_{d_s} and F_p functions. In general, the MGT method may be concluded to provide the best compromise in the presence of different control functions (Mehmet, 2001). By practically applying the MGT, the F_{d_s} and F_p are transformed into a single objective function. To obtain this single function, the procedure is defined as follows. First, a normalized bargaining model (NBM_{ij}) for the pair between PU i and SU j is constructed to compare the relative effectiveness.

$$NBM_{ij} = \prod_{k=1}^{2} \left[1 - f\_u_k\left(i, j\right) \right],$$

where $i \in \mathcal{M}$ and $j \in \mathbb{N}$ $\tag{6}$

where $f\_u_1(i,j)$ is $F_{d\_s}(i,j)$ and $f\_u_2(i,j)$ is F_p (i,j). This bargaining model gives a normalized indication value ($0 \leq NBM_{ij} \leq 1$) as to how far a function is from its worst value. Therefore, the solution is optimized by maximizing the bargaining model (Mehmet, 2001), (Kim, 2010). Second, a weighted average (WA_{ij}) for the pair between PU player i and SU player j is formulated as follows.

$$WA_{ij} = \sum_{k=1}^{2} \left[\gamma_k \times f\_u_k\left(i, j\right) \right], \text{ with } \sum_{k=1}^{2} \gamma_k = 1 \tag{7}$$

The parameter γ_k ($k = 1$ or 2) controls the relative weights given to bandwidth amount ($k =$

1) and price ($k = 2$). In the *TMGBS* scheme, by considering the mutual-interaction relationship, the γ_2 is defined as $1 - \gamma_1$, and the value of γ_1 is dynamically adjusted based on the current user decision. Therefore, by using the real-time online monitoring, the system can be more responsive to current network conditions. Finally, according to (6) and (7), the multi-objective matching function ($Mat\,(i,j)$) of between PU i and SU j is given by

$$Mat\left(i,j\right) = \min_{i \in \mathcal{M}, j \in \mathbb{N}} \left(WA_{ij} - NBM_{ij}\right) \qquad (8)$$

where WA_{ij} has to be minimized and NBM_{ij} has to be maximized; a new objective function (Mat (i,j)) is created for minimization.

The main goal of the developed algorithm is to find the optimal set of pairs, which minimizes the total sum of all pairs' *Mat* values. To satisfy this goal, players are put into a random order, and each player in turn examines the players of the counterpart set. In the main loop of the matching algorithm, primary users find out the most suitable partners according to (8). In addition, the developed algorithm identifies all potential swaps throughout matching procedure execution. For example, if a player picks the counterpart player in the already matched pair, swapping can occur on the basis of *Mat* values; the new match by swapping should be lower *Mat* value than its present matching pair.

The Main Steps of the *TMGBS* Scheme

In cognitive radio networks, wireless bandwidth can be dynamically shared to improve bandwidth usage. When the initially assigned bandwidth is not fully utilized, the bandwidth owner (PU) has an opportunity to sell the bandwidth to generate extra-revenue. The bandwidth leaseholders (SU) can purchase bandwidth by using the adaptive

bargaining process. Each player's behavior might affect the behavior of other players. Therefore, players' decisions are coupled with one another.

For the efficient dynamic bandwidth sharing, intelligent match-making decision mechanism is a key factor to maximize the bandwidth seller's revenue and the bandwidth buyer's satisfaction. The *TMGBS* scheme is a new bandwidth sharing scheme, which is developed based on the two-way matching game and modified game theory. In the developed algorithm, primary and secondary users are assumed as game players; they examine their payoffs in a distributed fashion. Based on the bandwidth supply and demand functions, two-way matching process continues interactively until there is no player in $\mathcal{M}$ or $\mathbb{N}$ sets for matching game. To get the most effective bandwidth sharing solution, matching pairs are decided by using modified game theory. The main steps of the *TMGBS* scheme are given next.

Step 1: At the initial time, primary user set $\mathcal{M}$ $= \{m_1,..., m_g\}$ and secondary user set $\mathbb{N} =$ $\{n_1,..., n_f\}$ are established. The members of sets are assumed as players of the matching game.

Step 2: Each player in $\mathcal{M}$ has his own supply (S) function and price (P) for the bandwidth selling. In a distributed manner, players estimate the amount of selling bandwidth by using (4).

Step 3: Each player in $\mathbb{N}$ has his own demand (D) function and price (P) for the bandwidth buying. In a distributed manner, players estimate the amount of purchasing bandwidth by using (4).

Step 4: All possible PU-SU players' matching pairs estimate F_{d_s}, F_p, NBM_{ij}, and WA_{ij} functions values by using (5),(6) and (7).

Step 5: Player i ($i \in \mathcal{M}$) ranks each player in $\mathbb{N}$ according to (8), and proposes to its most-preferred player j ($j \in \mathbb{N}$). If player j gets more than one proposal, player j retains all these proposals.

Step 6: If all players in $\mathcal{M}$ offer their preference partners in $\mathbb{N}$, swapping process is triggered to find the best matching for all individuals.

Step 7: The SU player in $\mathbb{N}$, who has more than one proposal, selects its most preferred PU player according to (8). Finally, an effective matching-pair is decided.

Step 8: If a matching-pair is finally decided, the players of decided pairs are removed in $\mathcal{M}$ and $\mathbb{N}$ sets.

Step 9: If $\mathcal{M}$ and $\mathbb{N}$ sets are not empty, proceeds to Step 5 for the next matching iteration. This feedback matching procedure continues until one of both sets ($\mathcal{M}$ and $\mathbb{N}$) is empty.

Termination: If one of sets ($\mathcal{M}$ or $\mathbb{N}$) is empty, matching game processing is over.

Recently, several bandwidth sharing schemes for CR networks have been presented. The *Demand-Matching Spectrum Sharing* (*DMSS*) scheme is a non-cooperative game model for CR bandwidth sharing problems (Liu, 2009). This scheme enables each unlicensed user to access appropriate bandwidth by using the *Nelder-Mead* direct search method. In addition, matching factors between the user demand and the bandwidth char-

acteristics are built up and the *Nash* equilibrium is achieved by adopting demand matching factor. The *Dynamic Bandwidth Selection Game* (*DBSG*) scheme is designed as a game theoretic framework to evaluate bandwidth management functionalities in CR networks (Malanchini, 2009). In the *DBSG* scheme, different quality measures are considered to select the best bandwidth opportunity under the tight constraint. The simulation results shown in Figure 1 demonstrate that the performance comparison of the *TMGBS* scheme with the *DMSS* scheme and the *DBSG* scheme.

Discussion

To model the bandwidth sharing problem in CR networks, the *TMGBS* scheme is designed as a two-sided matching game by using the MGT technique. The developed matching game can be interpreted as a potential game. A game is considered a potential game if the incentive of all players to change their strategy can be expressed in one global function, i.e., the potential function. The primary advantage for modeling the considered bandwidth sharing scheme as a potential game is that there exists at least one Nash equilibrium

Figure 1. Performance evaluations of the TMGBS scheme

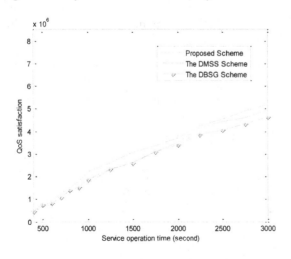

(a) QoS satisfaction

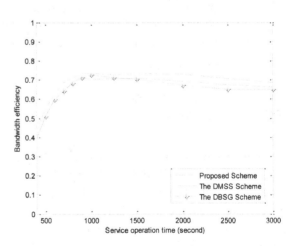

(b) Bandwidth efficiency

(Park, 2007); Nash equilibrium is a strategy set of all players' strategies with the property that each player has chosen a strategy and no player can benefit by changing his strategy while the other players keep their strategies unchanged (Park, 2007). Here, it is proved that the developed matching model is a potential game; hence, it has at least one Nash equilibrium. Congestion games, which were defined by Rosenthal, can be defined as follows:

Definition 1: A game model (*PG*) constitutes a tuple $(\Lambda, (\Omega_i)_{i \in \Lambda}, (U_i)_{i \in \Lambda})$, where Λ is a nonempty finite set of players. For each player $i \in \Lambda$, its collection of player action sets $(\Omega_i)_{i \in \Lambda}$, together with player utility functions $\{ U_i : \Omega_i \to \mathbb{R} \}$. The *PG* is a potential game if, for some potential function $\Phi : (\Omega_i)_{i \in \Lambda} \to \mathbb{R}$. (Marden, 2009).

$$U_i\left(a_i'', a_{-i}\right) - U_i\left(a_i', a_{-i}\right) = \Phi\left(a_i'', a_{-i}\right) - \Phi\left(a_i', a_{-i}\right), \tag{9}$$

s.t., $a_i', a_i'' \in \Omega_i$ and $a_{-i} \in \times_{j \neq i} \left(\Omega_j\right)_{j \in \Lambda}$

Therefore, a potential game requires perfect alignment between the global objective and the players' local objective functions. Because the incentives of all players are mapped into one function, the potential function is a useful tool to analyze equilibrium properties of games (Marden, 2009), (Park, 2007).

Here, it is showed that the developed two-sided matching game can be modeled as a potential game by appropriately defining the players' utilities. Therefore, if a player unilaterally changed its action, the change in its objective function would be equal to the change in the derived potential function.

Proposition: For bandwidth sharing, the two-sided game model in the *TMGBS* scheme is potential game.

Proof: Let $\mathbb{S}\left(i, j\right)_{i \in \mathcal{M}, j \in \mathbb{N}}$ denote the set of (i,j) pairs, which are selected by the two-sided matching game. We assume that (p,r) and (p', r') are elements of $\mathbb{S}\left(i, j\right)_{i \in \mathcal{M}}$ and $\mathbb{S}'_{p \mapsto p'}\left(i, j\right)_{i,p,p' \in \mathcal{M}, j \in \mathbb{N}}$ represents the $\mathbb{S}\left(i, j\right)_{i \in \mathcal{M}, j \in \mathbb{N}}$ but the p and p' are swapped in the pairs (p,r) and (p', r'). Based on these notations, we can define the pair set $(\mathbb{S}'_{p \mapsto p'})$ with swapping p and p' like as $\mathbb{S}'_{p \mapsto p'} = (p, r') + (p', r) + \mathbb{S}\left(i, j\right)_{i \in \mathcal{M} \setminus p, p', j \in \mathbb{N} \setminus r, r'}$ and denote each matching pair sets according to the p and p' swapping; $\mathbb{X}^1_{p \mapsto p'} = \{(p, r'), (p', r)\}$, $\mathbb{X}^0_{p \mapsto p'} = \{(p,r), (p', r')\}$ and $- \mathbb{X}_{p \mapsto p'} = \mathbb{S}\left((i, j)\right)_{i \in \mathcal{M} \setminus p, p', j \in \mathbb{N} \setminus r, r'}$. For the matching game model in the *TMGBS* scheme, the potential function can be expressed as follows:

$$\Phi\left(\mathbb{S}\left((i, j)\right)_{i \in \mathcal{M}, j \in \mathbb{N}}\right) = - \sum_{i \in \mathcal{M}} Mat\left(i, j\right), \text{ s.t.,} \quad j \in \mathbb{N}. \tag{10}$$

The change in the potential function by the p and p' swapping is

$$\Phi\left(\mathbb{S}'_{p \mapsto p'}\left(i, j\right)_{i,p,p' \in \mathcal{M}, j \in \mathbb{N}}\right) = - \left(Mat\left(p', r\right) - Mat\left(p, r'\right)\right) - \sum_{i \in \mathcal{M} \setminus p, p'} Mat\left(i, j\right)$$
$$\text{s.t., } j \in \mathbb{N} \tag{11}$$

The goal is to assign each player an utility function that is perfectly aligned with the global potential function in (10). To satisfy this goal, we should show that each player has an utility function that captures the player's marginal contribution to the potential function. In the two-sided matching game, each player being assigned the utility function like as

$$U_p\left(\mathbb{X}^1_{p\leftrightarrow p'}, -\mathbb{X}_{p\leftrightarrow p'}\right) = -\left(Mat\left(p', r\right) - Mat\left(p, r'\right)\right) \tag{12}$$

The change in the objective function of player p by the p and p' swapping, provided that other players collectively play $-\mathbb{X}_{p\leftrightarrow p'}$, is

$$U_p\left(\mathbb{X}^1_{p\leftrightarrow p'}, -\mathbb{X}_{p\leftrightarrow p'}\right) - U_p\left(\mathbb{X}^0_{p\leftrightarrow p'}, -\mathbb{X}_{p\leftrightarrow p'}\right) \tag{13}$$

$$= -\left(Mat\left(p', r\right) - Mat\left(p, r'\right)\right) - \left(Mat\left(p, r\right) - Mat\left(p', r'\right)\right)$$

$$= \Phi\left(\Phi^1_{p\leftrightarrow p'}, -\Phi_{p\leftrightarrow p'}\right) - \Phi\left(\mathbb{X}^0_{p\leftrightarrow p'}, -\mathbb{X}_{p\leftrightarrow p'}\right)$$

Finally, we can prove that the developed two-sided matching game is a potential game. It is concluded that the *TMGBS* scheme has at least one Nash equilibrium and converges to the equilibrium.

Summary

Nowadays, cognitive radio technique has been identified as a new paradigm for next generation wireless networks. In cognitive radio networks, adaptive bandwidth can be shared dynamically to enhance the overall system efficiency. The *TMGBS* scheme is a new cognitive radio bandwidth sharing scheme based on the two-sided matching game and modified game theory. Without much deviation from the original game theory, the *TMGBS* scheme is designed practically, and provides an effective matching-pair solution for the bandwidth sharing problem. In addition, it is proved that the two-sided matching game in the *TMGBS* scheme is a potential game. Therefore, the *TMGBS* scheme has at least one Nash equilibrium. The main objective of the *TMGBS* scheme is to effectively share the wireless bandwidth to maximize the bandwidth utilization and network performance.

MULTI-LEADER MULTI-FOLLOWER STACKELBERG (*MMS*) SCHEME FOR COGNITIVE RADIO NETWORKS

Radio spectrum is one of the most scarce and variable resources for wireless communications. Therefore, the proliferation of devices and rapid growth of wireless services continue to strain the limited radio spectrum resource. Cognitive Radio (CR) paradigm is a promising technology to solve the problem of spectrum scarcity. In 2012, S. Kim proposed a new Multi-leader Multi-follower Stackelberg (*MMS*) scheme, which is a fair-efficient spectrum sharing scheme for cognitive radio networks (Kim, 2012). Based on the multiple-leader multiple-follower Stackelberg game model, the *MMS* scheme increases opportunistic use of the licensed radio spectrum. To adaptively use the spectrum resource, control decisions are coupled with one another; the result of the each user's decisions is the input back to the other user's decision process. Under widely diverse network environments, this adaptive feedback process approach can provide an effective way of finding a suitable solution.

Development Motivation

The emergence of new wireless technologies has created huge demand of radio spectrum. However, radio spectrum is a naturally limited and expensive resource around the world. Due to the limitation of radio spectrum, wireless communication networks suffer from the scarcity in spectrum resource (Rohokale, Kulkarni, Prasad, & Cornean, 2010). Although almost all the spectrum has been allocated, the actual utilization measurement clearly shows that many portions of the radio spectrum are not used for a significant amount of time (Pal, 2007). It becomes obvious that the present fixed frequency allocation strategy cannot accommodate the new emerging multimedia services. To avoid the inefficiency of spectrum usage, opportunistic or dynamic spectrum access strategy has been considered an effective solution for wireless networks (Li, Wang, & Guizani, 2009).

For decades, research has been done to solve the problem of spectrum scarcity in a very dynamic environment. Cognitive Radio (CR) is widely regarded as one of the most promising technologies for improving the utilization of spectrum resources. CR is a paradigm for wireless communication that unlicensed users may access and use the spectrum when it is idle from licensed users. Therefore, the increased spectrum utilization in CR networks is achieved through spectrum sharing between licensed and unlicensed users (Li, 2009). For the proper spectrum sharing in CR systems, the spectrum trading process should be modeled effectively. Nowadays, the main idea of game theory has emerged as an effective way of designing the CR trading process (Bloem, Alpcan, & Başar, 2007).

Stackelberg games are a class of games in game theory; it is initially proposed by the German economist H. von Stackelberg in 1934 to explain some economic monopolization phenomena (Wang, Han, & Liu, 2006). In a Stackelberg game, one player acts as a leader and the rest as followers, and the main goal is to find an optimal strategy for the leader, assuming that the followers react in such a rational way that followers optimize their objective functions given the leader's actions. Therefore, it can be the static bilevel optimization model (Nie, & Zhang, 2008). In 1984, H.D. Sherali further extended the classical Stackelberg model by considering multiple leaders (Sherali, 1984). Multi-leader Stackelberg Game (MSG) model assumed the existence of more than one leader, with each leader's actions do not precipitate responses from other leaders. About MSG models, there are many applications in the field of economics, engineering and science. In particular, MSG model has some attractive features to understand

the behavior of self-regarding and independent CR users (Elias, & Martignon, 2010), (Xiao, Bi, & Niyato, 2010).

The *MMS* scheme is a new MSG based spectrum sharing scheme that solves the joint problem of licensed and unlicensed users in CR networks. The main challenge is to use spectrum as efficiently as possible while ensuring fairness. To achieve this design goal, the *MMS* scheme consists of two different algorithms; leader-level algorithm for the licensed users and follower-level algorithm for unlicensed users. In the leader-level algorithm, licensed users make their decisions based on the egalitarian bargaining solution (Matt, Toni, & Dionysiou, 2006). The result of licensed users' decision is the input back to the follower-level algorithm. In the follower-level algorithm, unlicensed users make their decisions by using the non-cooperative game (Dirani, & Chahed, 2006), (Nie, 2008). Therefore, control decisions of two algorithms are hierarchically interconnected and can cause cascade interactions. By using this dynamics of feedback loop, licensed and unlicensed users can be interacting with one another and make their decisions in a way to reach an efficient network equilibrium.

Related Work

Recently, several spectrum sharing schemes based on the game theory have been presented in research literature. The *Rate and Power Control (RPC)* scheme (Yang, Li, & Li, 2009) is a control algorithm based on game model for wireless communication. This scheme introduced the classic form of non-cooperative power control model as a new framework. By considering the joint transmission rate and power control issues, the Nash equilibrium solution for either the transmit rate or the transmit power is achieved in the cognitive radio. In addition, a pricing function that relates to both transmit rate and power is introduced for improving the Pareto efficiency and fairness of the obtained Nash equilibrium solution.

The *Game based Power Control* (*GPC*) scheme (Liu, Peng, Shao, Chen, & Wang, 2010) can regulate the transmitter power to meet the different SINR requirements and enhance the total throughput effectively. The *GPC* scheme adopted the game theory for power control modeling in cognitive radio system, and developed a new sigmoid efficiency function with non-liner pricing only related with user's SINR. In addition, non-cooperative power control game created by D. Goodman is applied for decentralized users. This approach is very suitable for cognitive radio system because of its regardless of the modulation of users' RAT.

The *Cognitive Radio Power Control* (*CRPC*) scheme is a multi-antenna cognitive radio power control algorithm with the idea of game theory (Hou, Wang, & Hu, 2010). In this scheme, every user improves the transmitting power selfishly not considering other users, and other users choose the corresponding strategies. This interactive and repeated process is actually a kind of non-cooperative game; it will reach a balanced state that is called Nash equilibrium. The *CRPC* scheme also shows that the proposed algorithm achieves the user transmitting power to make the global information transmission rate maximal after limited iterations, which proves the algorithm efficient.

Evolution Game based Spectrum Allocation (*EGSA*) scheme proposed an evolution game based spectrum allocation algorithm for cognitive radio networks (Song, Zhuang, & Zhang, 2011). In this scheme, a SU's behavior to select a PU was formulated as an evolution game problem. At a given spectrum price, the SU randomly chose a PU and rented spectrum from it at the first time, and then the SU selected a PU in an evolutionary way every time; PUs used a price game to adjust the price and amount of the leased spectrum to obtain maximum utility.

The *Demand-Matching Spectrum Sharing* (*DMSS*) scheme is a non-cooperative game model for CR spectrum sharing problems (Liu, 2009). This scheme enables each unlicensed user to access appropriate spectrum by using the *Nelder-Mead* direct search method. In addition, matching factors between the user demand and the spectrum characteristics are built up and the *Nash* equilibrium is achieved by adopting demand matching factors.

The *Dynamic Bandwidth Selection Game* (*DBSG*) scheme is designed as a game theoretic framework to evaluate spectrum management functionalities in CR networks (Malanchini, 2009). In the *DBSG* scheme, different quality measures are considered to select the best spectrum opportunity under the tight constraint.

Spectrum Sharing with Imperfect Sensing (*SSIS*) scheme addressed the problem of primary-secondary spectrum sharing in cognitive networks using discrete time Markov chain model (Gelabert, Sallent, Pérez-Romero, & Agustí, 2010). Model validation was achieved by means of a system-level simulator which captured the system behavior with high degree of accuracy. In addition, this work reflected the importance of time-sharing between spectrum sensing and data transmission.

Spectrum Sharing with Channel Heterogeneity (SSCH) scheme presented a cross-layer optimization framework to jointly design the spectrum sharing and routing with channel heterogeneity (Ma, & Tsang, 2009). This scheme considered heterogeneous channels and well captured the unique feature in cognitive radio networks. In addition, the SSCH scheme addressed a heuristic method by solving a relaxation of the original problem, followed by rounding and simple local optimization.

The *Pricing and Power Control for Bandwidth* (*PPCB*) scheme allocates spectrum between conflicting users and network provider as a non-cooperative game model (Feng, Mau, Mandayam, 2004). It is shown that the proposed strategy in the *PPCB* scheme results in a unique Nash equilibrium, and there exists a unique spectrum price that maximized the revenue of the network.

Previous proposed schemes have been designed to control the spectrum sharing problem in wireless networks. The interactions among users can be formally modeled as games. Therefore, the outcome of these game models can be predicted by using a game theoretic formulation. However, these schemes are designed for specific network environments, and focus on theoretical analysis, which provides no indication to users how to actually do these deals. In addition, these results do not address the real-world implementation problem. In addition, they rely on several assumptions that do not seem to be practical. Therefore, it is questionable whether these assumptions are satisfied under practical network operations.

Spectrum Sharing Algorithms in the *MMS* Scheme

Based on the multi-leader Stackelberg game model, the *MMS* scheme captures both economical and technical aspects of the spectrum sharing problem to improve the spectrum utilization and network revenue.

Network Model

A multi-leader multi-follower game is a general case of Stackelberg games (Mustika, Yamamoto, Murata, & Yoshida, 2010). In the *MMS* scheme, this methodology is adopted to solve the joint problem of revenue maximization and dynamic spectrum sharing in CR networks. There are a set $\mathbb{L} = \{l_1, l_2, \ldots, l_n\}$ of licensed users and a set $\mathbb{F} = \{f_1, f_2, \ldots, f_m\}$ of unlicensed users. In a realistic scenario, the licensed users have priority to the spectrum; unlicensed users make their reactions based on the licensed user's decision. Therefore, licensed users declare their strategies and play their roles as leaders and unlicensed

users must obey as followers. It is suitable assumption and proper modeling for practical CR network operations (Li, 2009), (Xiao, 2010). In the developed model, leaders decide the price independently, and followers respond to such price setting in order to optimize their utility functions. This is naturally a two-stage bilevel approach. The leader g ($g \in \mathbb{L}$) has a utility function (UL) as follows.

$$UL_g\left(p\_u_g, c_g\right) = p\_u_g \times Size\left(c_g\right), \quad \text{s.t.,}$$
$$p\_u_g = \begin{cases} \Delta_u \times p\_u_g, & \text{if } c_g \text{ is leased} \\ \Delta_d \times p\_u_g, & \text{otherwise} \end{cases}$$

(14)

where p_u_g is the price for spectrum unit (U_{nit}), and c_g is the spectrum channel, which is leased for unlicensed users. Δ_u and Δ_d are price control parameters. If the spectrum lease fails, the leader g can decrease the price (p_u_g) by multiplexing Δ_d (i.e., $0 < \Delta_d < 1$). When the available channel (c_g) can be successfully leased, the leader g can increase the price for the next bargain by multiplexing Δ_u (i.e., $1 < \Delta_u$). Therefore, the leader g can dynamically decide the p_u_g value to maximize $UL_g\left(p\_u_g, c_g\right)$.

The unlicensed user i ($i \in F$) has also a utility function. Strategies for the player i can be combined into a composite action $s_i = \{c_i, p_i\}$ where c_i ($c_i \in \mathbb{C}$) is a channel and p_i ($p_i \in \mathbb{P} = (p_1, p_2, \ldots, p_k)$) is a discrete power level, where $\mathbb{C}$ and $\mathbb{P}$ are the set of lease-available channels and power levels, respectively. In order to develop an algorithm over action spaces that include power level and transmission channel, the utility function for each unlicensed player i can be defined as follows (Bloem, 2007).

$$U_i\left(s_i, \boldsymbol{s}_{-i}\right) =$$

$$-\sum_{j=1, j\neq i}^{m} \left(p_j \times h_{ji} \times \delta\left(c_j, c_i\right)\right) - \sum_{j=1, j\neq i}^{m} \left(p_i \times h_{ij} \times \delta\left(c_i, c_j\right)\right)$$

$$+\left(\alpha \times \log\left(1 + p_i \times h_{ii}\right) + \beta / p_i\right) - \left(p_l \times h_{li} \times \delta\left(c_l, c_i\right)\right)$$

$$-\left(p_i \times h_{il} \times \delta\left(c_i, c_l\right)\right) - Pr_i\left(c_i\right) \quad (15)$$

s.t., $Pr_i\left(c_i\right) = \psi_i \times p\_u_g \times Size\left(c_i\right)$

and

$$\delta\left(c_i, c_j\right) = \begin{cases} 1, & \text{if } c_i = c_j \\ 0, & \text{otherwise} \end{cases}$$

where h_{ji} is the path gain from the transmitter of player j to the receiver of player i and $\boldsymbol{s}_{-i}$ is the current strategy set without the player i, i.e., $\boldsymbol{s}_{-i} = \left(s_1, \ldots, s_{i-1}, s_{i+1}, \ldots s_L\right)$. ψ_i is the price control factor and $Size\left(c_i\right)$ function returns the spectrum unit number of channel c_i. δ is the interference function characterizing the interference. In the formula (15), the first term captures the impact that other players have on the interference sensed by the receiver in the pair i, and the second term captures the impact of a potential action for player i on the interference observed by all other players (Bloem, 2007). The third term $\left(\text{i.e.}, \alpha \times \log\left(1 + p_i \times h_{ii}\right) + \beta / p_i\right)$ provides an incentive for individual players to increase their power levels. The fourth and fifth terms $\left(\text{i.e.}, p_l \times h_{li} \times \delta\left(c_l, c_i\right) \text{ and } p_i \times h_{il} \times \delta\left(c_i, c_l\right)\right)$ represent the impact that the player i's strategy has on the leader (i.e., player l). Finally, the last term ($Pr_i\left(c_i\right)$) is the price to pay by leasing a channel.

The Leader-Level Algorithm

In the cognitive radio spectrum sharing process, there exists a hierarchy of decision makers. Decisions are made at different levels with different goals in this hierarchy. Usually, those decisions are made independently of each other, but have to take into account decisions made by players of a different level. The strategies chosen by the followers depend on the strategy selected by the leaders. Therefore, the objective function of the leaders may depend not only on their own decisions but also on the followers (Wang, 2006).

The *MMS* scheme consists of two different control algorithms; leader-level algorithm and follower-level algorithm. The leader-level algorithm deals with the problem that maximizes the leader's utility function. By controlling the current price (p_u), the leaders try to maximize their revenues. However, there are multiple leaders. Therefore, fairness is another prominent issue for the leader-level algorithm. If the concept of fairness is not considered explicitly at the design stage of control algorithms, different leaders' revenues can result in very unfair. To implement fairness among multiple leaders, the *MMS* scheme adopted the Egalitarian Welfare Solution (EWS) (Bossert & Tan, 1995); EWS was developed by E. Kalai and R. Myerson in 1977 as one of cooperative bargaining models. The main feature of the EWS is a monotonicity with respect to expansions of the feasible set without using Nash's axiom of independence of scale of utility. Unlike other bargaining solutions, the egalitarian solution enjoys even stronger monotonicity requirements while satisfying independence conditions (Matt, 2006).

To design the EWS, the *MMS* scheme can assume that n leaders (i.e., n = $|\mathbb{L}|$) and m followers (i.e., m = $|\mathbb{F}|$) with leasable spectrum resources are involved in a spectrum sharing process. $A^{\{1..n, 1..m\}}$ is defined to represent the resource sharing to followers; it is a Boolean table of n lines and m columns (Matt, 2006).

$$A^{\{1..n,1..m\}} = \begin{pmatrix} A_{1,1}, A_{1,2} & \cdots & A_{1,m} \\ \cdots & \cdots & \cdots & \cdots \\ A_{n,1}, A_{n,2} & \cdots & A_{n,m} \end{pmatrix} \tag{16}$$

For simplicity, the *MMS* scheme assumes $A^{\{1..n,1..m\}}$ contains at most one element, which has 1, per row. It can say that f_j get the resource of l_i if and only if $A_{i,j} = 1$. Leaders can be characterized by their own preferences concerning their resources. These preferences are defined as utility functions $\left(UL_i \left(p\_u_i, c_i \right) \right)$ according to (14). It is measuring the contribution of the leasing spectrum resource (c_i) to the leader's welfare (Matt, 2006). At time t, the welfare of leader l_i resulting from allocation A is given by the equation:

$$w_i \left(A, t \right) = pc_i + \sum_{j=1}^{m} \left(UL_i \left(p\_u_i, c_i \right) \times A_{i,j} \right) \tag{17}$$

s.t., $1 \leq i \leq n$ and c_i is leased to f_j

where pc_i is a positive real-valued coefficient, representing the welfare of leader l_i prior to any allocation of resources (Matt, 2006). In the developed algorithm, each leader estimates his total received revenue, denoted by t_r_i, in a distributed manner.

$$t\_r_i = \int_{t_0}^{t_c} w_i \left(A, t \right) dt \tag{18}$$

where t_0 and t_c are the start and current times of system operations, respectively; the time period

$t_c - t_0$ is the duration of operations. Formally, the EWS ($s\_w_e \left(A^* \right)$) of an allocation A is defined as follows (Matt, 2006).

$$s_{we} \left(A^* \right) = \max_{1 \leq i \leq n} min \left\{ t_{ri} \right\} \tag{19}$$

Based on the social choice theories and welfare economics, an allocation A^* maximizes the EWS. It can be defined metaphorically as the welfare of the "unhappiest" or least "well-off" user in the system (Matt, 2006). To ensure fairness among multiple leaders, the developed leader-level algorithm is designed by using the EWS. To select a lending primary user, leaders are sorted in an increasing order based on the current total revenue value (t_r). The leader with the smallest t_r value is selected for the spectrum trading and the available spectrum (c) is leased to followers. If the price of selected leader is so high, there can be no follows, who want to borrow spectrum from the selected leader. In this case, the next smallest revenue leader is selected, and so on. The lease-failed leaders can decrease their spectrum price, and join to the next bargaining step. During step-by-step negotiation process, leaders are selected sequentially. When there are no leaders to lease the available spectrum or no followers to borrow the spectrum, network equilibrium is achieved. Finally, the leader-level algorithm operation is terminated.

The Follower-Level Algorithm

According to the price set by the leader, followers act solely and compete selfishly to maximize their individual utilities. Therefore, the *MMS* scheme adopted the non-cooperative game concept to develop the follower-level algorithm. In non-cooperative games, Nash Equilibrium (NE) is a fundamental solution concept; it is the most widely used method of predicting the outcome of strategic interactions (Srivastava, Neel, Mackenzie, Menon, Dasilva, Hicks, Reed, & Gilles,

2005). In the developed follower-level algorithm, an equilibrium-inducing algorithm is developed for unlicensed users.

Usually, the formal analysis of traditional non-cooperative game theory investigates the existence, uniqueness, and convergence to the NE. Therefore, it is convenient to concentrate on the possible group of games played repeatedly that always yields an NE (Mustika, 2010). In 1996, D. Monderer and L. Shapley proposed a class of games for which at least one NE exists (Monderer, & Shapley, 1996). These games, referred to as potential games, have been shown to always converge to a NE when the best response dynamics is performed. The best response dynamics is a dynamic process of updating strategies, in which a player chooses an strategy that maximizes his respective utility, given the current strategy of other players remain fixed (Mustika, 2010). Best response dynamics of the player i to the strategy profile s_{-i} at k+1 iteration (s_i^{k+1}) is an action that satisfies

$$s_i^{k+1} = \arg\max_{s_i' \in \mathcal{A}_i} U_i\left(s_i', \mathbf{s}_{-i}^k\right) \tag{20}$$

A game in game theory is considered a potential game if the incentive of all players to change their strategy can be expressed in one global function, the potential function. In potential games, it must be possible to construct a single-dimensional potential function where the change caused by any player's unilateral move is the same as the change in the potential, which may be viewed as a global objective function. Therefore, the existence of a potential function is the characteristic of a potential game (Mustika, 2010). A potential game $V: \mathcal{A} \to \mathbb{R}$ satisfies

$$\forall s_i' \in \mathcal{A}_i, \quad V\left(s_i', \mathbf{s}_{-i}\right) - V\left(s_i, \mathbf{s}_{-i}\right) = U_i\left(s_i', \mathbf{s}_{-i}\right) - U_i\left(s_i, \mathbf{s}_{-i}\right) \tag{21}$$

Since the potential of any strategy profile is finite, it follows that every sequence of improvement steps is finite, known as the finite improvement property (FIP). Therefore, any sequence of unilateral improvement steps converge to a pure strategy NE (Bloem, 2007). This NE is a local maximum (minimum) point of a global objective given by the potential function. Therefore, the potential function is a useful tool to analyze equilibrium properties of games, since the incentives of all players are mapped into one function, and the set of pure NE can be found by locating the local optima of the potential function. The *MMS* scheme demonstrates that the game with utility functions given by (15) is a potential game; this work already has been developed in (Mustika, 2010), (Nie & Comaniciu, 2006). To prove this, there exists a potential function, $V(s)$, which is a function with the property that

$$V\left(s_i, s_{-i}\right) - V\left(s_i', s_{-i}\right) = U_i\left(s_i, s_{-i}\right) - U_i\left(s_i', s_{-i}\right) \tag{22}$$

where s_i, $s_i' \in \mathcal{A}_i$. This formula means that when one player at a time changes his strategy, the change in the potential of the game is the same as the change in the utility of the acting player. Based on the utility functions given by (22), we can define the potential function as follows (Bloem, 2007) in Box 1.

Since $V_I\left(s_i, s_{-i}\right)$ has been proved as a potential function by Nie (Nie, 2006). Therefore, we only prove $V_{II}\left(s_i, s_{-i}\right)$, $V_{III}\left(s_i, s_{-i}\right)$ and $V_{IV}\left(s_i, s_{-i}\right)$ are potential functions. $V_{II}\left(s_i, s_{-i}\right)$ function can be derived as

$$V_{II}\left(s_i, s_{-i}\right) = \left(\alpha \times \log\left(1 + p_i \times h_{ii}\right) + \beta / p_i\right) + V_{II}\left(\mathbf{s}_{-i}\right) \tag{25}$$

Box 1.

$$V\left(s_i, s_{-i}\right) = \sum_{i=1}^{N}\left(-\frac{1}{2}\sum_{j=1,j\neq i}^{N}\left(p_j \times h_{ji} \times \delta\left(c_j, c_i\right)\right) - \frac{1}{2}\sum_{j=1,j\neq i}^{N}\left(p_i \times h_{ij} \times \delta\left(c_i, c_j\right)\right)\right)$$

$$+ \sum_{i=1}^{N}\left(\left(\alpha \times \log\left(1 + p_i \times h_{ii}\right)\right) + \beta / p_i\right). \tag{23}$$

$$- \sum_{i=1}^{N}\left(\left(p_l \times h_{li} \times \delta\left(c_l, c_i\right)\right) + \left(p_i \times h_{il} \times \delta\left(c_i, c_l\right)\right)\right) - \sum_{i=1}^{N} Pr_i\left(c_i\right)$$

The potential function $V\left(s_i, s_{-i}\right)$ can be rephrased as shown:

$$V\left(s_i, s_{-i}\right) = V_I\left(s_i, s_{-i}\right) + V_{II}\left(s_i, s_{-i}\right) + V_{III}\left(s_i, s_{-i}\right) + V_{IV}\left(s_i, s_{-i}\right)$$

$$\text{s.t.,} \quad V_I\left(s_i, s_{-i}\right) = \sum_{i=1}^{N}\left(-\frac{1}{2}\sum_{j=1,j\neq i}^{N}\left(p_j \times h_{ji} \times \delta_{c_j c_i}\right) - \frac{1}{2}\sum_{j=1,j\neq i}^{N}\left(p_i \times h_{ij} \times \delta_{c_i c_j}\right)\right)$$

$$V_{II}\left(s_i, s_{-i}\right) = \sum_{i=1}^{N}\left(\left(\alpha \times \log\left(1 + p_i \times h_{ii}\right)\right) + \beta / p_i\right) \tag{24}$$

$$V_{III}\left(s_i, s_{-i}\right) = -\sum_{i=1}^{N}\left(\left(p_l \times h_{li} \times \delta\left(c_l, c_i\right)\right) + \left(p_i \times h_{il} \times \delta\left(c_i, c_l\right)\right)\right)$$

$$V_{IV}\left(s_i, s_{-i}\right) = -\sum_{i=1}^{N} Pr_i\left(c_i\right)$$

$$\text{s.t.,} V_{II}\left(\mathbf{s}_{-i}\right) = \sum_{j=1,j\neq i}^{N}\left(\alpha \times \log\left(1 + p_j \times h_{jj}\right) + \beta / p_j\right)$$

$V_{III}\left(s_i, s_{-i}\right)$ function can be derived as

$$V_{III}\left(s_i, s_{-i}\right) =$$
$$-\left(p_l \times h_{li} \times \delta_{c_i c_i}\right) - \left(p_i \times h_{il} \times \delta_{c_i c_l}\right) - V_{III}\left(\mathbf{s}_{-i}\right) \tag{26}$$

$$\text{s.t.,} V_{II}\left(\mathbf{s}_{-i}\right) =$$
$$\sum_{j=1,j\neq i}^{N}\left(\left(p_l \times h_{lj} \times \delta\left(c_l, c_j\right)\right) + \left(p_j \times h_{jl} \times \delta\left(c_j, c_l\right)\right)\right)$$

$V_{IV}\left(s_i, s_{-i}\right)$ function can be derived as

$$V_{IV}\left(s_i, s_{-i}\right) = -\left(\psi_i \times p\_u_i \times Size\left(c_i\right)\right) - V_{IV}\left(\mathbf{s}_{-i}\right) \tag{27}$$

$$\text{s.t.,} V_{IV}\left(\mathbf{s}_{-i}\right) = \sum_{j=1,j\neq i}^{N}\left(\psi_j \times p\_u_j \times Size\left(c_j\right)\right)$$

The strategy of player i (s_i) is not depending on the strategies of other players ($\mathbf{s}_{-i}$) at functions $V_I\left(\mathbf{s}_{-i}\right)$, $V_{II}\left(\mathbf{s}_{-i}\right)$, $V_{III}\left(\mathbf{s}_{-i}\right)$ and $V_{IV}\left(\mathbf{s}_{-i}\right)$. Therefore, the function $T\_V\left(\mathbf{s}_{-i}\right)$ that corresponds to the action of other players ($\mathbf{s}_{-i}$) can be expressed as

$$T\_V\left(\mathbf{s}_{-i}\right) = V_I\left(\mathbf{s}_{-i}\right) + V_{II}\left(\mathbf{s}_{-i}\right) + V_{III}\left(\mathbf{s}_{-i}\right) + V_{IV}\left(\mathbf{s}_{-i}\right) \tag{28}$$

$T\_V\left(\boldsymbol{s}_{-i}\right)$ is also not affected by the strategy changing of the player i. Therefore, when the player i changes its strategy from s_i to $s_i^{'}$, the potential function can be obtained as follows.

$$V\left(s_i^{'},s_{-i}\right) = U_i\left(s_i^{'},\boldsymbol{s}_{-i}\right) + T\_V\left(\boldsymbol{s}_{-i}\right) \quad (29)$$

Hence,

$$V\left(s_i,\boldsymbol{s}_{-i}\right) - V\left(s_i^{'},\boldsymbol{s}_{-i}\right) =$$
$$\left(U_i\left(s_i,\boldsymbol{s}_{-i}\right) + T\_V\left(\boldsymbol{s}_{-i}\right)\right) - \left(U_i\left(s_i^{'},\boldsymbol{s}_{-i}\right) + T\_V\left(\boldsymbol{s}_{-i}\right)\right)$$

$$= U_i\left(s_i,\boldsymbol{s}_{-i}\right) - U_i\left(s_i^{'},\boldsymbol{s}_{-i}\right) \quad (30)$$

Finally, we prove the game in the follower-level algorithm can be formulated as a potential game with a potential function $V\left(s_i,\boldsymbol{s}_{-i}\right)$. It can guarantee that the follower's behavior converges to the Nash equilibrium.

Bi-Level Interactive Game Model in the *MMS* Scheme

The *MMS* scheme is a new fair-efficient spectrum sharing scheme based on the MSG model. In the *MMS* scheme, licensed and unlicensed users try to select their strategies to optimize their own payoffs. As leaders, multiple licensed users dynamically adapt their price settings in order to maximize their revenues, and play a cooperative game according to the egalitarian welfare model. Therefore, they act cooperatively and collaborate with each other to fairly distribute the outcome to each leader. As followers, multiple unlicensed users compete with each other, and play a non-cooperative game by using the self-interested strategy. Therefore, followers behave selfishly in order to maximize their utility functions.

The current selected strategy doesn't guarantee the best strategy for the future. Therefore, at the end of each game's iteration, players examine their payoffs periodically and dynamically adapt their decisions in an entirely distributed fashion. This procedure is defined as a feedback learning process. During the step-by-step iteration, this fine-grained feedback process is repeated until the best solution has been found. Based on the real-time interactive manner, this feedback process captures each player behavior, which is defined as a spectrum sharing algorithm in cognitive radio networks. The main steps of the *MMS* scheme are given next.

Step 1: At the initial iteration (k=0), all players set their utility parameters as starting values.

Step 2: In the leader-level algorithm, leaders are sorted in an increasing order based on their t_r values, and the leader with the smallest t_r value is selected for the spectrum sharing negotiation. If there are one more leaders with the smallest t_r values, one of them is selected randomly.

Step 3: If no followers want to borrow spectrum from the selected leader, the next smallest t_r value leader is selected for the next negotiation. The failed leader can decrease his p_u value for the next negotiation step.

Step 4: According to the price set by the leader, followers dynamically re-estimate their expected payoffs. The follower with the maximum payoff value is selected to borrow the spectrum from the leader, and spectrum trading process is executed.

Step 5: During step-by-step negotiation process, leaders are selected sequentially. Each game iteration, leaders adjust their p_u values by using (14). Based on the real-time interactive manner, this adjustment procedure is repeated until the best solution has been found.

Step 6: When there are no leaders to lease the available spectrum or no followers to borrow the spectrum, the game processing is terminated; the network equilibrium is achieved.

Step 7: Constantly, the system is self-monitoring the current network situation. When a new spectrum sharing request arrives, it can re-trigger the spectrum sharing algorithm; proceeds to Step 2 for the next iteration.

Recently, several Stackelberg game models for CR networks have been presented. The *Resource Pricing with Stackelberg Approach (RPSA)* scheme investigated the resource allocation problem in CR networks (Li, 2009). By using the Stackelberg model, this scheme solved the pricing process of licensed users and got the Nash Equilibrium point. In addition, the *RPSA* scheme introduced a control parameter to quantify the negative impact. Therefore, licensed users can guarantee their services by keeping this parameter below a predefined threshold. The *Power Control and Channel Allocation (PCCA)* scheme suggested a game theoretical approach that allowed master-slave cognitive radio pairs to update their transmission powers and frequencies, simultaneously (Bloem, 2009). Based on the Stackelberg game model, licensed frequency user became a leader and transmitted a virtual price for using the licensed frequency band. This approach was developed by constructing utility functions, which were potential functions. The *Distributed Optimization for Cognitive Radio (DOCR)* scheme was designed as a Stackelberg game based hierarchical framework to optimize the CR network performance (Xiao, 2010). By using a simple pricing function for licensed users, the *DOCR* scheme was implemented as a distributed algorithm to converge the Stackelberg equilibrium. In addition, the power allocation methods for unlicensed users had been derived, and the price for licensed users had been calculated. Figure 2 demonstrates that the performance of the proposed *MMS* scheme is generally superior to those of other existing schemes: the *RPSA* scheme, the *PCCA* scheme and the *DOCR* scheme. To reach a desirable system performance, our bilevel approach based on the Stackelberg model can be concluded to be an effective solution. Therefore, the proposed *MMS* scheme can maintain well-balanced network

Figure 2. Performance evaluations of the MMS scheme

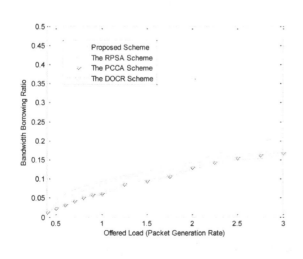

(a) Spectrum Borrowing Ratio

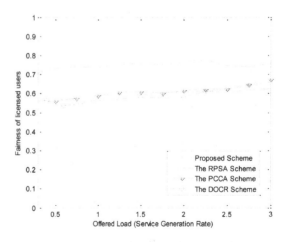

(b) System Fairness

performance under various network situations while existing schemes can not offer such an attractive trade off.

Summary

Game theory is useful in analyzing complex decision problems among self-regarding decision makers. It has been extensively applied in microeconomics, and recently has received attention as a solution for distributed network resource allocation problems. The *MMS* scheme is a new CR network spectrum sharing scheme based on the multi-leader multi-follower Stackelberg game model. To improve the spectrum utilization and users' satisfaction, unused spectrum is dynamically shared. In addition, control decisions are iteratively adjusted based on the feedback learning process. Therefore, the *MMS* scheme can capture the hierarchical interaction among players to get the desirable solution between two conflicting objectives - efficiency and fairness.

REVERSED STACKELBERG BANDWIDTH SHARING (*RSBS*) SCHEME FOR COGNITIVE MULTI-HOP CELLULAR NETWORKS

Multi-hop relaying cellular network is a recently proposed architecture to preserve the advantages of traditional single-hop cellular networks and ad hoc relaying networks. In MCNs, efficient bandwidth management plays an important role in determining network performance. Recently, S. Kim proposed a new Reversed Stackelberg Bandwidth Sharing (*RSBS*) scheme for cognitive multi-hop cellular networks (Kim, 2012b). In the *RSBS* scheme, base station and relay stations are hierarchically interconnected and interacting with one another to effectively share the wireless bandwidth. By using a trust model, the base station appropriately reacts to selfish relay stations

to maximize network performance. This approach can promote the cooperation with respect to adaptive bandwidth allocation.

Development Motivation

For the next generation wireless system, relay will play an important role by providing broader coverage to a large number of users. To support a wide range of services and applications in wireless networks, Multi-hop relaying Cellular Network (MCN) has been proposed as an extension to the conventional single-hop cellular network; it combines the fixed cellular infrastructure with the multi-hop relaying technology. MCN has greatly enhanced the network coverage and improved the overall network capacity [13-3-2]. In this technology, how to efficiently allocate bandwidth to relays is a crucial problem. However, choosing optimal bandwidth allocation in *a priori* is nearly impossible. Therefore, by taking the dynamic demand of each user, adaptive bandwidth allocation algorithms must be developed (Cho, & Haas, 2003).

Currently, it has been observed that allocated bandwidth bands are largely unused in any time and location; these are referred to as bandwidth holes (Niyato, 2007 & 2008). By detecting unoccupied bandwidth holes in the network environment, the Cognitive Radio (CR) technique can allow unlicensed users to use bandwidth holes opportunistically while they are idle from licensed users. Based on the CR technique, the bandwidth efficiency can be enhanced dramatically. However, one crucial assumption in the most previous CR work is that users can always be trusted. This assumption may not be valid in hostile real-world network environments (Zhu, Suo, & Gao, 2010). During CR network operations, selfish behaviors deter the trust among users and drastically bring down the system performance.

Nowadays, there has been increasing interest in integrating CR functionalities into MCNs. Combining bandwidth sharing and relaying technologies can significantly improve the network performance. To automatically cope with the ever-changing network environment, there is a need for a self-configuring control paradigm. In the past decade, game theory has emerged as an effective way to design proper self-configuring control algorithms. Game theory is a field of applied mathematics that provides an effective tool in modeling the interaction among independent decision makers. It can describe the possibility to react to the actions of the other decision makers and analyze the situations of conflict and cooperation in real world (Wang, 2006), (Nie, 2008), (Ho, Luh, & Muralidharan, 1981), (Le, 2007).

Stackelberg games are a class of games in game theory. In a Stackelberg game, one player acts as a leader and the rest acts as followers. The main goal is to find an optimal strategy for the leader, assuming that the followers react in such a rational way while optimizing their objective functions given the leader's actions. Therefore, it can be the static bilevel optimization model; the leader announces a strategy first and all the followers make their own decisions based on the knowledge of the leader's action. However, in this traditional Stackelberg approach, the followers can take advantage in a malicious manner (Zhu, 2010), (Nie, 2008). In 1981, R. Muralidbaran et al., further extended the classical Stackelberg model and developed a reversed Stackelberg model (Ho, 1981). Reversed Stackelberg model assumed that the leader has the right to announce first, and followers may be required to act before the leader. In other words, followers actually act first and the leader would decide the most probable strategy by given any of followers' actions. To optimize the leader's payoff, it is a reasonable scenario (Suo & Wen, 2009), (Wang, 2006), (Li, 2009).

The *RSBS* scheme is a new bandwidth sharing scheme for MCNs. In MCNs, each cell is serviced by a Base Station (BS), and Relay Stations (RSs) are deployed by BS for data delivery (Le, 2007). Therefore, the BS takes responsibility for the per-

formance of the whole system. The BS allocates bandwidth for each RS, and supervises whether the RSs cooperates or not by detecting the RS's misbehaviors. According to the BS decision, each RS can adaptively share the allocated bandwidth by using the CR technique. To maximize the system performance, the BS acts after RSs, knowing the actual choice of RSs; the BS's strategy can be a function of RSs' decisions. Such feature has inspired the study of the bandwidth sharing algorithm into a hierarchical game process based on the reversed Stackelberg game model.

In the developed game model, the BS plays the role of the leader and RSs become followers. Based on the sequence-dependent game process, the leader (BS) and followers (RSs) can be interacting with one another and select their strategies, which are hierarchically interconnected to cause the cascade effect. According to the cooperation contract between the BS and RSs, the BS can supervise and induce RSs to behave cooperatively. This situation leads us to develop an adaptive trust mechanism with focus on the Bayesian inference. Based on the trust values of RSs, the BS can promote the cooperation while discouraging RS's selfish behaviors with respect to give disadvantages in bandwidth allocation. This approach is possible to offer a more realistic model while appropriately reacting to selfish RSs.

The distinct novelties of the *RSBS* scheme are: 1) the BS can supervise the RS's misbehaviors, and adjust its strategies interactively in an online manner, 2) cooperative supervising approach based trust mechanism is introduced to optimize the BS's objectives, 3) the hierarchical and sequence dependent control procedure can consequently improves the system performance, and 4) the cooperation is progressed under the adaptive trust mechanism. These features of the *RSBS* scheme can maintain bandwidth efficiency as high as possible, and to increase the cell coverage while enhancing the throughput of MCNs.

Bandwidth Management Algorithms in the *RSBS* Scheme

Under CR network situations, bandwidth sharing process can be formulated as a hierarchical game. The *RSBS* scheme is developed as a reversed Stackelberg game model based on a repeated interactive manner.

Stackelberg Game Model

For next-generation wireless networks, MCN is a cost effective solution to support a wide range of services and applications. MCN system consists of a BS and RSs. In response to the demand from RSs, the BS can dynamically lease the available bandwidth (i.e, the BS allows RSs to access the leased bandwidth) (Jayaweera, Vazquez-Vilar, & Mosquera, 2010). RSs could act as a relay for the BS. During the relay work, a contract is required between the BS and RSs to ensure a certain Quality of Service (QoS) level and the cooperation should be progressed under the contract. After leasing the bandwidth, RSs are granted the rights to operate this leased bandwidth and can gain some payoffs. By using the CR technique, the leased bandwidth in RSs can be shared dynamically among local users (i.e., secondary users) to achieve maximum network throughput while not violating the QoS contract (Jayaweera, 2010). As a leader, the BS supervises RSs to detect the malicious behavior, which violates the QoS contract, and reacts adaptively after RSs' decisions.

In a reversed Stackelberg model, decision makers have their own hierarchy level, utility function and strategies. Therefore, this model is natural to be designed as a two-stage bilevel approach (Bloem, 2007). The *RSBS* scheme consists of leader-based and follower-based algorithms. In the leader-based algorithm, an appropriate bandwidth distribution is a critical issue; the BS adaptively decides the amount of leased bandwidth. Based on parameter α_i

$(\sum_{i=0}^{n} \pm_i = 1$, where n is number of RSs),

the total bandwidth (Γ) is divided. The ($\alpha_0 \times \Gamma$) bandwidth amount is assigned for the direct transmission mode in BS and the ($\alpha_{i,1 \leq i \leq n} \times \Gamma$) bandwidth amount is leased for the cooperative relay transmission mode in the i th RS. Therefore, how to determine α_i values needs to be made by the BS.

In the follower-based algorithm, each RS dynamically shares the leased bandwidth. Therefore, the leased bandwidth is divided into two fractions based on parameter β ($0 \leq \beta \leq 1$). For example, in the i th RS, the β_i ratio of the leased bandwidth ($\beta_i \times \pm_i \times \Gamma$) is used for the the cooperative relay to help the BS, and the (1- β_i) ratio of the leased bandwidth (($1 - \beta_i) \times \alpha_i \times \Gamma$) is dedicated to the i th RS for its own data transmission. A primary concern of RSs is to maximize their payoff while not violating QoS contract. Therefore, RSs dynamically adapt their β values in a distributed online manner. The outcome of RSs' decisions is the input back to the BS, and the BS adjusts the α values to determine the next round leased bandwidth amount. By using this dynamic iterative feedback loop, the BS and RSs can be interacting with one another and make their decisions in a way to get an effective network performance (Zhang, Chen, Gou, & Cheng, 2010), (Yi, Zhang, Zhang, Jiang, & Zhang, 2010).

In order to develop the leader-based algorithm, the utility function for the BS (U_{BS}) can be defined as follows.

$$U_{BS} = D_{UB}\left(\alpha_0 \times \Gamma\right) + \sum_{i=1}^{n} R_{UB}\left(\beta_i \times \alpha_i \times \Gamma\right)$$

(31)

where α_0 is a control parameter for the BS and α_i, β_i ($1 \leq i \leq n$) are control parameters for the

i^{th} RS. These parameters adaptively adjust the amount of available bandwidth. D_U_B is a function to account for the BS's direct transmission payoff, and R_U_B function estimates the cooperative relay transmission payoff with aid of the ith RS. Usually, payoff is defined as the number of information bits that are transmitted without error per unit-time. In wireless networks, it can be achieved with the SINR in the effective range (Kim, 2011). Based on the SINR (γ), these functions can be defined as

$$D\_U_B(\alpha_0 \times \Gamma) = (\alpha_0 \times \Gamma) \times \frac{1}{\rho_0} \times \log_2\left(1 + \frac{\gamma_0(\mathbb{P})}{\Omega}\right),$$

$$R\_U_B(\beta_i \times \alpha i \times \Gamma) = (\beta_i \times \alpha i \times \Gamma) \times \frac{1}{p_i} \times \log_2(1 + \frac{\gamma i(\mathbb{P})}{\Omega}$$

$$\text{s.t., } \gamma i(\mathbb{P}) = \frac{p_i h_{ii}}{\sigma_i + \sum_{j \neq i}^{n} p_j h_{ji}} \text{ s.t., } 0 \leq i \leq n \text{ and } \gamma_i^* \leq \gamma_i \mathbb{P}$$

$$(32)$$

where p_o and $p_{i,1 \leq i \leq n}$ are the power level of the BS and the ith RS, respectively. γ_o and $\gamma_{i,1 \leq i \leq n}$ are the SINR for the BS's and the ith RS's SINR, respectively. γ_i^* is the required QoS level by the contract between the BS and the ith RS. The utility function of the ith RS ($U_{RS}(i)$) can be defined in a similar way as

$$U_{RS}(i) = \left((1 - \beta_i) \times \alpha_i \times \Gamma\right) \times \frac{1}{p_i} \times \log_2\left(1 + \frac{\gamma_i(\mathbb{P})}{\Omega}\right),$$
$$s.t., 0 \leq i \leq n$$

$$(33)$$

As a leader, the BS monitors each RS's service QoS level (γ^*) and selects its strategy $\mathbb{S}_L = \{\alpha_0, \alpha_1, \alpha_2 \dots \alpha_n\}$, which is the vector of α values to maximize the payoff according to (31). As followers, the ith RS decides its strategy $S_{F(i)} = \{\beta_i \mid 0 \leq \beta_i \leq 1\}$. By being aware of the BS's strategy, the ith RS tries to optimize its payoff according to (33).

Trust Evaluation Mechanism

During the operation of networks, selfish behaviors deter the trust among nodes and drastically bring down the system performance. Therefore, cooperation among different nodes is essential for the effective wireless network operation (Refaei, DaSilva, Eltoweissy, & Nadeem, 2010). To satisfy this goal, an effective trust evaluation mechanism should be designed. In the *RSBS* scheme, trust is defined as BS's belief in RS's reliability. Based on the observation about the RS's past behavior within at a given time, the BS can estimate each RS's trust reputation as an expectation index of RS's behavior. With this information, the BS can distinguish between cooperative RSs and selfish RSs, and adaptively adjusts the amount of leased bandwidth. However, the future trust level about RSs is incompletely known to the BS. Therefore, scientific inference methods are necessary to predict the trust level of each RS.

Bayesian inference is a method of statistical inference to provide a logical, quantitative decision. Based on the Bayes' theorem and Bayesian probability rules, Bayesian inference summarizes all uncertainty by a 'posterior' distribution, and gives a 'posterior' belief, which may be used as the basis for inferential decisions. Therefore, the concept of Bayesian inference can be used to provide solutions to predict future values based on historical data (Pan, Klir, & Yuan, 1996), (Akkarajitsakul, Hossain, & Niyato, 2011). In this work, the BS predicts each RS's reliability by using Bayesian inference, and makes a decision for the next round bandwidth leasing amount. During each reversed Stackelberg game round, the BS has a chance to reconsider the current strategy with incoming information and reacts to maximize the expected payoff. According to the Bayes' theorem and updating rule, the Bayesian inference formula can be expressed as follows (Ishihara, Huang, & Sim, 2005).

$$P_t\left(H|e\right) = \frac{P_t\left(e|H\right) \times P_t\left(H\right)}{P_t\left(e\right)} \qquad (34)$$

where $P_t\left(H|e\right)$ is the posterior distribution of hypothesis H under the evidence e; t represents t^{th} round of game process. $P_t\left(H\right)$ and $P_t\left(e\right)$ are the prior probability of hypothesis H and evidence e, respectively. The *RSBS* scheme defines four hypotheses (i.e, bad, average, good and excellent) for RS trust levels. Each hypothesis takes shape as follows.

$$\begin{cases} H = (H_1 = 'bad') \text{ if } \gamma < (0.6 \times \gamma^*) \\ H = (H_2 = 'average'), \text{ if } (0.6 \times \gamma^*) \leq \gamma < (0.8 \times \gamma^*), \\ H = (H_3 = 'good'), \text{ if } (0.8 \times \gamma^*) \leq \gamma < \gamma^*, \\ H = (H_4 = 'excellent'), \text{ if } \gamma^* \leq \gamma \end{cases}$$
$$(35)$$

With four discrete RS's trust levels, there are three different evidences (i.e., low, medium and high evidences) about the bandwidth distribution; low (e_1), medium (e_2) and high (e_3) evidences mean that the lower, same and higher bandwidth is leased to a specific RS than the amount of the RS requested.

At first, the BS doesn't know each RS's behavior propensity, but can learn it based on the Bayesian model. In the *RSBS* scheme, $P_t\left(H_{l,1\leq l\leq 4}\right)$ represents the percentage of interactions that the RS provides H_l level trust; it is measured by the number of H_l level interactions divided by the total number of interactions (tn). $P_t\left(e_{j,1\leq j\leq 3}\right)$ represents the occurrence ratio of event e_j by the BS; it is measured by the occurrence number of e_j divided by the total number of event occurrences. $P_t(e_j | H_l)$ is the event conditional probability, given the trust level H_l; it can be computed as following formula

$$P_t\left(e_j|H_l\right) = \frac{P_t\left(H_l, e_j\right)}{P_t\left(H_l\right)}, \quad \text{s.t.,} P_t\left(H_l, e_j\right)$$
$$= \frac{h\_e_{lj}}{tn} \qquad (36)$$

where h_e_{lj} is the number of H_l level interactions when e_j event occurs. After each interaction, the BS dynamically updates its corresponding RS's probabilities. Finally, $P_t(H_l | e_j)$, which is the H_l conditional probability under e_j occurring circumstance, can be obtained as follows.

$$P_t\left(H_l|e_j\right) = \frac{P_t\left(e_j|H_l\right) \times P_t\left(H_l\right)}{P_t\left(e_j\right)} \qquad (37)$$

Once getting the RS's $P_t\left(H_l|e_j\right)$ probability, the BS can compute the $(t+1)^{th}$ round composite trust value of ith RS; it is defined as $T_i\left(t+1\right)$ and represents the trustworthiness of the ith RS.

$$T_i\left(t+1\right) = \sum_{l=1}^{4}\sum_{j=1}^{3}\left[P_t\left(H_l|e_j\right) \times \frac{\varphi_l}{\omega_j}\right] \qquad (38)$$

where φ_l and ω_j are control parameters to estimate the composite trust value. By using (38), we can easily get the average trust value (χ) of RSs as follows.

$$\chi\left(t+1\right) = \frac{1}{n} \times \sum_{i=1}^{n} T_i\left(t+1\right) \qquad (39)$$

The Main Steps of the *RSBS* Scheme

In the *RSBS* scheme, the BS first calculates the composite trust values ($T_{i,1\leq i\leq n}\left(t\right)$) and the average trust value ($\chi\left(t\right)$). And then, the BS announces this information to RSs. Based on $T_i(t)$ and $\chi(t)$ values, the ith RS ($i \in \mathcal{N}$) will choose individually a strategy $S^*_{F(i)}$ to maximize its own payoff $U_{RS}(i)$.

$$S^*_{F(i)} = arg \max_{S_{F(i)}} U_{RS}\left(S_{F(i)}|\{T_i(t), \chi(t)\}\right)$$

(40)

After knowing the reaction strategies $\left(S^*_{F(1)}, S^*_{F(2)} \dots S^*_{F(n)}\right)$ of RSs, the BS seeks a strategy $\mathbb{S}^*_L$ that optimizes its utility.

$$\mathbb{S}^*_L = arg \max_{\mathbb{S}_L} U_{BS}(\mathbb{S}_L \mid S^*_{F(1)}, S^*_{F(2)} \dots S^*_{F(n)})$$

(41)

Based on the reversed Stackelberg game model, the *RSBS* scheme focuses on working out a simple algorithm to implement the process of the bandwidth leasing mechanism. To reach a desirable system performance, the bilevel approach can be concluded to be an effective solution. At the end of each game's iteration, players examine their payoffs periodically and dynamically adapt their decisions in an entirely distributed fashion. During the step-by-step iteration, this feedback process is repeated until the best solution has been found. When either the leader or followers, given the strategy of the other, can not get any utility increase by deviating from its own strategy, network reaches an effective solution (Zhang, 2010), (Yi, 2010); it can be written as $\left(\mathbb{S}^*_L; S^*_{F(1)}, S^*_{F(2)} \dots S^*_{F(n)}\right)$. The main steps of the *RSBS* scheme are given next.

Step 1: At the initial iteration ($t = 0$), the composite trust values of all RSs are equally distributed. This starting guess guarantees that each RS enjoys the same benefit at the beginning of the game.

Step 2: According to (34),(35),(36),(37),(38) and (39), the BS can compute the $T(t)$ and $\chi(t)$ values, and announces this information to RSs.

Step 3: Based on $T(t)$ and $\chi(t)$ values, each RS will choose individually the best strategy to maximize its own payoff. By using (33) and (40), each RS dynamically adjusts β value to optimize its payoff while maintaining the QoS contract.

Step 4: According to RSs' responses, the BS recognizes the followers' strategies $\left(S^*_{F(1)}, S^*_{F(2)} \dots S^*_{F(n)}\right)$, and seeks an actual action to optimize its payoff. By using (31),(32) and (41), the BS adaptively adjusts α values.

Step 5: During step-by-step game process, BS and RSs are interacting with one another and reconsider the current strategy with incoming information. This fine-grained feedback process is repeated based on the real-time interactive manner.

Step 6: When either the BS or RSs can not get any payoff increase by deviating from their own strategies, network system reaches effective solution; game process is temporarily over.

Step 7: Constantly, the BS is self-monitoring the current network situation. If temporal or spatial traffic fluctuations occur, the bandwidth leasing algorithm is re-triggered; proceeds to Step 2 for the next game process.

Recently, several bandwidth sharing schemes for cognitive radio networks have been presented. The *Dynamic Spectrum Leasing for Spectrum Sharing* (*DSLSS*) scheme was designed as a dynamic spectrum leasing paradigm in cognitive radio networks (Jayaweera, 2010). This scheme developed a general game theoretic formulation to model the interactions among primary and secondary systems. The *DSLSS* scheme better captured the realities of a dynamic spectrum leas-

Figure 3. Performance evaluations of the RSBS scheme

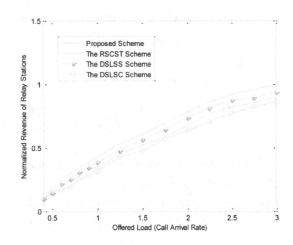

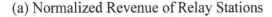

(a) Normalized Revenue of Relay Stations

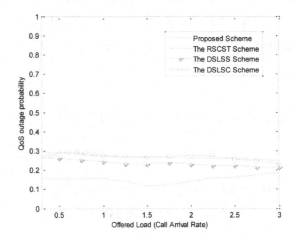

(b) QoS Outage Probability

ing network. In addition, this scheme proposed a general structure for a suitable class of utility functions that reflect the demand for spectrum access. The *Reversed Stackelberg-based Cooperative Spectrum Trading* (*RSCST*) scheme was proposed as a secure cooperative spectrum trading protocol based on a reversed Stackelberg game model (Zhu, 2010). With cross-level metrics and hierarchical gaming structures, the primary user can supervise whether the secondary user cooperates or not, and detect the compromised actions. The *RSCST* scheme also developed a supervising-cooperating mechanism to adjust its strategies interactively. The *Distributed Spectrum Leasing via Selective Cooperation* (*DSLSC*) scheme was developed as a game model for spectrum leasing in cognitive radio networks (Zhang, 2010). The *DSLSC* scheme described the dynamic interaction between the primary and secondary users based on a non-cooperative game model. In addition, this scheme proposed a simple distributed algorithm with two different selection criteria. Figure 3 demonstrates that the performance of the proposed *RSBS* scheme is generally superior to those of other existing schemes: the *RSCST*, *DSLSS* and

DSLSC schemes. In the adaptive feedback iteration manner, the proposed *RSBS* scheme is flexible, adaptable and able to sense the dynamic changing network environment; it is essential in order to be close to the optimized network performance.

Summary

For the effective operation of multi-hop cellular networks, adaptive bandwidth sharing algorithms should be developed to achieve maximum performance. The *RSBS* scheme is a hierarchical bandwidth sharing scheme based on a reversed Stackelberg game model. Taking into account that both the BS and RSs are selfish and rational, Stackelberg game is a powerful tool to model the bandwidth sharing problem in MCNs. The main objective of the *RSBS* scheme is to effectively allocate and share the wireless bandwidth to maximize the bandwidth utilization and network performance. By constantly monitoring the current network condition, the BS iteratively re-estimates RSs' trust levels and adaptively leases a fraction of the available bandwidth to RSs for relaying the data transmission.

TRUST-BASED RADIO SPECTRUM SHARING (*TRSS*) SCHEME FOR COGNITIVE RADIO NETWORKS

Recently, cooperative spectrum sensing is being studied to greatly improve the sensing performance of cognitive radio networks. To develop an adaptable cooperative sensing algorithm, an important issue is how to properly induce selfish users to participate in spectrum sensing work. By employing the trust-based bargaining model, S. Kim proposed a new Trust-based Radio Spectrum Sharing (*TRSS*) scheme for cognitive radio networks (Kim, 2012c). The *TRSS* scheme dynamically adjusts bargaining powers and adaptively shares the available spectrum in real-time online manner.

Development Motivation

Cognitive Radio (CR) technique has been developed to dramatically enhance the utilization of scarce spectrum resources. The main idea of CR is that the unlicensed users (i.e., secondary users: SUs) can dynamically sense the radio environment and opportunistically utilize the unused spectrum bands while causing no intolerable interference to licensed users (i.e., primary users: PUs). Since the CR functionality is initialized through spectrum sensing, spectrum sensing methods have gotten more and more attentions. Recently, the cooperative spectrum sensing technique has been presented as an effective sensing way to improve the performance of sensing in CR networks (Li, 2010).

Cooperative spectrum sensing occurs when a group of SUs voluntarily contribute to sensing and share their local sensing information to get a better picture of the spectrum usage. A fully cooperative scenario is assumed in most of the cooperative spectrum sensing schemes. However, sensing work of SU consumes a certain amount of energy and time. Therefore, selfish but rational

SUs do not serve a common sensing work and tend to be a free-rider to reduce their control overhead. In this instance, SUs face the risk of having no one sense the spectrum (Wang, Liu, & Clancy, 2010). Due to this reason, the key issue with the cooperative sensing method is how to make a selfish SU collaborate with others. But despite the concerns, not much work has been done in this direction.

Nowadays, the main idea of game theory has emerged as an effective way of designing the CR management process (Tembine, 2009). Cooperative games, also called bargaining solutions, are games in which players make binding commitments and find it beneficial to cooperate in the game. To reach an agreement that gives mutual advantage, players bargain with each other. In cooperative games, the main interest is to fairly distribute the outcome to each player according to their contributions to make joint-agreements. The *Kalai-Smorodinsky* bargaining solution (*KSBS*) is a well-known bargaining solution with a good balance between efficiency and fairness (Park, & Schaar, 2007b).

Motivated by the above discussion, the *TRSS* scheme is developed as a new spectrum sharing scheme based on the game theory. To induce the collaborative sensing work, a trust game model is developed. Based on the evaluating SU's behavior, the developed model estimates the trust level of each SU to distinguish between cooperative and selfish SUs. And then, the basic concept of *KSBS* is adopted to fairly distribute the spectrum resources among SUs. Usually, the *KSBS* bargaining solution is strongly dependent on the bargaining power. In the *TRSS* scheme, bargaining power of each SU is decided based on the SU's trust level, and the available spectrum is shared according to the *KSBS* model. This approach is possible to promote cooperation while discouraging selfish SUs, which can limit their negative impact on the total CR network performance.

Spectrum Sharing Algorithm in the *TRSS* Scheme

For the effective sensing operation, cooperation among different SUs is essential. During the operation of CR networks, selfish behaviors damage the profits of the other cooperative SUs and drastically bring down the system performance. Therefore, it is required that SUs cooperate together in the spectrum sensing process. In the *TRSS* scheme, a trust game model is designed to develop an effective cooperative sensing algorithm. The concept of trust game originates from the social sciences which study the actions between the human in the society, and then be applied into the psychology, sociology, economics, computer science, management science, etc. In particular, trust game model is an efficient method of constraining the selfish SU from enjoying a free ride in cooperative sensing process.

In the *TRSS* scheme, SUs sense the PU spectrum by using the centralized cooperative sensing method (Pei, Liang, & Li, 2011), where each SU senses the spectrum and sends the sensing information to the Cognitive Base Station (CBS). By using appropriate data fusion rules, the CBS makes a judgment whether or not the spectrum is idle. The cooperative sensing approach through multiple user cooperation can increase the sensing accuracy (Wang, 2010).

With the decision of spectrum idleness, the CBS can determine the trust level of each individual SU by considering the SU's actions. It is an index of cooperation behavior and used to distribute the available spectrum more efficiently. After the determination of trust level, the trust level of each SU is dynamically adjusted according to the users' behavior. Based on the trust level, the *TRSS* scheme categorizes SUs into three types: selfish SUs, cooperative SUs and faulty SUs. The selfish SUs refer to the users who do not serve a sensing work to avoid their control overheads. The cooperative SUs refer to the users who work cooperatively and collaborate with each other to sense the spectrum. The faulty SUs refer to the users send the wrong sensing results because their sensing ability had been impaired, or they are in the poor environment to correctly sense the spectrum.

Due to the dynamically changing CR network environment, SU behaviors can vary spatially and temporally. Therefore, SU type is dynamically changeable. To effectively adapt this fluctuation, the CBS needs to monitor the users' behavior constantly. For the implementation of time-dependent monitoring procedure, the *TRSS* scheme partitions the time-axis into equal intervals of length *unit_time*, and each SU's action is examined periodically at every *unit_time*. According to a sequence of SU action observations, trust value can be adaptively modified. Let $T_i(k)$ be the trust value of ith SU at the kth *unit_time* period.

$$T_i(k) = \begin{cases} (1-\alpha) \times T_i(k-1) + \alpha \times (-1)^{d^k + s_i^k}, & if\, s_i^k \neq 1 \\ (1-\beta) \times T_i(k-1) + \beta \times (-1)^{s_i^k}, & if\, s_i^k = 1 \end{cases}$$

(42)

$$\text{s.t.,}\quad d^k = \begin{cases} 0, & if\ spectrum\ is\ idle \\ 1, & else \end{cases}$$

and

$$s_i^k = \begin{cases} -1, if\ SU\ reports - spectrum\ is\ occupied \\ 0\ , if\ SU\ reports - spectrum\ is\ idle \\ 1\ , if\ SU\ reports - nothing\,(\text{selfish}) \end{cases}$$

where α and β control the relative weights given to recent and past behavior histories in trust value decision. s_i^k and d^k present the reporting result of the ith SU and the final judgment by the CBS at the kth *unit_time*, respectively. Repeatedly, this trust adjustment procedure is executed in a real-time online manner. Therefore, the CBS updates the trust value (T) of each SU according to the historical trust and the current trust evidence. In a constantly changing spectrum environment, this dynamic evaluation approach is very effective to make the CR network system much more flexible, adaptable and able to sense the current network environment.

In cooperative games, the main interest is to fairly distribute the outcome to each player according to their contributions to make joint-agreements. Therefore, the cooperative game model is attractive for network spectrum allocation problems. Among diverse cooperative bargaining game models, the *KSBS* has some good features to handle the spectrum allocation problem under diverse network conditions. In the *TRSS* scheme, a new *KSBS* based spectrum allocation algorithm is developed to achieve an efficient and fair solution. In the developed *KSBS* model, SUs are assumed as game players. Each player (i.e., SU) has its own utility function, which represents the amount of satisfaction of a player toward the outcome of the game. To quantify players' satisfaction, the utility function for player i can be derived as follows.

$$u_i\left(b_i\right) = \frac{1 - e^{-\gamma \times b_i}}{1 - e^{-\gamma \times Mb_i}} \tag{43}$$

where Mb_i and b_i is the maximum and the currently allocated spectrum amounts of the ith SU, respectively. The value γ is chosen to quantify the service adaptability based on the average slope of the linear utility function (Kim, & Varshney, 2005).

Assume $\mathbf{S} = \{(U_1, ..., U_n)\} \subset \mathbb{R}^n$ is a feasible utility set. The bargaining set $\boldsymbol{B}$ is the set of all individually rational, Pareto optimal payoff pairs in the cooperative payoff region $\boldsymbol{S}$. Therefore, in the solution set $\boldsymbol{B}$, one player cannot increase his utility without decreasing the utility of any other players (Park, 2007b). In the developed bargaining game, each player is a member of a team willing to compromise his own objective to gain a total optimal solution. By employing the *KSBS*

approach, the team players cooperate with each other and make a collective decision. If an agreement among the players cannot be reached, the payoff that the players will receive is given by the disagreement point $U_{1..n}^d = (U_1^d, ..., U_n^d)$. It is the minimum utility that each player expects by joining the game without cooperation (e.g., 0 in the system; it guarantees that players obtain nothing in case of disagreement point); $U_{1..n}^d$ can be the origin in the spectrum allocation problem. Based on the $U_{1..n}^d$ as a starting point, the line (L) is defined as the same manner in the *KSBBA* scheme (Kim, 2010). Usually, the bargaining solution is strongly dependent on the bargaining powers (Park, 2007b). If different bargaining powers are used, the player with a higher bargaining power obtains a larger amount spectrum than the other players. Therefore, bargaining power decision is an important factor and must be considered during the design of bargaining model. In the *TRSS* scheme, the bargaining power (ω) is defined based on the trust value (T). At the current time, the ith SU's bargaining power (ω_i) of is defined as follows.

$$\omega_i = \frac{T_i\left(c_t\right)}{\sum_{k=1}^n T_k\left(c_t\right)} \tag{44}$$

where n is the total number of SUs and c_t is the current time. By considering the dynamic changes of SU behaviors, the bargaining power (ω) can reflect the sequential trust ratio among SUs. Using the ω values, the *TRSS* scheme can give appropriate incentives or punishments to each individual SU.

Geometrically, the *KSBS* is the intersection point ($U_1^*, ..., U_n^*$) between the bargaining set $\mathbf{B}$ and the line L. Since the *KSBS* is located in the $\mathbf{B}$ as well as in the line L, the bargaining solution is also obtained in the *KSBBA* scheme (Kim, 2010). If $\omega_j < 0$, the jth SU is withdrawn from the spectrum allocation procedure. The benefit of SUs is closely related to the bargaining power, and the player with a higher trust value obtains the higher bargaining power. Therefore, SUs voluntarily participate in the sensing work to increase their higher trust values. By dynamically adapting the allocated spectrum amount, the *TRSS* scheme can appropriately react to selfish SUs.

The *TRSS* scheme is a new dynamic *KSBS* to solve the spectrum sharing problem in CR networks. To implement the dynamic bargaining process, the developed bargaining power adjustment algorithm is designed as a trust game. Based on the current and history of SU's behaviors, trust values and bargaining powers are dynamically modified. The main steps of the *TRSS* scheme are given next.

Step 1: At the initial time, the CBS assigns a same initial trust value to each SU. Each SU independently performs local spectrum sensing and this sensing information is sent to the CBS.

Step 2: After collecting the sensing result of each SU, the CBS makes a judgment whether or not the spectrum is idle.

Step 3: Every *unit_time*, each SU's action is examined periodically; at this time, detection of malicious users can take place. Thereofre, trust value is dynamically estimated according to (42). Based on the trust values, the CBS assigns a bargaining power to each SU by using (44).

Step 4: If the PU spectrum is idle, the idle spectrum is adaptively distributed to each SU according to the *KSBS*.

Step 5: After spectrum allocation, the obtained solution is examined periodically to maintain the finest solution. The developed repeated bargaining approach allows to model se-

quential decision making in a long-term interaction.

Step 6: Under widely diverse CR network environments, the CBS is self-monitoring constantly for the next iterative processing.

Recently, several spectrum sharing schemes have been presented for CR network systems. The *Dynamic Cooperative Spectrum Sensing* (*DCSS*) scheme is an evolutionary game-theoretical algorithm for distributed cooperative sensing over cognitive radio networks (Wang, 2010). By employing the theory of evolutionary game, the *DCSS* scheme modeled the interactions between selfish users in cooperative sensing and developed a distributed learning mechanism. This scheme can help the secondary users approach their optimal strategy with only their own payoff history. The *Dynamic Bargaining-based Spectrum Access* (*DBSA*) scheme is an opportunistic spectrum access algorithm using dynamic bargaining game theory (Tembine, 2009). This scheme covers time-dependent bargaining problems, long-term negotiations, and stochastic bargaining games, which are described as Markov decision processes with local resource states. The *DBSA* scheme examined the cost and the benefit of bargaining in the stochastic game model and showed the existence of equilibria and bargaining solution. Figure 4 demonstrates that the performance of the proposed *TRSS* scheme is generally superior to those of other existing schemes: the *DCSS* scheme and the *DBSA* scheme.

Summary

Due to the rapid increase in the variety of wireless communication services, the CR network system is becoming much more attractive. Usually, the performance of CR is characterized by both sensing accuracy and sharing efficiency. However, a lot of research has mainly focused on improving

Figure 4. Performance evaluations of the TRSS scheme

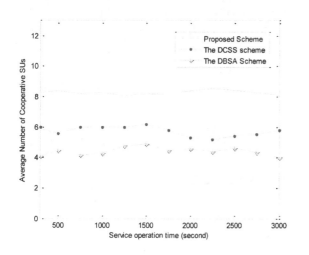

(a) Cooperative SUs

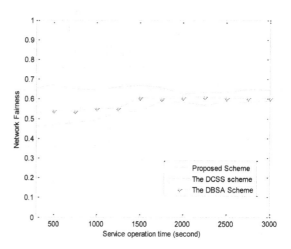

(b) Network Fairness

sensing accuracy while efficient sharing strategies have been largely ignored. The *TRSS* scheme is a new spectrum sharing scheme based on the trust-based dynamic *KSBS* model. The main design goal is to share the spectrum with a good balance between efficiency and fairness under widely diverse network situations. To satisfy this goal, the traditional bargaining concept is extended as a dynamic bargaining model based on the long-term behavior records of the SUs. By constantly monitoring the current network situations, the *TRSS* scheme yields good approximations of global system optimization.

REPEATED BAYESIAN-BASED SPECTRUM AUCTION (*RBSA*) SCHEME FOR COGNITIVE RADIO NETWORKS

Due to the remarkable growth in the number of users and the limited spectrum resource, an efficient spectrum sharing scheme is very important and has been an active area of research over the years. Auction model is a rich mathematical tool

and widely used to solve the spectrum allocation problem in cognitive radio networks. In 2013, S. Kim proposed a new Repeated Bayesian-based Spectrum Auction (*RBSA*) scheme for cognitive radio networks (Kim, 2013b). In the *RBSA* scheme, users adaptively decide their prices by using the Bayesian game approach and share spectrum bands based on the double auction protocol. According to a distributed control manner, the *RBSA* scheme is dynamic and flexible that can adaptively respond to current system conditions.

Development Motivation

Recently, researchers have proposed various algorithms to optimally share the spectrum resource using cognitive radio technologies. Auction game model was also proposed for efficient spectrum sharing in CRs (Akkarajitsakul, 2011), (Moham-madian & Abolhassani, 2010), (Xu & Wang, 2010). It is a significant and efficient market-based approach to solve allocation of the limited and rare resources for more requisitions. Therefore, the auction game model can provide better spectrum sharing by reducing the number of unallocated spectrum bands and increase the overall resource utilization; it is helpful in CR systems.

If all payoffs and set of strategies of users in a CR network system are completely known by all the users, auction mechanism can be simply modeled as a complete information game. However, in the real world, the information about characteristics of other users is incompletely known to a user (Akkarajitsakul, 2011). In this case, scientific inference methods are necessary to predict a current auction model. Bayesian inference is a method of statistical inference to provide a logical, quantitative decision; the accumulation of evidence is used to estimate parameters and predictions in a probability model. Based on the Bayes' theorem and Bayesian probability rules, Bayesian inference summarizes all uncertainty by a 'posterior' distribution, and gives a 'posterior' belief, which may be used as the basis for inferential decisions. Therefore, the concept of Bayesian inference can be used to provide solutions to predict future values based on historical data (Pan, 1996). During CR system operations, the auction information is unknown or partly known by users. Under this incomplete information situation, auction game can be modeled as a Bayesian game in which the outcome of the game can be predicted by using Bayesian inference (Akkarajitsakul, 2011). In addition, spectrum sharing auction procedure is operated iteratively. Therefore, it may be more reasonable to formulate the scenario as a repeated game model where users play multiple rounds periodically while remembering past experiences (Etkin, Parekh, & Tse, 2007).

Motivated by the above discussion, the *RBSA* scheme is designed as a repeated Bayesian auction game. In the *RBSA* scheme, primary and secondary users are assumed to be self-regarding game players and make their decisions for the goal of maximizing their perceived payoffs. To adaptively decide their strategies, the basic concept of Bayesian inference technique is adopted. During the step-by-step game iteration, the collection of fresh evidence repeatedly modifies an existing

probability distribution, whereas the modified belief is called the posterior probability. Usually, each player's behavior might affect the behavior of other players. Therefore, the result of the each user's decisions is the input back to the other user's decision process. This dynamics of the interactive feedback mechanism can cause cascade interactions of players and players can make their decisions to quickly find the most profitable solution.

Related Work

Recently, several auction-based spectrum sharing schemes have been presented. The *Strategy-Proof Spectrum Auction* (*SPSA*) scheme is a truthful and computationally efficient spectrum auction to support an eBay-like dynamic spectrum market (Zhou, X., Gandhi, S., Suri, S., & Zheng, H. (2008). This scheme allows wireless users to obtain and pay for the spectrum based on their demands. In addition, the *SPSA* scheme enables spectrum owners to maximize their revenues by assigning spectrum to the bidders who truly value it the most. However, the *SPSA* scheme is a single-sided spectrum auction only considering buyers. The *SPSA* scheme has been directly extended to the *Truthful Double Spectrum Auction* (*TDSA*) scheme (Zhou & Zheng, 2009). The *TDSA* scheme is developed to support truthful double spectrum auctions where multiple parties can trade spectrum based on their individual needs. This scheme applies a novel winner determination and pricing mechanism to select winning sellers and buyers. However, the *TDSA* scheme only assumes simple spectrum demand/request formats. In addition, this scheme is designed under the condition that the auctioneer has complete information. But, the question - how to obtain this information - is not answered.

As contrasted with the *SPSA* and *TDSA* schemes, CR spectrum sharing schemes have been developed according to the auction model. The *Repeated Auctions with Bayesian Learning* (*RABL*) Scheme is modeled as a repeated auction game

(Han, Zheng, & Poor, 2011). This scheme investigated the problem of spectrum access in cognitive radio systems with monitoring cost and access cost. Therefore, a repeated auction model has been adopted to maximize the tradeoff between the gain and cost in accessing spectrum bands. In addition, to design a formulation with incomplete information, a nonparametric belief update algorithm is constructed based on the Dirichlet process. The *Adaptive Auction-based Spectrum Sharing (AASS)* scheme is an auction based non-cooperative game model to characterize competitiveness among PUs and SUs (Mohammadian, 2010). In this scheme, the Hackner utility function is adopted to define selfish and self-interested secondary users' bids for frequency spectrum. In addition, the *AASS* scheme presented a dynamic updating algorithm for the cost function of each PU, which aids PUs to achieve more demands from SUs in each stage of the dynamic spectrum sharing game. The *Double Auction-based Spectrum Sharing (DASS)* scheme is a double auction based dynamic spectrum sharing scheme (Xu, 2010). This scheme allows free spectrum bands trading between operators to improve the efficiency of the spectrum utilization. The *DASS* scheme investigated the practical wireless communication model by using the adaptive adjustable bidding/asking strategies.

Spectrum Sharing Algorithms in the *RBSA* Scheme

When the spectrum resource is shared among multiple users with different objectives, the *RBSA* scheme can analyze the conflict network situation. To implement the dynamics of spectrum sharing process, PUs and SUs, who have own interests and capacities as sellers and buyers, are operated repeatedly to achieve their desired objectives.

Game Model for the *RBSA* Scheme

Game theory has many applications for resource allocation in wireless networks. However, traditional game models assume that all information needed by any player is known completely. However, in a real world situation, the information about other players' actions may be uncertain or unknown (Akkarajitsakul, 2011). Therefore, it is difficult to know a priori the action of players. Due to this reason, classical game model cannot be directly applied for real network operations. In 1967, John Harsanyi introduced the Bayesian game model, which is a control framework of strategic behavior under incomplete information. Bayesian game model relaxes the assumption that all information is completely known. This feasible approach can be used to predict the outcome of the uncertainty. To design a spectrum sharing auction algorithm under the incomplete information situation, it is the main advantage over traditional game models (Akkarajitsakul, 2011).

The *RBSA* scheme focuses on the Bayesian game approach to solve the spectrum sharing problem in CR systems. Generally, a Bayesian model is composed of a set of players, a set of actions, types of players and utility function for each player (Xu, 2010), (Pan, 1996). The Bayesian auction game in *RBSA* scheme can be formulated as follows:

- **Players:** PUs and SUs in CR systems; $\mathcal{N}$ = $\{1, 2, \cdots, N\}$ and $\mathcal{M}$ = $\{1, 2, \cdots, M\}$ are denoted as the PU set and the SU set, respectively. The PU $i \in \mathcal{N}$ operates on a spectrum band B_i that is non-overlapped with the spectrum bands of other PUs, i.e. $B_i \bigcap B_k = \Phi$, $\forall\ i,k \in \mathcal{N}$.
- **Sets of actions:** Any PU i has a set of all possible offers, which are expected prices of the selling B_i band. Any SU j has a set of all possible bids, which are affordable prices that SU i can pay.
- **Types of players:** The type of the player is a probability distribution, which is used to express the belief about uncertain or unknown information of the game players. Types are independent and dynami-

cally changed in repeated auction stages. Each player completely knows its own type while playing the game but not the types of other players. Therefore, a probability distribution is used to suppose the other players' types.

- **Utility functions:** A utility function can quantify the satisfaction that a player can get from a particular outcome. In the developed model, the utility function for PUs represents the monetary gains (e.g., revenue from spectrum trading). On the contrary, the higher auction price will result in a lower utility for SUs. Therefore, the utility function for SUs is defined as a reserved utility of PUs. If PUs or SUs fail to trade spectrum band, the payoff will remain 0.

The Bayesian auction model in the *RBSA* scheme can be formulated as a repeated game. In order to implement the repeated game model, the *RBSA* scheme partitions the time-axis into equal intervals of length, *time_period* (i.e., P_t, $t = 0,1,2....$). Within each *time_period*, PUs and SUs interact sequentially to share the spectrum resource. The assumption of multiple sequential interactions within a repeated game allows a player to infer about the behavior of other players (Dehnie, Guan, Gharai, & Ghanadan, 2009), (Yokoo, Sakurai, & Matsubara, 2001). Based on the Bayesian inference approach, the *RBSA* scheme characterizes a decision mechanism to know a priori the action of other players. In an effective distributed manner, it is operated in game stages, iteratively.

Repeated Double Auction Protocol

Conventional auctions mainly involve one auctioneer (seller) and multiple bidders (buyers). From the auction structure point of view, this one-to-many structure is called one-sided auction. However, in the spectrum sharing auction scenario, there are several buyers and sellers submit bids (i.e., the willing-to-pay prices) and offers (i.e.,

the expected selling prices) for spectrum bands. Based on this multi-seller multi-buyer situation, the auction mode in the *RBSA* scheme is designed as the many-to-many double auction structure.

In the *RBSA* scheme, system operator is defined as an auctioneer, who is in charge of pricing and trading spectrum bands. PUs in $\mathcal{N}$ can be a seller; sellers are allowed to make offers to auctioneer to show their preference in the selling price. SUs in $\mathcal{M}$ can be a bidder; bidders submit bids to purchase the spectrum band. Every *time_period*, spectrum auction among players (i.e., PUs and SUs) is operated periodically. For each auction stage, both bidder and seller estimate their values for the spectrum band based on their utility functions. When all offers and bids are sent to auctioneer, the auctioneer sets the trade-price for spectrum sharing and decides which bidder gets the spectrum band from which sellers. For this procedure, the standard double auction protocol (*Preston-McAfee Double Auction*: *PMDA*) is developed by Preston and McAfee (Kant & Grosu, 2005). In the *PMDA* protocol, the equilibrium auction price is determined by matching seller's prices with buyer's bid prices.

The *RBSA* scheme adopts the basic concept of the *PMDA* protocol to decide the trade-price. At the end of each auction round, the auctioneer collects all the information about offers and bids, and determines the trade-price by sorting and matching techniques (Kant, 2005). And then, the auctioneer announces the decided trade-price to all players. Therefore, the players learn the current spectrum sharing condition in CR systems. The SUs (i.e., bidders) who get the required spectrum band will not submit new bids in the next auction round. However, if some SUs fail to get the spectrum band, they will submit their new bids to the auctioneer. Simultaneously, if some PUs are also failed to sell their spectrum bands, they also will submit their new offers in the next auction period. Therefore, in each auction round, remaining players adjust their prices adaptively. This dynamic auction procedure is repeated sequentially every *time_period* (i.e., serial auction round) to reach an efficient auction consensus.

Bayesian Inference Formula and Learning Approach

In the Bayesian game model, players learn how to modify their prior knowledge and adaptively adjust their strategies. This approach does not assume that players always make optimal decisions with complete information. During the Bayesian game process, players have a chance to reconsider the current strategy and react to maximize the expected payoff. Therefore, it offers a more realistic model under the real world environment.

In general, a player's desire degree for spectrum trading as strong influence on player's decision in making price proposal. With the stronger desire, a player may make more concession to make narrow the difference between his price and the current trade-price, and vice versa (Ishihara, 2005). Usually, players don't know the other player's desire. However, it is actually hidden in the auctioneer's trade-price in each auction round. To submit new bids and offers, bidders or sellers infer the next round trade-price, which is referred to as the type of the auctioneer. In each auction round, players can learn the others' desire with incoming information from the auctioneer's proposal. From this inference, each player can make a better price decision for the next auction.

In the *RBSA* scheme, Bayesian learning approach is used to infer the others' desire level. According to the Bayes' theorem and updating rule, the Bayesian inference formula can be expressed as follows (Akkarajitsakul, 2011), (Ishihara, 2005).

$$P_t\left(A|B\right) = \frac{P_t\left(B|A\right) \times P_t\left(A\right)}{P_t\left(B\right)} \qquad (45)$$

where $P_t\left(A|B\right)$ is the posterior distribution of hypothesis A under the condition B; t represents tth period of game stage. $P_t\left(A\right)$ and $P_t\left(B\right)$ are

the probability of hypothesis A and B, respectively. Based on the Bayesian learning approach, each player's price adjustment procedure is developed. To infer the next trade-price, the *RBSA* scheme defines two parameters; auctioneer's concession ratio (CR_a) and desire level (η); they are used for the hypotheses in the Bayesian inference formula. The auctioneer's concession ratio (CR_a) is estimated as follows.

$$CR_a\left(t\right) = \frac{TP\left[t-1\right] - TP\left[t\right]}{TP\left[t-1\right]} \qquad (46)$$

where $TP[t]$, $TP[t$-$1]$ are the trade-price at the tth and (t-1)th game stage, respectively. If $CR_a\left(t\right)$ is negative value, it means the auctioneer increases the trade price with no concession. The auctioneer's desire level as at the tth game stage is denoted as $\eta\left(t\right)$; a higher value of $\eta\left(t\right)$ corresponds to a stronger desire to trade a spectrum band. For simplicity, the *RBSA* scheme assumes that η value ranges is fixed from -0.5 to 0.5 and uniformly divided to 10 intervals. Therefore, the value of η is an element of discrete set, i.e., $\eta \in \{ \eta_0 = -0.5, \eta_1 = -0.4, ..., \eta_9 = 0.4, \eta_{10} = 0.5\}$.

Let $P(CR_a\left(t\right) | \eta_i\left(t\right))$ be a conditional probability that the auctioneer's concession ratio under a given auctioneer's desire $\eta_i\left(t\right)$. A higher value of $P(CR_a\left(t\right) | \eta_i\left(t\right))$ means that the auctioneer's concession ratio is more likely to be $CR_a\left(t\right)$ when the given eagerness value is $\eta\left(t\right)$. The *RBSA* scheme follows the assumption in (Ishihara, 2005).. Therefore, the probability density function of $P(CR_a\left(t\right) | \eta_i\left(t\right))$ is defined having a normal distribution.

$$P\left(CR_a\left(t\right) | \eta_i\left(t\right)\right) =$$

$$\frac{1}{\sqrt{2\pi}\sigma}\exp\left\{-\frac{\left(CR_a\left(t\right)-\theta\right)^2}{2\sigma^2}\right\} \qquad (47)$$

s.t., $\theta = (1 - CR_p\left(t\right)) \times \eta_i\left(t\right)$

where $CR_p\left(t\right)$ is the concession ratio of player himself for the auction. The mean μ and the standard deviation σ yield different normal density curves; each player has different μ and σ values. By using (47), the *RBSA* scheme defines another conditional probability, $P(\eta_k\left(t\right)\mid CR_a\left(t\right))$, that auctioneer's desire is $\eta_k\left(t\right)$ under the condition of given $CR_a\left(t\right)$. According to the Bayesian updating rule, the $P(\eta_k\left(t\right)\mid CR_a\left(t\right))$ value can be given as follows.

$$P_t\left(\eta_k\left(t\right)\mid CR_a\left(t\right)\right)=$$

$$\frac{P_t(CR_a\left(t\right)\mid\eta_k\left(t\right))\times P_t\left(\eta_k\left(t\right)\right)}{P_t\left(CR_a\left(t\right)\right)} \qquad (48)$$

s.t.,

$$P_t\left(CR_a\left(t\right)\right)=\sum_{\eta_k}P_t(CR_a\left(t\right)\mid\eta_k\left(t\right))\times P_t\left(\eta_k\left(t\right)\right)$$

Based on the $P_t(\eta_k\left(t\right)\mid CR_a\left(t\right))$, $P_t\left(\eta_k\left(t\right)\right)$ value is obtained as follows.

$$P_t\left(\eta_k\left(t\right)\right)=$$

$$\frac{P_t\left(\eta_k\left(t\right)\mid CR_a\left(t\right)\right)}{\sum_{\eta_k}P_t\left(\eta_k\left(t\right)\mid CR_a\left(t\right)\right)}$$

where $\eta_k \in \{\eta_0, \eta_1,..., \eta_9, \eta_{10}\}$ \qquad (49)

According to the $P_t\left(\eta_k\left(t\right)\right)$, the probability distribution of $P_t\left(\eta\left(t\right)\right)$ is updated, and the current auctioneer's desire level (η^e) can be estimated as follows.

$$\eta^e = \sum_{\eta_k=\eta_0}^{\eta_{10}}\left(P_t\left(\eta_k\left(t\right)\right)\times\eta_k\left(t\right)\right) \text{ where } \sum_{\eta_k=\eta_0}^{\eta_{10}}P_t\left(\eta_k\left(t\right)\right)=1 \qquad (50)$$

To obtain a more precise η^e value, this Bayesian inference process repeats iteratively each *time_period*. Therefore, players constantly monitor the current auction situation in a distributed manner to decide their strategies. Finally, sellers and bidders can adjust their offer (Of_{t+1}) and bid (Bi_{t+1}) for the next auction round as follows.

$$Of_{t+1} \text{ (or } Bi_{t+1}) = \left(1-\eta^e\right)\times T\_P_t \qquad (51)$$

where T_P_t is the announced trade-price of the current (i.e., tth game stage) auction.

The Main Steps of the *RBSA* Scheme

In general, traditional game models have focused on investigating *which* decisions are made or *what* decisions should be made. To implement these models, the most fundamental assumption is rationality; it is assumed that the players know everything about the game and they can make the same deductions about the situation. However, due to its unrealistic premise, this rationality assumption has been widely criticized (Menasche, Figueiredo, & Silva, 2005). To overcome this drawback, the Bayesian game model investigates *how* decisions are made for control problems.

In the *RBSA* scheme, PUs and SUs (i.e., game players) adaptively select their auction prices to share spectrum bands. Based on the feedback learning process, players can capture how to adapt their price strategies to reach a consensus. This procedure is formulated as a repeated auction model. At the end of each auction round, players periodically examine the current trade-price and iteratively adjust their prices in an entirely distributed fashion. Therefore, computational complexity does not increase significantly when the number of players increases. This interactive feedback process continues until the consensus is obtained; it is a practical and suitable approach in real world system operations. The main steps of the *RBSA* scheme are given next.

Step 1: At the initial iteration ($t=0$), the initial probability for each auctioneer's desire level $P_t\left(\eta_k\right)$ is equally distributed ($P_t\left(\eta_k\right)$ = 1/| $\mathbb{L}$ |, $\forall i$ where | $\mathbb{L}$ | is the total number of η intervals). This starting guess guarantees that each player enjoys the same benefit at the beginning of the game.

Step 2: Each auction stage, spectrum seller $i \in \mathcal{N}$ = {1, 2, $\cdots$, N} and spectrum buyer $j \in \mathcal{M}$ = {1, 2, $\cdots$, M} send their offer o_i and bid b_j to the auctioneer.

Step 3: The auctioneer collects all the offers $\left\{o_1, o_2, \ldots, o_n\right\}$ and bids $\left\{b_1, b_2, \ldots, b_m\right\}$, and then sorts offers in increasing order and bids in decreasing order as follows.

$o_{\sigma(1)} \le o_{\sigma(2)} \le \ldots \le o_{\sigma(n)}$ and

$b_{\pi(1)} \ge b_{\pi(2)} \ge \ldots \ge b_{\pi(m)}$ (52)

where σ and π are the permutations defining the orders statistics above.

Step 4: The auctioneer finds k such that $b_{\pi(k)} \ge o_{\sigma(k)}$ and $b_{\pi(k+1)} < o_{\sigma(k+1)}$. If $b_{\pi(1)} < o_{\sigma(1)}$, proceed to Step 8. Otherwise, the auctioneer determines the current trade-price (T_P).

$$T\_P = \frac{1}{2}\left(b_{\pi(k)} + a_{\sigma(k)}\right)$$ (53)

Step 5: The sellers, who offer the price lower than the T_P, and the buyers, who bid the price higher than the T_P, are successfully trade the spectrum bands with the price T_P.

Step 6: The auctioneer announces the current T_P and sends reject messages to sellers and bidders who do not successfully trade spectrum bands at the current auction round.

Step 7: In a distributed manner, trade-failed sellers and bidders dynamically adjust their auction prices by using (46)-(13-51).

Step 8: If there are at least one seller and one bidder who will submit their new offers and bids, go to Step 3 for the next auction round. This iterative feedback procedure continues until sellers and bidders reach a consensus. Otherwise, proceed to Termination step.

Termination: Auction game processing time is temporarily over. However, constantly, the CR system is self-monitoring the current situation. When new spectrum sharing requests (i.e., offers and bids) arrive, it can re-trigger the spectrum sharing algorithm.

The simulation results shown in Figure 5 demonstrate that the performance comparison of the *RBSA* scheme with the *RABL* scheme, the *AASS* scheme and the *DASS* scheme. These existing schemes are also developed as spectrum sharing algorithms based on the auction game model; they have been attracted a lot of attention and introduced unique challenges for the adaptive spectrum sharing problem. However, the proposed *RBSA* scheme is more adaptively responsive to the constantly changing system environment, and well-scalable with the number of players. Therefore, the proposed *RBSA* scheme can maintain well-balanced system performance while existing schemes can not offer such an attractive trade off.

Figure 5. Performance evaluations of the RBSA scheme

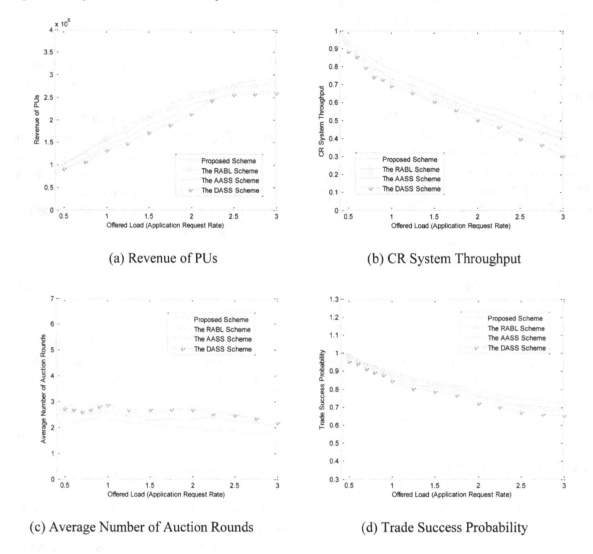

(a) Revenue of PUs

(b) CR System Throughput

(c) Average Number of Auction Rounds

(d) Trade Success Probability

Summary

Dynamic spectrum access has become a promising approach to improve spectrum efficiency by adaptively coordinating different users' access. The *RBSA* scheme is a novel spectrum sharing scheme, which is designed as a repeated Bayesian auction game. With the incomplete information, PUs and SUs adaptively decide their offering or bidding prices by using the Bayesian learning process. This auction process will be carried out periodically until the consensus is obtained. Due to the self-regarding feature, price adjustment decisions are made by an entirely distributed fashion. In real-world system operations, this distributed control approach is suitable and appropriate approach for ultimate practical implementation.

LEARNING BASED SPECTRUM SHARING (*LSS*) SCHEME FOR COGNITIVE RADIO NETWORKS

As the rapid development of wireless communication, the scarcity of spectrum become more and more prominent. Recently, Cognitive Radio (CR) technology is proposed to overcome the problem of low spectrum utilization brought by static spectrum allocation. Recently, S. Kim proposed a new Learning based Spectrum Sharing (*LSS*) scheme for CR networks. In the *LSS* scheme, a new CR spectrum sharing algorithm is developed by employing the dynamic coopetition game model. Coopetition game approach is an effective tool to describe CR sharing problems. The *LSS* scheme dynamically senses the spectrum based on the global game and efficiently re-allocates the available spectrum according to the trust-proportional bargaining approach. The main goal of *LSS* scheme is to greatly improve the sensing performance while maximizing the overall system capacity. Under widely different CR network situations, the *LSS* scheme is so dynamic and flexible that it can adaptively respond to current CR network conditions.

Development Motivation

To address the issue of inefficient spectrum management and the increasing demand of spectrum resources, Cognitive Radio (CR) is proposed to improve the spectrum utilization of wireless telecommunications. The main idea of CR technology is that the unlicensed users (i.e., secondary users: SUs) can dynamically sense the radio environment and opportunistically utilize the unused spectrum bands while causing no intolerable interference to licensed users (i.e., primary users: PUs). It is an important idea about spectrum sharing (Li, 2010).

In CR networks, SUs are expected to find available spectrum holes over a wide frequency range. Therefore, SUs are designed to monitor its surrounding radio environment and sense the unoccupied frequency bands (Qiao & Tan, 2011). However, sensing work of SU consumes a certain amount of energy and time. Therefore, selfish but rational SUs do not serve a common sensing work and tend to be a free-rider to reduce their control overhead. In this instance, SUs face the risk of having no one sense the spectrum (Wang, Liu & Clancy, 2010). Due to this reason, the major technical challenge of spectrum sensing problem is how to select sensing channels and to make a selfish SU collaborate with others. After sensing the spectrum to discover the available radio frequencies, these resources are to be dynamically shared among SUs to maximize the utilization of spectrum. To effectively improve the network capacity, spectrum sharing methods have gotten more and more attentions (Li, 2010), (Qiao, 2011), (Wang, Liu & Clancy, 2010).

Although many CR network management algorithms have recently drawn much attention, most work has assumed that the CR environment was perfectly recognized by SUs. However, this assumption has been widely criticized; realistic CR management shall be based on partial spectrum information. Therefore, traditional CR spectrum sharing approach practically unable to be implemented in real world CR network operations. Game theory is a field of applied mathematics that provides an effective tool in modeling the interactions among independent decision makers. It can describe the possibility to react to the actions of the other decision makers and analyze the situations of conflict and cooperation. The rational decision makers, referred to as 'players' in a game model, try to maximize their expected benefits through strategy set. Nowadays, game theory has emerged as an effective way of designing the CR management process and introduced well-fitted models to describe interaction among SUs in CR networks (Liu, Shen, Song, & Wang, 2009).

Usually, games can be divided into non-cooperative and cooperative games. In non-cooperative games, players are in conflict with each other and do not communicate or collaborate. Their preferences can be expressed as a utility function and players try to ensure the best possible consequence according to the utility function. Cooperative games, also called coalition games, are games in which players make binding commitments and find it beneficial to cooperate in the game. To reach an agreement that gives mutual advantage, players bargain with each other (Kim, 2012d). However, this two-binary classification has been questioned. Sometimes, the competition among players can be transformed into a cooperative competition. Nowadays, considerable efforts have been made to link the two type game models.

In 1996, N. Barry and B. Adam had introduced a new concept of game model, called coopetition game, which combined the characteristics of non-cooperative and cooperative games. The term 'coopetition' is a neologism coined to describe cooperative competition. Therefore, coopetition is defined as the phenomenon that differs from competition or cooperation, and stresses two faces (i.e., cooperation and competition) of one relationship in the same situation. In coopetition games, every player, who strengthens their competitive advantages by cooperation, can achieve greater and reciprocal advantages. An essential part in the coopetition game is the expression of individual decisions, which should cooperate while competing with each other game players. Recently, coopetition game model has been extensively discussed in economics and management science (Bouncken & Fredrich, 2011).

Motivated by the above discussion, the *LSS* scheme develops a new CR network spectrum sharing algorithm based on the coopetition game model. To model autonomous interacting SUs in CR networks, the coopetition game is a suitable approach to get an effective solution. At the first stage, the *LSS* scheme focuses attention on the spectrum sensing, which is the task of finding spectrum holes by sensing the radio spectrum. In the *LSS* scheme, spectrum sensing mechanism is developed as a non-cooperative global game. At the second stage, the detected idle spectrum is shared

based on the cooperative bargaining game. Under dynamically changing network environments, SUs compete and coordinate with each other in order to maximize their payoffs. Therefore, the *LSS* scheme approach is adaptable to get a globally desirable CR network performance.

The important features of the *LSS* scheme are i) appropriate incentive-based spectrum sharing to selfish SUs, ii) learning based respond to current CR network situations, iii) ability to provide a good tradeoff between the implementation complexity and optimized performance, iv) a practical and suitable approach under widely different and diversified CR network situations, and v) realistic assumption for practical CR network operations. During real world CR network operations, the *LSS* scheme can achieve an effective network performance while maintaining desirable properties of coopetition game model.

Related Work

Recently, several spectrum sharing schemes have been presented for CR network systems. The *Dynamic Cooperative Spectrum Sensing (DCSS)* scheme in (Wang, Liu & Clancy, 2010) is an evolutionary game-theoretical algorithm for distributed cooperative sensing over cognitive radio networks. By employing the theory of evolutionary game, the *DCSS* scheme modeled the interactions between selfish users in cooperative sensing and developed a distributed learning mechanism. This scheme can help the secondary users approach their optimal strategy with only their own payoff history. The *Dynamic Bargaining-based Spectrum Access (DBSA)* scheme in (Tembine, 2009) is an opportunistic spectrum access algorithm using dynamic bargaining game theory. This scheme covers time-dependent bargaining problems, long-term negotiations, and stochastic bargaining games, which are described as Markov decision processes with local resource states. The *DBSA* scheme examined the cost and the benefit of bargaining in the stochastic game model and showed the existence of equilibria and bargaining solution. The *Trust-based Bargaining Game Approach* (*TBGA*) scheme in (Kim, 2012c) is a new spectrum sharing scheme based on the trust game model. Based on the evaluating SU's behavior, this scheme estimates the trust level of each SU to distinguish between cooperative and selfish SUs. And then, the basic concept of *KSBS* is adopted to fairly distribute the spectrum resources among SUs. In the *TBGA* scheme, bargaining power of each SU is decided based on the SU's trust level, and the available spectrum is shared according to the *KSBS* model.

Spectrum Sharing Algorithms in the *LSS* Scheme

In this section, the *LSS* scheme is explained in detail. To reach a desirable CR system performance, the spectrum resource is effectively sensed and shared. The *LSS* scheme adopts the global game and trust-proportional bargaining methodologies to form a coopetition game model, which is a suitable approach to develop spectrum sharing algorithms.

Global Game Based Spectrum Sensing Algorithm

To share the CR network spectrum, the first task is to correctly sense the PUs' activities. The accuracy of spectrum sensing is a crucial factor for the CR network performance (Kim, 2012d). The *LSS* scheme designs a new spectrum sensing algorithm based on the concept of global game model.

Global games are games of incomplete information where players receive possibly-correlated signals of the underlying state of real world (Carlsson & Damme, 1993). Formally, global game is described by the following steps; i) a game ($\mathbb{G}$) can be described by its different payoff entries. At this time, a subgame ($g \in \mathbb{G}$) can be defined; it can be drawn from some subclass of $\mathbb{G}$, ii) each player have common prior beliefs represented by

a probability distribution and get additional private information in the form of a fuzzy observation of the actual g game to be played, iii) players independently choose actions simultaneously, and iv) payoffs are determined by g and the players' choices (Carlsson & Damme, 1993). The term *global* refers to the fact that, at each time, players can play any game selected from a subclass of all games, which adds an extra dimension to standard game-play. Therefore, global game is an ideal method for decentralized coordination amongst players (Krishnamurthy, 2010a).

The typical bar problem is a well-known example of global games (Krishnamurthy, 2010a, 2010b, 2010c). The bar problem example draws immediate parallels with the operation of decentralized spectrum sensing in CR networks. In 2009, V. Krishnamurthy had developed a new global game model for the CR spectrum sensing problem (Krishnamurthy, 2010b). However, the Krishnamurthy's global game makes the assumption that game players are perfectly intelligent. Intelligent players are assumed to know everything. This assumption is too strong to implement in the real world game player; it impossible to know everything about CR network environments. For the practical game operation, players should be modeled with bounded intelligence. The *LSS* scheme develops a new global game based on learning to play well where SU interact with an unknown environment. To reach an effective solution, the learning algorithm in the *LSS* scheme is designed as an iterative process in which each iteration involves three key steps performed by every SU; i) observing the current CR network environment, ii) estimating the prospective payoff, and iii) selecting a strategy to reach a certain desired game outcome.

The *LSS* scheme assumes a CR network system with N SUs and L channels. At a given time instant, each SU measures the L dimensional vector $\boldsymbol{X} = \left(X_1, \ldots, X_L \right)$, which consists of the quality of L channels. Each component in the vector $\boldsymbol{X}$ ($X_{l\in\{1,\ldots,L\}}$) maintains the appropriate-ness degree for each channel; X_l is the channel l's probability to be shared. It is measured as a sharing possibility rate per each sense and represents the expected quality of each channel. Let N_l be the number of SUs in the channel $l\in\left\{1,\ldots,L\right\}$, and denotes $\gamma_l = {N_l}\big/{N}$ as the fraction of SUs in a channel l (i.e., $\gamma_l \in \left[0,1\right]$ and $\sum_{l=1}^{L}\gamma_l = 1$). Based on the channel quality information $\boldsymbol{X}$ and $\gamma_{l,1\leq l\leq L}$, each SU decides whether to stay in its current channel $l \in \left\{1,\ldots,L\right\}$ or to move the other channel, or not to participate spectrum sharing process. To make this decision, each SU constantly monitors the CR network environments in a distributed online manner. In the *LSS* scheme, the interaction of all SUs can be modeled as a global game (Krishnamurthy, 2010a, 2010b). At each round of game, actively participating SUs consist of spectrum sharing subgame, and have involved learning to play optimally. Therefore, SUs make decision individually and opportunistically sense the spectrum. The payoff of the SU i in the channel l is be defined as follows.

$$P\_O_l^i\left(\boldsymbol{X},\gamma_l\right) = \alpha \times g(X_l) + \left(1-\alpha\right)\times f\left(\gamma_l\right) - p\left(\gamma_l\right) \qquad (54)$$

$$\text{s.t.,} \quad g(X_l) = \frac{1}{1+\exp\left(-X_l\right)},$$
$$f\left(\gamma_l\right) = 1-\gamma_l, \quad p\left(\gamma_l\right) = w\times log_2\left(1+\gamma_l\right)$$

where α denotes a positive constant to weigh the different components of the payoff. The quality function $g\left(\cdot\right)$ implies that the better the channel quality, the higher the payoff for that channel. The function $f\left(\cdot\right)$ measures the relative desirability

of channel. The function $p\left(\cdot\right)$ is the normalized price function for spectrum sharing. If too few SUs are in the channel (i.e., a lower value of γ), the resource of the channel is underutilized. If too many SUs are in the channel (i.e., a higher value of γ), network congestion occurs. Therefore, the *LSS* scheme develops the price function ($p\left(\cdot\right)$) to shape the γ distribution as a quasi-concave curve. By using (54), the SU i in the channel l rationally chooses an action $\mathcal{A}_l^{(i)} \in \left\{1,2,3\right\} = \{\text{stay, move, quit}\}$ to maximize its payoff. The reward payoff (U_l^i) list for the SU i in the channel l is defined as follows.

$$\begin{cases} U_l^i(X,\gamma_l,\mathcal{A}=1) = P\_O_l^i(X,\gamma_l), \\ U_l^i(X,\gamma_l,\mathcal{A}=2) = \sum_{1\leq n\leq L, n\neq l} \mathcal{P}(n)\times P\_O_l^i(\mathrm{X},\gamma_n) \\ U_l^i(X,\gamma_l,\mathcal{A}=3) = 0 \end{cases}$$

$$\text{s.t.,} \quad \mathcal{P}\left(n\right) = \frac{\left(1+\beta\right)^{P\_O_l^i\left(\boldsymbol{X},\gamma_n\right)}}{\sum_{1\leq n\leq L, n\neq l}\left(1+\beta\right)^{P\_O_l^i\left(\boldsymbol{X},\gamma_n\right)}}$$

where $\mathcal{P}\left(n\right)$ is the selection probability for the channel n; it is dynamically adjusted based on the exponential updating approach. After sensing the channel l, the SU i estimates reward payoffs according to (55) and selects its strategy ($\mathcal{A}_l^{(i)}$) like as;

$$\mathcal{A}_l^{(i)} = \max_{\mathcal{A}_l^{(i)}\rightarrow\left\{1\,(\text{stay}),\,2\,(\text{move}),\,3\,(\text{quit})\right\}} U_l^i\left(\boldsymbol{X},\ \gamma_l,\mathcal{A}\right) \qquad (56)$$

When the SU i in the channel l choses the strategy 1 (stay), the SU i does not change the current strategy and continuously senses the selected PU channel. When the SU i choses the strategy 2 (move), the SU i selects another PU channel based on the $\mathcal{P}(n)$ where $n \neq l$ and $1 \leq n \leq L$. Based on the $P\_O_l^i$ ratio, $\mathcal{P}(n)$ is dynamically adjusted. If the reward payoffs (U_l^i) of strategy 1 and 2 is less than 0, the SU i choses the strategy 3 (quit) and not to participate the spectrum sharing process. The *LSS* scheme formulates this channel sensing algorithm as a global game. Especially, global games study interaction of a continuum of players who choose actions independently based on the observation of common signal. This leads to a simple characterization of the competitive optimal behavior of the CR network system as a function of the prior probability distribution of spectrum channel occupancy and channel quality.

Trust Level Evaluation Mechanism

In CR systems, each SU senses the spectrum and sends the sensing information to the Cognitive Base Station (CBS). By using appropriate data fusion rules, the CBS makes a judgment whether or not the spectrum is idle. Therefore, the cooperative sensing approach through multiple user cooperation can increase the sensing accuracy (Zouridaki, Mark, Hejmo & Thomas, 2005). The *LSS* scheme designs a trust based spectrum sharing algorithm to induce selfish SUs to participate in cooperative sensing process. In particular, trust based spectrum sharing approach is an efficient method of constraining the selfish SU from enjoying a free ride in sensing process.

In the *LSS* scheme, the CBS determines the trust level (T) of each individual SU by considering its actions. Trust level is an index of cooperation behavior and used to distribute the available spectrum more efficiently. By using the Bayesian inference method, the trust level of SU i at the time k ($T_i(k)$) can be obtained as follows; it is equal to the mean value of the $Beta(\varepsilon_t, \eta_t)$ (Zouridaki, 2005),(Changiz, Halabian, Yu, Lambadaris & Tang, 2010).

$$T_i(k) = \frac{\varepsilon_t}{\varepsilon_t + \eta_t} \qquad (57)$$

where ε_t and η_t parameters represent the number of actively senses and free-rides, respectively. To effectively estimate the $T_i(k)$ value, the CBS constantly monitors the SUs' behaviors. Therefore, after the determination of trust level, it is dynamically adjusted according to the SUs' behavior.

Trust-Proportional Bargaining Based Spectrum Sharing Algorithm

In order to improve spectral efficiency, designing efficient spectrum sharing algorithm in CR networks is a challenging problem. But despite the concerns, not much work has been done in this direction. The *LSS* scheme develops a new resource sharing algorithm for available spectrum holes. Based on the SU's trust level, the available spectrum is adaptively shared according to the trust-proportional bargaining model. This approach is possible to promote cooperation while discouraging selfish SUs, which can limit their negative impact on the total CR network performance.

Usually, the main interest of bargaining games is to fairly distribute the outcome to each player according to their contributions to make joint-agreements. Therefore, the bargaining game model is attractive for spectrum allocation problems (Kim, 2012c). In 1977, E. Kalai and R. Myerson developed another interesting bargaining solution. It is the Egalitarian Bargaining Solution (EBS). Unlike other bargaining solutions, the egalitarian solution enjoys even stronger *monotonicity* requirements while satisfying independence conditions. Without using the Nash's axiom of *Invariance with respect to utility transformations*, the EBS attempts to grant equal gain to players. In other words, it is the point which maximizes the minimum payoff among players.

This characterization can be extended to a large class of solutions including the λ-proportional bargaining solution (Bossert, 1995).

Let $(\mathbb{S}, \mathrm{d})$ be a two-person bargaining problem where $\mathbb{S} \subseteq \mathbb{R}^2$ is the feasible set of payoff vectors and $\mathrm{d} \in \mathbb{R}^2$ is the disagreement point. The ideal point of a bargaining problem is simply defined by

$$F_i(\mathbb{S}, \mathrm{d}) = \max\{x_i | \boldsymbol{X} \in \mathbb{S}, \boldsymbol{X} \geq \mathrm{d}\}, \text{ s.t, } \forall i = 1, 2. \tag{58}$$

The egalitarian bargaining solution is defined by letting the unique point $(x_1, x_2) = \boldsymbol{X} \in \mathbb{S}$ such that

$$x_1 - d_1 = x_2 - d_2 \tag{59}$$

A generalization of the egalitarian solution is the class of λ-proportional bargaining solution. It is also defined as the unique point $\boldsymbol{X} \in \mathbb{S}$ such that

$$x_1 - d_1 = \lambda \times \left(x_2 - d_2\right) \tag{60}$$

Clearly, $\lambda = 1$ leads to the egalitarian bargaining solution (Bossert, 1995). To develop an adaptable spectrum sharing algorithm, an important issue is how to properly induce selfish users to participate in spectrum sensing work. The *LSS* scheme would set λ value as the current trust level of SU. Therefore, SUs have incentives to actively participate in spectrum sensing work.

In the *LSS* scheme, SUs in each channel are members of a team willing to compromise their own objective to gain a solution. By employing the trust-proportional bargaining approach, the team players cooperate with each other and make a collective decision. When m SUs are sensing the channel l, the sharing amount of channel l for SUs is given by $SA_{1..m}^l = \{(SA_1^l, .., SA_m^l)\}$. If an agreement among the SUs cannot be reached, the sharing amount that the SUs will receive is given by the disagreement point $SA_{1..m}^d = (SA_1^d, .., SA_m^d)$; it represents payoffs when the game fails. Finally, the desirable best solution for m SUs in the channel l ($SA_1^{l*}, .., SA_m^{l*}$) is obtained as follows.

$$\frac{1}{T_1(k)} \times$$
$$(SA_1^{l*} - SA_1^d) = ... = \frac{1}{T_m(k)} \times \left(SA_m^{l*} - SA_m^d\right),$$

$$\text{s.t. } SA_{1..m}^d = (0, ..., 0), \tag{61}$$

The Main Steps of the *LSS* Scheme

The *LSS* scheme develops a new coopetition game model based on the global game and proportional bargaining approach. By using this game model, CR spectrum can be shared effectively. During the step-by-step game iteration, SUs have a chance to reconsider their current strategies and react to maximize the expected payoff. Therefore, after selecting strategies, SUs examine their payoffs periodically in an entirely distributed fashion. This distributed learning approach can drastically reduce the computational complexity and control overhead. It is a good point for practical implementations. The main steps of the *LSS* scheme are given next.

Step 1: At the initial iteration ($k = 0$), the trust level (T) of each SU and the payoff of each channel are equally distributed. This starting guess guarantees that each SU enjoys the same benefit at the beginning of the game.

Step 2: Each SU maintains the channel quality vector ($\boldsymbol{X}$) and SU fraction information (γ) by step-by-step online manner.

Step 3: According to (54) and (55), each SU estimates reward payoffs and chooses its action

$\mathcal{A} \in \{1$ (stay), 2 (move), 3 (quit)$\}$ to maximize the payoff. This decision is made in the distributed manner.

Step 4: Based on the SUs, who participate the spectrum sensing process, a channel selection subgame is formulated.

Step 5: The CBS determines the trust level (T) of each game-participating SU by using (57).

Step 6: Based on the trust level information, the available spectrum is shared based on the trust-proportional bargaining model. According to (61), the available spectrum resource is dynamically distributed to SUs.

Step 7: SUs can be self-monitoring constantly the CR network environments; proceeds to Step 2 for the next iteration.

Summary

Recently, game theory based spectrum sharing approach has been presented as an effective sensing way to improve the performance of CR networks. The *LSS* scheme is a new CR spectrum sharing scheme based on the coopetition game model. The main design goal is to share the spectrum effectively under widely diverse network situations. To satisfy this goal, the traditional game concept is extended as a new paradigm. Coopetition game model combines the advantages of non-cooperative and cooperative games to shape the real world environment in a favorable way. Therefore, SUs in the *LSS* scheme compete and cooperative with each other in order to maximize their payoffs. This approach is suitable to get a globally desirable CR network performance. By using the feedback based learning algorithm, the *LSS* scheme can improve the sensing performance while maximizing the overall system capacity.

REFERENCES

Akkarajitsakul, K., Hossain, E., & Niyato, D. (2011). Distributed resource allocation in wireless networks under uncertainty and application of Bayesian game. *IEEE Communications Magazine*, *49*(8), 120–127. doi:10.1109/MCOM.2011.5978425

Bloem, M., Alpcan, T., & Başar, T. (2007). A Stackelberg game for power control and channel allocation in cognitive radio networks. In *Proceedings of IEEE international conference on Performance evaluation methodologies and tools*. IEEE.

Bossert, W., & Tan, G. (1995). An arbitration game and the egalitarian bargaining solution. *Social Choice and Welfare*, *12*(1), 29–41. doi:10.1007/BF00182191

Bouncken, R. B., & Fredrich, V. (2011). Coopetition: Its successful management in the nexus of dependency and trust. In *Proceedings of PICMET'11*. PICMET.

Carlsson, H., & Damme, E. V. (1993). Global games and equilibrium selection. *Econometrica*, *61*(5), 989–1018. doi:10.2307/2951491

Changiz, R., Halabian, H., Yu, F. R., Lambadaris, I., & Tang, H. (2010). Trust Management in Wireless Mobile Networks with Cooperative Communications. In *Proceedings of EUC*, (pp. 498-503). EUC.

Cho, J., & Haas, Z. J. (2003). Throughput enhancement by multi-hop relaying in cellular radio networks with non-uniform traffic distribution. In *Proceedings of IEEE Vehicular Technology Conference*, (pp. 3065-3069). IEEE.

Dehnie, S., Guan, K., Gharai, L., & Ghanadan, R. (2009). Kumar, S. Reliable data fusion in wireless sensor networks: A dynamic Bayesian game approach. In *Proceedings of IEEE Military Communications Conference 2009*. IEEE.

Dirani, M., & Chahed, T. (2006). Framework for Resource Allocation in Heterogeneous Wireless Networks Using Game Theory. In *Proceedings of EuroNGI Workshop*, (pp. 144-154). EuroNGI.

Elias, J., & Martignon, F. (2010). Joint QoS Routing and Dynamic Capacity Dimensioning with Elastic Traffic: A Game Theoretical Perspective. In *Proceedings of IEEE International Conference on Communications*. IEEE.

Etkin, R., Parekh, A., & Tse, D. (2007). Spectrum sharing for unlicensed bands. *IEEE Journal on Selected Areas in Communications, 25*(3), 517–528. doi:10.1109/JSAC.2007.070402

Feng, N., Mau, S. C., & Mandayam, N. B. (2004). Pricing and power control for joint network-centric and user-centric radio resource management. *IEEE Transactions on Communications, 52*(9), 1547–1557. doi:10.1109/TCOMM.2004.833191

Gelabert, X., Sallent, O., Pérez-Romero, J., & Agustí, R. (2010). Spectrum sharing in cognitive radio networks with imperfect sensing: A discrete-time Markov model. *Computer Networks, 54*(14), 2519–2536. doi:10.1016/j.comnet.2010.04.005

Han, Z., Zheng, R., & Poor, H. V. (2011). Repeated Auctions with Bayesian Nonparametric Learning for Spectrum Access in Cognitive Radio Networks. *IEEE Transactions on Wireless Communications, 10*(3), 890–900. doi:10.1109/TWC.2011.010411.100838

Heo, J. H., Shin, J. C., Nam, J. H., Lee, Y. T., Park, J. G., & Cho, H. S. (2008). Mathematical Analysis of Secondary User Traffic in Cognitive Radio System. In *Proceedings of IEEE VTC*. IEEE.

Ho, Y. C., Luh, P., & Muralidharan, R. (1981). Information structure, Stackelberg games, and incentive controllability. *IEEE Transactions on Automatic Control, 26*(2), 454–460. doi:10.1109/TAC.1981.1102652

Hou, Y., Wang, Y., & Hu, B. (2010). Research on power control algorithm based on game theory in cognitive radio system. In *Proceedings of International Conference on Signal Processing Systems,* (pp. 614-618). Academic Press.

Ishihara, Y., Huang, R., & Sim, K. M. (2005). Learning opponent's eagerness with Bayesian updating rule in a market-driven negotiation model. In *Proceedings of International Conference on Advanced Information Networking and Applications,* (pp. 903-908). Academic Press.

Jayaweera, S. K., Vazquez-Vilar, G., & Mosquera, C. (2010). Dynamic Spectrum Leasing: A New Paradigm for Spectrum Sharing in Cognitive Radio Networks. *IEEE Transactions on Vehicular Technology, 59*(5), 2328–2339. doi:10.1109/TVT.2010.2042741

Kant, U., & Grosu, D. (2005). Double auction protocols for resource allocation in grids. In *Proceedings of Information Technology Coding and Computing* (pp. 366–371). Academic Press. doi:10.1109/ITCC.2005.135

Kim, S. W. (2010). Game theoretic Multi-Objective Routing Scheme for Wireless Sensor Networks. *Ad Hoc & Sensor Wireless Networks, 10*(4), 343–359.

Kim, S. W. (2012a). Multi-leader multi-follower Stackelberg model for cognitive radio spectrum sharing scheme. *Computer Networks, 56*(17), 3682–3692. doi:10.1016/j.comnet.2012.08.004

Kim, S. W. (2012b). Reversed Stackelberg Bandwidth Sharing Game for Cognitive Multi-hop Cellular Networks. *IET Communications, 6*(17), 2907–2913. doi:10.1049/iet-com.2011.0782

Kim, S. W. (2012c). Trust-Based Bargaining Game Model for Cognitive Radio Spectrum Sharing Scheme. *IEICE Transactions, E95-B*(12), 3925-3928.

Kim, S. W. (2012d). Biform game based cognitive radio scheme for smart grid communications. *Journal of Communications and Networks, 14*(6), 614–618. doi:10.1109/JCN.2012.00027

Kim, S. W. (2013a). Cognitive Radio Bandwidth Sharing Scheme Based on the Two-way Matching Game. *Wireless Personal Communications, 68*(4), 893–905. doi:10.1007/s11277-011-0488-z

Kim, S. W. (2013b). A Repeated Bayesian Auction Game for Cognitive Radio Spectrum Sharing Scheme. *Computer Communications, 36*(8), 939–946. doi:10.1016/j.comcom.2013.02.003

Kim, S. W., & Varshney, P. K. (2005). An Adaptive Bandwidth Allocation Algorithm for QoS guaranteed Multimedia Networks. *Computer Communications, 28*(17), 1959–1969. doi:10.1016/j.comcom.2005.02.011

Kimbrough, S., & Kuo, A. (2010). On heuristics for two-sided matching: revisiting the stable marriage problem as a multiobjective problem. In *Proceedings of the 12th annual conference on Genetic and evolutionary computation*, (pp. 1283-1290). Academic Press.

Krishnamurthy, V. (2008). Decentralized Activation in Dense Sensor Networks via Global Games. *IEEE Transactions on Signal Processing, 56*(10), 4936–4950. doi:10.1109/TSP.2008.926978

Krishnamurthy, V. (2009). Decentralized Spectrum Access Amongst Cognitive Radios - An Interacting Multivariate Global Game-Theoretic Approach. *IEEE Transactions on Signal Processing, 57*(10), 3999–4013. doi:10.1109/TSP.2009.2022860

Krishnamurthy, V. (2010). Decentralized spectrum access via multivariate global games. In *Proceedings of International Workshop on Cognitive Information Processing,* (pp. 464-469). Academic Press.

Le, L., & Hossain, E. (2007). Multihop Cellular Networks: Potential Gains, Research Challenges, and a Resource Allocation Framework. *IEEE Communications Magazine, 45*(9), 66–73. doi:10.1109/MCOM.2007.4342859

Li, D., Xu, Y., Liu, J., Wang, X., & Han, Z. (2010). A Market Game for Dynamic Multi-Band Sharing in Cognitive Radio Networks. In *Proceedings of IEEE International Conference on Communications*. IEEE.

Li, Y., Wang, X., & Guizani, M. (2009). Resource Pricing with Primary Service Guarantees in Cognitive Radio Networks: A Stackelberg Game Approach. In *Proceedings of IEEE Global Telecommunications Conference*. IEEE.

Liu, J., Shen, L., Song, T., & Wang, X. (2009). Demand-matching spectrum sharing game for non-cooperative cognitive radio network. In *Proceedings of International Conference on Wireless Communications & Signal Processing*. Academic Press.

Liu, Y., Peng, Q. C., Shao, H. Z., Chen, X. F., & Wang, L. (2010). Power control algorithm based on game theory in cognitive radio networks. In *Proceedings of International Conference on Apperceiving Computing and Intelligence Analysis,* (pp. 164-168). Academic Press.

Ma, M., & Tsang, D. H. K. (2009). Joint design of spectrum sharing and routing with channel heterogeneity in cognitive radio networks. *Physical Communication, 2*(1), 127–137. doi:10.1016/j.phycom.2009.02.007

Malanchini, I., Cesana, M., & Gatti, N. (2009). On Spectrum Selection Games in Cognitive Radio Networks. In *Proceedings of IEEE GLOBECOM*. IEEE.

Marden, J., Arslan, G., & Shamma, J. S. (2009). Cooperative Control and Potential Games. *IEEE Transactions on Systems, Man, and Cybernetics*, *39*(6), 1393–1407. doi:10.1109/TSMCB.2009.2017273 PMID:19369160

Matt, P. A., Toni, F., & Dionysiou, D. (2006). The distributed negotiation of egalitarian resource allocations. In *Proceedings of the 1st International Workshop on Computational Social Choice*, (pp. 304-316). Academic Press.

Mehmet, S., & Ramazan, K. (2001). A Comparative Study of Multiobjective Optimization Methods in Structural Design. *Turkish Journal of Engineering and Environmental Sciences*, *25*(2), 69–78.

Menasche, D. S., Figueiredo, D. R., & Silva, E. S. (2005). An evolutionary game-theoretic approach to congestion control. *Performance Evaluation*, *62*(1-4), 295–312. doi:10.1016/j.peva.2005.07.028

Mohammadian, H. S., & Abolhassani, B. (2010). Auction-based spectrum sharing for multiple primary and secondary users in cognitive radio networks. In *Proceedings of IEEE Sarnoff Symposium*. IEEE.

Monderer, D., & Shapley, L. (1996). Fictitious Play Property for Games with Identical Interests. *Journal of Economic Theory*, *1*, 258–265. doi:10.1006/jeth.1996.0014

Mustika, I. W., Yamamoto, K., Murata, H., & Yoshida, S. (2010). Spectrum Sharing with Interference Management for Distributed Cognitive Radio Networks: A Potential Game Approach. In *Proceedings of IEEE Vehicular Technology Conference*. IEEE.

Nie, N., & Comaniciu, C. (2006). Adaptive Channel Allocation Spectrum Etiquette for Cognitive Radio Networks. *Mobile Networks and Applications*, *11*(6), 779–797. doi:10.1007/s11036-006-0049-y

Nie, P., & Zhang, P. (2008). A note on Stackelberg games. In *Proceedings of Chinese Control and Decision Conference*, (pp. 1201-1203). Academic Press.

Niyato, D., & Hossain, E. (2007). Hierarchical Spectrum Sharing in Cognitive Radio: A Microeconomic Approach. In *Proceedings of IEEE WCNC*, (pp. 3822-3826). IEEE.

Niyato, D., & Hossain, E. (2008). Spectrum trading in cognitive radio networks: A market-equilibrium-based approach. *IEEE Wireless Communications*, *15*(6), 71–80. doi:10.1109/MWC.2008.4749750

Pal, R. (2007). Efficient Routing Algorithms for Multi-Channel Dynamic Spectrum Access Networks. In *Proceedings of IEEE International Symposium on New Frontiers in Dynamic Spectrum Access Networks*, (pp. 288-291). IEEE.

Pan, Y., Klir, G. J., & Yuan, B. (1996). Bayesian inference based on fuzzy probabilities. In *Proceedings of IEEE International Conference on Fuzzy Systems*, (pp. 1693–1699). IEEE.

Park, H. G., & Schaar, M. V. D. (2007). Congestion game modeling for brokerage based multimedia resource management. *Packet Video*, 18-25.

Park, H. G., & Schaar, M. V. D. (2007b). Bargaining Strategies for Networked Multimedia Resource Management. *IEEE Transactions on Signal Processing*, 55(7), 3496–3511. doi:10.1109/TSP.2007.893755

Pei, Q., Liang, R., & Li, H. (2011). A Trust Management Model in Centralized Cognitive Radio Networks. In *Proceedings of International Conference on Cyber,* (pp. 491-496). Academic Press.

Qiao, X., & Tan, Z. (2011). Combination of spectrum sensing and allocation in cognitive radio networks based on compressive sampling. In *Proceedings of IEEE GLOBECOM Workshops,* (pp. 565-569). IEEE.

Refaei, M. T., DaSilva, L. A., Eltoweissy, M., & Nadeem, T. (2010). Adaptation of Reputation Management Systems to Dynamic Network Conditions in Ad Hoc Networks. *IEEE Transactions on Computers*, 59(5), 707–719. doi:10.1109/TC.2010.34

Rohokale, V., Kulkarni, N., Prasad, N., & Cornean, H. (2010). Cooperative Opportunistic Large Array Approach for Cognitive Radio Networks. In *Proceedings of International Conference on Communications*, (pp. 513-516). Academic Press.

Sherali, H. D. (1984). A multiple leader Stackelberg model and analysis. *Operations Research*, 32(2), 390–404. doi:10.1287/opre.32.2.390

Song, Q., Zhuang, J., & Zhang, L. (2011). Evolution Game Based Spectrum Allocation in Cognitive Radio Networks. In *Proceedings of Wireless Communications, Networking and Mobile Computing*. Academic Press. doi:10.1109/wicom.2011.6036695

Srivastava, V., Neel, J., Mackenzie, A. B., Menon, R., Dasilva, L. A., & Hicks, J. E. et al. (2005). Using game theory to analyze wireless ad hoc networks. *IEEE Communications Surveys & Tutorials*, 7(4), 46–56. doi:10.1109/COMST.2005.1593279

Suo, D., & Wen, F. (2009). A Reversed Stackelberg Approach to Electronic Commerce Logistics Based on Supernetwork Theory. In *Proceedings of International Symposium on Information Science and Engineering,* (pp. 114-118). Academic Press.

Tembine, H. (2009). Dynamic bargaining solutions for opportunistic spectrum access. In *Proceedings of IFIP Conference on Wireless Days*. Academic Press.

Wang, B., Han, Z., & Liu, K. J. R. (2006). Stackelberg game for distributed resource allocation over multiuser cooperative communication networks. In *Proceedings of IEEE Global Telecommunications Conference*. IEEE.

Wang, B., Liu, K., & Clancy, T. (2010). Evolutionary cooperative spectrum sensing game: how to collaborate? *IEEE Transactions on Communications*, 58(3), 890–900. doi:10.1109/TCOMM.2010.03.090084

Xiao, Y., Bi, G., & Niyato, D. (2010). Distributed optimization for cognitive radio networks using Stackelberg game. In *Proceedings of IEEE International Conference on Communication Systems*, (pp. 77 - 81). IEEE.

Xu, W., & Wang, J. (2010). Double auction based spectrum sharing for wireless operators. In *Proceedings of IEEE International Symposium on Personal Indoor and Mobile Radio Communications,* (pp. 2650-2654). IEEE.

Yang, C., Li, J., & Li, W. (2009). Joint rate and power control based on game theory in cognitive radio networks. In *Proceedings of Fourth International Conference on Communications and Networking*. Academic Press.

Yi, Y., Zhang, J., Zhang, Q., Jiang, T., & Zhang, J. (2010). Cooperative Communication-Aware Spectrum Leasing in Cognitive Radio Networks. In *Proceedings of IEEE Symposium on New Frontiers in Dynamic Spectrum*. IEEE.

Yokoo, M., Sakurai, Y., & Matsubara, S. (2001). Robust double auction protocol against false-name bids. In *Proceedings of International Conference on Distributed Computing Systems*, (pp. 137-145). Academic Press.

Zhang, B., Chen, K., Gou, X., & Cheng, S. (2010). Spectrum leasing via selective cooperation in distributed cognitive radio networks. In *Proceedings of IEEE International Conference on Network Infrastructure and Digital Content*, (pp. 16-20). IEEE.

Zhou, X., Gandhi, S., Suri, S., & Zheng, H. (2008). eBay in the sky: strategy-proof wireless spectrum auctions. In *Proceedings of ACM MobiCom*, (pp. 2-13). ACM.

Zhou, X., & Zheng, H. (2009). TRUST: A General Framework for Truthful Double Spectrum Auctions. In Proceedings of IEEE Infocom, (pp. 999-1007). IEEE.

Zhu, Y., Suo, D., & Gao, Z. (2010). Secure Cooperative Spectrum Trading in Cognitive Radio Networks: A Reversed Stackelberg Approach. In *Proceedings of International Conference on Multimedia Communications*, (pp. 202-205). Academic Press.

Zouridaki, C., Mark, B. L., Hejmo, M., & Thomas, R. K. (2005). A Quantitative Trust Establishment Framework for Reliable Data Packet Delivery in MANETs. In *Proceedings of ACM SASN*. ACM.

KEY TERMS AND DEFINITIONS

Band: A small section of the spectrum of radio communication frequencies, in which channels are usually used or set aside for the same purpose.

Radio Frequency (RF): A rate of oscillation in the range of around 3 kHz to 300 GHz, which corresponds to the frequency of radio waves, and the alternating currents which carry radio signals. RF usually refers to electrical rather than mechanical oscillations; however, mechanical RF systems do exist.

Radio Spectrum: The part of the electromagnetic spectrum corresponding to radio frequencies – that is, frequencies lower than around 300 GHz. Electromagnetic waves in this frequency range, called radio waves, are used for radio communication and various other applications, such as heating.

Spectrum Management: The process of regulating the use of radio frequencies to promote efficient use and gain a net social benefit. The term radio spectrum typically refers to the full frequency range from 3 kHz to 300 GHz that may be used for wireless communication.

Statistical Multiplexing: A type of communication link sharing, very similar to dynamic bandwidth allocation. In statistical multiplexing, a communication channel is divided into an arbitrary number of variable bit-rate digital channels or data streams. The link sharing is adapted to the instantaneous traffic demands of the data streams that are transferred over each channel.

Chapter 14
Economic Approach for Network Management

ABSTRACT

It is not surprising that researchers in network technology are utilizing ideas from the field of economics since it provides the conceptual understanding of underlying constructs such as usage and resource allocation. Proper resource allocation plays a key role in improving network performance. There are two primary approaches to economic resource allocation: quantity limits and pricing. Economic approaches can provide principles in situations and provide valuable guidelines and analysis. A concerted effort is needed from academia, the computer industry, network service providers, and businesses involved in electronic commerce to design new mechanisms for network operations that will be suitable for a new generation network applications. This chapter explores this economic approach for network management.

STACKELBERG GAME BASED PRICE CONTROL (*SGPC*) SCHEME FOR WIRELESS NETWORKS

Recently, game-theoretic approaches for network price problem have attracted much attention. In 2011, S. Kim proposed a new Stackelberg Game based Price Control (*SGPC*) scheme for wireless networks (Kim, 2011). To provide the most desirable network performance, the *SGPC* scheme consists of two different control mechanisms; user-based and operator-based mechanisms. By using the hierarchical interaction strategy, control decisions in each mechanism act cooperatively and collaborate with each other to satisfy conflicting performance criteria. In addition, the developed

dynamic online approach is practical for real network implementation.

Development Motivation

Nowadays, wireless/mobile networking is one of the strongest growth areas of communication technology. In view of the remarkable growth in the number of users, all performance guarantees in wireless networks are conditional on the current bandwidth capacity. However, in spite of the emergence of high network infrastructures, wireless bandwidth is still an extremely valuable and scarce resource. Therefore, efficient bandwidth management is very important for the wireless network performance (Niyato & Hossain, 2006)

DOI: 10.4018/978-1-4666-6050-2.ch014

One of the central issues for bandwidth managements is pricing; it can be used as a viable solution to improve network efficiency. Pricing strategy can have strong influence on the behavior of the users and lead the network system into a desirable state (Feng, Mau, Mandayam, 2004). Therefore, an adaptive pricing algorithm is an effective tool to solve the network control problem. Generally, pricing algorithms can be classified as either user-centric or operator-centric approaches. These two approaches tend to result in qualitatively different network performance. From the viewpoint of users, a personal payoff is a very important factor; traditionally, users act independently and selfishly without considering the existence of other users. Therefore, the user-centric approach tries to maximize the interest of individual users. From the operator's point of view, main interests are total network revenue and collective user-satisfaction. To get the globally desirable network performance, the operator-centric approach attempts to optimize these metrics simultaneously. For the ideal network management, it is necessary to effectively mediate between two different control approaches (Feng, 2004).

In the *SGPC* scheme, the main challenge is to design a price control algorithm to use bandwidth as efficiently as possible. To achieve this design goal, the *SGPC* scheme has developed a control scheme by using the game theory. A game model has some attractive features to understand the behavior of self-regarding applications or independent network users. However, due to some reasons, classical game theory cannot be directly applied to the network price control problem. First, players have very limited information. Therefore, it is usually impossible to delineate all conceivable strategies. Second, it is not easy to assign a payoff value to any given outcome, and also difficult to synchronize the activities of the different players. Third, due to the complexity of network situations, the mathematical modeling and numerical analysis have met with limited success (Wang & Schulzrinne, 2005), (Xiao, Shan, Ren, 2005).

In 1934, H. V. Stackelberg proposed a hierarchical game model based on two kinds of different decision makers; a leader and followers. Decision makers have their own hierarchy level, utility function and strategies; they are forced to act according to their hierarchy level. One higher-level decision-maker, who is referred to as a leader, makes his decisions by considering the possible reactions of followers. Many lower-level decision-makers, who are referred to as followers, react dependently based on the decision of the leader while attempting to maximize their satisfaction (Wang, Han, & Liu, 2006), (Anandalingam, 1988).

While developing a price control scheme, there is a tradeoff between a network operator and users' objectives. To arbitrate this conflicting relationship, the adopted methodology is the Stackelberg game theory. In general, it may be concluded to be a proper method for the best compromise in the presence of conflicting objectives. In a realistic scenario, the network operator has more global network information and users make their reactions based on the network operator's decision. Therefore, in the *SGPC* scheme, the network operator plays the role of the leader and users become followers.

By employing dynamic online and distributed approach, the *SGPC* scheme is a new adaptive online price control scheme based on the Stackelberg model. The *SGPC* scheme consists of two different control mechanisms; operator-based and user-based mechanisms. In the operator-based mechanism, an appropriate performance balance is a critical issue; the network operator adaptively decides the price to optimize diverse performance criteria, simultaneously. In the user-based mechanism, a primary concern is the user's payoff. Therefore, to maximize their expected payoff, price sensitive users dynamically adapt their bandwidth requests in a distributed online manner. The outcome of users' decisions is the input back to the network operator to adjust the current price. By using this dynamic iterative feedback loop, network operator and users can be interacting with one another and make their decisions in a way to reach an effective network equilibrium (Hofbauer & Sigmund, 2003).

Online Management Algorithm in the *SGPC* Scheme

Based on the current price, individual users follow selfish strategies to maximize their expected benefit. According to these decisions, the network operator adjusts the price to globally optimize the various performance metrics. This online interactive approach can provide a satisfactory solution for the network price problem.

User-Based and Operator-Based Mechanisms

The developed user-based mechanism deals with the problem that maximizes the user's utility function. By using the reciprocal relationship between benefit and price, the user's payoff corresponds to the received benefit minus the incurred cost (Wang, 2005). Based on the expected payoff, users can try to find the best actions. Therefore, the utility function of user i (U_i) is defined as follows:

$$U_i\left(x_i\right) = b_i\left(x_i\right) - c(p, x_i), \text{ where } p^{min} \le p \le p^{max} \tag{1}$$

where x_i is the allocated bandwidth and $b_i\left(x_i\right)$ is the received benefit for user i. The p is the denoted price for bandwidth unit (U_{nit}) and $c(p, x_i)$ is the cost function. The network operator decides the p between the pre-defined minimum (p^{min}) and the maximum (p^{max}) price boundaries. Usually, a received benefit typically follows a model of diminishing returns to scale; user's marginal benefit diminishes with increasing bandwidth (Wang, 2005). Based on this consideration, the received benefit can be represented in a general form as $b\left(x\right) = \omega \times logx$ where ω represents the payment a user would spend based on his perceived worth.

In a distributed self-regarding fashion, each individual user is independently interested in the sole goal of maximizing his utility function as follows:

$$\max_{x_i \ge 0} U_i\left(x_i\right) = \max_{x_i \ge 0}\left(\left(w_i \times logx_i\right) - c\left(x_i, p\right)\right) \tag{2}$$

In contrast to the user's interest, the most important criterion for the network operator is a network revenue; it is defined as the sum of payments from all the users (Feng, 2004). Based on the p and the amount of each user's throughput, the network revenue (λ) is given by

$$\lambda = \sum_{i=1}^{N} \lambda_i = \sum_{i=1}^{N}\left(p \times T_i\right) \tag{3}$$

where N is the total number of users and T_i is the received throughput of user i. Therefore, λ_i ($= p \times T_i$) is the payment of user i. The network operator adaptively controls the price (p) to maximize the network revenue. With the network revenue, the collective user-satisfaction (C_s) is another operator's objective (Yang, 1997 & 1997b). It is defined as the total sum of all users' payoffs ($\sum_{i=1}^{N} U_i\left(x_i\right)$), which reflects the total satisfaction degree of network resource usage. In the *SGPC* scheme, the operator-based mechanism is developed to optimize these two different objectives (λ and C_s) simultaneously by dynamically adjusting the price p.

Network Model and Performance Criteria

The *SGPC* scheme is designed based on the elastic-demand network paradigm; according to the current price (p), users can adapt their bandwidth requests. It is relevant in real world situations where the user request may be influenced by the price (Yang, 1997 & 1997b). In response to ω_i, the user i can derive the x_i ($= \omega_i / p$). Therefore, the total amount of the requested bandwidth for all users is defined as

$$\sum_{i=1}^{n} x_i = \frac{\sum_{i=1}^{n} w_i}{p} \tag{4}$$

Figure 1 depicts graphically the elastic-demand paradigm by using demand curve (D) and performance curve (P_S). Usually, the performance curve represents the price strategy. It describes the relationship between the user requests and the service price provided by the network system. Under different pricing strategies, the P_S characterizes how the generalized network price (p) increases with the user request (R). The demand curve shows the aggregated request of users, which is associated with any given level of the network price. Traditionally, the demand curve can be expected to be monotonically decreasing in the generalized service price while the performance curve is monotonically increasing in user requests (Yang, 1997 & 1997b). Under the fixed network capacity, the developed demand-performance network model is defined to describe the interactions between user requests and the generalized service price. By combining demand and performance curves, the equilibrium point can be determined for efficient network managements.

When the price is low, more users are attracted to participate network services due to the good satisfactory payoff. When the price is high, user requests are reduced due to the unsatisfactory payoff. In Figure 1, let assume that the P_S_1 and D_1 curves are selected for the current network operation. When the current price is P_1 (or P_2), the associated request amount is $X1$ (or $X2$). In order to toward the network equilibrium point (E_{0*}), the current price should increase (or decrease) by Δp_1 (or Δp_2). Under the network equilibrium state, the collective user-satisfaction (C_s) can be maximized. Therefore, the operator tries to reach the equilibrium point by adjusting the price. To maximize the C_s, a mathematical programming

Figure 1. Demand and performance curves in the elastic-demand model

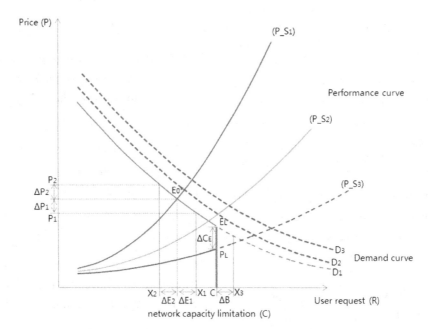

formulation can be described as follows (Yang, 1997 & 1997b).

$$\max_{i,k}(\int_0^{TR} D_i\left(R\right) dR - \int_0^{TR} P\_S_k\left(R\right) dR) \quad \text{s.t.}$$

$$\sum_j x_j = TR \tag{5}$$

where x_j is the requested bandwidth of user j and TR is the total amount of all users' requested bandwidths. In Figure 1, the solution of Eq. (5) can be viewed pictorially as a maximization of the area between curves; the area under the P_S curve minus the area under the D curve.

If the total amount of requests is $X3$, the available bandwidth is not enough to support all user requests; network congestion occurs. The over requests (Δ_B) should be rejected to meet the network capacity constraint (C). In the real world, the segment Δ_B represents a request blocking quantity. In the *SGPC* scheme, to deal with the network congestion problem, extra charge is used to match the capacity constraint. By substituting the over-requests (Δ_B) with an equivalent extra charge (ΔC_E), the potential demand can be reduced. Finally, the demand-supply balance is obtained.

Multi-Objective Optimization Process

Generally, control problems involve several objectives are conflicting in nature (Mehmet & Ramazan, 2001). As mentioned earlier, the network operator has two different objectives; network revenue (λ) and collective user-satisfaction (C_s). Obviously, there is a relevant tradeoff. Therefore, the network operator should find the most desirable duo-objective solution for this multi-criteria problem.

Usually, feasible solutions for multi-objective problems are most likely to have a continuous Pareto front (Mehmet, 2001). The *SGPC* scheme divides the possible Pareto front into a number of intervals depending of the number of solutions as

outcome. At each interval, λ and C_s values are normalized and a scalar solution is estimated. Eventually, among the available solutions, the most preferred solution is selected. The main steps are as follows. First, without considering the λ value, the *SGPC* scheme optimizes the C_s value; the price (P_{Mc}) for Eq. (5) is obtained. Second, without considering the C_s, the *SGPC* scheme optimizes the λ value; the price (P_{Mr}), which is to maximize the Eq. (2), is obtained. Third, the feasible price solution range ($|P_{M\_1} - P_{M\_2}|$) is divided into N intervals. At each interval point ($PT_{interval}$), the normalized values of the C_s and λ ($\overline{C\_S}$ and $\overline{N\_R}$) are calculated as follows

$$\overline{C\_S_i} = \frac{C\_S_{\Delta i}}{P_{Mc}} \text{ and } \overline{N\_R_i} = \frac{N\_R_{\Delta i}}{P_{Mr}} \tag{6}$$

where $C\_S_{\Delta i}$, $N\_R_{\Delta i}$ are the C_s and λ values at the ith $PT_{interval}$, respectively. Fourth, a scalar solution, a weighted average (WA_i) of $\overline{N\_R_i}$ and $\overline{C\_S_i}$, is obtained as follows:

$$WA_i = [\ \alpha \times \overline{N\_R_i}\ ] + [(1-\alpha) \times \overline{C\_S_i}\ ] \tag{7}$$

where α is a control parameter between two different objectives. After nth calculations, the n-element weighted average solution set can be obtained. Finally, the maximum weighted average is selected and the price for that interval point is taken as the most proper price to get the duo-objective network performance.

The parameter α controls the relative weights given to the C_s and λ objectives. Under dynamic network environments, a fixed value of α cannot effectively adapt to the changing conditions. Therefore, the *SGPC* scheme dynamically modifies the value of α by considering the current conditions. When the current network load is light, the network has sufficient bandwidth to support all service requests. In this case, the *SGPC* scheme can put more emphasis on the C_s, i.e., on $\overline{C\_S}$ value; a lower value of α is more suitable. When the current network load is heavy, the λ, i.e., on $\overline{N\_R}$ value is strongly considered as a primary factor. In this case, a higher value of α is more suitable. Based on the dynamic online manner, the α value is determined by the ratio of the amount of currently allocated bandwidth to the total bandwidth amount in the system. This online approach can make the system more responsive to the current network situation.

Bi-Level Interactive Game Model in the *SGPC* Scheme

The *SGPC* scheme is designed as a bi-level Stackelberg model. As a leader, the network operator adaptively decides the price (p) to get an attractive tradeoff between λ and C_s. By adjusting the p, the operator can translate the selfish motives of users into socially desirable actions. As followers, users attempt to maximize their utility function in a distributed online fashion. Users' decisions are applied as the input to the operator's price adjustment procedure. Therefore, control decisions are coupled with each other in a hierarchical interaction relationship. The network price depends not only on the operator's decision but also on the response actions of the follower. This feedback-based iterative process continues until a satisfactory solution is obtained.

Traditional game models have only focused on investigating *which* decisions are made or *what* decisions should be made (Menasche, Figueiredo, & Silva, 2005). However, the developed game model investigates *how* decisions are made in a distributed manner. Therefore, the developed control algorithm is formulated as a hierarchical repeated game model based on the real-time online approach. During the step-by-step iteration, a fair-balanced solution can be obtained. The main steps of the *SGPC* scheme are given next.

Step 1: At the initial iteration, all players start with the initial price (p^{init}) and same utility function. This starting guess guarantees that players enjoy the same benefit at the beginning of the game.

Step 2: Users try to optimize their payoff according to the utility function (2). These decisions are the input to the network operator.

Step 3: According to (3),(5),(6) and (7), the network operator adjust the p for pursuing a desirable duo-objective solution; the new price is announced to users.

Step 4: By using the currently announced price, users re-estimate their expected payoff and dynamically adapt their bandwidth requests.

Step 5: By using this iterative feedback loop, the online control procedure continues until network system reaches to an efficient equilibrium state.

Step 6: If the change of price is within a pre-defined bound (ε), this change is negligible; proceed to Termination step. Otherwise, proceed to Step 2 for the next iteration.

Termination: Game is over. Ultimately, the *SGPC* scheme finds the best compromise solution under widely diverse network environments.

Recently, several price control schemes for wireless networks have been presented. The *Pricing and Power Control for Bandwidth* (*PPCB*) scheme allocates bandwidth between conflicting users and network provider as a non-cooperative game model (Feng, 2004). It is shown that the proposed strategy in the *PPCB* scheme results in a unique Nash equilibrium, and there exists a unique bandwidth price that maximized the revenue of the network. The *Real-time Incentive Compatible Adaptation* (*RICA*) scheme dynamically decides the price based on a reasonable user utility function (Wang, 2005). Users adapt their sending rates and QoS requests in response to changes in service prices. Therefore, it can achieve significant gains in network availability, revenue, and user-perceived benefit. The simulation results shown in Figure 2

Figure 2. Performance evaluations of the SGPC scheme

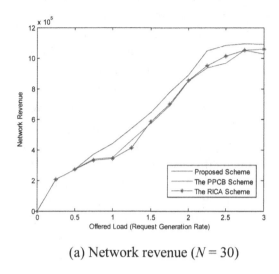

(a) Network revenue ($N = 30$)　　　　　　(b) C_s under different network load

demonstrate that the performance comparison of the *SGPC* scheme with the *PPCB* scheme and the *RICA* scheme. The simulation results demonstrate that the proposed *SGPC* scheme generally exhibits superior performance compared with the other existing schemes under widely different network situations.

Summary

In wireless network managements, price control strategy is one of the most fundamental problems. The *SGPC* scheme is an adaptive online price control scheme based on the bi-level Stackelberg game model. Usually, there is a tradeoff between a network operator and users' viewpoints. Users independently try to maximize individual payoffs. In contrast to the user's interest, the main concern for the network operator is to optimize network revenue and collective user-satisfaction, simultaneously. The design goal of the *SGPC* scheme is to drive the network system to an appropriate performance balance. By using the hierarchical interactive process, the developed game model in the *SGPC* scheme can adaptively decide the price while ensuring relevant balance among different objectives. In addition, the developed adaptive online approach can provide the adaptability and feasibility for practical implementation.

MARKET SHARING GAME BASED BANDWIDTH MANAGEMENT (*MSGBM*) SCHEME FOR WIRELESS NETWORKS

Nowadays, wireless networks have expanded significantly and being used by an increasing number of users to access multimedia information. However, wireless bandwidth is an extremely valuable and scarce resource. Therefore, efficient bandwidth management is a key factor in order to provide high-quality services to users in multimedia wireless/mobile networks. Recently, S. Kim proposed a new Market Sharing Game based Bandwidth Management (*MSGBM*) scheme that describes the interaction between several network access providers and their users. Competition among the access providers is formulated as the market sharing game based on the Bayesian inference and Nash bargaining approach. For the efficient bandwidth management, the *MSGBM* scheme is dynamic and flexible that can adaptively respond to current network conditions.

Development Motivation

Traffic service in wide area wireless networks is growing exponentially due to the increased users and new applications such as sports replays, news headlines, music videos, and movie trailers, etc. Therefore, there are many efforts underway to provide data services on wireless access networks. However, wireless bandwidth is a naturally limited and scarce resource. With the limited network capacity, next-generation wireless networks are expected to support multimedia services. Different multimedia services have different quality-of-service (QoS) requirements. Especially, QoS guarantee is very important issue for real-time multimedia applications. Therefore, efficient bandwidth management plays a critical role in determining network performance while ensuring different QoS requirements (Baslam, El-Azouzi, Sabir, & Echabbi, 2011), (Hosein, 2010).

Recently, there has been much debate about the effective management of wireless bandwidth that would support multiple types of services. Key issue of this debate is the technology that is employed to provide the tradeoff between costs and benefits. Pricing strategy can be used as a viable solution to that tradeoff. It can have strong influence on the behavior of the users and lead the network system into a desirable state. Based on the price of all access providers, users dynamically select the most adaptable access provider. To implement this mechanism, it faces some essential challenges; how to decide the price of bandwidth for each service provider and how to share the end users. However, it is really hard to give a blanket answer to these kinds of questions.

Wireless network systems involve a number of interacting intelligent agents, i.e., service providers and users. Each agent makes behavioral choices

in the context of a dynamic environment that is formed by the collective actions. To understand the behavior of self-regarding agents, game theory has some attractive features. In 1950, John Nash introduced the fundamental notion of the Nash Bargaining Solution (NBS) to allocate the resource fairly and optimally (Waslander, Inalhan, & Tomlin, 2004). The NBS is an effective tool to achieve a mutually desirable solution with a good balance between efficiency and fairness. Classical game theory makes the assumption that game players are perfectly rational. However, this supposition is too strong to implement in the real world game player. Therefore, for the practical game operation, players should be modeled with bounded rationality; bounded rational players have limits in their abilities to make their decisions. In 1967, John Harsanyi introduced the Bayesian inference game model, which is a control framework of strategic behaviors under incomplete information (Dehnie, Guan, Gharai, & Ghanadan, 2009), (Ishihara, Huang, & Sim, 2005). This feasible approach can be used to predict the outcome of the uncertainty.

Motivated by the facts presented in the above discussion, the *MSGBM* scheme develops new bandwidth management algorithms for wireless network operations. In the *MSGBM* scheme, several access providers serve a set of users and users pay the price per bandwidth unit to the corresponding AP access. This interaction mechanism among independent access providers and users is modeled as the market sharing game. To maximize the total network performance, the wireless bandwidth should be allocated appropriately to multiple access providers. For the implementation of bandwidth allocation algorithm, the basic concept of NBS is applied for the bandwidth allocation among APs. To select the most adaptable access provider, users estimate each provider's trust level by using the Bayesian inference. Under incomplete information situations, Bayesian inference can be used to make a logical, quantitative decision.

The *MSGBM* scheme considers the scenario where several access providers share a user market while maximizing the total network performance. The important feature of the *MSGBM* scheme is an ability to maintain bandwidth efficiency as high as possible by adaptively responding to current network system situations. In addition, the *MSGBM* scheme can provide a good tradeoff between the implementation complexity for the network management and optimized network performance. Under widely different and diversified wireless network situations, it is a practical and suitable approach in the real world wireless network operation.

Related Work

Recently, several bandwidth management schemes have been presented for wireless network systems. The *Market Share with Access Provider* (*MSAP*) scheme is a non-cooperative market share game, which is a competitive game model to describe the user interaction (Xiao, Zame, & Schaar, 2011). In the *MSAP* scheme, each access provider advertises some benchmark QoS by taking into account the generated demand, and determines the best price to maximize its own revenue. In addition, the numerical analysis between several competing access providers is provided. The *QoS based Pricing Control* (*QoSPC*) scheme investigates how pricing can be used to ensure that users continued to receive acceptable performance (Ma, He, & Zhang, 2012). When network capacity became limited, this scheme allows wireless operators to make a profit as much as possible. By considering the trending of the traffic distribution for wireless data, the *QoSPC* scheme also illustrates a suitable pricing algorithm for wireless bandwidth management.

Spectrum Management Algorithms in the *MSGBM* Scheme

The wireless bandwidth is allocated among multiple access providers and each user repeatedly

selects a service provider to achieve their desired objectives. To reach a desirable system performance, the *MSGBM* scheme adopts the NBS and Bayesian inference methodologies to control the bandwidth dynamically.

Network System and Bayesian Inference Model

In a wireless network system, there are Content Providers (CPs) and Access Providers (APs). The CP allocates the available bandwidth to APs and each AP leases the bandwidth among End Users (EUs) who registered that AP. The *MSGBM* scheme formalizes the bandwidth management algorithm abstractly in terms of a competitive market sharing model. In the market sharing model in the *MSGBM* scheme, there are a single CP, n APs ({ AP_1 ,, AP_i ,, AP_n }) and m EUs (i.e., $n \ll m$). Through an AP, multimedia data are serviced to EUs, and each EU dynamically selects an AP to maximize his payoff. For user selections, each AP advertises its service price and promised QoS to EUs (Xiao, 2011). Therefore, the competition among APs takes places in pricing as well as in the QoS they offer.

To select the most adaptable AP, EUs should distinguish between trustworthy and unreliable APs. Therefore, each EU estimates the AP's trust value (T) based on the evaluated AP's behavior. Usually, the concept of trust originally derives from social sciences and defined as the degree of subjective belief about the behaviors of a particular entity (Zouridaki, Mark, Hejmo, & Thomas, 2005). In this work, the T is a random variable taking values on the interval [0,1] and represents a notion of trust level associated with a given AP. The T value should help EUs to identify whether AP will be trustful for performing the packet transmission. If the AP behaves reliably, it does successfully transmit the data packets within the requested time deadline. Therefore, the T value for each AP is calculated based on its success rate and failure rate of packet transmissions (Changiz, Halabian, Yu, Lambadaris, & Tang, 2010).

For the T value calculation, the *MSGBM* scheme uses the Bayesian inference method. It is well-suited for stochastic problems. To model the Bayesian inference, some parameters should be defined. When the EU i monitors the behavior of AP j as an actor, a probability p_i^j is defined to estimate the AP j's faithful behavior; p_i^j represents the packet delivery success rate. Since p_i^j value can be drawn independently from observation, the p_i^j value for next time period is unknown. This uncertainty can be solved by assuming that p_i^j is drawn according to a prior distribution that is updated as new observations become available. As is commonly done (Zouridaki, 2005), (Changiz, 2010), the *MSGBM* scheme uses a Binomial distribution for this prior distribution. With parameters p_i^j and $q_i^j = 1 - p_i^j$, Binomial distribution suitably shows how confidence grows when the number of observations grows. Iteratively, the EU i updates this prior distribution by performing observations, i.e., counting the number of packets entering the AP j and the number of successfully serviced packets by that AP. In the developed model, there are n different APs. Therefore, each EU maintains n different distributions for each AP.

During the tth time period, suppose that the *MSGBM* scheme observes $N_i^{t,j}$ is the total number of packets that have been sent from the EU i to the AP j and let $M_i^{t,j}$ be the number of packets successfully serviced by the AP j. Also assume that the random variable p_i^j is derived from a prior distribution $f_{t-1}(p_i^j)$ (Zouridaki, 2005), (Changiz, 2010). Based on $N_i^{t,j}$, $M_i^{t,j}$ and $f_{t-1}(p_i^j)$, the EU i can derive the posterior distribution of random variable p_i^j via Bayes' rule. From the viewpoint of EU i, the AP j's trust value after the tth iteration ($T_i^j(t)$) is defined as

the expected value of p_i^j with respect to the corresponding distribution function $f_t(p_i^j)$ (Zouridaki, 2005), (Changiz, 2010); it is obtained as the same manner in the *NBGBM* scheme as follows.

$$T_i^j(t) = \frac{\alpha_t}{\alpha_t + \beta_t} \tag{8}$$

Wireless Network Market Sharing Game

The *MSGBM* scheme assumes that each EU dynamically selects a specific AP to maximize his payoff. By using the reciprocal relationship between benefit and price, the EU's payoff corresponds to the received benefit minus the incurred cost (Kim & Varshney, 2005). Based on the expected payoff, EUs can try to find the best actions. Therefore, the utility function (U_i^j) of EU i through AP j is defined as follows

$$U_i^j(x_i) = T_i^j(c) \times b_i(x_i) - c(p_j, x_i) \tag{9}$$

where x_i is the allocated bandwidth for the EU i and $T_i^j(c)$ is the current time trust value for the AP j. p_j is the AP j's price for bandwidth unit (U_{nit}) and $c(p, x_i)$ is the cost function. Usually, a received benefit typically follows a model of diminishing returns to scale; user's marginal benefit diminishes with increasing bandwidth (Kim, 2005). Based on this consideration, the received benefit can be represented in a general form as $b(x) = \omega \times logx$ where ω represents the payment a user would spend based on his perceived worth. In a distributed self-regarding fashion, each individual EU is independently interested in the sole goal of maximizing his utility function as follows.

$$\max_{1 \leq j \leq n} U_i\left(x_i\right) = \max_{1 \leq j \leq n} \left(T_i^j \times \left(w_i \times log x_i\right) - \left(x_i \times p_j\right)\right) \tag{10}$$

In contrast to the EU's interest, the most important criterion for APs is its revenue, which is defined as the sum of payments from the registered EUs. Based on the p_j and the amount of allocated bandwidth, the AP j's revenue (UA_j) is given by

$$UA_j = \sum_{i=1}^{k} \left(p_j \times x_i\right) \tag{11}$$

where k is the total number of EUs registered the AP j and ($p_j \times x_i$) is the payment of the EU i. To maximize its revenue, each AP controls the price (p) adaptively.

When the price of the AP j is low, more users are attracted to participate the AP j due to their good satisfactory payoff. When the price is high, user requests are reduced due to their unsatisfactory payoff. Therefore, by considering this tradeoff, APs adaptively select the most proper price strategy. In the *MSGBM* scheme, the set of price strategies ($\mathbb{S}$) is assumed as below.

$$\mathbb{S} = \left\{ \Pi_{1 \leq j \leq n} p_j \mid p_j \in \left[p_{min}, p_{max}\right] \right\} \tag{12}$$

where n is the number of APs and p_j is the price strategy of AP j. The p_{min}, p_{max} are the predefined minimum and maximum price levels, respectively. Each AP selects a single strategy from $\mathbb{S}$, and estimates the expected payoff through a utility function.

During the network operation, APs learn how to decide their price strategies like as a tournament play where losing strategies are eliminated and winning strategies remain. Therefore, APs have a chance to reconsider the current price strategy

and react to maximize the expected payoff. When an AP chooses a price, it can change the current network environment and triggers reactions by other APs. To maximize their expected payoffs, APs iteratively change their current price strategies and repeatedly interact with other APs. The price level is adjusted at a rate equal to the difference between the payoff of that price strategy and the average payoff of the whole APs. After making further changes among APs, this interaction mechanism gradually leads the network system into a stable state. When no individual AP can improve his payoff by unilaterally changing his strategy, this set of price strategies can be referred to as the price equilibrium (Kim, 2011b), (Altman, El-Azouzi, Hayel, & Tembine, 2008).

To represent the price control problem, let L be a number of possible price levels and x_i is the selection probability for the ith price level (strategy i). $\mathbb{X}$ is the L-dimensional vector ($x_1 \ldots x_i \ldots x_L$) and $\dot{x}_i$ stands for the variation of x_i, which is the changing rate for strategy i. $J(i, k)$ denotes the expected payoff for a AP using strategy i when it encounters a AP with strategy k, and $J(i, \mathbb{X})$ is the payoff for a AP using strategy i when it encounters the rest of other APs whose strategies are distributed in $\mathbb{X}$, which can be expressed like as $\sum_j (J(i,j) \times x_j)$ (Kim, 2011b), (Altman, 2008). Finally, the changing rate of price strategy i is defined as

$$\dot{x}_i = x_i \times \left(J\left(i, \mathbb{X}\right) - \sum_j x_j \times J\left(j, \mathbb{X}\right) \right)$$

$$= x_i \times \left(\sum_j x_j \times J\left(i, j\right) - \sum_j \sum_k x_j \times J\left(j, k\right) \times x_k \right) \tag{13}$$

By using (13), each AP maintains two variables, $J\left(i, \mathbb{X}\right)$ and $\dot{x}_i$, which are the basis for the next price strategy decision (Kim, 2011b), (Altman,

2008). Under all possible network scenarios, APs learn how to perform well by interacting with other APs and dynamically adjust their price levels. Therefore, without any impractical rationality assumptions, APs can modify their price strategies in an effort to maximize their own goals.

In the assumed network system, there is a single CP, which works as a gateway and is responsible for a set of *n* APs. To maximize its revenue, the CP allocates the different amount of bandwidth to each AP. To develop the bandwidth allocation algorithm, the methodology that the *MSGBM* scheme adopt is Nash Bargaining Solution (NBS). Based on the concept of NBS, the wireless bandwidth is shared effectively among multiple APs. Each AP has its own utility function according to (11), which represents the amount of satisfaction of an AP toward the outcome of the bandwidth allocation. Each AP is a member of a team willing to compromise its own objective to gain an effective solution. By employing the NBS approach, the team APs cooperate with each other and make a collective decision (Waslander, 2004). The total payoff (i.e., utility) for *n* APs is given by $TU_{1..n} = \{(UA_1,..,UA_n)\}$. If an agreement among the APs cannot be reached, the payoff that the APs will receive is given by the disagreement point $TU_{1..n}^d = (UA_1^d,...,UA_n^d)$; it represents payoffs when the compromise fails and the bandwidth allocation cannot be made (i.e., zero in the system) (Waslander, 2004). The desirable best solution for an utility vector ($UA_1^*,...,UA_n^*$) is obtained as follows.

$$\left(UA_1^*,...,UA_n^*\right) = \arg\max_{UA_j} \prod_j \left(UA_j - UA_j^d\right)^{\psi_j}, \text{where} \sum_{j=1}^n \psi_j = 1 \tag{14}$$

where ψ_j is the bargaining powers of the AP *j*. Based on the bandwidth efficiency, APs are asymmetric in their bargaining strengths. To maximize the system effectiveness, the higher bandwidth utilization becomes more preferable. Therefore,

the CP invests more bandwidth to the AP with higher bandwidth utilization. Due to this reason, the ψ value is dynamically adjustable according to the bandwidth utilization of corresponding AP. The bargaining power of AP *j* (ψ_j) is defined as follows.

$$\psi_j = \frac{B\_U_j}{\sum_{i=1}^n B\_U_i} \tag{15}$$

where *n* is the number of APs and B_U is the current bandwidth utilization. Based on the AP's revenue, the CP has its own objective. It is defined as the total sum of all APs' payoffs ($\sum_{j=1}^n UA_j$), which reflects the total satisfaction degree of network resource usage.

The Main Steps of the *MSGBM* Scheme

Classical game theory makes the assumption that game players are perfectly rational. In this assumption, each player must have knowledge of all relevant aspects of the environment, and enough computational power to choose the best strategy. However, it is the largely unrealistic assumption about players. Many studies have suggested that game players have very limited informaon and often do not behave in a perfect rational way. Therefore, for the practical game operation, players should be modeled with bounded rationality; bounded rational players have limits in their abilities to make their decisions (Zouridaki, 2005), (Changiz, 2010).

In the *MSGBM* scheme, both NBS and Bayesian inference approaches have been applied to model a market sharing game. During the step-by-step game iteration, game players (i.e., APs and EUs) have a chance to reconsider the current strategy and react to maximize the expected payoff. In general, traditional game models have focused on investigating *which* decisions are made or *what* decisions should be made. However, the *MSGBM* scheme investigates *how* decisions are made for control decision problems. This practical game-based approach is suitable in real world network operations. The main steps of the *MSGBM* scheme are given next.

Step 1: At the initial iteration ($t = 0$), the allocated bandwidth and price strategy selection probability in each AP are equally distributed. This starting guess guarantees that each AP enjoys the same benefit at the beginning of the game.

Step 2: By counting the number of entering and successfully serviced packets, each EU maintains n different distributions for APs. Based on this information, EUs estimates each AP's trust value according to (8).

Step 3: To maximize the payoff, each EU adaptively selects the most adaptable AP by using (10). This decision is made in a distributed manner.

Step 4: Each AP maintains two variables (i.e., $J\left(i, \mathbb{X}\right)$ and $\dot{x}_i$) and selects its price strategy according to the current selection probability.

Step 5: Bargaining power (ψ) is dynamically adjusted by using (15). Based on this information, the CP allocates the different amount of bandwidth to each AP according to (14).

Step 6: By considering the AP's revenue, the CP's objective is estimated as the total sum of all APs' payoffs ($\sum_{i=1}^{n} UA_i$). It is the total satisfaction degree of network resource usage.

Step 7: If all APs do not change their price strategy, game processing is temporarily over. However, constantly, the system is self-monitoring the current network situation.

Step 8: When an AP changes its current price strategy, it re-triggers the market sharing game process; proceeds to Step 2 for the next iteration.

Summary

Currently, game theoretic models have been developed for non-economic problems in telecommunication networks, such as flow, admission, and congestion control. Especially, game theory has been employed in the analysis of resource management in wireless networks. However, how to design the effective bandwidth allocation algorithms for network systems is still an open problem. The *MSGBM* scheme is developed as a new bandwidth management scheme based on market sharing game model. In the *MSGBM* scheme, the combined game theory approach is developed by using the Bayesian inference and Nash bargaining solution. To effectively handle the bandwidth under dynamically changing environments, the *MSGBM* scheme can adaptively respond to current system conditions and makes the system adaptable for the better network performance.

BARGAINING AND FICTITIOUS PLAY BASED BANDWIDTH MANAGEMNET (*BFPBM*) SCHEME FOR WIRELESS NETWORKS

With the Market Sharing Game based Bandwidth Management (*MSGBM*) scheme, S. Kim proposed a new Bargaining and Fictitious Play based Bandwidth Management (*BFPBM*) scheme for wireless networks. By using the fictitious play and Nash bargaining approach, the *BFPBM* scheme effectively formulates the competitive interaction situation between several access providers and their users.

Development Motivation

Classical game theory makes the assumption that game players are perfectly rational. However, this supposition is too strong to implement in the real world game player. For the practical game operation, players should be modeled with bounded rationality; bounded rational players have limits in their abilities to make their decisions (Kim, 2011), (Kim, 2012), (Kim, 2011c). Therefore, with the concept of equilibrium, another important issue in game-theoretic design is to develop learning algorithms that enable the players to reach a certain desired game outcome. To reach an effective solution, learning algorithms should be designed as an iterative process in which each iteration involves three key steps performed by every player; 1) observing the environment and current game state, 2) estimating the prospective utility, and 3) updating the strategy based on the observations (Young, 2005).

In 1951, G. Brown and J. Robinson introduced the fundamental concept of a fictitious play game as a learning algorithm. It is an iterative procedure applied to a finite non-cooperative game in which each of the players is faced with selecting a strategy from a finite set of available strategies. At each iteration of fictitious game, each player chooses a strategy which is a best reply to the other players' strategies, assuming they will be chosen based on the empirical probability distribution induced by the historical frequency of their decisions in all previous iterations. Therefore, fictitious game was designed to mimic the behavior of the players learning each others' strategies (Lambert, Epelman & Smith, 2005). There are many advantages about the fictitious game. First, it is extremely simple. Simplicity makes it easy to analyze and implement. Especially, this feature is useful in games whose normal form has exponential size, as long as best responses can be computed. Second, for large enough game iterations, it is guaranteed to get very close to exact an equilibrium. Third, fictitious game is a natural approach for learning

where the player is actually facing the natural randomness (Conitzer, 2009).

Motivated by the facts presented in the above discussion, the *BFPBM* scheme is developed as a new bandwidth management scheme by using fictitious game model. During wireless network operations, several Access Providers (APs) serve a set of users and users pay the price per bandwidth unit to the corresponding AP access. The *BFPBM* scheme considers the scenario where several access providers share a user market while maximizing the total network performance. The interaction mechanism among independent access providers and users is modeled as the market sharing game. For the implementation of bandwidth allocation algorithm, the basic concept of NBS is applied for the bandwidth allocation among APs. To select the most adaptable access provider, users estimate their payoffs by using the fictitious play game. Under incomplete information situations, fictitious play approach can be used to make a logical, quantitative decision. The important feature of the *BFPBM* scheme is an ability to maintain bandwidth efficiency as high as possible by adaptively responding to current network system situations. In addition, the *BFPBM* scheme can provide a good tradeoff between the implementation complexity for the network management and optimized network performance. Under widely different and diversified wireless network situations, it is a practical and suitable approach in the real world wireless network operation.

Recently, several bandwidth management schemes have been presented for wireless network systems. The *Market Share with Access Provider (MSAP)* scheme in (Xiao, Zame & van der Schaar, 2011) is a non-cooperative market share game, which is a competitive game model to describe the user interaction. In the *MSAP* scheme, each access provider advertises some benchmark QoS by taking into account the generated demand, and determines the best price to maximize its own revenue. In addition, the numerical analysis between several competing access providers is provided.

The *QoS based Pricing Control* (*QoSPC*) scheme (Ma, 2012) investigates how pricing can be used to ensure that users continued to receive acceptable performance. When network capacity became limited, this scheme allows wireless operators to make a profit as much as possible. By considering the trending of the traffic distribution for wireless data, the *QoSPC* scheme also illustrates a suitable pricing algorithm for wireless bandwidth management.

Spectrum Management Algorithms in the *BFPBM* Scheme

In this section, the *BFPBM* scheme is explained in detail. To reach a desirable system performance, the NBS and fictitious play methodologies are adopted to control the bandwidth dynamically.

Price Control Algorithm for APs

In a wireless network system, there are multiple Channel Providers (CPs) and Access Providers (APs). The CP allocates the available bandwidth to APs and each AP leases the bandwidth among End Users (EUs) who registered that AP. In the *BFPBM* scheme, a wireless network system, the utility function of EU i through AP j (UE_i^j), the AP's revenue (UA) and the set of price strategies ($\mathbb{S}$) are assumed as the same as the *MSGBM* scheme. To represent the price control problem, let L be a number of possible price strategies ($L=|\mathbb{S}|$). $p_i(t)$, $\psi_i(t)$ and $UA_i(t)$ are the price strategy, the mixed strategies and the estimated payoff of AP i at the time period t, respectively. In stage game of price control, the AP i selects its price level ($p_i(t)$) according to a probability distribution $\psi_i(t-1)$. The AP i neither knows the other APs' price strategy distribution $\psi_{-i}(t-1)$, but can get the current payoff by selecting its strategy ($p_i(t)$). In the *BFPBM* scheme, the AP i's attain-able payoff with price strategy p_k ($UA_i^k(t)$) is obtained as follows.

$$UA_i^k(t) = \begin{cases} UA_i^k(t-1) + \eta(\hat{\chi}_i^k), & if \ p_k = C_p(t) \\ UA_i^k(t-1), & otherwise \end{cases}$$

(16)

$$s.t., \hat{\chi}_i^k = \frac{UA_i^k(t-1) - \dfrac{1}{(L-1)} \times \sum_{l=1,l\neq k}^{L} UA_i^l(t-1)}{\dfrac{1}{(L-1)} \times \sum_{l=1,l\neq k}^{L} UA_i^l(t-1)}$$

ere $UA_i^{l,l\in\mathbb{S}}(t-1)$ is the observed average payoff of the strategy l. $\eta(\bullet)$ is a risk control function to control the speed of convergence, and $C_p(t)$ is the current (i.e., at the time period t) price strategy. To characterize the interaction manner of each player, the risk control function is concerned with the behavior of decision makers who face a choice. To implement the risk control function, the *BFPBM* scheme choses to use the constant absolute risk utility function of the expected utility theory (Byde, 2003). It is a well-known and effective method to solve a risk control problem. By applying this theory, players can be broadly classified as either *risk-averse* or *risk-seeking* players. The risk preference of a player is determined by assuming function's twice-differentiability ($\eta''(x)$). If $\eta''(x) < 0$ (*or* $\eta''(x) > 0$), a player is known as a *risk-averse* (*or* a *risk-seeking*) player (Byde, 2003). In the *BFPBM* scheme, for the adaptive convergence to a stable network equilibrium, the risk control function for player i ($\eta(\hat{\chi}_i^k)$) is defined as follows.

$$\eta(\hat{\chi}_i) = \frac{1}{\alpha}(e^{\alpha \times \hat{\chi}_i^k} - 1),$$

$$where \begin{cases} \alpha = -1, & if \ \hat{\chi}_i^k > 0 \\ \alpha = 1, & otherwise \end{cases}$$

(17)

When a player currently has the higher payoff than the average payoff of all strategies (i.e., $\hat{\chi}_i > 0$), he is most likely to be a *risk-averse* player; α is set to -1. Otherwise, a player will tend to be a *risk-seeking* player; α is set to 1. Under all possible network scenarios, players can dynamically decide the α value based on this online fine-grained approach and learn how to perform well by interacting with other players without any impractical rationality assumptions.

Based on the non-cooperative game model, each AP chooses a price strategy to maximize the payoff. In the *BFPBM* scheme, APs stochastically select the available strategies ($\mathbb{S}$). This idea was originally introduced to allow convergence of strategies to a mixed strategy Nash equilibrium. To implement this approach, smooth best response method is adopted; it is a proportionally probabilistic decision rule while mapping payoffs through a probabilistic choice function to a mixed strategy (Fudenberg & Levine, 1998), (Anderson, de Palma & Thisse, 1992), (Long, Zhang, Li, Yang & Guan, 2007). Therefore, a strategy of higher payoff is chosen with greater probability, and the strategy of player is uniquely determined in all cases. Using smoothed best response with fictitious play can result in players learning to play mixed strategy Nash equilibria (Fudenberg, 1998). There are some probabilistic choice functions that represent smoothed best response functions. In the *BFPBM* scheme, the fundamental idea of multinomial logit choice is adopted to predict the selection probabilities of the different possible strategies. It is known in statistical mechanics as the Boltzmann distribution, and used in typical specifications of smooth best response (Anderson, 1992). According to the stochastic fictitious game, the probability distribution vector over AP i's price strategies (ψ_i) is obtained like as

$$\psi_i^k(t+1) = \frac{\exp\left((1/\lambda) \times UA_i^k(t)\right)}{\sum_{k \in \mathbb{S}} \exp\left((1/\lambda) \times UA_i^k(t)\right)}, \text{ s.t., } \psi_i^{k,k \in \mathbb{S}} \in \psi_i$$

(18)

where λ is a control parameter. Strategies are chosen in proportion to their payoffs, but their relative probability is adjusted by λ. Value of λ close to zero allows very little randomization. It means that strategy is simply selected to maximize the payoff. Large value of λ results in complete randomization. It produces a uniform distribution across strategies, which results in the state of the system following a random selection. Metaphorically, the λ value is the current 'temperature' of the annealing process. At the beginning of the annealing algorithm run, the initialization temperature is high enough so that possibility of accepting any decision changes whether it improves the solution or not. While time is ticking away, the λ value decreases according to a cooling schedule. In the *BFPBM* scheme, the time-axis is partitioned into equal intervals of length *unit_time* to adjust the λ value; every *unit_time*, the λ value sequentially decreases. In a distributed manner, each AP periodically re-evaluates the current strategy and iteratively updates its own the probability distribution ($\psi_{i,1 \leq i \leq n}$).

AP Selection for EUs and Bandwidth Allocation among APs

To represent the AP selection problem, let $S_i(t)$, $\phi_i(t)$ and $UE_i(t)$ be the selection strategy, the mixed strategies and the estimated payoff of EU i at the time period t, respectively. In stage game of price control, the EU i selects its AP according to a probability distribution $\phi_i(t-1)$, and gets the payoff by selecting its strategy ($S_i(t)$). In the *BFPBM* scheme, the EU i's attainable payoff with selected jth AP ($UE_i^j(t)$) is obtained as follows.

$$UE_i^j(t) = \begin{cases} UE_i^j(t-1) + \eta\left(\hat{\nu}_i^j\right), & \text{if } S_i = j^{th} \text{ AP} \\ UE_i^j(t-1), & \text{otherwise} \end{cases}$$

(19)

$$\text{s.t., } \hat{v}_i^j = \frac{UE_i^j\left(t-1\right) - \dfrac{1}{\left(n-1\right)} \times \sum_{h=1, h \neq j}^{n} UE_i^h\left(t-1\right)}{\dfrac{1}{\left(n-1\right)} \times \sum_{h=1, h \neq j}^{n} UE_i^h\left(t-1\right)}$$

where n is the number of APs and $UE_i^{j, 1 \leq j \leq n}\left(t-1\right)$ is the observed average payoff from the jth AP. $\eta\left(\bullet\right)$ is the same risk control function in (17). Each EU also stochastically selects an AP to maximize his payoff. The probability distribution vector over EU i's selection strategies (ϕ_i) is obtained in the same manner based on (18). Therefore, EUs also learn how to perform well by interacting with other EUs and dynamically adjust their selections.

In the develop price control and AP selection algorithms, APs and EUs only observe their personal payoffs received at each stage and make decisions in a distributed manner. At each stage, their decisions are self-incentive with myopic best response correspondence. In particular, the *BFPBM* scheme does not need any information exchange or to observe other agents' private information to reduce the information tracking burden. This approach can avoid the complex mechanism implementations incurred by information exchange or observation; it is suitable in real world network operations.

In the *BFPBM* scheme, there is a single CP, which works as a gateway and is responsible for a set of n APs. To maximize its revenue, the CP allocates the different amount of bandwidth to each AP. To develop the bandwidth allocation algorithm, the methodology that the *BFPBM* scheme adopts is Nash Bargaining Solution (NBS). Bandwidth allocation algorithm among APs is developed as the same as the *MSGBM* scheme.

The Main Steps of the *BFPBM* Scheme

Under dynamically changing network environments, the traditional optimal approach is not applicable; the current optimal solution may not be an optimum result in the future. Therefore, control decisions should be made dynamically to effectively approximate an optimal network performance. The *BFPBM* scheme develops a new market sharing game model based on the NBS and fictitious play approach. During the step-by-step game iteration, players (i.e., EUs and APs) have a chance to reconsider the current strategy and react to maximize the expected payoff. Therefore, after selecting strategies, they repeatedly interact with other, and iteratively change their next strategies in a distributed way. This interactive feedback mechanism gradually leads the network system into a stable state. In addition, this distributed learning approach can drastically reduce the computational complexity and control overhead. It is a good point for practical implementations. The main steps of the *BFPBM* scheme are given next.

Step 1: At the initial iteration ($t = 0$), the allocated bandwidth and strategy selection probabilities in each AP and EU are equally distributed. This starting guess guarantees that each AP and EU enjoys the same benefit at the beginning of the game.

Step 2: Each AP and EU obtains the currently estimated payoffs according to (16) and (19) at each *unit_time*. At the same time, the λ value decreases in steps equal to $\Delta \lambda$ (the minimum value of λ is 0.2.). This information is the basis for the next strategy decision.

Step 3: Based on the received payoffs, each EU maintains n different distributions for APs by using (18). Each AP maintains L different distributions for price strategies at the same manner.

Step 4: To maximize the payoff, each EU and AP adaptively selects the most adaptable strategies. This decision is made in a distributed manner.

Step 5: Bargaining power (ξ) for each AP is dynamically adjusted by using (15). Based on this information, the CP allocates the different amount of bandwidth to each AP according to (14).

Step 6: By considering the AP's revenue, the CP's objective is estimated as the total sum of all APs' payoffs ($\sum_{i=1}^{n} UA_i$). It is the total satisfaction degree of network resource usage.

Step 7: If all APs and EUs do not change their strategy, it can converge to a subset of the mixed strategy Nash equilibria; game processing is temporarily over. However, constantly, the system is self-monitoring the current network situation.

Step 8: When an AP or EU changes its current strategy, it re-triggers the market sharing game process; proceeds to Step 2 for the next iteration.

Summary

Currently, game theoretic models have been developed for non-economic problems in telecommunication networks, such as flow, admission, and congestion control. Especially, game theory has been employed in the analysis of resource management in wireless networks. However, how to design the effective bandwidth allocation algorithms for network systems is still an open problem. The *BFPBM* scheme presents a new bandwidth management algorithm based on market sharing game model. The developed combined game theory approach is developed by using the fictitious play and Nash bargaining solution to avoid the largely unrealistic assumption of traditional game theory. In the *BFPBM* scheme, EU and APs iteratively observe their own information

and repeatedly change their current strategies to effectively handle the bandwidth under dynamically changing environments. This approach can adaptively respond to current system conditions and makes the system adaptable for the better network performance.

PUBLIC GOODS GAME BASED FILE SHARING (*PGGFS*) SCHEME FOR P2P NETWORKS

In recent years, Peer-to-Peer (P2P) network systems have been widely used in the Internet. Particularly, P2P file sharing mechanism has emerged popularity and attract millions of users. However, to create an efficient P2P system, users should share their resources among a group of other users. To satisfy this objective, S. Kim proposed a new Public Goods Game based File Sharing (*PGGFS*) scheme for P2P Networks. By adopting an interactive self-learning mechanism, the *PGGFS* scheme gradually leads the P2P system into an efficient network equilibrium. In a distributed manner, this approach is a practical and suitable method in real world P2P network operations.

Development Motivation

Recently, Peer-to-Peer (P2P) networking technology has caught a huge number of users to improve the end-to-end performance in network infrastructure. It does not use client/server paradigm but is a self-organizing, distributed resource-sharing network. Usually, P2P networks can be used for sharing contents such as audio, video, data, or anything in digital format files. Therefore, P2P networks can be thought as common goods in that they rely on voluntary provision of resources from individual participants to support the public service (Wang, Nakao and Ma, 2010), (Sun, Cheng, Lin, & Wang, 2006).

In P2P file sharing networks, all of the users, which are called peers, can download files from the other peers. Unfortunately, sharing files with others comes at a cost. By using energy, bandwidth, CPU, and other resources, peers can share their files. Therefore, there exists social dilemma in P2P resource provision. Since defectors outperform cooperators, many peers in P2P networks are intuitively reluctant to share files and would prefer to 'free-ride' without contributing anything (Wang, 2010). It is the well-known phenomenon 'Tragedy of the Commons' (Sun, 2006). To avoid the *Tragedy of the Commons* in P2P networks, incentive mechanism plays a crucial role to encourage cooperation among selfish peers. In recent years, lots of incentive mechanisms have been actively studied, and confirmed that cooperation could be sustained with direct or indirect reciprocity under suitable conditions (Xu & Fan, 2010). However, few attentions have been paid on the effects of trust on cooperation.

Game theory is a field of applied mathematics that provides an effective tool in modeling the interactions among independent decision makers. It can describe the possibility to react to the actions of the other decision makers and analyze the situations of conflict and cooperation. Traditionally, many applications of the game theory are related to economics. Nowadays, game theory becomes a sort of unified field theory for the rational side of social science, where 'social' is interpreted broadly, to include human as well as non-human players such as computers, animals and plants. Therefore, game theory can be a powerful tool to model the peer's behavior of in P2P file sharing networks.

In 1954, P. A. Samuelson proposed a fundamental concept of Public Goods (PG) game (Samuelson, 1954). It is one of the core economic game models and has challenged societies throughout the changing times. As a generalization of the prisoner's dilemma, PG game has become a classic paradigm for studying collective dilemma and describing competitive interactions (Xu & Fan,

2010), (Zhong, Chen, & Huang, 2008). In P2P networks, files can be regarded as public goods. Thus, the problem of file sharing can also be transformed as the modeling of PG game (Sun, 2006). Despite predictions of complete free riding in the traditional public good games, repeated interaction allows for any level of public provision, so long as it is feasible and Pareto superior to no provision at all. Therefore, the model of privately provided public goods within a repeated-game setting shows that it is possible to maintain cooperation (Samuelson, 1954), (Zhong, 2008).

Motivated by the above discussion, the *PG-GFS* scheme was developed as a new P2P file sharing scheme based on the repeated PG game model. To escape the social dilemma, the *PGGFS* scheme pays serious attention to trust evaluation, repeated interactions and iterative self-learning techniques. In the *PGGFS* scheme, such techniques have been incorporated into the original PG game, and trust-based P2P mechanism is developed to induce all peers to share files as many as possible (Zhong, 2008).

Related Work

Recently, several P2P file sharing schemes have been presented. The *Incentives File Sharing (IFS)* scheme in (Mawji & Hassanein, 2009) is an incentive algorithm for P2P mechanism. In *IFS* scheme, peers cooperate with one another based on their remaining energy, and the reputation of peer. Each peer has a reputation index which is based on how many times it has cooperated in the past, and agreeing to upload a file counts significantly toward the reputation. The *Credit based File Sharing (CFS)* scheme in (Li, Zuo, He, & Lu, 2008) proposes a credit mechanism based on automatic audit, which captures malicious behaviors through automatic detection in P2P network. In the *CFS* scheme, peers can detect malicious acts spontaneously and can resist free-riding effectively. All the earlier work has attracted a lot of attention and introduced unique challenges to efficiently solve the social dilemma in P2P networks. Compared to these schemes (Mawji, 2009), (Li, 2008), the *PGGFS* scheme attains better performance for P2P networks.

The Basic Concept of Public Goods Game

After introducing the basic concept of PG game, several public goods game models (e.g., iterative PG game, open PG game and PG game with punishment or reward) have been introduced (U & Li, 2010), (Isaac, Walker, & Williams, 1994). Usually, PG games can be thought as a natural extension of the prisoner's dilemma to an arbitrary number of players. In the original PG game, the players in a competition group are randomly chosen from the whole population and the benefits of the struggle are allocated equally among all the participants irrespective of their contributions (Zhong, 2008). This approach leads to the disappearance of cooperators in the population and defection becomes the dominating strategy. In this sense, the rational equilibrium solution prescribed to '*homo oeconomicus*' leads to economic stalemate. PG games are abundant in human and animal societies, and can be seen as basic examples of economic interactions (Hauert, De Monte, Hofbauer, & Sigmund, 2002).

Let consider a large population of players (N). Players can either contribute some fixed amount (c) or nothing at all. The return of the public good, i.e. the payoff to the players in the group, depends on the abundance of cooperators. If n_c denotes their number among the public goods players, the net payoff for cooperators ($\mathcal{P}_c$) and defectors $\left(\mathcal{P}_d\right)$ is given by

$$\mathcal{P}_c = \left(r \times c \times \frac{n_c}{N}\right) - c \text{ and } \mathcal{P}_d = r \times c \times \frac{n_c}{N}, \text{ s.t.,}$$
$$1 < r < N \tag{20}$$

where r denotes the interest rate on the common pool. The condition $1 < r$ states that if all players do the same, they are better off cooperating than defecting; it deserves the name of PG game. The condition $r < N$ states that each individual player is better off defecting than cooperating; selfish players will always avoid the cost of cooperation (c). Therefore, a collective of selfish players will never cooperate and defection is the dominating strategy (Hauert, 2002).

The volunteer's dilemma is an N-person public good game in which a public good is produced if and only if at least one player volunteers to pay a cost. The basic model of volunteer's dilemma is the following: each of N individuals can choose to cooperate or not. A public good is produced if and only if at least one individual cooperative player. Cooperation has a cost $c > 0$. Therefore, the cooperative players have a payoff $1 - c$ and the ones that do not have a payoff 1. If nobody cooperates, the public good is not produced; everybody pays a cost $a > c$ (i.e., payoff $1 - a$). Therefore, each individual prefers that the public good is produced, but also prefers that it is someone else to cooperate (Archetti, 2009). If $N = 2$, the game with the two strategies (i.e., cooperation and defect) has two asymmetric pure-strategy equilibria in which only one player cooperates, but they require coordination: it only works if the players decide in advance who is going to cooperate and when. The game has also a symmetric mixed-strategy equilibrium, which does not require coordination, in which $1 - c = \gamma \times (1 - a) + (1 - \gamma) \times 1$, where γ is the probability of defection. Therefore, at equilibrium $\gamma_{eq} = c / a$. The fitness of the pure cooperation strategy (W_{co}) is $W_{co} = 1 - c$ and the fitness of the pure defection strategy (W_d) is $W_d = \gamma^{N-1} \times (1 - a) + (1 - \gamma^{N-1})$. The fitness of the mixed strategy is

$W_{mix} = \gamma \times W_d + \left(1 - \gamma\right) \times W_{co}$. The mixed-strategy equilibrium (γ_{eq}) can be found by equating the fitness of the two pure strategies; $\gamma_{eq} = \left(c \, / \, a\right)^{1/\left(N-1\right)}$ (Archetti, 2009).

Generally, most conventional PG games have concentrated on the ideal scenarios, where players exhibit unbounded rationality and interact under complete and symmetric information. In addition, individual players are assumed to actually possess perfect information about their environments (Quek & Tay, 2007). This ideal scenario does not arise in reality. In addition, traditional approach of PG games only attempts to find an equilibrium solution. In an equilibrium, each player of the game has adopted a strategy that they are unlikely to change. This equilibrium concept is not free from criticism, and debates continue over the appropriateness and the usefulness of general mathematical models (U, 2010).

To draw close parallel with reality, the *PG-GFS* scheme was developed as a repeated PG game model under incomplete and asymmetric information. To effectively control P2P networks, bounded-rational peers individually adapt to the dynamic environment using an interactive self-learning algorithm. Therefore, the *PGGFS* scheme can provide a more holistic understanding of collective action and insights into how the predicament of social dilemma can be mitigated according to their true willingness.

P2P File Sharing Algorithm in the *PGGFS* Scheme

For the effective file sharing in P2P networks, the *PGGFS* scheme extends the original PG game to trust based repeated game. Based on the trust evaluation of each peer, the *PGGFS* scheme involves the PG game process over a series of rounds, and encourages each peer to have its own willingness to share the file resources.

Volunteer's Dilemma Model Based on the Trust Evaluation

Current research work for P2P control algorithms focused on the determination of optimal strategic behaviors of rational individuals. This payoff optimization approach is inspired from the classical forward-looking game model, and brings great burden to peer's cognitive ability. So, it is unfeasible for practical implementation (Wang, 2010). The *PGGFS* scheme adopts a backward-looking based iterative game model for the P2P file sharing. In the *PGGFS* scheme, peers learn from the iterative interactions with bounded rationality and local information. To maximize their payoffs, strategies of all peers are updated periodically to improve their strategies over time during the game period.

The *PGGFS* scheme assumes that there are two strategies for peers: cooperation (C) and defection (D). C strategy is willing to share their file resources with other peers and D strategy is to refuse a file sharing request from other peer. If contributing peers do not obtain profits as much as they do, they tend to reduce the amount of sharing files with others in next game round and vice versa. Therefore, the basic idea behind the *PGGFS* scheme is to guarantee an advantage of file sharing for cooperative peers; in each peer, the probability of choosing a strategy is proportional to the apparent profit gains. Thus, the peers' learning rule for strategy selection can be defined according to the volunteer's dilemma.

In many situations of P2P networks, each individual peer is genetically related to the neighbor peer's trust value (T) based on the evaluating it's behavior. T value represents a notion of trust level associated with a given P2P network and it is calculated based on its cooperation and defection rates of file sharing. The *PGGFS* scheme assumes that the T is a normalized value based on the Bayesian inference method. Let α and δ

be the rejected and accepted file amounts of sharing requests asked from other peers, respectively. Therefore, the trust value (T) of a peer i is defined as follows.

$$T_i = \frac{\delta_i}{\alpha_i + \delta_i} \tag{21}$$

The game model in the *PGGFS* scheme assumes that there is a set $N = \{1,...,n\}$ of peers with no central controller, and the cooperation cost is C_c. If no peer cooperate, every peers pay a defection cost C_d. Therefore, a peer who selects a cooperation (C) strategy has a payoff 1 - C_c. Based on the T value, the fitness of the C strategy ($F_{cooperation}$) can be written as (Archetti, 2009):

$$F_{cooperation} = \left(1 - C_c\right) +$$
$$Y \times \left\{\xi^{N-1} \times \left(N-1\right) \times 1 + \sum_{i=0}^{N-2}\left\{f\left(i\right) \times \left[\left(N-1-i\right) \times \left(1-C_c\right)\right]\right\} + \left(i \times 1\right)\right\} \tag{22}$$

where ξ is the probability of defection (i.e., probability of selection a D strategy) and Y is the average T value in the P2P network. The first term $\left(1 - C_c\right)$ means the peer i's payoff itself. In $\{\cdot\}$ terms, $\xi^{N-1} \times \left(N-1\right) \times 1$ represents the case of that no neighbor peers select C strategy and $\sum_{i=0}^{N-2}\left\{f\left(i\right) \times \left[\left(N-1-i\right) \times \left(1-C_c\right)\right]\right\} + \left(i \times 1\right)$ means that some neighbor peers select C strategies (Archetti, 2009). $f\left(i\right)$ is the probability that the peer i of the other N - 1 peers (other than self) do not select C strategy. $f\left(i\right)$ is obtained as follows:

C strategy has a direct payoff (1 - C_c) irrespective of the probability that someone else selects C strategy, whereas D strategy has a direct payoff 1 if other peers select C strategy, which happens with probability $\left(1-\xi\right)^{N-1}$, and (1 - C_d) if no peer selects C strategy, which happens with prob-

ability ξ^{N-1}. In addition, if no peers of the other $N-1$ neighbors selects C strategy, which happens with probability ξ^{N-1}, their payoff is 1 if the focal peer selects C strategy, and (1 - C_d) if the focal peer select D strategy. If i of these N - 1 peers select D strategy, instead, which happens with probability f_i, the payoff for those (N - 1 - i) that select C strategy it is (1 - C_c) and the payoff for the i peer that select D strategy is 1, irrespective of the strategy of the focal peer (Archetti, 2009). Finally, $f\left(i\right)$ is given by

$$f\left(i\right) = \binom{N-1}{i} \times \xi^i \times \left(1-\xi\right)^{N-1-i} \tag{23}$$

Similarly, the fitness of D strategy ($F_{defection}$) can be written as:

$$F_{defection} = \xi^{N-1} \times \left(1-C_d\right) + \left(1-\xi^{N-1}\right) \times 1 +$$

$$Y \times \left\{\xi^{N-1} \times \left(N-1\right) \times \left(1-C_d\right) + \sum_{i=0}^{N-2}\left\{f\left(i\right) \times \left[\left(N-1-i\right) \times \left(1-C_c\right)\right]\right\} + \left(i \times 1\right)\right\} \tag{24}$$

The first term $\xi^{N-1} \times \left(1-C_d\right)$ represents that no peers select C strategy and the second term $\left(1-\xi^{N-1}\right) \times 1$ represents the case of that some neighbor peers select C strategy. In $\{\cdot\}$ terms, $\xi^{N-1} \times \left(N-1\right) \times \left(1-C_d\right)$ represents that no neighbor peers select C strategy and $\sum_{i=0}^{N-2}\left\{f\left(i\right) \times \left[\left(N-1-i\right) \times \left(1-C_c\right)\right]\right\} + \left(i \times 1\right)$ means that some neighbor peers select C strategies (Archetti, 2009). Based on (22), (23) and (24), the mixed equilibrium can be found by equating

$F_{cooperation}$ and $F_{defection}$. The mixed equilibrium gives ξ value (ξ_{mix_eq}) as follows.

$$\xi_{mix\_eq} = \left\{ \frac{C_c}{C_d \times \left[1 + Y \times \left(N - 1 \right) \right]} \right\}^{1/(N-1)} \quad (25)$$

Repeated Public Goods Game

From the mixed equilibrium in (25), the *PGGFS* scheme can know that the probability of selecting *D* strategy increases with C_c and *N* while decreasing with C_d and *Y*. Usually, C_c and C_d are constant values. Therefore, to enforce the cooperation on peers in P2P networks, the *PGGFS* scheme should decrease *N* while increasing *Y*. To satisfy this goal, the *PGGFS* scheme adopts the repeated game approach and virtual clustering technique.

In P2P networks, each peer repeatedly interacts over time. This mechanism can be modeled as a repeated game. By repeating a decision-making process, peers may become aware of past behavior and change their strategies accordingly. This game model can encourage cooperation while punishing peers who deviate from the cooperative strategy. Note that for peers, maximizing their total payoff is the same as maximizing their average payoff. In the repeated game model, the average payoff ($\bar{U}$) to the peer *k* is given by:

$$\bar{U}_k = \left(1 - \beta \right) \sum_{t=1}^{\infty} \beta^{t-1} U_k \left(t \right) \quad (26)$$

where β is the discount factor and *t* is a time period. One way to interpret the discount factor β is as an expression of traditional time preference. The valuation of the game diminishes with time depending on the discount factor β ($0 < \beta \leq 1$).

Optimal method of playing a repeated game is to cooperate and play a socially optimum strat-

egy. According to the '*Folk Theorem*', we know that each player in an infinitely repeated game can obtain the better payoff than the Nash equilibrium. In particular, when β is sufficiently close to 1, the greedy players are forced to cooperate and have better payoffs. This is because the greedy player will get punishment from other players in the near future if he acts greedily. In other words, a player's cooperation can be rewarded in the future by others' cooperation.

To enforce cooperation among peers, the *PGGFS* scheme focuses how to define a game rule. The basic idea of the *PGGFS* scheme's rule is that the current defecting gains of the selfish peer will be outweighed by future punishment procedure. For rational peers, this threat of punishment prevents them from deviation, so the cooperation is enforced. To develop the punishment mechanism, the *PGGFS* scheme creates virtual clusters; peers are grouped together as clusters. Clusters can be used to organize a virtual overlay network. In existing literature the term clustering is often used to refer to identification of clusters in a network (Singh & Haahr, 2007). However, in the *PGGFS* scheme, the term clustering refers to the creation of clusters. According to the peer's trust level, peers are classified into three different clusters – High trustable cluster (H-cluster), Middle trustable cluster (M-cluster) and Low trustable cluster (L-cluster). In the *PGGFS* scheme, peers having certain characteristics about trust are grouped together. If a peer repeatedly defects, the *T* value of this selfish peer decreases and this peer has been forced to become a member of the M-cluster or L-cluster. For file sharing, peers only can interact with one another within their own cluster. Therefore, peers in H-cluster can access trustworthy peers. However, peers in L-cluster can interact with selfish peers; payoffs may be reduced. This clustering approach can provide enough threat to greedy peers so as to prevent them from deviating from cooperation. At the same time, the *PGGFS* scheme can decrease the *N* value in (25); it helps to decrease the probability of selecting D strategy from the mixed equilibrium.

The Main Steps of the *PGGFS* Scheme

Under dynamically changing P2P network environments, traditional static game approach is obviously not applicable. For bounded rational peers, they should have a chance to reconsider the current strategy and select the better strategy to maximize their expected payoff. Therefore, the *PGGFS* scheme studies the effects of the peers' strategy decisions, and answer the following two questions: i) what is an appropriate file sharing algorithm for the coexistence of cooperators and defectors? ii) how to induce the cooperative actions of peers with adaptive incentives? To answer these questions, the *PGGFS* scheme develops a more realistic P2P file sharing scheme by using trust-based repeated PG game model. The self-learning repeated game model let distributed peers learn the optimal strategy step by step, while within each step, the strategy of repeated game is applied to ensure the cooperation among peers. This approach can improve the non-cooperative outcomes and ensure a good tradeoff between the implementation complexity for the real world network management and optimized network performance.

The main steps in the *PGGFS* scheme are described in detail below: peers perform the below steps in a distributed manner.

Step 1: At the initial time, the self-learning repeated game model is setting with parameter (ψ, ω, P_T); ψ and ω are threshold values to classify peers. P_T is a predefined time period for each repeated game round.

Step 2: Peers select their strategies in a distributed manner. At the end of each game round, H, M and L clusters are dynamically formed. If the $T_{i,i\in N} \geq \psi$, the peer i is grouped as the H-cluster. If $\psi > T_{i,i\in N} \geq \psi$, the peer i is grouped as the M-cluster. If $\omega > T_{i,i\in N}$, the peer i is grouped as the L-cluster.

Step 3: Peers only can interact with one another within their own cluster. In each cluster, peers dynamically adjust their strategies to maximize their payoff. Therefore, the T value of each peer is dynamically changed.

Step 4: After the P_T time period, clusters are dynamically re-organized for the next game round. According to the current T value, peers leave the currently existing cluster and join a corresponding cluster.

Step 5: Based on the new clusters, repeated game is re-started. During this self-learning step, the current strategy of each peer is dynamically adjusted to optimize the payoff.

Step 6: To maximize the long-run payoffs over time, the cooperation can be enforced by the future repeated game step. So the game will converge to a stable P2P network equilibrium status.

Summary

Advancements in technology over the past decade have stimulated the development of P2P file sharing system. It has become popular as a new paradigm for information exchange. However, although P2P systems have huge potential, there are technical challenges. Usually, the decentralized and anonymous characteristics of P2P networks make the task of file sharing more difficult, which cannot be effectively done by traditional control approaches. As a solution of selfish free-riding problem, the *PGGFS* scheme develops a trust-based file sharing scheme. Based on the fundamental concept of public goods game, the *PGGFS* scheme effectively provides incentives to encourage peers to be cooperative in providing files. In addition, each peer iteratively re-estimates the other peers' trust levels and adjusts the strategy selection probability to maximize its payoff. The *PGGFS* scheme preserves P2P decentralized structure and peers' autonomy property while enabling collaboration between peers. By analyzing the simulation results, it concludes that the *PG-GFS* scheme deals with the *Tragedy of Common* problem effectively than other existing schemes.

REFERENCES

Altman, E., El-Azouzi, R., Hayel, Y., & Tembine, H. (2008). An Evolutionary Game approach for the design of congestion control protocols in wireless networks. In *Proceedings of Physicomnet Workshop*. Academic Press.

Anandalingam, G. (1988). A Mathematical Programming Model of Decentralized Multi-Level Systems. *The Journal of the Operational Research Society*, *39*(11), 1021–1033. doi:10.1057/jors.1988.172

Anderson, S. P., de Palma, A., & Thisse, J. (1992). *Discrete Choice Theory of Product Differentiation*. MIT Press.

Archetti, M. (2009). Cooperation as a volunteer's dilemma and the strategy of conflict in public goods games. *Journal of Evolutionary Biology*, *22*(11), 2192–2200. doi:10.1111/j.1420-9101.2009.01835.x PMID:19732256

Baslam, M., El-Azouzi, R., Sabir, E., & Echabbi, L. (2011). Market share game with adversarial Access providers: A neutral and a non-neutral network analysis. In *Proceedings of International Conference on Network Games, Control and Optimization*. Academic Press.

Byde, A. (2003). Applying evolutionary game theory to auction mechanism design. In *Proceedings of IEEE International Conference on E-Commerce*, (pp. 347- 354). IEEE.

Changiz, R., Halabian, H., Yu, F. R., Lambadaris, I., & Tang, H. (2010). Trust Management in Wireless Mobile Networks with Cooperative Communications. In *Proceedings of International Conference on Embedded and Ubiquitous Computing*, (pp. 498-503). Academic Press.

Conitzer, V. (2009). Approximation guarantees for fictitious play. In *Proceedings of the 47th Annual Allerton Conference on Communication, Control, and Computing*, (pp. 636-643). Academic Press.

Cui, G., Li, M., Wang, Z., Tian, L., & Ma, J. (2012). Analysis and Evaluation Framework Based on Spatial Evolutionary Game Theory for Incentive Mechanism in Peer-to-Peer Network. In *Proceedings of IEEE TrustCom*, (pp. 287-294). IEEE.

Dehnie, S., Guan, K., Gharai, L., & Ghanadan, R. (2009). Kumar, S. Reliable data fusion in wireless sensor networks: A dynamic Bayesian game approach. In *Proceedings of IEEE Military Communications Conference*. IEEE.

Feng, N., Mau, S. C., & Mandayam, N. B. (2004). Pricing and power control for joint network-centric and user-centric radio resource management. *IEEE Transactions on Communications*, *52*(9), 1547–1557. doi:10.1109/TCOMM.2004.833191

Fudenberg, D., & Levine, D. K. (1998). *The Theory of Learning in Games*. MIT Press.

Hauert, C., De Monte, S., Hofbauer, J., & Sigmund, K. (2002). Replicator dynamics in optional public goods games. *Journal of Theoretical Biology*, *218*(2), 187–194. doi:10.1006/jtbi.2002.3067 PMID:12381291

Hofbauer, J., & Sigmund, K. (2003). Evolutionary game dynamics. *Journal of Bulletin of the American Mathematical Society*, *40*, 479–519. doi:10.1090/S0273-0979-03-00988-1

Hosein, P. (2010). Pricing for QoS-based wireless data services and its impact on radio resource management. In *Proceedings of IEEE GLOBECOM*, (pp. 539-544). IEEE.

Isaac, R., Walker, J., & Williams, A. (1994). Group Size and the Voluntary Provision of Public Goods: Experimental Evidence Utilizing Large Groups. *Journal of Public Economics*, *54*(1), 1–36. doi:10.1016/0047-2727(94)90068-X

Ishihara, Y., Huang, R., & Sim, K. M. (2005). Learning opponent's eagerness with Bayesian updating rule in a market-driven negotiation model. In *Proceedings of International Conference on Advanced Information Networking and Applications,* (pp. 903-908). Academic Press.

Kim, S. W. (2011a). An Online Network Price Control Scheme by Using Stackelberg Game Model. *IEICE Transactions*, *94-B*(1), 322–325. doi:10.1587/transcom.E94.B.322

Kim, S. W. (2011b). An Adaptive Online Power Control Scheme based on the Evolutionary Game Theory. *IET Communications*, *5*(18), 2648–2655. doi:10.1049/iet-com.2011.0093

Kim, S. W. (2011c). Cellular Network Bandwidth Management Scheme by using Nash Bargaining Solution. *IET Communications*, *5*(3), 371–380. doi:10.1049/iet-com.2010.0309

Kim, S. W. (2012). Adaptive Ad-hoc Network Routing Scheme by Using Incentive-based Model. *Ad Hoc & Sensor Wireless Networks*, *15*(2), 107–125.

Kim, S. W., & Varshney, P. K. (2005). An Adaptive Fault Tolerance Algorithm for Multimedia Cellular Networks. *IEE Proceedings. Communications*, *152*(6), 932–938. doi:10.1049/ip-com:20045131

Lambert, T. J., Epelman, M. A., & Smith, R. L. (2005). A fictitious play approach to large-scale optimization. *Operations Research*, *53*(3), 477–489. doi:10.1287/opre.1040.0178

Li, R., Zuo, C., He, Y., & Lu, Z. (2008). A Credit Mechanism Based on Automatic Audit in P2P File Sharing Systems. In *Proceedings of ICYCS,* (pp. 2044-2049). ICYCS.

Long, C., Zhang, Q., Li, B., Yang, H., & Guan, X. (2007). Non-Cooperative Power Control for Wireless Ad Hoc Networks with Repeated Games. *IEEE Journal on Selected Areas in Communications*, *25*(6), 1101–1112. doi:10.1109/JSAC.2007.070805

Ma, S., He, J., & Zhang, Y. (2012). Trust Computation Based on Fuzzy Clustering Theory. *International Journal of Hybrid Information Technology*, *5*(2), 213–218.

Mawji, A., & Hassanein, H. (2009). Incentives for P2P File Sharing in Mobile Ad Hoc Networks. In *Proceedings of IEEE CCNC*. IEEE.

Mehmet, S., & Ramazan, K. (2001). A Comparative Study of Multiobjective Optimization Methods in Structural Design. *Turkish Journal of Engineering and Environmental Sciences*, *25*(2), 69–78.

Menasche, D. S., Figueiredo, D. R., & Silva, E. S. (2005). An evolutionary game-theoretic approach to congestion control. *Performance Evaluation*, *62*(1-4), 295–312. doi:10.1016/j.peva.2005.07.028

Niyato, D., & Hossain, E. (2006). A Cooperative Game Framework for Bandwidth Allocation in 4G Heterogeneous Wireless Networks. [IEEE.]. *Proceedings of the IEEE, ICC*, 4357–4362.

Quek, H. Y., & Tay, A. (2007). A evolutionary, game theoretic approach to the modeling, simulation and analysis of public goods provisioning under asymmetric information. In *Proceedings of IEEE CEC,* (pp. 4735-4742). IEEE.

Samuelson, P. A. (1954). The Pure Theory of Public Expenditure. *The Review of Economics and Statistics, 36*(4), 387–389. doi:10.2307/1925895

Singh, A., & Haahr, M. (2007). Decentralized Clustering In Pure P2P Overlay Networks Using Schelling's Model. [IEEE.]. *Proceedings of the IEEE, ICC,* 1860–1866.

Sun, L., Cheng, S., Lin, Y., & Wang, W. (2006). A Willing-to-Share Based Incentive Mechanism for File Sharing P2P Networks. In *Proceedings of IEEE CSCWD.* IEEE.

U, M., & Li, Z. (2010). Public Goods Game Simulator with Reinforcement Learning Agents. In *Proceedings of ICMLA,* (pp. 43-49). ICMLA.

Wang, B., Han, Z., & Liu, K. J. R. (2006). Stackelberg game for distributed resource allocation over multiuser cooperative communication networks. In *Proceedings of IEEE Global Telecommunications Conference.* IEEE.

Wang, X., & Schulzrinne, H. (2005). Incentive-Compatible Adaptation of Internet Real-Time Multimedia. *IEEE Journal on Selected Areas in Communications, 23*(2), 417–436. doi:10.1109/JSAC.2004.839399

Wang, Y., Nakao, A., & Ma, J. (2010). A Simple Public-Goods Game Based Incentive Mechanism for Resource Provision in P2P Networks. In *Proceedings of UIC 2010,* (pp. 352-365). UIC.

Waslander, S. L., Inalhan, G., & Tomlin, C. J. (2004). *Decentralized Optimization via Nash Bargaining.* Kluwer Academic Press.

Xiao, Y., Shan, X., & Ren, Y. (2005). Game theory models for IEEE 802.11 DCF in wireless ad hoc networks. *IEEE Communications Magazine, 43*(3), 22–26. doi:10.1109/MCOM.2005.1404594

Xiao, Y., Zame, W. R., & Schaar, M. V. D. (2011). Technology Choices and Pricing Policies in Wireless Networks. In *Proceedings of IEEE ICC.* IEEE.

Xu, B., & Fan, L. (2010). Information disclosing and cooperation in public goods game with punishment. In *Proceedings of ICISE,* (pp. 2896-2899). ICISE.

Yang, H. (1997a). Sensitivity analysis for the elastic-demand network equilibrium problem with applications. *Transportation Research, 31*(1), 55–70. doi:10.1016/S0191-2615(96)00015-X

Yang, H. (1997b). Traffic restraint, road pricing and network equilibrium. *Transportation Research Part B: Methodological, 31*(4), 303–314. doi:10.1016/S0191-2615(96)00030-6

Young, H. P. (2005). *Strategic Learning and Its Limits.* Oxford University Press.

Zhong, L. X., Chen, B. H., & Huang, C. Y. (2008). Networking Effects on Public Goods Game with Unequal Allocation. In *Proceedings of ICNC,* (pp. 217-221). ICNC.

Zouridaki, C., Mark, B. L., Hejmo, M., & Thomas, R. K. (2005). A Quantitative Trust Establishment Framework for Reliable Data Packet Delivery in MANETs. In *Proceedings of ACM SASN.* ACM.

KEY TERMS AND DEFINITIONS

Bayesian Inference: A method of inference in which Bayes' rule is used to update the probability estimate for a hypothesis as additional evidence is acquired. Bayesian updating is an important technique throughout statistics, and especially in mathematical statistics.

Multi-Objective Optimization: An area of multiple criteria decision making, that is concerned with mathematical optimization problems involving more than one objective function to be optimized simultaneously.

Public Good: A good that is both non-excludable and non-rivalrous in that individuals cannot be effectively excluded from use and where use by one individual does not reduce availability to others. Public goods that are available everywhere are sometimes referred to as global public goods.

Stackelberg Model: A strategic model in economics in which the leader firm moves first and then the follower firms move sequentially. It is named after the German economist, who published *Market Structure and Equilibrium* in 1934 which described the model.

Tradeoff: A situation that involves losing one quality or aspect of something in return for gaining another quality or aspect. More colloquially, if one thing increases, some other thing must decrease. The idea of a tradeoff often implies a decision to be made with full comprehension of both the upside and downside of a particular choice.

Chapter 15
Game–Based Control Approach for Smart Grid

ABSTRACT

The concept of smart grid to transform the old power grid into a smart and intelligent electric power distribution system is, currently, a hot research topic. Smart grid offers the merging of electrical power engineering technologies with network communications. Game theory has featured as an interesting technique, adopted by many researchers, to establish effective smart grid communications. The use of game theory has offered solutions to various decision-making problems, ranging from distributed load management to micro storage management in smart grid. Interestingly, different researchers have different objectives or problem scopes for adopting game theory in smart grid. This chapter explores the game-based approach.

BIFORM GAME BASED COGNITIVE RADIO CONTROL (BGCRC) SCHEME FOR SMART GRID COMMUNICATIONS

Smart grid is widely considered to be a next generation power grid, which will be integrated with information feedback communications. However, smart grid communication technologies are subject to inefficient spectrum allocation problems. Cognitive radio networks can solve the problem of spectrum scarcity by opening the under-utilized licensed bands to secondary users. In 2012, S. Kim proposed a new Biform Game based Cognitive Radio Control (*BGCRC*) scheme for smart grid environments (Kim, 2012). To enhance the effi-

ciency of spectrum usage, the concept of biform game model is adopted as a new spectrum control paradigm. This approach can make the system be close to the optimized network performance.

Development Motivation

Smart grid has become a global concern as the next generation power grid. A crucial factor to realize smart grid features is timely access to meter data via reliable communication infrastructure. Therefore, two-way feedback communication plays an important role in smart grid; it directly affects the performance of the whole system. To accommodate the growth of the numbers and types of data, a significant challenge for the future smart grid is

DOI: 10.4018/978-1-4666-6050-2.ch015

to ensure a large amount of bandwidth. Therefore, a key point in the success of smart grid technology is how to reduce the communication expenses as well as saving transmission bandwidth. Recently, many advanced wireless technologies are being investigated to be used for the communication layer of smart grid (Ghasemi, & Hosseini, 2010). Cognitive Radio (CR) is a new technique for wireless communications to improve the utilization of radio spectrum (Li, Xu, Liu, Wang, & Han, 2010).In the CR networks, unlicensed users (i.e., secondary users: SUs) are allowed to sense and temporarily access the unused bands originally allocated to the licensed users (i.e., primary users: PUs) when the PUs are inactive. For the accurate detection of idle spectrum bands, spectrum sensing is a crucial technology. Among spectrum sensing methods, cooperative sensing is an efficient and promising technique to obtain more trustable sensing results. This approach has been shown that sensing performance can be greatly improved (Liu, Shen, Song, & Wang, 2009).

Nowadays, the main idea of game theory has emerged as an effective way of designing this CR management process. Game theory is a field of applied mathematics that provides an effective tool in modeling the interaction among independent decision makers. In 1996, A. Brandenburger and H. Stuart introduced the fundamental notion of the biform game to shape the competitive environment in a favorable way. It is a hybrid noncooperative-cooperative game model to formalize the two-stage decision problem (Brandenburger, & Stuart, 2007). The first stage is the noncooperative component of a biform game. Each player chooses a strategy to maximize his expected payoff while regarding a subsequent effect of the chosen strategies on the second stage. The second stage is the cooperative component to model the resulting competitive environment. In this stage, players form a coalition to generate a surplus, which is shared fairly and optimally. Therefore, an actual payoff is realized after the second-stage game. Recently, it has been proven that the biform game model is

efficient when it is applied to a business strategy (Stuart, 2005).

The *BGCRC* scheme is designed as a new biform game model for smart grid system. To support the fast growing demand, the *BGCRC* scheme presents a biform game based CR communication algorithm, which is mainly motivated to use the unlicensed bandwidth while ensuring the need of explosive data traffic. At the first stage, SUs estimate the current network condition and adaptively form clusters for the cooperative spectrum sensing. Clusters are made up according to the non-cooperative game model. At the second stage, the detected idle spectrum is shared based on the cooperative bargaining model. The main feature of the *BGCRC* scheme is to maximize spectrum efficiency while ensuring the sharing fairness. Under dynamically changing network environments, SUs compete or coordinate with each other in order to maximize their payoffs. Therefore, the developed biform game approach is suitable to get a globally desirable network performance.

SPECTRUM MANAGEMENT ALGORITHMS IN THE *BGCRC* SCHEME

To reach a desirable system performance, the CR spectrum is sensed and shared based on the biform game model. This approach can be concluded to be an effective solution for the adaptive CR spectrum management in smart grid communications.

Non-Cooperative Game Based Spectrum Sensing Algorithm

The main concept of smart grid is the employment of intelligent two-way communication networks. Therefore, a key determining factor is timely access to meter data via an effective communication infrastructure. However, in harsh smart grid environments, communication infrastructure can provide limited bandwidth, which causes the spectrum scarcity problem. Nowadays, CR is recognized as a promising technology for bandwidth scarcity. To share the CR network spectrum, the first task is to correctly sense the PUs' activities. Therefore, the accuracy of sensing reports from SUs is critical to the CR network performance. However, the required sensitivity is very demanding since any individual SU may face fading and shadowing effects. To overcome these problems, cooperative spectrum sensing approach has been studied as a promising solution to improve the probabilities of detection and reduce the false alarm (Wang, Liu, & Clancy, 2010). In this approach, all SUs should be separated into a few clusters and some SUs, which are clustering together, cooperatively sense a small portion of the multiband. Each SU in each cluster performs local spectrum sensing independently and this sensing information is sent to the Cognitive Base Station (CBS), which makes a final decision to control the usage of the CR spectrum.

The *BGCRC* scheme is designed as a new cooperative spectrum sensing algorithm to provide reliable and effective service. The *BGCRC* scheme follows the system model where there are M SUs and K PUs; the multiband spectrum consists of K non-overlapping narrowband channels and each of them is used by each PU (Kim, Kim, You, Lee, & Lee, 2010). The multiband ($\mathbb{F}$) composed of narrowbands ($f^a : a \in \{1,2,...,K\}$) is given by

$$\mathbb{F} = \bigcup_{a=1}^{K} f^a \qquad (1)$$

where K is the number of PUs. Traditionally, multiband spectrum is divided into many narrowbands, which may carry data, independently. There should be no overlap among narrowband channels. Multiple cognitive SUs form a cluster to jointly access a narrowband and SU clusters do not interfere with each other. Each SU in a cluster can use only one narrowband at a time and each narrowband channel cannot be multiplexed by different SU clusters. In the developed algorithm, there can be K different SU clusters to the utmost. The set ($\mathbb{C}$) of clusters are defined as follows (Kim, 2010).

$$\mathbb{C} = \bigcup_{a=1}^{K} C^a, \text{ where } C^p \cap C^q = \varnothing \text{ and } \| \mathbb{C} \| \leq K \qquad (2)$$

The SUs in C^a cluster cooperatively sense the particular a^{th} narrowband (i.e., the ath PU band). Based on the sensing data from multiple SUs in each cluster, the decision about the spectrum idleness is made collaboratively. The sensed idle spectrum band is temporarily allocated to a specific SU in its cluster. Therefore, cooperative spectrum sensing becomes effective when SU clusters are formed adaptively. In the developed sensing algorithm, the fundamental concept of evolutionary game is adopted to form clusters.

Evolutionary game is a well-known non-cooperative game model and has been developed in biological sciences in order to explain the evolution of genetically determined social behavior. The payoffs in evolutionary game model depend on the actions of the co-players; strategies with high payoff will spread within the entire populations of players (Menasche, Figueiredo, & Silva, 2005). The *BGCRC* scheme practically applies the evolutionary game model to the clustering problem without much deviation from its original form. Each SU, as a non-cooperative game player, can constantly adapt the strategy (i.e., cluster selection) based on the evolutionary learning mechanism.

The player's payoff is defined as the amount of actually transmitted bits by using CR technique. Therefore, the utility function for player i (U_i, s.t., $i \in C^a$) with strategy s ($s \in \{1,2,...,K\}$) is given as follows (Long, Zhang, Li, Yang, & Guan, 2007).

$$U_i\left(s\right) = \frac{1}{p_i} \times W \times \log_2\left(1 + \frac{\gamma_i\left(\mathbb{P}\right)}{\Omega}\right) \times \psi_s$$

$$\text{(3)}$$

s.t.,

$$\begin{cases} \psi_s = 1, & \text{if } k^{th} \text{ PU band is allocated to the player } i \\ \psi_s = 0, & \text{otherwise} \end{cases}$$

and $\gamma_i\left(\mathbb{P}\right) = \dfrac{p_i h_{ii}}{\sigma_i + \sum_{j \neq i} p_j h_{ji}}$

where W is the PU channel bandwidth and $\gamma_i\left(\mathbb{P}\right)$ is the SINR of player i, respectively (Kim, 2011). p_i is the power level of player i to sense the sth PU band. The goal of each player is to maximize his own payoff by selecting a specific strategy where $\max_s: U_i(s) \rightarrow \mathfrak{R}, s \in \mathbb{A} = \{1,2,...,K\}$ and $\mathbb{A}$ is the set of PUs (Suris, DaSilva, Han, & MacKenzie, 2007).

During the evolutionary game, players learn how to select their strategies like as a tournament play where losing strategies are eliminated and winning strategies remain. Each player has the same strategy space, denoted by $\mathbb{A} = \{1,2,..,K\}$. If the payoff of strategy s ($s \in \mathbb{A}$) is small compared to other strategies, the selection probability for strategy s decreases in proportion to the expected payoff reduction. The *BGCRC* scheme tries to derive the *ESS* from the *RD*, especially by exploring different actions, adaptively learning during the strategic interactions, and approaching the best response strategy under changing conditions. The *RD* is defined as the same manner in the *MSGBM* scheme.

Cooperative Game Based Spectrum Allocation Algorithm

With the spectrum sensing technique, spectrum allocation is also important part for the CR network management. Traditionally, bargaining solution, which is a famous cooperative game theoretic concept, is an effective tool to solve resource allocation problems; it is a map that assigns a fair and optimal solution to a given cooperative game. In 1977, E. Kalai and R. Myerson developed the Egalitarian Bargaining Solution (*EBS*). Among various bargaining solutions, the main feature of the *EBS* is a monotonicity with respect to expansions of the feasible set without using Nash's axiom of independence of scale of utility. Therefore, unlike other bargaining solutions, the egalitarian solution enjoys even stronger monotonicity requirements while satisfying independence conditions (Matt, Toni, & Dionysiou, 2006), (Bossert, & Tan, 1995). To ensure fairness among multiple SUs, the *BGCRC* scheme adopts the *EBS* to develop the spectrum allocation algorithm.

In the developed model, K PUs and M SUs are involved in a spectrum sharing process. Therefore, $A^{\{1..K,1..M\}}$ can represent the cluster formation of SUs; it is a Boolean table of K lines and M columns (Matt, 2006), (Bossert, 1995).

$$A^{\{1..K,1..M\}} = \begin{pmatrix} A_{1,1}, & A_{1,2}, & \cdots & A_{1,M} \\ \vdots & \vdots & \ddots & \vdots \\ A_{K,1}, & A_{K,2} & \cdots & A_{K,M} \end{pmatrix}$$

$$\text{(4)}$$

$A^{\{1..K,1..M\}}$ contains at most one element, which has 1, per column. If $A_{k,i} = 1$, it can say that the ith SU ($1 \leq i \leq M$) is an element belonging to the kth cluster ($1 \leq k \leq K$) to sense the kth spectrum band. The *EBS* attempts to grant equal gain to players. In other words, it is the point which maximizes the minimum payoff among SUs in each cluster. Formally, in the cluster k, the allocation resulting from *EBS* ($E\_A_k\left(A^*\right)$) is defined as follows (Matt, 2006), (Bossert, 1995).

$$E_{Ak}\left(A^{*}\right) = \max_{1 \leq i \leq M} \min_{i \in C^{k}} \left\{ \int_{t_{i_s}}^{t_c} IB_i\left(k\right) dt \middle/ \left(t_c - t_{i_s}\right) \right\}$$

(5)

where $IB_i\left(k\right)$ is the kth cluster idle band, which is allocated for the player i. t_{i_s} is the start-time when the player i joins to the kth cluster. t_c is the current times of system operations. Therefore, the time period $t_c - t_{i\_s}$ is the sensing duration of kth band from the player i. In each cluster, this allocation mechanism is executed in a distributed manner. Based on the social choice theories and welfare economics, *EBS* based spectrum allocation mechanism can be defined metaphorically as the welfare of the "unhappiest" or least "well-off" user in the system (Matt, 2006), (Bossert, 1995).

The Main Steps of the BGCRC Scheme

In the *BGCRC* scheme, both non-cooperative and cooperative game models have been applied to spectrum sensing and allocation algorithms. This biform game approach is an effective way to control the CR spectrum. At first stage, SUs are clustered to jointly sense the same PU's presence. Each SU will act selfishly by pursuing as high an individual payoff as possible. Therefore, non-cooperative game approach is suitable for the cluster formation problem. The developed clustering procedure is designed based on the evolutionary game theory. This model offers a more realistic model for players with bounded rationality. During the evolutionary game, players have a chance to reconsider the current strategy and react to maximize the expected payoff. To implement the distributed learning algorithm, there is a little communications overhead. However, it is a controllable overhead for practical implementations. At second stage, the key issue is how to allocate the idle frequency band among SUs in each cluster. Cooperative bargaining solutions strive to understand the interplay between an efficient and a fair allocation. The problem of spectrum allocation in each cluster can be mapped into a bargaining game. In the *BGCRC* scheme, spectrum allocation mechanism is developed according to the Egalitarian bargaining solution. This approach fairly distributes the idle spectrum to each SU. The main steps of the *BGCRC* scheme are given next.

Step 1: At the initial iteration ($n = 0$), the selection probability for each strategy is equally distributed. ($x_i\left(n\right) = 1/\|\mathbb{A}\|$, $\forall i$ where $\|\mathbb{A}\|$ is the number of strategies, i.e., $\mathbb{A} = \{1, 2, .., K\}$). This starting guess guarantees that each player enjoys the same benefit at the beginning of the game.

Step 2: Each SU player selects a PS band ($f^i \in \mathbb{F}$ and $i \in \mathbb{A}$) according to the current selection probability.

Step 3: In each cluster, the sensed idle band is allocated according to (15-5). This allocation mechanism is executed in a distributed manner.

Step 4: Based on the individual self-interest, players re-estimate each strategy's selection probability according to the *RD*. For each player, the nth RD of the strategy s is obtained as follows.

$$\dot{x}_s\left(n+1\right) = x_s\left(n\right) \times$$
$$\left(\sum_j x_j\left(n\right) \times J\left(s,j\right) - \sum_j \sum_k x_j\left(n\right) \times J\left(j,k\right) \times x_k\left(n\right) \right)$$

(6)

Step 5: When the change of *RD* is within a predefined minimum bound (ε), this change can be negligible. Otherwise, proceeds to Step 2 for the next iteration. This iterative feedback procedure continues until network system reaches to an efficient equilibrium state.

Step 6: If all players do not change their current strategy, they remain the same cluster. All SUs have converged to the *ESS*.

Step 7: Constantly, the system is self-monitoring the current network situation. When the change of *RD* is larger than ε, it can re-trigger the cluster formation procedure; proceeds to Step 2 for the next iteration.

Recently, several CR management schemes have been presented for the next generation communication system. The *Dynamic Cooperative Spectrum Sensing (DCSS)* scheme is an evolutionary game-theoretical scheme for distributed cooperative sensing over cognitive radio networks (Wang, 2010). By employing the theory of evolutionary game, the *DCSS* scheme modeled the interactions between selfish users in cooperative sensing and developed a distributed learning algorithm that can help the secondary users approach their optimal strategy with only their own payoff history. The *Group-based Cooperative Spectrum Sensing (GCSS)* scheme is a cooperative spectrum sensing algorithm for multiband, where a number of clusters are formed to sense a small portion of

the multiband (Kim, 2010). The SUs belonging to the same cluster cooperatively sense the presence of PU in the narrowband. Based on the sensing results of SUs in a channel, the *GCSS* scheme assigned some of SUs to the channel which they can sense confidently. Compared to the *DCSS* and *GCSS* schemes, the proposed *BGCRC* scheme attains better performance for CR network systems. The simulation results shown in Figure 1 demonstrate that the performance comparison.

Summary

From the green IT point of view, smart grid has been being experimented as an intelligent solution to manage power consumption and distribution. A key point in the success of smart grid technology is how to set up the two-way communication mechanism. In this way, reliable and efficient communication should be guaranteed while taking care of the system expenses and bandwidth. However, the bandwidth requirement is increasing even more to manage the large amounts of data that smart devices will produce. Therefore, the main issue in smart grid is how to use the transmission bandwidth adaptively. As an effective solution for bandwidth scarcity, CR network is

Figure 1. Performance evaluations of the BGCRC scheme

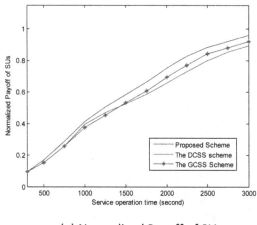

(a) Normalized Payoff of SUs

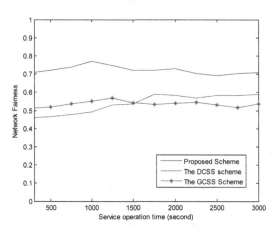

(b) Network Fairness

recognized as a promising technology to address the above question. Due to this reason, the *BGCRC* scheme adopts the CR technique to develop a new smart grid communication algorithm. In the *BGCRC* scheme, adaptive CR spectrum sensing and sharing algorithms are developed for smart grid communications. To implement the cognitive radio technique, the *BGCRC* scheme is designed as the biform game model to effectively control the scarce bandwidth resource. Due to the self-regarding game model feature, the *BGCRC* scheme effectively adapts to current communication conditions and approximates an optimal network performance under dynamically changing smart grid environments.

COOPETITION GAME BASED GROUPING AND SCHEDULING (CGGS) SCHEME FOR SMART GRID MANAGEMENT

The idea of smart grid has been gaining significant attention and becomes a hot research topic. In the smart grid, power appliances adaptively form groups. By exploiting multi-appliance diversity, appliances in each group are dynamically scheduled. For the efficient smart grid grouping and scheduling management, S. Kim proposed a new Coopetition Game based Grouping and Scheduling (CGGS) scheme for smart grid management (Kim, 2013). This coopetition game model can adaptively respond to current system conditions. The main feature is to maximize the overall system performance while satisfying the requirements of individual appliances.

Development Motivation

Nowadays, energy demand is exponentially increasing in many countries. Therefore, the issue of power energy management has directly impacted economics, society, industrial development and environment. However, electrical infrastructure has remained unchanged for about 100 years. Experiences have shown that the 20th century power grid is ill-suited to the current power needs. For the 21st century, the concept of smart grid has become a common choice to face future challenges. To adaptively support electric power generation, transmission, distribution, and control, the smart grid transforms the old power system into a smart and intelligent power system (Fadlullah, Nozaki, Takeuchi, & Kato, 2011).

Traditional power systems are generally used to carry power from a few central generators to a large number of customers. In contrast, the smart grid uses two-way flows of electricity and information to create an advanced energy delivery network (Fang, Misra, Xue, & Yang, 2012). Therefore, it is capable of delivering power in more efficient ways and automatically responding to wide ranging conditions and events that occur anywhere in the grid. To adaptively implement the smart grid system, current researches offer the fusion of electric power engineering technologies with network communications through smart meters, which are placed between the electricity provider and customers (Fadlullah, 2011).

For the future smart grid, the main goal is to develop an adaptive demand-side scheduling algorithm that enables efficient management of the power supply and demand (Saffre & Gedge, 2010). To satisfy this goal, we always face technical challenges such as pricing, regulations, adaptive decision making, appliances' interactions, and dynamic operation. All of these issues are ripe for game theory. Game theory is a conceptual framework with a set of mathematical tools enabling the study of complex interactions among independent rational players. Due to its many appealing properties, the basic concept of game theory has become an interesting research topic in smart grid and communication systems (Saad, Han, Poor, & Başar, 2012).

Traditionally, games can be divided into non-cooperative and cooperative games. In non-cooperative games, players are in conflict with each other and do not communicate or collaborate. Their preferences can be expressed as a utility function and players try to ensure the best possible consequence according to the utility function. On the contrary, cooperative games are games in which players make binding commitments and find it beneficial to cooperate in the game. To reach an agreement that gives mutual advantage, players bargain with each other. In cooperative games, the main interest is to fairly distribute the outcome to each player according to their contributions (Suris, 2007).

In 1996, A. Brandenburger and B. Nalebuff had introduced a new concept of game model, called coopetition game, which combined the characteristics of non-cooperative and cooperative games. The coopetition game model is understood to achieve greater and reciprocal advantages for every player, who can strengthen their competitive advantages by cooperation (Guan, Yuan, & Zhang, 2008), (Bossert & Tan, 1995). Specifically, the concept of coopetition describes the fact that most game players can achieve more success than they ever could working alone. Recently, it has been proven that the coopetition game model is efficient when it is applied to a business strategy in a dynamic industry field (Sun & Xu, 2005).

Motivated by the facts presented in the above discussion, a new Coopetition Game based Grouping and Scheduling (*CGGS*) scheme was developed as a new smart grid management scheme. To maximize the overall system performance while satisfying the requirements of the individual appliances, this *CGGS* scheme consists of competitive grouping algorithm and cooperative scheduling algorithm. Therefore, this model is part competition and part cooperation. The grouping algorithm allows power appliances to constitute groups of interest. Groups are adaptively formed according to the non-cooperative hedonic game model. In order to jointly reach the objective together, the scheduling algorithm is designed to schedule power appliances dynamically. In each group, multi-appliance diversity is exploited and

flexible appliances are shifted in a cooperative manner. This distributed power scheduling approach can provide an effective solution to the current power generation and distribution problem. The important feature of the scheme is an ability to maintain energy efficiency as high as possible by adaptively responding to current system situations. Under widely different and diversified smart grid situations, the coopetition approach in the *CGGS* scheme is suitable to get a globally desirable system performance. To the best of our knowledge, there have not been any studies on the coopetition control paradigm for the smart grid power management problem.

Related Work

Recently, several smart grid management schemes have been proposed. Quanyan Zhu et al., proposed a distribution demand side management scheme by using the framework of dynamic games (Zhu, Han, & Basar, 2012). In this scheme, a two-layer optimization framework is established. At the lower level, for each player (such as one household), different appliances are scheduled for energy consumption. At the upper level, the dynamic game is used to capture the interaction among different players in their demand responses through the market price. Shengrong Bu et al., presented a novel game-theoretical decision-making scheme for electricity retailers in the smart grid (Bu, Yu, & Liu, 2011). They modeled and analyzed the interactions between the retailer and electricity customers as a four-stage Stackelberg game. S. Lambotharan et al., proposed a consumption scheduling mechanism for home area load management in smart grid (Zhu, Tang, Lambotharan, 2012). The aim of this scheduling is to minimize the peak hourly load in order to achieve an optimal daily load schedule. It is able to schedule both the optimal power and the optimal operation time for power-shiftable appliances and time-shiftable appliances respectively according to the power consumption patterns of all the individual appliances. T. Logenthiran et al., proposed a demand side management algorithm based on load shifting technique for demand side management of future smart grids with a large number of devices of several types (Logenthiran, Srinivasan, & Shun, 2012). By using the day-ahead load shifting technique, this algorithm mathematically formulated as a minimization problem. D. Miorandi et al., designed a game-theoretical demand side management scheme (Miorandi, & De Pellegrini, 2012). Leveraging on concepts and results from evolutionary game theory, they have shown that in the first case there exists a phase transition in the eventual adoption of demand side management. In the second case, at the opposite, the system converges towards a mixed equilibrium, in which only a fraction of the agents' population uses demand side management. Most existing schemes were developed using dynamic programming or linear programming; these programming techniques cannot handle a large number of controllable devices from several types of devices which have several computation patterns and heuristics. Therefore, they handled only a limited number of controllable loads of limited types. Due to this reason, most existing literatures are not suitable to apply to the real world.

The *Autonomous Energy Consumption Scheduling* (*AECS*) scheme is a game theoretic demand side management algorithm for the future smart grid (Li, Jayaweera, & Naseri, 2011). The *AECS* scheme presented a distributed energy management system that took advantage of a two-way digital communication infrastructure. In this system, power appliances had the incentives to participate the energy consumption scheduling game. The strategy in the *AECS* scheme required each customer to simply apply its best response to the current total load and tariffs in the power distribution system. The *Auctioning based Smart Grid Scheduling* (*ASGS*) scheme proposed a decoupling approach which divided the two objectives - utility cost minimization and customers' social welfare maximization (Mohsenian-Rad,

Wong, Jatskevich, Schober, & Leon-Garcia, 2010). This approach gave better description of electricity networks. On receiving the initially submitted load demands from customers, the utility generated an optimal load profile over time that minimized its cost under the generation capacity constraint. And then, repeated auctions were adopted to allocate loads among customers in the system to maximize the social welfare.

Smart Grid Management Algorithms in the *CGGS* Scheme

In this section, the *CGGS* scheme is explained in detail. Based on the adaptive coopetition game model, power appliances in the smart grid form a group and scheduled to approximate an optimal system performance.

Grouping Algorithm in Smart Grid

Electrical energy is an important material foundation of the economical and social development in the world. Due to the growth of higher electric demands, the total electric energy consumption is still growing. However, most electrical energy is generated by burning a huge amount of fossil fuel, which causes environment degradation and global warming. In order to solve this problem, a lot of research has been conducted in renewable energy sources such as wind turbines and solar panels. However, these renewable energy sources are characterized by their high intermittence. Therefore, their energy outputs are not always available where and when needed. To efficiently and reliably operate these renewable energy sources, a number of new challenges have been introduced (Roossien, Noort, Kamphuis, Bliek, Eijgelaar, & Wit, 2011).

Smart grid has become a concern as the next generation power grid, which is defined as electricity networks that can intelligently integrate the power generators and consumers in order to efficiently deliver sustainable, economic and secure electricity supplies. Currently, advances in technology enable the integration of renewable energy sources into the emerging smart grid. To combine renewable energy sources in the smart grid, the key issue is to mitigate the impact of frequency fluctuations within a power system.

In the *CGGS* scheme, a new smart grid control algorithm was developed with renewable energy sources. The main goal of the developed algorithm is to match adaptively the requested energy power and the realized power production. To satisfy this goal, the *CGGS* scheme classify power generation units into renewable power units (RPUs; e.g., sunlight, wind, and geothermal heat plants) and non-renewable power units (NPUs; fossil fuels and nuclear power plants). With power units, power consumers (i.e., electrical appliances) are clustered as a customer unit (CU) and measured by the smart meter. To maintain the power balance between power demand and supply, entities of smart grid (i.e., RPUs and CUs) are autonomously self-organized into disjoint groups. Therefore, a power provider and end-users can be grouped together. However, renewable power units are highly stochastic and often uncontrollable (de Haan, Frunt, & Kling, 2010). Therefore, in each group, it is difficult to balance between energy load and generation at all times. When the energy generation of RPUs cannot able to match the total CU requests of their corresponding groups, NPUs compensate for these power shortfalls and keep the power system stable. With the flexibility offered by NPUs, the power imbalance is reduced in each group. In the *CGGS* scheme, CUs can act as a single virtual energy consumer and the cooperative combination of RPU and NPU can act as a virtual power plant (Vinyals, Bistaffa, Farinelli, & Rogers, 2012).

To form CU groups, the methodology adopted in the *CGGS* scheme is a hedonic game. This game model has previously been studied in Economics to model a variety of settings ranging from multi-agent coordination to group formation in social networks (Saad, Han, Hjorungnes, Ni-

yato, & Hossain, 2011), (Génin & Aknine, 2010). Hedonic games describe the situation where player's utility depends only on the identity of the members of the group. This is a general class of games which encompasses many matching problems. The *CGGS* scheme assumes that there are n CUs, i.e., $\mathcal{N} = \left\{ c_1, ..., c_n \right\}$. CU groups are defined as the set $\Pi = \left\{ S_1, ..., S_l \right\}$, s.t., $l << n$. The set Π partitions the CUs' set $\mathcal{N}$, i.e., $\forall k$, $S_{k, 1 \leq k \leq l} \subseteq \mathcal{N}$ are disjoint groups such that $\bigcup_{k=1}^{l} S_k = \mathcal{N}$ and $S_i \cap S_j = \varnothing, i \neq j$. For a CU (i.e., c_i and $c_i \in \mathcal{N}$), the *CGGS* scheme denotes $S_\Pi \left(c_i \right)$ as a group $S_k \in \Pi$, such that $c_i \in S_k$ (Saad, 2011), (Génin, 2010).

In each group, RPUs, NPUs and CUs are connected and self-adapt to environmental changes such as a change in the power demand and supply. When a group S_k is formed, the c_i in S_k gets a certain satisfaction and this satisfaction is defined by a utility function (U_{c_i}). This function induces a preference order $\succsim_i$ on groups in the set Π. In hedonic games, the preference order ($\succsim$) is defined based on the payoff value. For example, let A and B be groups and p be a player. According to a player p's utility function (U_p), if $U_p \left(A \right) \geq U_p \left(B \right)$, it is denoted by $A \succsim_p B$ and the p prefers a group A to B. In the *CGGS* scheme, each CU has preferences over its own set and can compare and order its potential groups. When the c_i prefers a group S_k to S_m if and only if $U_{c_i} \left(k \right) \geq U_{c_i} \left(m \right)$, it is denoted by $S_k \succsim_i S_m$. Using the preference-based group formation process, the developed grouping algorithm provides a solution (i.e., group structure Π) of a hedonic game. In a distributed online manner, each CU takes a decision individually to join a specific group. After groups are formed, smart grid situation is dynamically changed. In order to effectively adapt the current system conditions, formed groups should be re-configured. Therefore, the c_i can decide to quit its current group $S_{\Pi}(c_i) = S_k$, and join another group $S_{k'} \in \Pi$, if and only if $S_k \cup \{c_i\} \succ_i S_{k'} \cup \{c_i\}$.

The developed grouping algorithm is composed of three stages: demand and supply estimation, group formation, and group re-configuration. In the first stage, CUs and RPUs individually monitor their power demand and supply amounts throughout a time period. In order to implement the time-driven approach, the *CGGS* scheme partitions the duration of one day, i.e., 24 hours. Let $\mathbb{D}_{c_i}$ denote the energy consumption vector of c_i, and $\mathbb{S}_{RPU_j}$ denote the energy provisioning vector of RPU_j.

$$\mathbb{D}_{c_i} = [D_i^1, \ D_i^2, \dots D_i^H] \text{ and } \mathbb{S}_{RPU_j} = [S_j^1, \ S_j^2, \dots S_j^H], \text{ s.t., } H = 24 \tag{7}$$

where D_i^k (*or* S_j^k) is the amount of power demand (*or* supply) at the kth hour in a day. These vector values are dynamically modified in a real-time online fashion. In the second stage, the developed group formation procedure is triggered. In the *CGGS* scheme, each group consists of one RPU and some CUs. To implement grouping algorithm, each RPU maintains another $\mathbb{G}$ vector. At the initial time of grouping process, the values of $\mathbb{G}$ are assigned the same values of $\mathbb{S}$ (i.e., $\mathbb{G}_{RPU_j} = \mathbb{S}_{RPU_j} = [\ \mathcal{S}_j^1 = S_j^1, \ \ \mathcal{S}_j^2 = S_j^2, \dots, \mathcal{S}_j^H = S_j^H]$). For smart grid systems, it is an important issue to effectively distribute the power energy. Therefore, if a RPU has enough power energy, it is desirable that customers are enticed to get power energy from that RPU. In the *CGGS* scheme, according to $\mathbb{D}_{c_i}$ and $\mathbb{G}_{RPU_j}$, the c_i's utility function (U_{c_i}) is given by

$$U_{c_i} = \sum_{k=1}^{H} \left(\mathcal{S}_j^k - D_i^k \right), \text{s.t., } j \in \text{theset of RPUs} \tag{8}$$

At a point in grouping time, each CU discovers its neighbor RPUs and selects a RPU to maximize its expected payoff according to (15-8). If the c_i decides to join the jth group, which contains the RPU_j, $\mathbb{G}_{RPU_j}$ vector values are reduced by $\mathbb{D}_{c_i}$ values. This group formation process is repeated sequentially until all CUs are grouped. When the grouping procedure finishes, the topology of smart grid is represented by a collection of groups, which shape a two-level tree structure rooted at each RPU.

Due to the limitations in accuracy of forecasts, power energy yield from RPUs cannot be exactly predicted on a day-ahead market. In addition, the energy request of each power appliance is also dynamically changed. To adapt the current system situation, $\mathbb{D}$ and $\mathbb{S}$ vector values are adjusted periodically as follows.

$$\begin{cases} D_i^k = D_i^k + \alpha \times \left[D_i^{current} - D_i^k \right] \\ \\ S_j^k = S_j^k + \beta \times \left[S_j^{current} - S_j^k \right] \end{cases}, \text{ s.t., } k \in H \text{ and}$$
$$0 \leq \alpha, \beta \leq 1 \tag{9}$$

where the parameter α and β are learning rate to control the relative weights given to past and current information. Under diverse smart grid environments, a fixed value for α and β cannot effectively adapt to the changing conditions. The *CGGS* scheme treats it as an on-line decision problem and adaptively modify α and β values. When the power load difference ($D_i^{current} - D_i^k$) is small, the power load is uniformly distributed over time. Therefore, the *CGGS* scheme can put more emphasis on power request history, i.e., on D_i^k. In this case, a lower value of α is more suitable. But if power load distributions is non-uniform, due to temporal fluctuations, the *CGGS* scheme should strongly depend on the recent amount of power load differentiation, i.e., on ($D_i^{current} - D_i^k$). In this case, a higher value of α is more suitable. By the real-time monitoring, the value of α is adjusted based on the ratio of the current power differentiation to history, i.e. | $D_i^{current} - D_i^k$ |/ D_i^k . The value of β is also adaptively modified in the same manner, i.e., | $S_j^{current} - S_j^k$ |/ S_j^k .

Based on the adaptively adjusted $\mathbb{D}$ and $\mathbb{S}$ information, each CU has a chance to reconsider the previous grouping decision and can change its own group. Therefore, the third stage of grouping algorithm is developed as group re-configuration procedure. On a daily basis, each CU individually monitors the currently modification of its own $\mathbb{D}$ vector and neighbor RPUs' $\mathbb{S}$ vectors. If a CU can improve its payoff (i.e., the payoff in the new formed group is strictly preferred over the previous group), the CU can leave the current group and join a new group. For example, the c_i performs a switch operation from the current group S_k to the group $S_{k'}$ if the below condition is satisfied.

$$U_{c_i}\left(c_i \in S_k\right) < U_{c_i}\left(c_i \in S_{k'}\right) \text{ if}$$
$$S_k \cup \left\{c_i\right\} \succ_i S_{k'} \cup \left\{c_i\right\} \qquad (10)$$

By using the group switching operation, CUs can be re-grouped and the group structure Π is modified into a new grouping set $\Pi' = \left(\Pi \setminus \left\{S_k, S_{k'}\right\}\right) \cup \left\{S_k \setminus \left\{c_i\right\}, S_{k'} \cup \left\{c_i\right\}\right\}$. This dynamic re-configuration approach can make the smart grid more responsive to the current system situation.

$$N = \left\{c_1, ..., c_n\right\}.$$

Scheduling Algorithm in Smart Grid

Since energy cannot be stored efficiently on a large scale, the smart grid must perfectly balance the demand of all customers at any instant with supply. Therefore, next generation smart grids will use new monitoring and control technologies to balance supply and demand over a region more effectively than is done today. To improve energy efficiency, Demand Side Management (DSM) is one of the important functions and has been regarded as a promising technology in a smart grid. To accommodate the demand fluctuations over a daily cycle, DSM is developed to reshape the demand profile by shifting power consumption. Therefore, this technique can transfer as much of the flexible demand as possible away from peak time into the period of lower activity without impacting negatively on the system performance. However, most conventional DSM approaches are controlled in a centralized control manner, and too static to adapt the real world situation due to the lack of automation (Saffre, 2010).

Usually, power-appliance services can be categorized into two classes; shiftable (*S*) and non-shiftable (*NS*) services. For *S* services, such as washing machine and electric vehicle chargers, the *CGGS* scheme can schedule power requirements flexibly during the schedule-available period. Since *S* services need only to guarantee its deadline, the *S* services are amenable to adaptation with variable power levels between service request time and deadline. For *NS* services, such as TV and fridge which have fixed power requirements during the operation period, the *CGGS* scheme should ensure the continuous supply of power. Therefore, *NS* services should be executed immediately with a fixed power level. In the *CGGS* scheme, *S* and *NS* services are mixed and service scheduling is carried out in a cooperative manner.

We define Ψ_k as the set of requested services in the kth group, $\Psi_k = \left\{sr_1, ..., sr_i, ..., sr_m\right\}$ where m is the total number of requested services. The set Ψ_k consists of two different service types; S and NS. If the sr_i is a NS type service, sr_i is characterized by $\{a_i, r\_c_i\}$ where a_i is a service start time and r_c_i is the requested power level; a_i is the current time $(a_i = c_t)$, and r_c_i is a fixed value during service execution period. If the sr_i is a S type service, sr_i is characterized as $\{a_i, d_i, t\_c_i\}$ where a_i is a service request time, d_i is the service deadline ($s_i < d_i$) and t_c_i is the total power energy for the service sr_i. The assigned power level for the service sr_i at time t $\left(PS_i(t)\right)$ is defined as

$$PS_i(t) = \begin{cases} PS_i(t) = r\_c_i & \text{if } sr_i \in NS \\ 0 \le PS_i(t) \le t\_c_i & \text{if } sr_i \in S \end{cases}$$

(11)

At the current time, the total power consumption in the kth group $\left(TP_k(c_t)\right)$ is defined as the sum of all assigned power level for running services at the current time (c_t).

$$TP_k(c_t) = \sum_{i=1}^{m} PS_i(c_t), \text{s.t.}, sr_i \in_k, m = \Psi_k$$

(12)

The average $\left(AP_L\right)$ power levels during a day are defined as

$$AP_L = \frac{\int_1^H TP_k(t)dt}{H}, \text{s.t.}, H = 24$$

(13)

To potentially increase sustainability of the smart grid while lowering overall operational cost, the main goal of the scheduling algorithm is to minimize the $TP_k(c_t)$ while satisfying the constraints of all S services' deadlines. To satisfy this goal, the $CGGS$ scheme proposes an adaptive

online DSM scheduling approach – dynamically switches power levels based on the accumulated workload. When the power is supplied with a low level voltage, the service execution may be prolonged but the energy efficiency is very high. On the other hand, when the power can be set with a high level, service requests can be completed sooner with an expense of cost. Therefore, the $CGGS$ scheme tries to maintain each group's power level effectively while avoiding the adverse effect of running too slow to meet the required deadline demands.

To provide energy efficiency, the online scheduling strategy is to minimize the difference between $TP_k(c_t)$ and AP_L. Therefore, the $CGGS$ scheme adaptively reschedules the start times and power levels of shiftable services. There are two kinds of adaptive service techniques: for degradation and for upgradation. When the degradation (*or* upgradation) policy is applied to the shiftable services at the current time, the assigned power energy $(PS_i(c_t))$ decreases (*or* increases). This adaptive rescheduling technique based on real time feedback tries to balance the system load between the current and future times. Therefore, the developed scheduling algorithm can avoid abrupt power level changes over time as much as possible. Based on these requirements, the $CGGS$ scheme can formulate the following optimization problem:

Minimizw : $\min\left(TP_k(c_t) - AP_L\right)$ and

$$\min\left(\sum_{k=1}^{H}\max[S_j^k - \sum_{i=1}^{m}D_i^k, 0]\right)$$

(14)

subject to: $\int_{t_s}^{t_f} PS_i(t)dt = t_{ci}$

where $t_s \leq t_f \leq d_i$, if $sr_i \in S$

$$PS_i(t) = r \_ c_i, \text{if } sr_i \in NS$$

The scheduling algorithm in the *CGGS* scheme, which is distributedly executed in each group, can 1) mitigate the impact of power imbalance to facilitate the integration of renewable energy, 2) complete services just before its deadline, 3) reshape the energy consumption to reduce the overall operational cost, and 4) flatten the load over time by shaving the power peak.

The Main Steps of the *CGGS* Scheme

Due to the dynamics of smart grid environments, traditional DSM approaches are impractical to justify realistic system operations. The *CGGS* scheme adopts a coopetition paradigm by employing self-organizing grouping and flexible online scheduling algorithms. Therefore, the *CGGS* scheme defines the phenomenon that differs from competition or cooperation, and stresses two faces (i.e., cooperation and competition) of CUs. According to the grouping algorithm, self-concerned CUs can form groups in a competitive manner. In each group, scheduling is executed in a cooperative fashion. This combined approach suggests that a judicious mixture of collaboration and competition is advantageous in smart grid environments.

Based on the notion of coopetition game model, the algorithms in the *CGGS* scheme are developed to support decentralized smart grid system, which substantially powered by various forms of intermittent RPUs and stable NPUs. By a sophisticated combination of grouping and scheduling algorithms, the *CGGS* scheme dynamically adapts the current system condition and can effectively approximate an optimal system performance. Usually, the traditional optimal and centric algorithms have exponential time complexity. However, the distributed online algorithm in the *CGGS* scheme

has only polynomial time complexity. The main steps of the *CGGS* scheme are given next.

Step 1: At the initial stage, customer units (CUs) and renewable power units (RPUs) are autonomously self-organized into disjoint groups. Each CU discovers its neighbor RPUs and selects a specific RPU to maximize its expected payoff according to (15-8).

Step 2: After a CU joins a group, its corresponding $\mathbb{G}$ vector values are modified. In a distributed online manner, this group formation process is repeated recursively until all CUs are grouped.

Step 3: To adapt the current system situation, $\mathbb{D}$ and $\mathbb{S}$ vector values are adjusted periodically based on (15-9). In addition, the leaning parameter α and β are dynamically adjusted $|D_i^{current} - D_i^k| / D_i^k$ and $|S_j^{current} - S_j^k| / S_j^k$, respectively.

Step 4: In each group, the developed scheduling algorithm is triggered in a distributed manner.

Step 5: When a new *NS* service is requested in each group, this request is accepted without scheduling and executed immediately to guarantee required constraints.

Step 6: When a new *S* service is requested in each group, the developed algorithm schedules this request to minimize $(TP_k(c_t) - AP_L)$ while satisfying the deadline requirement.

Step 7: Every *unit_time*, $TP_k(c_t)$ value in each group is monitored constantly for load balancing over time and running services are dynamically rescheduled to approximately solve the optimization problem in (15-14).

7.1: The *CGGS* scheme sorts S services in a decreasing order based on their deadlines.

7.2: If $S_j^k - \sum_{i=1}^m D_i^k > 0$, ($c_t$ is in the kth time period), the *CGGS* scheme selects the

Figure 2. Performance evaluations of the CGGS scheme

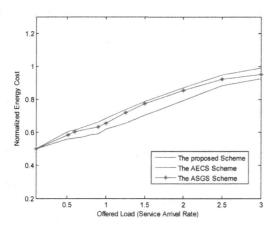

(a) Normalized Energy Cost

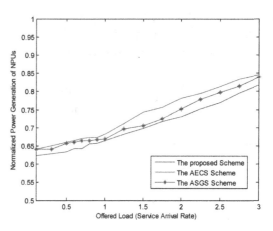

(b) Power Generation Amount of NPUs

sr_i ($sr_i \in S$) having the earliest deadline and the $PS_i\left(c_t\right)$ is upgraded by the power unit (P_U).

- Sequentially, next service is selected and power is upgraded in the same manner until $S_j^k - \sum_{i=1}^{m} D_i^k$ ≤ 0.

7.3: If $TP_k\left(c_t\right) - AP_L > 0$, currently executing S services are adaptively rescheduled.

- The *CGGS* scheme select a executing sr_i ($sr_i \in S$) having the latest deadline and the $PS_i\left(c_t\right)$ is degraded by the power unit (P_U) while satisfying the deadline requirement.
- Sequentially, next service is selected and power is degraded in the same manner until $TP_k\left(c_t\right) - AP_L \leq 0$.

Step 8: On a daily basis, group re-configuration procedure is triggered by considering the adaptively adjusted and $\mathbb{S}$ information. Ac-

cording to (15-10), a CU can leave the current group and join a new group.

Step 9: Constantly, the system is self-monitoring the current situation; proceeds to Step 3.

Figure 2 demonstrates that the performance of the proposed *CGGS* scheme is generally superior to those of other existing schemes: the *AECS* scheme and the *ASGS* scheme. The design goal of the *CGGS* scheme is to minimize energy cost while guaranteeing service requirements. To satisfy this goal, adaptive grouping and scheduling algorithms are developed and practically applied to smart grid management based on real time online manner.

Summary

Smart grid is the next-generation power system that incorporates power infrastructures with communication network technologies. However, due to the dynamic power demands and intermittent renewable energy resources, demand side management becomes a key factor in enhancing system performance. In the *CGGS* scheme, a new smart grid management scheme is developed by jointly employing the grouping and scheduling algorithms. Based on the basic concept of coopetition game, the developed approach can get an excellent solution for complex smart grid situation. Therefore, the *CGGS* scheme can minimize power generation cost while satisfying the requirements of individual appliances. In addition, the algorithms in the *CGGS* scheme are designed in a distributed online fashion without central controller. This approach is suitable for ultimate practical implementation in real world smart grid operations.

REFERENCES

Altman, E., El-Azouzi, R., Hayel, Y., & Tembine, H. (2008). An Evolutionary Game approach for the design of congestion control protocols in wireless networks. In *Proceedings of Physicomnet Workshop*. Academic Press.

Bossert, W., & Tan, G. (1995). An arbitration game and the egalitarian bargaining solution. *Social Choice and Welfare, 12*(1), 29–41. doi:10.1007/BF00182191

Bouncken, R. B., & Fredrich, V. (2011). Coopetition: Its successful management in the nexus of dependency and trust. In *Proceedings of PICMET'11*. PICMET.

Brandenburger, A., & Stuart, H. (2007). Biform Games. *Management Science, 53*, 537–549. doi:10.1287/mnsc.1060.0591

Bu, S., Yu, F. R., & Liu, P. X. (2011). A game-theoretical decision-making scheme for electricity retailers in the smart grid with demand-side management. In *Proceedings of IEEE SmartGridComm*, (pp. 387-391). IEEE.

de Haan, J. E. S., Frunt, J., & Kling, W. L. (2010). Mitigation of wind power fluctuations in smart grids. In *Proceedings of IEEE ISGT Europe*. IEEE.

Fadlullah, Z. M., Nozaki, Y., Takeuchi, A., & Kato, N. (2011). A survey of game theoretic approaches in smart grid. In *Proceedings of Wireless Communications and Signal Processing*. Academic Press. doi:10.1109/WCSP.2011.6096962

Fang, X., Misra, S., Xue, G., & Yang, D. (2012). The New and Improved Power Grid: A Survey. *IEEE Communications Surveys & Tutorials, 14*(4), 944–980. doi:10.1109/SURV.2011.101911.00087

Génin, T., & Aknine, S. (2010). Coalition Formation Strategies for Multiagent Hedonic Games. In *Proceedings of IEEE International Conference on Tools with Artificial Intelligence,* (pp. 465-472). IEEE.

Ghasemi, N., & Hosseini, S. M. (2010). Comparison of smart grid with cognitive radio: Solutions to spectrum scarcity. In *Proceedings of ICACT,* (pp. 898-903). ICACT.

Guan, Z., Yuan, D., & Zhang, H. (2008). Novel coopetition paradigm based on bargaining theory or collaborative multimedia resource management. In *Proceedings of IEEE PIMRC*. IEEE.

Kim, S. W. (2011). An Adaptive Online Power Control Scheme based on the Evolutionary Game Theory. *IET Communications, 5*(18), 2648–2655. doi:10.1049/iet-com.2011.0093

Kim, S. W. (2012). Biform Game based Cognitive Radio Scheme for Smart Grid Communications. *Journal of Communications and Networks, 14*(6), 614–618. doi:10.1109/JCN.2012.00027

Kim, S. W. (2013). Adaptive Smart Grid Management Scheme based on the Coopetition Game Model. *ETRI, 6*, 1–12.

Kim, Y. M., Kim, W. S., You, H. R., Lee, S. C., & Lee, H. J. (2010). Group-based management for cooperative spectrum sensing in cognitive radio networks. In *Proceedings of ICACT,* (pp. 119-123). ICACT.

Li, D., Jayaweera, S. K., & Naseri, A. (2011). Auctioning game based Demand Response scheduling in smart grid. In *Proceedings of IEEE Online Conference on Green Communications,* (pp. 58-63). IEEE.

Li, D., Xu, Y., Liu, J., Wang, X., & Han, Z. (2010). A Market Game for Dynamic Multi-Band Sharing in Cognitive Radio Networks. In *Proceedings of IEEE International Conference on Communications*. IEEE.

Liu, J., Shen, L., Song, T., & Wang, X. (2009). Demand-matching spectrum sharing game for non-cooperative cognitive radio network. In *Proceedings of International Conference on Wireless Communications & Signal Processing*. Academic Press.

Logenthiran, T., Srinivasan, D., & Shun, T. Z. (2012). Demand Side Management in Smart Grid Using Heuristic Optimization. *IEEE Transactions on Smart Grid*, *3*(3), 1244–1252. doi:10.1109/TSG.2012.2195686

Long, C., Zhang, Q., Li, B., Yang, H., & Guan, X. (2007). Non-Cooperative Power Control for Wireless Ad Hoc Networks with Repeated Games. *IEEE Journal on Selected Areas in Communications*, *25*(6), 1101–1112. doi:10.1109/JSAC.2007.070805

Matt, P. A., Toni, F., & Dionysiou, D. (2006). The distributed negotiation of egalitarian resource allocations. In *Proceedings of the 1st International Workshop on Computational Social Choice,* (pp. 304-316). Academic Press.

Menasche, D. S., Figueiredo, D. R., & Silva, E. S. (2005). An evolutionary game-theoretic approach to congestion control. *Performance Evaluation*, *62*(1-4), 295–312. doi:10.1016/j.peva.2005.07.028

Miorandi, D., & De Pellegrini, F. (2012). Demand-side management in smart grids: An evolutionary games perspective. In *Proceedings of Performance Evaluation Methodologies and Tools* (pp. 178–187). Academic Press. doi:10.4108/valuetools.2012.250351

Mohsenian-Rad, H., Wong, V. W. S., Jatskevich, J., Schober, R., & Leon-Garcia, A. (2010). Autonomous demand side management based on game-theoretic energy consumption scheduling for the future smart grid. *IEEE Trans. on Smart Grid*, *1*(3), 320–331. doi:10.1109/TSG.2010.2089069

Roossien, B., Noort, A. V. D., Kamphuis, R., Bliek, F., Eijgelaar, M., & Wit, J. (2011). Balancing wind power fluctuations with a domestic Virtual Power Plant in Europe's First Smart Grid. In *Proceedings of IEEE Trondheim PowerTech*. IEEE.

Saad, W., Han, Z., Hjorungnes, A., Niyato, D., & Hossain, E. (2011). Coalition Formation Games for Distributed Cooperation Among Roadside Units into implement Vehicular Networks. *IEEE Journal on Selected Areas in Communications*, *29*(1), 48–60. doi:10.1109/JSAC.2011.110106

Saad, W., Han, Z., Poor, H. V., & Başar, T. (2012). Game theoretic methods for the smart grid. *IEEE Signal Processing Magazine*, *29*(5), 86–105. doi:10.1109/MSP.2012.2186410

Saffre, F., & Gedge, R. (2010). Demand-Side Management for the Smart Grid. In *Proceedings of IEEE/IFIP Network Operations and Management Symposium Workshops,* (pp. 300-303). IEEE.

Stuart, H. W. (2005). Biform Analysis of Inventory Competition. *Manufacturing & Service Operations Management*, *7*(4), 347–359. doi:10.1287/msom.1050.0090

Sun, L., & Xu, X. (2005). Coopetitive game, equilibrium and their applications. In *Proceedings of International Conference on Algorithmic Applications in Management,* (pp. 104-111). Academic Press.

Suris, J., DaSilva, L., Han, Z., & MacKenzie, A. (2007). Cooperative game theory fordistributed spectrum sharing. In *Proceedings of the IEEE International Conference on Communications*, (pp. 5282–5287). IEEE.

Vinyals, M., Bistaffa, F., Farinelli, A., & Rogers, A. (2012). Stable coalition formation among energy consumers in the smart grid. In *Proceedings of AAMAS*. AAMAS.

Wang, B., Liu, K., & Clancy, T. (2010). Evolutionary cooperative spectrum sensing game: how to collaborate? *IEEE Transactions on Communications*, *58*(3), 890–900. doi:10.1109/TCOMM.2010.03.090084

Zhu, Q., Han, Z., & Basar, T. (2012). A differential game approach to distributed demand side management in smart grid. [IEEE.]. *Proceedings of the IEEE, ICC*, 3345–3350.

Zhu, Z., Tang, J., & Lambotharan, S. (2012). An integer linear programming based optimization for home demand-side management in smart grid. In *Proceedings of IEEE ISGT*. IEEE.

KEY TERMS AND DEFINITIONS

Demand Side Management (DSM): The modification of consumer demand for energy through various methods such as financial incentives and education. Usually, the goal of demand side management is to encourage the consumer to use less energy during peak hours, or to move the time of energy use to off-peak times such as nighttime and weekends.

Electricity Distribution: The final stage in the delivery of electricity to end users. A distribution system's network carries electricity from the transmission system and delivers it to consumers. Typically, the network would include medium-voltage (2kV to 34.5kV) power lines, substations and pole-mounted transformers, low-voltage (less than 1 kV) distribution writing and sometimes meters.

Energy Storage System: A device that stores electricity when the demand is low and provides stored electricity when the demand is high. This improves energy efficiency and stabilizes operations of the electricity grid.

Peak Demand: Used to refer to a historically high point in the sales record of a particular product. In terms of energy use, peak demand describes a period of simultaneous, strong consumer demand or a period of highest demand in a billing period.

Renewable Energy: Generally defined as energy that comes from resources which are naturally replenished on a human timescale such as sunlight, wind, rain, tides, waves and geothermal heat. Renewable energy replaces conventional fuels in four distinct areas: electricity generation, hot water/space heating, motor fuels, and rural (off-grid) energy services.

Scheduling: The method by which threads, processes or data flows are given access to system resources. This is usually done to load balance and share system resources effectively or achieve a target quality of service. The need for a scheduling algorithm arises from the requirement for most modern systems to perform multitasking and multiplexing.

Chapter 16
Game Paradigm for Wired Networks

ABSTRACT

There are a great number of situations in which a many agent system self-organizes by coordinating individual actions. Such coordination is usually achieved by agents with partial information about the system, and in some cases optimizing utility functions that conflict with each other. A similar situation is found in many network situations. An example of a frustrated multi-agent system is given by the evolutionary minority game in which many players have to make a binary choice and the winning option is the one made by the minority. In evolutionary minority game, players make decisions by evaluating the performance of their strategies from past experience, and hence, they can adapt. The players have access to global information, which is in turn generated by the actions of the agents themselves. As the game progresses, non-trivial fluctuations arise in the agents' collective decisions – these can be understood in terms of the dynamical formation of crowds consisting of agents using correlated strategies. This chapter explores the game paradigm for wired networks.

EVOLUTIONARY MINORITY GAME BASED CONGESTION CONTROL (*EMGCC*) SCHEME FOR WIRED NETWORKS

Telecommunication technology advances in the past decade have brought networking to another level in terms of reliability and link speeds. However, existing transmission control protocols do not provide satisfactory performance due to their inefficient congestion control mechanisms.

Recently, S. Kim proposed a new Evolutionary Minority Game based Congestion Control (*EMGCC*) scheme to provide QoS provisioning while ensuring bandwidth efficiency. Based on the evolutionary minority game model, the *EMGCC* scheme adaptively controls the packet transmission to converge a desirable network equilibrium. For the efficient network management, the evolutionary minority game approach is dynamic and flexible that can adaptively respond to current network conditions.

DOI: 10.4018/978-1-4666-6050-2.ch016

Development Motivation

Nowadays, the continuing growth of multimedia traffic raises the important issue of how to efficiently utilize network bandwidth. In addition, network systems should support widely different and diversified multimedia data services. Different data services require diverse Quality of Service (QoS). Usually heterogeneous multimedia data can be categorized into two classes according to the required QoS: class I (real time) and class II (non-real time). Class I data has a higher priority than class II data, so a multimedia network should take into account the prioritization among different multimedia traffic services. For the service differentiation, QoS provisioning strategy plays a crucial role (Mahapatra, Anand, & Agrawal, 2006). Therefore, the future network system is expected to provide a comprehensive solution where multimedia services can be delivered to the user with a satisfactory high data rate, premium quality and high security (Tao, & Yu, 2011), (Shaii, Ismail, Jais, & Manan, 2008).

Due to the shared nature of network bandwidth, all network users contend for medium access. If the traffic exceeds a network capacity, network congestion occurs. When congestion occurs, packets are dropped either because of collision or buffer overflow; it seriously penalizes the network throughput and coverage fidelity. In order to fully utilize the network bandwidth and effectively maximize the network performance, we have to control the traffic flow (Kutsuna & Fujita, 2011). Various congestion control algorithms have been developed to satisfy service requirements while maximizing network efficiency at the same time. However, due to the complexity of network structures, the nature of supported services, and the variety of involved dynamic parameters, the design of effective congestion control algorithms is a challenging problem (Shaii, 2008).

In network systems, a number of intelligent nodes interact with each other and make control decisions individually without centralized coordina-tion. To understand the behavior of self-regarding nodes, game theory has some attractive features (Shang, 2007), (Araujo & Lamb, 2004). Today, game theory is a sort of unified field theory for the rational side of social science, where 'social' is interpreted broadly, to include human as well as non-human players such as computers or network nodes. Therefore, game theory can describe the possibility to react to the actions of the other network nodes and analyze the situations of conflict and cooperation. However, classical game theory makes the assumption that game players are perfectly rational. In this assumption, each player must have knowledge of all relevant aspects of the environment, and enough computational power to choose the best strategy. However, this supposition is too strong to implement in the real world game player. Many studies have suggested that game players have very limited information and often do not behave in a perfect rational way. Therefore, for the practical game operation, players should be modeled with bounded rationality; bounded rational players have limits in their abilities to make their decisions (Shang, 2007), (Araujo, 2004).

In 1997, Challet and Zhang proposed a game model called Minority Game (MG) to study the effects of bounded rationality (Kutsuna, 2011). MG is a repeated coordination game where players use a number of different strategies in order to join one of the two available groups, and those who belong to the minority group are rewarded. Recently, MG models have been extended widely. The Evolutionary Minority Game (EMG) is regarded as a paradigmatic model of the evolutionary version of MG game. It allows players dynamically to adapt their strategy according to their past experiences (Shang, 2007). In the last few years, EMG has attracted considerable attentions and has been investigated extensively in many engineering fields (Araujo, 2004).

Motivated by the above discussion, the *EMGCC* scheme has been developed based on the EMG model. In the *EMGCC* scheme, sender nodes (i.e., source nodes for packet transmissions) estimate the current traffic condition and adaptively select the best packet transmission strategy based on the real-time online monitoring. The main goal is to maximize network efficiency while ensuring QoS prioritization. Under various QoS constraints and widely different and diversified traffic load situations, the *EMGCC* scheme can get a globally desirable network performance.

RELATED WORK

Recently, several congestion control schemes have been presented for complex network systems. The Multiple Class Congestion Avoidance (*MCCA*) scheme is a novel congestion control protocol (Mahapatra, 2006). It detects network congestion jointly by using dual buffer thresholds and weighted buffer difference. To ensure weighted fairness, the *MCCA* scheme dynamically estimates channel loading and maximizes channel utilization with an implicit manner. The Fair and Efficient Congestion Avoidance (*FECA*) scheme is also a congestion control scheme for high speed networks (Kutsuna, 2011). Based on the minority game model, this scheme realizes a selective reduction of the transmission speed of senders. On detecting any congestion, the *FECA* scheme starts a game among all senders who are participating in the communication. In this game, losers reduce the transmission speed by a multiplicative factor.

Congestion Control Algorithms in the *EMGCC* Scheme

Under dynamically changing network environments, the *EMGCC* scheme can be concluded to be an effective solution for the packet transmission system. By using adaptive evolutionary minority game approach, an effective network equilibrium can be obtained.

Minority Game Model

Minority Game (MG) is a game including the procedures used by the reasoning game players. Classical MG is designed for modeling the financial market made of bounded rational players with learning ability (Tanaka-Yamawaki & Tokuoka, 2006). The major function of those players is to decide one out of two possible actions, corresponding to buy or sell, and all players who have made the minority choice win the game (Araujo, 2004).

Let *G* be a set of an odd number of MG players; all players synchronously repeat a round, and receive a profit when it becomes a winner of a round. In each round, each player selects one of two groups. Then, the minority of players with respect to the selected groups is determined as the winner of the round (Kutsuna, 2011). This kind of game model could coarsely speaking be involved in a stock market where investors share information and make buy-or-sell decisions in order to gain profit. If the number of sellers of a particular stock is larger than the number of buyers, supply exceeds demand and one expects a decrease in the stock price. Then the buyers, being in minority, would win due to the low price levels. In the opposite case sellers would win, because excess demand would increase the price of the stock (Sysi-Aho, Saramäki, & Kaski, 2005). In the long run, the price of the stock eventually settles down to its equilibrium value, i.e. supply and demand are close to each other and the public information has been efficiently utilized. The MG can be viewed as simulating the performances of competing individuals and the welfare of the society they compose. Therefore, MG can be seen as a simplified model of a market economy. This approach is useful to analyze financial systems (Tanaka-Yamawaki, 2006).

In the last few years, MG has been extended by adding a simple evolutionary-based learning procedure (Mähönen & Petrova, 2008). The evolutionary learning, where underperforming results are discarded and new ones are generated for substitution, is well-known and effective method to solve a risk control problem. This approach allows players to adapt their strategy according to their past experiences. Therefore, players apply a very simple learning algorithm to discard bad strategies and create new ones (Shang, 2007), (Araujo, 2004). In the *EMGCC* scheme, a new network congestion control algorithms have been developed based on the Evolutionary Minority Game (EMG) model. In the *EMGCC* scheme, each node in a competitive network system is assumed as a bounded rational game player. To maximize the network performance, the *EMGCC* scheme aims at developing the effects of inductive learning. Through reasoning procedure, network system closely converges to a game-theoretic equilibrium. During the interactive EMG processing, an equilibrium can be obtained at a point where the sum of gains is maximum. At this time, the system is using the given resources in an efficient way by maximizing the number of satisfied players in each game round (Tanaka-Yamawaki, 2006).

Evolutionary Minority Game for Congestion Control Algorithm

When nodes send more packets than the network can accommodate, network congestion occurs in the form of router buffer overflows. Usually, congestion effect includes packet loss, which deteriorates network throughput and QoS. Therefore, various algorithms have been developed that prevent traffic congestion by setting controls on the sending systems. In the *EMGCC* scheme, the EMG model is adopted to design a congestion control scheme. Usually, in network systems, the sender's action is very similar to the behavior of selfish and bounded rational players. They decide to send a packet or not at each time step. These decisions are made independently, and without communicating with each other players. In the *EMGCC* scheme scenario, all players maintain a common look-up table, which has the outcome of the last *m* rounds of the game. It represents the

most recent trend, and is the only information that players have. At the end of each round, players belonging to the success-group are the winners, each of them gaining profit while players belonging to the fail-group loose profit. Success-group consists of sender nodes, which successfully transmit the latest packet and fail-group consists of sender nodes, whose latest packets are dropped. By referring to the history in the last *m* rounds, the player *i*'s total action value (T_i) is given by

$$T_i = \sum_{k=1}^{m} a_i(k),$$

$$where \begin{cases} a_i(k) = 1 & \text{If the player } i\text{'s packet} \\ & \text{is transmitted at the } k^{th} \text{ round} \\ a_i(k) = -1 & \text{If the player } i\text{'s packet} \\ & \text{is dropped at the } k^{th} \text{ round} \\ a_i(k) = 0 & \text{Otherwise} \\ & \text{(i.e., packet is halted)} \end{cases}$$

(1)

If network conditions are not conducive for a successful transmission, deferring packet transmission until conditions get better does no harm. In the *EMGCC* scheme, 'packet is halted' means that packet is not sent to avoid unnecessary packet loss. Routers determine the winner of an each game round. After receiving packets from sender nodes, each router forwards them by referring to the header of the packet. When network congestion occurs, a discard of packets happens in a router. To handle the overloaded traffic while providing diverse multimedia services, the *EMGCC* scheme also develops a buffer management algorithm by using reservation technique. To ensure the higher priority class I traffic, some buffer capacity is reserved. Under widely diverse network environments, this capacity should be dynamically adjusted based on the current network condition. To dynamically determine the capacity, the *EMGCC* scheme partitions the time axis into equal intervals of length *unit_time*. During every *unit_time*, each router adjusts individually the amount of reserved capacity (Res_c) based on real time measurements.

To maintain the Res_c close to the optimal value, the *EMGCC* scheme defines a traffic window which is used to keep the history of class I traffic requests (W_{class_I}). The traffic window is of size $[t_c - t_{class\_I}, t_c]$, where t_c is the current time, and t_{class_I} is the window length, which can be adjusted in time steps equal to *unit_time*. If the packet dropping probability for class I services is larger (*or* smaller) than its predefined target probability (P_{class_I}), t_{class_I} is increased (*or* decreased). By using the traffic window, the value of Res_c can be estimated as the sum of requested class I packet amounts in W_{class_I} as follows.

$$Res_c = \sum_{i \in W_{class\_I}} \left(B_i \times N_i \right), \text{ s.t., } i \text{ is class I data}$$

services (2)

where N_i and B_i are the number of packets and the corresponding packet size of data i, respectively. Therefore, by using this traffic window, the *EMGCC* scheme can adjust the amount of Res_c at every *unit_time*. This approach is more responsive to changes in the network condition.

With the aim of approximating optimal network performance while maintaining QoS guarantees, the *EMGCC* scheme adaptively adjusts two control parameters. In the *EMGCC* scheme, there are two buffer management parameters: queue range (Q_r) and packet marking probability (M_p). Q_r is a threshold for traffic buffering, and M_p is a probability to drop class II data packets in a randomized manner (Kim & Kim, 2007). Between class I and class II traffic services, the *EMGCC* scheme aims to ensure class I packet buffering until Q_r is reached. Therefore, Q_r is defined to be equal to the current Res_B. By inspecting the current reserved buffer capacity, the Q_r value can be adaptively adjusted at every *unit_time*. For effective buffer management, the ideal situation is that the current queue length (L) is the same as Q_r. Therefore, L is used as the main indicator for determining M_p. In the developed algorithm, M_p is also adaptively adjusted at every *unit_time*. According to the current queue situations, M_p is defined as follows.

$$M_p = \max \left(\frac{L - Q_r}{ML - Q_r}, 0 \right) \quad (3)$$

where ML is the maximum queue length. When packets are queued, the *EMGCC* scheme drops class II data packets with probability M_p. Dropping packets provides feedback information to source nodes. By monitoring the status of all packets passing through routers, sender nodes can detect the congestion level and count the total action value (T) in each round. Finally, player's payoff is defined based on the T value and the degree of current QoS. At the kth round, the player i's utility function ($U_i(k)$) is given by.

$$U_i(k) = \left(\left[\alpha \times \frac{T_i}{S_m} \right] + \left[(1 - \alpha) \times f(k) \right] \right) \text{ s . t . ,}$$

$$f(k) = \begin{cases} 1, & if\ QoS_m \geq QoS_R \\ \\ \dfrac{QoS_m}{QoS_R}, & if\ QoS_m < QoS_R \end{cases} \quad (4)$$

where S_m, QoS_m and QoS_R are the number of sending packets, the number of successfully sent packets and the number of required transmission packets during the latest m rounds, respectively. It is easy to see that T_i / S_m represents the reliability of data communications. The parameter α controls the relative weights given to network reliability or QoS degree. Under diverse network environments, a fixed value of α cannot effectively adapt to the changing conditions. The *EMGCC* scheme treats it as an online decision problem and adaptively modify α value. When the QoS_m is less than the QoS_R, the *EMGCC* scheme should put more emphasis on the QoS provisioning, i.e., on $f(k)$. In this case, a lower value of α is more suitable. When the current QoS degree is higher than the requirement ($QoS_m \geq QoS_R$), the *EMGCC* scheme should strongly depend on the network reliability, i.e., on T_i / S_m. In this case, a higher value of α is more suitable. In the developed algorithm, the α value is examined periodically, every game round, in order to approximate the best value. Therefore, the *EMGCC* scheme adjusts the value of α based on the current QoS degree as follows.

$$\alpha = \min(1, QoS_m / QoS_R) \qquad (5)$$

THE MAIN STEPS OF THE *EMGCC* SCHEME

The fundamental assumption of classical game theory is that players must be rational to determine their decisions. However, this assumption is obviously not satisfied under the real world network environment; experiments have shown that players do not always act rationally. The evolutionary approach offers a more realistic model for players with bounded rationality (Menasche, Figueiredo, & Silva, 2005), (Altman, El-Azouzi, Hayel, & Tembine, 2008). During the evolutionary minority game, players have a chance to reconsider the current strategy and react to maximize the expected payoff.

In the *EMGCC* scheme, players (i.e., sender nodes) have a simple inference algorithm to decide the strategy for the next round game. There are two different strategies for sender nodes – packet sending or packet halting. During the game process, the probabilities of *packet-send* strategy (P_{ps}) and *packet-halt* strategy (P_{hs}) are defined based on the $U_i(k)$ value. For example, if a sender node selected a packet sending strategy at the kth round and the payoff ($U(k)$) is small compared to the payoff ($U(k-1)$) of $(k-1)^{th}$ round, the P_{ps} for the $(k+1)^{th}$ game round decreases in proportion to the payoff reduction. Therefore, P_{ps} and P_{hs} are dynamically changed at a rate equal to the difference between the current payoff and the previous payoff. The *Packet-send* and *packet-halt* strategies for ($k+1$)th round ($P_{ps}(k+1)$ and $P_{hs}(k+1)$) are defined as follows.

$$
\begin{cases}
\begin{pmatrix} P_{ps}(k+1) - \min\{1, \max(0, P_{ps}(k)+\Delta_k)\} \\ P_{hs}(k+1) - 1 - P_{ps}(k+1) \end{pmatrix}, \\
\qquad \text{If } k^{th} \text{ strategy is a } packet\_send \\
or \\
\begin{pmatrix} P_{hs}(k+1) - \min\{1, \max(0, P_{hs}(k)+\Delta_k)\} \\ P_{ps}(k+1) - 1 - P_{hs}(k+1) \end{pmatrix}, \\
\qquad \text{If } k^{th} \text{ strategy is a } packet\_halt
\end{cases}
$$
$$(6)$$

$$\text{s.t., } \Delta_k = \left. \left(U_i(k) - U_i(k-1) \right) \middle/ U_i(k-1) \right.$$

When a sender node chooses a strategy, it can change the current network environment and triggers reactions by other players. Therefore, after selecting strategies, sender nodes repeatedly interact with other. This interaction mechanism can induce the cooperate behavior of sender nodes in spite of the individual selfishness, and gradually leads the network system into a stable state. Therefore, the *EMGCC* scheme dynamically adapts the current network condition and can effectively approximate an optimal network performance. In addition, sender nodes iteratively change their next strategies in a distributed way. This approach can drastically reduce the computational complexity and control overhead. It is a good point for practical implementations. The main steps of the *EMGCC* scheme are given next.

Step 1: At the initial iteration (k=0), each sender sends a packet ($P_{ps} = 1$). This starting guess guarantees that each player enjoys the same benefit at the beginning of the game.

Step 2: In a distributed online manner, each sender continuously observes the current network condition and QoS information while detecting the congestion occurrence.

Step 3: In each game round, sender nodes monitor the status of all packets passing through the router and count the T value according to (16-1).

Step 4: Individually, each router dynamically estimate the Res_c and M_p values by using (16-2) and (16-3), respectively. When network congestion occurs, packets are dropped based on the corresponding M_p.

Step 5: According to (16-4),(16-5) and (16-6), the next round strategy selection probability is dynamically adjusted. To maximize the expected payoff, sender nodes can change their next strategies, iteratively.

Step 6: When a sender node chooses a strategy, it can change the current network environment and triggers reactions by other sender nodes.

Step 7: After the strategy selection, sender nodes repeatedly interact with other; this interaction mechanism gradually leads the network system into a stable state.

Step 8: Under widely diverse network environments, each sender node is self-monitoring constantly to estimate the current network situation; proceeds to Step 2.

SUMMARY

Evolutionary minority game (EMG) has attracted considerable attentions and been investigated extensively in the last few years. It is a simple model of competition and evolution behaviors that occur with limited resources. In the *EMGCC* scheme, a new congestion control algorithms have been developed for multimedia networks. To get an excellent solution for complex network situation, the basic concept of EMG model is adopted. By using an interactive learning process, sender nodes can adaptively adjust their decisions to reach an effective network equilibrium. Due to the self-regarding feature, these control decisions are made by an entirely distributed fashion without central controller. In real world network operations, this distributed online approach is suitable for ultimate practical implementation. In addition, the developed learning paradigm in the *EMGCC* scheme is able to capture the effect of changes on simple parameters without directly referring to the decisions made by the other sender nodes.

REFERENCES

Altman, E., El-Azouzi, R., Hayel, Y., & Tembine, H. (2008). An Evolutionary Game approach for the design of congestion control protocols in wireless networks. In *Proceedings of Physicomnet Workshop*. Academic Press.

Araujo, R. M., & Lamb, L. C. (2004). Towards understanding the role of learning models in the dynamics of the minority game. In *Proceedings of IEEE International Conference on Tools with Artificial Intelligence,* (pp. 727-731). IEEE.

Kim, S. W., & Kim, S. C. (2007). An Online Buffer Management Algorithm for QoS-Sensitive Multimedia Networks. *ETRI Journal, 29*(5), 685–687. doi:10.4218/etrij.07.0207.0097

Kutsuna, H., & Fujita, S. (2011). A Fair and Efficient Congestion Avoidance Scheme Based on the Minority Game. *Journal of Information Processing Systems, 7*(3), 531–542. doi:10.3745/JIPS.2011.7.3.531

Mahapatra, A., Anand, K., & Agrawal, D. P. (2006). QoS and Energy Aware Routing for Real Time Traffic in Wireless Sensor Networks. *Computer Communications*, *29*(4), 437–445. doi:10.1016/j.comcom.2004.12.028

Mähönen, P., & Petrova, M. (2008). Minority game for cognitive radios: cooperating without cooperation. *Physical Communication*, *1*, 94–102. doi:10.1016/j.phycom.2008.03.001

Menasche, D. S., Figueiredo, D. R., & Silva, E. S. (2005). An evolutionary game-theoretic approach to congestion control. *Performance Evaluation*, *62*(1-4), 295–312. doi:10.1016/j.peva.2005.07.028

Shaii, A. Q., Ismail, R., Jais, J., & Manan, J. (2008). Congestion avoidance: Network based schemes solution. In *Proceedings of International Symposium on Information Technology*. Academic Press.

Shang, L. H. (2007). Self-organized Evolutionary Minority Game on Networks. In *Proceedings of IEEE International Conference on Control and Automation*, (pp. 1885-1889). IEEE.

Sysi-Aho, M., Saramäki, J., & Kaski, K. (2005). Invisible hand effect in an evolutionary minority game model. *Physica A*, *347*, 639–652. doi:10.1016/j.physa.2004.08.029

Tanaka-Yamawaki, M., & Tokuoka, S. (2006). Minority Game as a Model for the Artificial Financial Markets. In *Proceedings of IEEE Congress on Evolutionary Computation*, (pp. 2157-2162). IEEE.

Tao, L., & Yu, F. (2011). A Novel Congestion Detection and Avoidance Algorithm for Multiple Class of Traffic in Sensor Network. In *Proceedings of IEEE International Conference on Cyber Technology in Automation, Control, and Intelligent Systems*, (pp. 72-77). IEEE.

KEY TERMS AND DEFINITIONS

Evolutionary Game Theory (EGT): The application of game theory to evolving populations of lifeforms in biology. EGT is useful in this context by defining a framework of contests, strategies, and analytics into which Darwinian competition can be modelled.

Minority Game: Inspired by the El Farol bar problem, which is a simple model that shows how (selfish) players cooperate with each other in the absence of communication. In the minority game, an odd number of players have to choose one of two choices independently at each turn. The players who end up on the minority side win.

Network Packet: A formatted unit of data carried by a packet-switched network. Computer communications links that do not support packets, such as traditional point-to-point telecommunications links, simply transmit data as a bit stream.

Point-to-Point Link: A dedicated link that connects exactly two communication facilities (e.g., two nodes of a network, an intercom station at an entryway with a single internal intercom station, a radio path between two points, etc.).

Queuing Delay: The time a job waits in a queue until it can be executed. It is a key component of network delay. In a switched network, the time between the completion of signaling by the call originator and the arrival of a ringing signal at the call receiver. In a packet-switched network, the sum of the delays encountered by a packet between the time of insertion into the network and the time of delivery to the addressee.

Router: A device that forwards data packets between computer networks. This creates an overlay internetwork, as a router is connected to two or more data lines from different networks. When a data packet comes in one of the lines, the router reads the address information in the packet to determine its ultimate destination.

Chapter 17
Concluding Remarks

ABSTRACT

The main purpose of this chapter is to present a broad brush picture of the many areas of game theory researches and applications that have come into being. Therefore, this chapter can serve only as a minimal guide to the study of game theory and offer pointers towards future research. Although the discussion here has been primarily concerned with the present and future, it is desirable to have at least some understanding of the past. In addition, a rich reference is provided to help readers more fully appreciate the game theory developments of today.

READING LISTS FOR KEY ISSUES IN GAME THEORY

Since the 1950s, a broad coverage of game theory has successfully been extended. There are many subdisciplines in game theory. The breakneck speed of development of game theory calls for an appreciation of both the many realities of conflict, coordination and cooperation and the abstract investigation of all of them. Therefore, the boundaries among them are not firm, and there is a considerable mix involving, substantive areas (Shubik, 2011).

The purpose in this subsection is to present a broad brush picture of the many areas of game theory that have come into being. Some of the game theory developments may take place with many thousands of books and articles. They can be a minimal guide to key issues and main fields of game theory. The topics and fileds noted below touch on areas where formal models already exist, and special results have been obtained. Although the distinction is not tight all of the topics and fileds and the range of topics are clearly eclectic and sparse, we classify the main ideas of game theory into 19 topics. With no attempt at an in-depth discourse on the proliferation of subspecializations, a broad sketch of many of the current areas of game theory and reading lists are given as follows. In each instance one or a few references in reading lists are noted as early papers or exemplars of work in that specialty.

Introduction to Game Theory

Brown, G., & von Neumann J. (1950). Solutions of games by differential equations. *Annals of Mathematical Studies, 24*, 73-79.

DOI: 10.4018/978-1-4666-6050-2.ch017

Fort, M. (1950). Essential and non-essential fixed points. *American Journal of Mathematics,* 72, 315-322.

Fudenberg, D., & Tirole, J. (1991). *Game Theory.* MIT Press.

Goeree, J., & Holt, C. (2001). Ten little treasures of game theory and ten intuitive contradictions. *American Economic Review,* 91, 1402-1422.

Hart, S. (2002). Evolutionary dynamics and backward induction. *Games and Economic Behavior,* 41, 227-264.

Hart, S., & Mas-Colell, A. (2003). Uncoupled dynamics do not lead to Nash equilibrium. *American Economic Review,* 1830-1836.

Josephson, J. (2008). Stochastic better-reply dynamics in finite games. *Economic Theory,* 35, 381-389.

Josephson, J., & Matros, A. (2003). Stochastic imitation in finite games. *Games and Economic Behavior,* 49, 244-259.

Kohlberg E., & Mertens, J. F. (1986). On the strategic stability of equilibria. *Econometrica,* 54, 1003-1037.

Nagel, R. (1995). Unravelling in guessing games: An experimental study. *American Economic Review,* 85, 1313-1326.

Nash, J. (1950a). *Non-cooperative games* (Ph D thesis). Department of Mathematics, Princeton University.

Nash, J. (1950b). Equilibrium points in n-person games. *Proceedings of the National Academy of Sciences (USA),* 36, 48-49.

Nash, J. (1950c). The bargaining problem. *Econometrica,* 18, 155-162.

Osborne, M., & Rubinstein, A. (1994). *A Course in Game Theory.* MIT Press.

Ritzberger, K. (2002). *Foundations of Non-Cooperative Game Theory.* Oxford: University Press.

Rosenthal, R. (1981). Games of perfect information, predatory pricing and the chain-store paradox. *Journal of Economic Theory,* 25, 92-100.

Ross, D. (2008). Classical game theory, socialization and the rationalization of conventions. Topoi, 27: 57-72.

Sigmund, K. (1993). Games of Life. Oxford: Oxford University Press.

Sobel, J. (2005). Interdependent preferences and reciprocity. *Journal of Economic Literature,* 43, 392-436.

Tucker, A. W., & Luce, R. D. (1959). Contributions to the Theory of Games, Volume IV (Annals of Mathematics Studies, 40). Princeton: Princeton University Press.

Weibull, J. (2004). Testing game theory, in S. Huck (ed.), *Advances in Understanding Strategic Behaviour: Game Theory, Experiments, and Bounded Rationality: Essays in Honour of Werner Guth.* Palgrave.

Winter, S. (1971). Satisficing, selection, and the innovating remnant. *Quarterly Journal of Economics,* 85, 237-261.

Wu, W., & Jian, J. (1962). Essential equilibrium points of n-person non-cooperative games. *Science Sinica,* 11, 1307-1322.

Learning Algorithms for Game Theory

Angeletos, G-M., Hellwig, C., & Pavan, A. (2007). Dynamic Global Games of Regime Change: Learning, Multiplicity, and the Timing of Attacks. *Econometrica,* 75(3), 711-756.

Bergemann, D., & Valimaki, J. (1996). Learning and Strategic Pricing. *Econometrica,* 64(5), 1125-1149.

Fudenberg, D., & Levine, D. (1998). The Theory of Learning in Games. Cambridge, MA: MIT Press.

Hurkens, S. (1995). Learning by forgetful players. *Games and Economic Behavior,* 11, 304-329.

Selten, R. (1991). Evolution, learning, and economic behavior. *Games and Economic Behavior,* 3, 3-24.

Smith, L., & Sorensen, P. (2000). Pathological Outcomes of Observational Learning. *Econometrica,* 68(2), 371-398.

Game Strategy

Aumann, R. J. (1974), Subjectivity and Correlation in Randomized Strategies. *Journal of Mathematical Economics,* 1, 67-96.

Bernheim, B. D. (1984). Rationalizable Strategic Behavior. *Econometrica,* 52, 1007-1028.

Dixit, A., & Nalebuff, B. (1991). Thinking Strategically. New York: Norton.

Dixit, A., & Nalebuff, B. (2008). The Art of Strategy. New York: Norton.

Dixit, A., Skeath, S., & Reiley, D. (2009). Games of Strategy. (Third Edition). New York: W. W. Norton and Company.

Harsanyi, J. C. (1973). Games with Randomly Distured Payoffs: A New Rationale for Mixed Strategy Equilibrium Points. *International Journal of Game Theory,* 2, 1-23.

Hauk, E., & Hurkens, S. (2002). On forward induction and evolutionary and strategic stability. *Journal of Economic Theory,* 106, 66-90.

Hillas, J. (1990). On the definition of strategic stability of equilibria. *Econometrica,* 58, 1365-1390.

Hofbauer, J., & Weibull, J. (1996). Evolutionary selection against dominated strategies. *Journal of Economic Theory,* 71, 558-573.

Koons, R. (1992). Paradoxes of Belief and Strategic Rationality. Cambridge: Cambridge University Press.

McMillan, J. (1991). Games, Strategies and Managers. Oxford: Oxford University Press.

Pearce, D. G. (1984). Rationalizable Strategic Behavior and the Problem of Perfection. *Econometrica,* 52, 1029-1050.

Ross, D., & Dumouchel, P. (2004). Emotions as Strategic Signals. Rationality and Society, 16: 251–286.

Schelling, T. C. (1960). *The Strategy of Conflict.* Cambridge, MA: Harvard University Press.

Shubik, M. (1959), *Strategy and Market Structure: Competition, Oligopoly, and the Theory of Games.* New York: Wiley.

Young, H.P. (1998). Individual Strategy and Social Structure. Princeton: Princeton University Press.

General Theory for Game Applications

Bacharach, M. (2006). Beyond Individual Choice: Teams and Frames in Game Theory. Princeton: Princeton University Press.

Binmore, K. (1987). Modeling Rational Players I. Economics and Philosophy, 3, 179–214.

Binmore, K. (2007). Does Game Theory Work? The Bargaining Challenge. Cambridge, MA: MIT Press.

Binmore, K., Kirman, A., & Tani, P. (eds.) (1993). Frontiers of Game Theory. Cambridge, MA: MIT Press

Chew, S., & MaCrimmon, K. (1979). Alphanu Choice Theory: A Generalization of Expected Utility Theory. *University of Columbia Faculty of Commerce and Business Administration, Working Paper,* 686.

Ginits, H. (2000). Game Theory Evolving. Princeton: Princeton University Press.

Harsanyi, J. C. (1966). A General Theory of Rational Behavior in Game Situations. *Econometrica,* 34, 613-634.

Hendricks, V., & Hansen, P., (2007). Game Theory: 5 Questions. Automatic Press.

Kahneman, D., & Tversky, A. (1979). Prospect Theory: An Analysis of Decision Under Risk. Econometrica, 47: 263–291.

Kuhn, H. (1997). Classics in Game Theory. Princeton: Princeton University Press.

Kuhn, H. W. & Tucker, A. W. (1950). *Contributions to the Theory of Games, Volume I (Annals of Mathematics Studies, 24).* Princeton: Princeton University Press.

McKinsey, J. C. C. (1952). *Introduction to the Theory of Games*. New York: McGraw-Hill Book Co.

Melvin, D., Tucker A. W., & Wolfe, P. (1957). *Contributions to the Theory of Games, Volume III (Annals of Mathematics Studies, 39)*. Princeton: Princeton University Press.

Nozick, R. (1998). Socratic Puzzles. Cambridge, MA: Harvard University Press.

Poundstone, W. (1992). Prisoner's Dilemma. New York: Doubleday.

von Neumann, J., & Morgenstern, O. (1944). The Theory of Games and Economic Behavior. Princeton: Princeton University Press.

Yaari, M. (1987). The Dual Theory of Choice Under Risk. Econometrica, 55: 95–115.

Equilibrium in Games

Aumann R. (1990). *Nash equilibria are not self-enforcing, in J. Gabszewicz, J.-F. Richard and L. Wolsey, Economic Decision Making: Games, Econometrics, and Optimization*. The Netherlands: Elsevier.

Aumann, R., & Brandenburger, A. (1995). Epistemic conditions for Nash equilibrium, *Econometrica*, 63, 1161-1180.

Crawford, V. P. (1990). Equilibrium without Independence. *Journal of Economic Theory*, 50,127-154.

Cho I.-K., & Kreps, D. (1987). Signaling games and stable equilibria. *Quarterly Journal of Economics*, 102, 179-221.

Fudenberg, D., & Tirole, J. (1991). Perfect Bayesian Equilibrium and Sequential Equilibrium. *Journal of Economic Theory*, 53, 236-260.

Harsanyi, J. C., & Selten, R. (1988). *A General Theory of Equilibrium Selection in Games*. Cambridge, MA: MIT Press.

Jiang, J. H. (1963a). Essential equilibrium points of n-person non-cooperative games. *Science Sinica*, 12, 651-671.

Jiang, J. H. (1963b). Essential components of the set of fixed points in the multivalued map-pings and its application to the theory of games. *Science Sinica,* 12, 951-964.

Kohlberg, E. (1981). Some Problems with the Concept of Perfect Equilibria, Rapporteurs' Report of the NBER. *Conference on the Theory of General Economic Equilibrium, University of Californa Berkeley.*

Kohlberg, E., & Mertens, J. F. (1986). On the Strategic Stability of Equilibria. *Econometrica,* 54, 1003-1037.

Kreps, D. M., & Wison, R.B. (1982). Sequential Equilibria. *Econometrica,* 50, 863-894.

Lemke, C. E., & Howson, J. T. Jr. (1964). Equilibrium Points of Bimatrix Games. *Society for Industrial and Applied Mathematics Journal of Applied Mathematics,* 12, 413-423.

Myerson, R.B. (1978). Refinements of the Nash equilibrium concept. *International Journal of Game Theory,* 7, 73-80.

Nash, J. (1950a). Equilibrium Points in n-Person Games. Proceedings of the National Academy of Science, 36, 48–49.

Norde, H., Potters, J., Reijnierse, H., & Vermeulen, D. (1996). Equilibrium selection and consistency. *Games and Economic Behavior,* 12, 219-225.

Phelps, E., & Pollak, R. (1968). On second-best national savings and game equilibrium growth. *Review of Economic Studies,* 35, 201-208.

Rubinstein, A. (1982). Perfect Equilibrium in a Bargaining Model. *Econometrica,* 50, 97-109.

Samuelson, L. (1997). *Evolutionary Games and Equilibrium Selection.* MIT Press.

Selten, R. (1975). Reexamination of the Perfectness Concept for Equilibrium Points in Extensive Games. *International Journal of Game Theory,* 4, 25-55.

Smith, V. (1964). Effect of Market Organization on Competitive Equilibrium. Quarterly Journal of Economics, 78, 181–201.

van Damme, E. (1991). *Stability and Perfection of Nash Equilibria.* Berlin: Springer-Verlag.

Non-Cooperative Game Theory

Abreu, D., Pearce, D., & Stacchetti, E. (1990, September). Toward a Theory of Discounted Repeated Games with Imperfect Monitoring. *Econometrica,* 58(5), 1041-1063.

Brown, G. W. (1951). (T. C. Koopmans ed.). *Activity Analysis of Production and Allocation.* New York: Wiley.

Cournot, A. A. (1897). *Researches into the Mathematical Principles of the Theory of Wealth.* New York: Macmillan

Cripps, M. W., Mailath, G., & Samuelson, L. (2004, March). Imperfect Monitoring and Impermanent Reputations. *Econometrica,* 407-432.

Fudenberg, D., & Levine, D. K. (1992). Maintaining a Reputation when Strategies are Imperfectly Observed. *Review of Economic Studies,* 561-579.

Harsanyi, J. C. (1967-8). Games with Incomplete Information Played by 'Bayesian' Players, Parts I, II and III. *Management Science,* 14, 159-182, 320-334 & 486-502.

Kuhn, H. W., & Tucker, A. W. (1953). *Contributions to the Theory of Games.* (Volume II. Annals of Mathematics Studies, 28). Princeton: Princeton University Press.

Lucas, W. F. (1968). A Game with No Solution. *Bulletin of the American Mathematical Society,* 74, 237-239.

Mertens, J.-F., & Zamir, S. (1985). Formulation of Bayesian Analysis for Games with Incomplete Information. *International Journal of Games Theory,* 14, 1-29.

Nash, J. (1951). Non-Cooperative Games. *Annals of Mathematics,* 54, 286-295.

Shapley, L. S. (1953). *Contributions to the Theory of Games.* (Volume II. Annals of Mathematics Studies, 28. H. W. Kuhn and A. W. Tucker). Princeton: Princeton University Press.

Shapley, L. S. (1953). Stochastic Games. *Proceedings of the National Academy of Sciences of the United States of America,* 39, 1095-1100.

Cooperative Game Theory

Aumann, R. J. (1961). The Core of a Cooperative Game Without Side Payments. *Transactions of the American Mathematical Society,* 98, 539-552.

Aumann, R. J., & Peleg, B. (1960). Von Neumann-Morgenstern Solutions to Cooperative Games without Side Payments. *Bulletin of the American Mathematical Society,* 66, 173-179.

Debreu, G., & Scarf, H. (1963). A Limit Theorem on the Core of an Economy. *International Economic Review,* 4, 235-246.

Harsanyi, J. C. (1959). *Contributions to the Theory of Games Volume 4.* (A. W. Tucker and R. D. Luce). Princeton: Princeton University Press.

Nash, J. (1953). Two Person Cooperative Games. *Econometrica,* 21, 128-140.

Rawls, J. (1974). Some Reasons for the Maxmin Criterion. *The American Economic Review,* 64, 141-146.

Roemer, J. (1986). The Mismarriage of Bargaining Theory and Distributive Justice. *Ethics,* 97, 88-110.

Samet, D., & Safra, Z. (2005). A Family of Ordinal Solutions to Bargaining Problems with Many Players. *Games and Economic Behavior,* 50, 89-106.

Scarf, H. E. (1967). The Core of a N-Person Game. *Econometrica,* 35, 50-69.

Shapley, L. S. (1952). Rand Corporation research memorandum, *Notes on the NPerson Game III: Some Variants of the von-Neumann-Morgenstern Definition of Solution,* RM-817.

Shapley, L. S. (1953). *Contributions to the Theory of Games Volume 2.* (H. W. Kuhn and A. W. Tucker). Princeton: Princeton University Press.

Shapley, L. S. (1967). On Balanced Sets and Cores. *Naval Research Logistics Quarterly,* 14, 453-460.

von Neumann, J., & Morgenstern, O. (1944). *Theory of Games and Economic Behavior.* Princeton: Princeton University Press.

Yaari, M.E. (1981). Rawls, Edgeworth, Shapley, Nash: Theories of Distributive Justice Re-Examined. *Journal of Economic Theory*, 24, 1-39.

Market Games

Basu K., & Weibull, J. (1991). *S*trategy subsets closed under rational behavior. *Economics Letters,* 36, 140-146.

Binmore, K., & Klemperer, P. (2002). The Biggest Auction Ever: The Sale of British 3G Telcom Licenses. Economic Journal, 112, C74-C96.

Dan L. & James P. (2003, Autumn). To Grab for the Market or to Bide One's Time*: A Dynamic Model of Entry. RAND Journal of Economics*, 34(3), 536-556.

Gale, D., & Shapley, L. S. (1962). College Admissions and the Stability of Marriage. *American Mathematics Monthly,* 69, 9-15.

Horner, J., & Vieille, (2009). *N. Public vs. Private Offers in the Market for Lemons. Econometrica*, 29-70.

Peck, J., & Shell, K. (1990). Liquid markets and competition. *Games and Economic Behavior,* 2, 362-377.

Roth, A. E. (1984). The Evolution of the Labor Market for Medical Interns and Residents: A Case Study in Game Theory. *Journal of Political Economy,* 92, 991-1016.

Shapley, L. S., & Shubik M. (1969). On Market Games. *Journal of Economic Theory, 1,* 9-25.

Shapley, L. S., & Shubik, M. (1977). Trade using one commodity as a means of payment. J. Polit. *Econ,* 85, 937-968.

Shubik, M. (1959). *Contributions to the Theory of Games Volume IV.* (Annals of Mathematics Studies, 40. A. W. Tucker and R. D. Luce). Princeton: Princeton University Press.

Shubik, M. (1962). Incentives, Decentralized Control, the Assignment of Joint Costs and Internal Pricing. *Management Science,* 8, 325-343.

Smith, V. (1976). *Bidding and Auctioning Institutions: Experimental Results.* (Y. Amihud, ed.). New York: New York University Press.

Bargaining Solutions

Alexander, J., & Skyrms, B. (1999). Bargaining with Neighbors: Is Justice Contagious. *Journal of Philosophy,* 96(11), 588–598.

Aumann, R. J., & Maschler, M. (1964). *The Bargaining Set for Cooperative Games.*-(Annals of Mathematics Studies, 52. M. Dresher, L. S. Shapley and A. W. Tucker, eds.). Princeton: Princeton University Press.

Binmore, K., Rubinstein, A., & Wolinsky, A. (1986). The Nash Bargaining Solution in Economic Modelling. *RAND Journal of Economics,* 17. 176–188.

Chun, Y., & Peters, H. (1988). The lexicographic egalitarian solution. *Cahiers CERO 30,* 149–156

Chun, Y., & Thomson, W. (1990). Nash solution and uncertain disagreement points. *Games Econ Behavior,* 2, 213–223

Debreu, G., & Scarf, H. (1963). A Limit Theorem on the Core of an Economy. *International Economic Review,* 4, 235–246.

de Clippel, G. (2007). An Axiomatization of the Nash Bargaining Solution. *Social Choice and Welfare,* 29, 201-210.

Edgeworth, F. Y. (1881). *Mathematical Psychics: An Essay on the Application of Mathematics to the Moral Sciences.* London: Kegan Paul.

Harsanyi, J, C. (1959). *Contributions to the theory of Games IV.* (Tucker AW, Luce RD eds.). Princeton: Princeton University Press.

Kalai, E. & Smorodinsky, M. (1975). Other Solutions to Nash's Bargaining Problem. *Econometrica, 43*, 513-518.

Kalai, E. (1977). Proportional solutions to bargaining situations: Intertemporal utility comparisons. *Econometrica, 45*(7). 1623–1630.

Kalai, E., & Smorodinsky, M. (1975). Other solutions to Nash's bargaining problem. *Econometrica, 43*(3). 513–518.

Kalai, E. (1977). Proportional Solutions to Bargaining Situations: Interpersonal Utility Comparisons. *Econometrica, 45*, 1623-1630.

Kalai, E., & Smorodinsky, M. (1975). Other solutions to Nash's bargaining problem. *Econometrica, 43*, 513–518.

Thomson, W. (1994). Cooperative models of bargaining, *Handbook of game theory with economic applications, 2*, 1237–1284.

Lensberg, T. (1988). Stability and the Nash solution. *J Econ Theory, 45*, 330–341.

Mariotti, M. (1999). Fair bargains: Distributive justice and Nash bargaining theory. *Rev Econ Stud, 66*, 733–741.

Mariotti, M. (2000). Maximal symmetry and the Nash solution. *Soc Choice Welfare, 17*, 45–53.

Muthoo, A. (1999). *Bargaining theory with applications*. Cambridge University Press.

Nash, J. (1950). The Bargaining Problem. *Econometrica, 18*, 155-162.

Perles, M. A., & Maschler, M. (1981), *The Super-Additive Solution for the Nash Bargaining Game. International Journal of Game Theory, 10*, 163-193.

Perles M., & Maschler M. (1981). A super-additive solution for the Nash bargaining games. *Int J. Game Theory, 10*, 163–193.

Peters, H. (1986a). Characterizations of bargaining solutions by properties of their status quo. *Research Memorandum*, 86-012, University of Limburg

Peters, H. (1986b). Simultaneity of issues and additivity in bargaining. *Econometrica, 54*, 153–169.

Peters, H., & van Damme E. (1991). Characterizing the Nash and Raiffa bargaining solutions by disagreement point axioms. *Math Oper Res*, 16(3), 447–461.

Rubinstein, A. (1982). Perfect equilibrium in a bargaining model. *Econometrica, 50*, 97–110.

Shubik, M. (1959). *Contributions to the Theory of Games, Volume 4.* (Annals of Mathematics Studies, 40). Princeton: Princeton University Press.

Repeated Games

Benoit J. P., & Krishna, V. (1993). Renegotiation in finitely repeated games. *Econometrica, 61*, 303-323.

Dal B. P. (2005). Cooperation under the shadow of the future: Experimental evidence from infinitely repeated games. *American Economic Review, 95*, 1591-1604.

Maynard, S. J. (1982). Evolution and the Theory of Games. Cambridge: Cambridge University Press.

Neyman, A. (1985). Bounded Complexity Jusifies Cooperation in the Finitely Repeated Prisoner's Dilemma. *Economic Letters, 19*, 227-229.

Ritzberger, K., & Weibull, J. (1995). Evolutionary selection in normal-form games. *Econometrica, 63*, 1371-1399.

Rubinstein, A. (1986). Finite Automata Play the Repeated Prisoner's Dilemma. *Journal of Economic Theory, 39*, 83-96.

Experimental Gaming

Huber, J., Shubik, M., & Sunder, S. (2007). *Everyone-a-banker or the Ideal Credit Acceptance Game: Theory and Evidence.* Cowles Foundation Discussion Paper-1622, Yale University.

Shubik, M. (1962). Some Experimental Non Zero Sum Games with Lack of Information about the Rules. *Management Science, 8*(2), 215–234.

Siegal. S., & Fouraker, L. S. (1960). *Bargaining and Group Decision Making.* New York: McGraw-Hill.

Smith, V. (1979). *Research in Experimental Economics. I,* Greenwich, CT: JAI Press.

Mechanism Design

Bergemann, D., & Morris, S. (2005). Robust Mechanism Design. *Econometrica,* 1771-1813.

Cremer, J., & McLean, R. (1988). Full extraction of the surplus in Bayesian and dominant strategy auctions. *Econometrica,* 1247-1258.

Hurwicz, L. (2008). But Who Will Guard the Guardians? *American Economic Review, 98*(3), 577–585.

Jackson, M. O., & Sonnenschein, H. (2007). Overcoming Incentive Constraints. *Econometrica, 75*(1), 241-258.

Maskin, E. S. (2008). Mechanism Design: How to Implement Social Goals. *American Economic Review, 98*(3), 567–576.

Myerson, R. (1981). Optimal Auction Design. *Mathematics of Operations Research, 6,* 58-73.

Myerson, R., & Satterthwaite, M. (1983). Efficient Mechanisms for Bilateral Trading. *Journal of Economic Theory, 29,* 265-281.

Social Structure of Game theory

Charness, G., & Rabin, M. (2002). Understanding social preferences with simple tests. *Quarterly Journal of Economics, 117,* 817-869.

Dawkins, R. (1976). *The Selfish Gene.* Oxford University Press.

Demichelis, S., & Ritzberger, K. (2003). From evolutionary to strategic stability. *Journal of Economic Theory, 113,* 51-75.

Demichelis, S., & Weibull, J. (2008). Language, meaning and games; a model of communication, coordination and evolution. *American Economic Review, 98,* 1292-1301.

Durlauf, S., & Young, H. P., eds. (2001). Social Dynamics. Cambridge, MA: MIT Press.

Fehr, E., & Schmidt, K. (1999). A theory of fairness, competition and cooperation. *Quarterly Journal of Economics, 114,* 817-868.

Fehr, E., & G¨achter, S. (2000). Cooperation and punishment in public goods experiments. *American Economic Review, 90,* 980-994.

Fudenberg, D., & Maskin, E. (1990). Evolution and cooperation in noisy repeated games. *American Economic Review, Papers and Proceedings, 80,* 274-279.

Skyrms, B. (2004). The Stag Hunt and the Evolution of Social Structure. Cambridge: Cambridge University Press.

Young, P. (1998). *Individual Strategy and Social Structure.* Princeton University Press.

Evolutionary Game Theory

Cressman, R. (2003). *Evolutionary Dynamics and Extensive Form Games.* MIT Press.

Fudenberg, D., & Levine, D. K. (1998). *The Theory of Learning in Games.* MIT Press.

Gintis, H. (2000). *Game Theory Evolving.* Princeton University Press.

Hammerstein, P., & Selten, R. (1994). Game Theory and Evolutionary Biology. *in Handbook of Game Theory, 2,* 929–993.

Hofbauer, J., & Sigmund, K. (1998). *Evolutionary Games and Population Dynamics.* Cambridge University Press.

Hofbauer, J., & Sigmund, K. (2003). Evolutionary Game Dynamics. *Bulletin of the American Mathematical Society, 40*(4), 479–519.

Lewontin, R. C. (1961). Evolution and the Theory of Games. *Journal of Theoretical Biology, 1,* 382-403.

Maynard S. J. (1982). *Evolution and the Theory of Games.* Cambridge University Press.

Robson, A. (1990). Efficiency in evolutionary games: Darwin, Nash and the secret handshake. *Journal of Theoretical Biology, 144,* 379-396.

Sandholm, W. (2007). Evolutionary game theory. *in Encyclopedia of Complexity and System Science.*

Sandholm, W. (2008). *Population Games and Evolutionary Dynamics.* Cambridge: MIT Press.

Selten, R. (1980). A note on evolutionarily stable strategies in asymmetric animal conflicts. *Journal of Theoretical Biology, 84,* 93-101.

Sethi, R., & Somanathan, E. (2001). Preference evolution and reciprocity. *Journal of Economic Theory, 97,* 273-297.

Sigmund, K. (1993). *Games of Life: Explorations in Ecology, Evolution and Behaviour.* Oxford University Press.

Swinkels, J. (1992a). Evolutionary stability with equilibrium entrants. *Journal of Economic Theory, 57,* 306-332.

Swinkels, J. (1992b). Evolution and Strategic Stability: from Maynard Smith to Kohlberg and Mertens. *Journal of Economic Theory, 57,* 333-342.

Taylor, P., & Jonker, L. (1978). Evolutionary stable strategies and game dynamics. *Mathematical Biosicences, 40,* 145-156.

Vega-Redondo, F. (1997). *Evolution, Games, and Economic Behavior.* Oxford University Press.

Weibull, J. W. (1995). *Evolutionary Game Theory.* MIT Press.

Weibull, J. (1995). *Evolutionary Game Theory.* MIT Press, Cambridge, USA.

Young, P. (1993a). Evolution of conventions. *Econometrica, 61,* 57-84.

Young, P. (1993b). An evolutionary model of bargaining. *Journal of Economic Theory, 59,* 145-168.

Voting Theory

Banzhaf, John F. (1965). Weighted Voting Doesn't Work: A Mathematical

Analysis. *Rutgers Law Review 19*(2), 317–343.

Farquharson, R. (1969). *Theory of Voting.* CT: Blackwell (Yale University Press in the U.S.).

Shapley, L. S. (1953). *Contributions to the Theory of Games.* (H. W. Kuhn and A. W.

Tucker), *2,* Princeton: Princeton University Press.

Shapley L. S., & Shubik, M. (1954). A method for evaluating the distribution of power in a committee system. *American Political Science Review 48*(3): 787–792.

Decision Theory for Game Models

Anbarci, N. (1998). Simple Characterizations of the Nash and Kalai/Smorodinsky Solutions. *Theory and Decision, 45,* 255-261.

Binmore, K. (2009). Rational Decisions. Princeton: Princeton University Press.

Camerer, C. (1995). *Individual Decision Making.* In Kagel, J., & Roth, A. eds., Handbook of Experimental Economics, 587–703. Princeton: Princeton University Press.

Glimcher, P. (2003). Decisions, Uncertainty and the Brain. Cambridge, MA: MIT Press.

Luce, R. D., & Howard, R. (1957). *Games and Decisions: Introduction and Critical Survey.* New York: Wiley.

Luce, R. D., & Rai_a, H. (1958). *Games and Decisions.* Wiley, New York.

Selten, R. (1978). The chain-store paradox. *Theory and Decision, 9,* 127-159.

Game Theory for Economics

Aumann, R. J., & Hart, S. (2002). *Handbook of Game Theory with Economic Applications. 3,* Amsterdam: North-Holland.

Ausubel, L. M., & Deneckere, R. (1992). Durable Goods Monopoly with Incomplete

Information. *Review of Economic Studies, 59,* 795-812.

Dasgupta, P., & Maskin, E. (1986). The existence of equilibrium in discontinuous economic games, II: Applications. *Review of Economic Studies, 53,* 27-41.

Gul, F., Sonnenschein, H., & Wilson, R. (1986). Foundations of Dynamic Monopoly and the Coase Conjecture. *Journal of Economic Theory, 39,* 155-190.

Levine, D. (1998). Modelling altruism and spitefulness in experiments. *Review of Economic Dynamics, 1,* 593-622.

Reynolds, S., & Wilson, B. J. (2000). Bertrand-Edgeworth Competition, Demand Uncertainty, and Asymmetric Outcomes. *Journal of Economic Theory, 92*(1), 122-141.

Robson, A. (2001a). The biological basis of economic behavior. *Journal of Economic Literature, 29,* 11-33.

Robson, A. (2001b). Why would nature give individuals utility functions? *Journal of Political Economy, 109,* 900-914.

Singh, N., & Vives, X. (1984). Price and Quantity Competition in a Differentiated Duopoly. *Rand Journal of Economics,* 546-554.

Behavioral Game Theory

Bagwell, K. (1995). Commitment and Observability in Games. *Games and Economic Behavior, 8*(2), 271-280.

Camerer, C. (2003). Behavioral Game Theory: Experiments in Strategic Interaction. Princeton: Princeton University Press.

Dugatkin, L., & Reeve, H. (1998). Game Theory and Animal Behavior. Oxford: Oxford University Press.

Falk, A., Fehr, E., & Fischbacher, U. (2003). On the nature of fair behavior. *Economic Inquiry, 41,* 20-26.

Ginits, H. (2004). Towards the Unity of the Human Behavioral Sciences. Philosophy, Politics and Economics, *31,* 37–57.

Krebs, J., & Davies, N. (1984). Behavioral Ecology: An Evolutionary Approach. Sunderland: Sinauer.

Pearce D. (1984). Rationalizable strategic behavior. *Econometrica, 52,* 1029-1050.

Smith, V. (1962). An Experimental Study of Competitive Market Behavior. Journal of Political Economy, *70,* 111–137.

Stahl, D. (1993). Evolution of smart n players. *Games and Economic Behavior, 5,* 604-617.

Vega-Redondo F. (1997). The evolution of Walrasian behavior. *Econometrica, 65,* 375-384.

Game Theory in Other Academic Research Fields

Arrow, K. J. (1973). Some Ordinalist-Utilitarian Notes on Rawls' Theory of Justice. *The Journal of Philosophy*, 70, 245-263.

Aumann, R. J. (1964). Markets with a Continuum of Traders. *Econometrica, 32,* 39-50.

Aumann, R. J., & Shapley, L. S. (1974), *Values of Non-Atomic Games.* Princeton: Princeton University Press.

Aumann, R. J., & Hart, S. (1994). *Handbook of Game Theory with Economic Applications, 2.* Amsterdam: North-Holland.

Baird, D. G., Gertner, R. H., & Picker, R. C. (1994). *Game Theory and the Law.* Cambridge Mass.: Harvard University Press.

Baron, D. P., & Ferejohn, J. A. (1989). Bargaining in Legislatures. *American Political Science Review, 83*(4), 1181-1206.

Battaglini, M. (2002). Multiple Referrals and Multidimensional Cheap Talk. *Econometrica, 70*(4), 1379-1401.

Binmore, K. (1994). Game Theory and the Social Contract. *1*: Playing Fair, Cambridge, MA: MIT Press.

Binmore, K. (1998). Game Theory and the Social Contract. *2*: Just Playing, Cambridge, MA: MIT Press.

Borch, K. (1962). Application of Game Theory to Some Problems in Automobile Insurance. *The Astin Bulletin 2 (part 2), 208*-221.

Braithwaite, R. B. (1955). *Theory of Games as a Tool for the Moral Philosopher.* Cambridge: Cambridge University Press.

Bulow, J., & Klemperer, P. (1999). The Generalized War of Attrition. *American Economic Review, 89*, 175-189.

Callander, S. (2005). Electoral Competition in Heterogeneous Districts. *Journal of Political Economy, 113*(5), 1116-1145.

Callander, S., & Horner, J. (2009). The Wisdom of the Minority. *Journal of Economic Theory*, 1421-1439.

Chamley, C., & Gale, D. (1994). Information Revelation and Strategic Delay in a Model of Investment. *Econometrica, 62*, 1065-1085.

Crawford, V. P., & Sobel, J. (1982). Strategic Information Transmission. *Econometrica, 50*(6), 1431-1451.

Dan, L., & James, P. (2008). Investment Dynamics with Common and Private Values. *Journal of Economic Theory, 143*(1), 114-139.

Ennis, H. M., & Keister, T. (2009). Run equilibria in the Green-Lin model of financial intermediation. *Journal of Economic Theory*, 1996-2020.

Feddersen, T. J., & Pesendorfer, W. (1996). The Swing Voter's Curse. *American Economic Review, 86*(3), 408-424.

Ghemawat, P. (1997). Games Businesses Play. Cambridge, MA: MIT Press.

Gibbard, A. (1973). Manipulation of Voting Schemes: A General Result. *Econometrica, 41*, 587-601.

Harsanyi, J. C. (1975). Can the Maxmin Principle Serve as a Basis for Morality? *The American Political Science Review, 69*, 594-606.

Krishna, V., & Morgan, J. (2001). A Model of Expertise. *Quarterly Journal of Economics, 116*(2), 747-775.

Lyons, D. (1972). Rawls Versus Utilitarianism. *The Journal of Philosophy, 69*, 535-545.

Schmeidler, D. (1969). The Nucleolus of a Characteristic Function Game. *Society for Industrial and Applied Mathematics Journal of Applied Mathematics, 17*, 1163-1170.

Shapley, L. S., & Shubik, M. (1954). A Method for Evaluating The Distribution of Power in a Committee System. *American Political Science Review, 48*, 787-792.

In this subsection, only a few of the many topics in game theory have been discussed. All of them are still expected to grow, many with increasing rates. Although the discussion here has been primarily concerned with specific topins, it is desirable to help us more fully appreciate thegame theory development of today.

DIRECTIONS FOR FUTURE RESERACH

Ironically, game theory has been a victim of its own successes; it is firmly entrenched as a method of analysis as a tool (Shubik, 2011). Therefore, its functionality may be limited. In addition, the competitive problems in economics, political science, law, social psychology, computer science and other disciplines cannot be analyzed with the help of game theory. Therefore, it is necessary to indicate the probable research directions of development and to suggest where some of the challenges lie ahead for future game theory. In this subsection, a few research issues are considered looking towards the future of game theory. For the further research expectation, the stress is on what we may want and expect, keeping in mind the distinction between desire and feasibility.

General Solution for Dynamic Games

In the development of dynamic games, one question might be the proof of the existence of a general solution for all game players. Due to the game environment changes, the development of a viable solution appears one of the greatest difficulties in applied dynamics. To solve this problem, a mixture of gaming, game theory, cognitive psychology and social psychology is needed; it depends on a joint understanding among professionals in different disciplines that has hardly been developed, and the role of expertise calls for considerable collaborative work in both of game theory and other fileds. This is emerging, but at this time is far from fully developed (Shubik, 2011).

The Role of Behavioral Science

Behavioural science encompasses all the disciplines that explore the activities of and interactions among organisms in the natural world. Behavioral science involves the systematic analysis and investigation of human and animal behaviour through controlled and naturalistic observation, and disciplined scientific experimentation. It attempts to accomplish legitimate, objective conclusions through rigorous formulations and observation. Examples of behavioural sciences include psychology, psychobiology, and cognitive science (Behavioral sciences, n.d.).

Game theory is central to understanding human behavior and relevant to all of the behavioral sciences - from biology and economics, to anthropology and political science. However, game theory alone cannot fully explain human behavior and should instead complement other key concepts championed by the behavioral disciplines. Game theory without broader social theory is merely technical bravado, and social theory without game theory is a handicapped enterprise. Usually, game theory lacks explanations for when and how rational agents share beliefs. Rather than construct a social epistemology or reasoning process that reflects the real world, game theorists make unwarranted assumptions which imply that rational agents enjoy a commonality of beliefs (Gintis, 2009). A critical, but as yet lightly studied aspect of game theory has been the treatment of behavioral science. By combining the strengths of

the classical, evolutionary, and behavioral fields, future research should reinvigorate an innovative thinking for the behavioral sciences and will offer the useful tool of game theory for a better understanding of human behavior.

Mass Player Game Theory

Games with infinite number of players are often called mass player games or population games. These game models consider games involving a population of decision makers, where the frequency with which a particular decision is made can change over time in response to the decisions made by all individuals in the population. In biology, this is intended to model biological evolution, where genetically programmed organisms pass along some of their strategy programming to their offspring. In economics, the same theory is intended to capture population changes because people play the game many times within their lifetime, and rationally switch strategies (Game theory, n.d.).

It is easy to comment on analogies between physics or biology and economics. The mass particle methods of physics may appear to be highly attractive to those economists concerned with mass anonymous markets. However, how far does the analogy stretch and how useful is it? The burgeoning topic of network game theory may be of relevance. In the future research, it may expect that experimental gaming and simulation will flourish, in the investigation of mass behavior games, utilizing simulation and agent-based modeling to beat through otherwise intractable heterogeneous population models (Shubik, 2011).

Multi-Level Hierarchical Games

Game theory has been applied in various areas to assist rational decision making. In real life, the situation can be so complicated that multi-level games are used to capture all the information. A multi-level hierarchical game is defined as a game in which one player plays first and set a series of rules for the other players to follow. It is extremely useful in modeling policy making problems such as the policy issues in natural resources and the environment. In addition, structures with two or more levels of decision-making taking place on different time spans provide a setting to provide a more satisfactory paradigm. It is worth noting that with this structure a mass of individual local optimizers could drive an evolving system that is continuously modifying the rules for the local optimizers with the system as a whole having no particular direction (Shubik, 2011). This game approach will provide some insights to the system design perspective of future researches.

Statistical Modeling and Simulation

Purely analytical methods in statistical modeling and simulation are usually of great help. But their use is by no means an easy goal to achieve. The growth of simulation methods and the cheapness and speed of computation are beginning to provide the game theory with a new form of viewing device akin to the telescope and microscope in other sciences. The computer provides not only a means for computation, but a means for investigation in the game theory whether the simulation involves different types of optimizing agents or minimal intelligence automata, animal fights, market struggles or political voting contests, multi-agent models can be constructed and employed to provide insights and to sweeten the intuition in a way that even a decade ago was unthinkable (Shubik, 2011). These methods have been developing with increasing speed. But they will often but not always be best utilized when linked with clear questions and analytical concern. In the near future, new modeling and simulation based methods will be suggested that places the stress on the dynamic evaluation and analysis.

Algorithmic Game Theory

The widespread adoption of the Internet and the emergence of the Web changed society's relationship with computers. The primary role of a computer evolved from a stand-alone, well-understood machine for executing software to a conduit for global communication, content-dissemination, and commerce. The algorithms and complexity theory community has responded to these changes by formulating novel problems, goals, and design and analysis techniques relevant for modern applications. Game theory plays a central role in these new developments. Research on the interface of theoretical computer science and game theory is an area now known as algorithmic game theory. Over the past ten years, it has exploded phenomenally (Roughgarden, 2010).

The astonishing rate of progress in algorithmic game theory, nourished by deep connections with other areas of theoretical computer science and a consistent infusion of new motivating applications, suggests that it will flourish for many years to come. There is a surfeit of important open research directions across all three areas such as developing theory for the design and analysis of mechanisms for multi-parameter problems, for minimizing the inefficiency of equilibria (e.g., via a mediating network protocol), and for the computation of approximate equilibria. It is easily expect that a broad challenge is to develop more appropriate algorithmic game models as a rich and relevant theory (Roughgarden, 2010).

Game Theory for Network Security

As networks become ubiquitous in people's lives, users depend on networks a lot for sufficient communication and convenient information access. However, networks suffer from security issues. Network security becomes a challenging topic of future research since numerous new network attacks have appeared increasingly sophisticated. Game theoretic approaches have been introduced as a useful tool to handle those tricky network attacks (Liang & Xiao, 2013). However, many of the current game-theoretic security game models are based on either static game models or games with perfect information or games with complete information. In reality, a network administrator often faces a dynamic game with incomplete and imperfect information against the attacker. Until now, few game models consider a realistic attack scenario involving dynamic game with incomplete and imperfect information (Roy, Ellis, Shiva, Dasgupta, Shandilya, & Wu, 2010).

Possible future research directions for network security can be summarized as follows. First, untl now, there are only a couple models addressing three or more players' interaction with a focus on including multiple defenders. Therefore, building game models involving three or more players for more network security application scenarios and addressing application problems in which multiple attackers can launch attacks in a non-competitive way is one of the future research directions. Second, improving the existing stochastic game models by adopting the more realistic approach. Note that the existing solutions to the stochastic game models are valid only when the state is finite. Third, studying the construction of payoff functions to determine a guideline for network security. In the existing security game models, the payoff functions seem to rely on ad hoc schemes. Improper payoff functions in a game model can reduce the effectiveness of the prediction of the attack-defense strategies (Liang & Xiao, 2013).

Nowadays, we witness an increasing number of applications of game theory for the network security problems. Absolutely, network security imposes future challenges for us to address security at a larger and more complex scale. Game theory can provide a preliminary tool that enables a quantitative study of such complex systems.

Operational Gaming and Practical Implementation

At the initial stage of game theory research, many scholars were deeply impressed by the power of the formal models and the mathematics of game theory, which is called a traditional game theory. There was little doubt that a considerable amount of formal mathematics could be developed. However, many subtle features of game players are not going to be mathematized easily, and this approach looses connections with operational gaming. Practically, the game theorists must set up and maintain a dialogue with the practitioners to stay in touch with the various realities of application. Based on the common knowledge, theory may influence practice, but practice must influence the development the appropriate models if the subject is to be more than an exercise in a minor branch of pure mathematics. The appropriate models cannot be built without an understanding of context and both the models and their formal analysis. It stimulats the study of development for the practical game theory, and is forcing us towards more and more collaborations across all of the realistic implementation techniques (Shubik, 2011). Therefore, the future research to growth in both theory and applications will be accelerating.

REFERENCES

Behavioral Sciences. (n.d.). Retrieved from http://en.wikipedia.org/wiki/Behavioural_sciences

Game Theory. (n.d.). Retrieved from http://en.wikipedia.org/wiki/Game_theory

Gintis, H. (2009). *The Bounds of Reason: Game Theory and the Unification of the Behavioral Sciences*. Princeton University Press.

Liang, X., & Xiao, Y. (2013). Game Theory for Network Security. *IEEE Communications Surveys & Tutorials*, *15*(1), 472–486. doi:10.1109/SURV.2012.062612.00056

Roughgarden, T. (2010). Algorithmic Game Theory. *Communications of the ACM*, *53*(7), 78–86. doi:10.1145/1785414.1785439

Roy, S., Ellis, C., Shiva, S., Dasgupta, D., Shandilya, V., & Wu, Q. (2010). A Survey of Game Theory as Applied to Network Security. In *Proceedings of IEEE HICSS*. IEEE.

Shubik, M. (2011). *The Present and Future of Game Theory*. Retrieved from http://cowles.econ.yale.edu/P/cd/d18a/d1808.pdf

KEY TERMS AND DEFINITIONS

Algorithmic Game Theory: It is an area in the intersection of game theory and algorithm design, whose objective is to design algorithms in strategic environments. Typically, in Algorithmic Game Theory problems, the input to a given algorithm is distributed among many players who have a personal interest in the output. In those situations, the agents might not report the input truthfully because of their own personal interests.

Behavioral Science: It is the systematic analysis and investigation of human and animal behavior through controlled and naturalistic observation, and disciplined scientific experimentation. It attempts to accomplish legitimate, objective conclusions through rigorous formulations and observation.

Cognitive Science: It is the interdisciplinary scientific study of the mind and its processes. It examines what cognition is, what it does and how it works. It includes research on intelligence and behavior, especially focusing on how information is represented, processed, and transformed within nervous systems and machines.

Management Game: It is a training exercise in which prospective decision makers act out managerial decision-making roles in a simulated environment. Also it is known as business game or operational game.

Operations Research: It is a discipline that deals with the application of advanced analytical methods to help make better decisions. It is often considered to be a sub-field of mathematics. The terms management science and decision science are sometimes used as synonyms.

Compilation of References

Afergan, M. (2006). Using Repeated Games to Design Incentive-Based Routing Systems. In *Proceedings of IEEE INFOCOM 2006*. IEEE. doi:10.1109/INFOCOM.2006.61

Agah, A., Basu, K., & Das, S. K. (2005). Enforcing security for prevention of DoS attack in wireless sensor networks using economical modeling. In *Proceedings of IEEE International Conference on Mobile Ad hoc and Sensor Systems Conference*, (pp. 528-535). IEEE.

Ahmad, I., & Habibi, D. (2012). Resource Management in 4G Wireless Communications at Vehicular Speeds: A Game Theory Solution. In *Proceedings of IEEE VTC*. IEEE.

Akkarajitsakul, K., Hossain, E., & Niyato, D. (2011). Distributed resource allocation in wireless networks under uncertainty and application of Bayesian game. *IEEE Communications Magazine, 49*(8), 120–127. doi:10.1109/MCOM.2011.5978425

Akkarajitsakul, K., Hossain, E., Niyato, D., & Kim, D. (2011). Game Theoretic Approaches for Multiple Access in Wireless Networks: A Survey. *IEEE Communications Surveys & Tutorials, 13*(3), 372–395. doi:10.1109/SURV.2011.122310.000119

Akkaya, K., & Younis, M. (2005). An Energy-Aware QoS Routing Protocol for Wireless Sensor Networks. *Cluster Computing, 8*(2-3), 179–188. doi:10.1007/s10586-005-6183-7

Akl, R., & Uttara, S. (2007). Grid-based Coordinated Routing in Wireless Sensor Networks. In *Proceedings of IEEE Consumer Communications and Networking Conference*, (pp. 860-864). IEEE.

Akyildiz, I. F., Lee, W., Vuran, M. C., & Mohanty, S. (2008). A survey on spectrum management in cognitive radio networks. *IEEE Communications Magazine, 46*(4), 40–48. doi:10.1109/MCOM.2008.4481339

Allen, F., & Morris, S. (2002). Game Theory Models in Finance International Series. *Operations Research & Management Science, 35*, 17–48.

Alpcan, T., & Basar, T. (2006). An intrusion detection game with limited observations. In *Proceedings of International Symposium on Dynamic Games and Applications*. Academic Press.

Alpcan, T., & Baser, T. (2004). A game theoretic analysis of intrusion detection in access control systems. In *Proceedings of IEEE Conference on Decision and Control*, (pp. 1568-1573).

Alpcan, T., Basar, T., Srikant, R., & Altman, E. (2002). CDMA Uplink Power Control as a Noncooperative Game. *Wireless Networks, 8*, 659–670. doi:10.1023/A:1020375225649

Altman, E., Avrachenkov, K., & Garnaev, A. (2008). Generalized α-fair resource allocation in wireless networks. In *Proceedings of IEEE CDC*, (pp. 2414-2419). IEEE.

Altman, E., Borkar, V. S., & Kherani, A. A. (2004). Optimal Random Access in Networks with Two-Way Traffic. In *Proceedings of IEEE PIMRC*, (pp. 609-613).

Altman, E., El-Azouzi, R., Hayel, Y., & Tembine, H. (2008). An Evolutionary Game approach for the design of congestion control protocols in wireless networks. In *Proceedings of Physicomnet workshop*. Academic Press.

Altmana, E., Boulognea, T., El-Azouzia, R., Jiménezb, T., & Wynterc, L. (2006). A survey on networking games in telecommunications. *Computers & Operations Research, 33*, 286–311. doi:10.1016/j.cor.2004.06.005

Altman, E., El-Azouzi, R., Hayel, Y., & Tembine, H. (2010). Evolutionary Games in Wireless Networks. *IEEE Transactions on Systems, Man, and Cybernetics, 40*(3), 634–646. doi:10.1109/TSMCB.2009.2034631 PMID:19963703

An, B. K., Lee, J. S., & Kim, N. S. (2011). An entropy based cooperative-aided routing protocol for mobile ad-hoc networks. In *Proceedings of IEEE ICUFN,* (pp. 31-36). IEEE.

An, B., Tambe, M., Ordóñez, F., Shieh, E. A., & Kiekintveld, C. (2011). Refinement of Strong Stackelberg Equilibria in Security Games. In *Proceedings of the Twenty-Fifth AAAI Conference on Artificial Intelligence,* (pp. 587-593). AAAI.

Anandalingam, G. (1988). A Mathematical Programming Model of Decentralized Multi-Level Systems. *The Journal of the Operational Research Society, 39*(11), 1021–1033. doi:10.1057/jors.1988.172

Anderegg, L., & Eidenbenz, S. (2003). Ad hoc-vcg: A truthful and cost-efficient routing protocol for mobile ad hoc networks with selfish agents. In *Proceedings of MobiCom* (pp. 245–259). MobiCom. doi:10.1145/939010.939011

Anderson, S. P., de Palma, A., & Thisse, J. (1992). *Discrete Choice Theory of Product Differentiation*. MIT Press.

Antoniou, J., & Pitsillides, A. (2008). 4G Converged Environment: Modeling Network Selection as a Game. In *Proceedings of Mobile and Wireless Communications Summit*. Academic Press.

Araujo, R. M., & Lamb, L. C. (2004). Towards understanding the role of learning models in the dynamics of the minority game. In *Proceedings of IEEE International Conference on Tools with Artificial Intelligence,* (pp. 727-731). IEEE.

Archetti, M. (2009). Cooperation as a volunteer's dilemma and the strategy of conflict in public goods games. *Journal of Evolutionary Biology, 22*(11), 2192–2200. doi:10.1111/j.1420-9101.2009.01835.x PMID:19732256

Aristidou, P., Dimeas, A., & Hatziargyriou, N. (2011). Microgrid Modelling and Analysis Using Game Theory Methods. *Lecture Notes of the Institute for Computer Sciences, Social Informatics, and Telecommunications Engineering, 54*(1), 12–19. doi:10.1007/978-3-642-19322-4_2

Asokan, R., Natarajan, A. M., & Nivetha, A. (2007). A Swarm-based Distance Vector Routing to Support Multiple Quality of Service (QoS) Metrics in Mobile Ad hoc Networks. *Journal of Computer Science, 3*(9), 700–707. doi:10.3844/jcssp.2007.700.707

Atzeni, I., Ordóñez, L. G., Scutari, G., Palomar, D. P., & Fonollosa, J. R. (2013). Noncooperative and Cooperative Optimization of Distributed Energy Generation and Storage in the Demand-Side of the Smart Grid. *IEEE Transactions on Signal Processing, 61*(10), 2454–2472. doi:10.1109/TSP.2013.2248002

Aumann, R. J., & Maschler, M. B. (1995). *Repeated Games With Incomplete Information*. Cambridge, MA: MIT Press.

Ayres, I. (1990). Playing Games with the Law. *Stanford Law Review, 42*, 1291–1317. doi:10.2307/1228971

Ayyadurai, V., Moessner, K., & Tafazolli, R. (2011). Multihop cellular network optimization using genetic algorithms. In *Proceedings of IEEE Network and Service Management*. IEEE.

Azar, Y. (1998). *Online Algorithms - The State of the Art*. Springer.

Bachrach, Y., & Elkind, E. (2008). Divide and Conquer: False-Name Manipulations in Weighted Voting Games. In *Proceedings of International Conference on Autonomous Agents and Multiagent Systems,* (pp. 975-982). Academic Press.

Bachrach, Y., Meir, R., Zuckerman, M., Rothe, J., & Rosenschein, J. S. (2009). The cost of stability in weighted voting games. In *Proceedings of AAMAS,* (pp. 1289-1290). AAMAS.

Baird, D. G., Gertner, R. H., & Picker, R. C. (1998). *Game Theory and the Law*. Cambridge, MA: Harvard University Press.

Banner, R., & Orda, A. (2007). Bottleneck routing games in communication networks. *IEEE Journal on Selected Areas in Communications, 25*, 1173–1179. doi:10.1109/JSAC.2007.070811

Barash, D. P. (2004). *The Survival Game*. New York: Times Books Henry Holt and Company.

Bargaining Problem. (n.d.). Retrieved from http://www.answers.com/topic/bargaining-problem

Barolli, L., Koyama, A., Suganuma, T., & Shiratori, N. (2003). GAMAN: A GA based QoS routing method for mobile ad hoc networks. *Journal of Interconnection Networks*, *4*(3), 251–270. doi:10.1142/S0219265903000866

Barran, M. (n.d.). *Game Theory: An Introductory Sketch*. Retrieved from http://scienceworld.wolfram.com/biography/Borel.html

Barr, N. (2012). *Economics of the Welfare State*. Oxford, UK: Oxford University Press.

Baslam, M., El-Azouzi, R., Sabir, E., & Echabbi, L. (2011). Market share game with adversarial Access providers: A neutral and a non-neutral network analysis. In *Proceedings of International Conference on Network Games, Control and Optimization*. Academic Press.

Becerra, R. L., & Coello, C. A. (2006). Solving Hard Multi-objective Optimization Problems Using ε-Constraint with Cultured Differential Evolution. *LNCS*, *4193*, 1611–3349.

Behavioral Sciences. (n.d.). Retrieved from http://en.wikipedia.org/wiki/Behavioural_sciences

Berlemann, L., Hiertz, G. R., Walke, B. H., & Mangold, S. (2005). Radio Resource Sharing Games: Enabling QoS Support in Unlicensed Bands. *IEEE Network*, *19*(4), 59–65. doi:10.1109/MNET.2005.1470684

Bian, Z. A., & Luo, J. Z. (2007). A Cooperative Game Theory Based Coalitional Agent Negotiation Model in Network Service. *Lecture Notes in Computer Science*, *4402*, 447–458. doi:10.1007/978-3-540-72863-4_46

Bi, Y., Li, N., & Sun, L. (2007). DAR: An energy-balanced data-gathering scheme for wireless sensor networks. *Computer Communications*, *30*(14-15), 2812–2825. doi:10.1016/j.comcom.2007.05.021

Black, F. (1976). Studies in stock price volatility changes. In *Proceedings of Meeting of the Business and Economic Statistics Section*, (pp. 177-181). American Statistical Association.

Bloem, M., Alpcan, T., & Basar, T. (2006). Intrusion Response as a Resource Allocation Problem. In *Proceedings of IEEE Conference on Decision and Control*, (pp. 6283-6288). IEEE.

Bloem, M., Alpcan, T., & Başar, T. (2007). A Stackelberg game for power control and channel allocation in cognitive radio networks. In *Proceedings of IEEE international conference on Performance evaluation methodologies and tools*. IEEE.

Blum, A. (2008). *Online Learning, Regret Minimization, and Game Theory*. Retrieved from http://videolectures.net/mlss08au_blum_org/

Blumenthal, J., Reichenbach, F., & Timmermann, D. (2006). Minimal Transmission Power vs. Signal Strength as Distance Estimation for Localization in Wireless Sensor Networks. In *Proceedings of IEEE SECON*, (pp. 761-766). IEEE.

Bommannavar, P., Alpan, T., & Bambos, N. (2011). Security Risk Management via Dynamic Games with Learning. In *Proceedings of IEEE International Conference on Communications*. IEEE.

Bossert, W., & Tan, G. (1995). An arbitration game and the egalitarian bargaining solution. *Social Choice and Welfare*, *12*, 29–41. doi:10.1007/BF00182191

Boukerche, A., Araujo, R. B., & Villas, L. (2006). A Wireless Actor and Sensor Networks QoS-Aware Routing Protocol for the Emergency Preparedness Class of Applications. In *Proceedings of Local Computer Networks* (pp. 832–839). IEEE. doi:10.1109/LCN.2006.322184

Bouleimen, K., & Lecocq, H. (2003). A new efficient simulated annealing algorithm for the resource-constrained project scheduling problem and its multiple mode version. *European Journal of Operational Research*, *149*(2), 268–281. doi:10.1016/S0377-2217(02)00761-0

Bouncken, R. B., & Fredrich, V. (2011). Coopetition: Its successful management in the nexus of dependency and trust. In *Proceedings of PICMET*. PICMET.

Bragg, A. (2000). Which network design tool is right for you? *IT Professional*, *2*(5), 23–32. doi:10.1109/6294.877494

Brandenburger, A., & Stuart, H. (2007). Biform Games. *Management Science*, *53*, 537–549. doi:10.1287/mnsc.1060.0591

Breit, W., & Hirsch, B. T. (2009). *Lives Of The Laureates: Twenty-three Nobel Economists*. Cambridge, MA: The MIT Press.

Brown, M., An, B., Kiekintveld, C., Ordóñez, F., & Tambe, M. (2012). Multi-Objective Optimization for Security Games.[AAMAS.]. *Proceedings of AAMAS*, *12*, 863–870.

Bruin, B. (2005). Game Theory in Philosophy. *Topoi*, *24*(2), 197–208. doi:10.1007/s11245-005-5055-3

Bu, S., & Yu, F. R. (2012). Dynamic energy-efficient resource allocation in cognitive heterogeneous wireless networks with the smart grid. In *Proceedings of IEEE GLOBECOM*, (pp. 3032-3036). IEEE.

Bu, S., Yu, F. R., & Liu, P. X. (2011). A game-theoretical decision-making scheme for electricity retailers in the smart grid with demand-side management. In *Proceedings of IEEE SmartGridComm*, (pp. 387-391). IEEE.

Buck, A. J. (n.d.). *An Introduction to Game Theory with Economic Applications*. Retrieved from http://courses.temple.edu/economics/Game%20Outline/index02.html

Burd, T. D., & Brodersen, R. W. (1996). Processor Design for Portable Systems. *The Journal of VLSI Signal Processing*, *13*, 203–221. doi:10.1007/BF01130406

Byde, A. (2003). Applying evolutionary game theory to auction mechanism design. In *Proceedings of IEEE International Conference on E-Commerce*, (pp. 347-354). IEEE.

Cai, J. (2004). Allocate fair payoff for cooperation in wireless ad hoc networks using Shapley Value. In *Proceedings of Parallel and Distributed Processing Symposium* (pp. 26-30). Academic Press.

Cai, J., & Pooch, U. (2004). Allocate Fair Payoff for Cooperation in Wireless Ad Hoc Networks Using Shapley Value. In *Proceedings of PDPS*, (pp. 219-227). PDPS.

Canales, M., & Gállego, J. R. (2010). Potential game for joint channel and power allocation in cognitive radio networks. *Electronics Letters*, *46*(24), 1632–1634. doi:10.1049/el.2010.2627

Cao, L., & Zheng, H. (2005). Distributed Spectrum Allocation via Local Bargaining. In *Proceedings of IEEE SECON*, (pp. 475- 486). IEEE.

Carin, L., Cybenko, G., & Hughes, J. (2008). Cyber security: The queries methodology. *IEEE Computer*, *41*(8), 20–26. doi:10.1109/MC.2008.295

Carlsson, H., & Damme, E. V. (1993). Global games and equilibrium selection. *Econometrica*, *61*(5), 989–1018. doi:10.2307/2951491

Chandrasekhar, V., Andrews, J., & Gatherer, A. (2008). Femtocell networks: a survey. *IEEE Communications Magazine*, *46*(9), 59–67. doi:10.1109/MCOM.2008.4623708

Changiz, R., Halabian, H., Yu, F. R., Lambadaris, I., & Tang, H. (2010). Trust Management in Wireless Mobile Networks with Cooperative Communications. In *Proceedings of EUC 2010*, (pp. 498-503). EUC.

Chatterjee, M., Haitao, L., Das, S. K., & Basu, K. (2003). A game theoretic approach for utility maximization in CDMA system.[IEEE.]. *Proceedings of the IEEE, ICC*, 412–416.

Chen, Q. B., Zhou, W. G., Chai, R., Tang, L., & Zhao, Y. L. (2010). A noncooperative game-theoretic vertical handoff in 4G heterogeneous wireless networks. In *Proceedings of International Conference on Communications and Networking*. Academic Press.

Chen, X., Xu, L., & Li, J. (2010). Bargaining Game and Cross-layer Design Based Optimization Strategy in Wireless Multi-hop Network. In *Proceedings of IEEE CIT*, (pp. 2570-2575). IEEE.

Chen, Y. M., & Su, C. L. (2007). Meeting QoS Requirements of Mobile Computing by Dual-Level Congestion Control. In *Proceedings of GPC*, (pp. 241-251). GPC.

Cheng, S. F., Reeves, D. M., Vorobeychik, Y., & Wellman, M. P. (2004). Notes on Equilibria in Symmetric Games. In *Proceedings of International Workshop on Game Theoretic and Decision Theoretic Agents*, (pp. 23-28). Academic Press.

Cheng, H., Yang, Q., Fu, F., & Kwak, K. S. (2011). Spectrum sharing with smooth supermodular game in cognitive radio networks. In *Proceedings of Communications and Information Technologies* (pp. 543–547). Academic Press. doi:10.1109/ISCIT.2011.6092168

Chenglin, Z., & Yan, G. (2009). A Novel Distributed Power Control Algorithm Based on Game Theory. In *Proceedings of International Conference on Wireless Communications, Networking and Mobile Computing.* Academic Press.

Chen, L., & Leneutre, J. (2009). A game theoretical framework on intrusion detection in heterogeneous networks. *IEEE Trans. Inf. Forens. Security, 4*(2), 165–178. doi:10.1109/TIFS.2009.2019154

Chen, X., Li, B., & Fang, Y. (2005). A Dynamic Multiple-Threshold Bandwidth Reservation (DMTBR) Scheme for QoS Provisioning in Multimedia Wireless Networks. *IEEE Transactions on Wireless Communications, 4*(2), 583–592. doi:10.1109/TWC.2004.843053

Cho, J., & Haas, Z. J. (2003). Throughput enhancement by multi-hop relaying in cellular radio networks with non-uniform traffic distribution. In *Proceedings of IEEE Vehicular Technology Conference,* (pp. 3065-3069). IEEE.

Cho, Y., & Tobagi, F. A. (2008). Cooperative and Non-Cooperative Aloha Games with Channel Capture Global Telecommunications Conference. In *Proceedings of IEEE GLOBECOM.* IEEE.

Chowdhury, M. Z., Bui, M. T., & Jang, Y. M. (2011). Neighbor cell list optimization for femtocell-to-femtocell handover in dense femtocellular networks. In *Proceedings of International Conference on Ubiquitous and Future Networks,* (pp. 241-245). Academic Press.

Chun, Y. S., & Lee, J. H. (2007). On the convergence of the random arrival rule in large claims problems. *International Journal of Game Theory, 36*(2), 259–273. doi:10.1007/s00182-007-0075-4

Colin, C. F. (2003). *Behavioral Game Theory: Experiments in Strategic Interaction.* Princeton University Press.

Conitzer, V. (2009). Approximation guarantees for fictitious play. In *Proceedings of the 47th Annual Allerton Conference on Communication, Control, and Computing,* (pp. 636-643). Academic Press.

Conley, J. P., & Wilkie, S. (1996). An Extension of the Nash Bargaining Solution to Nonconvex Problems. *Games and Economic Behavior, 13*(1), 26–38. doi:10.1006/game.1996.0023

Correa, J. R., & Stier-Moses, N. E. (2010). *Wardrop equilibria.* Retrieved from http://www.columbia.edu/~ns2224/papers/WEsurveyRev2public.pdf

Cox, J. C. (2006). *Perfect Bayesian Equilibrium.* Retrieved from http://www.econport.org/content/handbook/gametheory/useful/equilibrium/perfect.html

Crossman, A. (n.d.). *Game Theory.* Retrieved from http://sociology.about.com/od/Sociological-Theory/a/Game-Theory.htm

Cui, G., Li, M., Wang, Z., Tian, L., & Ma, J. (2012). Analysis and Evaluation Framework Based on Spatial Evolutionary Game Theory for Incentive Mechanism in Peer-to-Peer Network. In *Proceedings of IEEE TrustCom,* (pp. 287-294). IEEE.

Cui, W., & Bassiouni, M. A. (2003). Virtual private network bandwidth management with traffic prediction. *Computer Networks, 42*(6), 765–778. doi:10.1016/S1389-1286(03)00217-2

Dash, R., Parkes, D., & Jennings, N. (2003). Computational Mechanism Design: A Call to Arms. *IEEE Intelligent Systems, 18*(6), 40–47. doi:10.1109/MIS.2003.1249168

DaSilva, L. A., & Srivastava, V. (2004). Node Participation in Ad-hoc and Peer-to-peer Networks: A Game-theoretic Formulation. In *Proceedings of Workshop on Games and Emergent Behavior in Distributed Computing Environments.* Birmingham, UK: Academic Press.

Davila, J. (2009). *Kalai - Smorodinsky solution to bargaining problems.* Retrieved from http://cermsem.univ-paris1.fr/davila/teaching/BargTh/Bargaining%20slides%20-%202%20-%20Kalai-Smorodinsky.pdf

de Haan, J. E. S., Frunt, J., & Kling, W. L. (2010). Mitigation of wind power fluctuations in smart grids. In *Proceedings of IEEE ISGT Europe.* IEEE.

Deepalakshmi, P., & Radhakrishnan, S. (2009). QoS Routing Algorithm for Mobile Ad Hoc Networks Using ACO. In *Proceedings of International Conference on Control, Automation, Communication and Energy Conservation.* Academic Press.

Dehnie, S., Guan, K., Gharai, L., & Ghanadan, R. (2009). Kumar, S. Reliable data fusion in wireless sensor networks: A dynamic Bayesian game approach. In *Proceedings of IEEE Military Communications Conference 2009.* IEEE.

Denicolò, V., & Mariotti, M. (2000). Nash Bargaining Theory, Nonconvex Problems and Social Welfare Ordering. *Theory and Decision*, *48*(4), 351–358. doi:10.1023/A:1005278100070

Dharwadkar, P., Siegel, H. J., & Chong, E. K. P. (2000). *A Study of Dynamic Bandwidth Allocation with Preemption and Degradation for Prioritized Requests*. Purdue University, School of Electrical and Computer Engineering, Technical Report No. TR-ECE 00-9.

Dianati, M., Shen, X., & Naik, S. (2005). A New Fairness Index for Radio Resource Allocation in Wireless Networks. In *Proceedings of IEEE WCNC*, (pp. 712-715). IEEE.

Dirani, M., & Chahed, T. (2006). Framework for Resource Allocation in Heterogeneous Wireless Networks Using Game Theory. In *Proceedings of EuroNGI Workshop*, (pp. 144-154). EuroNGI.

Dixit, A., & Nalebuff, B. (n.d.). *Game Theory, the concise encyclopedia of economics*. Retrieved from http://www.econlib.org/library/Enc/GameTheory.html

Donmez, N. (2011). A game-theoretic approach to efficient power control in CDMA data networks. In *Proceedings of IEEE INISTA*, (pp. 248-252). IEEE.

Downs, A. (1957). *An economic theory of democracy*. New York: Harper and Row.

Dramitinos, M., & Lassous, I. G. (2009). A bandwidth allocation mechanism for 4G. In *Proceedings of European Wireless Technology Conference*, (pp. 96-99). Academic Press.

Duan, L., Gao, L., & Huang, J. (2011). Contract-based cooperative spectrum sharing. In *Proceedings of IEEE New Frontiers in Dynamic Spectrum Access Networks (DySPAN)*, (pp. 399-407). IEEE.

Dziong, Z., & Mason, L. G. (1996). Fair-efficient call admission control policies for broadband networks-a game theoretic framework. *IEEE/ACM Transactions on Networking*, *4*(1), 123–136. doi:10.1109/90.503768

Elias, J., & Martignon, F. (2010). Joint QoS Routing and Dynamic Capacity Dimensioning with Elastic Traffic: A Game Theoretical Perspective. In *Proceedings of IEEE International Conference on Communications*. IEEE.

Erhun, F., & Keskinocak, P. (2003). Game theory in Business application (Tech. rep.). Atlanta, GA: School of Industrial and system engineering, Georgia Inst. of Tech.

Etkin, R., Parekh, A., & Tse, D. (2007). Spectrum sharing for unlicensed bands. *IEEE Journal on Selected Areas in Communications*, *25*(3), 517–528. doi:10.1109/JSAC.2007.070402

Evolutionarily Stable Strategies . (n.d.). Retrieved from http://ess.nbb.cornell.edu/ess.html

Evolutionary Game Theory. (2009). *The Stanford Encyclopedia of Philosophy*. Retrieved from http://plato.stanford.edu/entries/game-evolutionary/

Fadlullah, Z. M., Nozaki, Y., Takeuchi, A., & Kato, N. (2011). A survey of game theoretic approaches in smart grid. In Proceedings of Wireless Communications and Signal Processing (WCSP). WCSP.

Fadlullah, Z. M., Nozaki, Y., Takeuchi, A., & Kato, N. (2011). A survey of game theoretic approaches in smart grid. In *Proceedings of Wireless Communications and Signal Processing*. Academic Press. doi:10.1109/WCSP.2011.6096962

Fang, X., Misra, S., Xue, G., & Yang, D. (2012). The New and Improved Power Grid: A Survey. *IEEE Communications Surveys & Tutorials*, *14*(4), 944–980. doi:10.1109/SURV.2011.101911.00087

Farquharson, R. (1969). *Theory of Voting*. New Haven, CT: Yale University Press.

Fattahi, A., Fu, F., Schaar, M., & Paganini, F. (2007). Mechanism-based resource allocation for multimedia transmission over spectrum agile wireless networks. *IEEE Journal on Selected Areas in Communications*, *25*(3), 601–612. doi:10.1109/JSAC.2007.070410

Felegyhazi, M., & Hubaux, J.-P. (2006). *Game Theory in Wireless Networks: A Tutorial* (EPFL Technical Report: LCA-REPORT-2006-002). Lausanne, Switzerland: Ecole Polytechnique F´ed´erale de Lausanne.

Felegyhazi, M., Hubaux, J., & Buttyan, L. (2006). Nash Equilibria of Packet Forwarding Strategies in Wireless Ad Hoc Networks. *IEEE Transactions on Mobile Computing*, *5*(5), 463–476. doi:10.1109/TMC.2006.68

Felemban, E., Lee, C. G., & Ekici, E. (2006). MMSPEED: multipath Multi-SPEED protocol for QoS guarantee of reliability and. Timeliness in wireless sensor networks. *IEEE Transactions on Mobile Computing, 5*(6), 738–754. doi:10.1109/TMC.2006.79

Feng, H., Zhang, S., Liu, C., Zhou, Q., & Zhang, M. (2008). TCP Veno Connection Game Model on Non-Cooperative Game Theory. In *Proceedings of IEEE WiCOM'08.* IEEE.

Feng, N., Mau, S. C., & Mandayam, N. B. (2004). Pricing and power control for joint network-centric and user-centric radio resource management. *IEEE Transactions on Communications, 52*(9), 1547–1557. doi:10.1109/TCOMM.2004.833191

Friedman, E. J., & Parkes, D. D. (2003). Pricing WiFi at Starbucks: issues in online mechanism design. In *Proceedings of ACM Conference on Electronic Commerce,* (pp. 240-241). ACM.

Fudenberg, D., & Levine, D. K. (1998). *The Theory of Learning in Games.* MIT Press.

Game Theoretical Linguistics. (n.d.). *From the Communication in Context.* Retrieved from http://www.cccom.ut.ee/?page_id=29

Game Theory and Ethics. (2010). Retrieved from http://plato.stanford.edu/entries/game-ethics/

Game Theory. (n.d.). Retrieved from http://en.wikipedia.org/wiki/Game_theory

Ganesan, G., & Li, Y. (2005). Cooperative spectrum sensing in cognitive radio networks. In *Proceedings of IEEE Int. Symp. on New Frontiers in Dynamic Spectrum Access Networks, DySPAN 2005.* IEEE.

Garg, D., Narahari, Y., & Gujar, S. (2008). Foundations of Mechanism Design: A Tutorial, Part 1: Key Concepts and Classical Results. *Sadhana. Indian Academy Proceedings in Engineering Sciences, 33*(2), 83–130.

Garroppo, R. G., Giordano, S., & Iacono, D. (2009). Radio-Aware Scheduler for WiMAX Systems Based on Time-Utility Function and Game Theory. In *Proceedings of IEEE GLOBECOM 2009.* IEEE.

Gelabert, X., Sallent, O., Pérez-Romero, J., & Agustí, R. (2010). Spectrum sharing in cognitive radio networks with imperfect sensing: A discrete-time Markov model. *Computer Networks, 54*(14), 2519–2536. doi:10.1016/j.comnet.2010.04.005

Génin, T., & Aknine, S. (2010). Coalition Formation Strategies for Multiagent Hedonic Games. In *Proceedings of IEEE International Conference on Tools with Artificial Intelligence,* (pp. 465-472). IEEE.

Ghasemi, N., & Hosseini, S. M. (2010). Comparison of smart grid with cognitive radio: Solutions to spectrum scarcity. In *Proceedings of ICACT,* (pp. 898-903). ICACT.

Ghazvini, M., Movahedinia, N., Jamshidi, K., & Moghim, N. (2010). Game Theory Applications in CSMA Methods. In *Proceedings of IEEE Communications Surveys & Tutorials.* IEEE.

Gibbons, R. (1992). *Game Theory for Applied Economists.* Princeton, NJ: Princeton University Press.

Ginde, S., Neel, J., & Buehrer, R. M. (2003). A game-theoretic analysis of joint link adaptation and distributed power control in GPRS. In *Proceedings of IEEE Vehicular Technology Conference,* (pp. 732-736). IEEE.

Gintis, H. (2009). *The Bounds of Reason: Game Theory and the Unification of the Behavioral Sciences.* Princeton University Press.

Goodman, D., & Mandayam, N. (1999). Power control for wireless data. In *Proceedings of IEEE Mobile Multimedia Communications (MoMuC'99),* (pp. 55-63). IEEE.

Gorji, A. E., Abolhassani, B., Honardar, K., Adibi, M., & Okhovat, M. (2010). Utility Fair Non-cooperative Game Approach for Resource Allocation in Multi-cell OFDM Systems. In *Proceedings of ICCMS,* (pp. 154-158). ICCMS.

Guan, Z., Yuan, D., & Zhang, H. (2008). Novel coopetition paradigm based on bargaining theory or collaborative multimedia resource management. In *Proceedings of IEEE PIMRC.* IEEE.

Gunes, M., Sorges, U., & Bouazizi, I. (2002). ARA - The ant-colony based routing algorithm for MANETs. In *Proceedings of the International Conference on Parallel Processing Workshops,* (pp. 79-85). Academic Press.

Halpern, J. Y. (2008). Computer science and game theory: A brief survey. In S. N. Durlauf, & L. E. Blume (Eds.), *Palgrave Dictionary of Economics.* Palgrave MacMillan. doi:10.1057/9780230226203.0287

Hamilton, S. N., Miller, W. L., Ott, A., & Saydjari, O. S. (2002). Challenges in applying game theory to the domain of information warfare. In *Proceedings of Information survivability workshop*. Academic Press.

Hamilton, S. N., Miller, W. L., Ott, A., & Saydjari, O. S. (2002). The role of game theory in information warfare. In *Proceedings of Information survivability workshop*. Academic Press.

Han, Z., Ji, Z., & Liu, K. J. R. (2004). Low-complexity OFDMA channel allocation with Nash bargaining solution fairness. *IEEE Global Telecommunication Conf., 6*, 3726–3731.

Han, Z., Ji, Z., & Liu, K. J. R. (2004). Power Minimization for Multi-Cell OFDM Networks using Distributed Non-Cooperative Game Approach. In *Proceedings of IEEE GLOBECOM*, (pp. 3742-3747). IEEE.

Han, Z., Niyato, D., Saad, W., Başar, T., & Hjørungnes, A. (2011). *Game Theory in Wireless and Communication Networks*. Cambridge, UK: Cambridge University Press. doi:10.1017/CBO9780511895043

Han, Z., Zheng, R., & Poor, H. V. (2011). Repeated Auctions with Bayesian Nonparametric Learning for Spectrum Access in Cognitive Radio Networks. *IEEE Transactions on Wireless Communications, 10*(3), 890–900. doi:10.1109/TWC.2011.010411.100838

Harsanyi, J. C., & Selten, R. (1988). A General Theory Of Equilibrium Selection. In *Games*. Cambridge, MA: MIT Press.

Hart, S., & Mas-Colell, A. (2000). A simple adaptive procedure leading to correlated equilibrium. *Econometrica, 68*(5), 1127–1150. doi:10.1111/1468-0262.00153

Hauert, C., De Monte, S., Hofbauer, J., & Sigmund, K. (2002). Replicator dynamics in optional public goods games. *Journal of Theoretical Biology, 218*(2), 187–194. doi:10.1006/jtbi.2002.3067 PMID:12381291

Heo, J. H., Shin, J. C., Nam, J. H., Lee, Y. T., Park, J. G., & Cho, H. S. (2008). Mathematical Analysis of Secondary User Traffic in Cognitive Radio System. In *Proceedings of IEEE VTC*. IEEE.

Hoekstra, K. (2003). Hobbes on Law, Nature and Reason. *Journal of the History of Philosophy, 41*(1), 111–120. doi:10.1353/hph.2002.0098

Hofbauer, J., & Sigmund, K. (2003). Evolutionary game dynamics. *Journal of Bulletin of the American Mathematical Society, 40*, 479–519. doi:10.1090/S0273-0979-03-00988-1

Holliday, T., Goldsmith, A. J., Glynn, P., & Bambos, N. (2004). Distributed. power and admission control for time varying wireless networks. In *Proceedings of IEEE GLOBECOM*, (pp. 768-774). IEEE.

Homo Economicus. (n.d.). Retrieved from http://rationalwiki.org/wiki/Homo_economicus

Hong, E. J., Yun, S. Y., & Cho, D. H. (2009). Decentralized power control scheme in femtocell networks: A game theoretic approach. In *Proceedings of IEEE Personal, Indoor and Mobile Radio Communications*, (pp. 415-419). IEEE.

Hongshun, Z., & Xiao, Y. (2010). Advanced Dynamic Spectrum Allocation Algorithm Based on Potential Game for Cognitive Radio. In *Proceedings of Information Engineering and Electronic Commerce*. Academic Press.

Hosein, P. (2010). Pricing for QoS-based wireless data services and its impact on radio resource management. In *Proceedings of IEEE GLOBECOM*, (pp. 539-544). IEEE.

Hou, Y., Wang, Y., & Hu, B. (2010). Research on power control algorithm based on game theory in cognitive radio system. In *Proceedings of International Conference on Signal Processing Systems*, (pp. 614-618). Academic Press.

Hou, J., Yang, J., & Papavassiliou, S. (2002). Integration of pricing with call admission control to meet qos requirements in cellular networks. *IEEE Transactions on Parallel and Distributed Systems, 13*, 898–909. doi:10.1109/TPDS.2002.1036064

Howard, N. (1971). *Paradoxes of Rationality*. MIT Press.

Ho, Y. C., Luh, P., & Muralidharan, R. (1981). Information structure, Stackelberg games, and incentive controllability. *IEEE Transactions on Automatic Control, 26*(2), 454–460. doi:10.1109/TAC.1981.1102652

Huang, J., Berry, R., & Honig, M. L. (2006). Auction-based Spectrum Sharing. *ACM/Springer Mobile Networks and Apps.,* 405–18.

Huang, C. M., Ku, H. H., & Kung, H. Y. (2009). Efficient power-consumption-based load-sharing topology control protocol for harsh environments in wireless sensor networks. *IET Communications, 3*(5), 859–870. doi:10.1049/iet-com.2008.0217

Huining, H., Yanikomeroglu, H., Falconer, D. D., & Periyalwar, S. (2004). Range extension without capacity penalty in cellular networks with digital fixed relays. In *Proceedings of IEEE GLOBECOM,* (pp. 3053-3057). IEEE.

Hurwicz, L., & Reiter, S. (2008). *Designing Economic Mechanisms.* Cambridge, UK: Cambridge University Press.

Hussain, T., & Habib, S. J. (2009). Optimization of network clustering and hierarchy through simulated annealing. In *Proceedings of ACS/IEEE International Conference on Computer Systems and Applications,* (pp. 712-716). ACS/IEEE.

Ibars, C., Navarro, M., & Giupponi, L. (2010). Distributed Demand Management in Smart Grid with a Congestion Game. In *Proceedings of IEEE SmartGridComm.* IEEE.

Iklé, F. (1964). *How Nations Negotiate.* New York: Harper and Row.

Iqbal, M., Gondal, I., & Dooley, L. (2006). An Energy-Aware Dynamic Clustering Algorithm for Load Balancing in Wireless Sensor Networks. *The Journal of Communication, 1*(3), 10–19.

Irani, S., Shukla, S., & Gupta, R. (2003). Online Strategies for Dynamic Power Management in Systems with Multiple Power-Saving States. *ACM Trans. Embedded Computing Syst., 2*(3), 325–346. doi:10.1145/860176.860180

Isaac, R., Walker, J., & Williams, A. (1994). Group Size and the Voluntary Provision of Public Goods: Experimental Evidence Utilizing Large Groups. *Journal of Public Economics, 54*(1), 1–36. doi:10.1016/0047-2727(94)90068-X

Ishihara, Y., Huang, R., & Sim, K. M. (2005). Learning opponent's eagerness with Bayesian updating rule in a market-driven negotiation model. In *Proceedings of International Conference on Advanced Information Networking and Applications,* (pp. 903-908). Academic Press.

Jaeger, G. (2008). Applications of Game Theory in Linguistics. *Language and Linguistics Compass, 2/3,* 406–421. doi:10.1111/j.1749-818X.2008.00053.x

Jayaweera, S. K., Vazquez-Vilar, G., & Mosquera, C. (2010). Dynamic Spectrum Leasing: A New Paradigm for Spectrum Sharing in Cognitive Radio Networks. *IEEE Transactions on Vehicular Technology, 59*(5), 2328–2339. doi:10.1109/TVT.2010.2042741

Jensen, M., & Meckling, W. (1976). Theory of the Firm: Managerial Behavior, Agency, Costs, and Ownership Structure. *Journal of Financial Economics,* 305–360. doi:10.1016/0304-405X(76)90026-X

Jeong, D. K., & Kim, D. (2013). Optimal access point switching with per-link threshold under nonhomogeneous bandwidth allocation. In Proceedings of Information and Communication Technology (ICoICT), (pp. 187-191). ICoICT.

Jiang, M., & Ward, P. A. S. (2011). A cooperative game-theory model for bandwidth allocation in multi-hop wireless networks. In *Proceedings of IEEE WiMob,* (pp. 222-229). IEEE.

Kamal, H., Coupechoux, M., & Godlewski, P. (2009). Inter-operator spectrum sharing for cellular networks using game theory. In *Proceedings of IEEE PIMRC,* (pp. 425-429). IEEE.

Kannan, R., Ray, L., Kalidindi, R., & Iyengar, S. (2004). Max-min length-energyconstrained routing in wireless sensor networks. In *Proc. 1st EWSN 2004,* (pp. 19–21, 234–249). EWSN.

Kant, U., & Grosu, D. (2005). Double auction protocols for resource allocation in grids. In *Proceedings of Information Technology Coding and Computing* (pp. 366–371). Academic Press. doi:10.1109/ITCC.2005.135

Khan, S. U., & Ardil, C. (2009). Energy Efficient Resource Allocation in Distributed Computing Systems. In Proceedings of Distributed, High-Performance and Grid Computing, (pp. 667-673). Academic Press.

Khan, A. H., Qadeer, M. A., Ansari, J. A., & Waheed, S. (2009). 4G as a Next Generation Wireless Network. In *Proceedings of Future Computer and Communication* (pp. 334–338). Academic Press. doi:10.1109/ICFCC.2009.108

Kiekintveld, C., & Tambe, M. (2009). Computing optimal randomized resource allocations for massive security games.[AAMAS.]. *Proceedings of AAMAS, 09,* 689–696.

Kim, E., Park, H., & Frossard, P. (2012). Low complexity iterative multimedia resource allocation based on game theoretic approach. In *Proceedings of IEEE ISCAS,* (pp. 1099-1102). IEEE.

Kim, S. W. (2010). Dynamic Online Bandwidth Adjustment Scheme Based on Kalai-Smorodinsky Bargaining Solution. *IEICE Trans. on Communications, E93.B*(7), 1935-1938.

Kim, S. W. (2011b). Stackelberg Game-Based Power Control Scheme for Efficiency and Fairness Tradeoff. *IEICE Transactions, E94-B*(8), 2427-2430.

Kim, S. W. (2011c). QoS-Sensitive Dynamic Voltage Scaling Algorithm for Wireless Multimedia Services. *IEICE Transactions, E96-B*(1), 1745-1345.

Kim, S. W. (2012c). Trust-Based Bargaining Game Model for Cognitive Radio Spectrum Sharing Scheme. *IEICE Transactions, E95-B*(12), 3925-3928.

Kim, Y. M., Kim, W. S., You, H. R., Lee, S. C., & Lee, H. J. (2010). Group-based management for cooperative spectrum sensing in cognitive radio networks. In *Proceedings of ICACT,* (pp. 119-123). ICACT.

Kimbrough, S., & Kuo, A. (2010). On heuristics for two-sided matching: revisiting the stable marriage problem as a multiobjective problem. In *Proceedings of the 12th annual conference on Genetic and evolutionary computation,* (pp. 1283-1290). Academic Press.

Kim, S. (2011). Cellular Network Bandwidth Management Scheme by using Nash Bargaining Solution. *IET Communications, 5*(3), 371–380. doi:10.1049/iet-com.2010.0309

Kim, S. W. (2008). Energy Efficient Online Routing Algorithm for QoS-Sensitive Sensor Networks. *IEICE Transactions on Communications. E (Norwalk, Conn.), 91-B*(7), 2401–2404.

Kim, S. W. (2009). Adaptive online processor management algorithms for multimedia data communication with QoS sensitivity. *International Journal of Communication Systems, 22*(4), 469–482. doi:10.1002/dac.979

Kim, S. W. (2010). QoS-Aware Bandwidth Allocation Algorithm for Multimedia Service Networks. *IEICE Transactions on Communications. E (Norwalk, Conn.), 94-B*(3), 810–812.

Kim, S. W. (2010a). Cooperative game theoretic online routing scheme for wireless network managements. *IET Communications, 4*(17), 2074–2083. doi:10.1049/iet-com.2009.0686

Kim, S. W. (2010b). Game theoretic Multi-Objective Routing Scheme for Wireless Sensor Networks. *Ad Hoc & Sensor Wireless Networks, 10*(4), 343–359.

Kim, S. W. (2011). Adaptive online power control scheme based on the evolutionary game theory. *IET Communications, 5*(18), 2648–2655. doi:10.1049/iet-com.2011.0093

Kim, S. W. (2011). Adaptive Online Voltage Scaling Scheme based on the Nash Bargaining Solution. *ETRI Journal, 33*(3), 407–414. doi:10.4218/etrij.11.0110.0417

Kim, S. W. (2011a). An Online Network Price Control Scheme by Using Stackelberg Game Model. *IEICE Transactions, 94-B*(1), 322–325. doi:10.1587/transcom.E94.B.322

Kim, S. W. (2012). An Online Bandwidth Allocation Scheme Based on Mechanism Design Model. *IEICE Transactions, 96-B*(1), 321–324.

Kim, S. W. (2012a). Adaptive Call Admission Control Scheme for Heterogeneous Overlay Networks. *Journal of Communications and Networks, 14*(4), 461–466. doi:10.1109/JCN.2012.6292253

Kim, S. W. (2012a). Multi-leader multi-follower Stackelberg model for cognitive radio spectrum sharing scheme. *Computer Networks, 56*(17), 3682–3692. doi:10.1016/j.comnet.2012.08.004

Kim, S. W. (2012b). Adaptive Ad-hoc Network Routing Scheme by Using Incentive-based Model. *Ad Hoc & Sensor Wireless Networks*, *15*(2), 107–125.

Kim, S. W. (2012b). Reversed Stackelberg Bandwidth Sharing Game for Cognitive Multi-hop Cellular Networks. *IET Communications*, *6*(17), 2907–2913. doi:10.1049/iet-com.2011.0782

Kim, S. W. (2012d). Biform game based cognitive radio scheme for smart grid communications. *Journal of Communications and Networks*, *14*(6), 614–618. doi:10.1109/JCN.2012.00027

Kim, S. W. (2013). Adaptive Smart Grid Management Scheme based on the Coopetition Game Model. *ETRI*, *6*, 1–12.

Kim, S. W. (2013). Femtocell Network Power Control Scheme based on the Weighted Voting Game. *EURASIP Journal on Wireless Communications and Networking*, *1*(44), 1–9.

Kim, S. W. (2013). Multi-hop Network Bandwidth Management Scheme based on Cooperrative Bargaining Models. *Wireless Personal Communications*. doi:10.1007/s11277-013-1199-4

Kim, S. W. (2013a). Cognitive Radio Bandwidth Sharing Scheme Based on the Two-way Matching Game. *Wireless Personal Communications*, *68*(4), 893–905. doi:10.1007/s11277-011-0488-z

Kim, S. W. (2013b). A Repeated Bayesian Auction Game for Cognitive Radio Spectrum Sharing Scheme. *Computer Communications*, *36*(8), 939–946. doi:10.1016/j.comcom.2013.02.003

Kim, S. W., & Kim, S. C. (2007). An Online Buffer Management Algorithm for QoS-Sensitive Multimedia Networks. *ETRI Journal*, *29*(5), 685–687. doi:10.4218/etrij.07.0207.0097

Kim, S. W., & Varshney, P. K. (2004). An Integrated Adaptive Bandwidth Management Framework for QoS sensitive Multimedia Cellular Networks. *IEEE Transactions on Vehicular Technology*, *53*(3), 835–846. doi:10.1109/TVT.2004.825704

Kim, S. W., & Varshney, P. K. (2005). An Adaptive Bandwidth Allocation Algorithm for QoS guaranteed Multimedia Networks. *Computer Communications*, *28*(17), 1959–1969. doi:10.1016/j.comcom.2005.02.011

Kim, S. W., & Varshney, P. K. (2005). An Adaptive Fault Tolerance Algorithm for Multimedia Cellular Networks. *IEE Proceedings. Communications*, *152*(6), 932–938. doi:10.1049/ip-com:20045131

Kimura, K., Yamamoto, K., Murata, H., & Yoshida, S. (2008). Fair channel and route selection algorithm using Nash bargaining solutions in multi-hop radio networks. In *Proceedings of IEEE International Workhop on Wireless Distributed Networks*. IEEE.

Klinkowski, M., Careglio, D., & Sole-Pareta, J. (2009). Reactive and proactive routing in labelled optical burst switching networks. *IET Communications*, *3*(3), 454–464. doi:10.1049/iet-com:20070498

Kondareddy, Y., & Agrawal, P. (2011). Enforcing Cooperative Spectrum Sensing in Cognitive Radio Networks. In *Proceedings of IEEE GLOBECOM*. IEEE.

Korad, U., & Sivalingam, K. M. (2006). Reliable data delivery in wireless sensor networks using distributed cluster monitoring. *International Journal of Sensor Networks*, *1*(1/2), 75–83. doi:10.1504/IJSNET.2006.010839

Korzhyk, D., Conitzer, V., & Parr, R. (2011). Security Games with Multiple Attacker Resources.[IJCAI.]. *Proceedings of IJCAI*, *11*, 273–279.

Koskie, S., & Gajic, Z. (2005). A Nash Game Algorithm for SIR-based Power Control in 3G Wireless CDMA Networks. *IEEE/ACM Transactions on Networking*, *13*(5), 1017–1026. doi:10.1109/TNET.2005.857068

Krebs, J. R., & Davies, N. B. (1997). *Behavioural Ecology: An Evolutionary Approach*. Wiley-Blackwell.

Krishnamurthy, V. (2010). Decentralized spectrum access via multivariate global games. In *Proceedings of International Workshop on Cognitive Information Processing*, (pp. 464-469). Academic Press.

Krishnamurthy, V. (2008). Decentralized Activation in Dense Sensor Networks via Global Games. *IEEE Transactions on Signal Processing*, *56*(10), 4936–4950. doi:10.1109/TSP.2008.926978

Krishnamurthy, V. (2009). Decentralized Spectrum Access Amongst Cognitive Radios - An Interacting Multivariate Global Game-Theoretic Approach. *IEEE Transactions on Signal Processing*, *57*(10), 3999–4013. doi:10.1109/TSP.2009.2022860

Krithikaivasan, B., Zeng, Y., Deka, K., & Medhi, D. (2007). ARCH-Based Traffic Forecasting and Dynamic Bandwidth Provisioning for Periodically Measured Non-stationary Traffic. *IEEE/ACM Transactions on Networking, 15*(3), 683–696. doi:10.1109/TNET.2007.893217

Kuhn, S. T. (2004). Reflections on Ethics and Game Theory. *Synthese, 141*(1), 1–44. doi:10.1023/B:SYNT.0000035846.91195.cb

Kumar, S., Kambhatla, K., Hu, F., Lifson, M., & Xiao, Y. (2008). Ubiquitous Computing for Remote Cardiac Patient Monitoring: A Survey. *International Journal of Telemedicine and Applications*, (4): 1–19. doi:10.1155/2008/459185 PMID:18604301

Kunnumkal, S. (2004). *Algorithmic Game Theory.* Retrieved from http://www.cs.cornell.edu/courses/cs684/2004sp/feb20.pdf

Kuo, Y. L., Wu, E. H. K., & Chen, G. H. (2004). Noncooperative admission control for differentiated services in IEEE 802.11 WLANs. In *Proceedings of IEEE GLOBECOM*, (pp. 2981-2986). IEEE.

Kutsuna, H., & Fujita, S. (2011). A Fair and Efficient Congestion Avoidance Scheme Based on the Minority Game. *Journal of Information Processing Systems, 7*(3), 531–542. doi:10.3745/JIPS.2011.7.3.531

Kwon, H., Lee, H., & Cioffi, J. M. (2009). Cooperative Strategy by Stackelberg Games under Energy Constraint in Multi-Hop Relay Networks. In *Proceedings of IEEE GLOBECOM*. IEEE.

Lafferty, R. (2001). *Practical applications of game theory in sociological research.* (Unpublished bachelor thesis). McGill University, Montreal, Canada.

Lambert, T. J., Epelman, M. A., & Smith, R. L. (2005). A fictitious play approach to large-scale optimization. *Operations Research, 53*(3), 477–489. doi:10.1287/opre.1040.0178

Latifa, B., Gao, Z., & Liu, S. (2012). No-Regret learning for simultaneous power control and channel allocation in cognitive radio networks. In *Proceedings of IEEE ComComAp*, (pp. 267- 271). IEEE.

Lecture Notes. (n.d.). Retrieved from http://www.gametheory.net/lectures/field.pl

Lei, D., Melodia, T., Batalama, S. N., & Matyjas, J. D. (2010). Distributed Routing, Relay Selection, and Spectrum Allocation in Cognitive and Cooperative Ad Hoc Networks. In *Proceedings of IEEE SECON*. IEEE.

Leino, J. (2003). *Applications of Game Theory in Ad Hoc Networks.* (Unpublished Master's Thesis). Helisnki University of Technology, Helisnki, Finland.

Le, L., & Hossain, E. (2007). Multihop Cellular Networks: Potential Gains, Research Challenges, and a Resource Allocation Framework. *IEEE Communications Magazine, 45*(9), 66–73. doi:10.1109/MCOM.2007.4342859

Lescanne, P., & Perrinel, M. (2012). Backward coinduction, Nash equilibrium and the rationality of escalation. *Acta Informatica, 49*(3), 117–137. doi:10.1007/s00236-012-0153-3

Leu, J. J. Y., Tsai, M. H., Chiang, T. C., & Huang, Y. M. (2006). Adaptive power aware clustering and multicasting protocol for mobile ad-hoc networks. In *Proceedings of Ubiquitous Intelligence and Computing* (pp. 331–340). Academic Press. doi:10.1007/11833529_34

Levine, D. K. (n.d.). *What is Game Theory?* Retrieved from http://levine.sscnet.ucla.edu/general/whatis.htm

Li, D., Jayaweera, S. K., & Naseri, A. (2011). Auctioning game based Demand Response scheduling in smart grid. In *Proceedings of IEEE Online Conference on Green Communications*, (pp. 58-63). IEEE.

Li, D., Xu, Y., Liu, J., Wang, X., & Han, Z. (2010). A Market Game for Dynamic Multi-Band Sharing in Cognitive Radio Networks. In *Proceedings of IEEE International Conference on Communications*. IEEE.

Li, H., Liu, Y., & Zhang, D. (2010). Dynamic spectrum access for cognitive radio systems with repeated games. In *Proceedings of IEEE Wireless Communications, Networking and Information Security*, (pp. 59-62). IEEE.

Li, J., Chen, D., Li, W., & Ma, J. (2007). Multiuser Power and Channel Allocation Algorithm in Cognitive Radio. In *Proceedings of ICCP*. ICCP.

Li, J., He, J., Zhang, Q., & Huang, S. (2009). A Game Theory Based WiMAX Uplink Power Control Algorithm. In *Proceedings of International Conference on Wireless Communications, Networking and Mobile Computing*. Academic Press.

Li, J., Shi, Z., Liu, W. Y., Yue, K., & Chen, R. J. (2010). No-Regret Learning for Cost Constrained Resource Selection Game. In *Proceedings of ICNC*, (pp. 2921-2925). ICNC.

Li, R., Zuo, C., He, Y., & Lu, Z. (2008). A Credit Mechanism Based on Automatic Audit in P2P File Sharing Systems. In *Proceedings of ICYCS*, (pp. 2044-2049). ICYCS.

Li, X., & Cui, J. (2009). Real-time water resources allocation: methodology and mechanism. In *Proceedings of IEEM*, (pp. 1637-1641). IEEM.

Li, Y., & Feng, Z. (2011). Enterprise femtocell network optimization based on neural network modeling. In *Proceedings of IEEE CCNC*, (pp. 1130-1131). IEEE.

Li, Y., Wang, X., & Guizani, M. (2009). Resource Pricing with Primary Service Guarantees in Cognitive Radio Networks: A Stackelberg Game Approach. In *Proceedings of IEEE Global Telecommunications Conference*. IEEE.

Liang, X., & Xiao, Y. (2013). Game Theory for Network Security. *IEEE Communications Surveys & Tutorials*, *15*(1), 472–486. doi:10.1109/SURV.2012.062612.00056

Lin, X. H., & Wang, H. (2012). On using game theory to balance energy consumption in heterogeneous wireless sensor networks. In *Proceedings of IEEE Conference on Local Computer Networks*, (pp. 568-576). IEEE.

Lin, H., Chatterjee, M., Das, S. K., & Basu, K. (2005). ARC: An Integrated Admission and Rate Control Framework for Competitive Wireless CDMA Data Networks Using Noncooperative Games. *IEEE Transactions on Mobile Computing*, *4*(3), 243–258. doi:10.1109/TMC.2005.35

Liu, J., Shen, L., Song, T., & Wang, X. (2009). Demand-matching spectrum sharing game for non-cooperative cognitive radio network. In *Proceedings of International Conference on Wireless Communications & Signal Processing*. Academic Press.

Liu, Y., Peng, Q. C., Shao, H. Z., Chen, X. F., & Wang, L. (2010). Power control algorithm based on game theory in cognitive radio networks. In *Proceedings of International Conference on Apperceiving Computing and Intelligence Analysis*, (pp. 164-168). Academic Press.

Liu, P., Zang, W., & Yu, M. (2005). Incentive-based modeling and inference of attacker intent, objectives, and strategies. *ACM Transactions on Information and System Security*, *8*(1), 78–118. doi:10.1145/1053283.1053288

Liu, Y., Comaniciu, C., & Man, H. (2006). A Bayesian game approach for intrusion detection in wireless ad hoc networks. In *Game theory for communications and networks*. Academic Press. doi:10.1145/1190195.1190198

Li, X., Qian, L., & Kataria, D. (2009). Downlink power control in co-channel macrocell femtocell overlay. In *Proceedings of Information Sciences and Systems* (pp. 383–388). Academic Press. doi:10.1109/CISS.2009.5054750

Logenthiran, T., Srinivasan, D., & Shun, T. Z. (2012). Demand Side Management in Smart Grid Using Heuristic Optimization. *IEEE Transactions on Smart Grid*, *3*(3), 1244–1252. doi:10.1109/TSG.2012.2195686

Lohi, M., Weerakoon, D., & Aghvami, A. H. (1999). Trends in multi-layer cellular system design and handover design. In *Proceedings of IEEE Wireless Communications and Networking Conference*, (pp. 898 - 902). IEEE.

Long, C., Zhang, Q., Li, B., Yang, H., & Guan, X. (2007). Non-Cooperative Power Control for Wireless Ad Hoc Networks with Repeated Games. *IEEE Journal on Selected Areas in Communications*, *25*(6), 1101–1112. doi:10.1109/JSAC.2007.070805

Lu, Z., Sun, Y., Wen, X., Su, T., & Ling, D. (2012). An energy-efficient power control algorithm in femtocell networks. In *Proceedings of IEEE ICCSE*, (pp. 395-400). IEEE.

Luo, C., Ji, H., & Li, Y. (2009). Utility-Based Multi-Service Bandwidth Allocation in the 4G Heterogeneous Wireless Access Networks. In *Proceedings of IEEE WCNC*. IEEE.

Lye, K., & Wing, J. (2005). Game strategies in network security. *International Journal of Information Security*, *4*(1-2), 71–86. doi:10.1007/s10207-004-0060-x

MacKenzie, A. B., & Wicker, S. B. (2001). Game theory in communications: motivation, explanation, and application to power control.[IEEE.]. *Proceedings of IEEE GLOBECOM*, *01*, 821–826.

Mahapatra, A., Anand, K., & Agrawal, D. P. (2006). QoS and Energy Aware Routing for Real Time Traffic in Wireless Sensor Networks. *Computer Communications*, *29*(4), 437–445. doi:10.1016/j.comcom.2004.12.028

Maharjan, S., Zhu, Q., Zhang, Y., Gjessing, S., & Basar, T. (2013). Dependable Demand Response Management in the Smart Grid: A Stackelberg Game Approach. *IEEE Transactions on Smart Grid, 4*(1), 120–132. doi:10.1109/TSG.2012.2223766

Mähönen, P., & Petrova, M. (2008). Minority game for cognitive radios: cooperating without cooperation. *Physical Communication, 1*, 94–102. doi:10.1016/j.phycom.2008.03.001

Malanchini, I., Cesana, M., & Gatti, N. (2009). On Spectrum Selection Games in Cognitive Radio Networks. In *Proceedings of IEEE GLOBECOM*. IEEE.

Malanchini, I., Cesana, M., & Gatti, N. (2012). Network Selection and Resource Allocation Games for Wireless Access Networks. *IEEE Transactions on Mobile Computing*, 1–14.

Ma, M., & Tsang, D. H. K. (2009). Joint design of spectrum sharing and routing with channel heterogeneity in cognitive radio networks. *Physical Communication, 2*(1), 127–137. doi:10.1016/j.phycom.2009.02.007

Marden, J., Arslan, G., & Shamma, J. S. (2009). Cooperative Control and Potential Games. *IEEE Transactions on Systems, Man, and Cybernetics, 39*(6), 1393–1407. doi:10.1109/TSMCB.2009.2017273 PMID:19369160

Ma, S., He, J., & Zhang, Y. (2012). Trust Computation Based on Fuzzy Clustering Theory. *International Journal of Hybrid Information Technology, 5*(2), 213–218.

Mathur, S., Sankaranarayanan, L., & Mandayam, N. (2006). Coalitional games in Gaussian interference channels. In *Proceedings of IEEE ISIT*, (pp. 2210–2214). IEEE.

Matt, P. A., Toni, F., & Dionysiou, D. (2006). The distributed negotiation of egalitarian resource allocations. In *Proceedings of the 1st International Workshop on Computational Social Choice*, (pp. 304-316). Academic Press.

Mawji, A., & Hassanein, H. (2009). Incentives for P2P File Sharing in Mobile Ad Hoc Networks. In *Proceedings of IEEE CCNC*. IEEE.

McCain, R. A. (n.d.). *Émile Borel*. Retrieved from http://faculty.lebow.drexel.edu/McCainR/top/eco/game/nash.html

Mehmet, S., & Ramazan, K. (2001). A Comparative Study of Multiobjective Optimization Methods in Structural Design. *Turkish Journal of Engineering and Environmental Sciences, 25*(2), 69–78.

Mehta, S., & Kwak, K. S. (2009). Game Theory and Cognitive Radio Based Wireless Networks.[KES-AMSTA.]. *Proceedings of KES-AMSTA, 09*, 803–812.

Menasche, D. S., Figueiredo, D. R., & Silva, E. S. (2005). An evolutionary game-theoretic approach to congestion control. *Performance Evaluation, 62*(1-4), 295–312. doi:10.1016/j.peva.2005.07.028

Meshkati, F., Poor, H. V., Schwartz, S. C., & Balan, R. V. (2006). Energy-efficient power and rate control with QoS constraints: a game-theoretic approach. In *Proceedings of IWCMC*, (pp. 1435-1440). IWCMC.

Miorandi, D., & De Pellegrini, F. (2012). Demand-side management in smart grids: An evolutionary games perspective. In *Performance Evaluation Methodologies and Tools* (pp. 178–187). Academic Press. doi:10.4108/valuetools.2012.250351

Mizuno, H., Okamoto, T., Koakutsu, S., & Hirata, H. (2012). A growing complex network design method with an adaptive multi-objective genetic algorithm and an inner link restructuring method. In *Proceedings of SICE Annual Conference (SICE)*, (pp. 1525–1531). SICE.

Mochocki, B., Hu, X. S., & Quan, G. (2002). A Realistic Variable Voltage Scheduling Model for Real-Time Applications. In *Proceedings of Computer Aided Design* (pp. 726–731). Academic Press. doi:10.1109/IC-CAD.2002.1167612

Mochocki, B., Hu, X. S., & Quan, G. (2007). Transition-Overhead-Aware Voltage Scheduling for Fixed-Priority Real-Time Systems. *ACM Transactions on Design Automation of Electronic Systems, 12*(2), 1–12. doi:10.1145/1230800.1230803

Mohammadian, H. S., & Abolhassani, B. (2010). Auction-based spectrum sharing for multiple primary and secondary users in cognitive radio networks. In *Proceedings of IEEE Sarnoff Symposium*. IEEE.

Mohsenian-Rad, H., Wong, V. W. S., Jatskevich, J., Schober, R., & Leon-Garcia, A. (2010). Autonomous demand side management based on game-theoretic energy consumption scheduling for the future smart grid. *IEEE Trans. on Smart Grid, 1*(3), 320–331. doi:10.1109/TSG.2010.2089069

Mo, J., & Walrand, J. (2000). Fair end-to-end window-based congestion control. *IEEE/ACM Transactions on Networking, 8*(5), 556–567. doi:10.1109/90.879343

Monderer, D., & Shapley, L. (1996). Fictitious Play Property for Games with Identical Interests. *Journal of Economic Theory, 1*, 258–265. doi:10.1006/jeth.1996.0014

Musku, M. R., Chronopoulos, A. T., Popescu, D. C., & Stefanescu, A. (2010). A game-theoretic approach to joint rate and power control for uplink CDMA communications. *IEEE Transactions on Communications, 58*(3), 923–932. doi:10.1109/TCOMM.2010.03.070205

Mustika, I. W., Yamamoto, K., Murata, H., & Yoshida, S. (2010). Spectrum Sharing with Interference Management for Distributed Cognitive Radio Networks: A Potential Game Approach. In *Proceedings of IEEE Vehicular Technology Conference*. IEEE.

Myerson, R. B. (1997). *Game Theory: Analysis of Conflict*. Cambridge, MA: Harvard University Press.

Nagel, J. (1975). *Descriptive Analysis of Power*. New Haven, CT: Yale University Press.

Nash Equilibrium. (n.d.). Retrieved from http://economics.about.com/cs/economicsglossary/g/nashequilibrium.htm

Neumann, J. V., & Morgenstern, O. (1944). *Theory of games and economic behavior*. Princeton University Press.

Newton, M., Thompson, J. S., & Naden, J. M. (2008). Wireless systems Resource allocation in the downlink of cellular multi-hop networks. *European Transactions on Telecommunications, 19*(3), 299–314. doi:10.1002/ett.1264

Nguyen, K. C., Alpcan, T., & Basar, T. (2009). Security games with incomplete information. In *Proceedings of IEEE ICC*. IEEE.

Nguyen, K. C., Alpcan, T., & Basar, T. (2009). Stochastic games for security in networks with interdependent nodes. In *Proceedings of GameNets* (pp. 697–703). GameNets. doi:10.1109/GAMENETS.2009.5137463

Nie, P., & Zhang, P. (2008). A note on Stackelberg games. In *Proceedings of Chinese Control and Decision Conference*, (pp. 1201-1203). Academic Press.

Nie, N., & Comaniciu, C. (2006). Adaptive Channel Allocation Spectrum Etiquette for Cognitive Radio Networks. *Mobile Networks and Applications, 11*(6), 779–797. doi:10.1007/s11036-006-0049-y

Ning, G., Zhu, G., Li, Q., & Wu, R. (2006). Dynamic Load Balancing Based on Sojourn Time in Multitier Cellular Systems. In *Proceedings of IEEE Vehicular Technology Conference*, (pp. 111-116). IEEE.

Nisan, N., & Ronen, A. (2000). Computationally feasible VCG mechanisms. In *Proceedings of ACM Conference on Electronic Commerce*, (pp. 242-252). ACM.

Niu, L., & Quan, G. (2009). Energy-Aware Scheduling for Practical Mode Real-Time Systems with QoS Guarantee. In *Proceedings of World Congress on Computer Science and Information Engineering*, (pp. 428 - 432). Academic Press.

Niu, L., & Quan, G. (2006). Energy minimization for real-time systems with (m,k)-guarantee. *IEEE Transactions on VLSI Systems, 14*(7), 717–729. doi:10.1109/TVLSI.2006.878337

Niyato, D., & Hossain, E. (2006). WLC04-5: Bandwidth Allocation in 4G Heterogeneous Wireless Access Networks: A Noncooperative Game Theoretical Approach. In *Proceedings of IEEE GLOBECOM*. IEEE.

Niyato, D., & Hossain, E. (2007). Hierarchical Spectrum Sharing in Cognitive Radio: A Microeconomic Approach. In *Proceedings of IEEE WCNC*, (pp. 3822-3826). IEEE.

Niyato, D., & Hossain, E. (2006). A Cooperative Game Framework for Bandwidth Allocation in 4G Heterogeneous Wireless Networks.[IEEE.]. *Proceedings of the IEEE, ICC, 4357*–4362.

Niyato, D., & Hossain, E. (2007). Radio resource management games in wireless networks: an approach to bandwidth allocation and admission control for polling service in IEEE 802.16. *IEEE Wireless Communications, 14*(1), 27–35. doi:10.1109/MWC.2007.314548

Niyato, D., & Hossain, E. (2008). A noncooperative game-theoretic framework for radio resource management in 4G heterogeneous wireless access networks. *IEEE Transactions on Mobile Computing, 7*(3), 332–345. doi:10.1109/TMC.2007.70727

Niyato, D., & Hossain, E. (2008). Spectrum trading in cognitive radio networks: A market-equilibrium-based approach. *IEEE Wireless Communications, 15*(6), 71–80. doi:10.1109/MWC.2008.4749750

Niyato, D., & Hossain, E. (2009). Dynamics of Network Selection in Heterogeneous Wireless Networks: An Evolutionary Game Approach. *IEEE Transactions on Vehicular Technology, 58*(4), 2008–2017. doi:10.1109/TVT.2008.2004588

Niyato, D., Hossain, E., & Han, Z. (2009). Dynamics of Multiple-Seller and Multiple-Buyer Spectrum Trading in Cognitive Radio Networks: A Game-Theoretic Modeling Approach. *IEEE Transactions on Mobile Computing, 8*(8), 1009–1022. doi:10.1109/TMC.2008.157

Nokleby, M., & Aazhang, B. (2010). User Cooperation for Energy-Efficient Cellular Communications. In *Proceedings of IEEE ICC'2010*. IEEE.

Nurmi, P. (2004). Modelling routing in wireless ad hoc networks with dynamic bayesian games. In *Proc. 1st SECON 2004*, (pp. 63–70). SECON.

Oh, H., Lee, J., & Choi, J. (2013). Energy-efficient dynamic load distribution for heterogeneous access networks. In *Proceedings of ICT Convergence (ICTC)*, (pp. 18-23). ICTC.

Osborne, M. J., & Rubinstein, A. (1994). *A Course in Game Theory*. Cambridge, MA: MIT Press.

Otrok, H., Debbabi, M., Assi, C., & Bhattacharya, P. (2007). A Cooperative Approach for Analyzing Intrusions in Mobile Ad hoc Networks. In *Proceedings of ICDCSW'07*. ICDCSW.

Overill, R. E. (2001). Information warfare: battles in cyberspace. *Computing & Control Engineering Journal, 12*(3), 125–128. doi:10.1049/cce:20010304

Pal, R. (2007). Efficient Routing Algorithms for Multi-Channel Dynamic Spectrum Access Networks. In *Proceedings of IEEE International Symposium on New Frontiers in Dynamic Spectrum Access Networks*, (pp. 288-291). IEEE.

Pan, M., & Fang, Y. (2008). Bargaining based pairwise cooperative spectrum sensing for Cognitive Radio networks. In *Proceedings of IEEE MILCOM*. IEEE.

Pan, Y., Klir, G. J., & Yuan, B. (1996). Bayesian inference based on fuzzy probabilities. In *Proceedings of IEEE International Conference on Fuzzy Systems*, (pp. 1693–1699). IEEE.

Pan, R., & Xu, C. (2010). Research on Decision of Cyber Security Investment Based on Evolutionary Game Model. In *Proceedings of Multimedia Information Networking and Security* (pp. 491–495). Academic Press. doi:10.1109/MINES.2010.110

Pareto Optimality . (n.d.). Retrieved from http://www.economyprofessor.com/pareto-optimality-1906

Park, H. G., & Schaar, M. V. D. (2007). Congestion game modeling for brokerage based multimedia resource management. *Packet Video*, 18-25.

Park, H. G., & Schaar, M. V. D. (2007b). Multi-User Multimedia Resource Management using Nash Bargaining Solution. In *Proceedings of IEEE ICASSP*, (pp. 717-720). IEEE.

Park, Y. S., & Jung, E. S. (2007). Resource-Aware Routing Algorithms for Multi-hop Cellular Networks. In *Proceedings of International Conference on Multimedia and Ubiquitous Engineering*, (pp. 1164-1167). Academic Press.

Parkes, D. C., Singh, S. P., & Yanovsky, D. (2004). Approximately efficient online mechanism design. In *Proceedings of Conference on Neural Information Processing Systems*. Academic Press.

Parkes, D. C., Singh, S. P., & Yanovsky, D. (2004). Approximately efficient online mechanism design. In *Proceedings of Neural Information Processing Systems*. Academic Press.

Park, H. G., & Schaar, M. V. D. (2007). Bargaining Strategies for Networked Multimedia Resource Management. *IEEE Transactions on Signal Processing, 55*(7), 3496–3511. doi:10.1109/TSP.2007.893755

Park, J. O., & Schaar, M. V. D. (2012). The Theory of Intervention Games for Resource Sharing in Wireless Communications. *IEEE Journal on Selected Areas in Communications, 30*(1), 165–175. doi:10.1109/JSAC.2012.120115

Park, J. O., & Scharr, M. V. D. (2011). *A Note on the Intervention Framework*. Los Angeles: University of California.

Paruchuri, P., Pearce, J. P., Marecki, J., Tambe, M., Ordóñez, F., & Kraus, S. (2008). Paying games for security: An efficient exact algorithm for solving Bayesian Stackelberg games.[). AAMAS.]. *Proceedings of AAMAS, 2*, 895–902.

Paschalidis, I. C., & Tsitsiklis, J. N. (2000). Congestion-dependent pricing of network services. *IEEE/ACM Transactions on Networking, 8*(2), 171–184. doi:10.1109/90.842140

Patcha, A., & Park, D. J. (2004). A game theoretic approach to modeling intrusion detection in mobile ad hoc networks. In *Proceedings of IEEE workshop on Information Assurance and Security*, (pp. 280-284). IEEE.

Pati, H. K. (2007). A distributed adaptive guard channel reservation scheme for cellular networks. *International Journal of Communication Systems, 20*(9), 1037–1058. doi:10.1002/dac.857

Pavlidou, F. N., & Koltsidas, G. (2008). Game theory for routing modeling in communication networks — A survey. *Journal of Communications and Networks, 10*(3), 268–286. doi:10.1109/JCN.2008.6388348

Pei, Q., Liang, R., & Li, H. (2011). A Trust Management Model in Centralized Cognitive Radio Networks. In *Proceedings of International Conference on Cyber*, (pp. 491-496). Academic Press.

Pell, B. D. (1993). *Strategy Generation and Evaluation for Meta-Game Playing*. (Ph.D dissertation). University of Cambridge, Cambridge, UK.

Persone, V. N., & Campagna, E. (2009). Adaptive bandwidth allocation and admission control for wireless integrated service networks with flexible QoS. In *Proceedings of International Conference on Simulation Tools and Techniques*, (pp. 85-95). Academic Press.

Postigo-Boix, M., & Melús-Moreno, J. (2007). Performance evaluation of RSVP extensions for a guaranteed delivery scenario. *Computer Communications, 30*(9), 2113–2121. doi:10.1016/j.comcom.2007.04.015

Prisoner's Dilemma . (n.d.). Retrieved from http://en.wikipedia.org/wiki/Prisoner's_dilemma

Qiao, X., & Tan, Z. (2011). Combination of spectrum sensing and allocation in cognitive radio networks based on compressive sampling. In *Proceedings of IEEE GLOBECOM Workshops*, (pp. 565-569). IEEE.

Qin, F., & Liu, Y. (2009). Multipath Routing for Mobile Ad Hoc Network. *Journal of Networks, 4*(8), 771–778.

Qiu, Y., Chen, Z., & Xu, L. (2010). Active Defense Model of Wireless Sensor Networks Based on Evolutionary Game Theory. In *Proceedings of Wireless Communications Networking and Mobile Computing*. Academic Press. doi:10.1109/WICOM.2010.5601100

Quek, H. Y., & Tay, A. (2007). A evolutionary, game theoretic approach to the modeling, simulation and analysis of public goods provisioning under asymmetric information. In *Proceedings of IEEE CEC*, (pp. 4735-4742). IEEE.

Ramchurn, S. D., Mezzetti, C., Giovannucci, A., Rodriguez, J. A., Dash, R. K., & Jennings, N. R. (2009). Trust-Based Mechanisms for Robust and Efficient Task Allocation in the Presence of Execution Uncertainty. *Journal of Artificial Intelligence Research, 35*(1), 119–159.

Randall, M., McMahon, G., & Sugden, S. (2002). A Simulated Annealing Approach to Communication Network Design. *Journal of Combinatorial Optimization, 6*, 55–65. doi:10.1023/A:1013337324030

Rapoport, A. (1960). *Fights, Games and Debates*. Ann Arbor, MI: The University of Michigan Press.

Refaei, M. T., DaSilva, L. A., Eltoweissy, M., & Nadeem, T. (2010). Adaptation of Reputation Management Systems to Dynamic Network Conditions in Ad Hoc Networks. *IEEE Transactions on Computers, 59*(5), 707–719. doi:10.1109/TC.2010.34

Rextin, A. T., Irfan, Z., & Uzmi, Z. A. (2004). Games Networks Play A Game Theoretic Approach to Networks. In *Proceedings of International Symposium on Parallel Architectures, Algorithms, and Networks*, (pp. 451-457). Academic Press.

Rhee, S. H., Yoon, J. W., Choi, H. J., & Choi, I. S. (2001). Dynamic Capacity Resizing of Virtual Backbone Network. In *Proceedings of the First International Conference on Networking*, (pp. 698-708). Academic Press.

Riker, W. H. (1962). *The Theory of Political Coalitions*. New Haven, CT: Yale University Press.

Rogers, A., David, E., & Jennings, N. R. (2005). Self-organized routing for wireless microsensor networks. *IEEE Transactions on Systems, Man, and Cybernetics*, 35(3), 349–359. doi:10.1109/TSMCA.2005.846382

Rohokale, V., Kulkarni, N., Prasad, N., & Cornean, H. (2010). Cooperative Opportunistic Large Array Approach for Cognitive Radio Networks. In *Proceedings of International Conference on Communications*, (pp. 513-516). Academic Press.

Roossien, B., Noort, A. V. D., Kamphuis, R., Bliek, F., Eijgelaar, M., & Wit, J. (2011). Balancing wind power fluctuations with a domestic Virtual Power Plant in Europe's First Smart Grid. In *Proceedings of IEEE Trondheim PowerTech*. IEEE.

Ross, S. A. (1977). The Determination of Financial Structure: The Incentive-Signalling Approach. *The Bell Journal of Economics*, 8(1), 23–40. doi:10.2307/3003485

Roth, A. E. (2002). The Economist as Engineer: Game Theory, Experimentation, and Computation as Tools for Design Economics. *Econometrica, 70*(4), 1341-1378.

Roughgarden, T. (2010). Algorithmic Game Theory. *Communications of the ACM*, 53(7), 78–86. doi:10.1145/1785414.1785439

Roy, S., Ellis, C., Shiva, S., Dasgupta, D., Shandilya, V., & Wu, Q. (2010). A Survey of Game Theory as Applied to Network Security. In *Proceedings of IEEE HICSS*. IEEE.

Roy, S., Wu, L., & Zawodniok, M. (2011). Spectrum management for wireless networks using adaptive control and game theory. In *Proceedings of IEEE WCNC*, (pp. 1062-1067). IEEE.

Rubinstein, A. (1982). Perfect equilibrium in a bargaining model. *Econometrica*, 50, 97–109. doi:10.2307/1912531

Saad, W., Alpcan, T., Basar, T., & Hjørungnes, A. (2010). Coalitional game theory for security risk management. In *Proceedings of Conf. on Internet Monitoring and Protection*, (pp. 35-40). Academic Press.

Saad, W., Han, Z., Basar, T., Debbah, M., & Hjørungnes, A. (2009). Physical layer security: Coalitional games for distributed cooperation. In *Proceedings of WiOPT*. WiOPT.

Saad, W., Zhu, Q., Basar, T., Han, Z., & Hjorungnes, A. (2009). Hierarchical Network Formation Games in the Uplink of Multi-Hop Wireless Networks. In *Proceedings of IEEE GLOBECOM*. IEEE.

Saad, W., Han, Z., Debbah, M., Hjørungnes, A., & Basar, T. (2009). Coalitional games for distributed collaborative spectrum sensing in cognitive radio networks. In *Proceedings of IEEE INFOCOM* (pp. 2114–2122). IEEE. doi:10.1109/INFCOM.2009.5062135

Saad, W., Han, Z., Hjorungnes, A., Niyato, D., & Hossain, E. (2011). Coalition Formation Games for Distributed Cooperation Among Roadside Units into implement Vehicular Networks. *IEEE Journal on Selected Areas in Communications*, 29(1), 48–60. doi:10.1109/JSAC.2011.110106

Saad, W., Han, Z., Poor, H. V., & Başar, T. (2012). Game-Theoretic Methods for the Smart Grid: An Overview of Microgrid Systems, Demand-Side Management, and Smart Grid Communications. *IEEE Signal Processing Magazine*, 29(5), 86–105. doi:10.1109/MSP.2012.2186410

Sabir, E., El-Azouzi, R., & Hayel, Y. (2009). A hierarchical slotted aloha game. In *Proceedings of International Conference on Game Theory for Networks*, (pp. 222-231). Academic Press.

Saffre, F., & Gedge, R. (2010). Demand-Side Management for the Smart Grid. In *Proceedings of IEEE/IFIP Network Operations and Management Symposium Workshops*, (pp. 300-303). IEEE.

Sagduyu, Y., Berry, R., & Ephremides, A. (2011). Jamming games in wireless networks with incomplete information. *IEEE Communications Magazine*, 49(8), 112–118. doi:10.1109/MCOM.2011.5978424

Sallhammar, K., Knapskog, S., & Helvik, B. (2005). Using stochastic game theory to compute the expected behavior of attackers. In *Proceedings of International Symposium on Applications and the Internet Workshops (Saint2005)*, (pp. 102-105). Saint.

Samuelson, P. A. (1954). The Pure Theory of Public Expenditure. *The Review of Economics and Statistics*, *36*(4), 387–389. doi:10.2307/1925895

Sandholm, W. H. (2007). *Evolutionary Game Theory*. Retrieved from http://www.ssc.wisc.edu/~whs/research/egt.pdf

Sato, Y., Ryusuke, M., Obara, T., & Adachi, F. (2012). Nash bargaining solution based subcarrier allocation for uplink SC-FDMA distributed antenna network. In *Proceedings of IEEE International Network Infrastructure and Digital Content*, (pp. 76-80). IEEE.

Schmidt, C. (Ed.). (2002). *Game Theory and Economic Analysis: A Quiet Revolution in Economics*. New York: Routledge. doi:10.4324/9780203167403

Shaii, A. Q., Ismail, R., Jais, J., & Manan, J. (2008). Congestion avoidance: Network based schemes solution. In *Proceedings of International Symposium on Information Technology*. Academic Press.

Shang, L. H. (2007). Self-organized Evolutionary Minority Game on Networks. In *Proceedings of IEEE International Conference on Control and Automation*, (pp. 1885-1889). IEEE.

Shapley Value. (n.d.). Retrieved from http://www.answers.com/topic/shapley-value

Shapley, L. S., & Shubik, M. (1966). Quasi-cores in a monetary economy with non-convex preferences. *Econometrica*, *34*(4), 805–827. doi:10.2307/1910101

Sherali, H. D. (1984). A multiple leader Stackelberg model and analysis. *Operations Research*, *32*(2), 390–404. doi:10.1287/opre.32.2.390

Shneidman, J., & Parkes, D. (2003). Rationality and self-interest in peer-to-peer networks. In *Proceedings of IPTPS*, (pp. 139-148). IPTPS.

Shubik, M. (1973). *Game Theory and Political Science* (Cowles Foundation Discussion Paper No.351). Department of Economics, Yale University.

Shubik, M. (2011). *The Present and Future of Game Theory*. Retrieved from http://cowles.econ.yale.edu/P/cd/d18a/d1808.pdf

Sierra, C., Faratin, P., & Jennings, N. R. (1997). A Service-Oriented Negotiation Model between Autonomous Agents. In *Proceedings of European Workshop on Modeling Autonomous Agents in a Multi-Agent World*, (pp. 17-35). Academic Press.

Simon, M. H., & Kevin, J. S. Z. (2013). Methodology in Biological Game Theory. *The British Journal for the Philosophy of Science*, 1–22. PMID:23526835

Singh, A., & Haahr, M. (2007). Decentralized Clustering In Pure P2P Overlay Networks Using Schelling's Model. [IEEE.]. *Proceedings of the IEEE, ICC*, 1860–1866.

Smith, J. M., & Price, G. R. (1973). The logic of animal conflict. *Nature*, *246*(5427), 15–18. doi:10.1038/246015a0

Sodagari, S., Attar, A., & Bilen, S. G. (2010). Strategies to Achieve Truthful Spectrum Auctions for Cognitive Radio Networks Based on Mechanism Design. In *Proceedings of IEEE New Frontiers in Dynamic Spectrum*. IEEE.

SongHuai, D., Xinghua, Z., Lu, M., & Hui, X. (2006). A novel nucleolus-based loss allocation method in bilateral electricity markets. *IEEE Transactions on Power Systems*, *21*(1), 28–33. doi:10.1109/TPWRS.2005.860932

Song, Q., Zhuang, J., & Zhang, L. (2011). Evolution Game Based Spectrum Allocation in Cognitive Radio Networks. In *Proceedings of Wireless Communications, Networking and Mobile Computing*. Academic Press. doi:10.1109/wicom.2011.6036695

Song, W., Zhuang, W., & Cheng, Y. (2007). Load balancing for cellular/WLAN integrated networks. *IEEE Network*, *21*(1), 27–34. doi:10.1109/MNET.2007.314535

Spangler, B. (2003). *Positive-Sum, Zero-Sum, and Negative-Sum Situations*. Retrieved from http://www.beyondintractability.org/essay/sum

Srinivasan, V., Nuggehalli, P., Chiasserini, C. F., & Rao, R. R. (2003). Cooperation in wireless ad hoc networks. In *Proceedings of IEEE INFOCOM* (pp. 808–817). IEEE.

Srivastava, V., Neel, J., MacKenzie, A. B., & Menon, R. (2005). Using game theory to analyze wireless ad hoc networks. *IEEE Communications Surveys & Tutorials*, *7*(4), 46–56. doi:10.1109/COMST.2005.1593279

Strategy . (n.d.). Retrieved from http://en.wikipedia.org/wiki/Strategy_(game_theory)

Stuart, H. W. (2005). Biform Analysis of Inventory Competition. *Manufacturing & Service Operations Management*, *7*(4), 347–359. doi:10.1287/msom.1050.0090

Sun, L., & Xu, X. (2005). Coopetitive game, equilibrium and their applications. In *Proceedings of International Conference on Algorithmic Applications in Management*, (pp. 104-111). Academic Press.

Sun, L., Cheng, S., Lin, Y., & Wang, W. (2006). A Willing-to-Share Based Incentive Mechanism for File Sharing P2P Networks. In *Proceedings of IEEE CSCWD*. IEEE.

Sun, T., Zhu, Q., Li, S., & Zhou, M. (2007). Open, Dynamic and Continuous One-to-Many Negotiation System. In *Proceedings of BIC-TA 2007*, (pp. 87-93). BIC-TA.

Sun, W., Kong, X., He, D., & You, X. (2008). Information security problem research based on game theory. In *Proceedings of International Symposium on Publication Electronic Commerce and Security*, (pp. 554-557). Academic Press.

Sun, B., & Li, L. (2006). Distributed QoS multicast routing protocol in ad-hoc networks. *Journal of Systems Engineering and Electronics*, *17*(3), 692–698. doi:10.1016/S1004-4132(06)60118-7

Suo, D., & Wen, F. (2009). A Reversed Stackelberg Approach to Electronic Commerce Logistics Based on Supernetwork Theory. In *Proceedings of International Symposium on Information Science and Engineering*, (pp. 114-118). Academic Press.

Suris, J., DaSilva, L., Han, Z., & MacKenzie, A. (2007). Cooperative game theory for distributed spectrum sharing. In *Proceedings of the IEEE International Conference on Communications*, (pp. 5282–5287). IEEE.

Suris, J., DaSilva, L., Han, Z., & MacKenzie, A. (2007). Cooperative game theory for distributed spectrum sharing.[IEEE.]. *Proceedings of the IEEE, ICC*, 5282–5287.

Swedberg, R. (2001). Sociology and Game Theory: Contemporary and Historical Perspectives. *Theory and Society*, *30*(3), 301–335. doi:10.1023/A:1017532512350

Sysi-Aho, M., Saramäki, J., & Kaski, K. (2005). Invisible hand effect in an evolutionary minority game model. *Physica A*, *347*, 639–652. doi:10.1016/j.physa.2004.08.029

Tambe, M., Jain, M., Pita, J. A., & Jiang, A. X. (2012). Game theory for security: Key algorithmic principles, deployed systems, lessons learned. In *Proceedings of Annual Allerton Conference*, (pp. 1822-1829). Academic Press.

Tan, G., & Guttag, J. (2005). The 802.11 MAC Protocol Leads to Inefficient Equilibria. In *Proc. IEEE INFOCOM*. IEEE.

Tanaka-Yamawaki, M., & Tokuoka, S. (2006). Minority Game as a Model for the Artificial Financial Markets. In *Proceedings of IEEE Congress on Evolutionary Computation*, (pp. 2157-2162). IEEE.

Tan, C. K., Sim, M. L., & Chuah, T. C. (2010). Fair power control for wireless ad hoc networks using game theory with pricing scheme. *IET Communications*, *4*(3), 322–333. doi:10.1049/iet-com.2009.0225

Tao, L., & Yu, F. (2011). A Novel Congestion Detection and Avoidance Algorithm for Multiple Class of Traffic in Sensor Network. In *Proceedings of IEEE International Conference on Cyber Technology in Automation, Control, and Intelligent Systems*, (pp. 72-77). IEEE.

Tao, Y., & Wang, Z. (1997). Effect of time delay and evolutionarily stable strategy. *Journal of Theoretical Biology*, *187*, 111–116. doi:10.1006/jtbi.1997.0427 PMID:9236113

Tembine, H. (2009). Dynamic bargaining solutions for opportunistic spectrum access. In *Proceedings of IFIP Conference on Wireless Days*. Academic Press.

Tembine, H., Altman, E., ElAzouzi, E. R., & Sandholm, W. H. (2008). Evolutionary game dynamics with migration for hybrid power control in wireless communications. In *Proceedings of IEEE CDC*, (pp. 4479-4484). IEEE.

Trivedi, N., Elangovan, G., Iyengar, S. S., & Balakrishnan, N. (2006). A Message-Efficient, Distributed Clustering Algorithm for Wireless Sensor and Actor Networks. In *Proceedings of IEEE International Conference on Multisensor Fusion and Integration for Intelligent Systems*, (pp. 53-58). IEEE.

U, M., & Li, Z. (2010). Public Goods Game Simulator with Reinforcement Learning Agents. In *Proceedings of ICMLA,* (pp. 43-49). ICMLA.

Ullman-Margalit, E. (1977). *The Emergence of Norms.* Oxford, UK: Oxford University Press.

Urpi, A., Bonuccelli, M., & Giodano, S. (2003). Modeling cooperation in mobile ad-hoc networks: A formal description of selfishness. In *Proc. Model. Optim. Mobile Ad Hoc Wireless Netw.* Academic Press.

Vane, H. R., & Mulhearn, C. (2010). *James A. Mirrlees, William S. Vickrey, George A. Akerlof, A. Michael Spence and Joseph E. Stiglitz.* Edward Elgar Publishing.

Vejandla, P., Dasgupta, D., Kaushal, A., & Nino, F. (2010). Evolving Gaming Strategies for Attacker-Defender in a Simulated Network Environment. In *Proceedings of IEEE International Conference on Social Computing,* (pp. 889-896). IEEE.

Viduto, V., Maple, C., Huang, W., & Bochenkov, A. (2012). A multi-objective genetic algorithm for minimising network security risk and cost. In *Proceedings of IEEE HPCS,* (pp. 462-467). IEEE.

Viet-Anh, L., Pitaval, R. A., Blostein, S., Riihonen, T., & Wichman, R. (2010). Green cooperative communication using threshold-based relay selection protocols.[ICGCS.]. *Proceedings of ICGCS, 2010,* 521–526.

Vinyals, M., Bistaffa, F., Farinelli, A., & Rogers, A. (2012). Stable coalition formation among energy consumers in the smart grid. In *Proceedings of AAMAS.* AAMAS.

Virapanicharoen, J., & Benjapolakul, W. (2004). Fair-Efficient Guard Bandwidth Coefficients Selection in Call Admission Control for Mobile Multimedia Communications using Game Theoretic Framework.[IEEE.]. *Proceedings of the IEEE, ICC,* 80–84.

Walker, P. (2012). *A Chronology of Game Theory.* Retrieved from http://www.econ.canterbury.ac.nz/personal_pages/paul_walker/gt/hist.htm

Wang, B., Han, Z., & Liu, K. J. R. (2006). Stackelberg game for distributed resource allocation over multiuser cooperative communication networks. In *Proceedings of IEEE Global Telecommunications Conference.* IEEE.

Wang, B., Han, Z., & Liu, K. J. R. (2009). Peer-to-Peer File Sharing Game using Correlated Equilibrium. In *Proceedings of Annual Conference on Information Sciences and Systems,* (pp. 729-734). Academic Press.

Wang, B., Jij, Z., & Liu, K. J. R. (2007). Self-Learning Repeated Game Framework for Distributed Primary-Prioritized Dynamic Spectrum Access. In *Proceedings of IEEE SECON,* (pp. 631 - 638). IEEE.

Wang, G., Cao, J., Zhang, L., Chan, K. C. C., & Wu, J. (2005). A novel QoS multicast model in mobile ad-hoc networks. In *Proc. IEEE IPDPS,* (pp. 206-211). IEEE.

Wang, H. J., Katz, R. H., & Giese, J. (1999). Policy-enabled handoffs across heterogeneous wireless networks. In *Proceedings of IEEE Workshop on Mobile Computing Systems and Applications,* (pp. 51-60). IEEE.

Wang, H. M., Choi, H. S., & Kim, J. T. (2008). Workload-Based Dynamic Voltage Scaling with the QoS for Streaming Video. In *Proceedings of IEEE International Symposium on Electronic Design, Test and Applications,* (pp. 236 - 239). IEEE.

Wang, H., Choi, H., & Kim, J. (2008). Workload-Based Dynamic Voltage Scaling with the QoS for Streaming Video. In *Proceedings of IEEE International Symposium on Electronic Design, Test and Applications,* (pp. 236-239). IEEE.

Wang, H., Gao, L., Gan, X., Wang, X., & Hossain, E. (2010). Cooperative Spectrum Sharing in Cognitive Radio Networks: A Game-Theoretic Approach. In *Proceedings of IEEE ICC.* IEEE.

Wang, L., Xue, Y., & Schulz, E. (2006). Resource Allocation in Multicell OFDM Systems Based on Noncooperative Game. In *Proceedings of IEEE PIMRC.* IEEE.

Wang, Y., Martonosi, M., & Peh, L. S. (2006). A supervised learning approach for routing optimizations in wireless sensor networks. In *Proceedings of International Symposium on Mobile Ad Hoc Networking & Computing,* (pp. 79–86). Academic Press.

Wang, Y., Nakao, A., & Ma, J. (2010). A Simple Public-Goods Game Based Incentive Mechanism for Resource Provision in P2P Networks. In *Proceedings of UIC 2010,* (pp. 352-365). UIC.

Wang, B., Liu, K., & Clancy, T. (2010). Evolutionary cooperative spectrum sensing game: how to collaborate? *IEEE Transactions on Communications, 58*(3), 890–900. doi:10.1109/TCOMM.2010.03.090084

Wang, B., Wu, Y., Ji, Z., Liu, K. J. R., & Clancy, T. C. (2008). Game theoretical mechanism design methods: suppressing cheating in cognitive radio networks. *IEEE Signal Processing Magazine, 25*(6), 74–84. doi:10.1109/MSP.2008.929552

Wang, B., Wu, Y., & Liu, K. J. R. (2010). Game theory for cognitive radio networks: An overview. *Computer Networks, 54*, 2537–2561. doi:10.1016/j.comnet.2010.04.004

Wang, B., Wu, Y., Liu, K. J. R., & Clancy, T. C. (2011). An anti-jamming stochastic game for cognitive radio networks. *IEEE Journal on Selected Areas in Communications, 29*(4), 877–889. doi:10.1109/JSAC.2011.110418

Wang, H., Wang, F., Ke, Z., & Guo, Z. (2009). QoS-Adaptive Bandwidth Allocation Scheme Based on Measurement Report Real-Time Analysis.[WiCom.]. *Proceedings of WiCom, 09*, 4278–4281.

Wang, T., Song, L., Han, Z., Cheng, X., & Jiao, B. (2012). Power Allocation using Vickrey Auction and Sequential First-Price Auction Games for Physical Layer Security in Cognitive Relay Networks.[IEEE.]. *Proceedings of the IEEE, ICC*, 1683–1687.

Wang, X., & Schulzrinne, H. (2005). Incentive-Compatible Adaptation of Internet Real-Time Multimedia. *IEEE Journal on Selected Areas in Communications, 23*(2), 417–436. doi:10.1109/JSAC.2004.839399

Waslander, S. L., Inalhan, G., & Tomlin, C. J. (2004). *Decentralized Optimization via Nash Bargaining*. Kluwer Academic Press.

Wen, S., & Wu, H. (2012). A Novel Resource Allocation Scheme for Station Area. In *Proceedings of IEEE Wireless Communications, Networking and Mobile Computing*. IEEE.

Wittman, M. D. (2011). *Solving the Blotto Game: A Computational Approach*. MIT.

Woodard, C. J., & Parkes, D. C. (2003). Strategyproof mechanisms for ad hoc network formation. In *Proceedings of IEEE IPTPS*. IEEE.

Wooldridge, M. (2012). Does Game Theory Work? *IEEE Intelligent Systems, 27*(6), 76–80. doi:10.1109/MIS.2012.108

Wu, M. Y., & Shu, W. (2004). RPP: a distributed routing mechanism for strategic wireless ad hoc networks. In *Proceedings of IEEE GLOBECOM*, (pp. 2885-2889). IEEE.

Wu, C., Mohsenian-Rad, H., Huang, J., & Wang, A. Y. (2011). Demand side management for Wind Power Integration in microgrid using dynamic potential game theory.[IEEE.]. *Proceedings of IEEE GLOBECOM, 2011*, 1199–1204.

Wu, Y., Wang, B., Liu, K. J. R., & Clancy, T. C. (2009). A scalable collusion-resistant multi-winner cognitive spectrum auction game. *IEEE Transactions on Communications, 57*(12), 3805–3816. doi:10.1109/TCOMM.2009.12.080578

Wu, Y., Wang, B., Ray Liu, K. J., & Clancy, T. C. (2009). Repeated open spectrum sharing game with cheat-proof strategies. *IEEE Transactions on Wireless Communications*, 1922–1933.

Xiang, M. (2013). *Trust-based energy aware geographical routing for smart grid communications networks*. (Master's Thesis). Auckland University of Technology.

Xiao, Y., Bi, G., & Niyato, D. (2010). Distributed optimization for cognitive radio networks using Stackelberg game. In *Proceedings of IEEE International Conference on Communication Systems*, (pp. 77 - 81). IEEE.

Xiao, Y., Zame, W. R., & Schaar, M. V. D. (2011). Technology Choices and Pricing Policies in Wireless Networks. In *Proceedings of IEEE ICC*. IEEE.

Xiaolin, C., Xiaobin, T., Yong, Z., & Hongsheng, X. (2008). A Markov game theory-based risk assessment model for network information systems. In *Proceedings of International conference on computer science and software engineering*, (pp. 1057-1061). Academic Press.

Xiao, Y., Park, J., & Schaar, M. V. D. (2012). Intervention in Power Control Games With Selfish Users. *IEEE Journal on Selected Areas in Communications, 6*(2), 165–179.

Xiao, Y., Shan, X., & Ren, Y. (2005). Game theory models for IEEE 802.11 DCF in wireless ad hoc networks. *IEEE Communications Magazine, 43*(3), 22–26. doi:10.1109/MCOM.2005.1404594

Xie, B., Zhou, W., Hao, C., Ai, X., & Song, J. (2010). A Novel Bargaining Based Relay Selection and Power Allocation Scheme for Distributed Cooperative Communication Networks. In *Proceedings of IEEE VTC*. IEEE.

Xu, B., & Fan, L. (2010). Information disclosing and cooperation in public goods game with punishment. In *Proceedings of ICISE*, (pp. 2896-2899). ICISE.

Xu, F., Zhang, L., Zhou, Z., & Liang, Q. (2007). Adaptive Power Control for Cooperative UWB Network Using Potential Game Theory. In *Proceedings of IEEE WCNC*, (pp. 1620-1624). IEEE.

Xu, W., & Wang, J. (2010). Double auction based spectrum sharing for wireless operators. In *Proceedings of IEEE International Symposium on Personal Indoor and Mobile Radio Communications (PIMRC)*, (pp. 2650–2654). IEEE.

Yang, C., Li, J., & Li, W. (2009). Joint rate and power control based on game theory in cognitive radio networks. In *Proceedings of Fourth International Conference on Communications and Networking*. Academic Press.

Yang, H. (1997a). Sensitivity analysis for the elastic-demand network equilibrium problem with applications. *Transportation Research*, *31*(1), 55–70. doi:10.1016/S0191-2615(96)00015-X

Yang, H. (1997b). Traffic restraint, road pricing and network equilibrium. *Transportation Research Part B: Methodological*, *31*(4), 303–314. doi:10.1016/S0191-2615(96)00030-6

Yang, K., Ou, S., Guild, K., & Chen, H. H. (2009). Convergence of ethernet PON and IEEE 802.16 broadband access networks and its QoS-aware dynamic bandwidth allocation scheme. *IEEE JSAC*, *27*(2), 101–116.

Yarvis, M., & Zorzi, M. (2008). Ad hoc networks: Special issue on energy efficient design in wireless ad hoc and sensor networks. *Ad Hoc Networks*, *6*(8), 1183–1184. doi:10.1016/j.adhoc.2007.11.005

Yasuda, Y. (2010). *Game Theory in Finance*. Retrieved from http://yyasuda.blogspot.kr/2010/10/game-theory-in-finance.html

Yee, Y. C., Choong, K. N., Low, A. L. Y., Tan, S. W., & Chien, S. F. (2007). A conservative approach to adaptive call admission control for QoS provisioning in multimedia wireless networks. *Computer Communications Archive*, *30*(2), 249–260. doi:10.1016/j.comcom.2006.08.025

Yi, Y., Zhang, J., Zhang, Q., Jiang, T., & Zhang, J. (2010). Cooperative Communication-Aware Spectrum Leasing in Cognitive Radio Networks. In *Proceedings of IEEE Symposium on New Frontiers in Dynamic Spectrum*. IEEE.

Yokoo, M., Sakurai, Y., & Matsubara, S. (2001). Robust double auction protocol against false-name bids. In *Proceedings of International Conference on Distributed Computing Systems*, (pp. 137-145). Academic Press.

Young, H. P. (2005). *Strategic Learning and Its Limits*. Oxford University Press.

Younis, M., Youssef, M., & Arisha, K. (2002). Energy-Aware Routing in Cluster-Based Sensor Networks. In *Proceedings of MASCOTS*, (pp. 129-136). MASCOTS.

Younis, O., Krunz, M., & Ramasubramanian, S. (2006). Node clustering in wireless sensor networks: recent developments and deployment challenges. *IEEE Network*, *20*(3), 20–25. doi:10.1109/MNET.2006.1637928

Zafar, H., Harle, D., Andonovic, I., & Khawaja, Y. (2009). Performance evaluation of shortest multipath source routing scheme. *IET Communications*, *3*(5), 700–713. doi:10.1049/iet-com.2008.0328

Zagare, F. C. (1986). Recent Advances in Game Theory and Political Science. In S. Long (Ed.), *Annual Review of Political Science*. Norwood, NJ: Ablex Publishing Corporation.

Zakiuddina, I., Hawkins, T., & Moffat, N. (2005). Towards a game theoretic understanding of ad-hoc routing. *Electronic Notes in Theoretical Computer Science*, *11*, 67–92. doi:10.1016/j.entcs.2004.07.009

Zaluski, W. (n.d.). *On the Applications of Game Theory in Contract Law*. Retrieved from http://www.academia.edu/505649/On_the_Applications_of_Game_Theory_in_Contract_Law

Zappone, A., Buzzi, S., & Jorswieck, E. (2011). Energy-Efficient Power Control and Receiver Design in Relay-Assisted DS/CDMA Wireless Networks via Game Theory. In *Proceedings of IEEE Communications Letters*. IEEE.

Zhang, B., Chen, K., Gou, X., & Cheng, S. (2010). Spectrum leasing via selective cooperation in distributed cognitive radio networks. In *Proceedings of IEEE International Conference on Network Infrastructure and Digital Content*, (pp. 16-20). IEEE.

Zhang, H., Fang, X., & Yuan, Q. (2007). A Game Theory-based Fairness Call Admission Control Scheme for CDMA Systems. In *Proceedings of CHINACOM*, (pp. 1021-1025). CHINACOM.

Zhang, T., & Yu, X. (2010). Spectrum Sharing in Cognitive Radio Using Game Theory-A Survey. In *Proceedings of WiCOM*. WiCOM.

Zhang, T., Zeng, Z., Feng, C., Zheng, J., & Ma, D. (2007). Utility Fair Resource Allocation Based on Game Theory in OFDM Systems. In *Proceedings of IEEE ICCCN*, (pp. 414-418). IEEE.

Zhang, G., Yang, K., Liu, P., & Enjie, D. (2011). Achieving User Cooperation Diversity in TDMA-Based Wireless Networks Using Cooperative Game Theory. *IEEE Communications Letters*, 15(2), 154–156. doi:10.1109/LCOMM.2011.122010.100629

Zhanjun, L., Chengchao, L., Yun, C., Huan, D., & Cong, R. (2010). An interference avoidance power control algorithm based on game theory. In *Proceedings of Second Pacific-Asia Conference on Circuits, Communications and System*, (pp. 414- 416). Academic Press.

Zhao, L., Zhang, H., & Zhang, J. (2008). Using Incompletely Cooperative Game Theory in Wireless Sensor Networks. In *Proceedings of IEEE WCNC*, (pp. 1483-1488). IEEE.

Zhao, Y., & Zhao, H. (2002). Study on negotiation strategy. In *Proceedings of International Conference On Power System Technology*, (pp. 1335-1338). Academic Press.

Zheng, Y., & Feng, Z. (2001). Evolutionary game and resources competition in the Internet. In *Proceedings of SIBCOM*, (pp. 51-52). SIBCOM.

Zhong, L. X., Chen, B. H., & Huang, C. Y. (2008). Networking Effects on Public Goods Game with Unequal Allocation. In *Proceedings of ICNC*, (pp. 217-221). ICNC.

Zhong, S., Chen, J., & Yang, Y. (2003). Sprite: A Simple, Cheat-Proof, Credit-Based System for Mobile Ad-Hoc Networks. In Proceedings of IEEE INFOCOM, (pp. 1987–1997). IEEE.

Zhou, X., & Zheng, H. (2009). TRUST: A General Framework for Truthful Double Spectrum Auctions. In Proceedings of IEEE Infocom, (pp. 999-1007). IEEE.

Zhou, X., Gandhi, S., Suri, S., & Zheng, H. (2008). eBay in the sky: strategy-proof wireless spectrum auctions. In *Proceedings of ACM MobiCom*, (pp. 2-13). ACM.

Zhu, Q., & Basar, T. (2011). A multi-resolution large population game framework for smart grid demand response management. In *Proceedings of International Conference on Control and Optimization (NetGCooP)*. NetGCooP.

Zhu, Y., Suo, D., & Gao, Z. (2010). Secure Cooperative Spectrum Trading in Cognitive Radio Networks: A Reversed Stackelberg Approach. In *Proceedings of International Conference on Multimedia Communications*, (pp. 202-205). Academic Press.

Zhu, Z., Tang, J., & Lambotharan, S. (2012). An integer linear programming based optimization for home demand-side management in smart grid. In *Proceedings of IEEE ISGT*. IEEE.

Zhu, Q., Han, Z., & Basar, T. (2012). A differential game approach to distributed demand side management in smart grid.[IEEE.]. *Proceedings of the IEEE, ICC*, 3345–3350.

Zou, Y., Mi, Z., & Xu, M. (2006). Dynamic Load Balancing Based on Roulette Wheel Selection. In *Proceedings of International Conference on Communications, Circuits and Systems*, (pp. 1732-1734). Academic Press.

Zouridaki, C., Mark, B. L., Hejmo, M., & Thomas, R. K. (2005). A Quantitative Trust Establishment Framework for Reliable Data Packet Delivery in MANETs. In *Proceedings of ACM SASN*. ACM.

Zuckerman, M., Faliszewski, P., Bachrach, Y., & Elkind, E. (2008). Manipulating the Quota in Weighted Voting Games. In *Proceedings of Conference on Artificial Intelligence*, (pp. 13–17). Academic Press.

About the Author

Sungwook Kim received the BS and MS degrees in Computer Science from the Sogang University, Seoul, in 1993 and 1995, respectively. From 1995 to 1998, he was a Member of Technical Staff at A. I. Soft. Company Ltd., Seoul, Korea. In 2003, he received the PhD degree in Computer Science from the Syracuse University, Syracuse, New York, supervised by Prof. Pramod K. Varshney. After that, he held faculty positions at the Department of Computer Science of Chung-Ang University, Seoul. In 2006, he returned to Sogang University, where he is currently an Associate Professor of Department of Computer Science and Engineering, and is a Research Director of the Internet Communication Control research laboratory (ICC Lab).

Index